SCHOENBERG
HIS LIFE, WORLD AND WORK

Also by H. H. Stuckenschmidt

Maurice Ravel
Feruccio Busoni

H. H. STUCKENSCHMIDT

SCHOENBERG

HIS LIFE, WORLD AND WORK

Translated from the German by
Humphrey Searle

John Calder
London

For my old friends Nuria and Luigi Nono

First published in Great Britain 1977
by John Calder (Publishers) Ltd
18 Brewer Street London W1

© this translation John Calder (Publishers) Ltd 1977

Originally published as SCHOENBERG, LEBEN, UMWELT, WERK

© Atlantis Musikbuch-Verlag Zurich 1974

ISBN 0 7145 3532x Casebound

Type set in 10 on 11 point Baskerville by Woolaston Parker Ltd Leicester
Printed in Great Britain by M. & A. Thomson Litho Ltd. East Kilbride
Bound by Hunter & Foulis Ltd., Edinburgh, Scotland

CONTENTS

	Page
Preface	vii
The Second District	15
Schoenberg at the Überbrettl	47
Relations with Strauss	61
Vienna, teaching and crises	77
Relations with Mahler	101
Air from another planet	115
Flight	127
Berlin for the second time	145
Up to the First World War	167
Three times seven recitations	195
Schoenberg and Busoni	219
The faith of the disillusioned man	233
Mödling, new conditions and a new life	249
The great call	303
Homeless and speechlessness	365
Los Angeles	403
Changes due to war	437
Last years and death	473
The primal cell	525
APPENDIX	535
Documents	536
Chronological list of works	558
Select Bibliography	563
Index	564

LIST OF ILLUSTRATIONS

Pauline Schoenberg, née Nachod, with Ottilie and Arnold, 1879	19
Schoenberg at ten with Edmund, Rudolf and Malva Goldschmied	24
A cheerful quintet, Vienna 1895–1898	32
'Two Songs', 1895 (Autograph)	36
Verklärte Nacht, 1899 (Autograph of the String Sextet)	41

The Wolzogen Theatre Berlin 1901   57
Alban Berg, 1909   82
Anton von Webern, 1912   89
Villa Lepcke, Berlin-Zehlendorf   147
Group Photograph at the 'Gurrelieder' performance,
    Leipzig 1914   147
Schoenberg with Alexander von Zemlinsky, Prague 1912   162
Schoenberg in St. Petersburg, 1912   182
Programme of the orchestral concert in Vienna,
    13 March 1913   186
Albertine Zehme, 1912   197
Schoenberg's programme of work, 1919   256
Programme of the Johann Strauss concert, 27 May 1921   273
Villa Josef in Traunkirchen   276
Mathilde and Arnold Schoenberg with Francis Poulenc   280
Programme of the private première of the Serenade
    opus 24 in Vienna, 2 May 1924   296
Gertrud Kolisch, 1924   298
Schoenberg with a moustache, 1925   305
Schoenberg's reply to a request   314
Rudolf Kolisch, 1926   318
Schoenberg with Josef Rufer, Berlin 1927   323
The Schoenbergs with Oskar Kokoschka and Adolf Loos,
    1927   323
Von heute auf morgen, 1929 (Facsimile of the piano score)   327
Telegram from Franz Lehar, 1930   338
Arnold and Gertrud Schoenberg at Lugano, 1930   338
Programme of the première of Moses and Aaron,
    Hamburg 1954   356
Schoenberg's return to the Jewish faith, Paris 1933   369
Arnold and Gertrud Schoenberg in Los Angeles, 1935   417
Schoenberg with his daughter Nuria, 1937   425
Eduard Steuermann, 1940   447
Schoenberg with his family, 1946   477
Schoenberg with Erika Stiedry von Wagner, 1940   516
Schoenberg with Fritz Stiedry, 1949   516
The Workroom in Brentwood Park   522
Programme of the first performance of the Three Songs
    opus 48 in London, 5 June 1952   527
Note on Webern, after 1910   538

vi

PREFACE

Arnold Schoenberg's life, surroundings and works form an indissoluble unity. To speak of the man is to point out the countless connections which link him with his artistic, religious, economic and political surroundings and is to recognize his works, musical as well as literary and pictorial, as the reflection of this link. The recognition of this fact gave my work its purpose and proportion from the beginning. Since my schooldays (to be exact since the summer of 1917, when I bought the score of the Five Orchestral Pieces Op. 16) I have never ceased to study Schoenberg's music and his book on harmony. I first met Schoenberg himself in Hamburg in January 1924 and then frequently in Vienna and Berlin, and for the last time in 1949 in Los Angeles. I owe much of my insight into artistic matters to my visits to his Course of Analysis and Rehearsals and also to conversations with him. I know how he lived, made music, played ping-pong, and I have seen him delightful and angry, affectionate and scornful, but never indifferent.

Josef Rufer, who introduced me to him, became my friend for life; Hanns Eisler was a close friend in the 1920s. Alban Berg and Anton von Webern, Erwin Ratz and Eduard Steuermann opened many avenues to the understanding of his music to me. Through Margot Hinnenberg-Lefèbre, the favourite singer of his works from 1926 until his emigration and my wife since 1932, I came nearer to him and his circle than before. His brother-in-law Rudolf Kolisch became my friend, and Gertrud, Schoenberg's second wife, gave me her confidence, as did her three children, Nuria Nono, Rudolf Ronald and Adam Lawrence. I am indebted to them for allowing me access to his complete estate, which I was able to work through in November and December 1971, both in his house at 116 North Rockingham Avenue, Los Angeles, and also in the Library of Congress, Washington. Assisted by my wife I evaluated and partly copied thousands of documents, letters, photographs and manuscripts. We looked through the library and music collection piece by piece, and deciphered the marginal notes Schoenberg wrote in them. I would like to thank Adam Lawrence Schoenberg for his continual help during my weeks in Los Angeles and also for his letter to the Library of Congress which authorized me to study there all the letters from and to Schoenberg, especially the correspondence with Vassily Kandinsky and Ferruccio Busoni. In this work, as in previous years, Dr. Harold Spiwacke, who was then Director of the Music Department, was helpful to me in the kindest possible way. Conversations which I had later in Boston with Rudolf Kolisch and in New York with Felix Greissle gave me important leads for further research.

For the whole of his life Schoenberg threw practically nothing away which came into his possession. So it was possible to follow the course of his life right back to his youth from letters and documents. The biographical value of the correspondence is uneven. The numerous letters from Alma Maria Mahler-Gropius-Werfel, which are extremely interesting from a personal point of view, are undated, and so are most of Alexander von Zemlinsky's. Schoenberg himself wrote in his own hand until his friends and pupils gave him a typewriter for Christmas 1922. Carbon copies of all his letters exist from that date; before that he only occasionally used a copy-book.

The numerous sheets and little pieces of paper, which he used for notes, are mostly undated. Until his emigration in May 1933 he employed the German cursive writing, after that only Roman letters. Changes in spelling like the use of k's instead of c's in foreign words cannot be dated exactly, as relapses into the older method of writing are liable to fluctuate. The old fashioned *th* instead of *t* appears at times even in his later years. In many cases the date can be approximately established through comparison of the different papers. So a more detailed research should not rely entirely on photo-copies and xerox. With such a complex personality as Schoenberg the knowledge of the sources themselves (and not only of copies of them) is as indispensible for his biography and the complete publication of his works as is the knowledge of the peculiar aura which surrounded and still surrounds him and the work he left behind.

As the arrangement and cataloguing of letters and manuscripts were still incomplete in 1971 and some of the letters were in the post to the Library of Congress, there are some documents

viii

which I have not been through. I had to look round the large circle of Schoenberg's correspondents in order not to leave out anything important. For his childhood and the years until his first move to Berlin in 1901 the sources were very sparse. His school reports were found in the archive of the Bundesreal-gymnasium in Vienna II; I am grateful to Magister Johannes Wurth for the discovery and copying of these documents, which have been supplemented by some letters from former school companions of Schoenberg.

From Schoenberg's correspondence with his sister Ottilie Blumauer I discovered that two love-letters of Schoenberg as a sixteen-year-old to his cousin Malvina Goldschmied were in Rio de Janeiro. At my request the Austrian Consul-General in West Berlin, Dr. F. W. Hoess, established contact through his embassy in Brasilia with the descendants of Malvina Bodanzky, née Goldschmied. Through her daughter, Frau Renate Neschling-Bodanzky, and her son John Luciano Neschling I obtained copies of these Schoenberg letters, which must be the earliest preserved; I hereby thank everyone who took part in this detective work.

In 1902 Schoenberg met Richard Strauss, who was his ener-getic supporter for years. The correspondence of the two com-posers is preserved in the archive of the Villa Strauss at Garmisch-Partenkirchen. Frau Dr. Alice Strauss allowed me to see these documents and gave me photo-copies of them; I thank her as well.

The late Professor Dr. Egon Wellesz, the last witness of Schoenberg's early teaching activity from 1904 onwards, gave me during many years the most valuable information and advice both in letters and orally. As Schoenberg's first biographer he already had access to manuscripts and sketch books in 1920, and I thank him for a great deal of information about Schoenberg's life and work.

I am obliged to Professor Dr. Werner Haftmann for the dis-covery of sources about Schoenberg's relations to the Blaue Reiter and the Munich Circle round Kandinsky.

Universal Edition in Vienna was Schoenberg's chief publisher from 1903. Director Alfred Schlee gave me access to the import-ant and numerous documents in their archives. I found there not only the piano scores which Schoenberg made of Rossini, Lortzing and Schubert, but also the correspondence – although it has not been preserved entirely complete – which Schoenberg carried on with the publishing firm and its director Emil Hertzka from 1910 until his American years. A most important biographical source was the voluminous, still unpublished correspondence between Alban Berg and Anton von Webern which Herr Schlee put at my disposal. Together with Schoenberg's diary from the beginning of 1912 and 1915 this provides information for practically every day in certain periods of his life. As both these correspondents were almost pedantically accurate, the dates of this correspondence can be regarded as reliable. Schoenberg himself sometimes made mistakes about the day, month and even the year.

From 1911 till 1915 he lived in Berlin again. One of the most important meetings of this time was that with Albertine Zehme, who commissioned and performed his *Pierrot Lunaire*, and was also a motherly friend and patroness. Up till now research knew very little about her. I am grateful to the tireless activity of Klaus Thiel of Leipzig for all the dates of her important life; together with the many letters in Schoenberg's estate they give an exact picture of her as woman and artist.

I am especially grateful to Professor Dr. Hans Sittner, the President of the International Schoenberg Society, for the evaluation of the Viennese sources regarding Schoenberg's relations with the Music Academy. He has searched the documents for me and copied them in his own hand. Important dates can also be found in the letters and cards which Schoenberg exchanged between 1913 and 1918 with Alexander Jemnitz and which Professor Denis Dille of the Béla Bartók Archive in Budapest put at my disposal.

After Schoenberg's demobilization from the army in 1917 and his move to Mödling in 1918 witnesses of his activities became more numerous. Among the pupils who came to him after the war Max Deutsch of Paris, the late Erwin Ratz, Hans Swarowsky and Joseph Trauneck gave me a great deal of information. For me the most important witness of this year was Josef Rufer; for years he collected material for a planned book on Schoenberg, but had to give up the project. He generously put the material at my disposal. It contains documents of great importance from Schoenberg's teaching in Mödling and The Viennese Society for Private Musical Performances. I thank him with all my heart for his help.

During his years in Mödling Schoenberg began his friendship with Dr. Fritz Stiedry and his wife Erika von Wagner. Schoenberg corresponded with both of them from 1922 up till his death;

the letters are among the most important sources. My thanks to Frau Erika Stiedry for much advice. In 1962, shortly before his death, Francis Poulenc from Paris sent me copies of the photographs he took in 1922 in Schoenberg's house at Mödling. In 1970 I got copies of his correspondence with Schoenberg from Darius Milhaud.

Professor Joachim Stutschewsky of Tel Aviv, and Professor Friedrich Wührer of Mannheim gave me many details from their reminiscences of the Spanish tour of *Pierrot Lunaire* in 1925; and I am also grateful to them for programmes of this tour. I was unable to contact those who took part in the Italian tour of 1924. However, Luigi Dallapiccola, to whom I am also grateful for other information, described to me Schoenberg's meeting with Puccini in Florence, at which he was present. Fedele d'Amico kindly provided me with photo-copies of the programmes of that time and of Alfredo Casella's article about *Pierrot Lunaire*; Signora Yvonne Casella showed me letters and signed photographs that Schoenberg had sent to her late husband.

The Archives of the Prussian Academy of Arts contain many documents relating to the Berlin master classes of 1926–1933; the Director Dr. Walter Huder gave me access to them, for which I thank him. Schoenberg's correspondence with Frau Maria Seligman-Kolisch from San Francisco contains many valuable details about this time; and I am grateful to her for sending me copies. Else C. Kraus, a zealous interpreter of Schoenberg's piano works and friend of his family gave me some information.

From East Berlin came information from Max Butting and Paul Dessau; the Arnold Zweig Archive of the German Academy of Arts there answered my questions in a friendly manner, but their Musical Department left my letters unanswered.

There are many reminiscences of Schoenberg as a teacher apart from my own participation in the analysis courses; these were published in many languages. The most important article dealing with him was from the Swiss conductor Erich Schmid, Schoenberg's pupil from 1930.

Frau Maria Schreker has retained many personal reminiscences of this time and related them in conversations with many valuable suggestions.

Frau Marketa Královcová, who died in 1972, was an always willing helper in Prague; she found a number of documents which had disappeared in the archives and libraries regarding Schoenberg's mother's family and performances of his works.

Professor Dr. Hans Frischauf of the University of Vienna gave me information and details about his mother, Frau Dr. Marie Pappenheim, who wrote the text of *Erwartung*.

Very little research had been done up till now on Schoenberg's first years in America, that is to say the time before he moved to California in 1934. From Miss Beatrice Malkin of New York I obtained the parts relating to Schoenberg of the unpublished reminiscences of her late father Joseph Malkin, who brought the Master to America. Her uncle too, Dr. I. Malkin, gave me information. An important and very extensive source in addition was given me by Dr. Hans W. Heinsheimer, who also helped me with many problems about my work, and gave me Schoenberg's very large correspondence with Carl Engel, and I am grateful for access to this to the publishers G. Schirmer of New York. Among Schoenberg's pupils in his early years in America in Boston and New York, Mrs. Lois Lautner and Mr. Lowndes Maury gave me much information. Miss Sheila Schultz sent me photo-copies of the article about Schoenberg in *Musical America*. Rudolf Kolisch and Gunter Schuller found some material about Schoenberg's life and working conditions in Boston itself.

Much has been written about Schoenberg's years in California, especially from the personal viewpoint of Dika Newlin. I was given information from letters and orally by Richard Hoffmann and Leonard Stein, who together with Gerald Strang were Schoenberg's closest collaborators. Professor John Ulric Nef authorized me to obtain copies of the letters which were in the Joseph Regenstein Library in the University of Chicago; these were sent to him and his first wife by Schoenberg, and I am grateful to the librarian Hans Lenneberg for these. I am also grateful to Mrs. Monica Mann for descriptions of her meetings with Schoenberg. Clara Steuermann and Salka Viertel-Steuermann helped to obtain photos and dates. Walter Goehr, one of Schoenberg's last pupils in Berlin, gave me access to his correspondence with Schoenberg from 1933–1949. Peter Yates gave me information about the 'Evenings on the Roof' arranged by him. Miss Sonja Lane, catalogued Schoenberg's literary estate in Los Angeles, helped with photo-copies.

But I am especially grateful to members of the Schoenberg family for their help. Frau Susanne Remus from Berlin gave me Schoenberg's correspondence with her mother Ottilie Blumauer, Schoenberg's sister, and much information. She and Frau Bertel

Schoenberg in Aigen, the widow of Schoenberg's brother Heinrich, gave me photos from Schoenberg's youthful days.

Nuria Nono was the most important source of help. In January 1973, together with my wife and myself, she read the manuscript and augmented my book with some corrections, additions and suggestions. Together we looked through the many photos and copies of manuscripts, of which several were put into the book. She gave us reminiscences of her father from her childhood and youth and conjured up the atmosphere of the house in Brentwood Park in such a lively manner that it no longer seemed to be a dead place. I am grateful to her for an insight into the most private domain of the Schoenberg family, especially during his last years up to 1951. And it was just these private and intimate insights which gave me a closer view of Schoenberg's creative process and justified my recognition of the fact that his life, surroundings and works were indissolubly linked together.

The list of those who contributed to the documentation of my work can hardly be given complete, as countless letters and conversations in the course of many years led to paths which I often followed with success. I will mention only the late Higino Anglès, Michael Gielen, Peter Gradenwitz, Karl Holl, Thomas-M. Langner, Friedrich Luft, Willi Reich, Willi Schuh, Nicolas Slonimsky and Fritz Zweig. In the tracing and translation of Russian and Ukrainian texts I was helped by Boris Blacher, Gottfried Eberle and Grigory Schneerson.

In Vienna I was helped by the Austrian Portrait Gallery, the Evangelical Church in the Dorotheergasse, and the Jewish Religious Centre (Dr. David Alpern). In Berlin I was helped by the Telephone Department of the Post Office which allowed me to see telephone books from 1901–1933, by the Prussian State Archive, which found dates in address books of the same period, and Dr. Rudolf Elvers made it possible to evaluate the Schoenberg autographs which are kept there; also the Senator for Housing. The U.S. Mission in West Berlin (Mr. Terence F. Catherman) was always helpful in finding documents in American universities. The Town Council of Gmunden in the Salzkammergut and the Archive of the Hessian Radio in Frankfurt gave me important dates. I would specially like to thank the editorial staff and publishers of the *Frankfurter Allgemeine Zeitung* for financial support in my exploratory journey in 1971 to the United States and for the help which my colleagues Friedrich Hommel and Hildegard Weber gave me.

In the British Museum in London I was able to see Schoenberg's letters, especially the important ones to Edward Clark between 1921–1933.

I would like to say a final word of thanks to Dr. Daniel Bodmer of the Atlantis Verlag, whose lively interest and untiring advice demanded and made possible the carrying out of this ambitious plan from 1970 till now.

I know that even in my work not all sources concerning Schoenberg's life and works have as yet been followed up and exhausted. However, most of the gaps have been filled and many mistakes corrected which can be found in the previous literature (including my own books and articles from 1920 to 1972), and have often been reproduced without further research. So I think I have come a step further forward.

H. H. Stuckenschmidt.
Berlin-Grunewald, January 1974

THE SECOND DISTRICT

In its North-Eastern frontier districts Austria–Hungary stretched deep into the Slavonic world. The Bohemian, Moravian and Slovak lands were not only the breeding ground of many-sided cultural events and spiritual manifestations. They were also filled with a feeling for music which had been practised for hundreds of years, the roots of which were based principally on native song and dance. In the chiefly peasant population of these districts singing and playing on musical instruments was a festive part of everyday life. From the village this widely spread musical culture found its way to the smaller and larger towns.

Among the Slavonic communities, which were divided by various languages and dialects, there were old-established Jewish minorities, which took over much of the culture of their host peoples, without sacrificing their own traditions. In the large towns the Jewish community was particularly creative culturally. In addition, in spite of all its close links with the large Slavonic majorities, the Jewish community had a very individual national function. In language it belonged to the German community, which also formed an old-established minority within the Slavonic society.

In the nineteenth and also the twentieth century countless good musicians came from this German-speaking Jewish people. Gustav Mahler belonged to it and so did the violinist Bronislaw Huberman, and Artur Schnabel as well as Alexander von Zemlinksy.

The Slovak capital Bratislava, Pressburg in German and Pozsony in Hungarian, was once a German settlement and was later ruled by noble Hungarian families. Its old cultural life was taken over by the Slovak majority and could boast of important results in the realms of the university and the theatre.

On the 20 September 1838 Samuel Schoenberg was born in

Szecseny, a member of a Jewish family. Like many of his compatriots he sought his fortune in Vienna. At the age of fourteen in 1852 he left his native land and in the capital of the Hapsburg monarchy he became an apprentice to a commercial firm. Samuel Schoenberg had a good voice and joined a choral society, attending their rehearsals and performances in the evenings after his work. One of his nephews, Hans Nachod, describes him as a sort of anarchistic wit. He had a brother, Ignaz Schoenberg, whose son Arthur became an engineer.

Samuel Schoenberg was thirty-two years old when in 1870 he married Pauline Nachod, who was ten years younger than himself. She was born on 7 April 1848 in Prague, the daughter of Joseph Nachod and Caroline, née Hutter. The Nachods were an old Jewish Prague family, whose male members for many generations had been cantors of the Altneuschul, Prague's chief synagogue. They inherited vocal and musical talent. Pauline had two sisters and three brothers. All six children seemed to have come with their parents to Vienna when they were young. Pauline's brother Gottlieb had two sons of whom the elder, Walter Josef Nachod, became an operatic singer. Another brother of hers, Friedrich Nachod, also had two sons of whom Hans had a notable career as an operatic tenor. The newly married couple opened a shoe shop which more or less supported the family. A first baby boy died immediately after his birth. A second arrived on 13 September 1874. In the register of the Viennese Jewish Religious Community, which survived the Nazi occupation in the Second World War by a miracle, the birth is numbered 8023. The circumcision ceremony took place a week later, showing the strong and healthy constitution of the boy, who was given the name Arnold.

The Schoenbergs were then living in the Second District at No. 393 Obere Donaustrasse. The Second District of Vienna, the Leopoldstadt, is a large island. It lies between the River Danube, which flows past its circumference, and the Danube canal which borders on the centre of the city. The Obere Donaustrasse runs along this canal. Its houses of three to five stories face the water and the city buildings on the other bank. On the Leopoldstadt island there are large green spaces like parks planted with fine old trees. The largest and most famous are the Augarten and the Prater. Between them and through them there are main streets like the old Jägerzeile, later called Praterstrasse, and the Taborstrasse where the Schoenbergs moved a few years after Arnold's birth. The name Leopoldstadt derives from the Emperor Leopold I, who was a humanist and an artistic man. Like many members of the House of Hapsburg he also loved music. He played the piano well and composed some attractive songs. But one day this cultured man ordered that this island with its beautiful parks, pleasure grounds and hunting fields should be cleared of all the Jewish inhabitants who had settled there. There were many of them there at the time. It was not till Maria Theresa's liberally minded son, the Emperor Joseph II, reigned in the Vienna Hofburg that the Jews were again allowed to live in the district, which was now called Leopoldstadt. On a house in the Obere Augartenstrasse there is a plaque of the year 1775. On it is written what the Emperor Joseph II ordered when he opened the Augarten and the Prater – which up till then had been reserved for the nobility – to the common people and gave it to his subjects: 'A pleasure ground dedicated to all people by him who esteems them.' The Monarch valued his people and they honoured him for it.

We know little more about Arnold Schoenberg's early childhood than the memories he told his wife Gertrud when he was an old man and also wrote down in short notes in a fragmentary way on paper. But we can imagine that he went for walks with his father or his mother in the Leopoldstadt. Perhaps these walks took place down the long Taborstrasse. There Schoenberg's father may have shown his son the large paddle steamers which linked Bratislava with Vienna and one of which had brought him as a young man from the provinces into the imperial capital. Perhaps his father also sang him songs from his native Slovakia, melodies in a Slavonic language which the child did not understand. Other walks could have led them to the Flossgasse, where once the violinist and waltz king Johann Strauss the elder was born in a beer tavern called 'Zum Heiligen Florian'.

Schoenberg himself told us, in a commentary on his string quartets written in 1937, that as a small boy he was terrified by the picture of a scene from the fairy tale 'The Ghost Ship' by Wilhelm Hauff. It showed the captain of the ship nailed to the mast through his head by the mutinous crew. The remembrance of this pursued him during the composition of his third string quartet of 1927, especially in the first movement.

Schoenberg was a great lover of animals. This love was already evident in his early childhood. When Gertrud Schoenberg sketched out a biography of the Master in the form of notes after

1951 in Los Angeles, the love of animals was one of the first characteristics of his which she mentioned. She wrote of the milk cart in the Prater and quoted a childish saying, 'Horse b'longs to Arnold'. After 1918 he always had dogs around him, and even shared his meagre wartime ration with his German Shepherd dog. Names of dogs mentioned by Gertrud were Wulli, Witz, Snowy, Rudi, Chris, and Laddie.

I have already mentioned Pauline's brother Friedrich, known as Fritz in the family circle. It was this uncle who as well as his parents influenced the boy's development most strongly. Arnold loved him, and also went for walks with him, sometimes in the Augarten, sometimes in the Prater. The boy learnt many things from his uncle long before he went to school. This widely-travelled man spoke good French and taught the language to Arnold. It is possible that Arnold learnt the French form of his first name, Arnaud, from him, and used it in one of his earliest compositions. Like Schoenberg's father Fritz Nachod was an idealistic freethinker. He loved poetry, especially Schiller's, and he wrote some poems himself. In contrast to the two men Pauline Schoenberg maintained the conservative principle in the family. She clung to the old practices which had been followed by the pious Nachod family in Prague for centuries. One can easily imagine the lively conversations which took place in the Schoenberg house when Uncle Fritz came to visit them. In these the political revolutions of the eighteenth and the nineteenth centuries were animatedly discussed and also the position of the Jews in modern society. Arnold Schoenberg remembered these childhood impressions later in Berlin and California and often spoke about them. In these conversations within the family circle the mother tried to calm down the two rebellious men and put up arguments against their expressed beliefs, of which the child took notice. In his mature character we find the strict preservationist and in his later years also the pious Jewish feelings of his mother together with the stimulating views of his father, who took a critical standpoint on all matters; the father lost this early and his rôle as educator of the boy was taken over by the uncle.

The family was increased on 9 of June 1876 by a sister for Arnold called Ottilie. Six years later a second son was born and called Heinrich Samuel. An old photograph shows Pauline Schoenberg with her two children Arnold and Ottilie. The picture was taken by the photographic shop Matzner, Vienna II, Lilienbrunhgasse 19, later the Sperlgasse. Mrs. Schoenberg

Pauline Schoenberg, née Nachod, with Ottilie and Arnold, 1879

dressed herself and her children very grandly. Comfortably plump, she sits there in her dark silk dress with a big white bow over her bosom, her hair piled up in plaits on her head, with a lorgnette on a chain. Ottilie stands on her right, her hands clasped, her face serious and attentive. On the left stands Arnold, with his hand in his mother's. Like his sister he is in Sunday dress with white stockings and dark boots. His slightly slanting, almost ironical mouth is unmistakable. The children must have been five and three years old, as the photograph was taken in 1879.

In April 1880 Arnold entered the Volksschule of the Second District. His father wanted him to take technical studies so that he could later become an engineer. In the Volksschule Arnold became friendly with two of his schoolmates. One was called Friedrich Eichberg and later acquired a considerable reputation and prosperity as an engineer and inventor. The other, Arnold Steiner, wrote in 1944 from Buenos Aires to Schoenberg, who was then seventy years old. He said that he had entirely parted from Eichberg, who had formerly been his best friend, over twenty years ago; he said that Eichberg had become too rich and had taken on the manners of West Berlin too much. The teacher who taught the three friends at school was called Starek. Steiner describes Schoenberg as a boy in his letter: 'You sat next to me in the school under Starek and every five minutes you fell on the ground, you made your trousers dirty at the knees and then scratched the dust off with your pocket knife. So you were already a nervous creature at that stage.' When Schoenberg moved to Berlin in September 1911 Dr. Friedrich Eichberg was living in New West End. The old school comrades met several times. And they corresponded again after 1939 in exile. In 1937 Eichberg went to America and sold an invention which he had patented to General Electric. He died in the university town of Ann Arbor on 29 July 1941. 'How much lies between our school years and now,' he wrote at Christmas 1940 to Schoenberg in Brentwood Park.

It seems that there was no music-making in Schoenberg's parents' house. Even after the father had opened a collection agency the family remained in modest conditions and did not own a piano. In her book *Bruckner, Mahler, Schoenberg*, published in New York in 1947, and based on information from Schoenberg, Dika Newlin spoke of Schoenberg's mother Pauline as a piano teacher. Hans Nachod's statements are to the contrary. However, we can imagine that the mother, who came from an old Prague family of cantors, was probably musically gifted. All the three children already showed musical gifts at a tender age. If there had been a piano in the house they would probably have played it. Arnold Schoenberg certainly made himself familiar with the technique of all instruments. But the only instrument that he learned as a child was the violin. It seems that at any rate in his youth he did not play the piano.

In the autumn of 1885 he entered the first class of the Real-schule Vienna II as a 'student coming from outside'. He went through all the classes and left on 2 January 1891. His results at school seemed to have been average. He was not a very willing pupil. Anyone who knows the descriptions of the Austrian 'middle schools' at the turn of the century in Stefan Zweig's *The World of Yesterday* will understand why. The Realschule of the Second District, today the admirable Bundesrealgymnasium of Vienna II, in those days was regarded as not even a leading school. A person with such strong instincts for teaching and inborn capacity for learning as Schoenberg must have been forced into early criticism and rebellion.

He himself wrote nothing about his school years and hardly ever spoke of them. What he learnt from them was certainly only a paltry foundation for the later development of his personality. In his writing he used up till the time of his leaving Germany in 1933 a clear and correct German cursive hand, sprinkled with Roman letters for certain words. After 1933 he used only the Roman script. Modern languages, especially French, were not difficult for him. In America after troublesome beginnings he acquired a wide knowledge of English, reaching even into idiomatic phrases. The fact that he had little knowledge of Greek mythology is due to his modern training in the Realschule. Stefan Zweig wrote about the 'evaluation of aesthetics carried to absurd lengths' practised by the boys of his generation (he was born in Vienna in 1881) and about the prison atmosphere of an Austrian Gymnasium. Perhaps Schoenberg also found his school years oppressive. His artistic favourites were certainly not of such a literary and intellectual kind as Stefan Zweig's or of Hugo von Hofmannsthal, who was born in 1874, and at the age of sixteen, under the pseudonym of 'Loris', startled the literary world by the maturity of his poems.

During his schooldays Schoenberg started a friendship with Oskar Adler, the highly intellectual philospher and admirable violinist, who wrote in 1948 from his London exile: 'My recollections of youth had remained very much alive. I often think back to the time when we played quartets together in the messenger boys' room in the Augartenstrasse on Sunday afternoons, followed by walks in the Prater with philosophical discussions and of the time when we admired Komzak's conducting.[1] Many figures come back to me – Eichberg, Herzl, Heim, who died here two years ago of a serious illness . . .'

The young musicians lacked a cello for their Sunday concerts in the messenger boys' room. Oskar Adler produced a large viola. It was fitted with four zither strings which were tuned like a cello. Schoenberg played on this curious instrument. He used violin fingering, which was the only one he knew. So things remained for the moment, even when he bought a cello out of his meagre pocket money at the 'Tandelmarkt', a second-hand market in Vienna. Again Adler came to the rescue. He asked the cellist of the Vienna Philharmonic, Friedrich Buxbaum, to show him the right fingering and in turn showed this to his friend.

As well as Karl Komzak's orchestra there were other musical events on the island of the Second District. In the First coffee-house of the Prater a military band played under the direction of Grossmann. His repertory ranged from Viennese Waltzes to Wagner. Here, on the main street of the Prater, the seventeen- or eighteen-year-old Schoenberg used to walk 'in order to hear music free', as he said himself. This information comes from another friend of his youth, David Josef Bach. He was the same age as Schoenberg, and they became friends in the summer of 1893, when they spent some weeks' holiday together in Kierling near Vienna. During this summer Schoenberg wrote his earliest song which still survives, 'In hellen Träumen hab ich dich oft geschaut', on a text of Alfred Gold. It was shown in 1924 at the Vienna Music and Theatre Festival. Schoenberg remained friend-ly with Bach when they were both emigrés. In his article 'From my Youth', which Bach contributed in 1924 to the book in celebration of Schoenberg's fiftieth birthday, he describes Schoenberg as a young student in a bright yellow, short overcoat.

There were several coffee-houses in the Second District. Bach mentioned the First one on the Prater. From other witnesses we know that the Third one was especially famous for its music. The

---

[1] Karl Komzak (1851–1905) studied at the Prague Conservatorium, and was a military bandmaster and later conductor of the Spa Band in Baden near Vienna.

English writer on music Alan Pryce-Jones speaks of the Swoboda Café, the 'Eisvogel' and also of the Third Coffee-house as the best loved musical restaurant in the Prater.

The Prater, with its noisy roundabouts, its swings, and from 1897 onwards the famous giant wheel built by an English engineer, had a magical attraction for the young intellectuals before and after the turn of the century. Among the young idlers from rich families who were attracted by this was Richard Engländer, who took the name of Peter Altenberg, and under this name wrote a new kind of short impressionistic prose pieces which are among the most original products of the Austrian literature of that time. Arthur Schnitzler, the doctor and poet, was one of the first admirers of Altenberg's gifts; Schnitzler's grandparents lived in the Carl-Theater in the Second District. In his 'Cultural History of Modern Times' Egon Friedell wrote that Peter Altenberg, in the telegraphic style of his pointillistic miniatures, created a topography of Viennese spiritual conditions about 1900, just as Schnitzler dramatized psychoanalysis and in his novels and plays captured the Vienna of the end of the century.

At that time Schoenberg knew neither Schnitzler nor Altenberg. Both were older than he was. But that was not the only thing which divided him from the two writers. Like Stefan Zweig later on they came from rich bourgeois Jewish families. Altenberg's whole existence as a loafing medical student without other practical ability, except for scrawling his prose pieces on the marble tops of coffee-house tables could only be thought of against a background of great wealth. Schnitzler was certainly not a loafer himself but he was a young man with a gilded childhood. Stefan Zweig's father was able to lead a luxurious life as a successful manufacturer. None of this was the case with the Schoenbergs. With their small shoe-shop in the Second District they never became wealthy. 'My parents' marriage seems to have been quite normal, at the worst troubled by material cares', as Schoenberg wrote later. During his whole life he was characterized by a strong need to achieve results. As soon as he began any work, he was the true son of his mother, and he said himself that he had inherited from her his feeling for duty. This work was not always of a musical or artistic nature. He had a capacity for simple manual activities.

The families of Schoenberg and Nachod, with their wide ramifications, mostly lived in the Leopoldstadt. A sister of Pauline

The ten-year-old Arnold Schoenberg with Edmund, Rudolf
and Malva Goldschmied

Schoenberg, Arnold's mother, married a Sigmund Goldschmied. Of this marriage were born three sons and a daughter. The latter, called Malvina, was born at the beginning of 1877. She seems to have been a pretty, pale and very intelligent girl. At the age of sixteen-and-a-half Arnold developed a strong affection for his cousin.

In December 1890 Samuel Schoenberg was attacked by the influenza epidemic which caused countless deaths in Vienna. By nature he was not very resistant, and suffered from emphysema, asthmatic attacks and corporeal swellings, and he died on New Year's Eve 1890/1, leaving his family in difficult circumstances. So Arnold had to leave the Realschule without completing his studies. His mother obtained for him a position as an apprentice in the Private Bank of Werner and Company, Vienna I, Wipplinger Strasse 39.

At the beginning of February Malvina Goldschmied turned fourteen. In May she travelled to Nikolsburg, a little town in southern Moravia. Her cousin Arnold remained in Vienna, loving and desiring her. On 16 May he sent her a four-page letter. He complains that she did not say goodbye to him and hopes for a regular correspondence. He praises a letter which she had sent to his mother for its excellent style, its great dexterity of form and its profusion of thoughts. He will be pleased if she feels well in Nikolsburg; however he will be still more pleased if she is bored there. He meant by that that he hoped that she was missing him.

He went on to say that he had at last begun to work in his job 'at the till', and that 'yesterday after a long period I have at last written something new – a Song without Words.' He hopes for another happy creative period. Then he asks Malvina why she does not believe in the existence of a Higher Being, and continues ironically that the blows of fate, which had caused her to give up 'these million consoling thoughts', were to be found in novels which she had read in the winter.

In the letter, which was written at half past ten in the evening, the young lover put some flowers which he had picked in the Prater on the way to the bank. The scent of the flowers was to remind her of the sound of a cheerful voice, he said. He asked her to address her answer to the bank.

Her answer disappointed him.

'*Ma chére cousine!*'

begins his letter of the 25th of May.

'*Your letter did not satisfy me in any way. You say for example that I have rejoiced too early that you are not going to amuse yourself. – Now that is a nice phrase, but badly used here. For, firstly, so far as I remember, I wrote that out of malice it would be nicer for me if you did not amuse yourself too much; secondly, I have not rejoiced at all. You go on to say that you have only disputed the amount of nonsense that is in the Bible; now I must oppose you, as an unbeliever myself, by saying that nowhere in the Bible is there any nonsense. For in it all the most difficult questions concerning Morals, Law-making, Industry and Medical Science are resolved in the most simple way, often treated from a contemporary point of view; in general the Bible really gives us the foundation of all our state institutions (except the telephone and the railway).'*

Then follows a discussion about God and Nature, and another one about right and subjective opinions. He would like to keep the basket which she had given him for more flowers. He can't understand why she doesn't want to continue the correspondence. He thinks he does not write boringly, and from their previous meetings he imagines that she does not hate him. He hopes that she will be healthy and well in Nikolsburg and change her green colour for red cheeks. Then comes the final turn:

'While waiting for an answer from you soon, I remain your cousin, Arnold Schoenberg (I. l. Y.!)'

A strange love letter, which contains no word of love and only at the end in a bracket comes the phrase which he has treated with shameful silence (I love you!) and then only in initial letters. Schoenberg added three postscripts to this letter. In the first he says that she must read his letters more attentively, in order to see that in every sentence he has something quite definite to say. 'If perhaps the surface seems smooth to you, the water is very deep and often the smoother the surface the deeper the water.' He says that he has thought out in the Prater exactly what he was going to write and would answer every point of her letter, which he now knew almost by heart. In the last postscript he says:

'For the moment I can't think any more, for it is half past eleven at night and my head is buzzing. So thank you, goodbye (as one says on the telephone) and rings off ting-a-ling-a-ling.'

On the last line to the left and right there are in brackets

'(I . . l . . . . D . .!).'

And in order to say it three times Schoenberg adds; 'Arnold Ild'. And thinking that this is not enough the original letter ends:

'I have now got a new waltz theme – A Green Bedspread – I am going to sleep soon – (I . . l . . . . D . . .!).'

This is the most curious mixture of bright intellect, lively irony and disappointed young love that one could ever think of. Schoenberg's character is shown to us clearly in this letter in many ways. In the second letter he calls himself an unbeliever; and yet survival was the foundation of nearly everything for him. He was more and more concerned with the Bible later on, especially after his experiences in the First World War. One can see that as a child and as a young man he admired it as much as he did in his very last days.

The idea of hiding deep perceptions behind simple and smooth conversational formulae also comes back in many later phases of Schoenberg's life. It was remarkable that he was shy enough to show his feelings to the girl he loved only through flowers, and another remarkable feature is the business-like final formula in the second letter which parodies Malvina's answering letter somewhat maliciously.

Malvina, called Malva for short, married Robert Bodanzky, who wrote the libretti of the operettas *Count of Luxemburg* and *Gipsy Love* for Franz Léhar and died in Berlin in 1923. She had three brothers who all made music, and Schoenberg often played music with them and visited the Goldschmied house. Her daughter, Renate Neschling-Bodanzky, wrote to me in 1972 from Rio de Janeiro that Robert Bodanzky had been a great admirer and follower of Schoenberg and had always believed in him firmly.

At the age of seventy Malva Bodanzky resumed relations with her cousin. Her letter from Rio in February 1947 describes their early relationship: 'A childhood binds us together. My shyness as a child prevented my coming nearer to you in friendship. I was not old enough for your irony even if it was "delightful" . . . Today you are a recognized genius but even as a child I believed in your greatness . . . You once tried to give me German lessons, and to help me; I asked you to do it. But my mind was so muddled up, so unfree that you gave me up then . . .'

Another small document of Schoenberg's youthful love has come down to us, a little book of verses written under a picture of fruit-bearing branches. In all naïveté it testifies to Schoenberg's poetic efforts.

Robert Bodanzky's brother Arthur was a musician. He was born in Vienna on 16 December 1877, went to the Gymnasium and the Conservatory there and became a violinist in the Court Opera Orchestra. His conducting career began in Budweis, where he conducted operettas. In 1903 he became a Chorus

Repetiteur in the Vienna Court Opera, and in 1904 he conducted operettas at the Carl Theatre and the Theater an der Wien. In 1906 he was employed by the short-lived Berlin Lortzing-Oper, and a year later he went to the German Landestheater in Prague as first Kapellmeister. In 1909 he became conductor of the Mannheim National theatre and also of the Academy concerts there and of the Musikverein. In 1915 he went to the Metropolitan Opera in New York, and died there in 1939, a famous man.

Schoenberg's sister Ottilie survived him by three years. She died on 7 December 1954 in Berlin, where she had spent much of her life. Ottilie inherited musical and vocal qualities from her mother's family. She studied singing and appeared in public on many Austrian stages in operas and operettas. In 1899 she married the Bank Director Emil Kramer, the brother of Leopold Kramer who as Director of the new German theatre in Prague carried on the great tradition of Angelo Neumann. Two children were born of the marriage in Vienna, a son in 1900 and in 1907 a daughter Susanne, who also became a singer and lives in Berlin. After her divorce from Emil Kramer, Ottilie married the writer Oskar Blumauer, who wrote stories, operetta texts and plays under the pseudonym of Oskar Felix. In a memorial broadcast on 13 September 1952 in the Berlin RIAS Station Ottilie Blumauer-Felix held a conversation with Josef Rufer in memory of her brother: 'There were three of us, Arnold was the eldest and my other brother Heinrich the youngest. Arnold and I had violin lessons very early, he was eight then and I was six. I can still remember the zeal with which he practised from the beginning and the rapid progress which he made. At the age of ten he began his first attempts at composition, and when he was twelve he wrote a waltz which he dedicated to our grandmother and called it Karoline Waltz after her.[1]

I can still see him in front of me playing it over and over again and dancing through the room at the same time. You can imagine how at the age of ten I was very proud of my brother. One day I secretly took the music of the Waltz to the well known music publisher Weinberger, who kept it to examine it. After a week I got an answer from him. The waltz was very nice, but not yet ready for publication. He said that my brother should learn studiously and come back to him later. My brother never heard this story himself.'

---

[1] Karoline Nachod, née Hutter, was Pauline Schoenberg's mother.

Schoenberg's sister's stories agree with the reminiscences which Schoenberg published in 1949 in his often quoted 'Rückblick' in the monthly musical paper *Stimmen*, edited by Josef Rufer and myself. Ottilie went on to say: 'My mother, who . . . had to look after us all was against Arnold becoming a musician and sent him to the bank as a supernumerary clerk. But already after a few months the Director sent for his mother and said that he did not know what he could do with her son, for he was covering all his papers with music. It would be best for him to become a musician. Now my mother gave in and Arnold was naturally overjoyed . . . soon we had a quartet evening every week at our house.'

Schoenberg's end of being employed at the bank has been described in various differing ways. Hans Nachod said in 1952 that one day Arnold came back home and declared to the horror of his family that he would not go back to the bank, but would become a musician. The friend of his youth, David Josef Bach, writes that the bank went bankrupt and Schoenberg was very pleased by this. Ostensibly his employment there lasted till 1895.

In 1892 the Prater, which was already a beloved visiting-place for all the Viennese, even if they lived far from the Leopoldstadt, was turned into a cultural centre for some months. At the beginning of May an International Theatre and Music Exhibition was opened, which was described by Eduard Hanslick in his autobiography *From my Life* from its beginning. It was originally planned as an exhibition in honour of the centenary of Mozart's death in July 1891, but at the wish of the Countess Metternich it was considerably enlarged. According to Hanslick's testimony it had an imposing appearance: 'In the great rotunda there was shown the history of Music and the Theatre of all nations and periods through an enormous richness of musical instruments, manuscripts, prints, illustrations and portraits . . . A pretty, large theatre was built in the Park, and national operas and comedies were played by French, Italians, Poles, Hungarians and Czechs.'

When Schoenberg was working at the bank he must have visited this exhibition and heard many performances. We know from his own mouth that he used every opportunity of listening to music. Vienna was the right place to satisfy a young man's hunger for music. Hanslick, the leading Critic of the period wrote about some of the performances during the Theatre Exhibition, for instance about Mascagni's *Cavalleria Rusticana* and Richard Strauss's symphonic poem *Don Juan*. His criticisms give a very clear picture of the events of the musical life in that year. Schoenberg probably heard the *Don Juan* performance in 1892, and in 1893 that of *Tod und Verklärung*. In the same year Brahms's Piano Pieces opus 116 to 119 were also played in Vienna. Hanslick describes them as music which in its strength and lack of compromise does not speak immediately to the listener but has more prospect of a lasting effect than in any successful fashionable compositions. These are small forms which Brahms himself called Fantasies, or simply Piano Pieces. 'A Breviary of Pessimism', says Hanslick, 'not a single joyful or cheerful piece. Almost throughout Brahms speaks a harsh and hard language here, which leads even to cutting dissonances . . . It displays the claw of the lion throughout'.

In 1894 Schoenberg wrote three piano pieces which, the friend of his youth, Bach especially mentions along with some compositions for four hands. These have been included in the collected edition of Schoenberg's works as his earliest piano pieces and bear the date 'Vienna October 1894'. The first is an Andantino in C Sharp Minor. Brahms's influence is unmistakable in this piece and also in the paradoxical notation. The theme is in 6/8 rhythm, but is notated by Schoenberg in 2/4 bars, leading to charming displacements of the rhythmical centres of gravity. The piece is 41 bars long and shows nothing special in the way of harmonic ideas.

The second piece is an 'andantino grazioso' in F Major, 72 bars long, modulating in a lively or conventional manner, with an elegant transition shortly before the reprise. The piano writing is rich, mainly homophonic and often doubled in thirds and sixths in Brahms's manner.

A brilliant Presto in A Minor ends this little group of pieces. At 101 bars long it is the largest of the three pieces, virtuoso music, beginning with chromaticism which is ornamental and applied from outside but gradually entering into the substance of the piece and leading to surprising modulations. The piece is in three parts with a middle section in E Major. The character is one of aspiration, with a triple fortissimo in a late climax, after which octaves slide down chromatically. The detailed motivic work of Schoenberg's style emerges more here than in the first two pieces.

Although the three pieces are not what Hanslick calls: 'either wildly passionate or gloomily resigned', they clearly stem from Brahms's small pieces. D. J. Bach relates that at round about this time Schoenberg was advised by Richard Heuberger to devote himself entirely to music. Heuberger also suggested to Schoenberg the writing of the four hand pieces – It was the year in which Heuberger's opera *Miriam* to a libretto by Ludwig Ganghofer was performed in Vienna.

Ottilie continues in her reminiscences: 'My brother did not want to be dependent on my mother and he took a position as a Chorus master with some workers' choral societies. There he met Zemlinsky and together with him and other young musicians founded the 'Polyhymnia' where they performed their compositions. As time went by other possibilities of work turned up, especially the orchestration of operettas. My brother did more of this later on during his first stay in Berlin, but he did begin it in Vienna. So together with Zemlinsky he undertook the orchestration of the well-known operetta *The Operaball* by Heuberger, and he wrote the score of the third act'.

The interesting news that her brother and Zemlinsky orchestrated Heuberger's *Operaball* has not been able to be confirmed or denied up till now.

Hans Nachod (1883–1966) described this year in an article in *The Listener* in 1952: 'They are almost all dead. One of the last was my cousin and dear friend Arnold Schoenberg. They are all gone. Zemlinsky, Bodanzky, Edmund Eisler, Pieau, Carl Weigl, the Jonas brothers and many others. They were rebels, attractive rebels, especially attractive to the younger generation, to which I belonged in those days, because they were unconventional in the conventional surroundings of old traditional Vienna. They used to meet in the old café Griensteidl or in the Winterbierhaus. Every night they discussed their problems until dawn and then went home drunk. One of the gayest and liveliest of the band was my cousin Arnold . . . He was a wild and energetic young man and even in his early days was already known for his witty and pert replies . . . If his musical gifts came from the Nachod family, I am certain that his genius was inherited from his father; his father was a dreamer and a thinker and a kind of anarchistic idealist.'

The most important witness of his time, Zemlinsky himself, wrote in 1934, in the book for Schoenberg's sixtieth birthday: 'It is now thirty years ago since enthusiastic music students found an amateur orchestra, proudly called it "Polyhymnia" and chose me as their conductor . . . We were all young and hungry for music and made music as well as we could every week . . . At the only cello desk sat a young man who handled his instrument both

A cheerful quintet during the period 1895–1898 in Vienna. The celloist is Schoenberg, the violinist with moustache Fritz Kreisler fierily and wrongly (in any case the instrument deserved nothing better – it had been bought by its player for a thriftily saved three gulden in the so-called Tändelmarkt in Vienna) and this cello player was Arnold Schoenberg. At that time Schoenberg had a modest job in a bank, but did not make much use of his profession and preferred his musical notes to the notes in his bank. This was how I met Schoenberg . . .' Among compositions of this time Zemlinsky mentions from memory violin sonatas, duets, choruses, songs and a string quartet influenced by Brahms. As a member of the Committee of the Vienna Society of Musicians he recommended this quartet for performance. From the records of the Society of Musicians from 1897/98 it has been discovered that the performance took place on 17 March 1898.

The names in Hans Nachod's article are mostly known. Edmund Eisler, who later called himself Eysler, was the same age as Schoenberg, studied at the Vienna Conservatorium and started with operas and a ballet before he turned to operetta. *Bruder Straubinger*, with its famous song 'Küssen ist keine Sünd' (Kissing is not a sin), began his important career, which ended in 1927 with the *Gold'ne Meisterin*.

Carl Weigl, born in 1881, was also a composer, a student at the Conservatorium and the University and later a private pupil of Zemlinsky's. He achieved fame as a theoretician, left Austria in 1938 and died in New York in 1949 – From the Jonas family came the pianist Etta Jonas-Werndorff, who gave the first performance of Schoenberg's opus 2 in 1910 in Vienna.

Through Zemlinsky Schoenberg got to know Wagner's works. Later he told his American pupil and biographer Dika Newlin that at the age of twenty-five he had already heard all the Wagner operas twenty or thirty times. As he came under Zemlinsky's influence in 1893, in the years up till 1899 he must have seen twenty or thirty performances of *The Ring* cycle, *Tristan*, *Meistersinger*, *Parsifal* and probably other works of Wagner as well. That makes two hundred evenings at the opera! An astonishing figure, which, however, seems believable if one recognizes in Schoenberg's works of that time the flame with which Wagner's harmonic and melodic formations burnt away earlier forms and procedures.

In the D Major string quartet the spirit of Brahms is still predominant. This work, completed in 1897 in Vienna, is in four movements and is devoid of chromaticism and rhetoric. One can hardly doubt that Schoenberg carried on an inner battle against Wagner's influence for years, and never really got rid of it. His inner development between 1894 and 1899 was one of the most dramatic times in Schoenberg's life. Not only because he made friendships with men at that time who remained linked with him and influenced his spiritual position: also because his horizon was broadened in all artistic matters and in conditions of life and because spiritual worlds were opened to him which had a fruitful influence on his thinking and creativity for all time.

An undated 'Report of the Schoenberg Family about their Life during and immediately before the War', in which Franz Werfel's death on 26 August 1945 is mentioned as having happened a few months earlier, states that, 'about 1898' Schoenberg played string quartets with Arthur Bodanzky, Hugo Riesenfeld and Edward Falck, 'several times a week, each time for five to seven hours.'

In these years his position with regard to religion also changed. Schoenberg's education by his pious Jewish mother on the one hand and his free-thinking father on the other had taught him to regard these questions from a dialectical point of view. He knew the arguments of both parties. In his letter to his cousin Malvina Goldschmied in 1891 he called himself an unbeliever: but at the same time he defended the Bible. Among the friends of his youth was Walter Pieau, mentioned by Hans Nachod; he was an opera singer who also took part in the concerts of the Ansorge-Vorein in 1907 and sang songs by Zemlinsky and Schoenberg. Pieau was a Protestant. Under his influence Schoenberg seems to have obtained a thorough knowledge of the Christian religion and its evangelical faith. Biographies of Schoenberg have said that he left the Jewish community somewhere between his seventeenth and twenty-first year. In fact he freed himself from the beliefs of his fathers on 21 March 1898, as is shown by an entry in the registry of the Vienna community. Four days later he was baptized. The entry in the church book of the Protestant Doro-theer Community (Augsburger Konfession), Vienna I, Doro-theergasse 18, runs: 'Arnold Franz Walter Schoenberg, Vienna II, Leopoldgasse 9. Baptism 25 March 1898: Priest Alfred For-mey, Godfather Walter Pieau, Opera singer, Vienna I, Bauern-markt 3.'

Little is known about Schoenberg's work with the Workers' Choruses. It is only certain that he did conduct choral societies in Mödling and Meidling. He himself said that at that time he had a great sympathy for the political aims of the Workers' movement. His singers called him 'Comrade'. However, he does not seem ever to have written any compositions for these choruses or in the spirit of the Socialist movement.

His spiritual situation at that time can be interpreted by two things. One is the kind of literary models which he chose for his vocal music and which also had a formative effect on his instrumental music in part. The other is his musical language itself, in its harmonic, melodic and rhythmical nature, which was subjected to quite definite tendencies of which the main one could only be discovered afterwards.

The first songs that we know of use traditional texts such as the 'Schilflied' of Lenau, written in 1893, or poems of authors like Alfred Gold and Ludwig Pfau. Schoenberg's first meeting with an important literary contemporary came through the poems of Richard Dehmel. This North German poet, eleven years older than Schoenberg, was one of the most fascinating and influential phenomena of German literature in the 1890s. His view of the world, rich in tensions and contradictions, came from the philosophy of Friedrich Nietzsche, whose concepts of the superman Dehmel accepted, without, however, overlooking the fact that it could not be combined with the Socialist ideas of the industrial age. Dehmel was as much influenced by the conditions of modern society as by Nietzsche's Superman. His ecstatic spirit, which psychologists try to explain by hereditary epilepsy, gave him a lyrical style of expression, of concise diction and of irregular metres which influenced a whole generation. Dehmel had a large and important circle of friends, which included men like August Strindberg and his neighbour Detlev von Liliencron, who was later to be his neighbour at Blankenese, as well as Otto Erich Hartleben and Gustav Mahler, who was very much admired by Dehmel. In the eighties and nineties the growing spread of workers' poetry found in Dehmel a leader of genius who understood the tension of modern society extremely well. He struggled for an art and a literature which could be understood by everybody and he believed that he could overcome the creative loneliness which affected most of the great poets by devotion to humanity.

One of the most important driving forces in his work was love, the relations between man and woman, which he had tried to demythologize and found formulae for it which shocked the prudish nineteenth century. He was an unashamed advocate of naturalistic functions, no less than Gerhart Hauptmann, who

Two songs by Ludwig Pfau set to music by Arnold Schoenberg.
'Fraulein Gisela Cohn for 11 September 1895.'
Opening of the first song (Autograph)

was slightly older, or the group of North German writers which included Johannes Schlaf and the brothers Hart. The most important elements in his poems are problems of workers' marriages, free love and so-called erotic companionship. Dehmel was a passionate yes-sayer, an enlightened man trained in socialism who also published metaphysical and religious ideas with increasing maturity.

In 1896 his collection of poems, *Woman and World*, was published and aroused excitement and passionate opposition in the whole German-speaking world. Even the censors took notice of some of the poems in this volume which they found offensive, until the poet was rehabilitated after long-drawn out lawsuits. This collection was followed in 1903 by a verse novel *Two People*, which soon became famous.

Schoenberg seems to have got to know *Woman and World* soon after it was published, and he was influenced by Dehmel from 1897 onwards. His first Dehmel song, 'Mädchenfrühling', was written on 15 September of that year. At the same time he was writing traditional kinds of orchestral and chamber music – Gavotte and Musette for String Orchestra in March with the title 'In the old style' and in the summer a Scherzo and Trio for string quartet, followed in October by the D Major Quartet.

In 1898 his musical horizon broadened. In July he wrote a fragment of a symphonic poem *Frühlingstod* (Death of Spring) after a poem of Lenau for large orchestra. This shows for the first time his leaving Brahms's path of absolute music and turning to the New German ideals of descriptive, symphonic music after literary models. The inner conflict between the apparently inimical worlds of Wagner and Brahms had begun; this lasted until after Brahms's death in 1897. Soon Schoenberg had composed the first songs which he considered worthy of publication; he gave them to the Berlin Drei-Lilien-Verlag with the opus numbers 1 to 3, and they published them in 1904. Two songs for baritone and piano, dedicated like all Schoenberg's early works to his friend Zemlinsky, are undated. But a Viennese singer, Professor Eduard Gärtner, sang them in 1898 in a recital. The poems are by Karl von Levetzow whom we shall meet again in the surroundings of Wolzogen's Überbrettl. The titles are 'Dank' and 'Abschied'. The verses move in a somewhat elocutory emotional language which is nearer to Wagner's sphere than the poems set by Brahms. However, Brahms dominates the musical setting. Rich chords, parallel thirds and sixths, and heavy bass octaves all appear. But there are new methods as well. The sound of the piano is broadened in an orchestral manner; before the powerful end of the first song tremolos appear in both hands, as if in a piano score of a string work. Chromatic alterations in the chords show Wagner's influence. Many details anticipate the language of the 'Gurrelieder' which Schoenberg began two years later. The dynamic range in both songs is remarkable, and in 'Abschied' between bars 21 and 24 it goes from *ppp* to *ff*. The marks of expression also show the passionate character of both these extensive songs; 'working up, broad, holding back, with passionate movement, very broad with great expression.'

In 1899 Schoenberg found a text of Hugo von Hofmannsthal, who was the same age as himself; he set it without writing down the title. A remarkable thing about the piece is the expression marked 'less sung than declaimed, to be performed in a descriptive manner like reading about an old picture.'

Perhaps we can find here the kernel of the recitations which appear again and again in Schoenberg's work from the 'Gurrelieder' right up until the last unfinished modern Psalm of 1950.

Until his meeting with Zemlinsky Schoenberg had no technical or theoretical education. As he tells us himself, he looked up in the encyclopaedia in his parents' bookcase musical terms like 'sonata movement' and suchlike and formed his own conceptions according to the explanations of them given there. This was changed when Zemlinsky began to give him instruction in all theoretical questions. 'Zemlinsky is the person whom I thank for practically all my knowledge of technique and the problems of composition', Schoenberg said in 1949. Literary sources also gave him equally important impressions. When in December 1912 Dehmel thanked Schoenberg for the impression which his *Verklärte Nacht* had made on him, Schoenberg answered in a long letter full of veneration:

'Your poems had a decisive influence on my musical development. They made me look for a new note in lyrical poetry for the first time. That means I found this without looking for it, when I mirrored in my music what your verses aroused in me. People who know my music will be able to tell you that in my first attempts to set your poems more remains of what was to develop in me later than in many much later works.'

Among the Dehmel songs of opus 2 and 3, 'Warnung' is dated 17 May 1899. The song is marked: 'Quick, with restrained vehemence,' and is one of the most typical of Schoenberg's early works. For the first time we find an aggressive passion which sticks at nothing, which is as characteristic of Dehmel's poetic attitude as that of the spiritual condition of the twenty-five-year-old musician, who set this verse to music.

> *My dog has merely snarled at you,*
> *And I have poisoned him;*
> *And I hate every person,*
> *Who causes disunion.*

That is the exposition; concise, sparing, and emotional. Schoenberg's song is written in B Flat Minor in 6/8 tempo. The first two bars in quick tempo modulate like lightning from E Flat Minor through B Flat Minor and F Minor to C Minor. In falling fourths the harmonies twist in a paradoxical manner from one dominant to another. E Flat–B Flat–F–C – that is a pile of falling fourths which anticipates by years what Schoenberg carried out in a radical manner in 1906 in his first chamber symphony. It is a precedent which causes the scaffolding of conventional tonality to totter. And the piano writing, with its big melodic lines in the right hand and the short rhythmical figures in semi-quavers in the left, with the voice coming in later with only two intervals, a semitone and a fourth, anticipates methods which Schoenberg later used consciously. This makes us understand what Schoenberg means in his letter sent to Dehmel in 1912.

After the exposition the lyrical middle section of the poem begins no less passionately than the first section.

> *I send you two blood-red carnations, my blood, you,*
> *With a bud on one of them; be good to the three, you,*
> *Till I come – I come again tonight, be alone, be alone, you!*

The music at once takes up the change to a lyrical tone. The rhythm remains the same, but the upper part shows an intimate melodic character, which suddenly sounds like a scene from Wagner's *Tristan and Isolde*. The middle and bass lines are strongly chromatic; the key remains B Flat Major, until in the 19th bar an unexpected modulation leads back to the beginning of the song. Dehmel's poem ends with a brutal warning:

> *You; think of my dog!*

There Schoenberg finds a synthesis. Brahms's law of motivic unity and the development of various themes from small intervals and small rhythms remains in force. At the same time the expressive capacity of the harmony is broadened under the influence of Wagner. The chromaticism of *Tristan* is married to the classic symphonic procedure which Brahms had brought into the field of song.

1899 was also important for Schoenberg's personal life. His sister Ottilie left her parents' house to marry the Bank Director Emil Kramer. Schoenberg's friendship with Zemlinsky became closer. They spent the summer months together in Payerbach near Semmering. And here Schoenberg's relations with Zemlinsky's sister Mathilde began. All the erotic glow expressed in the Dehmel songs of this year can be traced back to this great passion, and to Schoenberg's connection with this clever woman who was highly educated musically and an excellent pianist, the sister of the man from whom Schoenberg had received the only methodical instruction in composition in his life. As with Robert Schumann, so with Schoenberg this great love experience increased his creativity. In the songs of 1899, especially in 'Erwartung' which was written on 9 August, there are harmonic discoveries which lead into the as yet unknown territory of polytonality and atonality.

According to Egon Wellesz Schoenberg wrote the string sextet *Verklärte Nacht* in Payerbach in three weeks; it bears the termination date of 1 December. This work too is remarkable in the double sense of being a new orientation of literature and ethics and a changed idea of musical form. Dehmel's poem from *Woman and World*, which is the basis of the work, describes the conversation of a lover with a girl who is bearing a child by another man. It is a characteristic Dehmel subject, full of the expression of a new, anti-bourgeois morality, and carried along entirely by the idea of love which overcomes everything and sweeps all conventions aside.

The musical style and form of the sextet belongs to the field of programme music, i.e. music which seeks to describe the musical events in sound. But while the followers of Franz Liszt and the new German school wrote their symphonic poems for a large orchestra, as for instance Richard Strauss's *Don Juan, Tod und Verklärung, Till Eulenspiegel* and *Also sprach Zarathustra*, Schoenberg, like Smetana before him, applied the descriptive principle to chamber music for an ensemble of six strings. Anton Webern not only spoke of the unusual independence of this step, leading to programmatic chamber music, but also excitedly praised the richness of themes, the free architecture and the novelty of the melodic and harmonic events. *Verklärte Nacht*, opus 4 in the list of Schoenberg's works, was first performed on 18 March 1902 in

Verklärte Nacht, op. 4. First page of the score of the original version for the string sextet (Autograph)

Vienna by the Rosé Quartet with extra players. Dehmel heard a performance in Hamburg in 1912 with the violinist Heinrich Bandler, and wrote Schoenberg the letter of thanks mentioned above.

When Schoenberg ended his employment at the bank he had to earn his living by musical work. His work with the choruses he found pleasant and it brought him some good personal contacts. The only snag was that he could not play the piano and he therefore had to use the services of a friendly pianist for the preparation of rehearsals from time to time. Zemlinsky gave him advice about conducting at that time and remained in every respect his reliable adviser and helper. The friendship between the two musicians, which became deeper through Schoenberg's love for Zemlinsky's sister Mathilde, continued for years. But the two men were quite different in their relations to their art. Zemlinsky was a practical musician and had prepared his conducting career with basic technical studies, also remaining bound up with the theatre. He was born in 1871 in the same Second District of Vienna and was only three years older than Schoenberg. Schoenberg, though self-taught and never good in practical musical activity, was superior to his friend in quick appreciation and following the consequences of artistic ideas. This difference between them helped them to enjoy a mutual fruitfulness and effort, which continued until Schoenberg began to draw more radical consequences from his experiences in composition. These were in 1908 in works outside the bounds of tonality and in 1921 with his 'new order', the twelve-note technique. As a composer Zemlinsky was one of the most peculiar musicians of his generation in Austria. In 1897 he wrote an opera *Zarema*, for which Schoenberg made the piano score. Although the work was awarded the Luitpold Prize, its first performance in Munich in 1908 had no success. In 1900 Gustav Mahler put on Zemlinsky's second opera *Es war einmal* at the Vienna Court Opera. The text was based on a story of Hans Andersen and written by the Danish poet Holger Drachmann, an interesting and original Scandinavian writer, who in his novel *Forskrevet* put forward ideas which were later used by Ernst von Wolzogen in his Überbrettl.

It was clear that in *Verklärte Nacht* Schoenberg was developing as a follower of Wagner under the influence of Strauss. In March 1900 he began working on one of the largest works that he ever wrote, the *Gurrelieder*. Alban Berg says in his guide to the work that Schoenberg told him that the dates of composition were between

March 1900 and March 1901. The orchestration was begun in
August 1901, still in Vienna, and was continued in the middle of
1902 in Berlin; in 1903 it was interrupted and given up entirely
for the moment. But in Vienna in July 1910 Schoenberg resumed
working on the score, and finished it in 1911 in Berlin–Zehlendorf
right up to the final chorus. The latter was in the form of a
sketch of the most important voice-parts and the whole form; it
merely needed to be written out in full score. The poems are by
Jens Peter Jacobsen.

The *Gurrelieder* were written for an enormous ensemble. The
work demands a solo soprano for Tove, a solo mezzo-soprano for
the Wood-Dove, two tenors for Waldemar and Klaus the Fool,
a solo bass for the peasant and a speaker for the recitation in the
third part. Waldemar's men are sung by three four-part male
choruses and an eight-part mixed chorus. The orchestra consists
of eight flutes (four of them also play piccolo), five oboes (two of
them also play English horn), seven clarinets in A (three of them
also in B flat, two in E flat and two bass clarinets in B flat), three
bassoons and two contra-bassoons. The brass section contains ten
horns in F (four also play Wagner tubas), six trumpets in F, B
flat and C, a bass trumpet in E flat, an alto trombone, four
tenor-bass trombones, a bass trombone in E flat, a double bass
trombone and a double bass tuba. New tone colours are found in
the percussion. This consists of six timpani, a large tenor drum,
cymbals, triangle, glockenspiel, side drum, bass drum, xylophone,
rattle, some large iron chains and a tam-tam. In addition there
are four harps, celesta and an enormous string orchestra, in which
the first and second violins are each divided into ten parts and the
violas and cellos into eight parts each. A comparable number of
double basses are also required.

Schoenberg's life made it necessary for this composition to be
continually interrupted by bread-and-butter jobs, and it was not
finished until 1911. However the work was substantially complete
in 1901. An event in the early summer of 1900 shows how strongly
the supposedly 'abstract constructionist' Schoenberg was inspired in his work by live impressions. In Mödling a concert was
given by a workers' chorus conducted by Schoenberg. As usual
there was a celebration afterwards, at which the company drank
wine until dawn. And in the first light of a beautiful summer
morning they decided to climb the Anningerberg in order to see
the sun rise from there. The impression must have been marvellous for all those who took part. It made such a strong effect on

Schoenberg that the vision of a sunrise scene at the end of the *Gurrelieder* was inspired by it.

Other compositions of the year 1900 were understandably few. In August Schoenberg wrote a song *Gruss in die Ferne* on the text of Hermann Lingg, and at Christmas a fragment of a piano piece. Portions of literary texts from this time of the turn of the century have also been preserved.

At Advent Schoenberg was sent a copy of the *Deutsche Chansons* which had already appeared in Berlin; they were a collection of Brettl songs, and he set several of these in the course of the next year. These will be discussed later.

In June and July 1901 Schoenberg wrote an opera text *Die Schildbürger* after a story in Gustav Schwab's *Die deutschen Volksbücher*; only two acts of this have been preserved.

On 7 October Schoenberg's marriage to Mathilde von Zemlinsky was solemnized in the church of the Dorotheer Community.

Two young musicians whom Schoenberg met in the 1890s later became world-famous: Fritz Kreisler and Artur Schnabel. Kreisler was the older; born in Vienna in 1875, he showed his gifts as a violinist early on. After a limited education he appeared as a prodigy and in 1890, when he was only fifteen, he did his first tour of the United States. Kreisler was not only one of the greatest violinists of his age but also a considerable composer in a conservative style. In 1894 he wrote two cadenzas for Beethoven's Violin Concerto which were often played by him and became famous. At that time he became friendly with Schoenberg. His biographer Louis P. Lochner quotes what he said about Schoenberg: 'In no way was he the revolutionary of his later years. He was very interested in my Beethoven cadenzas and especially admired my fugal combination of several themes. At this time he was also a convinced follower of Wagner.' In his book on Kreisler Lochner published a photo of a comic Tyrolese band in which Kreisler can be seen as violinist and Schoenberg as cellist; this picture must have been taken between 1895 and 1898.

Artur Schnabel, born in Lipnik in 1882, had been living with his parents in Vienna since 1888, at first modestly in the Grossen Schiffgasse, later in the Herminengasse in the Leopoldstadt, near the Danube Canal like Schoenberg. Among his student companions were Eugen d'Albert, Teresa Carreno and Ossip Gabrilowitsch. They went to the Philharmonic concerts conducted by Hans Richter, heard Brahms conduct his Academic Festival Overture and stood in the queues for the opera box-office. César Saerchinger writes about this in his biography of Schnabel in 1957: 'A visit to the opera – that means to an unreserved seat in the gods – took at least eight hours. The young enthusiasts stood from three in the afternoon until seven, when the doors were opened. Then followed a wild rush up four staircases and a *mêlée* to get the best seats. This standing in a queue for hours was a community event where the young hopefuls met each other and exchanged ideas. Among other later colleagues Schnabel met Arnold Schoenberg here, and Schoenberg often chased him up the stairs.' Schnabel also shared with Schoenberg an enthusiasm for the new opera director Gustav Mahler, who was the idol of the progressive youth in Vienna. In 1900 Schnabel moved from Vienna to Berlin, but does not seem to have seen Schoenberg when the latter lived there from 1901 till 1903. The two great musicians came together again in 1912. Schnabel was immediately impressed by Schoenberg's piano pieces opus 11 and his orchestral pieces opus 16. He seems also to have helped Schoenberg financially in 1913. The conversations between the two of them often lasted till late into the night. Saerchinger writes that these did not only rob the busy pianist of his sleep but they also seriously disquieted his spiritual peace of mind. In his teaching he discussed Schoenberg's piano music; but he never played it in public.

SCHOENBERG AT THE ÜBERBRETTL

During the German romantic period the difference between serious and popular art had reached an unbridgeable gap. The elevated nature of the artistic profession, according to the concepts of that time, would not endure any mixing in the spheres which served to entertain wider sections of the public. Opera and operettas were regarded as being in different categories, and were served by completely independent theatres. There was no common ground between Offenbach and Wagner. The followers of serious art looked upon her lighter sister with disdainful contempt, and were parodied by the latter for the solemnity of their tragic art.

The first notable reaction against this position took place in Paris in the eighties and nineties. In 1881 Rodolphe Salis, who was actually Baron de la Tour de Neintre, founded the Chat Noir in Montmartre. It was a literary cabaret. Those who took part in in it were well-known writers and painters and the audience were not so much men of the world as intellectuals. A few years later the Auberge du Clou was opened as a rival to the Chat Noir, and a series of other enterprises followed soon, in the wake of the extraordinary success of this newly discovered genre. Among the stars of these ambitious small literary theatres was the actress Yvette Guilbert, whose portrait was painted by many famous artists from Toulouse-Lautrec to Kokoschka. After 1900 she made frequent guest appearances in Berlin as well as other German cities.

The idea of the literary cabaret was soon followed up in European literature. In 1890 the Norwegian writer Holger Drachmann published his novel *Forskrevet* in which he advocated the popularization of literature. In 1897 the poet and writer Otto Julius Bierbaum made a cabaret artist of the Parisian type the principal character in his novel *Stilpe*. In Berlin these tendencies from the socialist point of view, fitted in with the efforts to create an artistic education of the people. About 1899 the concept of a reform of the Tingel-Tangel began. The dangerous trend of variety and cabaret to grow shallow and lose their blood streams aroused opposing tendencies. The great poet Richard Dehmel wanted the 'strong demand of the people for the theatre' to be ennobled, in order 'to develop from the raw pleasures of the senses of modern theatrical tricks a unity which was more refined spiritually, broader in outlook, and something which could be taken seriously artistically.'

In Munich too in the nineties a group of writers had come together with similar aims. Among them were Frank Wedekind and Baron Ernst von Wolzogen, whom we know as a friend and the librettist of Richard Strauss for his opera *Feuersnot*. He was a restless man who spent much time travelling; he was also extremely productive and extraordinarily good at organization. After some disappointments he left Munich in the winter of 1899–1900 in order to find fertile soil for his cabaret plans in Berlin. On a journey to Paris in the summer of 1900 he studied the Chat Noir and the Grand Guignol on the spot; and from this he developed his own ideas further. In Berlin, from quite another quarter, these had been prepared for by the 'Galgenbergbund' of Christian Morgenstern, the writer of the 'Galgenlieder' (Gallows Songs). The ideas of the Munich Academic-Dramatic Society had found supporters in the capital. An article 'Style in Variety' by Oskar Panizza was much discussed here, and the Munich paper *Simplicissimus* was eagerly read.

In the slim volume of poetry *Deutsche Chansons*, which appeared in the autumn of 1900 and went through many editions in a short time, one can find the names of the young writers who believed in the new literary cabaret. These were Bierbaum, Dehmel, Gustav Falke, Ludwig Finckh, Alfred Walter Heymel, Arno Holz, Detlev von Liliencron, Rudolf Alexander Schröder, Wedekind and Wolzogen.

The actress Hedda Somin, who at that time was known as Käthe Kruse and had worked out a very popular type of puppet theatre, said about the countless discussions in the Berlin literary cafés, especially in the Café des Westens; 'For long weeks and months every evening hopes were demolished if the patrons were suddenly worried about the viability of the enterprise and went back on previous commitments . . . Utopia became a reality. In the Café Grössenwahn contracts were signed and all business was concluded. And with the opening of the Überbrettl a joyful wind was felt throughout Berlin.'

Early in 1901 a house became free in the Alexanderplatz which Wolzogen described as 'a superior theatrical barn and extremely practical from the point of stage and wardrobe . . . it was handed over to me cheaply by the direction of the Sezession stage which at that time had its home there.' The rehearsals took place in Wolzogen's house in the Burggrafenstrasse. The première was on 18 January 1901. It was an enormous success. The noble founder of this 'Überbrettl', Wolzogen, went on to the stage in a blue tail coat and grey trousers and greeted his guests as 'My noble lords'. Some poets read their own poems. Christian Morgernstern got the audience on his side with a parody of d'Annunzio and after that amused his listeners with a parody of an imaginary criticism by Alfred Kerr of the evening which they were attending at that moment. Poems by Liliencron were applauded, and the chief success was Bierbaum's scene 'The Happy Bride-groom' set by Oskar Straus; this had to be repeated three times. The Überbrettl had started with a hit and was sold out for weeks in advance.

At Easter the company went on tour, and the Berlin success was repeated in Hamburg, Leipzig, Dresden, Vienna, Prague and Breslau. Meanwhile Wolzogen's well-born child had sired children of its own. In April a cabaret 'Schall und Rauch' (Sound and Smoke) was opened in Berlin. In Munich the modern writers had come together as 'Elf Scharfrichter' (Eleven Execu-tioners). While part of the ensemble was on tour the Überbrettl continued to play on the temporary stage on the Alexanderplatz. As a replacement for Wolzogen the writer Hanns Heinz Ewers took over as director. Later he made himself independent with his own ensemble, while the Berlin group continued to work under the direction of Count Karl Michael von Levetzow.

Meanwhile Wolzogen had developed more ambitious plans. He wanted to have his own house, and fate helped him because a rival company settled in the old Spiellokal on 1 September 1901. So the Überbrettl went on its second tour which again led to Vienna. On 23 September an event happened which Wolzogen wrote about twenty years later in his book of memoirs *Wie ich mich ums Leben brachte*. 'The Jewish Day of Atonement fell during the time that we were doing guest performances at the Karl-theater in Vienna and Oskar Straus was not able to appear on the evening of this day by the command of his rich uncle. As a replacement for this evening he brought me a young musician of small stature, strong features and dark hair, whose name,

Arnold Schoenberg, at that time was completely unknown. As a proof of his talents he played me some little songs, including a charming setting of Falke's poem 'Rechts Luischen, links Marie und voran die Musici', which I immediately took for my Überbrettl.'

The Carltheater was built on a site of an old baroque theatre in the Leopoldstadt. At the beginning of the nineteenth century it enjoyed the reputation of being a meeting-place for whores and was also in a scandalous condition from the structural point of view, when the director Carl Carl took it over and had it rebuilt. It was opened in 1847 on 10 December with Johann Nestroy's extravaganza *Die schlimmen Buben* and it was carried on by Carl until his death in 1854 with the greatest success. It catered exclusively for light music and, next to the Theater an der Wien, was the place where modern Austrian operettas were presented. In 1858 with the *Hochzeit beim Laternenschein* the era of the great German-speaking success of Offenbach began. Johann Strauss brought out one of his many stage pieces, *Prinz Methusalem* in 1873, without, however, repeating the success of *Fledermaus.* Early in 1883 Gustav Mahler, whose contract as the conductor of the theatre in Olmütz had ended, looked for work in Vienna. He found it for two months at the Karltheater where he rehearsed the choruses for a touring Italian opera company. In May he signed a contract with the Kassel Opera House as Musical Director.

At the end of the century the theatre began a new lease of life. In December *Wiener Blut* (Vienna Blood) by Johann Strauss, who had died in May 1899 leaving it unfinished, was given its first performance. In 1900 Alexander von Zemlinsky took over the musical direction for six years. During this period Oscar Straus's *Die Lustigen Nibelungen* (November 1904) and *Hugdietrichs Brautfahrt* (March 1906) were performed. The *Lustigen Nibelungen* is a piece in the spirit of the Wolzogen Überbrettl. The text was written by Rideamus, a pseudonym for Fritz Oliven, a successful writer of comedies and revues who lived in Berlin.

In 1907 Straus had a considerable international success with his *Waltz Dream* shortly after Zemlinsky had gone to the Volksoper. Two other operas by him, *Die kleine Freundin* (1911) and *Die schöne Unbekannte* (1915) were also performed at the Karltheater.

While Zemlinsky was still director Edmund Eysler had successes in this theatre in the Leopoldstadt with *Schützenliesel* (1905) and *Künsterblut* (1906), though they did not achieve the triumph of *Bruder Straubinger*, which was given its first performance in 1903.

Both Straus, who lived from 1870 to 1954, and Eysler, who was the same age as Schoenberg and died in Vienna in 1949, were professionally trained musicians. Straus had studied in Vienna with Hermann Grädener and in Berlin with Max Bruch. Eysler had studied at the Vienna Conservatorium with Robert Fuchs. Both began as composers of opera and chamber music and then turned to the lighter medium. They belonged to the circle of the young artists of the Second District of Vienna who carried on conversations in coffee-houses with Schoenberg and Zemlinsky.

Besides Straus and Schoenberg Wolzogen had as his collaborators two musicians who had changed over from other activities and then made a transitory success in good light entertainment music. One was Waldemar Wendland, born in 1873 in Liegnitz, who gave up his medical studies to enter a bank. He was self-taught musically, and was taken on as a pupil by Engelbert Humperdinck, to whom he had been recommended by Ernst von Schuch. He was Wolzogen's conductor and later worked in opera houses. His wife was the writer Olga Wohlbrück. He died in 1947 in Zeitz. The other musician, Bogumil Zepler, came from Breslau, changed from architecture to medicine, and in 1886, after becoming a Doctor of Medicine was a composition pupil of Heinrich Urban's in Berlin. After a parody of Mascagni's *Cavalleria Berolina* (1891), the one-act comic opera *Der Brautmarkt zu Hira* (1892 Krolloper Berlin) and the comic opera *Der Vicomte von Letorière* (Hamburg 1899) he turned to cabaret and operetta. Schoenberg met him in Wolzogen's company and orchestrated several works of his. A 'Girl's song' for three women's voices by Zepler is preserved in Schoenberg's orchestration in the Library of Congress in Washington and bears the date 21 April 1902. The opera *Diogenes*, written in the same year, was also orchestrated by Schoenberg. Together with Ernst von Wolzogen Zepler wrote a Singspiel *Die Bäder von Lucca* (after Heinrich Heine's Travel Pictures) for Wolzogen's attempt to found a Berlin comic opera in 1905 which quickly came to grief. It had indeed forty-nine successful performances but could not prevent the ruin of this ambitious enterprise. The idea of this comic opera was taken over from the season of 1905/6 onwards with the greatest success by Hans Gregor, who continued it for six years. It showed a broadening of the idea of offering entertaining art on a high technical level which was also tasteful. In this it embodied the success of the Überbrettl.

Zepler, who was one of Schoenberg's most important employers in 1902/3, died in 1918 in Krummhübel. Of the six thousand pages of score which Schoenberg had to write about the turn of the century when commissioned by other musicians in order to earn his living, a large part is based on music by Zepler. The manuscripts have mostly disappeared, including one which we know of from a printed copy printed by the Dreililienverlag. It is the instrumentation of one of the very successful songs of Heinrich von Eyken, *Lied der Walküre*. The copy found in Schoenberg's library carries the handwritten remark 'Orchestrated at the request of the Dreililienverlag! Arnold Schoenberg'. The Dreililienverlag published Schoenberg's first works, the songs opus 1, 2, 3 and 6, the strong sextet *Verklärte Nacht*, the symphonic poem *Pelleas und Melisande* and the First String Quartet, opus 7.

As we know from his own writings, Wolzogen was an aristocrat who kept all the prejudices of his class against Jews, but after the manner of the old German nationalists made a distinction between those whom he called Jewish business people and those whom he called Jews of talent. So in his Überbrettl theatre he surrounded himself with poets and composers many of whom were Jews. In his own formulation, which can be read in the symposium *Ansichten und Aussichten* (1908), he wrote: 'I indeed wanted to teach the German bear to dance, and without pain, for its own pleasure – so I could not use the old cruel method of putting this bear on a hot grill, but I preferred to use the mild and as it were proven method of education by arousing its ambition of imitation by presenting other animals which by nature are able to dance.' Later Wolzogen became a propagandist for a Nordic German spirit, which brought untold misery into this world, and after the First War he was one of those who prepared the way for National Socialism. But his important function as a stimulator of the German cultural life at the beginning of the nineteenth century is not lessened thereby.

Oscar Straus was one of his first and best known collaborators and long before he became famous in 1907 through the *Waltz Dream* he laid the foundations of the sensational success of the première of the Überbrettl. Wolzogen, who later attacked him as an intolerable and quarrelsome collaborator, was one of the first to recognize his gifts. The dance duet 'The Happy Bridegroom' was published in the theatrical library of Eduard Bloch and apart from Straus's music gives 'Dance directions to Bierbaum's Verses', which correspond to the first performance given by the dancer Koppell and the young star of the Überbrettl, the dancer and singer Bozena Bradsky. 'The Dance', it says, 'is performed by a couple not as a social dance but as an exhibition on festive occasions. Because of the text, which has to be sung simultaneously, and because of the elegant tenderness of the dancing couple the dance is suitable for performance at weddings. Its entire character demands that during the whole performance the dancing couple look at each other's face with blushing tenderness.'

From these directions we can see how Wolzogen's Überbrettl looked in practice. 'The Happy Bridegroom', to which Oscar Straus gave the opus number 61, was written with piano accompaniment. The cover was drawn by Edmund Edel, an artist very popular at that time, and together with the fashionable garlands of Art Nouveau it shows on the back cover the characteristic picture of the Clown, laughing in a melancholy manner and playing a guitar. Other Überbrettl songs are mentioned there, 'Die Haselnuss' and 'Der Starr' by Straus, and by James Rothstein, another of Wolzogen's composers, 'Madame Adele' after a 'Poem' by Wolzogen, 'Die Spinne im Wald' (Wilhelm Schulz), 'Das Lied von den lieben, süssen Mädeln' (Wolzogen) and 'Der schöne Alfred'. What is remarkable about this last piece is that the poem was written by Rudolf Alexander Schröder, who later made marvellous translations from Greek and Latin and was a staunch Protestant Christian.

How Oscar Straus and Schoenberg met each other and in what year we do not know. However Straus was Viennese like Schoenberg, and his house in the Untere Augartenstrasse 27 in the Second District was not far from Schoenberg's birthplace in the Obere Donaustrasse. As Straus had professional connections with the Karltheater, with which Alexander von Zemlinsky was also connected, the two men could have met some time earlier. Among his acquaintances in the intellectual cafés Schoenberg had many representatives of light music. All through his life he retained a certain love for the classical Viennese operetta; he was glad to hear good performances of works by Franz Lehar and transmitted this taste to some of his pupils. In contrast to Anton von Webern, who hated any kind of entertainment music.[1] Alban Berg was very interested in it. He wrote in a letter to his wife Helene about a performance of the *Waltz Dream,* and added that

---

[1] But Webern conducted waltzes by Johann Strauss in his concert tours in Germany and England in the early 1930s, and he also admired Lortzing. H. S.

the work pleased him. From this unusual cross-connection there resulted an addition which he himself put in Georg Büchner's play text when he was writing the opera *Wozzeck*. The last scene with the playing of noisy children in front of Marie's house begins with the words 'Ringel, ringel, Rosenkranz'. This is exactly the beginning of the 'Happy Bridegroom' by Otto Julius Bierbaum – though, of course, the music is entirely different!

Since Christmas 1900 Schoenberg had owned a copy of the *Deutsche Chansons*, in which Bierbaum's 'Happy Bridegroom' appears as the second poem. A few months after the sensational Berlin première success of the Überbrettl he set some poems from this collection while in Vienna, including the 'Gigerlette' by Bierbaum, the first poem in the book, the 'Galathea' of Frank Wedekind, and the 'Nachtwandler' of Gustav Falke, the refrain of which 'Rechts Luischen, links Marie und voran die Musici' (Luisa on the right, Marie on the left and the musicians in front) pleased Wolzogen so much that he engaged both the composition and the composer on the spot. Schoenberg set Falke's text for high voice accompanied by piccolo, trumpet in F, side drum and piano. He told his first biographer Egon Wellesz that the performance in Berlin was a failure because of too great difficulties for the trumpeter, and it had no further performances. In his memoirs, written twenty years later, Wolzogen said that the occasion of his début at the Carltheater in Vienna on that Jewish Day of Atonement had already led to Schoenberg's break with the theatre. Here it seems that Wolzogen's memory failed him, for Schoenberg followed the company to Berlin in December 1901 and in the Berlin address book of 1903 he was still mentioned as the conductor of the Überbrettl. The 'Nachtwandler', which was performed again in Hamburg in 1954 and printed in Los Angeles in 1969, displays a musical appearance which has little in common with the novelties and boldnesses of Schoenberg's style of that time. Apart from some chromatic runs and altered harmonies, perhaps also a few syncopations, the song is entertainment music with great verve and good from the technical point of view. It shows how cleverly Schoenberg – who was then living in the elevated world of the 'Gurrelieder' – knew how to meet the demands of the popularization of literature and music which he also was striving for.

Meanwhile things had changed for Wolzogen in Berlin. The dream of his own theatre was nearing fulfilment. Money had to be raised for this; the business transactions were taken over by a

board of directors of the Überbrettl company, in whose documents dating from autumn 1901 there is recorded among other
things the engagement of the conductors Oscar Straus and
Arnold Schoenberg. A plot in the Köpenicker Strasse was bought,
and August Endell was engaged as the architect. He was famous
in the then flourishing Art Nouveau style. In 1897–98 he had
caused a sensation with the building of the Munich studio
Elviera, and he was one of the first architects who, like Adolf
Loos in Vienna, loved plain roofs and simple ground plans, but
decorated the facades of his buildings with fantastic Chinoiseries
in the taste of Art Nouveau. Endell built the theatre in a short
time at a relatively small cost. It became the meeting-place of the
elegant Berlin world and was regarded by its contemporaries as
the first theatre in an individual style since Schinkel's Schauspielhaus. All the colours of the rainbow were spread out in clear hues
in the interior, and were varied in the different colours of the rows
of seats and even in the aprons of the young girls who sold programmes. The floor was covered with Smyrna carpets, the roof
was painted pointillistically and the lamps had fashionable
shapes. But above all there was a modern large stage and a small
orchestra pit. The theatre soon became the most exclusive one in
Berlin.

There Schoenberg began a short period of activity as a musician
in a literary cabaret. The opening of the 'Bunte Theater', as the
enterprise was now called, took place after several postponements
on 28 November 1901. Schoenberg went there from Vienna later.

In spite of the elegant public which met there, Wolzogen's
own theatre was a commercial failure. He came out of this
enterprise very much in debt. The tour which he made to St.
Petersburg and Riga in February 1902 could not help his
situation. In May of the same year there was a bitter discussion
with the Board of Directors and in June the founder of the
Überbrettl, which had begun so triumphantly, retired, disappointed and embittered.

In the meantime his idea had been take up by others and remained to ferment the literary and musical situation during the
first years of the twentieth century. Schoenberg had nothing to
do with this. It was not till ten years later, when the singing
actress Albertine Zehme asked him to write recitations for her
programmes, that he returned to some stylistic elements of
Wolzogen's stage. The 'Pierrot-Lunaire' – poems by Albert
Giraud are unmistakably related to Art Nouveau in the trans-

lation of Otto Erich Hartleben (who was close to the Wolzogen circle). From the description of the first performance in October 1912 people agreed that Frl. Zehme had made some of the Überbrettl performance tricks her own.

But it is a mistake to imagine that the use of the recitation technique, i.e. speaking with musical accompaniment, came from the Überbrettl. It was often used around the turn of the century, and Schoenberg himself had included it from the beginning in the plan of his 'Gurrelieder', which had been conceived in all essentials in 1900, that is a year before the creation of the Wolzogen cabaret. Also the Überbrettl did not include the type of the diseuse, as has recently been stated. This is a speciality of French cabaret, in fact that of the 'Chat Noir', and remains so. Its most prominent representative was Yvette Guilbert, who did not appear in German cabarets. In the Überbrettl either the poets themselves spoke their own verses, like Ernst von Wolzogen, Hanns Heinz Ewers, Christian Morgenstern and others, or singers of Chansons like Bozena Bradsky, who danced simultaneously, and Elsa Laura von Wolzogen performed. The latter continued her activity with success for many years after the break up of the 'Bunte Theater'; she sang to a lute and had nothing in common with the French diseuse type. I heard her myself in my youth and was very pleased with her pretty, small voice and witty method of entertainment. In a few exceptional cases women recited in Wolzogen's cabaret. One of them was the novelist Olga Wohlbrück, who was famous at that time and was the wife of the composer Waldemar Wendland.

All seven of Schoenberg's Brettl songs were written before he got to know Wolzogen's cabaret, and so were not written for it specially but at best were influenced by its new reputation. None of the songs uses speech-song or contains even episodes of recitation.

Albertine Zehme, who came from the straight stage and at one time wanted to be an opera singer, was not influenced by Wolzogen's cabaret, even if she knew it.

When Schoenberg moved with his young wife Mathilde from Vienna to Berlin, she was far gone in pregnancy. The couple found furnished lodgings in the Lettestrasse 9, not too far from Wolzogen's Bunte Theater in the Köpenickerstrasse. We can assume that the move took place in the middle of December 1901, for on the 23rd Wolzogen and Moritz Muszkat signed the contract (see appendix) which engaged Schoenberg as conductor from 16 December 1901 to 31 July 1902. In return for a monthly

The Wohlzogen Theatre, Schoenberg's first place of work
in Berlin, 1901

payment of 300 marks he had to provide all compositions which were suitable for the Überbrettl, and if the director found them suitable, to allow them to perform them for one year. He also had to give the publishers, who were in liaison with the theatre, preferential treatment in obtaining publication rights. For travel expenses with the theatre he was allowed five marks a day. Breach of contract was penalized by a fine of 3000 marks.

The remarkable thing about this contract is that, in spite of being called professionally 'Kapellmeister', there was no mention of his activity as a conductor. Schoenberg was bound to 'fulfil those duties which correspond to his artistic capabilities', but only duties as a composer were mentioned. However the direction made no further use of his compositions, for his name cannot be found in the programmes or press notices about the Bunte Theater.

A monthly wage of 300 marks was a moderate income at that time; compared to the salaries earned by conductors in large opera houses it was very small. The young Richard Strauss had already in 1897 been given by Ernst von Possart 1000 marks a month plus living expenses in Munich. As against this Schoenberg's own duties were also fairly modest. He would have liked an extension of his contract. Since the birth of his daughter Trudi on 8 January 1902 the struggle for existence for the small family was extremely hard especially as his young wife was often ill. Schoenberg then remembered a rich acquaintance in Vienna. This was the composer Adalbert von Goldschmidt, in whose parents' house in the Opernring 6 gifted musicians were always welcome; Hugo Wolf was an intimate friend of his. After highly dramatic and idealistic attempts at opera, such as a trilogy *Gaea*, Goldschmidt turned to operetta. His *Fromme Helene* after Wilhelm Busch was rejected in 1897 in Hamburg. Apparently Wolzogen was interested in the piece and Schoenberg was also interested in realizing a plan to perform it in the Bunte Theater. On 2 May 1902 the influential and socially popular Goldschmidt, wrote to him at the Lettestrasse: 'Of course it would be very good if W. would really perform the F. H.; wouldn't he extend your engagement? Will you negotiate with another theatre about this? I will then make your engagement a condition of performance. W. will only get the score if there is a new contract with a penalty clause. I don't trust him with the score any more. Write to me what you think about a performance somewhere else in Berlin, talk about it to Nikisch in connection with an engagement for you for this; or with Tappert. I enclose a letter of recommendation to

Tappert.' (Arthur Nikisch was the director of the Berlin Philharmonic, Wilhelm Tappert was a leading music writer and
critic in Berlin).

The plan seemed to have foundered on the fact that Wolzogen
broke with the Bunte Theater in June. Schoenberg sent the
scores and text-books of the *Fromme Helene* back to Goldschmidt
without having achieved his object.

Meanwhile the Vienna Society of Musicians had given the first
performance of *Verklärte Nacht*. Arnold Rosé played the work
with his quartet and two additional players from the Vienna
Philharmonic on 18 March 1902 before an unappreciative public
which included among others the young Anton von Webern.
Schoenberg was not able to come. However, the German Society
of Musicians in Berlin now became interested in the work. Karl
Halir, to whom Schoenberg offered the score on the advice of
Richard Strauss, refused it. But the well-known violinist and
chamber music player Professor Waldemar Meyer, together with
the members of his quartet, Max Heinecke, Berthold Heinz and
Albrecht Löffler, as well as the viola player Willibald Wagner
and the cellist Max Schulz-Fürstenburg, played the quartet on
30 October 1902 in the large hall of the Architects' House in the
Wilhelmstrasse. The concert, which was put on by the Society of
Musicians, began with Ferruccio Busoni's String Quartet in D
Minor, opus 26 and Richard Strauss's Quartet in A Major, opus
2. Wilhelm Altmann's report in the *Musik* was cautiously negative.
The concert was announced in No. 3 of the *Deutsche Tonkünstler-
zeitung* of 21 October. For this Schoenberg wrote a short biography
in which he said; 'As I was originally supposed to be an engineer,
I was rather late in following my early inclination embracing
music as a profession.'

Perhaps it was in the Society of Musicians that he met Max
Marschalk. In 1903 he signed a contract with the Dreililienverlag,
which belonged to the enterprising composer and music critic
Marschalk; it brought out Schoenberg's first printed works in
1904. A postcard of 25 April 1903 asks Schoenberg to visit
Marshalk the following morning at Berlin-Halensee, Georg
Wilhelmstrasse 22. He was asked to bring scores and other things.
It was a Sunday; they had plenty of time. Further visits followed
on 28 May and 2 June. Marschalk acquired Schoenberg's first
twelve songs opus 1–3 and the strong sextet *Verklärte Nacht*. He
paid him 820 marks in advance, as are shown by the first accounts
at the end of 1903.

Schoenberg had already begun relations with the Vienna Universal Edition in 1902. But at that time, as is shown by a letter to him on 16 April in reply to his letter of 13 April these had only led to a discussion in their executive committee.

In Vienna at the beginning of the century a circle of young people was formed around Conrad Ansorge, the pianist and composer of Franz Liszt's school. The young critic Paul Stefan-Grünfeld met Schoenberg in Berlin in 1903 on a visit there during a rehearsal of a work of Ansorge's at the Philharmonic. Since then he never failed to attend any Schoenberg performance that he could reach.

In the autumn of 1902 Ferruccio Busoni had given his first two orchestral concerts of modern music. Schoenberg did not know him personally, but offered him in the spring of 1903 the score of *Pelléas and Mélisande* which was finished on 28 February. Busoni asked him to send him the score but did not perform it.

Among the pupils whom Schoenberg taught at the Stern Conservatory was a young Viennese, Josef Reitler, born in 1883. In 1907 he became, together with Julius Korngold, the music critic of the *Neue Freie Presse* in Vienna and in 1915 he was director of the Neues Wiener Konservatorium. In exile in California on 4 June 1944 he reminded Schoenberg that the latter had been responsible for his 'first steps in harmony' in 1903 in Berlin.

We do not know if Schoenberg, who was always a great lover of the theatre, took part in the very exciting Berlin cultural life from 1902–3. The Court Opera Unter den Linden, to which Richard Strauss certainly gave him access, performed very few novelties which were important to him apart from *Feuersnot* by Strauss-Wolzogen, *Pfeifertag* by Max Schillings and Gustave Charpentier's *Louise*. And Strauss gave programmes of modern music with the Tonkünstler-Orchester in the winter of 1902/3. In October and November of 1902 Sarah Bernhardt, who was then fifty-eight and still of legendary fame, gave guest performances in the Schauspielhaus. We do not know which of these Schoenberg attended.

Since Wolzogen's departure from the Bunte Theater there was no thought of his contract being extended after 31 July. The young composer used all his energies in order to keep his family in commissioned musical work such as copying and orchestration of works by other composers. In the summer of 1903 he realized that it would be better to go home to Vienna.

RELATIONS WITH STRAUSS

Richard Strauss, who had been appointed as royal conductor of the Berlin Court Opera in the Unter den Linden in 1898, met Ernst von Wolzogen in Munich at the end of 1898 or the beginning of 1899; the latter also had the idea of moving to Berlin. Both had found artistic opposition in Munich, and this gave them the feeling of a defiant offensive kind of collaboration. 'And so we sat down', says Wolzogen in his book of memoirs in 1922, 'and worked out a plan of revenge, which later took artistic form in *Feuersnot*.' The libretto, which was written in a few days on holiday on Rügen, was sent to the composer early in 1900. Strauss worked on the score until the summer of 1901, and Ernst von Schuch gave the first performance of it in Dresden as early as 21 November; Gustav Mahler had tried without success to obtain this for Vienna.

The work shows the spirit of the times which was dominant in German literature about 1900 and was taken over by Strauss in his music. 'In the *Feuersnot*', so the eighty-five-year-old composer wrote in a diary, 'there is the tone of irony, of protest against normal opera texts and the individual new element.' It is the spirit which won over some of the best German poets at that time to the idea of 'literary variety'. Wolzogen was one of these and brought the idea to fruition in the Berlin Überbrettl.

When the newly married Schoenberg came to Berlin in December 1901, in order to begin his work with Wolzogen, he was well acquainted with the music of Richard Strauss. He must have written to the older colleague, whom he much admired, in April 1902; possibly Wolzogen gave him an introduction to him. Strauss answered with a postcard dated 15 April from Charlottenburg to Schoenberg's address at Berlin 2, Letterstrasse 9; 'Dear Sir, you can see me every day from three till four at home. Yours sincerely, Richard Strauss.'

The contact seems to have become closer, so that no more

letters or postcards were needed. However, on 19 July 1902 Strauss wrote again from the summer resort of Marquartstein, in upper Bavaria. 'I shall take pleasure in supporting your application to Direktor Holländer, if he asks me for this. Your score of *Pelléas and Mélisande*, which I look forward to with interest, I would have to receive at the latest by the beginning of September in Berlin, if it will be possible for me to consider it.' And in a postscript Strauss advised him to send his sextet to Professor Halir; he said that Rosé would also make a special recommendation to him.

Clearly Schoenberg had spoken about his difficulties in earning a living. The tone of the letters between the two men quickly became warmer, and in September Strauss ended a postcard with the words 'Best greetings'. At that time he was writing the enormous score of the choral work *Taillefer* for an orchestra of 24 woodwind, 20 brass, 12 percussion players and 90 strings, which Strauss wrote in gratitude for the doctorate the Heidelberg University had bestowed on him. Schoenberg copied the parts of this for Strauss. On 6 November 1902 a card arrived at his new address Berlin W, Augsburger Strasse 48, in which Strauss asked him to bring part of the score on the same day ('where the 4/4 bar in G minor with the trombone begins'); he also introduced Schoenberg to the chief of the copying department, Herr Dessau, at the General Intendant's office. And on 26 November he asked Schoenberg to come punctually at 5 o'clock to fetch a further part of the *Taillefer* score, as Strauss was going away that evening for ten days.

Meanwhile Strauss introduced his Viennese colleague, whom he much admired, and who had asked his advice about an opera text, to Maurice Maeterlinck's *Pelléas and Mélisande*. Schoenberg took up the idea – certainly without knowing about Debussy's opera on the same text and its first performance in Paris on 30 April – and on 4 July wrote down the first sketches of his symphonic poem of the same name, finishing the score in 1903. In the Augsburger Strasse he was much nearer to Strauss, who was living in Charlottenburg, than he was in the Lettetrasse, though the latter was not too far from the 'Bunte Theater' in the Köpenickerstrasse. The house, No. 48, was only a few steps away from No. 55, where Ferruccio Busoni was living at least from May 1902 onwards. However, the two musicians did not know each other at this time.

On 21 April Schoenberg orchestrated a song for Bogumil

Zepler, for whom he had already orchestrated whole operettas. However, work of this kind was not sufficient to ease his financial worries – not to speak of the distaste with which it filled him. So he followed his vocation to be a teacher and must have spoken to Strauss about this. On 6 December 1902, immediately after his return from the journey mentioned above, Strauss wrote to Schoenberg: 'Dear Herr Schoenberg. Today I saw Direktor Holländer: he sincerely promised to take you on. He will arrange a small class for you now (so that at least you can call yourself a teacher at the Stern Conservatoire). But from 1 January onwards he hopes to give you a larger class: he also has copying work for you. Meanwhile, if you have any troubles, please turn for more detailed information to Inspector Pohl, who is a dear and true friend of mine, and will help you with advice and action.'

Since 1895 Gustav Holländer was the director of this important teaching academy, which was founded in 1850 as the first private institution for higher musical education. In 1897 he engaged Hans Pfitzner as a composition teacher, who carried on his work there till 1907. At that time it seems as though it was not possible to arrange a class for Schoenberg.

However, Strauss had other ideas and continues: 'If you are really in need, write a request for support to me as the President of the General German Musical Society: I could tide you over the worst patch with 50 marks. So good luck! Best greetings from Richard Strauss.'

Strauss also attempted by other means to help the young couple. In a letter of 18 December 1902 to his friend Max von Schillings in Munich Strauss wrote: 'I have recommended a man who lives in the most dire poverty and is *very* talented, to be given urgently a scholarship of 1000 marks a year for some years. Please support me and write a splendid testimonial for him. You will find that his works, if a bit overcharged at the moment, show great talent and gifts . . .'

The scholarship mentioned above was part of the Liszt Foundation, which had been given to the General German Musical Society by Countess Hohenlohe (a daughter of Franz Liszt's mistress and heiress Countess Carolyne Sayn-Wittgenstein). The money was given to composers or pianists. The seat of the Foundation was Weimar; the trustees were Strauss and Schillings as well as Hans von Vignau, who sent Schoenberg's scores to Schillings for consideration. Through Strauss's recommendation Schoenberg twice obtained this scholarship.

Besides working on larger pieces such as the orchestration of the 'Gurrelieder', which had been begun in Vienna in 1900 and was finished as a composition in 1901, and the symphonic poem *Pelléas and Mélisande*, on 3 January 1903 Schoenberg wrote a song from Goethe's *Westöstliche Diwan* 'Deinem Blick mich zu bequemen'; this was not published at the time.

Strauss's next card asked Schoenberg to send back the *Taillefer* score, as he wished to work on it further. There is also a mention of early music by Alexander von Zemlinsky. Probably Schoenberg had recommended the work of his friend, teacher and brother-in-law to Strauss for performance. Strauss asks if he has the parts for 16 each of first and second violins, 10 violas, 8 celli and 8 double basses. He asks for Schoenberg's advice as to which two of the three movements he found the best. Strauss hopes to conduct them in his next concert at the beginning of February. The card is dated 19 January 1903; on the 14th the untiringly active Strauss had founded the Society of German Composers.

The list of Zemlinsky's works does not show which work this was. In 1902 he wrote a ballet *The Triumph of Time* with Hugo von Hofmannsthal but it remained unfinished. Possibly these were pieces from this work. In any case the proposed performance did not take place.

On 28 February Schoenberg put the final date to his *Pelléas* score. It was the first orchestral work which he had finished, and it was as large in its duration – the work takes about three quarters of an hour to perform – as in its instrumental demands. There is a string orchestra of 32 violins, 12 violas, 12 celli and 8 double basses and also 17 woodwind, 18 brass and 2 harps, more or less the orchestra of Strauss's *Taillefer*. The latter work was further mentioned in a card of 21 April in which Strauss asks Schoenberg to come the following morning at eleven 'to fetch new pages of *Taillefer*, which was nearly ready'. It was finished on 3 May, and the first performance took place in October at the opening of the Heidelberg Stadthalle.

In 1920 Alban Berg wrote a short thematic analysis of *Pelléas and Mélisande*, which was published by Universal Edition. In contrast to Anton von Webern, who had written about the symphonic poem in 1911 in the Piper book dedicated to Schoenberg, saying that its structure was entirely free, Berg recognized the four movements of a symphony in this one-movement work. These follow the course of Maeterlinck's drama. The first section is a large sonata movement with an introduction ('In the Forest'), followed by the exposition of the 'Fate Motive' (a rising major seventh and a falling major chord), the themes of Mélisande and Golo, the main section with the theme of marriage which grows from this, the transition and the subsidiary passage representing Pelléas, and the final section, 'Mélisande's Awakening Love'. Next comes a second main section in three parts, introduced by a scherzo ('The Spring in the Park'), followed by the scene at the castle tower (Mélisande combs her long hair at the window; Pelléas kisses it, until Golo appears), ending in the vaults under the castle. Here Berg only mentions the whole-tone chords in thirds which also return in the final scene, but not the glissandi on two muted trombones which Schoenberg was the first to use here. The third section is an adagio with an introduction in the form of a development section; farewell-love scene between Pelléas and Mélisande. The concluding section with Mélisande's death forms a finale constructed as a reprise – The work, in which the tonality of D minor predominates, is unique among Schoenberg's works because of its complex polyphony. Both the harmony and the contrapuntal combinations of motives are similar to Max Reger's music. Chords built in fourths appear already from time to time.

On 18 April Schoenberg composed a small choral piece: *Darthulas Grabgesang,* on a text by Goethe after Ossian. It remained unperformed and unpublished. Schoenberg's circumstances in the Prussian capital remained extremely difficult. He did not break off his connections with Vienna. Friends of his, especially Alexander von Zemlinsky, had good contacts with Universal Edition, which was founded in June 1901. He was advised to look for possibilities of work in Vienna. So he accepted an invitation to spend the summer with the Zemlinskys in Payerbach. He knew the little Lower Austrian summer resort in the Schwarzatal from a previous stay with his future brother-in-law in 1899, and had worked there on the sextet *Verklärte Nacht* and songs.

In order to say good-bye to Strauss he looked him up at the beginning of July, but did not meet him. A long letter from Payerbach dated 10 September 1903, informs us about this and the changes in his life. It was the first letter of Schoenberg's to Strauss which has been preserved, and gives a good account of the still unaltered relationship between the two men. '*Honoured Herr Hofcapellmeister, On the 2nd or 3rd July I went to your house to pay my respects to you – at a time when the opera was still performing.*

I was told that you had already gone away, and I could not obtain your summer address from the porter: therefore, I could not even pay my respects by letter. Meanwhile I accepted an invitation to go to Vienna and was a guest of relations in Payerbach for the summer. So I had to leave this letter till now, and I imagine that you have now begun your work at the opera again.

Now I must tell you something. I am going to remain in Vienna. Some friends have taken trouble on my behalf, so that I can earn my living here to a certain extent. Naturally I have no fixed employment, unfortunately, but I will have a lot of work for Universal Edition, the new Viennese publishing house, and if this goes only half way, it will at least be bearable.

So I must say good-bye to you for a long time. I would like to take this opportunity to thank you, honoured master, once again for all the help you have given me at a sacrifice to yourself in the most sincere manner. I will not forget this for the whole of my life and will always be thankful to you for it – If I ask you to keep a good memory of me, I hope you will forget the great amount of trouble that I have caused you.

I ask you to give my best regards to Frau Strauss and remain, again with thanks, yours very sincerely, Arnold Schoenberg.'

The work which was waiting for Schoenberg in Vienna was of several kinds. In the catalogue of 1903 Universal Edition mentioned new publications of four-hand piano scores, arranged by Arnold Schoenberg and Alexander Zemlinsky. However Schoenberg had to wait another six years for the conclusion of a copyright contract for original works, by which the publishers, through buying the firm of Joseph Aibl in Munich, obtained the complete chamber music, songs, symphonic poems and choral works of Richard Strauss.

Zemlinsky had many contacts in Vienna. As conductor of the Carltheater he lived in the theatrical world, especially that of comic opera and operetta. Through his composition pupil, the beautiful young Alma Maria Schindler, who in 1902 became Gustav Mahler's wife, his relations with the great composer and the director of the Court Opera were strengthened.

At the beginning of 1904 there was a plan to found a 'Society of Creative Musicians' of which the members were Rudolf St. Hoffmann, Arnold Schoenberg, Karl Weigl, Alexander von Zemlinsky and other Viennese musicians. During the season of 1904/5, as well as works of their own members, they performed pieces by Siegmund von Hausegger, Gustav Mahler and Richard Strauss. Mahler became their honorary president. On 26 January

1905 Schoenberg himself conducted the first performance of *Pelléas and Mélisande*, a performance which gave him little satisfaction. On 23 November the *Sinfonia Domestica* of Strauss had been performed. Schoenberg corresponded with him about a planned repetition of the performance in March 1905. Strauss was interested: 'If it is at all possible for me, I will certainly come on 11 March, but I can't . . . promise definitely', he wrote on 11 November, and asked Schoenberg to give him full details of the performance on 23 November. The tone of the letter of 22 February is somewhat cooler; Strauss says he has heard no more from 'your society' and imagined that the plan had been abandoned. In any case he could not come as his work at the theatre and various other commitments were piling up in March. However, Schoenberg seems to have repeated his proposal and also expressed the wish to acquaint Strauss with his own new compositions. Strauss's answer, written on 26 February in Leipzig, Hotel de Prusse, was brief but polite; '. . . impossible to come this year. If you will and can play the works to me, perhaps next year! Very sorry. Best greetings and thanks.' This was followed by an obscure postscript: 'Save your friends their money!' Perhaps Schoenberg had suggested that Strauss's journey to Vienna should be financed by patrons.

The contact between the two men seems to have been interrupted for a year and half. It was the time when Schoenberg 'discovered' Mahler's works. But we know from many sources that he continued to occupy himself with Strauss's music with undiminished interest. Egon Wellesz visited him in 1905 at his house in the Liechtensteinstrasse and saw on his piano the newly published piano score of *Salome*, given to him by Mahler. Mahler had tried in vain to obtain permission from the Royal and Imperial censorship authorities to give the first Austrian performance of *Salome* in the Vienna Court Opera. So this première in fact took place on 16 May 1906 in Graz. It was a definite success for Strauss. Among those present, as the composer wrote the next day to his wife, were not only Gustav and Alma Maria Mahler but the widow of Johann Strauss: '. . . the Italian composer Puccini came expressly from Pest, and many young people from Vienna, whose only luggage was a piano score . . .' We know that Schoenberg and Zemlinsky as well as Alban Berg were among these young people from Vienna.

On 31 August of the same year Schoenberg wrote a long letter to Strauss, in which he recommended some of his works to him

for Strauss's concerts with the Vienna Philharmonic. He mentioned *Pelléas and Mélisande*, the songs with orchestra opus 8 and
the chamber symphony. He called the songs 'much more mature,
calmer and cleaner' than the symphonic poem.

Strauss, who was very busy and was travelling a lot, answered
from the Grand Hotel in Milan with a postcard, saying that for
the moment he was only conducting two Philharmonic concerts
in which he would 'as it were introduce himself for the first time'
in Vienna and therefore couldn't introduce any novelties. However, he had long had the idea of performing works of Schoenberg
at the Musicians' Congress, but things did not always happen as
he wanted them to. If Schoenberg could leave the first performances of the songs with orchestra and the chamber symphony
till the summer of 1907, Schoenberg should send the scores to Dr.
Aloys Obrist in Weimar. Strauss would then look at them himself
and take a personal interest in Schoenberg's works.

Schoenberg's undated answer to this card of 11 September is
both thankful and reserved; it begins indeed with 'Honoured
Master', but ends in an extremely formal manner. Schoenberg
says that he has had the score of the chamber symphony returned
to him by Ferdinand Löwe (who was the director of the Vienna
Konzertvereins), because 'in spite of intensive study of the score'
Löwe did not understand it. 'So I will probably still have a lot to
do in order to get performances of these pieces. Rosé won't play
my new quartet and Schalk turned down my songs with orchestra
last year. I have more songs as well. So I have certainly enough
material for "premières".' Schoenberg did not wait for the date
suggested by Strauss; probably the Allgemeine Deutsche Musikverein did not want to perform the works. So the first performance of the chamber symphony was given by the Rosé Quartet
and the wind ensemble of the Vienna Philharmonic as early as
the spring of 1907.

A year later Schoenberg again applied to Strauss for performances, but received a reply, written on 20 May 1908 in
Lyon, that the programmes for the winter of 1908/1909 were
already finished and published. 'However, I will be pleased if
towards autumn you will send me a few (not too long) pieces to
have a look at and would be very happy if I could find something
among them which I could serve to the Berlin Opera House
public, which unfortunately is madly conservative, without too
great a risk.'

Schoenberg kept to the new date and on 27 September 1908

he received an answer from Garmisch. Strauss wrote that he had read the works with great interest. They would not do for the big orchestral concerts without soloists in the Berlin Opera House. The chamber symphony must definitely be performed in a smaller hall; with the bad accoustics of the Opera House it would not have its desired effect. However, he would try to put it on the programme of the next Tonkünstlerfest.

Meanwhile with the last two movements of the F Sharp Minor String Quartet, finished on 11 July 1908, and the Stefan George songs, (first date 27 September 1908) Schoenberg had undertaken his voyages of discovery in the territory of music which was free from key. The three piano pieces opus II were written in 1909, Nos. 1 and 2 in February, the third in August. Did Schoenberg remember Strauss's suggestion of writing 'a few not too long' pieces for orchestra? The letter of 14 July 1909, which Schoenberg sent from Steinakirchen am Forst in Lower Austria to Strauss supports this supposition, even if it is not the concerts of the Hofkapelle but those of the Berlin Philharmonic which are mentioned. Schoenberg offers something which 'should correspond to your conditions as regards length. These are short orchestral pieces (duration between 1 and 3 minutes) without any cyclical connections. Up till now I have written 3, a fourth one can be added in a few days at most and perhaps two or three more will come to life afterwards.'

There is no doubt that Schoenberg is talking about the pieces, five of which form his opus 16. The short score of the first one bears the date of completion 23 May 1909; the fourth one was finished on 17 July. Numbers 2, 3 and 5 are not dated. The first, second and fifth pieces are written on similar music paper, sized 26.5 × 35 centimetres; the other two are written on various kinds of paper of different shapes.

Schoenberg put these pieces into full score shortly after sketching out the short score. The dates of completion are 9 June for the first, 15 June for the second, 1 July for the third, 18 July for the fourth and 11 August for the fifth piece. This corresponds to the information in Schoenberg's letter to Strauss; on 14 July the first three pieces had been written and the fourth followed four days later. However, Schoenberg was planning two or three more pieces; the total would then have become six or seven. (In a letter later to Strauss he speaks of four pieces and the fifth one which was almost ready.)

The letter of 14 July gives further details of Schoenberg's

proposals. 'As they do not hang together, as I told you one can easily perform only three or four of them. I think it would be necessary to do three so that the whole work would not fizzle out too much. The orchestration is not larger than "normal" – but the difficulty of them is.'

Then follows the most interesting section of the letter: 'I believe that this time it is really impossible to hear the music from the score. It would almost be necessary to perform it "with blind judgement". I expect a great deal of it, specially as regards sound and mood. For it is these that the pieces are about – certainly not symphonic, they are the absolute opposite of this, there is no architecture and no build-up. Just a colourful, uninterrupted variation of colours, rhythms and moods. But, and this is the advantage of them, which perhaps will make you take the risk of conducting them; *very short*! the shortest perhaps 3/4 minutes, the longest which is finished yet hardly 2 minutes. One will be longer, but I have not yet begun this one.'

This description: the opposite of the symphonic, neither architecture nor build-up; then – speaking positively – colours, rhythms, moods in varied uninterrupted change is very important as the expression of Schoenberg's aesthetic at that time. Also his doubts about the readability of the score which Mahler later also agreed with.

Strauss answered on 22 July from Garmisch, that his winter programme was already complete. But he asked Schoenberg to send him the score 'provided that I can decipher it.' And he would gladly try everything possible to have the work performed. 'In any case it interests me very much to see everything that you write.'

Schoenberg was still at the summer resort of Steinakirchen. From there he wrote the letter of 28 July 1909, which accompanied the sending of the four orchestral pieces to Strauss. He says that the fifth, which was still unfinished, would be 'more cheerful than Nos. 1 and 4, and so together with 2 and 3 could give the balance of a lighter tone against Nos. 1 and 4 which are perhaps too dark.' He says that he is sorry to make Strauss undertake the deciphering of his music, but hopes to impress him in such a way that he will decide to perform it.

He continues:

'*In Vienna I am at loggerheads with everything that goes on. I can only be amiable when I respect people; and so for this reason I only have a few friends in Vienna . . . I know no one in foreign countries, and the tight clique of the General German Musical Society treated me very badly at the musical festival, so that I have very little confidence in sending them further works. – So it comes about that I, now 35 years old, have only had one single orchestral performance!! You are the best person to understand what this means and you can see from this how thankful I would be if you were able to perform the pieces. You are also the person who could best risk taking somebody like myself under his protection. People in Europe believe in you, and even if you made a mistake it would not be taken too badly. Perhaps you can decide in my favour this time.'*

After Strauss acknowledged the receipt of the music on 30 July, Universal Edition, which had made a copyright contract with Schoenberg in 1909, seems to have become interested in the orchestral pieces. Schoenberg, while still staying in Steinakirchen, asks Strauss to send the scores back, but remarks that a promise of performance from Strauss would help him very much both with the publishers and also in dealing with the Conservatorium. He doesn't want to press Strauss, but does need the music immediately. The letter is undated; it must have been sent off at the end of August, as Strauss answered it on 2 September.

Clearly Strauss could not understand this music, or any of Schoenberg's works after the liquidation of tonality. In its form his rejection of the work was extremely friendly, but in fact it was negative: 'I am very sorry to have to send your scores back to you without a promise of performance. You know I am glad to help people and I also have courage. But your pieces are such daring experiments in content and sound that for the moment I dare not introduce them to the more than conservative Berlin public.'

But Strauss's thoughts went further than he admitted in public; he really doubted if Schoenberg could anticipate the effect of these pieces. For he says: 'If you would take well-meant advice from me I suggest that you ask a friendly conductor, perhaps Löwe or Nedbal, to try them out in a few rehearsals, or you yourself hire a good orchestra for this purpose in order to try out the pieces; for I am afraid that you will not find any conductor who will take them for performance without further ado.'

Schoenberg must have been very disappointed by this rejection and Strauss' clearly apparent doubts about his 'daring experiments in content and sound'. But this letter reached him when he was setting Marie Pappenheim's text for the melodrama *Erwartung* in a real rush of composition; the short score of nineteen pages was written in seventeen days between 27 August and 12 September 1909.

The relations between Strauss and Schoenberg were interrupted for two years, but not yet finally broken off. In his Harmony Book, which he wrote between 1910 and 1911, Schoenberg describes Strauss as 'a great master of our time' and mentions him more frequently than any other living composer, even more frequently than Mahler, to whose memory this book was dedicated. After finishing the preface in July 1911 Schoenberg went to Berg on the Starnberger See. He had learnt to love Bavaria since 1906, when he spent the summer in Egern-Rottach, and he looked forward to exchanges of views with Kandinsky, who lived in Murnau, and with other members of the 'Blaue Reiter'. In Berg he stayed with the master carpenter Widl. On 21 August he wrote a very polite letter ('Very honoured Herr Generalmusik-direktor') suggesting that he should visit Strauss in Garmisch. He ended with an extremely formal phrase. He said he would be there for two weeks more, that is later than 4 September. Strauss wrote a much more friendly letter and asked him to visit him between 2 and 6 September, but recommended him to telephone in advance, as he might be off on a trip.

Whether the visit took place and what was discussed there we do not know. But the two letters are the last which were exchanged between the two musicians. However, they had a personal meeting again in 1912. Strauss was conducting a concert with the Berlin Philharmonic in Berlin. Schoenberg was invited and went to it with Webern. His diary for 14 February has the following entry:

'*Went with Webern to the Strauss concert. Haussegger-Sinfonie. Very pretty. Warm melodically, fairly honest, but overdone and not very intelligent. Very well orchestrated. Very Straussian. A good deal of applause with some hissing. Webern and I were sitting in the stage box but went into the hall itself in order to applaud strongly. I am always annoyed by hissing. A fat old man laughed at us and asked if I would like to take his stick to help things. I would like to have said to him:* "What right have you to speak to me?" *But instead I said in my anger,* "You haven't introduced yourself to me!" *But that was enough, for the chief thing is that I shouted loudly and frightened the old man sufficiently. Strauss makes music very sympathetically in general. But the ensemble is very slovenly.* 'The Kaisermarsch': *a very beautiful piece of music! It is real Wagner! Yesterday we played part of* Siegfried. *That is wonderful too!*

'*After the last piece I went to see Strauss. He was very friendly. But I was clumsy. I was embarrassed like a young fifteen-year-old boy, I*

stammered and certainly made on Strauss the impression of an un-
sympathetic devotion. I lost all my dignity, because I wanted to be
certain that I was not promoting myself as a "Selfian" in the presence
of Strauss.[1]

'*But I didn't need to do that. On the contrary it would have been*
better to have shown myself as a "Selfian" in order to get at least
halfway towards him. However I am not too worried about it. I know
how it was and that is enough for me.

'*I introduced Webern. But I couldn't say anything on his behalf*
because I was stammering too much.'

After Mahler's death a foundation was set up bearing his name,
and his widow Alma Maria suggested to the trustees that Schoenberg should be paid a sum of 3000 kronen. Strauss agreed
'. . . For one never knows what posterity will think about it.' But
his rejection of the more recent Schoenberg composition was
shown in his remark: '. . . I . . . believe, that it would be better for
him to be shovelling snow than scrawling on music paper . . .'

Schoenberg heard about this and also about Strauss's remark:
'Nowadays only an alienist can help poor Schoenberg.' When
Schoenberg was asked in 1914 to write about Strauss's fiftieth
birthday, he refused emphatically, referring to these remarks. It
was not only the understandable bitterness which he felt at such
insults; Schoenberg also mentioned artistic motives. He disliked
the 'banality like the themes of a song' and found that the themes
of *Heldenleben* and *Zarathustra* contained the same themes as
were 'unashamedly prattled in the song themes and the letters of
the Mahler foundation.' And he continues: '. . . since I have
understood Mahler, I have inwardly rejected Strauss.'

Later Schoenberg never denied what he had learnt from
Strauss. *Salome* and *Elektra* were and remained masterpieces for
him, and in his book, *Structural Functions of Harmony*, which he
finished in 1948, he quoted four bars from *Salome* as an example of
expanded tonality. He even preferred Strauss to all modern
French composers, including Debussy.

After 1912 Strauss had very little interest in modern music. As
he said once, he found it unnecessary to occupy himself with it, so
long as there was still a lot of good old music which he did not
know. However, when he was Director of the Vienna Opera
he was basically in favour of performances of works of Schoenberg's and Ernst Krenek's, and in a letter to the critic Dr.

[1] Schoenberg was referring to the anecdote when Strauss was asked if he was a
Wagnerian or a Brahmsian and he answered that he was a Selfian.

Heinrich von Kralik of 16 November 1924 he wrote: 'I can say that I would also have performed Schoenberg and Krenek, for I do not subscribe to the point of view that the novelties which I perform should be personally pleasing to me.' Richard Strauss Junior, the grandson of the composer, who was born in 1927, told me that his grandfather, who gave him his musical education, had used Schoenberg's Harmony Book in this.

Strauss and Schoenberg, born respectively in 1864 and 1874, were divided in age by half a generation. What united and what separated them?

Strauss came from a musical family in upper bourgeois circumstances. His father was a horn-player in the Court Opera Orchestra in Munich, conservative musically, and an important figure in the anti-Wagner and anti-Bülow party. Music was played in the family; the household gods were Mozart, Haydn and Beethoven, as well as Mendelssohn and Spohr. Richard's mother came from the Pschorr family and brought the prosperity of this powerful brewing family with her. Their outlook was Bavarian, Royalist and Catholic.

Strauss's musical education as well as his school work was strict, methodical and conventional. In spite of the Munich people's liking for Wagner, and in spite of his early study of the *Tristan* score he came to Wagner much later. He was introduced by Hans von Bülow to Brahms, and Brahms's music influenced him very much from his twenty-third to his twenty-fifth year. He was introduced to Wagner and to his admiration of Berlioz and Liszt in 1885/6 by Alexander Ritter in Meiningen. This gradually superseded his admiration for Brahms, whom the mature Strauss regarded as an embodiment of talent, whereas to him Wagner was a genius.

In 1894 Strauss became Conductor in his home town for the second time. Here he came into the company of the rebellious and ironical literary men, who carried their dislike of romantic rhetoric even into the fields of opera. In Weimar Strauss's rhetorical tribute to the spirit of Wagner, the opera *Guntram*, was a failure. So he took up his earlier work on a comic opera again. Since 1893 he had been fascinated by the *Till Eulenspiegel* story, and clung specially to the idea of bringing the rogue to Schilda. In a letter of 1 February 1894 he wrote: 'Now I am going to get to grips with *Till Eulenspiegel with the Schildbürgers* (Philistines). A year later he wrote *Till Eulenspiegel's Merry Pranks* for orchestra, and in 1896 the Munich poet and friend of Strauss, Count

Ferdinand von Sporck, wrote an *Eulenspiegel* libretto for him. He also had plans for ballets and operas with Frank Wedekind and Otto Julius Bierbaum. However the first text he found that he was able to compose was Ernst von Wolzogen's *Feuersnot*. It remained his only contribution to an opera form taken over from the spirit of the Uberbrettl.

Schoenberg, as we know, was self taught in music. Alexander Zemlinsky played a similar role as mentor in his development to what Alexander Ritter did for Strauss. Their work together in the orchestral society 'Polyhymnia' was influenced equally by Brahms and Wagner. In 1895, while still a Brahmsian through and through, Schoenberg was introduced to Wagner by Zemlinsky and from then on admired both masters. So at the age of twenty-one he underwent the same course of development as Strauss had done ten years earlier when he himself was twenty-one.

Schoenberg's circle of friends did not include the type of the rebellious literary man in the same way as Strauss' circle in the nineties in Munich. We know about Schoenberg's discussions in coffee-houses, and also his walks in the Prater, where military bands sometimes even played Wagner.

It was through these concerts that Schoenberg learnt that besides the symphonic and highly dramatic worlds of Brahms and Wagner there could be good entertainment music. The appearance of the 'Deutsche Chansons' at Advent 1900 led him to occupy himself with the entertainment genre. Between April and September 1901 he not only wrote seven cheerful songs of this kind, three of them with texts from the 'Deutsche Chansons' by Bierbaum, Falke and Wedekind, but between 18 June and 28 July he also wrote the text of a comic opera *Die Schildbürger*. So this brought him near, doubtless without his knowledge, to Strauss's *Till Eulenspiegel with the Schildbürgers* of 1894. The work of both composers was influenced stylistically by Brahms and Wagner. Chromatic harmony leading to the limits of tonality was predominant in Strauss's music since *Guntram* in 1894 and also in Schoenberg's Songs opus 1 to 3 of 1897. Strauss started writing programme music of a Lisztian type in 1889 with *Macbeth* and his following symphonic poems. However, Schoenberg's attachment to chamber music was so strong that he used the idea of the symphonic poem first in his string sextet *Verklärte Nacht* of 1899. He adopted the Liszt-Berlioz principle for the first time in *Pelléas and Mélisande* in 1903, but later gave it up in favour of 'absolute music'. Strauss and Schoenberg both shared a taste for large orchestral forces, which Mahler had also demanded.

What separated the two men was principally their relation to practical musical work. As a pianist and a conductor Strauss reached an early level of virtuosity; he enjoyed instrumental brilliance and showed himself to be a composer of extrovert and 'stormy youthful' character, which often had to conceal inner tensions. Schoenberg never became a virtuoso on any instrument and he had difficulties manually as a conductor. His musical language is hardly ever influenced by the intention of writing brilliant vocal or instrumental effects or even of making them possible. His language is dematerialized from his first works onwards and later deliberately avoids the ideals of pleasing people or general popularity.

The parting of the artistic careers of Strauss and Schoenberg can be dated. In September 1908 Strauss finished the score of *Elektra*, in which for the last time he experimented in the world of harmony free of key. On 27 September 1908 Schoenberg wrote the Stefan George song 'Du lehnest wider eine Silberweide' and with it began the way to non-tonal composition, which led to new technical and formal freedom.

VIENNA, TEACHING, CRISES

When Schoenberg returned to Vienna in the late summer of
1903, his position had improved in so far as a certain amount of
bread and butter work was in prospect for him. Here Zemlinsky's
helpful friendship had paved the way for him. Zemlinsky, as
permanent conductor of the Carltheater, helped Schoenberg in
this work. As before these were orchestrations, arrangements for
piano, two or four hands, and also making fair copies of works.
As a conductor Zemlinsky's tasks were normally far below his
artistic level. He rehearsed operettas and conducted them every
evening *en suite*, mostly for months, often for years. This continued
until Rainer Simons sent for him to go to the Volksoper in 1906,
and in a short time Zemlinsky raised this from a modest undertaking to an artistic institute of high rank. Finally Gustav Mahler
engaged him at the Vienna Court Opera shortly before his own
departure from there, but Zemlinsky returned disappointed from
there to the Volksoper, and in September 1911 went to the New
German Theatre in Prague. As we know Schoenberg had been
his friend since 1895, and since 1901 his brother-in-law, and he
spent some summers with him in the country, and lived in the
same house in Vienna with him for years and admired him as a
musician all his life. 'He was my teacher, I became his friend, and
later his brother-in-law, and in the many years which have passed
by he has remained the one person to whom I can always turn
when I need advice,' Schoenberg wrote in 1921 in a special
Zemlinsky issue of the Prague magazine *Auftak*', which appeared
shortly after Zemlinsky's fiftieth birthday – he was born in
1871.

In a letter to Richard Strauss, which I have already reproduced, Schoenberg mentions as one of his future employers in
Vienna Universal Edition. This publishing firm, which soon
became one of the leading ones in Europe, had begun publication
in January 1901, and by the end of the year their first catalogue

already contained four hundred items. The constituent general assembly took place on 1 June; at the beginning of July the Austrian Ministry of Education issued a decree which recommended publications of this firm to all musical educational institutes and schools. This naturally helped the commercial success of the enterprise. The later director of the firm Emil Hertzka (since 1908) had an inborn feeling for creative gifts and hardly let himself be hampered by the often great risks in promoting these. – Among Schoenberg's first works for Universal Edition were four-hand piano scores, made in 1903, of Rossini's opera *The Barber of Seville*, the 'Waffenschmied' of Lortzing and the 'Rosamunde' of Schubert.

After Schoenberg had obtained a three-room flat for himself, his wife and his one-year-old daughter Gertrud in the Liechtensteinstrasse, No. 68/70, where the Zemlinskys were also living, he went on a short holiday with his brother-in-law to Payerbach. The important school reformer, Frau Dr. Eugenie Schwarzwald, had introduced courses of music in her schools. Zemlinsky gave lectures on musical form and orchestration, Frau Dr. Elsa Bienenfeld taught musical history. At Zemlinsky's recommendation Schoenberg was asked to teach harmony and counterpoint.

The Rosé Quartet had already given the first performance of *Verklärte Nacht* on 18 March 1902. This aroused attention in both a positive and a negative way. Now, a year and a half later, Rosé decided to repeat the sextet in a concert of his own. As the leader of the Vienna Philharmonic he was allowed to rehearse in a practice room in the Court Opera. Gustav Mahler, who had been Director of the Opera for six years, came to a rehearsal. There Rosé introduced Schoenberg to him.

Schoenberg's work as a composer was necessarily lessened by his practical occupations. But in December he wrote two songs one after another, on 18 'Traumlegen' on a poem of Julius Hart and on 19 'Verlassen' after Hermann Conradi. 'Traumleben' is significant for Schoenberg's style of harmonic thinking at this time. The melodic line lives in a twilight on the borders of keys E and F. In addition it shows an extravagant affection for large intervals, with a rising minor seventh right at the beginning, expanded in the third bar to a major seventh and in the fifth to a minor ninth, and then this minor ninth is used as a falling interval. The piano accompaniment is mostly in four parts and is predominated by lines which move up and down in semitones, often in several parts, and these are concentrated, as it were casually,

into chords. Brahms's motivic working and Wagner's chromaticism are combined and dovetailed, and the apparently
conventional ending with another confrontation of F and E, is
influenced by the central motive, which had already been exposed
in the first two bars. In another song 'Verlassen' semitones and
fifths predominate in a specific way which Schoenberg later used
in another connection. Schoenberg continued the work on these
songs and his orchestral songs opus 8 in January 1904. On 23 he
wrote 'Ghasel' on Gottfried Keller's poem, which with its dove-
tailing of motives and its technique of rhythmical augmentations
and diminutions is one of the songs which embodies in an exemplary way Schoenberg's strict method of writing, which was
always concentrated on one motive from the beginning of the
song.

The Circle of Friends Of Modern Musicians met on 12 January
1904 in the Festival Room of the Hotel Continental, where the
Ansorge Society together with the Artists' Society of Hagen
performed songs by modern composers, including some by
Zemlinsky. Zemlinsky himself accompanied the opera singer
Walter Pieau, a friend of Schoenberg's from his youth. On 11
February the Ansorge-Verein gave in the festival room of the
Lower Austrian Industrial Society a 'Performance of Modern
Works.' This time the three songs of Schoenberg which were on
the programme were also sung by Pieau, 'Schenk mir deinen
goldenen Kamm' and 'Erwartung' from opus 2 as well as 'Hoch-
zeitslied' from opus 3. Zemlinsky accompanied. In March 1904
Schoenberg bought the first of his sketchbooks in which from now
on he wrote many of his compositions, sometimes already as large
scale works. The first book with sixty numbered pages went on till
20 April 1905. It contains part of the D minor string quartet opus
7 and the orchestral songs opus 8. Among the poems which
Schoenberg used as texts for his songs the collection *Des Knaben
Wunderhorn* now appears with 'Sehnsucht' written on 7 April
(opus 8, No. 3) and 'Wappenschild', written on 25 May. Schoenberg also set two sonnets of Petrarch in this year, the first 'Nie
ward ich, Herrin, müd' on 3 July in Mödling, the other one, 'Voll
jener Süsse', in November in Vienna.

On 15 April Zemlinsky opened the Vienna Volksoper with a
performance of *Freischütz*.

A student, Anton von Webern, who had matriculated in the
winter term of 1902, had been working for some time in the
musicological seminar of Professor Dr. Guido Adler, a friend of

Mahler's from his youth. The scientific and philosophical lectures as well as practical music lessons on the cello had only satisfied part of his hunger for education. He had composed since his early youth and looked for a teacher to help him to solve his creative problems. Together with his colleague Heinrich Jalowetz Webern went to Berlin early in 1904, in order to study with Hans Pfitzner at the Stern Conservatorium. Guido Adler had probably learnt to admire the composer of 'Armen Heinrich' and the 'Rose vom Liebesgarten' through Mahler and recommended his two composition students to him. But their meeting in Berlin turned out to be negative. Webern never talked about it later on. However, it seems that Pfitzner so annoyed him with biting remarks about Mahler that he and Jalowetz went straight back to Vienna. It appears that after this Adler sent the two young people to Schoenberg. Webern, who later said that he had been among the audience at the first performance of Schoenberg's *Verklärte Nacht*, showed Schoenberg some of his works in the summer of 1904, probably songs. In the autumn he became Schoenberg's pupil. In order to increase the number of his composition pupils Schoenberg put a notice in a Vienna newspaper. In the summer of 1904 the nineteen-year-old Alban Maria Johannes Berg, the son of a merchant, passed his final school examination after a first failure. In October, against his own wishes, he took a job in the Lower Austrian government office. But all his leanings were towards cultural things. Henrik Ibsen's plays, Gustav Mahler's music and the paintings of the Sezessionists. And since his years of puberty he had been writing songs and duets. His brother Charly, who knew Alban's most secret wishes, read Schoenberg's notice, sent Berg's compositions to him without letting him know and arranged that in the autumn Schoenberg made Alban too one of his private pupils. Together with Egon Wellesz, Erwin Stein and Heinrich Jalowetz, Berg and Webern were the strongest pillars of the young group of musicians which now called themselves with pride and defiance the School of Schoenberg.

Schoenberg, who of course was tied up with the educational plan of the Schwarzwald School, spent one summer holiday from 1 July in the Mödling house of the parents of his friend David Josef Bach. His financial position had not improved greatly in the first year of his stay in Vienna. Through Richard Strauss's recommendation he had already received a thousand marks in Berlin on 19 March 1903 from the General German Musical Society in Bremen, given to him by the Board of the Liszt

Foundation. He received the same amount again in 1904. On 21
March of the same year he filled up a questionnaire 'showing need
of support' to the 'Sisters of the Fröhlich Foundation' in order to
demand a pension. Apart from exact dates for himself, his wife
Mathilde and his daughter Gertrud the questionnaire gives
details about the flat, which consisted of three rooms, a hall and a
kitchen, and cost 250 kronen a quarter. Besides this 24 kronen a
month were set aside for a servant girl. This is typical of that
time: a servant girl belonged so much to the living conditions of
a composer that one could put down her wages in a request for a
pension. The request was granted on 6 July; Schoenberg received
a pension, once and for all, of 1000 kronen. The authority was
signed by two people: E. Mandyczewski, Curator and Dr. Karl
Lueger, Mayor. (Dr. Karl Lueger, who lived in Vienna from
1844 to 1910, was a lawyer, a democratic anti-Semite, attacked
by the Court, President of the Christian Socialist Party and mayor
of Vienna since 1897. He coined the phrase: 'I decide who is a
Jew'. Eusebius Mandyczewski, 1857–1929, musical scholar and
choir master, taught at the Vienna Conservatorium and was a
friend of Brahms.)

In 1903 Schoenberg had drawn up his first publishing contract
with Max Marshalk, the Director of the Drei-Lilien-Verlag in
Berlin. Marschalk, who was the brother-in-law of Gerhart
Hauptmann, also wrote incidental music for several of Hauptmann's plays, including *Und Pippa tanzt*, which both Schoenberg
and Berg later thought of setting as an opera. In a letter of 21
July 1904 to a colleague who asked for information Schoenberg
praised Marshalk especially for his work as a publisher.

In composition the first half of 1905 was dominated by work
on the first string quartet in D minor. During that summer the
Schoenbergs took a long holiday on the Traunsee, whose landscape always attracted them. The little town of Gmunden must
have been much loved by the nobility as a summer resort in these
years. The list of visitors of 12 July 1905 begins with the names of
Duke Albrecht of Württemberg with princes and princesses,
entourage and servants, Prince Johann Georg of Saxony and
Prince Max of Baden, also with entourage and servants. Under
the entry No. 321 we find: Herr Schoenberg, Arnold, musician
from Vienna, with family and servant, Traunstein II. Traunstein,
not to be confused with the town of the same name in Upper
Bavaria, was situated outside Gmunden. The Schoenbergs lived
at the Hois'n-Wirt. As the number of persons in the list of visitors

Alban Berg, Vienna 1909

is given as five, probably Schoenberg's mother Pauline was there as well. Here Schoenberg wrote on 6 September his Dehmel setting 'Alles', and here on 26 September he ended the D minor quartet. Schoenberg had always loved the quartet medium from his earliest composing days to his old age. But only four of his quartets seemed good enough to him to be published. The first of these, written in 1905, is in one movement and lasts forty-five minutes. Through its continuous course, however, the outlines of the classical four movements can be observed, as in many symphonies, concertos and symphonic poems of early and late romantic composers, such as Berlioz, Schumann, Mendelssohn, Liszt and Richard Strauss. Schoenberg's own analysis in the programme of the Dresden Music Festival of 1907 says: 'The four sections are not like four movements which are separated by pauses, but are sections which lead from one to another. The types of themes of the four movements are indeed used in this work, but their variously interlaced order seeks to present an unbroken and unified movement.' And then he details the four sections, 'Main movement, scherzo and trio, adagio and rondo-finale.

Webern's analysis in the Schoenberg book of 1912 probes rather deeper and speaks of a fusion of the classical four movements 'into a single big movement, in the middle of which is a large development section. It is the central section of this fusion. Before it there is a section which corresponds to a main sonata movement with a long fugato between the main theme and secondary section and the scherzo (with trio); after it comes the reprise of the main theme, the adagio section which follows immediately, the repetition of the secondary section and finally the rondo-finale, the themes of which are variations of those of the previous sections. Basically the form of this quartet is that of a large sonata movement. Between the first development and the reprise comes the scherzo and the big development section, and the reprise is lengthened by the adagio which comes between the main theme and the secondary theme. In this case one could regard the rondo-finale as an extended coda.'

Alban Berg went even further into the details of the construction of this work in 1924 in his article 'Why is Schoenberg's music so difficult to understand?' which concludes the 'Anbruch's' special publication to celebrate Schoenberg's fiftieth birthday. Starting from the first ten bars of the work he shows the motivic and polyphonic connections, the invention of all the thematic ideas together with all the subsidiary parts, and the technique of variation. With this he confirms Webern's remark: 'There is no note, so to speak, in this work which is not thematic. There is no other example of this. The nearest resemblance is to Johannes Brahms.'

In the writing for the instruments the first quartet goes much further than the sextet *Verklärte Nacht*, written six years earlier. In spite of the smaller number of instruments the colour effects are stronger in this extraordinary work. Webern discussed them: 'The use of new possibilities of sound derived from a modern orchestra on strings: mutes, writing on the bridge, col legno, harmonics etc. One can't speak here of outside instrumental effects. These new means of sound are born from the expression of the music. And in addition there is a wonderful use of the sound of strings in various registers.'

In her book *Bruckner, Mahler, Schoenberg* Dika Newlin reports a self-critical remark of Schoenberg's in his lectures at the U.C.L.A. He said that in his first quartet he had still gone in for 'dense writing', perhaps under the influence of Brahms, and had not left enough rests in the parts of the individual instruments. It was not till his later quartets that he had come near to the Mozartian ideal of transparency.

The D minor quartet shows a close connection with the first chamber symphony, whose six-note series of fourths seems to be anticipated by the cello part in bars 8 to 10 of the quartet: E flat–A flat–C–f–a–d–F sharp, also in its rhythmical course.

On 21 April 1905 Schoenberg used for the first time the second of the sketch books, whose 116 numbered pages contain, apart from the work on the quartet, also the songs opus 6 and many fragments of the first chamber symphony, which was written later. There were also unfinished works, the beginning of songs with texts by Hölderlin and the second movement of a chamber music work in it. This piece is again written on a poem by Dehmel, Stelldichein', and is dated 21 October, i.e. shortly after Schoenberg finished the quartet. The instrumental combination is remarkable: oboe, clarinet, violin, cello and piano, because it is almost the same (oboe instead of flute) as that of *Pierrot Lunaire* which was not written till 1912.

In the autumn of 1905 Schoenberg wrote two more songs from opus 6, on 6 September in Traunstein in Austria 'Alles' on a poem by Dehmel, and on 15 October 'Der Wanderer' on a text of Friedrich Nietzsche. The second sketch book also contains

Schoenberg's first canons. Their texts were taken from the *West-Ostliche Divan* by Goethe. Two are complete, both written in four parts for mixed choir unaccompanied, the first on the poem 'Oh, dass der Seinnen doch so viele sind!' the other on 'Wenn der schwer Gedrückte klagt'. Schoenberg increasingly used the canon form as a method of following the strictest contrapuntal rules. In this he shows a great sympathy with Johannes Brahms, whose words he often quoted: 'If I don't feel like composing, I write some counterpoint.' But in his article of 1947 'Heart and Brain in Music' he said that without any inspiration he could not even write any good counterpoint. Some of his pupils were better at this than he was. 'There are times when I am not in the position even to write a single example of simple counterpoint in two parts, of the kind that I demand from the advanced students in my class. In order to write a *good* example of this kind I need to work hand in hand with inspiration.'

In Schoenberg's legacy thirty canons were found, written between 1905 and 1951, the year of his death. These are often written for festive occasions, such as one at Christmas 1926 for Erwin Stein or on 7 March 1928 for the jubilee of the Concertgebouw Orchestra. The collection, which was published in 1963 by Bärenreiter, edited and with a commentary by Josef Rufer, who discovered the manuscripts in Schoenberg's legacy, is a document of great artistic and biographical value.

Art always comes from the connection between intuition and construction. The degree of their fusion changes. In addition logic can become automatic and inspiration can fail.

Schoenberg was an extraordinarily complicated mixture of imagination which broke out in an aggressive manner and a cerebral power of combination which reminds one almost of a computer. Spontaneity and a violent creative tempo are important in many of his works. But he also wrote canonic games of the old Netherlands type during his whole life with the same zeal with which he played chess, whist and tarock. Apart from the canons at the end of the 'Gurrelieder' and in some parts of *Pierrot Lunaire* there are also some in the Three Satires, opus 28, which end with the six-part birthday greeting for the seventy-year-old Bernard Shaw. He sent his friend Alban Berg for his fiftieth birthday a canon with quotations from Berg's opera *Lulu*. The strictest pieces in Rufer's collection sound like works from the sixteenth century. However, there are also polytonal ones like the three-part ones in G major, D major and E flat major for the

Society of German Musicians. The most interesting one was written for Thomas Mann's seventieth birthday, a non-tonal and very dissonant string quartet. However, one cannot measure purely polyphonic music with the criteria of colour and interesting sound. For with shop characteristics of this kind it goes beyond the boundaries of the workshop, and the pure play of glass beads is destroyed by the intervention of genius.

The chief work of 1906 was the completion of the first chamber symphony. We find a short score of it almost complete in the second and third sketch books. The latter, which consisted of 175 numbered pages, was begun in April 1906 and contains fragments of a number of unfinished works. Among these are four pages of sketches for Schoenberg's planned opera after Gerhard Hauptmann's *Und Pippa tanzt*. The reason why this was not finished was the large financial demands which Hauptmann and his publisher S. Fischer demanded for the libretto of the play.

The chamber symphony was finished on 25 July in Rottach-Egern on the Tegernsee. Three days later Webern, who had spent the summer on his father's estate at Preglhof, asked in a letter whether the chorales which Schoenberg had given him should be simply harmonized or worked out contrapuntally. In one of his lectures, which were published in 1960 under the title of 'Paths to New Music' by Willi Reich, Webern spoke on 2 February 1932 about Schoenberg's new works: 'In 1906 Schoenberg came back from a stay in the country with the chamber symphony. The impression of it was colossal. At that time I had been his pupil for three years and I immediately had the wish: 'You too must write something like that!' – Under the impression of this work the very next day I wrote a sonata movement – In this movement I went to the furthest limits of tonality – Schoenberg was enormously prolific at that time. Each time we pupils went to him there was something new there.'

With the score of the chamber symphony, which still bears the key signature of E major and the opus No. 9, Schoenberg had found a new synthesis of symphonic form and the spirit of chamber music. The piece is written for fifteen solo instruments, flute (alternating with piccolo), oboe, English horn, D and E flat clarinet, A and B flat clarinet, bass clarinet in A and B, bassoon, double bassoon, two horns, a string quartet and double bass. If necessary the strings can be doubled up. Like the *Verklärte Nacht*, *Pelléas and Mélisande* and the D minor string quartet the chamber symphony is in one movement. In 1912 Webern discussed the construction of the work as a fusion of the classical movements into a single movement. In this Schoenberg continues the idea of the D minor quartet. In both cases the development section is extended, according to the significance which Schoenberg gave to the principle of development in classical symphonic and chamber music, in general. But every analysis of the chamber symphony brings us to the point where we cannot make any distinction between a purely formal examination and the observation of harmonic, melodic and contrapuntal events. If one compares the chamber symphony with works of other composers written at the same time, like Mahler's Sixth Symphony or the compositions of Max Reger, the harmony is always in the foreground. For the first time Schoenberg wishes to replace the construction of chords in thirds of a traditional kind by a system of fourths. Right at the beginning of the symphony there is a six-part fourth chord G–C–F–B flat–E flat–A flat, but these notes are still used as an alteration of a conventional chord, and resolve into F major. Immediately after this comes the theme in fourths, sounding like a rocket in the first horn: D–G–C–F–B flat–E flat.

We have seen Schoenberg's inclination to leave the opening tonality in a descent to the dominant in his Dehmel song 'Warnung'. Without using any actual fourth-chords, by the three-fold falling fourths E flat–B flat–F–C he created a tonal instability, which dominates the whole sound as a kind of tension and climate. But it needed seven years, from 1899 to 1906, for him to 'emancipate' the interval into fourths, i.e. to release it from its tonal functions and give it a feeling as musical material, which happened for the first time in the chamber symphony. How strong Schoenberg's links with tradition were, how hesitantly and how unwillingly he gave in to his own development, is shown by the rather forcible alterations of meaning of the new sounds derived from traditional chords.

The chamber symphony does not only show this new type of six-layer chords in fourths and its three- four- and five-layer derivatives. It takes over and develops from Schoenberg's earlier works, especially from *Pelléas and Mélisande*, the chain of whole tones and the significance of the traditional 'augmented triad' as a combination of thirds in the whole tone scale. The whole-tone harmonies and melodies, which were important in French music at that time, especially that of Paul Dukas and Claude Debussy, only play an ephemeral part in Schoenberg's musical language and really only in connection with the layers of fourths which are more important constructively. In this Alexander Scriabin with his 'Prometheus Chord' of 1909–10 is much nearer to Schoenberg. For in this chord there is a combination of pure, diminished and augmented fourths in a similar way to Schoenberg's chamber symphony. The inner function of the augmented fourths, the 'tritone' in the development of Schoenberg's language will be discussed in more detail later. In any case the fourths, tritones, semitone relations and series of whole tones were important fermenting elements in the liquidation and replacement of the pillars on which traditional tonality rested.

Schoenberg himself said in his Harmony Book of 1911: 'The fourth-chords, like everything else which later became generally used as technical means, at their first appearance in music were regarded as impressionistic means of expression.' Increased expressiveness became more and more the normal condition of Schoenberg's language. 'Middle of the road experiences', he wrote in 1904 to Mahler, 'do not happen to me.'

There were certainly times when personal experiences multiplied with the expressive power of his music. Up to the time of his second marriage Schoenberg prevented third persons, not only people who were on the outer edge of his large circle of acquaintances, but even friends, from having a glimpse of his private life. His marriage of 1901 with Mathilde von Zemlinsky was blessed by the birth of a daughter in 1902, and Mathilde devoted herself to her duties as housewife and mother all the more because the external existence of the young couple was a continual struggle with material circumstances and perpetual worries. Schoenberg kept her apart from his circle of friends; she did not accept invitations to Mahler's house and her name was not mentioned in Schoenberg's exchange of letters with Strauss. However, in Schoenberg's letter to Mahler in 1906 he said in answering an invitation to Maiernigg: 'The condition of my wife – she will be having a child at the beginning of September – saps all my pleasure because I am worried about her'. The child was born on 22 September; a son called Georg. With this increase in the family Schoenberg's troubles also increased. Perhaps at this time there was already some tension between the couple.

In the summer of 1906 Anton von Webern ended his studies at the university with promotion to Doctor of Philosophy. His dissertation was on the Flemish-Austrian Renaissance musician Heinrich Isaac. The choice of this subject shows the interest which Webern had for the strict forms of counterpoint and canon,

Anton von Webern shortly after completing his studies with
Schoenberg, Stettin 1912

an interest which had first been aroused through Schoenberg's instruction. We know indeed that Schoenberg had already written canons of the strictest kind in 1905. But he only had a very limited interest in the purely musicological work of his oldest pupil. To regard music as science or to get interested in the history of music lay outside his inclinations. And even if we regard his remark in his Harmony Book of 1911 'I have never read a history of music' as a paradoxical and provocative exaggeration, we also know the scepticism which he felt during the whole of his life about the discipline of musicology and almost all its academic representatives. In this he was very near to the other of his two favourite pupils, Alban Berg.

Otherwise 1906 provided no larger and more important experiences in Schoenberg's life. His brother-in-law Zemlinsky continued his work as chief conductor at the Volksoper on the Währinger Gürtel, where through the brilliant musical results of his premières he soon aroused attention.

1907 began with preparations for two concerts of great importance. On 8 February Rosé gave the first performance of the Chamber Symphony with his quartet and the wind ensemble of the Vienna Philharmonic; shortly before, on 5 February, he had given the first performance of the 1st string quartet in the Bösendorfer Room. Gustav Mahler, who was present, made a strong attack on an angry listener who showed his displeasure by whistling on a doorkey. The impression of the work was so strong that Mahler wrote the following letter to Richard Strauss:

'Dear Friend! Yesterday I heard Schoenberg's new quartet, and I had such an important and enormous impression from it that I cannot prevent myself from suggesting it to you urgently for the Musicians' Meeting in Dresden. I am sending the score herewith, and hope that you will have time to look at it – The Rosé Quartet offers to play the work if their travel expenses are met.

Please forgive me, for I know that you are very busy, for putting this upon you, but I think that you yourself will enjoy the work. With best wishes and in haste your friend M. Thank you very much for *Salome*. It never leaves my writing desk.'

In March and April 1907 Schoenberg wrote two large ballads for voice and piano, which were published together as opus 12. They were written for a competition which the Berlin publisher August Scherl had arranged for his well-known magazine 'Die Woche'. There had already been a competition for ballad poems in 1906, in which among others Josef Lauff, Otto Ernst, Hermann Löns, Max Geissler and Ernst Zahn had taken part and the results of which appeared as *A New Treasury of German Ballads.* Three prizes of 3000, 2000 and 1000 marks were offered for settings of these poems. The judges were Wilhelm Berger, Carl Krebs, Felix Schmidt, Georg Schumann and Max Schillings. 742 compositions were sent in; Schoenberg was among the competitors with 'Jane Grey' (text by Heinrich Ammann) and 'Der verlorene Haufen' (text by Victor Klemperer). However the prizes were given to Hans Hermann, Heinrich Eckl and Gustav Lazarus. In the volume *Prize-winning Ballads, composed for the Woche* in 1908 twelve other compositions were also published, including a setting of 'Jane Grey' by Philipp Rödelberger and one of 'Verlorener Haufen' by Hugo Kaun.

Schoenberg's 'Verlorener Haufen' was begun on 15 March and was finished at the end of April. 'Jane Grey' was finished on 28 April. Schoenberg began to set a third text from the *New German Treasury of Ballads* but left it after four pages; 'Jeduch' by Löns.

Schoenberg himself in *Looking back* described the ballads as 'immediate predecessors of the 2nd string quartet'. Both are written in his favourite key of D minor, but the negation of it goes further in 'Jane Grey' than in the 'Verlorene Haufen'. Both contain the melodic and harmonic combinations of a fourth, a semitone and a tritone, which act as elements of fermentation against diatonicism and tonality.

Mahler's letter to Strauss had the desired result; at the beginning of June the Rosé Quartet played Schoenberg's D minor quartet at a matinée of the Musicians' Meeting in Dresden. Schoenberg accepted the invitation of the General German Musicians' Society. Afterwards he thanked Rosé on a postcard 'for the very splendid performance'. It was necessary for him to repeat his thanks and give expression to his joy at the sensational success of the performance. 'You have been praised in all the papers with all the strongest expressions of appreciation. I am even more glad, as the gentlemen of the Petri Quartet described the work as unperformable. It is very important, that these haughty people have been shown for once what one means by quartet playing . . . !' Schoenberg spent the summers of 1907 and 1908 in Gmunden on the Traunsee.

Both Mahler and Schoenberg knew little about the events which were taking place round the turn of the century in the artistic scene. When the young Alma-Maria Schindler and her stepfather Carl Moll entered the circle of musicians a new world was opened to Mahler and soon to Schoenberg too. In 1897 the most modern spirits amongst the Viennese painters, architects and sculptors formed a society, which was called Sezession after the Munich prototype of 1892. The leading figures were Gustav Klimt and Alfred Roller, who both were later the first to leave the group again in the restless year of 1905. In 1899 Roller became a teacher at the School of Industrial Art, where he educated a series of important pupils. In the art of Germany and Austria at that time the tendency was to lead away from naturalism to a new style. This was closely related to the development of Art Nouveau, which had appeared in Belgium, France and Spain and was as effective and fruitful there as in the German-speaking and the West Slavonic worlds, Schoenberg's only meeting with the spirit of Art Nouveau in 1901 in Berlin did not have any traceable results. The Wolzogen Theater was built by August Endell, one of the most successful and original architects of the modern movement. For Art Nouveau, especially for Gustav Klimt and also for the English painter and designer Aubrey Beardsley, who was very much related to him spiritually, a plant was no longer an object to be observed as a manifestation of nature, but led exclusively to the drawing of ornaments which were called floreal.

In 1902 Roller became a friend and collaborator of Mahler's. Their work together in the Court Opera began on 21 February 1903 with an entirely new kind of production of Wagner's *Tristan and Isolde*. The première aroused a great deal of attention. In contrast to the Viennese tradition of well-worked-out scenic naturalism, which had specially been brought to a high level by Antonio Brioschi, one now saw a stage picture and a stage set which both in its details and in its larger conception fitted the dramatic and musical essence of the work. The giving up of naturalism and turning to a new consciously formed style had entered scenic design. Schoenberg, who did not come back to Vienna until the summer of 1903, got to know this performance in a later revival. In it he saw a new way of using stage lighting. The 'Light-Music', which Oskar Bie, one of the most important Berlin music critics of the epoch, described in connection with the Mahler-Roller *Tristan*, certainly aroused or strengthened tendencies in Schoenberg which later produced creative results. Mahler and Roller carried their scenic reform through in such a radical way that they even had to think of the disturbing effect of the lights on the desks in the orchestra. This was one of the reasons which led to a deepening of the orchestra pit in 1903, soon after the *Tristan* première.

Mahler's most important production with Alfred Roller came on 7 October 1904, Beethoven's *Fidelio*. A year later Mozart's *Don Giovanni* followed, and in 1905 a new production of Wagner's *Ring of the Nibelungs* was begun, which took several years to complete. Schoenberg went to all of these performances. In 1905 he also heard the first performance of Hans Pfitzner's *Rose vom Liebesgarten*, whose scenic demands came halfway to meet Roller's ideas.

A close friendship joined Schoenberg and Zemlinsky in these years to Mahler. Alma, the housewife and very gifted artist, had been friendly with painters and painting through her father Schindler and also her stepfather Carl Moll since her childhood. A strong youthful love had tied her to the much older Gustav Klimt. She took a lively part in the development of the arts, specially since the foundation of the Viennese Sezession. And so in her house – and this corresponded entirely to the wide cultural horizon of Gustav Mahler's – there were meetings of as many painters, sculptors and architects as there were musicians and opera people. Schoenberg, who had had hardly any contact in his youth with art, looked with growing interest into a world which opened his eyes in a new way. His later friendship with the architect Adolf Loos, and the painters Oskar Kokoschka, Max Oppenheimer and Vassily Kandinsky had their foundations in these years.

In 1906 artistic Vienna was put in a state of excitement by an exhibition of forty-five pictures by Vincent van Gogh in the Miethke Gallery. The painter's temperament and his glowing imagination in colour of this man who died in 1890 at the age of thirty-three by suicide met the feeling for art of a generation which had already been set in uproar by the Sezessionist movement. Amont the young artists who felt themselves electrified by this Van Gogh exhibition was Richard Gerstl. He was born on 14 September 1883 in Vienna, was a difficult child and left high school before his final examination. In 1903 he became a pupil of the Vienna Academy of Arts, but only for a short time. About this time his first self-portrait was painted, still in an academic style. After studying on his own and working as an apprentice in the studio of other older painters, he became independent artistically and in a studio in the Liechentstein Park he began to paint a series of his highly original pictures, which brought him belated fame. As well as urban pictures like the 'Inn in the

Liechtenstein Park' and the 'Danube Canal', and landscapes like 'Tree in the Garden' he painted especially portraits, double portraits like the 'Two Sisters' and group pictures, in which he found his own style. In it the influence of Van Gogh was recognizable and also that of the Norwegian Edvard Munch. The exhibition of pictures by Paul Gauguin at the Miethke Gallery in 1907 impressed him very much.

Like the somewhat younger Kokoschka Gerstl was gifted in many directions. He had studied philosophy and classical languages and from his youth onwards seems to have had a great interest in modern music. He joined musicians' circles as a keen concert-goer. We do not know if he knew the two Mahlers and Alfred Roller, but at least from 1907 onwards he became a friend of Zemlinsky and the Schoenberg family.

About this time Schoenberg, for whom a single art was not sufficient to express his powerful ideas, was looking for possibilities of translating his inner visions into reality. Just as once Zemlinsky as a friend had instructed him in counterpoint, now Gerstl showed him the elements of painting. Mathilde too, Schoenberg's wife, was captivated by the personality of the much younger painter. Like Schoenberg himself she became his pupil. And she was his model as well.

In 1908 the Schoenbergs were still living in the Liechtenstrasse 68–70 in the 9th District. Gerstl moved into a studio in the same house. The pictures which he painted of Schoenberg, Mathilde and the whole family have an extraordinarily spiritualized and immaterial expression. They are premonitions of German expressionism which came somewhat later, embodied by Emil Nolde and Karl Schmidt-Rottluff. The colour is laid on in pastel as in the pictures by Kokoschka painted at the same time. Portrait likeness is subordinated to a visionary stylization of the heads. The same is also true of his pictures of Alban Berg and Alexander von Zemlinsky.

Gerstl was seized by a passionate affection for Mathilde Schoenberg. It is certain that in 1907, probably soon after the birth of his son Georg in September 1906, Schoenberg's marriage had reached a critical situation. Because of Mahler's departure from Vienna at the end of 1907 Schoenberg was in a state of inner confusion and spiritual unrest, of which we can find traces in his work. And the altered creative position as the result of his activities as a painter made him turn away from the realities of life into complete isolation.

On 9 March 1907 Schoenberg wrote the beginning of a new composition in the third of his sketchbooks. It was the second string quartet in F sharp minor, which was given the opus number 10. Work on it was interrupted several times by other compositions. On the same day in March Schoenberg had finished his chorus 'Friede auf Erden' on a poem of Conrad Ferdinand Mayer; the two ballads were written in March and April. The four movements of the F sharp minor quartet were not written in chronological order. The third, 'Litanei' which adds a singing voice to the quartet, bears the date of completion 11 July 1908. However, the second movement, the curious scherzo, was not finished until 27 July. In this summer Schoenberg's marriage broke up. However, Mathilde came back to Schoenberg from flight with Gerstl. Mutual friends, specially Webern, had worked as intermediaries and had appealed particularly to Mathilde's maternal feelings, for she had left behind two young children, the six-year-old Gertrud and Georg, who was only just two.

The F sharp minor quartet is dedicated to Mathilde Schoenberg, 'My Wife'. In the third and fourth movement the voice increases the number of performers to a quintet. Both movements are settings of poems by Stefan George. The 'Litanei' begins with the words:

> *Deep is the mourning which clouds round me,*
> *again I enter, Lord! Into your house.*
> *Long was the journey, faint are the limbs,*
> *Empty my coffers, full alone my pain.*

And it ends:

> *Kill my longings, close my wounds!*
> *Give me love, give me your joy!*

The finale of the work is formed by the 'Entrückung' (turning the back), a vision of a trip into space, the feeling of 'air from another planet', an enigmatic expression of setting oneself free from all earthly bonds. The two vocal movements of this quartet are the last steps in a world of music which is turning away from key and musical consonance.

In the first movement of the work, which was written more than a year before the others, Schoenberg does not go beyond the harmonic and tonal limits of the chamber symphony of 1906. However, his deep inner crisis, after it had been overcome, finds an ironic expression in the second movement. This begins with a very quick motoric movement on a cello pedal of D. A somewhat crabbed scherzo-character is presented; the ostinato D in the bass returns. Between passages in free tonality there are paradoxical triads, sometimes major, sometimes minor. Then, after 106 bars of allabreve, a trio begins in a slower 3/4 time. The second violin plays the popular song 'Ach, Du lieber Augustin', developed in a few variations. In the cello the bass part circles round the unrelated tonalities of D and A flat, leading to a monotonous falling fifths figure on the notes B–E–E and A–D–D in a banal manner. One does not need much imagination to think of the words of the text of the song 'alles ist hin' (all is lost). This may have meant for Schoenberg not only the breaking up of a domestic situation but also a musical surrender. The ironic and bitter gallows humour would hardly be possible for him to have written if the catastrophe in his personal relations had not been repaired, so that the final vocal movements seem to presage a new beginning. In any case this passage is only an episode in the second movement, and after 28 bars the motoric movement of the earlier part is taken up again in a short transitional passage and leads in a very quick stretta to a big dynamic outbreak on the ostinato D in the bass.

Autumn 1908. Schoenberg finds new consolation in his teaching work. Alban Berg had already finished his counterpoint studies in 1907 and began to study composition. Schoenberg's circle of friends became closer and closer. On 27 September 1908 he set the Stefan George poem 'Du lehnest wider eine Silberweide', the first composition in which all connections with traditional conceptions of key and consonances are left behind. This is one of the big cycle of fifteen poems from *Das Buch der Hängenden Gärten* by Stefan George, op. 15, in which it is the thirteenth song. Perhaps this began Schoenberg's peculiar superstitious relation to the number 13, which disquieted him right up to the last hours of his life.

Richard Gerstl could not bear the final break with the Schoenbergs. On 4 November 1908, at the age of 25, he committed suicide. Before this he destroyed the letters and drawings from which posterity could have had information about his last months, and also part of his output as a painter. He left life young and incomplete, like the Viennese philosopher Otto Weininger, who shortly after the appearance of his famous book *Geschlecht und Character* in 1903 also committed suicide at the age of twenty-three.

As a painter Schoenberg was spiritually akin to Gerstl, nine years younger than himself. Schoenberg's portraits and self portraits, especially that of Helene Berg, are nearer to nature than Gerstl's more abstract and stylized portrait visions. But the pictures which he himself called visions and caricatures like the 'Vision of Christ' or the 'Portrait of a Critic', start from similar artistic principles. The way of using colours without transition and with a ruthless hardness, is common to both. But in the course of his development as a painter Schoenberg had a tendency towards the grotesque and to ironic distortion, which one does not find with Gerstl. It is a characteristic which was first found rather late in his music, especially in some pieces in *Pierrot Lunaire*. This was anticipated by the song of Klaus the Fool in the 'Gurrelieder', but the years of his important development in musical language, that is to say the time between 1906 and 1909, only provide a single but very important example: the 'Augustin' passage in the F sharp minor quartet.

In order to introduce his pupils to the public and to give them a chance of hearing their own works, Schoenberg gave a concert on 7 November 1907 in the Hall of the Viennese Merchants' Corporation. Works were performed by Berg, Horwitz, Ivanov, Jalowetz, Stein, Wilma von Webenau and Webern. Schoenberg's work as a teacher was praised in an article in the *Neue Wiener Journal*. Among the performers was Marietta Jonasz, who shortly afterwards married the orthopaedic surgeon Dr. Werndorff; she was an excellent young pianist, whom Schoenberg thanked warmly for her performance on a postcard.

Almost a year later to the day, on 8 November 1908, Schoenberg gave an orchestral concert in the large Musikvereinssaal, in which he conducted Webern's Passacaglia and Irène Bien performed Berg's piano variations.

A few weeks later, on 21 December 1908, Rosé gave the first performance of Schoenberg's second quartet at one of his concerts in the Bösendorfersaal. This led to powerful protests, laughter, and a great deal of disturbance. Marie Gutheil-Schoder, the singer of the soprano part in the last two movements, carried out her task in tears. But the work was heard without disturbance at a later performance given by the Ansorge Society.

In Schoenberg's circle from this time onwards the opening motive of the quartet in F sharp minor, which played backwards is similar to the introduction of the second act of *Tristan*, became a whistle of recognition like Siegfried's horn call used once to be with the Wagnerians. So at least in this piece Schoenberg's dream was fulfilled, that his melodies would become the folk songs of later generations.

At the time when Schoenberg was turning away from conventional aesthetics to new aims and became a scandal in Europe, he found a number of important interpreters of both sexes who learnt and performed his works. Through Mahler he had met Anna von Mildenburg, the dramatic mezzo-soprano and a fine interpreter of Wagner's and Strauss's scores. Born in 1872, from 1898 to 1917 she was a member of the Vienna Opera company. She was admired by Cosima Wagner, who studied Kundry with her in 1897, and in 1909 in Bayreuth she sang Ortrud in some *Lohengrin* performances. The biographical notice in the Bayreuth Festival guide of 1909 says: 'As a concert singer she prefers Beethoven, Schubert, Schumann, Wagner, Brahms, Hugo Wolf, Mahler, Pfitzner, Walter, Schoenberg and Strauss.' Her recognition of Schoenberg at this time was very audacious. Schoenberg admired Mildenburg as a singer and respected her as a person.

Among the Viennese writers at that time Hermann Bahr was like a prophet of the new spirit. In all fields of art he helped and propagated the position which was called Sezessionistic. He encouraged youth and attacked convention; he was an Austrian who understood the European mission of his country. 'In 1899 I was in Rome and Naples, in 1900 in Paris again, in 1904 and 1905 in Athens, in 1907 and 1908 in Berlin again as a producer in Reinhardt's German theatre, and for five years every summer I spent a month in Venice, in 1909 two months in Bayreuth, in 1910 I spent the winter in London, the spring in Paris and the autumn in London again. In foreign countries I always recognized again that all nations are capable of turning themselves into one new nation'; this he wrote in 1913 at the age of fifty. His musical roots came from Wagner; in the year that Wagner died, in 1883, he met Hugo Wolf. In 1902 he was entranced by Richard Strauss's *Feuersnot*.

On 24 March 1909 Bahr heard the new Viennese production of *Elektra* with stage designs by Alfred Roller. Anna von Mildenburg sang Clytemnestra. From this day on the poet fell for her; shortly afterwards she became his wife.

Bahr knew Schoenberg at that time from his Viennese performances and scandals. He helped him artistically and as a person. He had set up a foundation for the support of fighting artists, to which many rich Viennese gave their services or money. After one Schoenberg scandal the dentist Dr. Alois Botstiber, who had treated the composer, refused to accept any fee; this was his contribution to the 'Hermann Bahr Foundation for misunderstood Heroes of the Spirit.'

Since his marriage to Anna von Mildenburg Bahr himself realized the tenuousness of his musical knowledge. On 10 April 1909 he wrote to Schoenberg that he would like to begin theoretical studies with him in the autumn. In June he accompanied Anna to Bayreuth. The spirit of the rehearsals and the performances, and the meetings with conductors and singers fascinated him. He enjoyed the 'Magic of Bayreuth' (the title of an article he wrote in July) in spite of the anti-modernist spirit which reigned there. For he was on the side of Mildenburg, whom Siegfried Wagner 'described with a suspicious look of appraisal the Goddess of the Sezession.'

The Bahrs spent the autumn in Vienna. Nothing came of his planned studies with Schoenberg. But on 10 October Bahr wrote that an admirer who wanted to remain unnamed had given him some money for the composer; he wanted Schoenberg to come to him on Sunday at four o'clock. Two days later he sent him 3000 kronen.

Anna Bahr-Mildenburg had sung Schoenberg's early songs. For the first performance of the 'Gurrelieder' in 1913 he thought of her as the Wood Dove. She studied the score: 'Dramatically I cannot understand it at all – I mean all greatness and strength comes to me from peace. This I will have to use all alone in the Wood Dove part. But there is greatness, much greatness in it, and you must hope that I will be able to bring it to expression;' so she wrote to him.

Schoenberg's friendship with Hermann and Anna Bahr did not prevent him from keeping in contact with Karl Kraus. Kraus and Bahr had been implacable enemies for years. Like Berg and Webern Schoenberg read the 'Fackel' regularly. (The 'Fackel' was a literary magazine edited by Kraus.) Schoenberg sent Kraus an article attacking musical criticism, which Kraus sent back to him on 21 January 1909. A year later Schoenberg tried some aphorisms. Kraus answered on 18 March 1910: 'I thank you very much for your literary contribution. Unfortunately, although it interested me very much I cannot publish it in the 'Fackel'. Aphorisms should not in fact be a heading in the 'Fackel' but only a necessity of life for me. I would like to discuss this with you soon verbally – perhaps in the Café Imperial one afternoon.'

Marie Gutheil-Schoder (1874–1935) was one of Mahler's

company in Vienna from 1901 onwards; she was the brave interpreter of the soprano part in the first performance of the second string quartet. In January 1909 Marschalk sent her the songs which had been published by the Drei-Lilienverlag at Schoenberg's request. In 1921 she studied *Pierrot* with Steuermann and Erwin Stein for a performance which Paul von Klenau conducted in Copenhagen. In 1924 she sang the first performance of 'Erwartung' under Zemlinsky in Prague; Zemlinsky preferred her to Marya Freund, who had been suggested by Schoenberg.

Schoenberg met Marya Freund (1876–1966) on a summer holiday in Gmunden on the Traunsee, in 1908. As a child she had studied the violin with Pablo de Sarasate, later learnt singing and became a member of the opera company in her home town of Breslau (the present Wroczlaw). Schoenberg admired her musicality and quickly became a friend of this attractive woman. At his request she sang Tove in the first performance of the 'Gurrelieder', and later performed *Pierrot* in Paris and the Stefan George songs op 15. From 1925 onwards she lived permanently in Paris, where she died at the age of 90. She corresponded with Schoenberg from 1912 to 1949. From some undetermined date they addressed each other in the second person.

RELATIONS WITH MAHLER

From his early youth, that is to say from 1897 to the very last years of his life, the artistic and human personality of Gustav Mahler strongly attracted Schoenberg. We do not know when he got to know Mahler's music. But we do know that Alexander von Zemlinsky, whom he met for the first time in 1895, was one of Mahler's greatest admirers at that time. Schoenberg was twenty-one years old when he played the cello in the orchestral society 'Polyhymnia' in those days and was still working in a bank. It is very probable that his increased occupation with music and his friendship with Zemlinsky made it easier for him to leave his employment. His work as a composer began to increase about this time with songs and piano pieces and became more important. From 1896 it became more intensive when he gave up his work at the bank. A serenade for small orchestra, written at the beginning of September of this year and his works in 1897, which ranged from songs to an orchestral piece and a string quartet, testify to this. All these compositions were still influenced by Brahms; Wagner's influence was more gradual and was clearly recognizable from the songs of 1899 onwards.

Schoenberg's path towards Mahler ran its course in curious curves due to personal influences, which again were due to Zemlinsky. In Vienna, the painter Schindler had a young daughter, Alma-Maria, who from her childhood onwards showed unusual musical gifts. In 1899 she became a pupil of Alexander von Zemlinsky. The strange relationship between the small, gnome-like but gifted musician and the beautiful, happy twenty-year-old girl was later described by Alma-Maria Mahler-Werfel in her reminiscences with great frankness.

In 1900 Franz Schalk conducted the first Viennese performance of Mahler's first symphony, which had previously had its première in Budapest. Alma-Maria describes the excited discussions which took place after the concert. The symphony by the director of the Opera, who was certainly admired by her at

that time, had in her words 'filled us with anger'. Shortly afterwards Zemlinsky introduced her to his pupil and friend, the
twenty-six-year-old Schoenberg. She did not conceal from
Zemlinsky her lack of sympathy for him, to which Zemlinsky
answered: 'Have a good look at him; the world will have a lot to
say about him.' Since then she met Schoenberg every time she
went for a lesson at Zemlinsky's. It was the time when he had
finished writing the string sextet *Verklärte Nacht* and had begun
the 'Gurrelieder'. We know that in Alma-Maria's memoirs, as
also in her book on Mahler, fantasy and truth are often mixed up
together. In her memoirs she muddled up dates and also artistic
events. But her memory is reliable in one thing, and her judgment
is not much influenced by either hate or love: that is the charac-
terization of people whom she knew well. And, therefore, her
description of the young Schoenberg can be treated as a reliable
source. She speaks of him as suffering from inexhaustible
Bohemianism, from being original, prone to paradoxes, aggressive
in conversation and taking pleasure in argument.

On 9 November 1901 in the Viennese house of the famous
anatomist Emil Zuckerkandl there took place the fateful meeting
of the twenty-two-year-old Alma-Maria with Gustav Mahler,
who was nineteen years older. Shortly afterwards she met Schoenberg again, just before his move to Berlin. When she asked if he
would go to the first Viennese performance of Mahler's Fourth
Symphony on 12 January 1902, Schoenberg replied bitingly:
'How can Mahler do something in his Fourth Symphony which
he could not already do in his First.' There was no mention of the
fact that at this time he would be working in Berlin.

On 9 March 1902 the marriage of the director of the Opera to
the beautiful young Alma-Maria, a marriage which was much
discussed in Viennese society, took place in the Karlskirche.
Schoenberg was living in Berlin; he had close personal contacts
with Richard Strauss and did not return to Vienna until September 1903, after a longish summer holiday in Payerbach. In
Vienna he had possibilities of work. He had missed the performance of Mahler's Fourth Symphony; we do not know whether
he got to know other works of Mahler in Berlin.

Zemlinsky remained in friendly contact with the newly-
married Mahlers. He visited them both in 1904 in Maiernigg on
the Wörthersee, where from 1903 to 1907 they regularly spent
their holidays. In December of this year Mahler's Third Symphony was given its first Viennese performance, two years after

its première in Krefeld in 1902. Schoenberg, who had previously been opposed to Mahler's music, as we know, attended the concert. On 12 December 1904, immediately after the concert, he wrote his first letter to Mahler. It is an unreserved confession and in addition a document which unmistakably reveals Schoenberg's mode of expression, which can be found in all his important letters.

'In order to speak of the unheard-of impression which your symphony made on me, I cannot talk as one musician to another but I must speak as man to man. For: I have seen your soul naked, stark naked. It lay before me like a wild mysterious landscape with its horror-provoking shadows and ravines, and, next to these, joyful charming sunny meadows, idyllic resting places. I felt the symphony to be an experience of nature with its horror and evil and its transfiguring, tranquillizing rainbows.

And then follows a defence against something which Schoenberg does not allow to be forced upon him: the defence against the famous and much discussed 'Programme', which Mahler attached to his symphony. 'Does it matter', asks Schoenberg further 'whether I am a good or bad interpreter of the feelings which an experience arouses in me? Must I frankly *understand*, where I have experienced and felt?'

Finally the description of his own feelings: 'I felt they were battles about illusions; I felt the grief of a disillusioned man, I saw good and evil forces struggling with each other, I saw a man in torturing agitation seeking for inner harmony; I could see it, a man, a drama, *truth*, most reckless truth!'

And at the end Schoenberg made a personal confession: 'I had to let off steam, please forgive me, I do not have medium feelings, it is either – or!'

So this was the thunderbolt. The despiser became the admirer, and the mocker a passionate follower, and even spoke of Mahler as a saint. Their personal relationship now became close and friendly. But there were still some crises. In her Mahler book Alma-Maria described how dramatically events occurred in the relationship between Mahler on the one side and their two friends Zemlinsky and Schoenberg on the other. In her diary of 26 January 1905 she wrote: 'Yesterday a concert of Zemlinsky and Schoenberg. My feelings were justified. Zemlinsky is . . . not as strong as Schoenberg, who is indeed an intricate and very interesting person. People walked out *en masse* and banged the doors during the music. Much hissing – but his talent convinced us both.' This was the evening on which Schoenberg himself conducted the first performance of his symphonic poem *Pelléas and Mélisande*.

It was Zemlinsky who took Schoenberg to Mahler's house. As Alma-Maria says, he was full of youthful protests against the older artists, whom he also admired. After a frugal meal music was played or discussed: 'at the beginning quite peaceably, but suddenly some arrogant remark by Schoenberg, a reprimand from on high by Mahler, and a row broke out in all directions. Schoenberg produced paradoxes of the most wicked kind, but Mahler answered in a doctrinaire and lecturing manner; Schoenberg jumped up and ran out with a short word of thanks. Zemlinsky followed shaking his head.' Mahler forbade any future invitations to the 'conceited fellow'. Schoenberg swore never to enter the house again. But after a while Mahler missed something: 'Why don't "Eisele and Beisele"[1] come to us any more?' And soon the two inseparables came back again.

In 1906 Zemlinsky exchanged his position as director at the popular Carltheater in Vienna for the artistically more satisfying one of principal conductor at the Volksoper. But he was aiming higher. Mahler, whom he had never himself approached with a request, knew this quite clearly and in the summer of 1906 offered him a position as conductor at the Court Opera, a job which Zemlinsky took on in 1908. Schoenberg heard of this and thanked Mahler with a spontaneous, extravagant letter on 14 June 1906: '*How wonderful, how marvellous of you this was; I must say this to you, that there is only one person in the world and that is Mahler. I have always liked you very very much – you perhaps don't know this – but today I know why! I kiss your hands a thousand times.*'

Mahler answered him straight away and invited him to spend the summer holidays at Maiernigg. Schoenberg was spending the summer of 1906 in Rottach-Egern on the Tegernsee and wrote on 18 July to Mahler that he had been busy finishing his chamber symphony and so had had to delay his reply. Mahler's letter, in which the older man confirmed that they had drawn nearer together, had pleased Schoenberg very much: '*I . . . am more proud of this than if you had pra sed a work of mine, although I have the greatest regard for your judgement. Personal affection is the most important thing to me in relationships between people.*' Then he mentions the invitation to visit Mahler, which he had almost accepted spontaneously but later had to refuse it. Mathilde, his wife, was pregnant and was awaiting the birth of her second

---

[1] Eisele and Beisele were Viennese comic figures of the time.

child. So he could not make so long a journey as fourteen hours. But he suggested to Mahler that he should visit him at the Mozart Festival in Salzburg in August, which was only two hours away. He also asks him to give greetings to Alma and to say to her 'that I am happy that she has at last come round to the view that I am "a nice fellow" – I have always maintained it myself, but unfortunately very few people believe me.' And finally he says he would like to send the chamber symphony to Mahler in case the latter had the time and the desire to look at it.

In 1903 Schoenberg had begun his composition courses at the Schwarzwald schools. In 1904 Alban Berg, Anton von Webern, Egon Wellsez, Erwin Stein and Dr. Heinrich Jalowetz became his private pupils. Some of these had been sent to Schoenberg by the Professor of Musicology at the Vienna University, Professor Dr. Guido Adler. Adler was one of Mahler's closest friends. The young composers, who looked on Schoenberg with indescribable enthusiasm, were also passionate partisans of Mahler's. Among them Alban Berg became friendly with the great man and his young wife. This relationship lasted long after Mahler's death up to the last year of Berg's life. Alma-Maria's daughter Manon from her marriage with Walter Gropius was greatly honoured by Berg; when she died at the age of eighteen he wrote his violin concerto in her memory.

Together with the growing circle of Schoenberg's students Mahler was one of those who applauded all Vienna performances of Schoenberg which he was able to attend. He missed no opportunity of taking the side of his younger friend, even if he could not entirely follow his development as a composer. The D minor String Quartet he still found approachable; and when it was hissed at the Viennese performance, Mahler went up to one of those who were protesting against it and reprimanded him. It was only the intervention of friends which prevented them from coming to blows. He behaved in the same way at the performance of the chamber symphony by the Rosé Quartet and the wind ensemble of the Vienna Philharmonic. When the audience became restless, Mahler caused peace to be restored at a word. However, the work remained strange to him. He said to Alma-Maria: 'I don't understand his music, but he is young; perhaps he is right. I am old, and perhaps do not have the ear for his music any more.'

This incident happened only six months before Mahler's departure from Vienna. In October he left the Court Opera and began his various activities in New York. But before this he wanted to have a good conversation with his two friends 'Eisele and Beisele' and their friends. Alma-Maria describes the conversation around the table in the Grinzing in the 'Zum Schutzengel', at which she was not present herself, but which Mahler described to her when he came home late at night laughing. It must have been a cheerful and noisy affair, and Mahler's attempt to go away secretly with Schoenberg and Zemlinsky from the larger circle misfired, after which it became still noisier.

Alma-Maria also described their departure from Vienna: 'Schoenberg and Zemlinsky had collected their pupils and Mahler's friends on the station platform. They were all standing there when we arrived, with their hands full of flowers and their eyes full of tears; they got into our carriage, and decorated it, the seats, the floor, everything.'

During Mahler's American years from 1907 to 1911 Schoenberg and his pupils began the fateful development of musical language which was the beginning of the New Music in the twentieth century. Mahler and Alma came back to Europe every summer and spent their summer holidays regularly in Toblach in the Tyrol. In 1908 Schoenberg had written the first of his nontonal songs on a text of Stefan George. He spent the summer of 1909 in Steinakirchen in Lower Austria, and there wrote the Five Orchestral Pieces, opus 16. After he had offered it in vain to Richard Strauss for performance, he also showed the score to Mahler. Mahler said openly that he could not read it, for he was not able to translate the optical impression of the pieces into the acoustical. In the same year Mahler's Seventh Symphony, which had had its première in Prague in 1908, was performed in Vienna. Schoenberg was there and let some time elapse before he wrote to Mahler about it on 29 December 1909. The Seventh and Third Symphonies had lasting effects on him, he says. He had felt the element of the sensational and of the whipping up of excitement less than before. His impression was of a perfect calm, founded on artistic harmony: 'I have regarded you as a classic. But a classic which is still a *model* for me.' Then follow remarks about rumours that Mahler was writing a Theseus opera – it was never planned or written. However Schoenberg takes this opportunity of asking what Theseus really is:

> '*I only know him from the Temple of Theseus. He has no other space in my consciousness, as I have already forgotten the results of my history lessons.*'

This remark is typical of Schoenberg's indifference to classical literature. In all his works and in all his letters and literary articles Greek and Roman antiquity are completely eclipsed by the world of the Bible. He was similarly indifferent to the works of Shakespeare. The letter, which was sent to New York, contains a postscript to Alma-Maria, who seems to have complained that he never wrote to her.

On Mahler's fiftieth birthday Schoenberg, who had recently moved into a larger apartment in the Hietzinger Haupstrasse 113, wrote him a long letter. It is a statement of his admiration for him and also of his repentance for having annoyed the person he so much admired with so much argumentation. He says he has a right as the younger man to be different, even if imperfect:

'*But there is one thing which I have to bow down to: the essential thing which comes out of great men, that unnamable element which I have found in your presence and which to me is the power of a genius . . . If in spite of this I have contradicted you . . . perhaps it was short-sightedness, perhaps obstinacy? Perhaps it was love too, for I have always respected you enormously. It was like a young girl: love, which pursues with hate.*'

And he hopes that Mahler will soon finally return to the hated loved Vienna. The rabble do not deserve to have him conducting there, but perhaps his circle of friends do. He will certainly find so much warm admiration that all the earlier ill-will will be forgotten.

In the summer of 1910 the lack of money which afflicted Schoenberg nearly all the time was so great that he asked Mahler for help. Not for himself, but for his wife and the two children. He could not pay the rent, and asked for a loan of 300–400 Gulden, which he would certainly be able to repay next year when he was in the Conservatorium. The request was so urgent that he asked for a reply by telegram, and if possible that the money should be sent telegraphically. Mahler's answer came the next day: he sent Schoenberg 800 kronen.

Schoenberg wrote to thank Mahler on 3 August 1910 in his own special and remarkable way. He speaks of goodness, 'which to the truly superior person is natural, and does not even require an outside stimulus.' He wishes to keep his admiration for Mahler independent of his gratitude to him. He feels 'an expression of that power, to approach which is the sole object of my self-education.' And he justifies his exaggeration as the 'fever which removes impurities from the soul. And to be as pure as you is my

concern, because it is impossible for me to be as great as you.'
This was the last letter that we know was addressed by Schoenberg to Mahler. The event which caused it to be written charac-
terizes both men.

Alma-Maria does not give us very full information about the
last year before Mahler's death in 1911. She was present at the
conversation in which Schoenberg defended his idea of using
varying instrumentation of a single note in order to obtain a kind
of melodic event. Mahler did not understand this at all. Then
came his fatal illness and his return from America in April 1911,
his period in a Paris sanatorium, and the transfer of the dying
man to Vienna. Mahler's mental powers were still untouched,
but physically he was already near to death. Even on his death-
bed he worried about Schoenberg: 'If I go, he has no one left.'
Alma remembered this remark when she created the Gustav
Mahler Foundation after his death. Schoenberg received money
from this for several years.

Mahler died on 18 May, mourned by a large circle of admirers.
A few weeks later, on 17 June 1911, Schoenberg wrote the last of
his Little Piano Pieces, opus 19, and later said that it was written
in memory of Mahler's death. The wide-spaced chord A–F sharp–
B sounds like a reflection of Mahler's late works.

In July of the same year Schoenberg's work on his harmony
book, which was more than 500 pages long, was finished in Ober
St. Veit. Schoenberg dedicated it to the memory of Mahler. And
he added: 'He was a truly great man.' Ten years later he omitted
these words. In the preface to the second edition he said that they
are now superfluous: 'These were words written in deep emotion
after Mahler's death, which echoed my grief for the man who had
been taken from us and my anger at the disproportion between his
value and the recognition which he got. These were troubled,
passionate words, fighting words, which today have a lessened
effect as young people almost fulfil their duty of placing his
work alongside that of our greatest composers.' Mahler's works
are often mentioned in the book, mostly in connection with
Strauss, Pfitzner and Reger. Schoenberg also quotes as a musical
example the eight-part chord from the Sixth Symphony, which
today we regard as an expression of bitonality. On 30 October
1912 in Berlin Schoenberg wrote an article about Mahler which
was the origin of the big chapter in *Style and Idea*. He also wrote
about Mahler's Ninth Symphony in 1917, and in a fragment of an
article on the twenty-fifth anniversary of Mahler's death in 1936.

Three years before his death Schoenberg entered energetically into a discussion about Mahler with two letters written in English to the New York music critic Olin Downes. Downes had written in the *New York Times* about the Seventh Symphony, which had been performed under Dimitri Mitropulos. Schoenberg recommended the critic to study the score so that he could recognize the beauty of the work:

'*After one single hearing, you pronounce your sentence of life and death, regardless of all the experience your trade has gone through when history turned to the absolute contrary of your judgement.*'

He says that probably Downes was afraid to deviate from his earlier unfriendly judgement on Mahler:

'*You are not so old that you dare not change your mind. I am at least ten to twenty years older than you. I can assure you that I am still ready to change my opinions, to learn something new, to accept the contrary and to digest it, the contrary of all I had believed in my whole life.*'

Downes had the nobility to publish Schoenberg's long letter in the *New York Times*. He added his own answer to it. Schoenberg returned to the discussion in a second letter of 21 December. He attacked Downes above everything for ending his review with the words '*Chacun a son gout*'. This appeal to personal taste Schoenberg found wrong, although Downes had admitted that his ideas about music were not unchangeable. And then comes the important section in Schoenberg's letter: '*I hope you will now understand why your condemnation of a great man and composer on the basis of personal taste enraged me. Then I will gladly admit that another cause of this fury derived from the fact that between 1898 and 1908 I had spoken about Mahler in the same manner that you do today. For that I made good subsequently by adoration.*' The dates quoted are striking. Had Schoenberg forgotten the enthusiasm with which he had written in 1904 to Mahler about the latter's Third Symphony? Or did he sometimes relapse into his earlier reserve as regards Mahler's music, relapses that we know nothing about? One might almost believe this if one reads his letter to Downes to the end. For in the descriptions of his opinions at various phases of his life up to maturity he makes a confession: 'Between 1925 and 1935 I did not dare read or listen to Mahler's music. I was afraid that my aversion to it in a preceding period might return. Fortunately when I heard in Los Angeles a moderately satisfactory performance of the Second Symphony I was just as enchanted as ever before.'

The big Mahler chapter in *Style and Idea* was translated into

English by the editor Dika Newlin. One of its chief ideas is the defence of Mahler against the reproach that his themes were banal. Schoenberg admits that he thought so himself at the beginning. But then he reaches the conclusion that a single detail of a work of art could not be banal but only the complete shape of the spiritual approach of its creator. And in a detailed enquiry Schoenberg shows with what art Mahler's themes are built, such as the first one of the Andante of the Sixth Symphony. The whole chapter is not only a creed on a man whom he admired, but also an expression of Schoenberg's view of the world at that time. In this the personal picture of Mahler as the essence of a great man becomes more and more clear. Schoenberg sees him as a genius, and everything which a great man of that kind does was for him an expression of his genius. Half jokingly he once told one of his pupils that he only had to see how Mahler tied his tie in order to learn something from him about the purpose of art. In his innermost being Schoenberg was always a religious man. Belief in genius could not be separated from his view of art. He wanted to admire and honour, and did this with unbounded devotion, if he recognized greatness in other people. His relationship with Richard Strauss also contained this admiration, up to his disappointing experiences from 1909 onwards.

Mahler's and Schoenberg's background and origins were not unlike. Both their fathers were small tradesmen, Mahler's in Iglau, Schoenberg's in Vienna after his move from Bratislava. Both families were gifted musically. Mahler's talent was so developed by lessons in his early childhood that at the age of eleven he was able to appear publicly as a pianist in Iglau. He then had a regular education at the Vienna Conservatorium.

Schoenberg too was attracted to music as a boy. But then his characteristic wish for independence and individuality set in so energetically that he refused the guiding hand of his teacher and became self-taught. However, his work as a composer went a great deal beyond all conventional theories. Schoenberg said later that he had written his harmony book because he had not studied harmony at all. Mahler's school education was also more organized and more complete than Schoenberg's; while Mahler was studying at the Conservatory in Vienna he also matriculated at the university.

The difference between them in age was fourteen years – less than a generation and yet more than was able to give them unanimity in questions of aesthetics and views of art. Musically they were both affected by the quarrel between the Brahms and Wagner parties; Mahler was subjected to the influence of *Tristan* earlier than Schoenberg. Both had the desire to express extra-musical events in music. This increased with Mahler in the course of his development more than with Schoenberg, for whom the idea of absolute music was important at all times.

Mahler grew up in the country and in small provincial towns. In his childhood he was impressed by folk songs, dances and military music from a neighbouring barracks. The whole ethnical variety of colour of the Hapsburg monarchy lives in these primitive melodies. Their reflection can be found in many marches, trumpet calls and dance movements in his symphonies. From his very beginning his spirit was stimulated by metaphysical events. Metaphysical thoughts, searching for God, fear of Eternity, the glory of Heaven all calmed and entranced him.

When Mahler was writing his 'Lieder eines fahrenden Gesellen', Schoenberg was still at school and making his first attempts at composition for one or two violins. He got to know Mahler's First Symphony relatively late through its first Viennese performance. At that time he was very much against music of this kind, because he was very little interested in using folk songs as themes. This was 1900, the year in which he himself sketched out his giant 'Gurrelieder' score and began to write the music. But these 'Gurrelieder' have a definite affinity with the titanic symphonies of Mahler, not only in their time-length but also in the size of the orchestra. In the world of legends and of spirits in the choral work there are points of rest with intimate melodic lines which are close to folksong; these have few points of contact with the folksong-like tone of Mahler, but they have a similar connection with nature. This applies especially to the tender D major song 'So tanzen die Engel vor Gottes Thron nicht', with which Waldemar expresses his love for Tove.

More important than the purely musical differences which separated the young Schoenberg from the maturer Mahler were those of their respective views of the world. The choice of text for the 'Gurrelieder' from the youthful poems of the Dane Jens Peter Jacobsen shows a love of the unreal, saga, fairy-tale and legends and also that of Nordic material and Nordic nature. About the turn of the century Schoenberg shared this love with many representatives of German literature. It was the time when Germany discovered Henrik Ibsen, and the Berlin publisher S. Fischer won him a larger platform in German-speaking countries than he had had in his Norwegian home. Also the novels of Knut Hamsun and slightly later the dramas and prose writings of the Swede August Strindberg enjoyed considerable respect at that time in Central Europe.

Mahler stood completely apart from these tendencies. In Vienna as a student, together with his association with musicians like Hugo Wolf and Anton Bruckner, whose university lectures he attended, he came together more with representatives of socialist ideas than with literary men. But his inborn metaphysical inclinations soon contradicted these influences. The deeply religious character, which was a mark of Mahler together with an increasingly overpowering experience of nature, was already shown in many of his youthful songs, and then burst into powerful flame in 1894 with the Resurrection Symphony. Schoenberg's youthful years too were not free from religious considerations. However, at the age of twenty-four he had freed himself so much from the influence of his Jewish parents that he became a Christian. His music at this time was completely free from metaphysical connections and thoughts. In the 'Gurrelieder' we find supernatural scenes, but these belong more to the scene of saga, like the great vision of the 'Wild Hunt' in the third part.

Up to 1904 Schoenberg, who was still strongly under the influence of Richard Strauss, remained indifferent to Mahler's music. Then came the overpowering impression of the Third Symphony which ascended from human surroundings to deification. When Mahler left Vienna in December 1907, the great crisis in Schoenberg's whole spiritual condition had already been anticipated. It led to an eruption immediately afterwards.

It is not an uncommon phenomenon, especially among romantic spirits, that a creative artist goes beyond the boundaries of his own territory. Schumann was gifted in both music and poetry and so was Wagner. E. T. A. Hoffmann was an interesting writer and a remarkable composer and brilliant draughtsman. Felix Mendelssohn-Bartholdy drew in crayons in many periods of his life and left us his impressions of nature in wonderful little works of art.

In 1907 Schoenberg unexpectedly began to draw and paint. His first pictures are nature studies and portraits. He painted a remarkable picture of Gustav Mahler with his thatch of black hair and in 1911 he portrayed the burial of the man whom he had admired. Most of Schoenberg's ninety or so paintings date from between 1907 and 1910; these were shown in 1964 in Florence at an exhibition at the Maggio Musicale. There are a great number of self-portraits, in which Schoenberg as it were illuminates himself and allows us to recognize many of the peculiarities of his nature.

In the same years his literary activities also began to increase beyond normal day-to-day needs. In his private life he had complications and difficulties which led to the brink of catastrophe. The only man with whom he could perhaps have discussed his problems and from whom he could have had advice and help was Gustav Mahler. And he was living in faraway America, and only came to Austria in the summer months in order to compose.

A few days after Mahler's departure from the South Station Schoenberg wrote on 17 December 1907 a song which is important as showing the direction of his future creation. The text comes from the volume *Wanderer in the Snow* by Stefan George. It is the first of several settings of George written by Schoenberg and shows a new orientation in his relation to contemporary literature. It begins with the lines:

> *I cannot sink down to you with thanks*
> *You are from the spirit of the plain, from which we have*
>   *climbed:*
> *If my consolation will cringe before your sorrow,*
> *Then this will jerk in sign of refusal.*

A strange text, remote from life, and completely different from anything which Schoenberg had set up till then.

But it is not the text alone which differs so much from the thought world which Schoenberg had used up till now for his settings. The song speaks a musical language which leaves all previous experiments behind it, even the Chamber Symphony, opus 9 which had been written not long before. In place of triads appear perfect or altered fourth chords which are connected without any relations in the sense of traditional harmony and only on occasions, like an anchorage, reach a triad which resolves them. However, freedom from tonality is not complete; one can still clearly feel the sub-current which leads to tonal points. And the whole song ends with a chord in B minor. But the critical zone on the frontiers of traditional European music has been reached and is only left exceptionally during the whole duration of the thirty bars which make up the song. The situation is something like the joke which Schoenberg once made: 'That is quite strict counterpoint; consonances only come on the unaccentuated beats of the bar.'

If one compares this song and the opus 14, No. 2 on a text by Paul Henckel, written only a few weeks later, with the paintings which Schoenberg was producing at the time, their unity is clear. In both forms of expression reality is only used as a not yet indispensable starting point. Both arts show an inclination towards subconscious events and visions, whose laws can only be recognized and followed by feeling. Everything which follows now is music of a freely formed kind, which was the mark of a whole epoch. With it Schoenberg has finally left the path of comfortable conventions. He had to put up with the fact that musicians whom he admired, like Richard Strauss and Max Reger, turned away from him.

For Mahler too, who spent the next four winters in America and only renewed his old friendly contacts with Zemlinsky, Schoenberg and their circle in the summer months, this world was a book with seven seals. After the Chamber Symphony he no longer had any access to it. But – and this divides his position essentially from that of Strauss and Reger – his belief in Schoenberg was not shaken by this. He continued to support the musician, whom he trusted because of his earlier works, and he knew that Schoenberg depended very much on his help. The strength of character expressed by such a position is remarkable, and Schoenberg gave no bounds to his admiration. Mahler's belief in him was the answer to his belief in Mahler. And it was not only human relations which were important in this. Mahler's death hit him as a blow of fate more strongly artistically than personally; 'I believe strongly and unshakably that Mahler was one of the greatest men and musicians', he said in his memorial speech, which was written and pronounced in 1912. This also contains sentences which do not only refer to Mahler but formulate Schoenberg's view of art in general: 'Talent is the capacity for learning, genius the capacity for developing oneself. Talent increases, in that it appropriates things and capabilities which are outside it already, assimilates them and finally even possesses them. Genius possesses all its future capabilities in advance. It merely develops them, unrolls them, unfolds them. Where talent, which has to learn a limited field, namely that which is already there, soon reaches its climax, and after this usually sinks back, the development of genius, which looks for new ways into uncharted territory, stretches itself out over the whole of life.'

AIR FROM ANOTHER PLANET

In October 1908 Gustav and Alma-Maria Mahler went to New York for the second time. Shortly before this, in September, he had conducted the first performance of his Seventh Symphony in Prague. Many of his friends, including Alban Berg, were present. Schoenberg was not. The events of the summer had uprooted him in his innermost being and put him in a state of creative and psychic exaltation, as is shown by the manuscript of the thirteenth George song. The progress beyond all the bounds of a past aesthetic, of which he later spoke in connection with his album of songs, had already been shown in the F Sharp Minor Quartet. There was no way back from here. Now there came a time of almost feverish production, which produced four important works in the year. The George songs are only dated here and there. The latest entry runs: 28 February 1909. On 23 May Schoenberg began to work on the orchestral pieces, whose number was not decided at this point. We know from his correspondence with Richard Strauss that he had planned up to seven, but then contented himself with the set of five pieces. He ended his work in Steinakirchen am Forst, in Lower Austria, where since July he had been on holiday.

During the months which were mainly devoted to the composition of the George songs and these orchestral pieces, Schoenberg wrote his first mature work for piano after the youthful pieces of 1894 which were strongly influenced by Brahms; these were often interrupted. These are the three pieces which appeared as opus 11 in the Universal Edition and in which the new language which is not bound to tonality is used with masterly freedom and abstraction. The first piece bears as date of completion 19 February, the second 22 February, the third 7 August 1909. So these works were composed between the other two to which Schoenberg later gave the opus numbers 15 and 16. This fact is even more remarkable, because each of the three works has its own individual style which cannot be exchanged with that of any of the others which were written at the same time. Though Schoenberg uses similar means for them all in free harmonies and the melodic line, in their metrical and rhythmical condition and also in their form, which avoids symmetries and almost excludes repetitions, we must look for reasons for such differences in other things. The most notable difference is in the spiritual starting-point. The George songs, like all vocal music, are conditioned by the text. Schoenberg, whose beginnings as a composer of songs were very much influenced by Richard Dehmel's revolutionary world of ideas, had discovered Stefan George's esoteric and hieratic poem in the autumn of 1907. In the summer of 1908 there followed the two vocal movements of the F Sharp Minor Quartet, also settings of two George poems. And finally there came the cycle of songs from the *Book of the Hanging Gardens* of 1908 to 1909.

The contrast between the spirit of George's poems, which were strict and conservative in form, and the inner tumult of Schoenberg's music has often been criticized. In reality this contrast does not exist. In this phase of his musical development, and in the overpowering experience of the aesthetic freedom which he had reached himself, Schoenberg needed a supporting counter-weight. Dehmel's or Rilke's poems would not have attracted him, nor would the Impressionist prose poems of Peter Altenberg, whom he had read at this time and much enjoyed. Stefan George's function in German literature of that era was of someone who called to order and was the priest of the absolute spirit. Order and measure were the maxims which he set up against naturalism and its social connections. Nietzsche's aristocratic manner and the concept of the Master, which Dehmel contrasted with his democratic brotherly love, were over-accentuated in George's art. Some of the best writers in Germany and Austria, including the young Hugo von Hofmannsthal, orientated themselves to this model. For Schoenberg, for whom conventional order had been broken, George was the aesthetic and even pedagogic authority whom he needed. Like the poet, since 1904 he had had a small exclusive circle of pupils and fanatical supporters around him for whom he himself was the highest authority in all spheres of spiritual utterance.

If one reads the fifteen poems from the *Book of the Hanging Gardens*, one recognizes in the figure of the woman, which emerges from it, the spirit of priestly authority and the immaterial spirituality which George himself embodies. The tragic ending, which the verses hint at rather than state precisely, corresponds to Schoenberg's feeling about life at that time. It is this that links this cycle with the big romantic song cycles of Schubert and Schumann. And it is just this human and spiritual tension, from which the songs are born, which gives them their individual character. In spite of complete independence each of the fifteen songs contains very subtle reminiscences which allow the cycle to appear as a work which is linked together. Even some reminiscences of key and cadence, consonances and triads which appear fleetingly, accompany like reflexes from the subconscious the path of this interpretation of the text. George's strict metres are as it were unmasked by Schoenberg. Where on the surface of the poem order and strict measure are set by an act of power, Schoenberg's sounds and rhythms shine behind this order and disclose the spiritual organism which hides behind it. – The orchestral pieces begin from another point of view. In his correspondence with the Leipzig publisher Peters, where the pieces appeared in 1912, Schoenberg spoke about the problem of giving them titles.

'*Whatever was to be said has been said by the music. Why then have words as well? If words were necessary they would have been there in the first place. An art says more than words.*'

This Schoenberg wrote in his diary. But how did he describe the pieces to Strauss? 'Sound and mood. This is what it is all about – absolutely not symphonic, the direct opposite of it, no architecture, no construction.' However, Schoenberg remembers the impressions of nature which influenced him when writing the piece. The third piece, which he first wanted to call 'Chord Colours', in the revised score of 1950 again published by Peters (who was now in New York), was called 'Summer Morning by a Lake' and carries in brackets the sub-title 'Colours'. The other titles are less impressionistic. These are 'Premonitions', 'Past', 'Peripetie', and 'The Obligato Recitative'. Such an attempt at giving the pieces titles and the results of it show a similar spiritual position to the George songs. All that the orchestral pieces lack is an explanatory text. Instead of this there appears what Schoenberg calls mood in this connection and differs from the conception of a poetic content. Schoenberg recognizes that the idea of the publisher was not sympathetic to him. People have secrets which one may not even recognize oneself. But one does not like to talk about them. Nevertheless this remark of Schoenberg shows that he had such secrets and they were with him when he wrote these pieces.

They belong to the period of freedom in which Schoenberg made himself independent of thematic writing. His technique of inventing motivic material for each part ends in a method of writing which he called 'permanent variation'. The first piece, full of wild dramatic tension, is the development of two contrasting thoughts, which are exposed in a short passage. The first idea is played by muted celli, later strengthened by two oboes, the second is played by celli spiccato, with the character of a crescendo, which goes through the whole piece. The next movement, which is freer from symphonic traditions, begins broadly and meditatively. The pedal in fifths D–A suggests a tonality. The solo cello plays a Cantilena, against which the horn and bass clarinet play a counter-theme. This latter theme ends the movement in a canon on the celesta diminished into semi-quavers. In 1912 Webern admired the polyphonic middle section in 3/8 with violas, celli and flute as an example of Schoenberg's orchestration. The third movement is a text-book example of what Schoenberg called melody of tone colour. It begins with changing colours on five-part chords which remain stationary.

The fourth movement is a ghostly scherzo in the spirit of Mahler with a chorale-like resting-point of chords which returns from time to time. Like the first piece it is of aphoristic brevity and became a model for Webern.

In the fifth movement we see an example of melodic development from a germ cell and a complex Schoenbergian polyphony in which the arts of imitation, contrary motion and the division of the weight of the intervals all serve to give a new feeling of sound. It condenses itself to real six-part writing. For the performance of opus 16 Schoenberg added to the usual marks in the score by marking the main part with H⁻, subsidiary parts with N⁻, and the end of a part with ⌐.

In the three piano pieces opus 11 Schoenberg's language of the time is shown most clearly. Here there was no relation to a text or any other connection with natural impressions or extra-musical events. The pieces differ from the songs opus 15 and the orchestral pieces opus 16 externally through their greater length. The tendency towards complete compression of the forms, which Schoenberg had been doing since the autumn of 1908, had led to specific formal sequences and vice versa. The lack of repetition, even varied repetition, struck at the foundations of Western musical development. The three piano pieces contain repetitions, some of which are varied and some hardly varied, and also the elements of ostinato and pedal points, which had been almost completely eliminated from Schoenberg's other music at that time. While the orchestral pieces use an extraordinarily rich palette of colours in a completely new way, also compressing and moulding them together, the pieces opus 11 do not go beyond a piano sound which is characteristic of Schumann and Brahms. What divides these pieces from Brahms's later piano works, is strictly speaking only the lack of tonal tensions, and the avoidance of the unsettling effect of dissonances and the relaxing effect of their resolution into consonances. The atmospheric side of this music, which is its charm, was isolated and increased by Ferruccio Busoni in his 'Concert Interpretation' of the second piece of opus 11. Although this arrangement differs from the spirit of Schoenberg's compositions it does show that there are latent impulses in the music which Schoenberg was not conscious of when he wrote it. Busoni's interpretation at least brings the second of the piano pieces near to the spirit of the third orchestral piece.

From Bratislava a young medical student came to Vienna to finish her studies. Marie Pappenheim, born in 1882, entered the circle of Schoenberg, Zemlinsky and Alban Berg about 1908. She took her degree in 1910 as a specialist in skin diseases, and in the General Neurological Hospital she met Dr. Hermann Frischauf, who she later married. Both were not only very interested in cultural affairs, but were also active in literature. Poems of the young Marie Pappenheim were published in the 'Fackel' of Karl Kraus, a great honour at that time.

In 1909 Schoenberg met Marie Pappenheim in Steinakirchen and asked her if she would write an opera text for him. According to her own account, which she gave to the musicologist Helmut Kirchmeyer about 1960 (see the text of this on the Wergo record of Schoenberg's *Erwartung*) she answered: 'At the most I could write a monodrama.' She then went to friends in Traunkirchen and wrote the text of *Erwartung* there. She came back to Steinakirchen three weeks later and gave Schoenberg the libretto. He set it to music at once. In an astonishingly short time he had finished his first stage work, which only contains one character, the woman. She looks for her lover in a wood at night, and finds him at the end of the piece, but he is dead. *Erwartung* is a passionate monologue full of anguish, premature joy, jealousy, hate and again anguish. The expressionistically concentrated language of the text expresses all the feelings and spiritual unrest which a woman like Marie Pappenheim, with her experience of psychology and psycho-analysis, had lived through spiritually and put into an artistic form. For a musician of highly tense expression like Schoenberg it was the ideal text. What he was looking for, the concentration of dramatic action to the minimum of characters, was provided here. The monologues of the woman drew from him an imagination in sound beyond all the limits which he had set himself in the vocal movements in the George songs and the instrumental writing in the orchestral pieces. In spite of its very short length of twenty-eight minutes *Erwartung* is a piece which seems to mirror an entire life. Its performance by a singer and a producer did not take place until fifteen years after it was composed.

Erwartung, a music-drama of the highest psychical expression, for a long time was regarded as a work unsusceptible to analysis and representative of tonal anarchy, of themelessness, and of creative wilfulness. But here our distance in history has opened our eyes. What once seemed anarchical and merely a product of feeling as regards form, can now be seen as a series of analysable events, a train of motives bound together for long stretches, and partly as the product of an extremely bold and radical type of variation.

Of course this kind of motivic connection cannot be analysed by the methods of traditional symphonic writing or of the Wagnerian leitmotif technique. One cannot find 'thematic working' in the sense of the New German School or the followers of Brahms. But the more one studies the score the easier it is to recognize the connections of the variants. Even the first phrases of the voice part in the third to the sixth bar show a subtle technique of variation. The beginning to the words 'hier hinein?' (E sharp–B–C) are immediately taken up with a slight variant (E–F–E flat–E), and this variation is quoted almost exactly in bar 26. This motive wanders through the entire score; it also appears in the aria in bars 389 to 390 as an accompanying oboe figure.

This thinking in motivic connections becomes even clearer if one compares the beginning of the second scene, bars 38 to 45, with the first. Here in the voice part practically everything comes into relation. The sequence D–E–G–C sharp–A sharp at 'ist das noch der Weg?' corresponds to the notes D–E–G–E–G sharp at 'man sieht den Weg nicht'. From the sequence C–A–A sharp–G sharp–E sharp at 'schimmern wie Birken' through changing over two notes and a slight rhythmical variation a new form comes C–B flat–A–G sharp–E sharp at 'um Gottes Willen'. These are only some examples from hundreds.

An especially individual role, almost that of a leitmotif is played for long stretches by the sequence of notes D–F–C sharp, which rises like a rocket, with its passionately climbing variants D—F—E and D–F–G (a ninth), not to speak of transpositions and inversions. It first appears as a figure in the double basses in the introduction to the second scene (bar 38), and shortly afterwards appears slightly varied as C sharp–D–F–C – in the violins (bar 49). From bar 150 onwards its role becomes dominant; the soprano has hardly given the cue with her excited 'Es ist noch nass, es ist von dort', when the orchestra starts on a seven-bar symphonic whirlwind, which extracts all possibilities of variation, inversion, change of register and diminution from the D–F–C sharp. In bar 173 the motive is again predominant; in bar 330 it is heard fortissimo in the trombones, and in bar 385 – in the variant D–F–E–C sharp – it becomes a clarinet melody. In 411, expanded and varied rhythmically, it becomes a bass figure. These bars are in any case taken from the song 'Am Wegrand' opus 6; the reason for this quotation is that the words in both works are the same 'Tausend Menschen ziehn vorüber'.

Harmonic events are also repeated. The famous 12-note chord in bar 269, for instance, which really only consists of ten different notes and two repeated ones (B flat–E flat–A–D–G–C sharp–G–B–D sharp–G flat–C–F), is heard again rather later in bars 382–383 with the notes arranged in a different order, certainly, but it is still recognizable, most clearly in the groups B–D sharp and G flat–C–F.

Marie Pappenheim herself was very worried about her work. On 3 October she wrote to Schoenberg at Steinakirchen: 'I am writing out the last alterations on a separate piece of paper. Naturally I didn't want you to have to work any more. I have not shown it to anybody, not even Zemlinsky. I am not happy with it. I did not write before as I was very agitated. Now I am halfway. The fact that you have finished already gives me new courage. This was not her only attempt at dramatic collaboration; three years later she wrote a letter to Schoenberg in which she asked him for his permission to send somewhere, probably to a publisher or a theatre three or four scenes and to add *Erwartung* to them. The volume of her own poetry, which she published in 1962 under the title *Verspätete Ernte zerstreuter Saat* (The Destroyed Sowing of a Late Harvest), shows that she had an important lyrical gift and a very individual kind of language. Clearly this woman fought against all sorts of difficulties, for she complains in this letter to

Schoenberg that she could not finish anything. Her high ethical convictions as a doctor are shown by the fact that during the Balkan war of 1912 she went of her own free will to Constantinople (Istanbul) as a cholera doctor, and repeated her attempt to do the same in Bulgaria, when she was refused in Turkey. During the Second World War Marie Pappenheim-Frischauf was in Mexico; she came back to Vienna in 1950 and died there in 1966. Her son, Professor Dr. Hans Frischauf, is a specialist for Internal Medicine in Vienna.

This monodrama had a predecessor which goes back to 11 October 1908. On this day Schoenberg wrote down some musical ideas for a dramatic work which he finished much later, and for which he wrote the text himself. This was called *Die Glückliche Hand* (The Lucky Hand) and was described as a drama with music. The final text, the previous version of which we do not know, was finished by Schoenberg in the last days of June 1910. Here again he sees only one singing character, the Man, who is joined by a Woman and a Gentleman in silent parts. A chorus of twelve singing and speaking voices comments on the action after the model of Greek tragedy and contributes dialogue. The action, which varies between mystical, realistic and fairy-tale-like scenes takes place in six scenes. The *Glückliche Hand*, like *Erwartung*, is a drama of destroyed love. The man embodies the genius, the creative person who can succeed in wonderful miracle works like the producing of a diadem. But what his creative work gives him is denied to him in life; the Woman leaves him and turns to the Gentleman, who is described in the text as 'dressed in elegant fashionable clothes, distinguished and good-looking in figure.' The final words are sung by the chorus of six men and six women: 'Did you have to experience again what you have been through so often before? Did you have to? Can you not refrain from it? Can you not finally refuse?' And further on: 'Can you only feel what you touch, your wounds only in your flesh, your pain only in your body?'

The *Glückliche Hand* was also not performed until long after it was completed. For a later revival at the Berlin Kroll Opera in 1930 Schoenberg wrote some instructions for it. He says in these that above all it is a question of a play of light and colour. Colours and stage lighting are strictly prescribed in the text book and worked out according to an exact plan, which transfers the concept of the crescendo into the world of optics.

There is no doubt that the opera reflects symbolic experiences from Schoenberg's own most personal world. The work was written in several stages, often dragged with difficulty out of his creative spirit, and the score was not finished until 1913 in Berlin. Schoenberg himself spoke of the symbolic character of the title, to which he attributed magical powers.

Die Glückliche Hand is an important document of atonality; the score, which is written for a large orchestra of 25 wind instruments, at least 30 strings, harp, celesta, xylophone, glockenspiel and many other percussion instruments, like *Erwartung* avoids keynotes and consonances. The use of all the semitones leads as early as the second bar to a nine-note ostinato which continues throughout the entire scene, to which the bassoon adds two further notes.

As well as the solo baritone and the mime parts of the Woman and the Gentleman, Schoenberg writes for a chorus of six women's and six men's voices. These both sing and speak and carry the first and last scene by themselves. The remarkable counterpoint, which begins in the third bar with two-part speaking with women's and men's voices, and increases in the tenth bar to three each of singing and speaking voices, in the final scene turns into a sung three-part canon, the soprano part of which is in augmentation. And this canonic movement too is finally taken over by speaking voices. Together with the fantastic many-coloured sound of the orchestra the vocal line is as original as Schoenberg's paintings of the same time, about 1910, in their geometrical dissolution of human shapes.

The baritone part of the Man develops the content in motivic cells, out of which the whole score grows according to the principle of perpetual variation.

In addition to musical innovations there is a new scenic aesthetic. In the third scene a wind is prescribed, the crescendo of which takes place simultaneously with the crescendo of the lighting. The scale of colours goes from pale red through brown to a dirty green light, then from blue-grey and violet to a red which is dark at first but becomes brighter all the time, and is mixed with orange and bright yellow. Symbols and apparitions which are difficult to explain like the cat-like fabulous beast on the nape of the man's neck or the severed Turk's heads on his belt show Schoenberg's aesthetic standpoint: in a transition from naturalism and symbolism he anticipates the expressionistic method of working which later became prominent in the operas of Alban Berg, Ernst Krenek and Luigi Dallapiccolo. The combination of colours, sounds and words reminds us of similar tendencies in

Alexander Scriabin, especially in his *Prometheus*. Schoenberg also
sketched out some stage designs for the *Glückliche Hand*, which were
used at the performance in Florence in 1964 at the Maggio
Musicale and worked very well from a scenic point of views.

The text of the *Glückliche Hand*, which Schoenberg sent immediately after its publication in the summer of 1910 to some
acquaintances who were of importance to him, received very
varying criticisms. Hermann Bahr, who was himself a successful
and very experienced dramatist, thanked Schoenberg on 29 July,
but objected to the figure of the Gentleman in the overcoat, 'who
seems to me to bring an unpleasantly real day-to-day character
into the work whose effect through its compression is otherwise
that of eternity.'

A quite different reaction came from Rainer Simons, the
director of the Vienna Volksoper, who read both one-act plays
with the view to giving the first performance of them in his
theatre. After receiving the text he wrote on 15 August 1910 that
the new piece, which Schoenberg had not yet written the music
for, had pleased him much better than the monodrama. 'While
I did not find the latter approachable (I also know why now,
because it was unsatisfactory for the stage) I feel much more
sympathetic to the new opus because of its stage effectiveness.
This has a plot and a serious purpose! I will take a lot of trouble
about it and rehearse the work personally myself.'

The 'Air from another Planet', of which George's 'Entrückung'
speaks, had summoned up a real pandemonium of sounds,
rhythms and forms. From 1908 the new musical language which
avoided key and consonance was seen as a warning signpost in
the field of Western music. Its creator had said over and over
again that he had gone extremely unwillingly into the unknown
and the uncertain. He felt himself under the command of higher
powers who had sent him on this path. The act of complete
emancipation from all traditional rules, which Schoenberg performed at this time, worked in two directions. Those to whom
Schoenberg had become uncomfortable for some time, now finally
turned away from him, including people who had admired and
helped him. But the much smaller circle of people who believed
in him surrounded him now more closely and more fanatically.
Above all these were his pupils, but also Mahler as well; Mahler
trusted him without being able to understand him. And in this
field of force between angry dismissal and enthusiastic recognition
Schoenberg's life took its course during the next few years.

He himself was far from looking at his own development in an uncritical manner. In his work with the young students whom he had educated, a large number of theoretical and pedagogic discoveries were being made. His chief task in 1910 and 1911 was to work these out and put them in an intelligible form. He had long recognized his vocation as a great teacher and tried to find a position in Vienna which would establish him as a teacher and broaden his possibilities of working. In connection with these plans and tendencies, at the request of Emil Hertzka, he wrote his Harmony Book.

In 1909 Hertzka drew up contracts with Mahler, Schreker and Schoenberg. On 7 October began the voluminous correspondence which Schoenberg carried on with Universal Edition and its director. The first letter announced a visit together with Anton von Webern, at which Schoenberg's own works and works by Webern were to be produced.

This correspondence lasted right up to Schoenberg's American years. It not only gives a gripping and often moving picture of the troubles and plans which beset Schoenberg during these decades, but it is also a true portrait of his emotions and passions, his self-knowledge and the pretensions which he was allowed by the conviction of his creative role. Unfortunately lack of money also played a big part in this for a long time.

THE FLIGHT

In 1910 Schoenberg had exchanged his dark apartment in the Liechtensteinstrasse for the larger and nicer Hietzinger Haupstrasse 113. The suburb of Hietzing, which he had already come to love in 1908 at the time of his first stay in the Gloriettegasse 43, coincided with his desire to live in the country and work in fresh air. Through the birth of his son Georg in 1906 the family now consisted of four people; and this meant that they needed larger space. And Schoenberg's superstitious fear of the number 13 had not gone so far as to make him avoid Hietzing (the thirteenth district) and a house numbered 113. But the high rent made things difficult for him, and in the summer he sent off the letter to Mahler asking for help; Mahler immediately replied with assistance.

On 14 January 1910 the 'Society for Art and Culture' put on an evening of Schoenberg first performances in the Ehrbar-Saal. In this the first part of the 'Gurrelieder' was performed in an arrangement made by Webern for eight hands for the preludes and the interludes and with a two-hand accompaniment for the songs. These were followed by the Stefan George lieder from the *Book of the Hanging Gardens* and the three piano pieces opus 11. The main part of the performance was carried out by two women: Martha Winternitz-Dorda sang the fifteen George songs and the soprano songs in the 'Gurrelieder'; Etta Werndorff played the piano part of the George songs and opus 11. Hans Nachod sang the tenor parts. The other pianists were Arnold Winternitz, Anton von Webern and Dr. Rudolf Weirich. The programme contained an oft-quoted explanation of Schoenberg about his breaking all the bonds of a past aesthetic.

Martha Winternitz-Dorda (1880–1958), daughter of a Viennese writer, made her way as an actress and operatic singer through the Burgtheater, provincial Austrian theatres, the Comic Opera and the Viennese Raimund-Theater to Hamburg. Here she was a member of the opera as a coloratura-soprano from 1908 to 1931.

Her first marriage was to the conductor and pianist Arnold Winternitz (1874–1928), and her second to the pianist Richard Goldschmied. Her repertory stretched from Verdi's *Traviata* and *Aida*, Mozart's Elvira, Meyerbeer's Margarete in the *Huguenots* and the three principal roles in Offenbach's *The Tales of Hoffmann* to the Marschallin in Richard Strauss's *Rosenkavalier*.

Etta Werndorff, née Jonasz, since her youth had been close to Schoenberg's circle and since 1907 had taken part in performances of works by Berg, Webern and Schoenberg.

Dr. Rudolf Weirich (born in 1886 in Vienna) had studied with Schoenberg from 1904 to 1910 and had worked in Austrian theatres since 1910, more recently in the Vienna State Opera as conductor and repetiteur.

On 8 February Schoenberg wrote to Hertzka about a concert he planned of works by his pupils, in which Etta Werndorff was to play Alban Berg's Piano Sonata opus 1. At the same time he asked if he could become a member of the Author's Society. And on the same day he wrote down some astonishing pieces, which – like so many of his works – remained unfinished and unpublished and only came to light after his death. These are miniatures for chamber orchestra, very expressive, tender studies, steps into the unexplored land beyond tonality. The melodic lines have a pure and concentrated expression, consisting of very small and very large intervals alternately. The harmony is ruled by wandering chords which have no tonal connections, chords of up to seven notes used in chains of complementary notes, so that repetitions of notes are reduced to an extreme. Motives and themes, in so far as one can talk of them, are hardly ever repeated and are not developed. A floating rhythm which is against the bar line is present in these forms which are reduced to aphorisms.

The colour is the most remarkable element. The extreme registers of the four woodwind and the horn predominate. The five solo strings (two violins, viola, cello and bass), as well as bowed and pizzicato notes, also use harmonics and striking or bowing with the wood of the bow. The first piece uses only oboe, B flat clarinet, horn and strings; the second uses a double quintet. In the third, which remained a fragment, celesta and organ (or harmonium) are added. These pieces are clearly related to the Orchestral Pieces which had been written shortly before. However, in the unfinished third piece a sound was anticipated which was later used in 1911 in the song 'Herzgewächse'. Over a six-part chord in fourths the celesta plays four ostinato notes in a dreamlike and hushed manner. The tendency to the compression of the forms which had already been seen in the first chamber symphony and the F Sharp Minor Quartet, and increased in the Stefan George songs and the orchestral pieces, here leads to structures of explosive shortness. The first piece lasts 35 seconds, the second piece 31, and the third 25.

However, Schoenberg's conditions of life had not yet been stabilized. The existence of his family was hardly ensured for the next few months, and worries about food, rent and clothes upset his creative powers. Since 1908 his daughter Trudi had been going to school. Mathilde's health was poor. She was inclined to colds and lung infections. – However, Schoenberg was no longer so much alone as in 1903, when he returned home from Berlin. At that time Zemlinsky was the only one of his friends who shared his daily worries. Since 1904 the circle of his pupils had grown incessantly. And some of these young men regarded it as an important duty to help their master in his needs.

Schoenberg's occasional work for Universal Edition grew into an important connection. Schoenberg, whose optional contract with Marschalk's Dreililienverlag was still valid, had been able to sell some works to Hertzka since 1909 and make a general contract with Universal Edition in the Karlsplatz. In addition to this he asked Hertzka for work. When the first generation of his pupils were fledged, there were many gaps in Schoenberg's teaching hours. On 7 March 1910 he poured his heart out to his publisher. He suggested that Hertzka should recommend him as a portrait painter and get some well-known patrons to buy his pictures. He said that it would be much more interesting to have one's portrait painted by a musician of his reputation than to be painted by some mere practitioner of painting. 'For a life-size portrait I want from two to six sittings and 200 to 400 kronen. That is really very cheap, considering that in twenty years people will pay ten times as much, and in forty years a hundred times as much for these paintings.' As a sample he offered to paint Hertzka without fee. Clearly this plan did not work out in practice. In material things Schoenberg often had an unreal, fantastic imagination, even when he had long been a famous man and the director of a master class in Berlin.

Among the Viennese conductors whom Mahler had helped was Schoenberg's friend Artur Bodanzky, who was three years younger. His career had risen quickly from Vienna through Prague and Berlin to Mannheim. Since 1906 the National Theatre there had one of the most progressive German intendants, Dr. Carl Hagemann, a promoter of new stylistic ideas and an admirer of artistic experiments.

As a pupil of Zemlinsky Bodanzky knew about the tendencies of Schoenberg and his school. Immediately after taking up his post in Mannheim he sent for the piano score of *Erwartung*. On 16 December 1909 Schoenberg was able to tell Hertzka that Intendant Hagemann wanted to give the first performance of the monodrama at a matinée. Anna Bahr-Mildenburg could not undertake the part, but Martha Winternitz-Dorda had been engaged. At Christmas Bodanzky and Hagemann came to Vienna to hear her.

On this visit the two men from Mannheim asked Schoenberg to conduct the work himself. On 14 February 1910 Schoenberg made detailed suggestions to Bodanzky about copying the orchestral parts and about rehearsals. The plan continued until the end of November 1913 and foundered on the fact that the orchestra pit was not big enough to hold the number of players demanded by Schoenberg. – Hertzka had not been able to take over the publication of *Erwartung*, until Max Marschalk – to whom Schoenberg had to offer it because of his previous contract with him – had released it. This took place in December 1909.

Soon after Hagemann and Bodanzky, the director of the Vienna Volksoper, Rainer Simons, also showed interest in *Erwartung*. On 8 August 1910 Schoenberg asked the painter Max Oppenheimer (1885–1954), who was a friend of his, to visit him. 'I would very much like you to do the décor for my monodrama, which will be performed at the Volksoper'. Universal Edition lingered over the discussions with Simons so much that on 28 September Schoenberg pressed the publisher to make an agreement with the Volksoper; he also asked that the performance should not be endangered by their charging too much money for the material.

VENIA LEGENDI

Supported by Hertzka, Schoenberg now undertook his often discussed plan of teaching composition at the Vienna Music Academy. He wanted a professorship, but got wind of the opposition which arose against him when rumours that he might be appointed began to spread. So he lowered his sights somewhat and on 19 February 1910 he wrote to the president of the Academy, a Professor Dr. Karl von Wiener, a letter with the proposal that he should obtain permission to be a private teacher (venia legendi) in the theory of music. He obtained this in the winter term.

The path which led to this office was circumstantial. In a session of the Kuratorium on 19 March the director of the Academy, Wilhelm Bopp, pleaded for Schoenberg. In April and May they received the opinions of Karl Goldmark, Felix von Weingartner, Ferdinand Löwe and Gustav Mahler. These were all positive for him; only Weingartner voiced a few small doubts. On 20 June the Kuratorium made a unanimous decision to ask the Royal and Imperial Ministry of Culture and Education to agree to Schoenberg's request and to grant him his wish. On 28 June the authorities declared themselves in agreement.

It must be said for the Institute that its leading men had discussed Schoenberg's request very seriously. Bopp mentioned the sterility of the composition classes, spoke of the negotiations with Engelbert Humperdinck and Max Reger, which had fallen through, and finally said, 'Let us try Schoenberg and so let a little fresh air into the stifling life of the composition school'. The president of the Kuratorium, Karl von Wiener, said that the composition teachers had not produced any pupils of importance. And one would also have to remember, if Schoenberg's request were turned down, that he might be regarded by some as one of the many martyrs.

Schoenberg had said that he wanted no salary. However the Kuratorium decided to pay him 400 kronen a year for his course, especially in view of the notoriously bad conditions which he had endured for years.

When Schoenberg was appointed a professor two years later one of the members of the Kuratorium, the barrister Dr. E Kraus, said in his report on the harmony course which he had taken part in that it was 'very stimulating and interesting', also that 'it hadn't once happened that any person taking part had had a feeling of boredom or of pedantic and dry teaching.'

Dr. Kraus says: 'Schoenberg lectures freely, without any notes, his speech is fluent, his lecturing very rich in examples, he uses fine comparisons, he has a wide positive knowledge of the whole of musical production and theory, and his aim is to arouse in his pupils pleasure in independent thought and creation; he also demands expressly that every step in harmony should have an inner motivation and can be motivated by the pupils. If the pupils cannot state the motivation for a step in harmony which is blameless in itself he must not use it.'

The report continues: 'Schoenberg gives his pupils many exercises; in looking through them he is so strict that he regards mistakes, especially serious ones, as personal insults . . . Schoenberg never speaks about himself and his compositions; I have never heard him make a critical remark about anyone who is regarded historically as a great man . . . Schoenberg evidently goes on the principle that every age has its own art and theories of art.'

Kraus further praised the cordial and pleasant relations between teacher and pupils, who continued to listen to him teaching harmony of their own free will, waited for him at the tram stop and after the lesson went on long walks with him. 'One can never leave a meeting with him without having been stimulated.'

The author of this report probably meant Berg, when he spoke of those who listened to his harmony lessons of their own free will. Berg wrote a letter to Webern in December, describing how he used to wait for Schoenberg twice a week before his lessons on the Karlsplatz. Then they would walk through the town for a quarter or half an hour, and the street noises 'became inaudible behind the sound of his words.'

In this winter and spring Schoenberg again began to paint in oils and water-colours. He continued the work which he had begun in the critical year of 1907. Unfortunately he gave exact dates to only a few of his paintings. However, among the works which he showed in 1910 ten oil paintings and one small water-colour ('Vision of Christ') bear the date 1910. Two of them, which Schoenberg gave the same title 'Red Glance', were painted in the spring of 1910, one on 26 March and one in May. In the same month he also painted one of his many self-portraits; two painted in 1910 are called 'Blue Self-portrait' and 'Green Self-portrait'. And the vision of Gustav Mahler is also one of the dated portraits of the year. Two were given the title 'Glance', one is called 'Hands', and a landscape is called 'Night'.

His money troubles continued. On 3 May 1910 Schoenberg wrote to the Royal and Imperial Ministry for Culture and Education and asked for help because of a financial crisis. He based his request on the poor health of his entire family, which was caused by bad sanitary conditions in Vienna. Because of his teaching he was compelled to keep up a large apartment. He had enough pupils, but not many of them were in a position to pay him. However, he regarded it as his duty to pass on his knowledge even to those who could not pay him for it. His request was passed on 7 May.

It seems that Schoenberg found no peace in Hietzing for his work on the Harmony Book. The new task lay like a mountain in front of him. He needed physical help. Emil Hertzka offered to send him a typewriter and a secretary to dictate to. Schoenberg agreed, but kept on having to remind Hertzka about it, in order that the work could continue. In May he asked Hertzka impatiently about the machine and the secretary. On 26 July he also said that he was worried about the secretary; he wanted to finish the dictation, had composed nothing for a year and was planning some fairly large works. In a week he could dictate 30 to 40 pages at most. Of the 450 pages at least which the book would need to have, only 130 were finished. In the eight weeks up till the time when he had agreed to deliver the book he would have to write another 320.

In spite of all his concentration on the book he found time for other plans. He sent Hertzka an idea for a musical journal ('if I could be the editor'). To Mahler, who was again in Toblach to recover from his fatiguing months in America, he wrote one of his warmest letters for his fiftieth birthday.

He was also visited by pupils. For his Piano Sonata opus 1 and his songs on texts of Hebbel and Alfred Mombert opus 2 Alban Berg had designed his own title pages, with which they were published in Berlin by Robert Lienau. He showed Schoenberg the sketches for these and was able to report in a letter to Webern: 'Schoenberg very pleased with my title pages'. They are in the soft, plantlike style of the *Art Nouveau* of 1900.

In addition there were pressing problems with publishers. The Chamber Symphony was still not printed and had to be sent off. The parts of the F Sharp Minor Quartet had to be copied. Proofs of the Three Piano Pieces opus 11 had to be read. Busoni had given his arrangement of the second piece to Universal Edition; how was the problem of the division of royalties to be solved?

These things took up valuable time. Schoenberg needed greater isolation than he had in Hietzing. In the summer of 1910 he found a place to live in a country house at Ober St. Veit. It was not far from Hietzing but was very much a country district. Here he created an oasis which could only be entered by his closest friends and pupils. The seventeen-year-old Fritz Zweig appeared at that time, and he was entrusted with the decoration of the house with Schoenberg's pictures. The Harmony Book was finished in September. But the pressure of work continued. Hugo Heller's bookshop became interested in Schoenberg's pictures and arranged an exhibition of them. According to an advertisement in the *Neue Freie Presse* of 2 October 1910 this opened on 8 October. At the opening Arnold Rosé and his colleagues played the two quartets opus 7 and 10. The soprano part in the second one was sung by Marie Gutheil-Schoder. Mahler came to the final rehearsal. He also saw the exhibition and was enthusiastic about Schoenberg's artistic visions and colours.

Carl Moll had again acted as artistic adviser in this. From him Schoenberg learnt one day to his great and joyful surprise that a stranger, who did not want his name to be known, had bought three of his pictures.

Shortly after this event, which was important for Schoenberg, but was received by most of the critics with their usual lack of understanding, Oskar Fried performed *Pelléas and Mélisande* in Berlin with the Blüthner Orchestra. (In the *Vossische Zeitung* of 30 October 1910 there was an advertisement: 'Society of the Friends of Music and the Stern Choral Society, Blüthner-Saal, 31 October at 8 p.m., 2nd Subscription Concert with the Blüthner Orchestra, Conductor Oskar Fried, Soloist Arrigo Serato. Arnold Schoenberg: *Pelléas and Mélisande*). The composer came to the final rehearsals; he stayed in the Hotel Friederich. Webern also came to Berlin from Danzig, where he occupied a modest position as a conductor at the theatre. He reported to Berg that the performance was very fine, and above all the work: 'This sound; this content; this tragedy! Marvellous!' He complained how much he missed in Danzig the company of his admired teacher. He said that the finest times had been when he had gone for walks with him, as in September.

After the concert Fried introduced to Schoenberg a young English pupil of his. He was called Edward Clark (1888–1962), was enthusiastic about *Pelléas* and from then on became a devoted advocate of Schoenberg's.

Although Berg had finished his studies in 1909 he continued to have further sessions with his admired master. He wrote to Webern: 'Twice a week to Schoenberg himself in Ober St. Veit, where I always bring the next section of the 'Gurrelieder' to the lesson, see his new paintings, and look at Mahler songs.' (Berg was working on the piano score of the 'Gurrelieder'. In the spring of 1910 he was also asked to make a piano score of Schoenberg's Songs with Orchestra opus 8, but gave up the task because of other work, and it was finished by Webern.)

1910 was nearing its end. As always about this time Schoenberg summed up his compositions for the year in the autumn seclusion of his Viennese suburb. There were fewer than in previous years. Too much energy had been taken up with teaching. Also for many years he had mainly composed during his summer holiday in the country, the last time being in 1909 in Steinakirchen. This year Schoenberg had not gone to a summer resort, in order to finish the Harmony Book. Apart from this large theoretical book Schoenberg did not do much literary work this year. The most important was an article 'Problems of Artistic Education', which was published about Christmas time in the *Musical Handbook* for 1911. Schoenberg had given the Berlin magazine 'Die Musik' some ideas from this article, supplemented by his aphorisms of the previous year. At the end of June, during his work on the Harmony Book, he finished the text of the *Glückliche Hand*. He began to write the music for it on 9 September, but had to stop work on it, until he took up the score again in 1913 in view of a performance which had been planned in Dresden, and finished it on 18 November.

After the strong impression made by the first part of the 'Gurrelieder' at the makeshift performance in the Ehrbarsaal, Schoenberg was convinced that it was necessary for him to take up the enormous task of orchestrating it and finishing it. In 1903 he had got as far as page 118 of the score, for which the Waldheim-Eberle Press had printed 48 stave paper for him. Then he resignedly gave up work on it. Now, after hearing its actual sound, he realized how important this music was to him. 'This work is the key to my development', he wrote on 19 August 1912 to Hertzka in a letter from Zehlendorf. In July 1910 the enormous music sheets were again on his writing table and were rapidly filled with notes. Schoenberg had already begun to orchestrate the third part, the 'Wild Hunt', in 1903 and had stopped in the song of the Peasant. Now followed the choruses of Waldemar's men and the recitation 'The Summer Wind's Wild Chase' up to the final chorus, which had only been sketched in 1901. Now Schoenberg again had to put aside the almost finished score and dictate the Harmony Book to its end instead. He began the rest of the work on the final chorus again in the autumn of 1911. The score bears the date of completion: Berlin-Zehlendorf, 7 November 1911.

It is one of the characteristics of his spiritual nature, that pure vision went hand in hand with intellectual calculation. At no time in his development did these two traits of his character, which would seem to be mutually exclusive, appear so clearly as in 1910. There was the Harmony Book with its brilliant and surprising conclusions, its very practical reasoning, its correction of many traditional errors, its demythologization of the concept of tonality with its important consequences. And at the same time Schoenberg painted the glowing colours of his insights into a world of optical imagination, visions which took a most bizarre dramatic form in the text of the *Glückliche Hand*, finished in June 1910.

Yes, this discoverer of unknown regions of art, who as a teacher began from impressive analyses of classical works, and in his theoretical teaching warned his pupils against all prejudices and uncontrolled procedures, in decisive moments appealed to his artistic feeling as a final resort.

Schoenberg was still busy with the Harmony Book at the beginning of 1911. He had written a preface to it with which he was not satisfied. He asked for the manuscript back and did not find the final form of the preface till the summer.

In the middle of correcting proofs and of discussions with his publisher about *Pelléas*, the 'Gurrelieder' and the Songs with Orchestra opus 8, Schoenberg wrote five little piano pieces as if in creative intoxication on a single day (19 February), structures of only a few bars, the first consisting of seventeen and the second and third of only nine.

Each of these miniature pieces has a complete form of its own, and each one is a combination of several new methods of writing. Although all the pieces fundamentally avoid thematic repetitions, the second is an ostinato on the major third G–B, which is played 26 times and forms a kind of inflexible tonal double centre of gravity. In the third piece bitonality is predominant; it also uses a four part chord in different positions at the beginning and the end: D–F sharp–B–C sharp and B flat–D–G–A. In the first piece, the most complex and longest of them, mostly based on five-part chords, one of its best interpreters, Eduard Steuermann, described the long-drawn-out line as 'endless melody'.

The ends of the piece show a tendency to change from tension to relaxation similar to the endings of the George songs. Schoenberg takes over from the tonal cadence the 'pressing' effect of the leading note, which he uses both upwards and downwards. The first, third and fifth pieces end with notes or intervals sliding up or down chromatically; among the latter the major third predominates. Rising leading notes form a cadence in the last bars of the third and fourth pieces, and in the third one the progression C sharp–D comes in the tenor register.

The language of the pieces is similar to that of the ones for chamber orchestra, which Schoenberg had written almost exactly a year before. The piano writing is much less ambitious than that of the three pieces opus 11 of 1909.

At the end of February Schoenberg received a letter from Webern in Danzig. He said he had married his cousin Wilhelmine Mörtl, after waiting for months for the marriage dispensation which was made necessary by their relationship.

Berg was also occupied with marriage plans. Since 1907 he and the beautiful Helene Nahowsky had been bound together with a mutual passion. For a time he was so occupied by this that even his admiring friendship with Schoenberg had to take second place. The marriage was celebrated on 3 May 1911.

Meanwhile disquieting rumours about Mahler had reached Vienna. He had already suffered from a fever during his last American concerts. His journey back at the end of April, on which he was accompanied by Busoni, seemed to have done him good. But in Paris his condition became so serious that Alma brought him back to Vienna on the fastest possible train. There he died on 18 May in the Löw Sanatorium. His funeral was on the 21 May and was attended by hundreds of his friends and admirers, including Schoenberg.

The death of the great man was a severe blow to him. The little piano piece, which he wrote on 17 June as the sixth of the set opus 19, was a reaction to this shattering experience. It was different from the other five and has a static, hardly moving form; it ends with a whispered falling ninth in the base under a widely spread chord, without any real conclusion. More eloquent than this delicate homage is the dedication of the Harmony Book, which testifies to a great artistic love:

'This book is dedicated to the memory of Gustav Mahler. The dedication was intended to give him some slight pleasure while he was alive. And it wished to express admiration of his works, his immortal compositions, and to testify that, while educated musicians pass them by with exaggerated shrugs of the shoulders, and even with contempt, these works are admired by somebody who also perhaps has some understanding. – Gustav Mahler had to do without greater pleasures than this dedication would have given him. This martyr, this saint had to leave us before he was able to do so much for his works that he was able to hand them happily over to his friends. – I would have been contented with giving him pleasure. But now that he is dead I would like my book to bring me some esteem, so that no-one can disregard me when I say: He was a truly great man.'

The printing of the Harmony Book continued. Schoenberg was helped in the proof-reading by several of his colleagues and especially Berg, who compiled the index with the greatest care. Schoenberg gave the preface its final form in July. It begins with the sentence that has become famous: 'I have learnt this book from my pupils.' It is a confession of an exploring nature which turns against the modern desire to be comfortable and to put on one side everything which is tendentious, unpleasant or causes feelings of guilt. And Schoenberg mentions the names of thinkers who also explored the problems in the way he did himself: Strindberg, Maeterlinck and Weininger.

Universal Edition took trouble to bring out the book, with its more than 500 pages and numerous musical examples, in a worthy manner. Schoenberg had less anxiety about this than about the printing of his compositions. On 2 May he had to remind Hertzka that he had had his F Sharp Minor Quartet printed at his own expense; he protested in the same letter about the 'nasty' covers, which had been used instead of his own ones. The Harmony Book aroused great interest even before its publication, and not only in Vienna, where the magazine 'Der Merker' wanted to print a chapter from it, but also in Berlin, where Schoenberg had a supporter in Bernhard Schuster, the editor of 'Musik'. The publisher Paul Cassirer asked for an advance copy and even wanted to take over the whole book. His magazine 'Pan', edited since 1910 by Alfred Kerr, had already shown interest in printing a Schoenberg song in March. It appeared in facsimile in the issue of 16 March 1911: 'Wenn ich heut nicht deinen Leib berühre' from the George songs opus 15.

This increasing fame was in agonizing contrast to Schoenberg's material conditions, which had become even more difficult since the summer of 1911. The sales of his works published by the

Dreililienverlag, which included some that were very successful and were often performed, left much to be desired. Marschalk was naturally upset by Schoenberg's contract with Universal Edition, but behaved correctly. On 13 March 1911 he sent Schoenberg a statement of accounts which demonstrates the situation. The sales were:

Songs opus 1, No. 1	17 Copies	Sextet opus 4	Score	57	Copies
No. 2	14 Copies		Parts	9	Copies
opus 2, No. 1	18 Copies	Songs opus 6	Complete	19	Copies
No. 2	17 Copies		No. 1	3	C
No. 3	17 Copies		No. 2	2	Copies
No. 4	28 Copies		No. 3	4	Copies
opus 3, No. 1	16 Copies		No. 4	2	Copies
No. 2	18 Copies		No. 5	1	Copy
No. 3	17 Copies		No. 6	1	Copy
No. 4	13 Copies		No. 7	1	Copy
No. 5	16 Copies		No. 8	8	Copies
No. 6	10 Copies	Quartet opus 7	Score	52	Copies
			Parts	12	Copies

The most popular of the songs was the 'Waldsonne' from opus 2; opus 6 was frequently thought complete. 57 copies of the sextet were sold and 52 of the quartet. This was a shameful result for four to seven years after publication. However when one thinks that Debussy's Piano Arabesque No. 1, with its tiny edition of 400 copies, took 13 years – from 1891 to 1903 – to sell out (as Arthur Honegger has told us in 'Je suis compositeur') this is not surprising. Schoenberg could not nearly live on the 400 kronen for his lectures at the Music Academy. Webern, who often went from Danzig to Berlin, believed he could find openings for him there.

At the beginning of August there were new troubles. Mathilde Schoenberg was ill with catarrh of the lung, and Schoenberg himself had violent toothache. Of his closest friends Webern was far away. He had had a misunderstanding with Berg which Webern was trying to clear up. Only Josef Polnauer, who was living and studying with him in Ober St. Veit was present and helpful.

There an event occurred to which Schoenberg reacted with violent action. An engineer, who was living in the same house, threatened his life in a fit of madness. In a kind of panic Schoenberg went away and hired an apartment in Berg on the Starnberger See.

It was a flight, and not only from the mad attacker. Schoenberg felt himself disappointed in Vienna. The path which he took led him over the frontiers of his country. In Germany he hoped to find friends and people of like mind. Munich was considered the most important and progressive city culturally. These were probably the unconscious motives of his journey, which surprised all his friends and which he really could not afford.

Webern, who was taking a holiday on the small estate of his family in Carinthia, the Preglhof near Bleiburg, sent details of this in a letter to Alban Berg on 11 August. 'Together we must collect 1000 kronen'. Berg, Webern, Jalowetz, Horwitz and Stein should each contribute 200. Schoenberg had offered to sell them his pictures. Berg drew up an appeal and collected forty signatures. After a few days Schoenberg thanked them all for their rapid help. He asked Mathilde and the children to join him.

Since his flight he had been corresponding with Hertzka. On 5 August he asked the publisher to visit him at the Starnberger See. Already in Vienna he had appealed for his patronage at the end of July. He said that in similar circumstances Marschalk would have paid him twice as much as Hertzka was paying him. What he needed was 1500 kronen. He was planning new theoretical books which could all be ready in five years. One on counterpoint. One on orchestration (methods of writing for orchestra). A preliminary study of form (discussion of formal principles and their effect on modern compositions); this would probably only be about Mahler's works. Analysis of forms and rules which arise from them. A treatise on form.

All of these plans were postponed, but some of them came to fruition much later in America. In his Bavarian exile Schoenberg was thinking of quite other things. However, he was pleased that the sales of the piano pieces opus 11, the string quartets and the songs with orchestra had exceeded expectations. And he was able to tell Hertzka on 20 August that Gerhard von Keussler in Prague and Siegfried Ochs in Berlin were planning performances of his chorus *Friede auf Erden*.

More important for him were new meetings and contacts with people who understood his thoughts or tried to understand them. Oskar Fried wrote him a card from Nikolassee on 28 August 1911. He said that on Thursday the 31st he would be in Munich at the Hotel Leinfelder, and in the evening would see the *Oresteia*. Schoenberg went there and was introduced to Max Reinhardt. The great producer had put on Aeschylus's drama for summer performances on the Theresien-Wiese and had asked

Otto Klemperer to write incidental music for it. The latter says
in his memoirs: 'I met Schoenberg in 1911 in Munich, on the
occasion of the performance of the *Oresteia* of Aeschylus, for which
I had written some music which Schoenberg did not like at all.
He made the impression on me of being a very angry man. At
that time I did not know a single note of his music.'

Fried had already spoken to the Berlin publisher and art dealer
Cassirer in July about Schoenberg and had got the impression
that Cassirer would help Schoenberg financially. 2000 marks
would be a bit too much for him, but he should certainly pay more
than 1000 marks. – As usual Schoenberg informed his friend
Webern about his meetings in Munich, and his plans to
meet Richard Strauss and Vassily Kandinsky in Bavaria. 'Do you
know about him?' Webern asked Alban Berg on 5 September.

Kandinsky, the great Russian painter, was living with the artist
Gabriele Münter at that time in Murnau and was preparing the
first exhibition of the 'Blaue Reiter' in Munich. In a letter of 1936
he reminded Schoenberg of their first meeting: '. . . on the
Starnberger See – I arrived by steamer and had short Lederhosen
on and I saw a black and white drawing – you were dressed
entirely in white and your face was deep black'. The meeting had
a previous history.

On 1 January 1911 there was a Schoenberg concert in Munich.
The Rosé Quartet played the two string quartets – with Marie
Gutheil-Schoder as the singer in the last two movements of opus
10, and Etta Werndorff played the Three Piano Pieces opus 11.
Soon after this Schoenberg received a letter in a writing unknown
to him. It came from Vassily Kandinsky, Munich-Schwabing,
Ainmillerstrasse 36 I. The painter excused himself for writing to
him as an unknown person. He said that the concert had caused
him great pleasure. He confirmed that their endeavours and their
ways of thinking and feeling had so much in common that he felt
himself justified in expressing his sympathy. This spark of sympathy was reciprocated. Schoenberg reacted in a letter and this
led to a correspondence in which Kandinsky developed plan after
plan.

The idea of going to the concert came from Franz Marc, who
like Kandinsky belonged to the new Society of Artists in Munich,
which was founded in 1909. 'I persuaded the Society to come with
me', he wrote to his friend August Macke on 14 January. 'The
public behaved vulgarly like schoolboys, sneezed and cleared their
throats with titters and moving their chairs about, so that it was

very difficult to follow the music at all. Can you think of a music in which tonality (that is the maintenance of a key) is completely removed? I almost had to think of Kandinsky's great composition . . . and of Kandinsky's "springing spots" when I listen to this music, in which each tone is sounded, is allowed to speak for itself (a kind of white linen wall between the spots of colour!) . . . Schoenberg, like our society, seems convinced of the continuous dissolution of the laws of European art and harmony.' Together with Alexey von Jawlensky, Kandinsky, his friend Gabriele Münter and Marianne von Werefkin, Marc sat over 'some bottles' afterwards in the Ratskeller.

Maria Franck too, who later became Marc's wife, was deeply moved by Schoenberg's music; she 'is struggling with the strong angel' Marc wrote to his friend Macke in February. She wrote about the music herself in a letter to Frau Macke.

The second and longer personal meeting between Schoenberg and Kadinsky, who both liked their close contact by correspondence, took place at the beginning of September in Murnau. The Marcs were there too. After this the friendship between the musician and the Russian increased. Macke did not share the enthusiasm of his Munich colleagues. When Schoenberg was represented in the first exhibition of the 'Blaue Reiter', founded about the 'green-eyed water-bread with its astral appearance'. The only one he liked was the self-portrait from behind.

Marc visited Schoenberg on Sunday, 28 January 1912 in Zehlendorf. Schoenberg's diary says on 2 February:

'*Then came Marc (without his wife, who was ill). He praised Cassirer in spite of my strong opposition . . . Marc showed me a letter from Loos, who is annoyed about Oppenheimer, calls him a cheat and a copyer of Kokoschka and warns people about him. It is wrong to do this to Oppenheimer: he is unoriginal, but one does not have to call him a cheat for that . . . Marc is a nice person. A bit unclear and not very important. He won't go along with Kandinsky much longer . . .*'

Of the Munich circle the only one who kept contact in correspondence with Schoenberg, apart from Kandinsky, was Gabriele Münter. She wanted to get him to give a lecture in Munich, and Schoenberg suggested that he should speak about Mahler. However, the plan did not come off.

On 8 September Webern told his friend Berg that Schoenberg's plan to move to Berlin was very much alive again. An appeal was coming out in 'Pan' in the middle of the month, drawn up by Oskar Fried and Alfred Kerr and which would be signed by all important people in Berlin, to raise a fund for Schoenberg as a teacher. All the Berlin papers were due to publish this. Edward Clark, the English admirer of Schoenberg, took part in this enterprise and looked for patrons to set up a guarantee fund.

Among the influential Viennese intellectuals who believed in Schoenberg was Hermann Bahr, whose writings about modern tendencies and the way beyond naturalism were as successful as his novels and his comedy *The Concert*. Webern had spoken to him when Bahr lectured in Danzig and had asked him to give greetings to Schoenberg. Schoenberg asked Alban Berg in September to look him up and to ask for his support and help.

13 September was Schoenberg's thirty-seventh birthday. He spent it with his relations and far from his friends; he probably took his usual morning walk on the shores of the lake, where in 1886 Ludwig II, King of Bavaria, who had a passion for music and deified Wagner, mentally confused, committed suicide at the age of forty-one. Schoenberg sent a few bitter words to his publisher in Vienna.

Among the many letters of greeting Webern's moved him very much. His friend wrote to him on 10 September:

> *Dear Herr Schoenberg, I am very glad to be able to tell you the following. Since yesterday evening I know who the buyer of your pictures was.*
> *He did not want you to know it.*
> *Now he has gone to eternal rest.*
> *I do not think that he wants you not to know of it.*
> *If so, and I hope he pardons me, for telling you now.*
> *But to know it, and not to do this, is impossible for me.*
> *Your pictures were bought by*
>   *GUSTAV MAHLER.*
>
>   *Your Webern.*

However Schoenberg's immediate future was uncertain. His day-to-day life was full of minor worries. On 18 September he sent a card to Zemlinsky in Prague '. . . today I had to go with Trudi to Munich to see a doctor. She has trouble with her skin, something like five years ago, when Professor Sp. looked after her.' About this time he was also negotiating with his friend and brother-in-law about a concert in Prague, to which he had been invited to conduct one of his own works. Zemlinsky wanted him to conduct in the new German theatre on 29 February 1912. As Pablo Casals was the soloist it would be sold out in advance.

Then Schoenberg had to make his decision. His conversation with Reinhardt had strengthened his wish to seek his fortune in Berlin for the second time. On 20 September he wrote to Hertzka that he would probably leave at the end of the week to discuss performances of *Erwartung* and *Glückliche Hand*, which he was to conduct himself. 'Reinhardt is very interested in this.' Five days later he gave as his address Edward Clark, Berlin-Friedenau, Rheingaustrasse 16. The latter found a room for him in the Pension Philipson.

His flight was of great importance. In the loneliness of his late summer days on the Starnberger See Schoenberg had realized the results of many experiences and disappointments of the last few years. Perhaps his meeting with Kandinsky, who had many contacts with Berlin, also led to his decision.

If one wants to explain this fateful flight, it must be regarded from a distance in time and with regard to earlier connections. For more than a year Schoenberg, supported by Hertzka and some of his friends, had tried to get a permanent teaching post at the Academy. A Professorship would not only have removed all his financial difficulties but would have made him a person of importance. Of course his position as a private teacher was an important step towards this goal. However, there were forces which worked against his activity in his capacity as lecturer which Schoenberg recognized more instinctively than consciously. In this the Antisemitic tendencies of the Christian Socialist Society, incorporated in the Mayor Dr. Karl Lueger, played an important part.

In spite of his friendship with Dr. David Josef Bach Schoenberg felt himself no longer allied to Austrian social democracy. Indeed his political convictions were developing more clearly in the direction of a tolerant monarchy with social reforms.

After Mahler's death Vienna had become impoverished musically for him. His favourite pupils Webern and Berg had become independent and were married. There was nothing much more to bind him to his native city, and much which repelled him. He had sensed what he was fleeing from. In the summer weeks in Bavaria it became clear to him he would go.

BERLIN FOR THE SECOND TIME

Among Berlin's suburbs in 1911 Zehlendorf, in the south-west of the city, was one of the most distant. The woods with their pines and birches grew right into the gardens and parks of the houses which were built there. This was different from the comfortable parts of the city, Grunewald and Dahlem, where the Prussian nobility and Jewish bankers had built their villas on the shores of the many lakes; this was populated by some intellectuals and nature lovers who wanted to get away from the insolent metropolis. The Wannsee railway, of which Berlin was as proud as it was of the underground railway in the central districts, only ran as far as the middle of the suburb. At its station the long avenue began, which ended at the Machnower Schleuse. It ran through solitary stretches of wood in which there were little fish-ponds. In the spring lovers went walking there and listened to the nightingales.

In this solitary area a colony had grown up about 1910, in which people of a special kind lived. The rich merchant Oscar Lepcke built there for himself and his brother, the sculptor Ferdinand Lepcke (1866–1909), a villa on the corner of the Machnower Chaussee and the Dietloffstrasse, an elegant, large two storied building with an attic, and the cap roof of Art Nouveau. The park-like garden surrounded a pond, on the banks of which there was a stately pavilion made of birch wood with a thatched roof. People could swim and row in a boat.

It was not difficult to get there. A few times a day a two-horse post-omnibus ran from the Wannsee station to the Schleuse. On the way was the rifle club, built in 1894, with a restaurant and rifle range. On Sunday people drank beer here and shot at targets. It survived two world wars; the Villa Lepcke was destroyed in 1945 towards the end of the war.

Here Schoenberg lived from 1 October 1911 to May 1913. A whole large storey was put at his disposal, so that there was plenty of room not only for the family of four, but for visitors as well. In the Villa Lepcke Schoenberg finished the score of the 'Gurrelieder'; here he also wrote *Pierrot Lunaire*, the song 'Herzgewächse' and parts of the music for the *Glückliche Hand*. In spite of many disappointments this was a time of optimism. Schoenberg found himself esteemed. He enjoyed the company and admiration of many important people from the worlds of music, literature, the theatre and the plastic arts.

Edward Clark, the Berlin correspondent of the *Musical Times* of London, had done propaganda everywhere for him as a teacher. From 1912 onwards Schoenberg's name appeared in the Berlin telephone book with an extension of the Lepcke number; Zehlendorf 249. The entry reads 'Arnold Schoenberg, Composer and Composition Teacher, Office Hours 1–2.'

One of his first guests was Webern. He had been discharged from his job at the Danzig Theatre in the summer, had had a holiday in Carinthia and then found lodgings with relations in Vienna. Schoenberg invited him to come to Berlin, and on 10 October he wrote overjoyed to Berg. Two days later he also found lodgings in Zehlendorf, not far from the Villa Lepcke.

Schoenberg had concluded a contract with the Stern Conservatory, to which Richard Strauss had recommended him in 1902, to give a course of lectures. The Conservatory put a lecture room at his disposal and advertised the lectures; in return Schoenberg had to give them a third of his earnings. At this time he had no private pupils. But Berlin patrons put 2000 marks at his disposal.

The lectures were on aesthetics and composition. They took place on Monday afternoons, beginning on 20 November. There were to be eight to ten of them. Schoenberg hoped for more results from them than they actually produced. He kept on pressing Vienna to hurry up with the printing of the Harmony Book, so that at least the first copies should be ready at the beginning of the course. Meanwhile he received the printed scores of *Pelléas and Mélisande*. He was delighted with the fine print. The enormous 48-stave pages of the 'Gurrelieder' score lay on his writing desk. The orchestration was finished on 7 November.

In his first weeks in Berlin Schoenberg had already met some people who were important to him for the propagation of his works. Among these were acquaintances from previous years such as Artur Schnabel, Oskar Fried and Ferruccio Busoni, with whom

Villa Lepcke, Berlin-Zehlendorf, 1912.
Here *Pierrot Lunaire* was composed

In the background Villa Zehme, Leipzig 1914 on the occasion of
the 'Gurrelieder' performance. Back row: Polnauer, Steuermann,
Webern, Königer, Marya Freund, Jalowetz, (?), Helene Berg,
Clark with Görgy, Stein. Front row: Trude Schoenberg, Mathilde
Schoenberg, Hertzka, Albertine Zehme, May, Smaragda Berg (?)

he had corresponded; these all admired his music, worked on his behalf and gave him help when his situation became difficult. Busoni introduced him to the circle of the magazine 'Pan', the dramatic critic Alfred Kerr and the publisher Cassirer. His most important meeting was with Louise Wolff. Since the death of her husband Hermann Wolff in 1902 she was the soul of the powerful concert agency which he had founded in 1880. This woman, who was clever, energetic, and important in society, came from Brno, spent her youth in Vienna and studied at the Theatre Academy. As a young actress she met Hermann Wolff and accompanied him in his rise to fame. 'Queen Louise', as the fifty-six-year-old lady was called then, had made Berlin the world centre of musical life from her office in the Flottwellstrasse. Busoni, Fried and Schnabel told her about Schoenberg. She asked him to visit her, and he came. It was 30 October, a Monday. In a letter written on the next day he said to Hertska:

'*The Wolff Concert Agency wants to "take me in hand". I saw Frau Wolff yesterday and she wants to do an enormous amount for me and my pieces. She has already spoken to Nikisch. This evening she will tell Rose that he should bring my quartets to Berlin now (even this year) . . . then she will say to Lula Gmeiner* (a German alto singer 1876-1948; later after her marriage, Mysz-Gmeiner) *that she should sing my songs this year. Naturally not only in Berlin. Siloti* (Alexander Siloti 1863-1945, Liszt pupil pianist, conductor of the Philharmonic concerts in St. Petersburg which were named after him) *is performing "Pelléas" in Petersburg at her request.* Please send him the score straight away. *And she also wants to put on the "Gurrelieder". And she is going to show the five orchestral pieces to Nikisch. She suggests that Nikisch should meanwhile first perform the Songs with Orchestra. Now we must find a tenor for them.* Please send her the piano scores of the Songs with Orchestra straight away.

'*I don't believe everything that she promises me, and indeed only believe part of it. But I seem to have made a very big impression on her . . . In addition she has also prepared to put on a concert of my works. But I am not very much for that . . .*'

There is no doubt that he made a great impression on her. On 3 November she wrote to him: 'You can count on my readiness to help in all things, very honoured Herr Schoenberg.' Meanwhile she had already acted. The Rosé Quartet played in the Bechsteinsaal on 31 October. After this there was a large party in the nearby Rheingold Winehouse on the Potsdamer Platz, where the Onyx Room was reserved for the company. Schoenberg and

Webern were able to send a card together to Hertska, saying: 'Have just been with Rosé. He is playing the D minor quartet on 12 December.'

Siloti kept his word too. *Pelléas and Mélisande* was in his programmes for the season 1912–13. However it was not he who conducted the performance, but Schoenberg himself.

Lula Mysz-Gmeiner performed some of the early Schoenberg songs in her concerts. Nikisch took longer than the others. He did not conduct the orchestral pieces or the songs opus 8. But in January 1914 he gave a performance of the first chamber symphony in the Leipzig Gewandhaus Concerts. Schoenberg heard the final rehearsal and thanked the conductor for 'performing his work with great love and warm interest.'

Webern had also told Berg about Schoenberg's visit to Louise Wolff. The two friends were worried about Schoenberg, who found more fame in Berlin than means of existence. Berg prepared an 'Action for Schoenberg'. The two of them thought of possible subscribers: Rothschild, Alma Mahler, Carl Moll, Redlich (Josef Redlich, 1869–1936, lawyer, University Professor in Vienna, Privy Councillor, from 1907 to 1918 Member of Parliament for the German Progressive Party, 1918 Minister of Finance, 1926 Professor at Harvard University, a friend of Hugo von Hofmannsthal; his correspondence with the latter was published in 1971) and Bahr were mentioned.

And another plan was worked out in this correspondence. There was to be a book about Schoenberg. Webern had already written his contribution; it was on Schoenberg's compositions. On 7 November he came with his wife and their five-month-old daughter Amalia to supper in the Villa Lepcke. He showed Schoenberg his article. The Weberns spent the night in the guest room, because it was too far to walk home and the post-omnibus was not running so late.

The idea of the book came from Berg. Webern had given his enthusiastic agreement to it in September. Paul Stefan was called in as adviser. Schoenberg's pupil Karl Linke would be asked to collaborate. The preliminary work went on for months.

In November there was to be an important event in Munich. Mahler's *Song of the Earth* was to be given its first performance on 20 November under Bruno Walter. 'For the first time since Mahler's death there is a new work by him. And we shan't be there?', Webern wrote to Berg. And they decided, together with Erwin Stein, Karl Horwitz and Heinrich Jalowetz to collect money so that Schoenberg could visit the Munich Festival as well. In a few days the necessary sum was raised. 'Milliards here for this man!' said Webern joyfully. But on 15 November he had to tell Berg that Schoenberg would be prevented from coming because he was beginning his lectures at the Stern Conservatory. And so Schoenberg was not present at the Munich performance, and Webern was not present at his first lecture in Berlin.

The Englishman Edward Clark was the vanguard of the Schoenberg group in Berlin. At the beginning he was Schoenberg's only pupil, till Leo Perelman appeared; Fritz Zweig followed Schoenberg from Vienna and Eduard Steuermann joined him in 1912. Clark went to all Schoenberg's lectures in the Stern Conservatory and later described them as a 'sensational success'. His description gives a good picture of them: 'Schoenberg never prepared the text of his lectures and did not stand on a platform. He walked up and down between the rows of seats, smoking the whole time, talked about his experiences and theoretical procedures in musical composition and answered questions. The result was not great from the material point of view, but Schoenberg's stay in Berlin had perceptible results.'

Webern hastened back from his trip to Munich. He spent most of Wednesday, 22 November, with Schoenberg and in the morning he played him through the *Song of the Earth*. Both were deeply affected: 'We couldn't speak!' Between 24 and 26 November Adolf Loos was in Berlin. In spite of his deafness he was an admirer of Schoenberg and his pupils, missed no concert in which their works were performed and promoted their compositions so far as he could. He gave lectures every year in Berlin, where there were like-minded people among the young architects and painters, and where Herwarth Walden and the 'Storm' group fought for similar aims with their radical modern magazine. This time he talked about 'Walking, sitting, sleeping, eating and drinking'. The hall of the Architects' House was filled by an illustrious company. Afterwards in the Rheingold Restaurant they sent a card to the poet Else Lasker-Schüler. Schoenberg, Webern, Loos, Ludwig and Lene Kainer, Ada and Emil Nolde, Herwarth Walden, Alfred Döblin and Albert Ehrenstein all signed it. Karin Michaelis, who was then at the height of her fame as a poet, wrote a long letter to her colleague, who was much admired by Loos and Karl Kraus; Else Lasker-Schüler reproduced the complete contents of the 'Mass Postcard' in her autobiographical novel *Mein Herz* of 1912. Two days later, on 27 November 1911, Schoenberg gave his second lecture at the Conservatory. But in spite of the enthusiastic applause Schoenberg was disappointed with Berlin. No pupils had yet appeared.

Hertzka came to Berlin at the end of the month, and Schoenberg spoke to him about plans in Vienna. Berg and Webern believed sincerely that he would be appointed to succeed Bruno Walter, who had resigned from the directorship of the Vienna Singakademie. The possibility of a professorship at the Academy was mooted again. One of the most progressive groups of intellectuals had formed themselves into the 'Academic Society for Literature and Music in Vienna'. They wrote to Schoenberg about a magazine which was due to appear under the direction of Dr. Paul Stefan, Ludwig Ullmann and Erhard Buschbeck. The first number, which was called 'Carnival', was planned for February. Schoenberg sent them some aphorisms which he had already published in 1910 in the Berlin magazine 'Musik'.

At the beginning of December Webern was taken ill with serious bronchitis, fever and headaches. Schoenberg visited him every day. At this time he wrote the song 'Herzgewächse' on a text from the *Serres Chaudes* by Maurice Maeterlinck, for high soprano, celesta, harmonium and harp. 'This is the highest quality in music!', said Webern, 'the vocal part goes right up to F in alto with coloratura passages. And it goes down to G' (actually G sharp). Schoenberg wanted it to be performed by Martha Winternitz-Dorda at a concert of songs in Berlin – perhaps at a matinée in Max Reinhardt's Chamber Theatre.

'Herzgewächse' was finished on 9 December. On the same day Schoenberg acknowledged to Universal Edition the receipt of the first three copies of his Harmony Book. He himself experienced nausea on looking at his text, as he wrote. However, he suggested that they should send the book to Kandinsky, Carl Einstein (the art historian of the 'Blaue Reiter' circle), Alma Mahler, Mahler's sister Justine Rosé, Carl Möller, Karl Kraus and Alexander von Zemlinsky. Also to art magazines, but as few as possible to musical critics. And later he said on receiving bound copies: 'They really look very nice.'

The publishers were behindhand in printing earlier compositions. Schoenberg had to admonish them. Of the works which had been printed he asked copies to be sent to Erich J. Wolff, who, as an outstanding song accompanist, was in touch with important singers, to the music critic Georg Gräner of the *Vossische Zeitung* and Hermann W. Draber of the 'Signale für die musikalische Welt'. He also asked for them to be sent the Harmony Book.

Franz Schreker, who had founded the Philharmonic Choir in Vienna in 1908 and put it at the service of contemporary music, was interested in the unaccompanied chorus, *Friede auf Erden*, which had been written as early as the beginning of 1907 but was still unpublished. However, Schreker found difficulties of intonation in performing this very contrapuntal work which was also very bold harmonically. So Schoenberg decided to write an *ad. lib.* accompaniment for it, which he finished on 6 October in the Villa Lepcke. Written for double woodwind, horns and string quartet it should, according to a note to the conductor, make correct intonation for the choir possible without being noticed by the audience. Now Schreker asked Schoenberg for the parts of the accompaniment and Schoenberg warned Hertzka about this. He said that his pupils Berg, Polnauer and Linke would correct them.

As regards performances, he wrote contentedly to Hertzka, things were not too bad. *Pelléas* was about to be done in Prague, and *Friede auf Erden* in Vienna. The sextet, the quartets and songs were due to be performed in Berlin by the Rosé Quartet, and in Prague and Budapest by the Waldbauer Quartet.

Preparations for the Schoenberg book continued. A publisher had been found for it, Reinhard Piper in Munich, who also published the collective volume of the 'Blaue Reiter' edited by Kandinsky and Franz Marc. Kandinsky had promised an article on Schoenberg's pictures by the end of December. Webern's article on Schoenberg's music had already appeared in the Cologne paper *Rheinische Musik und Theaterzeitung*, published by Tischer and Jagenberg, before the Schoenberg book actually appeared. This publisher also negotiated for a short time with Webern about his own compositions. In 1913 Tischer and Jagenberg published Schoenberg's *Friede auf Erden*. The first performance of this had taken place under Franz Schreker with the Philharmonic Choir in Vienna on 9 December 1911. He wrote on the next day: 'Dear Herr Schoenberg, Don't be worried: Your work had an undoubted success – I was called back three times. No hissing or anything like that. The choir consisted of more than 120 ladies, 30 tenors and more than 50 basses. It sounded *wonderful*, and you would certainly have been pleased by the performance, for it was the best one which our choir has yet given. No impure notes. I was very happy about it.'

1911 drew to its close. Schoenberg looked back on it with mixed feelings. He did not regret his flight from Vienna. 'You cannot imagine how famous I am here', he wrote on 31 October in a five-page long letter in neat German cursive script to Hertzka. 'I am almost too embarrassed to mention it. I am known to everyone. I am recognized by my photographs. People know my "Biography", all about me, all about the ":scenes" I have occasioned, indeed almost more than I, who forgets such things very quickly.' Never had there been so many prospects of performances of his chief works.

And yet he was worried about his daily existence. Fortunately the house in Zehlendorf was cheap. Alma Mahler described a visit there in these words: 'Again I found a true, important person. My visit seemed to please him and his wife. For a long time he couldn't speak for excitement. Schoenberg had made his house into something rare and special with the cheapest materials. He likes tinkering, binds books and music himself, and has divided large rooms by wooden partitions which he covers with material. Against this he puts boxes of books and hangs his own very interesting pictures on them – each room has its individual colour and its own atmosphere.'

But materially little had changed. Four people had to be fed. Trudi was going to school and in 1912 Georg was also due to go to school. The lectures in the Conservatory brought practically nothing in; twice a week Clark and Leo Perelman came as private pupils.

Among the few people who came to Schoenberg's lecture at the Conservatory on 4 December were Emil and Ada Nolde. The painter, who for a short time belonged to the 'Brücke' circle, was then regarded as the most important representative of German expressionism. Franz Marc, who visited him in Berlin, had persuaded him also to collaborate with the 'Blaue Reiter' movement. After Schoenberg's lecture there seems to have been a discussion. On 9 December Nolde wrote him a card: 'We hope you didn't take our frank words about your lecture amiss. We would very much like to get to know you and your art better; would you like to visit us on Monday evening the 11th?' The Noldes lived in Tauentzienstrasse 8, near the house where Busoni had lived until 1902.

Busoni, who had returnea on the same ship as Mahler in his serious illness in April from New York, was busy until October with work on his first full-length opera *Die Brautwahl*. 1911 was a very full year for him, because he had to play a cycle of six piano recitals in the Beethoven-saal in celebration of Liszt's hundredth birthday. The last of these took place on 12 December.

The hard Berlin winter depressed Schoenberg very much: in spite of everything he was attached to his native Vienna. It was the same with Webern. So the two families spent Christmas together. Schoenberg gave his friend his Harmony Book with an intimate dedication. In return the latter gave Schoenberg Plato's *Republic*.

At that time Schoenberg hardly ever went to concerts and opera performances. They did not interest him very much, and in addition it was difficult to get from Zehlendorf into the city and back late in the evening.

Busoni was only able to attend two of his lectures in the Stern Conservatory, but had a very favourable impression of them.

On 19 January 1912 the Society of Friends of Music, which had been founded by Oskar Fried in 1907 and was directed by him, put on an evening of Busoni's music. Three works were in the programme: the *Fantasia Contrappuntistica*, the *Berceuse Elégiaque* and the concerto for piano, orchestra and male chorus which had been written much earlier. Schoenberg was in the audience, and also Hertzka. And the concert was also attended by Busoni's large circle of friends, including a new pupil whom he had met in 1910 at a summer school in Basel, Eduard Steuermann. In the autumn of 1963, more than fifty years later, Steuermann gave an account of this concert in a conversation with Gunther Schuller and described how he was introduced to Schoenberg. He mentioned the Busoni concert at the end of 1911 or the beginning of 1912 and the party afterwards in the Link Hotel on the Potsdamer Platz. He meant the Huth Wine House in the Potsdamer Strasse, on the corner of the Linkstrasse, which Busoni often liked to visit. Suddenly, so he said, Busoni got up, took him by the arm and led him to Schoenberg, who was sitting with Frau Schoenberg and Hertzka. 'May I introduce to you Herr Steuermann, a pupil of mine, who would like to study with you?' Schoenberg immediately took out his diary and asked: 'When would you like to come?' Two days later he had his first lesson in Zehlendorf.

This account contains some mistakes. But there is a more reliable one describing the same evening. This was written by Schoenberg himself. For on the day after the Busoni concert he began to keep a diary, something he had been meaning to do for a long time. There is an account of every day from 19 January to 12 March 1912. The first entry runs:

'*Good. Begun at last. Have had it in mind for a long time. But I couldn't get rid of the conception that I would first have to write down what comes into my head about my early life. So that is why I have neglected it for ten years or more. But now it will go on. While I have decided to delude myself by persuading myself only to make short notes in it for which I can find time every day.*'

This is the preamble, which is typical of Schoenberg's irony about himself. It is followed by this description:

'*Went to Fried's concert last night. Busoni's compositions hadn't pleased me until now. But I liked the* Berceuse *yesterday. It was a directly affecting piece. I was really moved. I had been very wrong about him. Another one! – On the other hand Fried: he pleases me less and less. He is only a carver. Since I have been treating him with coolness, he woos me a great deal. But I am deaf to him. Afterwards met Kousse-vitzky* (Sergej Koussevitzky, 1874–1951, contrabass player, conductor, gave concerts from 1909 onwards with his own orchestra in Moscow, founded the Russian Music Publishing Firm. From 1924 he was conductor of the Boston Symphony Orchestra, and in 1944 he gave the first performance of Schoenberg's *Theme and Variations*, opus 43b in Boston.) *Guttmann* (Emil Gutmann, concert agent, admirer of Mahler's, who put on the first performance of Mahler's Eighth Symphony in 1910) *led me up to him. Koussevitzky wants to perform* Pelléas *in St. Petersburg and Moscow next year. That would be very nice; I hope so. Foreign countries are beginning to get interested in me very intensively this year. K. says that my second quartet will be done in St. Petersburg in two weeks.*'

Then met van Dieren (Bernard van Dieren 1884–1936, Dutch composer and writer, friend of Busoni's). *Seems to be very interesting. Am curious about him. He will visit me and show me his compositions.*

After the concert went with Guttmann, Hertzka, Webern and Clark to the Heidelberg Restaurant. Guttmann very sportive. But he has sworn (!!) to perform Gurrelieder *in the autumn! We'll see. Hertzka beamed!*

Also spoke to Petri in the concert (Egon Petri, 1881–1962, violinist and pianist, pupil of Busoni). *Sloppy. Is supposed to perform my songs and piano pieces (on 28th). Without directly disliking him, I don't like him very much. Asked Busoni if he will take part in the piano arrangement of my orchestral pieces. He turned it down: no time (probably no wish!)*. *As a result Petri also has no wish to do it. A little master! Will take other people.*

This is the first entry in the diary. It shows the high-handed self-centred way in which Schoenberg reacted to people. But it also shows that he was ready to revise his own judgements, as in the case of Busoni's compositions. The performance of songs and piano pieces, in which Petri was supposed to take part, was included in a concert of Schoenberg's works which had been planned for 28 January and after many difficulties took place on 4 February in the Harmoniumsaal. The programme also included Webern's arrangement of some of the orchestral pieces opus 16 for two pianos and eight hands.

The diary mentions preparations and rehearsals for this concert nearly every day. Schoenberg's latest composition, the song 'Herzgewächse', was due to have its first performance. The harpsichord player decided not to play. Martha Winternitz-Dorda hesitated about agreeing to sing, agreed and then gave up the part. On 22 January Schoenberg went to Egon Petri, who played him through the piano pieces opus 19.

'He will probably play the pieces very well. At least pianistically. In general he took everything too fast; or rather too hastily. I said to Webern: One must have time in my music. It is not for people who have other things to do. At any rate it is a great pleasure to hear one's pieces played by someone who can master them perfectly from a technical point of view. It seems that the concert will be very good. I am hoping for the best from the eight-hand arrangement of the orchestral pieces!'

On the same afternoon he gave another lecture in the Conservatory. He kept the audience, which included the Busonis with their elder son Benvenuto, Clark and Van Dieren, waiting for a quarter of an hour. On 29 January he gave the last of these lectures; the paltry attendance at them embittered Schoenberg and Webern.

The first rehearsal for the orchestral pieces, arranged for eight hands, was on Tuesday, the 23rd. The two pianos were played by Louis Closson, Louis T. Grünberg, Eduard Steuermann (all three pupils of Busoni) and Anton von Webern. Schoenberg notes:

'Great disappointment. My pupils are better than Busoni's. They are much more musicians. I believe they are also more intelligent people. Grünberg especially is very bad. No rhythm. Closson is very good. Steuermann not bad . . . it is difficult to rehearse something like that. It often makes it difficult for me to say if they were together. I will be able to decide when it begins to become clearer. I miss the sounds! The

colours. The piano is after all only one instrument. But less for musicians than for pianists. Perhaps that's why it's so popular!?'

The next day brought new difficulties. Winternitz is prevented from coming, and Petri cannot change the date. Schoenberg postponed the concert till 4 February, on which Winternitz is free. But she cannot come to a rehearsal. Schoenberg wants to ask Leo Blech whether Frieda Hempel (dramatic coloratura-soprano in the Berlin Court Opera, 1885–1955) can take over the songs. Winternitz is annoyed by a stiff letter which Emil Gutmann had written her on this occasion, and reproaches Schoenberg with all that she had done for him in the past.

Rehearsals for the orchestral pieces go on. Closson will play the piano pieces opus 19 instead of Petri; the song accompaniments are taken over by Steuermann. After the rehearsal of 30 January of the orchestral pieces (of which only the first, second and the fourth were played) Schoenberg was very pleased with the performance. He was also pleased with the accompaniment of the 'Herzgewächse', with Webern and Closson for harmonium and celesta. The placing of the instruments caused problems – two pianos, harmonium, celesta and harp – on the small stage of the Harmoniumsaal.

In the evening a telegram arrived: Winternitz cannot sing the 'Herzgewächse'. The conductor Ivan Fröbe, who had already been helpful at the rehearsals, will try to find a young singer who could take over the part in 24 hours. On 3 February Schoenberg rehearsed the accompaniment in the morning with Webern and Closson, and then cancelled the performance.

'Loos comes to the rehearsal. Is very nice. Especially to Webern. He finds a similarity between himself and me in that I make alterations in my compositions at rehearsals. But this is wrong: I don't work out the composition during the building, as he says, but on the contrary such alterations are very rare with me and are mostly only concerned with notation marks. But I didn't contradict him, because he was very amiable; and then, above all, he is so deaf that one can hardly talk to him; it would be exhausting for me to contradict him. At the rehearsal minor arguments between Webern and Clark. Webern is impatient if Clark doesn't pull the stops at the right moment and is awkward. I mediate! It was very funny!'

In the afternoon there was a rehearsal with the four pianists.

'Calvocoressi (Michel Dimitri Calvocoressi, 1877–1944, Franco-Greek writer on music and critic, lived in Paris, after 1914 in London, a friend of Ravel, biographer of Debussy) *came to it. A*

man of very adroit, amiable behaviour. Otherwise not very impressive at the moment. He liked my orchestral pieces very much and he promises to come to the concert, which he is very pleased about.'

At ten o'clock on the Sunday of the performance there was the only rehearsal with Winternitz, who had just arrived.

'She is rather embarrassed in front of me, and tries to hush this up with many speeches. I cannot do anything but be rather cold with her. I can't forgive her so quickly. At the rehearsal I was astonished again at how musical she is. And her voice sounds very beautiful. Against this she is hoarse at present.'

There are several descriptions of the matinée, which was greeted with great applause, apart from those of the numerous critics of the daily press. Among those who attended the concert were Ferruccio and Gerda Busoni, Louise Wolff, Adolf Loos, Oskar Fried, Dr. Eugenie Schwarzwald with her husband, Karl Horwitz, Georg Gräner, Emil Gutmann, Ivan Fröbe, Calvocoressi, Amalie Webern and her sister, the poet Dr. Albert Ehrenstein (an intimate friend of Kokoschka's, who illustrated his novel *Tubutsch*) and the actress Frau Albertine Zehme. After dining in the Hotel Frederich they all went to her apartment on the Olivaer Platz 5–6.

The programme consisted of some of the early songs including 'Waldsonne' from opus 2, the Stefan George Songs opus 15, three of the Orchestral Pieces opus 16 and the Six Little Piano Pieces opus 19. Schoenberg found Winternitz's singing 'much too dramatic (rather ordinary), taking everything from the words instead of from the music'. He could not understand his own George Songs in part. He was also disappointed by Closson; he played the Six Little Piano Pieces too quickly and without pauses. He was pleased with the Orchestral Pieces, apart from a mistake by Grünberg in the fourth one.

Busoni pleased him by the warmth of his reception. And he was able to write on a post-card to Hertzka (with the wrong date 2 February 1912) that his concert had definitely been a good and great success as many people said; much applause, much attention and a very nice atmosphere. He recommended to him Calvocoressi, who had interrupted a trip to Russia in order to visit him.

Webern, whose admiration certainly did Schoenberg good in this concert ('as always the one I like the most!') wrote a few words to his friend Berg in Vienna, saying that the concert – without 'Herzgewächse' – had been a success.

The next 'Pan' printed Busoni's short comment on the concert; from it we learn that Schoenberg conducted the Orchestral Pieces: 'At the keyboard sat four youngsters with fine, characteristic heads; it was gripping to see how they put their young intelligences at the service of something which has not yet been deciphered, devoted and capable. In the background of the little stage two eyes were gleaming in an unquiet manner, and a baton was moving with short, nervous gestures. – One can only see Schoenberg's head and hand, making suggestions to the four brave young men, and communicating more and more of his fever to them. – An unusual picture, supported by an unusual sound, caused a fascinating atmosphere.'

Meanwhile the publisher Peters in Leipzig had taken the Orchestral Pieces. The fee of 600 marks was modest, but Schoenberg was satisfied with being taken up by the famous Peters Edition and with the guarantee of a printed score. He also negotiated with Marschalk, who had got in contact with him again, and with Dr. Tischer in Cologne. He asked Hertzka about the works of his which were still free.

Peters hastened to pay him the fee. On 31 January the Director of the famous publishing house, Henri Hinrichsen, came to Berlin and entertained Schoenberg in the Weinstube Habel on the Unter den Linden with caviare and Rhine wine. Schoenberg turned down his proposal to give up his contract with Universal Edition and come to him 'indirectly, in that I praised Hertzka very greatly (overcoming my own prejudices)'. When Hinrichsen asked him if he should melt down the printing plates of Mahler's Fifth Symphony Schoenberg was horrified. He answered that the young people adored Mahler, and that his time would come in five to ten years at the latest. And he decided to write something soon about Mahler.

On the next day he wrote to Universal Edition, asking for a renewal of his first contract of 1909, which had become a general contract. In February they came to an agreement, and also with Marschalk; the works published by the Dreililienverlag were later taken over by Universal Edition.

The chief music critic of the *Berliner Tageblatt*, Dr. Leopold Schmidt, wrote a notice of the concert in the Harmoniumsaal which hurt Schoenberg deeply. His pupils Clark and Perelman assured him that Schmidt had only heard a small part of the programme. He replied with a satirical article 'Sleepwalker', which Cassirer published in 'Pan'. 'I must show this Berlin critic, this arrogant fool, how one should talk to artists' he wrote in his diary of 11 February.

'*The Viennese mob has a pleasing quality of laughability, which has at any rate a half-conciliatory effect. One can despise them but not hate them. But these people here, every one of whom wants to be something better, stir one up to the highest degree. For in reality they are the same as the others. Only their colour is different, and the reason perhaps why they write better German comes from their barrenness. They don't risk anything.*'

On 21 February the 'Sleepwalker' article appeared in 'Pan'. Schmidt answered on the 24th in the Saturday number of the *Tageblatt*. Schoenberg was sent the cutting in Prague and on Zemlinsky's advice replied straight away. 'Pan' published his answer on the 29th. Schoenberg wrote:

'*The affair has stirred up a lot of dust and made me many enemies. The kind that I deserve!*'

Eduard Steuermann first came to Zehlendorf on 27 January, a holiday, in celebration of Kaiser Wilhelm II's birthday. Schoenberg found that the compositions which he played to him were so full of talent that he said that he was ready to teach him. He wrote in his diary:

'*If he studies with me, and Zweig comes, then I'll earn perhaps 200 marks a month. And above all I'll have pupils again. I told Steuermann that I would even teach him for nothing..*'

This was a week after Busoni had introduced them in the Heidelberg Restaurant. Steuermann remained Schoenberg's pupil and became the most important interpreter of all his piano works. Fritz Zweig had already come to Schoenberg in 1910 in Vienna at the age of seventeen after basic theoretical training, and wrote in a letter from Los Angeles on 1 September 1971: 'At that time he was living in a suburb of Vienna, Ober St. Veit. – The apartment was decorated with his pictures. – I showed him some of my very conservative compositions, whereupon he said: "You are pure Kuhlau". – As far as I remember his teaching was not at all systematic, but it consisted of very valuable suggestions. – We never analysed one of his own compositions, but classical works, especially Mendelssohn and Brahms, and in the latter – as he said – one could see the seams much better than in Beethoven. – Then I followed him to Berlin; we never had a break-up in our relationship, and his instruction stopped because of my job at the Mannheim Court Theatre (1913).'

In February Schoenberg undertook a journey, the preparations for which cost him a good deal of work. Since the autumn of 1911 Alexander von Zemlinsky had been musical director of the German Opera in Prague. He invited Schoenberg to share the conducting of a concert with him. Schoenberg was to conduct his *Pelléas* and before that the Bach Suite, which Mahler had put together from three of J. S. Bach's orchestral suites. His pupil Dr. Karl Horwitz, who was also employed at the Prague Opera, brought news of Zemlinsky on occasional visits to Berlin. On 21 February the Schoenbergs and Webern travelled to Prague. His diary shows how fascinated he was by the journey through the Elbe Valley, which Schoenberg did not know. He and Mathilde stayed with Zemlinsky, who met them at the station together with Horwitz. The next days were very exhausting. Schoenberg had to spend every evening at social functions, slept badly and too little, and was also worried about a few difficult places in his *Pelléas* score. On the second evening Zemlinsky took him to the theatre to see a performance of Wilhelm Kienzl's *Kuhreigen*, because it was conducted by the young Hungarian conductor István Strasser, whom Schoenberg found very sympathetic. Gerhard von Keussler, at that time the director of the Prague Choral Society and an admirer of Schoenberg, was also introduced to him. On Friday 23 February he had his first rehearsal with the wind, and found difficulty with a complicated 12/8 bar. On Sunday, after a night which he slept through with the help of veronal, he had a string rehearsal. On Sunday morning Zemlinsky and Schoenberg visited the director of the theatre Heinrich Teweles. In the evening there was a big party at Zemlinsky's, at which Webern was present with Berg, who had just arrived from Vienna. 26 February, a Monday, was filled with rehearsals and functions, and so was the Tuesday. More and more friends and pupils of Schoenberg arrived in Prague, including Josef Polnauer, Paul Königer, Karl Linke, and Berg's pupil Josef Schmied.

Schoenberg began to feel more secure at the rehearsals, and admired Zemlinsky's practical capabilities such as reading a cello concerto by Saint-Saens at sight; in this he had to accompany Pablo Casals in the same concert. Schoenberg made a few alterations to the Bach-Mahler score. A social evening on the night before the concert with his friends and pupils made him very happy.

Meanwhile after preparations which had taken months of work and anxiety, the Book of Homage by Schoenberg's friends arranged by Webern and Berg was published by R. Piper and

Arnold Schoenberg and Alexander von Zemlinsky,
February 1912

Co. in Munich. Webern gave Schoenberg the first copy. Schoenberg wrote in his diary:

> '*How moved he was, when he handed the book to me. Solemn and yet so simple. Almost like a schoolboy; but one who has learnt enough not to let himself be overpowered.*'

This solemn ceremony took place during the reception at Zemlinsky's. Schoenberg seemed to feel that his brother-in-law was a little bit put out of countenance by so much praise and homage. He himself felt a bit unquiet about the enormous amount of passionate admiration which was already shown in his dedication; 'To Arnold Schoenberg with the greatest admiration'. It seems that this gift even led him to a critical revision of his relationships with his most important and dearest pupils, Webern and Berg. We shall return to this later.

On Thursday, 29 February (1912 was a Leap Year), were the final rehearsal and the concert in the evening. After the seven rehearsals which had been held in the little Ständetheater, where Mozart's *Don Giovanni* had been given its first performance, the final rehearsal took place in the large hall. Hertzka and Gutmann were impressed by Schoenberg's conducting. The friends had had luncheon together, and the concert in the evening was very successful. Schoenberg conducted the first half, and aroused much applause with his *Pelléas*; the second half belonged to Casals and Zemlinsky. Berg sent enthusiastic impressions to his wife Helene, who had remained in Vienna. On 1 March Schoenberg's friends took leave of him. At mid-day he went with Mathilde and the Weberns to Berlin. Webern went direct from the station to a concert in which Julia Culp, accompanied by Oskar Fried and the Blüthner Orchestra, was singing 'Adelaide' by Beethoven, orchestrated for her by Schoenberg, in a programme of songs.

While in Prague Schoenberg was invited by the Lese- and Rede-halle to give a lecture on Mahler on 25 March. On the day before that Zemlinsky was to give the first performance of Mahler's Eighth Symphony in Prague.

Schoenberg received many offers and invitations during these winter months. The Academic Society for Literature and Music in Vienna consisted predominately of young people who admired Schoenberg. He was invited by them to speak in Vienna. About the same time a similar invitation came from the Vienna Urania. Both these projects came to nothing, principally because the fees offered were not big enough. On 14 February he received the first number of the magazine published by the Academic Society under the title 'The Call' (Der Ruf). It was a carnival number and contained the aphorisms which Schoenberg mentioned previously, as well as articles by Erich Mühsam, Hermann Bahr, Stefan Zweig, Christian Morgenstern, Albert Ehrenstein, Frank Wedekind, Adolf Loos, Bernard Shaw, Egon Friedell, Alfred Polgar, Roda Roda, Berthold Viertel and others. It announced events due to take place in the near future: an Altenberg evening with Friedell, Mimi Marlow and Ida Orloff; Frank Wedekind reading his mystery *Franziska*, the first performance of his *Schloss Wetterstein*; an evening of Schoenberg's music and lectures by Friedell, Alfred Roller, Schoénberg, Professor Töply and Stefan Zweig. And an advertisement by Universal Edition announced the *Pelléas* score and the Harmony Book as newly published; previous publications mentioned were the Orchestral Songs opus 8, the String Quartet in F sharp minor opus 10, Three Piano Pieces opus 11 and Busoni's concert arrangement of opus 11 No. 2; in preparation were the 'Gurrelieder' and the First Chamber Symphony. This magazine, 70 pages long, contained illustrations by Gustav Klimt and Oskar Kokoschka. It gives a remarkable picture of the Viennese modernists at that time. The further four numbers of 'Ruf', which were published by different firms up till October 1913, contained some interesting contributions. In the second one of March 1912 as well as the authors mentioned above one can find articles by Emile Verhaeren, Franz Schreker (Pantomime *The Blue Flower* or *Pierrot's Heart*), Karl von Levetzow, Georg Trakl, Paul Zech, Franz Werfel, Franz Theodor Csokor, Emil Ludwig, and Else Lasker-Schüler as well as the publication of the first of the Four Pieces for Violin and Piano, opus 7 (1910) by Webern. Events put on by the Society were announced: On 11 April 1912 a Shaw Evening with Egon Friedell, on 16 April a Schoenberg Concert in the Bösendorfer Saal with the Rosé Quartet and on 2 May a Nestroy Festival with Karl Kraus as speaker in the large Musikvereinssaal. The third number, in the autumn of 1912, announces as events for the season of 1912/13 a chamber concert in the Festsaal of the Kaufmannschaft on 20 November containing works by Schoenberg, Bartók, Wellesz, Berg and Webern played by Arnold Rosé, Hermann Gürtler, Rudolf Réti, Norah Drewett and Etta Werndorff. For 23 February 1913 an orchestral concert in the big Musikvereinssaal conducted by Schoenberg was announced, containing the Chamber Symphony and *Pelléas*. No date is given for an evening of Schoenberg Songs by Martha Winternitz-

Dorda, or for the first performance of the monodrama *Erwartung* and the performance of a drama by Kokoschka. The fourth number of May 1913 contains another Webern composition in facsimile. Here it was called 'No. 3 from Four Pieces for String Quartet'. This was actually the fourth of the six bagatelles opus 9, a piece which has the extremely short length of 8 bars.

Schoenberg was rather annoyed about the first number, because his article had been cut down and his name was only mentioned on the cover after the more attractive ones of Bahr, Wedekind and Shaw. The Berlin 'Pan' had treated him better, and he drew the conclusion from this that he had been quite right to move from Vienna to Berlin.

Only some of the events planned by the Academic Society took place. *Erwartung* had to wait another twelve years for its first performance, which finally took place in Prague. The concert in the large Musikvereinssaal took place not on 23 February, but on 31 March 1913. We shall speak about this later.

1912 brought Schoenberg more European fame than any previous year. His early songs and chamber music got more and more performances. On 16 February the thirty-one-year-old American pianist Richard Buhlig (1880–1952) gave a recital in the Berlin Beethovensaal, a programme which, besides works by Liszt, Busoni and Erich Wolfgang Korngold contained the Three Piano Pieces opus 11. Holland and Russia asked Schoenberg to conduct his own works. He wrote to Hertzka about these plans with understandable pride. Webern was kept informed by Schoenberg about all these plans and passed on the news to his friend Berg.

In Berlin Artur Schnabel was Schoenberg's most zealous advocate. On 4 January he wrote to the banker and wealthy patron Eduard Arnhold, the founder of the German Academy in Rome (in the Villa Massimo), about a projected Berlin performance of the 'Gurrelieder'. The latter answered by return of post that he was willing to contribute 1000 marks to the cost of the performance. Arnhold also wrote to Emil Gutmann, the organizer of this plan, with the same information. The concert did not take place.

Several music publishers were getting interested in the famous and notorious man. In March he had a correspondence with Bote and Bock about the publication of one of his works. Dr. Gerhard Tischer, the proprietor of the publishing firm Tischer and Jagenberg in Cologne, asked him on 14 February to ask Universal Edition if they would allow him to publish the choral work *Friede auf Erden*. The contract was signed in June, and Tischer wrote to Schoenberg about the opus number (13) and a piano part which Schoenberg wanted printed under the score. The printing was finished on 12 July; complimentary copies were sent to Bodanzky, Keussler, Ochs, Schreker and Zemlinsky. Strauss's publisher Adolph Fürstner also began negotiations with Schoenberg, as is shown by a letter from this firm of 12 June.

The diary gives information of many kinds about the private life of Schoenberg's family. On 23 January Schoenberg notes that he was getting to know many new people. He does not mention names; one of them was certainly Ivan Fröbe, a conductor, very good-looking, who gave concerts in his house in Wannsee, Hohenzollernstrasse 3, and who on 21 January invited Schoenberg and his family to a performance of the six-part Ricercare from Bach's *Musical Offering* 'in our circle'. Webern kept in almost daily contact with Schoenberg. The two families visited each other. On 6 February the Schoenbergs visited Webern; two days later the two friends went for a walk together.

A school friend from the Leopoldstadt, Dr. Friedrich Eichberg, was living in Berlin. The physicist and inventor had a flat in the superior Ahornallee in the West End. The Schoenbergs invited him to lunch on Sunday, 28 January. The diary reads:

'Is still the same person, who falls from one embarrassing thing to another . . . When he speaks about his profession he speaks very cleverly. I wish he would only speak about it more, because he knows that I am so interested in all techniques . . . Eichberg kept on making opportunities of drawing attention to my productions . . . He looked through my printed music and books. He wondered if he would understand my Harmony Book. He asked about my lectures. He spoke of his intention of buying my printed songs. (Rather forced!) And he repeatedly praised one of my pictures. Finally he expressed a wish to buy it from me (a little winter landscape which I once painted because I had a headache). I answered evasively, for I did not want him to buy reconciliation from me. Afterwards Webern came in.'

On the next day Schoenberg sent the picture to Eichberg as a gift. He thought that as a rich man he could have afforded a bigger one; he did not want to be grateful to him so cheaply!

The final visitor on this eventful day was the painter Franz Marc, who appeared in the afternoon.

A week before Webern had been the cause of a quarrel between the Schoenbergs. Schoenberg was sorry that his friend could not be in Berlin on 5 March, when Rosé was playing his first quartet.

'He is going to Vienna', he wrote in his diary, *'to hear Mahler's Eighth Symphony. I would have liked to do that too. However it shows that he is not so dependent on me as he would like me to believe. In the evening I had a discussion about this with Mathilde. The result was that we quarrelled. Naturally she goes much too far; for she has for certain reasons (G) a need to attack Webern. I said to her that often I myself didn't behave any better to Mahler; that parents*

behaved badly to children and children to parents. That goodness is an *abstraction and not an absolute. That there are no men who are ab-* *solutely good and spotless. And that I will not forget how marvellously* *Webern has behaved to me at other times. But she won't agree to this.* *She remains firm in her convictions and hardly listens to me'.*

One can see from this that Schoenberg had not forgotten the tragic Gerstl affair, shown by the capital G in brackets. However, as in all marriages there could be much more trivial reasons for friction. On 9 February the central heating broke down, and this led to a quarrel. The winter of 1911/12 was very cold in Berlin; in January Schoenberg had a restless night because little Georg was suffering from chilblains and cried. But the quarrel about the central heating was soon forgotten. Next day the two Schoen-bergs went for a walk near Zehlendorf; on the way they met Webern. Schoenberg's daughter Trudi, who was ten on 8 January, was at the Zehlendorf Waldschule. One day she went on a school expedition to Berlin to look at the State pictures.

'I was very worried about this', Schoenberg wrote; *'she came* *home late. So we went to meet her. She confessed timidly that she had* *lost her purse with 1 mark 60 in it. She does this every time.'*

There is little about composition in the diary. On 27 January Schoenberg corrected proofs of continuo parts for Professor Dr. Guido Adler; on 6 February this tiring work was finished and the music was sent off to Vienna. Schoenberg had written the harpsichord part for the G minor Concerto for cello and orchestra by Georg Matthias Monn and some other works for the 'Denkmaler der Tonkunst in Osterreich' edited by Adler. He was clearly interested in the work, for in the summer he asked Adler for further jobs of this kind; Adler promised him some in a letter of 3 September. Schoenberg also wanted to put a continuo part into the Andante of the Bach-Mahler Suite which he conducted in Prague in February.

There is an interesting entry about his pupil Edward Clark, who had a lesson with him on 10 February in the afternoon:

'Remarkable: he knows no Wagner operas, nothing by Mozart, *nothing by Beethoven. But he wants to be a conductor!! And he has* *often seen* Elektra*! This is another example of how little one should* *take for granted: I thought that the young people of today grew up* *with Wagner! Seems to be an exception. He blames it on musical* *conditions in England.'*

The invitations to give lectures in Vienna for the Urania and the Academic Society were turned down in February. Not only because the fees offered were too small. Schoenberg wanted to know nothing of Vienna, and was happy to be away from it. He would certainly have been able to give the Mahler lecture somewhere else, in Berlin or Munich. This was the lecture which he had been invited to give by the Prague Lese-and-Redehalle. Gutmann arranged a repetition of it in Berlin, on 13 October 1912.

Schoenberg was pleased with his new pupil Steuermann. The diary mentions one afternoon (Tuesday, 13 February 1912), on which Beethoven's C minor Variations were analysed: 'He pleased me again today.'

Steuermann's sister Salome, called Salka, lived in Berlin and worked in Max Reinhardt's theatre. She used to visit Schoenberg and wrote in her memoirs *Das unbelehrbare Herz* about this. 'On Sundays, when I was not playing, I often went with Edward to Zehlendorf, where we also met other Schoenberg pupils . . . There was always marvellous coffee and homebaked cakes, which we enjoyed very much. Schoenberg dominated the conversation. He was very vital, full of inexhaustible ideas, an inspired teacher. Not only music or literature, but also the most ordinary things in daily life could fascinate him and draw brilliant remarks from him. His wife Mathilde, small and sickly, sat on the sofa, always shivering and wrapped in a shawl, and listening to the conversation. Two good-looking, frolicsome children, a boy and a girl, ran through the room.'

The Strindbergian idea of soon having to suffer for wrongs done in the past, returns again. On 18 February Schoenberg notices a 'great diminution of all the things which have appeared so well up till now. Remarkable: since I turned down the Mahler lecture. Have I done a wrong by this for which I will be punished?' The reason for this self-criticism was a letter from Hertzka which arrived on 16 February. One can see how much Schoenberg valued Mathilde's advice from the fact that he discussed all problems of this kind w th her and also the drawing-up of his replies, which were often subjected to her corrections to make them less harsh. He also shared his financial worries with her. Carl Moll had aroused hopes in him that he would receive money from the Foundation which Alma Mahler had set up after Gustav Mahler's death for the support of musicians and had brought into being with the help of rich friends. The trustees were Richard Strauss, Ferruccio Busoni and Bruno Walter; Alma Mahler saw to it that the payments went to Schoenberg several times. The news that a memorial to Mahler in Vienna had been planned, annoyed Mathilde because the money from the Foundation might be used for it. Schoenberg discusses this in the diary of 17 February and intends to turn down the grant from the Foundation – which he had already counted on in January – if it was offered to him. Later he changed his mind. The Weberns came on the evening of 17 February, and Schoenberg was very impressed by a song of his friend's. Webern came again on the next day, a Sunday, looking for a score of his orchestral pieces (probably opus 6, which is dedicated to Schoenberg). The diary reads:

'*Webern came to me in the morning. We looked (on the roof, in all the boxes) for Webern's orchestral pieces which he had given to me in his own handwriting, very clearly and carefully written. . . . But we can't find them. I am very unhappy about this, because I am very careful about manuscripts and I don't like doing this to anybody; but I don't know where it can have got to . . . At last we thought that our previous house maid Mathilde Stepanek . . . might have taken it with her "as a souvenir" just to be annoying or perhaps has misplaced it somewhere.*'

In the afternoon it was so warm that Schoenberg was able to walk with Mathilde without a coat. Finally he studied the Bach-Mahler score right through to its end:

'*Discovered some interesting thematic relationships. (Episodes in the Fugue, Flute solo, are variations of the theme.)*'

Even before Schoenberg's journey to Prague a very convenient commission came from the singer Julia Culp, passed on by her accompanist Erich J. Wolff, to orchestrate Beethoven's 'Adelaide'. He received the music of the song on the morning of 20 February; Frau Culp sang the song to him, and he asked for 200/300 marks, – help in a moment of financial need. His diary says:

'*Frau Culp has a beautiful voice, rather over-used, but unfortunately she is not very musical.*'

He was also asked to do further orchestrations of classical songs. He wrote half the score of 'Adelaide' on the same day, working till eight o'clock at night, and the rest in Prague. The score reached Berlin on the 24; Culp's concert was on the 29, conducted by Fried.

Schoenberg did not go on with his diary until his return from Prague and began it on 11 March. The entry takes eight pages and looks back at his time in Prague. This has already been described here.

In Berlin there was a newspaper battle between Schoenberg and Leopold Schmidt, who had written an answer in the *Berliner Tageblatt* to Schoenberg's article in 'Pan', and was again answered by Schoenberg. On 3 March the Schoenbergs dined at Marschalk's house together with the writer Eduard Stucken (1865–1936), his wife and Dr. Georg Gräner, the music critic of the *Vossischen Zeitung*. Two days later the Rosé Quartet played Schoenberg's opus 7, which was greeted with hisses and applause. After this a large company dined in the Rheingold Restaurant. Paul Stefan had come over with his wife from Vienna. Schoenberg met the pianist Carl Friedberg and his wife Gerda and liked them very much. On this 5 March 1912 he addressed Webern in the second person for the first time.

Sunday 10 March was a fine day; the Schoenbergs had received some money from Albertine Zehme, went on a trip to Wannsee and ended with a fine walk from Klein-Machnow to their house. On Monday the ten-year-old Trudi had an examination in her school; her parents were present.

The long diary entry of 11 March ends here. On the 12th there was a notice which was concerned with the problems of Schoenberg's followers and important thoughts about the Schoenberg school, more important than any other remarks in his writing before his American years:

'*This morning I suddenly had a great desire to compose. Since a long time! I'd often thought about the possibility that I might never be able to compose again. There seemed to be many reasons for this. The obstinacy with which my pupils are at my heels, and try to surpass what I have to offer, brings me into danger of becoming an imitator of them and prevents me from building up quietly in the place where I am. They increase everything tenfold. And it is right! It is really good. But I don't know if it is really necessary. And so I am compelled to decide with much more care if I must write, than I did before. For this is not so much concerned with my originality; but it gives me pleasure very often and in any case I prefer it to unoriginality.*

Then my theoretical work came. This certainly dries one up. And perhaps this is the reason why, for the last two years, I suddenly don't feel so young. I have become remarkably quiet! This was shown even in my conducting. I lack the aggressive element. The rapid exceeding of myself and seizing, over-reaching.

Perhaps it will be better if I compose again now. Or: it is better. I remember writing a poem ten to twelve years ago in which I wanted to be old, unambitious and quiet. Now when I suddenly see the old possibilities of unrest again, I almost have a longing for them. Or are they still there?

I really ought to finish my lecture on Mahler, which I am giving in Prague on the 25th. But in the next few days I will certainly compose.' And the entry ends: *'I know now where this comes from: "Spring", always my best time. I already feel things stirring in me. In this I am almost like a plant. It is the same every year. I have nearly always composed something in the spring.'*

This is as far as the diary goes. Schoenberg's lecture in Prague gave him no time for composition. He worked on the manuscript of the speech about Mahler, which acquired many alterations and additions in the following years. Schoenberg read it in its first version on 25 March 1912 in Prague. Webern, who had gone there with him, wrote the next day to Berg: 'It was marvellous yesterday at Schoenberg's lecture. Unheard-of.'

When Schoenberg returned to Berlin with Webern at the end of March he had a great deal to do there, principally the composision of the 'Pierrot' songs. The Academic Society of Vienna was putting on an evening of Schoenberg's works; the latter did not want Etta Werndorff to play his new piano pieces, opus 19. Visitors came from Vienna. Webern's father, the sixty-two-year-old Carl von Webern, who was a mining engineer and a Chief of Section in the Ministry of Agriculture, came to Berlin, as well as Schoenberg's former pupil Paul Königer. With these three Schoenberg visited the exhibition of the 'Blaue Reiter' in Herwarth Walden's Gallery 'Der Sturm' on Sunday, 7 April. He himself had withdrawn his pictures; instead there were many of Oskar Kokoschka's to be seen. In conversation with Webern he worked out the plan for a 'Week of Unofficial Music in Austria.'

This plan was the subject of Schoenberg's first letter to Béla Bartók which has been preserved, dated 7 May 1912:

'The original idea was to put up a counter-weight to the Austrian Vienna Music Festival, which only performed dead composers' works, under the title of "Music Festival of unofficial Austrian Art." This was to perform works of the modern Austrian composers, including Germans, Hungarians and Czechs, in 2–3 concerts if possible. The Hungarians and Czechs were to send contributions to this and to increase the reputations of those writers in the most modern style which they wished to have performed on this occasion.'

Bartók's answer is not known; but the whole plan came to nothing in this form.

Schoenberg had letters to answer, especially from Kandinsky and Gabriele Münter. In May he received an enthusiastic letter· from Scheveningen from the twenty-one-year-old Hungarian conductor and composer Alexander Jemnitz, who thanked Schoenberg for the opportunity of having got to know him: 'You are just like I imagined you, and I am yours for ever.' Then followed a long discussion about counterpoint and harmony. This correspondence went on till August 1912; when in despair about his career as a conductor, Jemnitz asked on 17 June for advice as to what he should do.

The diary remained untouched after 12 March. Schoenberg had already had doubts about whether he could continue it. In 1912 there was only one more entry, on 23 October; the last one was on 24 May 1915. However, Webern's letters to Berg keep us informed about the next few months. On 24 April he was furious about a Viennese criticism of the Schoenberg concert; on the 28th he talks of the possibility of Schoenberg being offered the position of teacher of a master class of composition at the Vienna Academy. In fact there was some truth in this. Robert Fuchs (1847–1927) was to retire, on reaching his sixty-fifth birthday, on 1 September. President Wiener and some other admirers of Schoenberg had suggested him as Fuchs's successor. Schoenberg agreed in principle. In May he saw an announcement in the *Berliner Tageblatt* that the Prague composer Vitézslav Novák had been appointed director of the composition class for the autumn of 1912. He wrote to Wiener saying that he would not take second place in any event; it was only Wiener's indication that he would be able to take over the Concert Society that had made him say yes. But as there had been publicity about the appointment of Schreker and Novák and not about his own, he would certainly withdraw. Wiener calmed him down at once, and Schoenberg wrote with warm thanks on 22 May. Novák did not go to Vienna.

The appointment came in June. Schoenberg thought about the position for some time and finally on 29 June 1912 he sent a detailed refusal, which has been published in Erwin Stein's collection of Schoenberg's letters. Two reasons decided him; he did not want to live in Vienna and he was afraid he would have to teach harmony and counterpoint as well as composition.

Meanwhile his friends in Vienna had made great plans for him. Webern, who left Zehlendorf in the middle of May, asked Berg on the 29th in a letter from Klagenfurt to find a really nice house for the Master in Hüttelsdorf. At the beginning of June he came back to Berlin and stayed with Schoenberg at the Villa Lepcke until he left for Stettin on the 21st.

The summer weeks were darkened by a loss. On 12 June Mathilde's mother, Klara von Zemlinsky, née Semo, died at the age of sixty-three during a visit to Berlin. Schoenberg's work on *Pierrot* was nearing its end. At the beginning of July the Schoenbergs went for six weeks to Carlshagen on the Baltic Sea island of Usedom. Webern, who had found a post as conductor in Stettin nearby, was happy at this. In any case he was disgusted at his work in the theatre, and it needed the whole authority of his friend to persuade him to continue with it.

Schoenberg's correspondence with Hertzka continued. On 11 June he pressed him to print the George songs. He said that Bote and Bock had offered him 500 marks for the Chamber Symphony but he had refused it, thinking of Universal Edition. However, according to their first, old contract he should ask for 1000 kronen for the two works. 'I am sending you the text of the monodrama today and ask you to do something energetic about it. (Brecher would certainly have it). In December I am conducting in the Hague and Amsterdam for a fee of 1000 marks.' Gustav Brecher (1879–1940) had been first conductor of the Cologne Opera since 1911. On 1 July Schoenberg announced the completion of the 'Gurrelieder' on a card. Two days later he gave his address in Carlshagen: Villa Concordia. At the same time he asks about the 'Gurrelieder', Chamber Symphony and George Songs. In Carlshagen he also received from the Austrian Boden-Credit-Anstalt the eagerly awaited cheque of 850 marks, which Commercial Chancellor Fritz Redlich had paid into the account of the Gustav Mahler Foundation.

On 16 July Schoenberg asks Hertzka to acknowledge the receipt of seven manuscripts, sent from Zehlendorf to Vienna: the whole 'Gurelieder' score, the Chamber Symphony, piano score and text of the monodrama, six new piano pieces, three songs, two ballads and 'Herzgewächse'. On 14 July he received a letter from Alban Berg; the latter was very upset that Schoenberg had refused the appointment in Vienna. The news had already appeared in the papers.

Webern took every opportunity to visit Carlshagen. Schoenberg was working on a stage work after Balzac's *Seraphita*; he had intended in the winter to combine this with Strindberg's *Jacob ringt*, which Berg already knew about. After a visit on

Monday 29 and Tuesday 30 July Webern wrote to Berg: 'We bathed in the sea and in the afternoon went for a sail. In the evening there was a champagne party, given by Stein and Jalowetz.'

These two friends were both working in North German theatres, and Jalowetz was with Webern in Stettin. Zemlinsky too, who had had a quarrel with Schoenberg in July, came to the Baltic island to see his brother-in-law. However Webern was happiest alone with Schoenberg. 'Next morning I walked with Schoenberg on the beach. He was happy to have turned down Vienna, but is worried about next winter. Unfortunately he does not have much calm for working. He is composing the *Glückliche Hand* and is planning *Seraphita* . . . He had just received the second proofs of the second and third parts of the "Gurrelieder" when I was there. The proof which was lost has not yet been found.'

Schoenberg was concerned with other things besides composition while on the Baltic Sea. His inventive mind, which had already produced a musical typewriter in 1909, which he had patented, was occupied in Carlshagen with an attempt to reproduce autograph manuscripts and drawings. He wrote about this to Hertzka, and at the same time asked for twenty-five sheets of uncut music paper with forty staves. This letter is dated 4 August. On Saturday the 10th the family went to Stettin, where they stayed in Webern's house for two days. On Sunday afternoon Webern conducted *The Dollar Princess*, an operetta much loved at the time, in the theatre (this was first performed in Vienna in 1907 and was by Leo Fall (1873–1925)). Schoenberg went to the performance. 'He was very pleased with me' Webern wrote to Berg. And he added that the master was thinking about the future, and above everything else would like to conduct.

In Berlin, where the family arrived on the afternoon of Monday, 12 August, preparations had to be made for the rehearsals of *Pierrot*, which had been arranged for the end of the month. Schoenberg was also worried about the printing of the 'Gurrelieder'. A new translation of the text demanded rhythmical alterations, which he inveighed against in a long letter to Hertzka because, if he was going to 'tailor' his melody to these, the unity of his musical thought would be destroyed.

> '*Anyone who knows my method of setting texts knows that it is not the same for the structure of my melody if there is one syllable more or less, and if a strongly accented important word comes in one place or*

*another. As all translations are imperfect, I could not decide because
of these small improvements to impoverish my melodies (for in those days
I was writing melodies). So the first version of my work is its basis.'*
And then followed an important paragraph:

'*This work is the key to my whole development. It shows facets of me
which I do not now show, or at any rate on another basis. It explains
how everything later had to come, and this is enormously important for
my work: that people can follow my character and development from
here onwards.'*

Meanwhile Henri Hinrichsen had been doing some work for
the Five Orchestral Pieces which had been published by him.
At Schoenberg's request scores had been sent to the conductors
Alexander von Zemlinsky in Prague, Oskar Fried in Berlin,
Arthur Bodanzky in Mannheim, Oskar Nedbal in Vienna,
Sigmund von Hausegger and Gustav Brecher in Hamburg and
also to Richard Strauss. Without Schoenberg's knowledge Sir
Henry Wood had also got hold of the work in London; he
quickly decided to give the first performance of it. Schoenberg
was surprised to read in an announcement in the *Daily Telegraph*
that this would take place at the beginning of September, and he
wrote a vexed letter about it to the publishers. He regarded it as
almost inconceivable that the performance would be good without his personal presence and advice. What sort of a conductor
and what sort of an orchestra would give the performance?
Who had given them the right to give the first performance?
Would the minimum five rehearsals needed be possible? Hinrichsen answered, calming him down, and remarked that
Schoenberg would have been able to travel to London at Hinrichsen's expense, if he had realized that Schoenberg was worried
about this.

In fact the first performance took place on 3 September 1912
in a Promenade Concert conducted by Sir Henry Wood. The
Queen's Hall Orchestra played the work. It was received by
both public and press with little understanding, but not without
applause. Among the notices the most important and relatively
the most understanding was that of Ernest Newman in the
'Nation'. This ran: 'It does not often happen that an English
public hisses when it does not like a piece of music; but a good
third of the people allowed themselves this luxury after the
performance of the Five Orchestral Pieces by Schoenberg.
Another third of the public did not hiss, because it was laughing,
and the remaining third seemed too non-plussed either to laugh

or to hiss . . . Nevertheless, I allow myself to say that Schoenberg is not the lunatic that he is generally taken for. Could it not be that the new composer sees a logic in tonal relations which amount to chaos for the rest of us at present, but whose connection could be clear enough to us one day?'

Strauss, Hausegger and Brecher sent the scores back to the publishers. Schillings showed willingness to try out the pieces: 'This music, which has points of contact only in a few moments with everything that has existed up till now, interests me extraordinarily artistically', he wrote to the publisher. He asked to be allowed to borrow the material and played the work through with the Stuttgart Court Orchestra. However, on 20 December 1912 he wrote to the publisher Peters: 'I got the firm impression that a performance here would be the opposite of a pleasure for the composer. Our public lacks understanding and judgement of these pieces and I and the whole Court Orchestra do not feel we are in a position to follow Schoenberg's feelings in this music. – The failure of this piece, which would certainly happen here, would give a hard blow to the whole cult of modern music to which I dedicate myself as much as I can. – Believe me when I say that I took these pieces very seriously; but I feel that I am too much a man of the present to be able to put myself at the service of this musical futurism with proper understanding.'

Alexander Siloti in St. Petersburg was interested in the pieces, but then invited Schoenberg to conduct *Pélleas and Mélisande* instead of them. Later the expectation of Hinrichsen was justified in that the Five Orchestral Pieces belong to the repertory of the great orchestras all over the world. Only the Vienna Philharmonic took over half a century before they played them in 1969 in the Musikvereinssaal.

Schreker was looking for soloists for the first performance of 'Gurrelieder' in Vienna. Waldemar Schoenberg suggested his cousin, the tenor Hans Nachod, and had written to him in Kiel, where as first Helden tenor he received a monthly salary of 1600 marks. Nachod agreed to sing the part, but demanded 700 marks. At the end of August Schoenberg had a letter from the music teacher Emile Jaques-Dalcroze, the inventor of rhythmical gymnastics. His July Festival in Hellerau near Dresden had been such a success that he was going to repeat it in 1913, and he invited Schoenberg to come.

Old and new pupils wrote to Schoenberg. Leo Perelman wrote from Doberan; in November 1911 he had abandoned his studies with Wilhelm Klatte in order to study with Schoenberg. He remembered his lessons well, but he felt that Schoenberg had treated him badly. In any case he could not pay him at present. The young Fritz Zweig wrote in a letter of 9 September that he was full of regret for having behaved insolently. He wanted to come to Berlin on the 16th to start lessons again. Another Viennese acquaintance, Rudolf Réti (1885–1957), a composer and a brilliant performer of the Piano Pieces opus 11, wanted to speak to Schoenberg on the 18th.

A letter came from Guido Adler, on holiday on the Ausse. The musicologist regrets Schoenberg's refusal to join the Academy. He is ready to speak on a favourable opportunity to Hermann Kretzschmar, the then director of the Berlin Royal Musikhochschule. Kretzschmar would know that he, Adler, had suggested Schoenberg as a teacher of harmony and counterpoint in Vienna. He could not get on very well with reading the Harmony Book. He agreed with many things, but other things repelled him. Schoenberg must have written to his old patron that he would gladly have a position in the Berlin Hochschule.

From Munich and Koblenz came greetings from his brother Heinrich, who had at last, thanks to Schoenberg's recommendation, received an engagement from Zemlinsky for 1913 in Prague. Paul Schwers asked for an article on Strauss for his *Allgemeine Musikzeitung,* – later he became one of the bitterest enemies of Schoenberg.

Important news came from Emil Gutmann. He engaged Schoenberg to give his Prague speech on Mahler on 13 October in the Harmonium Room in Berlin. Koussevitzky had postponed the planned Moscow performance of *Pelléas and Mélisande* to the season of 1913/14. However an agreement had been reached with Alexander Siloti. On 27 September Gutmann writes: 'Further to our telephone conversation, I ask you to regard your engagement to conduct your *Pelléas* in Siloti's concert in St. Petersburg on Saturday, 21 December, (our calendar) as definite. You will receive a fee of 500 roubles and three rehearsals are arranged, the dates of which I will let you know later.' Siloti also wrote to Schoenberg.

On 13 September Schoenberg's thirty-eighth birthday was celebrated in Zehlendorf. Webern rang up from Stettin. Heinrich Jalowetz came as a visitor. He found Schoenberg orchestrating Schubert songs for Julia Culp. As Fritz Zweig had arrived he now had four pupils. For May of 1913 Schoenberg planned to wander down the Rhine from Mainz to Cologne, together with Berg, Jalowetz and Webern, who sent the news joyfully to his friend Berg in Vienna on 14 September.

Schoenberg was so busy at this time that it is impossible to imagine how he kept his enormous correspondence going as well as his musical work. But these were not his only activities. He needed new furniture for his apartment in Zehlendorf. The old furniture, which he had partly made and designed himself, was now to be modernized. He turned to the famous store of N. Israel, sent them his drawings and asked them for an estimate. On 26 October 1912 the firm sent a letter to 'Herr Artist A. Schoenberg, Highly born' with the estimate ('Errors and omissions excepted') for building sideboards, reconstructing a writing-table which was there already and modernizing a table which was also there.

Now the date of the Mahler lecture was approaching. Hermann Scherchen, the critic Arno Nadel and the Busoni pupil Gisella Selden-Goth asked for tickets. Marie Pappenheim wrote from Vienna that she would not be in Berlin before December. Schoenberg must have asked her to visit him. The lecture, which took place a few days before *Pierrot*, aroused attention and was received by the press with much enthusiastic agreement and also much bitter rejection. The factions for and against Schoenberg hardened. But Schoenberg's work on the rehearsals of the recitations and the much discussed first performance left him no time to reiterate his standpoint again.

In November, immediately after the *Pierrot* concerts in Hamburg, Breslau and Vienna, Schoenberg had to leave the ensemble and travel via Berlin to Amsterdam. In Zehlendorf Webern spent two days with him. Erwin Stein had said that he would attend the rehearsals and concerts in Holland. Stein was in Osnabruck as conductor and remembered with regret his fine days with Jalowetz in Danzig. Schoenberg arrived in Amsterdam on the 25th. For the first time he was conducting the Concertgebouw Orchestra, whose conductor Willem Mengelberg was a champion of Mahler. The performances of *Pelléas and Mélisande*, which had been prepared in three rehearsals taken by Mengelberg and three taken by Schoenberg, were a great success on 28 and 30 November; thereafter Schoenberg was often invited to give performances as a guest conductor.

In Berlin letters had piled up. Schoenberg had to answer them. Meanwhile the *Pierrot* ensemble had returned from Frankfurt.

The two matinées on 1 and 8 December had to be prepared. On the 15th Schoenberg began his journey to St. Petersburg. Mathilde and the children had gone to Stettin to stay with Webern; she felt very well there. But she was worried about Webern's condition: 'He looks terrible and is incredibly weak. When he goes up the stairs he has to hold on to the banisters with both hands, and in the room he sways from one chair to another,' she wrote in her first letter.

Schoenberg had sent a telegram and cards from the frontier. Mathilde begs him not to catch cold: 'Think of your stiff neck in the train!'

He stayed modestly in the Dagmar Hotel in St. Petersburg, not in the expensive Europe opposite the Philharmonia, where Bodanzky and other conductors usually stayed. The first rehearsal of *Pelléas*, about which he wrote to Webern, went very well and he found the orchestra excellent.

He got on well with Siloti; because it was so cold the latter lent Schoenberg a magnificent fur coat in which he was photographed. The performance was on 21 December. Schoenberg already had a small public of admirers in this beautiful city. In 1911 the nineteen-year-old Sergei Prokofiev had played his piano pieces opus 11. The young literary and musical people were interested in this and a performance of the F Sharp Minor Quartet in February 1912 was much discussed. The soprano solo was sung by Sandra Belling, whom Schoenberg also met and who later lived in Damascus. His strongest propagandist was the Finnish composer Ernest Pingoud (1888–1942), a pupil of Siloti and Max Reger, who later published an analytical article in the *Petersburger Zeitung*. He was not able to attend the concert. The leading critic Vyatcheslav Gavrilovitch Karatygin was present and wrote in No. 339 of the liberal paper *Retsch* (Speech): 'There was a remarkable event on the podium; a little man with a bald head and a burning, restless look, nervous gestures and demonic passion even in calmer moments, appeared. He is as lively as quicksilver, a small man who reminds one of a little Chinese Buddha. One thinks of figures from Hoffmann's fairy tales or the sinister stories of Edgar Allan Poe. However, the programme, which I have in front of me, says nothing about Poe's imaginations. What was performed was the symphonic poem *Pelléas and Mélisande* by the very paradoxical, daring and perhaps the most important of German modernists, Arnold Schoenberg.'

Schoenberg wearing Alexander Siloti's fur coat in the courtyard
of the St. Petersburg Philarmonic, December 1912

He returned home on the 22nd. Siloti was greatly impressed and thanked him in a letter. Schoenberg sent him a small Christmas present and Siloti was highly delighted with the 'wonderful pencil'.

In Berlin the festivities of the end of the year were in preparation, for the first time without money worries. Amsterdam and Petersburg had brought in nearly 2000 marks, and in January a second contribution from the Mahler Foundation was due to come. Schoenberg celebrated Christmas in the family circle. On 27 December he wrote down some music for the opera he planned on *Seraphita*. Adolf Loos came again from Vienna and they all ate with him, Webern and Herwarth Walden in the 'Rheingold'. The Schoenbergs spent the New Year with Erwin Stein, who had come on a visit from Osnabruck. So the year ended in harmonious company.

Schoenberg used a few weeks which were free of concerts in January 1913 to put his library in order. On 23rd he finished a catalogue of the books, which he bound himself. This shows which authors he preferred. Balzac was represented with twelve volumes (mostly in German translations), Richard Dehmel with ten, Rilke with nine, Karl Kraus with twelve, Ibsen with five, Stefan George with eleven, Gerhart Hauptmann with six, Maeterlinck with eighteen, Strindberg with twenty-eight! Among the philosophers Kant leads with eleven; then follows Schopenhauer with six, Bergson, Nietzsche and Plato with four each, Aristotle with two. There was also a volume of Swedenborg's letters. Schoenberg possessed classical and romantic literature in the popular Meyer Edition.

The catalogue was expanded several times at irregular intervals, in June and December 1914, in June 1915, in March 1918 and – for the last time – in December 1919. Up till 1932 Schoenberg contented himself with the old Meyer Conversation Lexicon of 1885 from his parents' house; then he bought Knaur's Lexicon. In 1918 he bought Ullstein's History of the World in six volumes. He had the complete works of Peter Altenberg, Kandinsky, Kokoschka, Otto Weininger and Karl Kraus. In 1971 in the house in Brentwood Park no psychological or psychoanlaytical books could be found.

The Schoenberg Concert of the Academic Society in Vienna on 20 November had aroused attention. Erhard Buschbeck and Marie Pappenheim wrote to Schoenberg about the stormy applause which Rudolf Réti aroused with the Piano Pieces opus

11 and 19. The orchestral concert with *Pelléas* and the Chamber Symphony, conducted by Schoenberg, was finally arranged for the end of March. Meanwhile Schreker was preparing the first performance of the 'Gurrelieder'. He had difficulties with the material, which was full of mistakes. Schoenberg was annoyed because Schreker let him know through Hertzka that he wanted Schoenberg to attend the rehearsals. Ten rehearsals with the 'bad Tonkünstler Orchestra' seemed too little to him. But if his expenses were paid he said he would come on the 18th and direct the premiere on the 23rd – He did come, but Schreker conducted. Before this there was an unpleasant event: Dr. Königer, the father of his pupil Paul Königer, served a writ on him on the day before the final rehearsal because of an old debt.

The tremendous success of the performance soon made him forget his vexation. The concert on Sunday in the big Musik-vereinssaal was full. With Martha Winternitz-Dorda (Tove), Marya Freund – instead of Anna Bahr-Mildenburg who should have sung in the first place – (Wood Dove), Hans Nachod (Waldemar), Alfred J. Boruttau (Klaus the Fool) and Ferdinand Gregori from the Burg Theatre as Speaker. It was a triumph. All Schoenberg's friends and former pupils came to it, including Webern, who was taking a cure in Dr. Vecsey's Sanatorium at Semmering. Schoenberg was given a laurel crown, – the first one he had had.

Returning to Zehlendorf, Schoenberg had to think about the programme for the orchestral concert on 31 March. Apart from his own pieces, *Pelléas* and the Chamber Symphony, Mahler's 'Kindertotenlieder,' Songs with Orchestra by Zemlinsky and works by Berg and Webern were to be performed. Marya Freund, who had already spoken to Schoenberg about this in January in Berlin, was against doing the Peter Altenberg Songs of Berg. 'I *can't* sing the Berg, don't be angry with me – it is not pleasant', she wrote. Schoenberg reacted sourly:

'Dear Frau Freund, you can't do this! Because something doesn't please one straight away you don't throw it away for that reason,'
he wrote on 24 January. But Boruttau sang the songs.

The concert in the large Musikvereinssaal on 31 March 1913 ended with one of the greatest tumults in modern musical history, comparable only with that of the first performance of Igor Stravinsky's *Rite of Spring* in the Paris Champs Elysées Theatre on 28 May in the same year. The 'Musik-blätter des Anbruch' printed in 1924 in the special number for Schoenberg's fiftieth birthday the report of a Viennese paper, which ran:

'Yesterday's concert of the Academic Society for Literature and Music led to unexampled scenes of tumult . . . Immediately after the first part of the programme, an orchestral piece by Anton Webern, the applauders and hissers carried on a battle, which, however, remained within the limits of what we know only too well from other Schoenberg performances. After the second orchestral piece[1] a storm of laughter went through the hall, which was overpowered by the admirers of this nerveracking and provocative music with thunderous applause. And the remaining four pieces contribute to make the atmosphere in the hall such that one feared the worst. Four beautiful songs with orchestra by Alexander von Zemlinsky on texts of poems of Maeterlinck apparently calmed down those who were heated and eager for battle. After Schoenberg's opus 9, his Chamber Symphony which had already been a failure some years ago, one could hear the shrill sound of door keys among the violent clapping and in the second gallery the first fight of the evening began. In all directions people were now taking sides with wild shouting and in the unnaturally long pause between the works the enemies formed up against each other. Two songs with orchestra on picture postcard texts by Peter Altenberg set by Alban Berg removed all control from those who had previously been sensible . . . The music . . . goes beyond anything heard so far and one can only hand it to the good nature of the Viennese that they were content to listen with hearty laughter. However, when Schoenberg knocked on the desk in the middle of the song and shouted to the public that anyone disturbing the peace would be removed by the police, insults, fisticuffs and challenges broke out again. Herr von Webern shouted from his box that the whole lot should be pushed out, and the public answered immediately that the admirers of this misguided kind of music should be sent off to Steinhof.[2] The shouting and bawling in the hall now would not stop. It was not an unusual occurrence when one of the public with breathless haste and with ape-like agility climbed over several rows of seats in order to box the object of his anger on the ears.

The police officer who came in could do nothing with this chaos of wildly whipped-up passions. If he wanted to create any kind of peace, one could hear at the same time the sound of

[1] These were Webern's Six Pieces opus 6.
[2] Steinhof is the local lunatic asylum.

Montag, den 31. März 1913, ½8 Uhr abends
im grossen Musikvereinssaal

ORCHESTER-KONZERT

Dirigent: ARNOLD SCHÖNBERG

Orchester des Wiener Konzertvereins

Gesang: A. Boruttau, Margarete Bum, Maria Freund

1. ANTON VON WEBERN: Sechs Stücke für Orchester op. 4*

2. ALEXANDER VON ZEMLINSKY: Vier Orchesterlieder nach Gedichten von Maeterlinck

    Margarete Bum

3. ARNOLD SCHÖNBERG: Kammersymphonie op. 9 in einem Satz

4. ALBAN BERG: Zwei Orchesterlieder nach Ansichtskartentexten von Peter Altenberg (aus einem Zyklus)

    Alfred J. Boruttau

5. GUSTAV MAHLER: Kindertotenlieder*

    Maria Freund

* Die einzelnen Teile bilden ein einheitliches Ganzes und es muss daher die Kontinuität (auch durch Hintanhaltung von Beifallsbezeugungen u. dgl.) aufrecht erhalten werden.

==== PREIS DES PROGRAMMES 30 HELLER ====

Programme of the Orchestral concert in Vienna, 13 March 1913 fisticuffs in all directions. Finally the President of the Academic Society[1] went onto the conductor's stand and asked that Mahler's memory should be honoured and his "Kindertotenlieder" listened to. This request only led to a general series of insults which the President again replied to with ear-boxing. All the public now stormed on to the platform, in front of the musicians, who were pale with fear and trembling, determined to clear the platform and end the concert. However, it still took another half hour, till the last brawlers left the hall in a fury . . .'

Egon Wellesz says in his book on Schoenberg, that part of the public had clearly come looking for sensation and scandal. A law-suit followed, in which the operetta composer Oscar Straus said as a witness that he had laughed too, because it really was comic. A doctor who was also called as a witness regarded the effect of such music on a large part of the public as 'enervating and injurious to the nervous system . . . and that many of the audience showed exterior signs of deep mental depression.'

Paul Stefan says in his Schoenberg book that the papers reported the scandal as a 'Pub' sensation to all the world. On 2 April the poet George Trakl heard about the affair in Innsbruck and wrote to his friend Buschbeck: 'I read in today's Innsbruck papers about the dreadful scandal at the Schoenberg concert. What a terrible disgrace for an artist who is prevented by the vulgarity of the mob from presenting the works of his pupils.'

Schoenberg returned to Berlin embittered. Webern continued his convalescence in Portorose on the Adriatic, 'almost rid of all those terrible things', he wrote on 7 April to Berg, and: 'Think of the fine time of the rehearsals, of the Chamber Symphony, of the wonderful evening with Altenberg, of Loos's villa'.

In Berlin the Schoenbergs had to look for a new apartment; the Villa Lepcke was needed for other purposes. After an attempt in Schlachtensee Albertine Zehme offered them her house in the South End. They moved in at the end of May. Their first visitor was Alban Berg on 4 June. He remained for a week and had daily conversations with his friend, and spent some evenings in the theatre and at the opera, where he saw Strauss's *Ariadne auf Naxos*. Shortly before his departure there was an argument between the two, when Schoenberg censured him for lack of good qualities in his latest works. However, Berg accepted thankfully even this stern criticism.

The planned 'Gurrelieder' performance in Berlin did not take

[1] Erhard Buschbeck.

place. At the beginning of July 1913 Schoenberg sought out the director of the Philharmonic Choir, Siegfried Ochs, and wanted clarification about the financial prospects of the concert. This led to an argument. Schoenberg turned his back on Ochs and left. The Schoenbergs spent their summer holidays at Göhren on Rügen Island. At the end of August they were back in South End. Because of his enormous correspondence Schoenberg was not able to compose; the score of the *Glückliche Hand* was still waiting to be completed. From Mannheim came a request from Bodanzky, who wanted to perform *Erwartung*. Schoenberg turned to Marie Gutheil-Schoder, the brave interpreter of the soprano part in the second string quartet which was hissed at the first performance in 1908. He sent her Marie Pappenheim's text and asked whether she liked it, whether she would like to perform the piece in Mannheim and would be able to get leave to do it. He said that the work was very difficult musically. Gutheil was ready; but the performance of the monodrama did not take place until 1924 under Zemlinsky in Prague.

Schoenberg had to correspond with publishers about the orchestrations for Julia Culp. He had already received permission from Peters in Göhren to orchestrate Hugo Wolf songs 'as an exceptional case and for the personal use of Culp'; Simrock also agreed that Schoenberg could arrange Brahms songs for the singer. A correspondence with Schotts', to whom he had offered manuscripts, ended on 25 August with a refusal.

Compared with the winter and spring the autumn of 1913 was peaceful. A frequent visitor from October onwards was Alexander Jemnitz, who had theory lessons with Schoenberg and discussed general musical problems with him.

To a singer, Maria Schoeffer, who wanted to perform Schoenberg songs, he gave information about the method of performance:

> '*Not too accented pronunciation of the text ("declamation") but a musical working out of the melodic lines! – So don't emphasize a word which is not emphasized in my melody, and no "intelligent" caesuras which arise from the text. Where a "comma" is necessary, I have already composed it'.*

This letter, four pages long, in small writing is dated 12 November. Schoenberg's chief work was finishing the *Glückliche Hand*. The final bar was written on 20 November but on the 18th Schoenberg had already told the tenor Fritz Soot, who was going to sing Waldemar in a performance of the 'Gurrelieder' planned by Bruno Walter in Munich, about finishing the piece.

During his work on the music-drama Schoenberg wrote a song with orchestra on the poem 'Seraphita' by Ernest Dowson, translated by Stefan George. (Ernest Christopher Dowson, 1867–1900, was the most original representative of the 'décadents' in England who were influenced by French symbolism.) There are two versions of it, dated 6 October and 9 November 1913. The form of the score, which is concentrated on to a few staves, was used for publication by Schoenberg for the first time in the four songs with orchestra, of which the first was 'Seraphita'.

On 23 November he told Bodanzky that the Mannheim Orchestra, which only had six violas, was too small for *Erwartung*. Now Ernest von Schuch became interested in giving the first performance of both the one-act operas. For some reason Schoenberg wanted Fritz Soot, the Munich Heldentenor, who sang the Drum Major in the first performance of Berg's *Wozzeck* in 1925, to sing the Man in the *Glückliche Hand*, a baritone part. Hertzka was planning to get a film producer interested in this work. Schoenberg here saw a possibility of representing things for which there were only poor expedients on the stage. He wanted to have 'the greatest unreality' and a 'play with apparitions of colours and forms'. As the designer he suggested Kokoschka, Kandinsky or Roller. But there must be no alterations in the music, which must be properly performed! As there were no sound films in 1913 he was thinking of a performance with orchestra, chorus and soloists.

In January 1914 Schoenberg accepted Sir Henry Wood's invitation to conduct his Orchestral Pieces in the Queen's Hall in London. He got on extremely well with the orchestra, and the London musicians were as enthusiastic about their guest as he was about them. He also appeared again in Amsterdam to perform the same work with Mengelberg's orchestra. It was a great success. Both Wood and Mengelberg planned to give the 'Gurrelieder' under his direction. Meanwhile these had been rehearsed in Leipzig (where Arthur Nikisch had conducted the Chamber Symphony opus 9 thereby giving Schoenberg great pleasure); we have heard about their enthusiastic reception. Hinrichsen, the director of the Peters Publishing Firm, was so pleased by this and by the Amsterdam success of the Orchestral Pieces that he immediately paid Schoenberg his remaining fee of 600 marks for opus 16.

At the end of January there was a small assembly of Schoenbergians in Prague. Zemlinsky had performed the Songs with

Orchestra opus 8. The soloist was the Heldentenor Hans Winkelmann, the son of Hermann Winkelmann, the first Bayreuth Parsifal. He sang only three of the six songs: 'Das Wappenschild', 'Voll jener Süsse', and 'Wenn Vöglein klagen'. Beside Arnold and Mathilde Schoenberg, Berg, Königer, Stein, Webern and Gerhard von Keussler came to the final rehearsal and the concert on 29 January.

In the Spring of 1914 Schoenberg went to Dresden. Steuermann, who accompanied him, told Günther Schuller about it on 20 May 1964; Ernst von Schuch and the Intendant Count Nikolaus Seebach wanted to get to know Schoenberg's operas in order to propose them for performance. Steuermann played *Erwartung*, and Schuch followed the score. Then Schoenberg described the content of the *Glückliche Hand*. Seebach interrupted him and he himself related the plot extremely well. Steuermann was surprised at his exact knowledge of the work.

In Prague Schoenberg had not only heard three of his Songs with Orchestra, but also *Parsifal* under Zemlinsky, so well performed that in a letter to Hertzka he described him as the greatest living conductor. In a letter to his brother-in-law of 16 April he speaks about *Parsifal*. 'I have the idea of becoming a good old Wagnerian again. No music has stirred me so much as this for a long time.'

On 27 May 1914 he wrote the theme of a scherzo of a symphony which he planned. This consists of twelve notes without any repetitions. In his letter to Nicolas Slonimsky of 3 June 1937 he called it an attempt on the way to the twelve-note method, and wrongly dated it too late, at the turn of the year 1914/15.

Regarding Strauss he said, in a refusal to write something for the latter's fiftieth birthday, that he was now estranged from him.

In May and June Schoenberg had an extensive correspondence with Kandinsky, who invited him to spend the summer with him in Murnau. The Schoenbergs went there in July and also met Heinrich Jalowetz. This idyll in Upper Bavaria was interrupted by the news of the outbreak of war between Austria and Serbia, and later between the Central Powers and half of Europe. At the end of August Schoenberg returned to South End; as a curiosity he told his brother-in-law in Prague that his English pupil Clark had volunteered to join the German army and was trying to acquire German nationality.

Hertzka did not let himself be diverted from his larger plans.

On 1 September he suggested to the representative of Breitkopf and Härtel in New York that there should be a series of 'Gurrelieder' performances. Schoenberg, who wished to conduct them, wanted to have five performances at a fee of 5000 dollars plus travelling expenses and living expenses for three months with his wife and children.

Schoenberg lost all his pupils through the outbreak of war. Although his income was high compared with previous years, he was worried about the immediate future. His tax return of 1914 informs us about his position exactly. It shows us income from foundations of 5700 marks, (of which 1300 came from the Mahler Foundation); a person who contributed 400 marks monthly from February till December is unknown. Six months' teaching (from January till the end of June) brought in 1320 marks. As a conductor he earned 500 marks in London, and the same in Amsterdam and Leipzig, of which 450 marks were spent on living expenses. The sale of his works in the first half of the year brought in 500 marks; Universal Edition paid him a similar sum as an advance. His total income of 9070 marks came mainly from foundation contributions.

If Schoenberg was worried about his own future for the coming year of 1915, he also hoped confidently that the war would soon be over. He had reached his fortieth birthday in September. He had had a healthy constitution since his youth. From his father he had inherited a tendency towards asthmatic disturbances, which had been increased by smoking cigarettes and cigars and regular drinking of alcohol. We know with what care Mathilde warned him not to catch cold on his travels and not to bring back a 'stiff neck'. But he had never thought to escape military service on account of troubles of this kind. He was a patriot and felt, as a German-Austrian, committed to the cause of his country.

However, the military authorities left him alone for the moment. His life in South End continued peacefully. He finished two of the Songs with Orchestra opus 22 between 1 and 14 January. He had chosen two poems from Rilke's *Stundenbuch*. One of them, 'Alle, welche dich suchen', had already been sketched on 30 November and was finished on 3 December. In the New Year he wrote the beginning of the second one, 'Mach mich zum Wächter deiner Weiten', and a week after he wrote a second fair copy of the first song. The second song was finished on 14 January. Schoenberg wrote a piano score of 'Alle welche dich suchen'. This was published in May 1915 in No. 14 of the 'Zeit-Echo', a magazine published by the Graphik-Verlag in Munich, which called itself 'A War Diary of Artists'. The dedication 'To my dear friend Anton von Webern' was omitted in the latter score published by Universal Edition.

Immediately after this work, which was not completed till 1916 in Vienna with 'Vorgefühl' from Rilke's *Buch der Bilder*, Schoenberg wrote the text of the 'Totentanz der Prinzipien' (Dance of Death of the Principles), which was completed on 15 January. Beginning with strokes of the bell in the tower which remind one of Strindberg's *Inferno*, and ending with its thirteenth stroke, it is the most mysterious and gloomy of all his texts. In language and thought it is similar to *Jacob's Ladder*; Schoenberg wrote the first sketch of the text three days later. The two sketches for the music of *Jacob's Ladder* were probably also written in 1915.

At that time Schoenberg had few connections with the outside world. The flood of letters had almost dried up since the outbreak of war. Once there was an enquiry from Peters in Leipzig; Sigfried Karg-Elert, who at that time was still a supporter of Schoenberg, had arranged the second of the Orchestral Pieces opus 16 for a harmonium album. Schoenberg did not allow him to print it.

News came regularly from Vienna. Berg was made very unhappy by the impact of war, but remained free from military service till August 1915. Oskar Kokoschka was one of the first to volunteer and was fighting as a cavalryman in Russia. Alma Mahler had become friendly with the architect Walter Gropius. He was in a Berlin hospital with a nervous breakdown. Alma Mahler visited him there and remained in the capital for a few weeks. Schoenberg suggested to her that he should conduct a concert in Vienna with Beethoven's Ninth Symphony in Mahler's revised version. This concert, which was financed by Alma's rich friend, Frau Lieser, took place in April 1915.

At Easter the Schoenbergs went to Stettin. There Schoenberg wrote a letter about the Strindberg biography by Adolf Paul to Webern, who had volunteered for military service and was doing basic training in Görz. Schoenberg sent the Rilke song in a blue volume which he had bound himself to his faithful friend, who was worried about his master being called up.

On 10 April Berg informed Schoenberg that his calling up was due on 10 May. Webern was eager that he should definitely be stopped from becoming a soldier, even against his will. And he said that Adolf Loos had already done something about this. Schoenberg saw matters more calmly. He wanted to volunteer himself in order that he could choose his own regiment. In April he went to Vienna to rehearse and perform the Ninth Symphony on the 26th. It was not such a great success as Alma Mahler had hoped.

There were new worries about the grant from the Mahler Foundation. Berg had intervened with Alma in May. On 20 May 1915 Schoenberg was enrolled but left free at the moment. Back in South End he made his last entry in the diary. This concerns his correspondence with Alma Mahler, and he protests against her warning that he should be thankful to her. He had heard from her that Julius Bittner would be the next recipient of the grant. Schoenberg saw forthcoming troubles in his financial circumstances and adopted for a while his peculiar defensive position which suspected enmity and neglect all round him. He even suspected Alban Berg and Erwin Stein of lack of interest in his existence; anything they did for him was only done with regard to what posterity might think of it. (This is shown in Berg's letter to Webern of 13 June 1915.)

His indignation soon calmed down. On 20 June he told Zemlinsky about his reconciliation with Alma Mahler and Frau Lieser. As regards the war, he was certain that it would be over by October. He had no doubt of the victory of the Central Powers.

In August the reconciliation was confirmed: Schoenberg visited Alma at Semmering. Webern and Stein visited him. Frau Lieser showed herself at her most helpful. She invited Schoenberg, who was awaiting his enrolment, and his family to take an apartment in her house at Hietzing, Gloriettegasse 43. The move took place at the beginning of September; this ended Schoenberg's second period in Berlin. In four years he had increased his activity as a composer and performer all over Europe. The history of music for generations had been enriched by a new kind of language and new forms. Apart from finishing the score of the 'Gurrelieder', the arrangements of baroque works for Guido Adler, the orchestration of songs for Julia Culp, and considerable activity as a teacher and conductor Schoenberg wrote two important works in this period: *Pierrot Lunaire* and the music of the *Glückliche Hand*. The 'Herzgewächse' and the Orchestral Songs opus 22 enlarged instrumental colour and anticipated future developments for decades. Even the literary works of these years in Berlin, especially the texts for the choral works which he planned, show Schoenberg at the height of his inspiration and poetic imagination.

THREE TIMES SEVEN RECITATIONS.

On 25 January 1912 Schoenberg heard from Emil Gutmann, with whom he was discussing a large number of concert plans, that Frau Dr. Albertine Zehme wanted to commission him to write a cycle of recitations on poems from *Pierrot Lunaire* by Albert Giraud, in the translation by Otto Erich Hartleben which had appeared in 1892 and had later become very success- ful. The fee suggested was 1000 marks. Schoenberg wrote in his diary on 28 January:

> '*Have read the preface, looked at the poems, am enthusiastic. A marvellous idea, quite right for me. Would do it even without a fee. So have made another suggestion: instead of fee a share of performing rights. Better for me, because I can't work to a commission. So: I will finish the recitations, then she will perform them and give me the agreed share of the performing rights for 20 to 30 performances. This should be agreeable.*'

After the concert in the Harmoniumsaal he went with the company to Albertine Zehme's apartment. She was enthusiastic, he found her very sympathetic.

> '*Reminds me somewhat of Mildenburg and somewhat of Gutheil (cordial, smooth) so of people whom I like. But I will give her different tasks from Friedlander's music (bad!).*'

In fact Zehme was a remarkable woman. She was Viennese, born on 7 January 1857, with the maiden name of Albertine Aman; she was fifty-five when Schoenberg first met her. She was trained in Vienna as an actress, and got her first engagement in Oldenburg, from where she went to the Leipzig Stadttheater after a few years. In Leipzig she played roles like Thekla in *Wallenstein* and Desdemona in *Othello* with great success. Soon after her marriage to the lawyer Dr. Felix Zehme she said farewell to the stage as Oberon in *Midsummer Night's Dream*. Her husband's family regarded his marriage with a woman who had no means and came from a modest background as a misalliance.

Dr. Zehme became famous and rich through a lawsuit which caused a lot of publicity about 1900. The Saxon Crown Princess Luise, a member of the Imperial House of Hapsburg, fell in love with a young Italian violinist and composer Enrico Toselli, whose 'Serenade' was a kind of popular hit from 1900 onwards. It seemed impossible to dissolve a Catholic marriage. However, finally the efforts of Dr. Zehme to get permission for the divorce in Rome were successful. Through the fortunate result of the lawsuit he became one of the most prominent lawyers in Leipzig and built his wife the luxurious Villa Albertine in Gautzsch (today called Markkleeberg-West).

In 1891 Albertine Zehme became a pupil of Cosima Wagner in Bayreuth; she studied with her and the famous repetiteur Julius Kniese the parts of Venus in *Tannhäuser* (the Paris version), the three Brünnhilde parts in *The Ring* and Kundry till 1893. In 1904 she returned to the stage to play women's parts in an Ibsen cycle in Leipzig. When she met Schoenberg she was an advocate of melodrama, of words spoken to music, a form loved by Richard Strauss, Max Schillings, Engelbert Humperdinck and other composers and often performed in concerts. The 'Pierrot Lunaire' songs by Otto Vrieslander date from 1904 and some of them were performed by her. In 1908 she had aroused attention in Leipzig in recitations of poems by Ujelski to Chopin's piano pieces and also with Liszt's composition *Lenore* (Bürger).

The comparison with Anna Bahr-Mildenburg and Marie Gutheil-Schoder shows what a great impression this woman made on Schoenberg. She took on the commission after long negotiations, and she fitted in with all his unexpected ideas while he was working on the composition and in the rehearsals.

The first of Schoenberg's friends to be informed about this plan was Webern; the latter told Berg about it on 11 February. On the following afternoon there was a second discussion with Gutmann about the recitation project. Schoenberg suggested a royalty of 50 marks and a guarantee of 30 performances, which would bring in 1500 marks, of which 10 % would go to Gutmann. Zehme was annoyed. Schoenberg's diary says:

'Very unpleasant, because I had hoped very much for the money. However, I feel that things are easier for me, because it depressed me very much to have to compose something, which I am not really forced to do.' Then a Strindbergian thought follows: *'It seems that my fate will protect me from even such a small artistic sin. For if I don't have the courage to turn down an offer of money which I need very much,*

Albertine Zehme, Summer 1912

then nothing will come from the affair. So that I can remain pure and only have a sin of thought.'

This was written on 18 February. He did not come to terms with Zehme until after his journey to Prague, on 9 March. And on the 12th he wrote the first of his recitations, 'Gebet an Pierrot', No. 9 in the final order of the work. Note in the diary:

'I think it has worked very well. It gives me many stimuli. And I think that I am approaching a new kind of expression. The sounds become an almost too animal and immediate expression of sensual and spiritual emotions. Almost as if everything was translated directly. I am curious to see how it goes on.'

It did not go on at once. On 1 April Schoenberg took up work again on it, and worked almost without interruption on it from 17 April till the end of May. The verse technique of the poems must have had a great attraction for him. Giraud-Hartleben use a form of thirteen lines, of which the first comes back like a motto as the seventh and the last line. The second line is repeated as the eighth line. This gives a formal scheme A–B–C–D–F–A–B–G–H–I–K–A. This means that a musical form, the reprise, is translated into a poetic form. The *Pierrot* cycle consists of three parts of seven recitations each. Its total length, on the record conducted by Schoenberg in 1940, is only thirty-three minutes, and each poem on the average is hardly a hundred seconds long. Some of them are aphoristic and fleeting structures like the 'Song of the Gallows', which only lasts thirteen seconds, the twelfth in the cycle, and larger ones like No. 5, the 'Valse de Chopin', or the passacaglia 'Night', which is the first piece in the second part as No. 8.

This passacaglia, the darkest nocturne in the cycle, is a compendium of thematic and motivic writing. The responsible use of every single note without concessions, which increasingly became a sign of Schoenberg's music with his greater maturity, can clearly be seen in this piece. From the three-note motive E–G–E flat in the first bars a three-part canon in stretto is developed, and this is also used in the form of chords; the semitone between the two lowest notes in the motive is then developed into a six-note chromatic descent in crotchets, which together with the principal motive forms the theme of the passacaglia, – this is a masterpiece, in the smallest space, of which Schoenberg once called the form of developing variation. And this is only the beginning! In a hundred variations, in diminutions in crotchet and quaver movement, in three-part chords with fixed rhythmical construction, produced contrapuntally and in canon, mirrored in retrograde inversion, the three-note motive appears, surrounded by the chromatic steps upwards and downwards, the movement increases and the dynamics go from a hardly audible ppp to fff; suddenly the dramatic life stops abruptly, and we reach the quiet pace of the beginning again. But this is not just a musical form for its own sake; it becomes a suggestive interpretation and exultation in sound of the extraordinary image in the words of the text, of dark black giant moths, which kill the light of the sun and sink on to mens' hearts as invisible monsters with heavy wings from heaven down to earth. The American writer James Huneker, deeply impressed and tortured by this music, called this passacaglia a vision of prehistoric night; it uses only bass clarinet, cello and piano to make extraordinary tone colours.

Schoenberg uses all the arts of refined contrapuntal technique in the eighteenth of the pieces, the 'Mondfleck'. The text shows Pierrot, walking one warm evening, with a white spot of the bright moon on the back of his dark coat. As he is vain and looking for adventure, something worries him about his dress. He looks round at himself and indeed finds the white spot of the bright moon. He rubs the supposed spot of plaster furiously, but cannot get rid of it, and rubs it until the early morning.

From this wonderful episode Schoenberg produces a moment which stimulated his musical imagination. It was the place where Pierrot turns round and discovers the spot on his back. It is a very unusual situation that a person can see himself from behind. This had inspired Schoenberg before in quite a different way. Among the pictures which he had painted in 1907 and 1910 are several self-portraits. One of them shows him from behind climbing a mountain. In order to paint it Schoenberg must have made studies in a mirror. He observed himself so exactly, that the portrait shows his stance and his head from behind with his round bald patch like a tonsure unmistakably.

He transfers the same method of mirror writing to the musical form. The whole piece is a double mirror or retrograde canon in the parts of the piccolo and the clarinet on one side and the violin and the cello on the other. This means that the four instruments, linked in pairs, go forwards up to a certain point and then backwards. The place at which the movement goes through the mirror comes between the words in the text *richtig* and *einen weissen Fleck*. In this as well as the content of the poem Giraud's 'reprise construction' may have inspired Schoenberg's imagination. Against the canon in the wind and strings the piano plays a fugal but not a mirror part.

Canonic and fugal writing of this kind, which reminds one of the methods of the Netherlands polyphonists in the fifteenth and sixteenth century, is also found in other pieces in the cycle, expecially in the second part. The piece which comes before 'Mondfleck', 'Parodie', begins straight away with a canon in inversion between viola and clarinet, and the voice of the speaker imitates the viola as a third part; later on there is a similar imitation between speaker and piccolo.

Together with these purely contrapuntal forms, which always arise out of the text, the very complex score also contains other, homophonic pieces like the 'Serenade', which has to be played freely in the rhythm of a slow waltz with a virtuoso cello part, whose cantilenas and cadenzas are accompanied by the piano with chords or figures. In a similar way the No. 9, 'Gebet an Pierrot', combines flute, clarinet and piano, and No. 2, 'Colombine', combines flute, clarinet, violin and piano. A purely concertante piece is No. 7, 'Der kranke Mond', where a wide-ranging speaking part is accompanied by a tender flute.

One of the greatest means of contrast in *Pierrot Lunaire* is the instrumental colour, which is tried out in all pieces in different combinations. The five players have eight instruments, i.e. the violin also plays viola, the flute plays piccolo, the clarinet plays bass clarinet. The individuality of Schoenberg's instrumentation resides in its capability of as it were distilling the quintessence of the individual tone-colour of each instrument. While classical and romantic orchestration is mainly dominated by the endeavour to find a common denominator, and to reach the highest possible degree of blending (even if contrasted colours are used so to speak as dissonances), Schoenberg's palette of sound is based on the emphasizing of contrasts. One can say that in *Pierrot* each instrument is discovered anew in its extremes of colour. This is true of the wind and strings as well as the piano, which is the most used instrument in the cycle. The colours are divided in the score as follows: The piano is used in 17 pieces, clarinet and cello in 14 each, violin and flute in 12 each, piccolo in 7, bass clarinet in 6 and viola in 5 pieces.

The predominant rôle of the piano made it necessary for it to have as much variation as possible. The piano writing ranges from the most complex polyphony to simple and broken chords, a ranged differently for each individual piece, from roaring fullness of sound to naked writing, from soloistic predominance to simple accompaniments.

All the eight instrumental colours appear in the last piece 'O alter Duft'. It is the simplest example of a predominantly homophonic song in varied strophies. However, each strophe of the poem does not correspond to one in the composition. Through continual variation of the periods there are surprises from one bar to another; the simple main theme appears in diminution, in inversion, in three-part chords, turned into figures and in a canon between its own diminution and its inversion. The speaking part, which gives out the theme in the first bar as it were in unison with the piano, does the same thing in canon in the 14th bar. The impression of simplicity is strengthened by the fact that the theme appears in thirds. Moreover it is in E major, with a 6/4 chord in the third and sixteenth bars. The end is a variant of a major cadence. The E in the bass, with which the piano ends the piece, is as it were the resolution of a dissonance; as it was preceded by an augmented triad E flat–G–B, the human ear has the understandable weakness of adding the lacking notes G sharp and B to the E. – The simplicity of this last piece is also due to the text. Hartleben writes: 'A happy wish makes me aspire to joys which I have long despised'. Perhaps tonality, a triad, consonances belonged to these despised joys at that time, at a critical stage in Schoenberg's development? Later in an article *On revient toujours* he commented on the tonal compositions of his American years. The last of the *Pierrot* recitations, and the passages in the text about 'happy wishes', may remind us of Schoenberg's later remarks.

Albertine Zehme had thought of only having a piano accompaniment. But in the first piece written, 'Gebet an Pierrot', Schoenberg had already added a clarinet.

Steuermann was engaged to play the accompaniment and for the rehearsals. Fifty-one years later (in the Juilliard News Bulletin of 1963) he described the growth of the composition and the work at rehearsals. Each time that Schoenberg wanted to include a further instrument, he asked Frau Zehme if she was agreeable to it. So the performance became more expensive because of this. Thus in 'Dandy' (composed on 1–2 April) he added a flute, in 'Eine blasse Wäscherin' (18 April) a violin, and in 'Mondestrunken' (17–29 April) a cello. 'Now Schoenberg's restless imagination was sufficiently in flight', Steuermann wrote; 'why not alternate flute with piccolo, violin with viola, clarinet with bass clarinet?

And, with all these possibilities at his disposal, why not orchestrate each number differently?'

In fact in the 'Rote Messe' (22–24 April) all the alternative instruments, apart from cello and piano, are used, so that the combination is: Piccolo, bass clarinet, viola, cello and piano. The full quintet appears several times, but almost always in different combinations.

Schoenberg took till 9 July to finish the cycle with the 'Kreuzen'. 'As far as I am concerned', Steuermann wrote, 'I shall never forget these weeks and months, when every few days the eight-o'clock post brought me manuscript sheets of a new piece from the work. I rehearsed it feverishly on the piano and rushed to Frau Zehme's studio to undertake the fairly difficult task of rehearsing it with her. She was an intelligent and artistic woman, but an actress by profession and only as musical as the well educated German ladies of that time. I remember how I, doubting if I could show her the exact difference between 3–4 and 4–4 rhythms, asked her to dance a few bars of a waltz and then a polka, with shorter and shorter intervals between the two and finally trying out the first bars of "Dandy".'

From the beginning of July the Schoenberg family was at Carlshagen on the Usedom. On the 5th Schoenberg wrote to Hertzka about the printing of the cycle of recitations. It could only be printed in full score; 'a piano score is unthinkable, because of the polyphony. Especially in this work where colour is everything and the notes mean nothing.'

Zehme was in her house, the Villa Albertine in Gautzsch Leipzig, and she continued to work. On 17 August she was worried about a manuscript of Schoenberg's which had been lost. She wanted to be in Berlin on Monday the 19th. Karl Essberger, the clarinettist, was to rehearse with her again on the Friday. Before that she would like to speak to Schoenberg, but would ring him up. 'Two copyists are waiting for the music here', she warned him and said that she was working very hard with Dr. Georg Göhler, the director of the Riedel Society and the Musical Society in Leipzig, who supervised things marvellously for her, showed her the rhythms and helped her a great deal.

Two days later the manuscript was found. She said she would ring up on the 21st to find out when she could come to Schoenberg in Zehlendorf. She felt that she was now steady in keeping the time and was in touch with Essberger. She was sorry that Steuermann and the cellist Hans Kindler could not come before the 20th. The violinist, Jakob Maliniak, was not mentioned.

Meanwhile Gutmann had arranged a tour, which was to take in as many German cities as possible, immediately after the first performance in Berlin in October. On 28 August Zehme sent Schoenberg a list of the cities and said that still more would be added to it. There were also discussions with Gutmann about money. The two wind players, Essberger and H. W. de Vries, both musicians in the Royal Band, would get 70 marks a concert, second-class travel expenses and ten marks a day living expenses. Zehme said that the hire of the hall and other arrangements cost a thousand marks for each concert, and her own personal expenses were not covered by this. However, Schoenberg should dispose of things according to his own discretion. 'The most important thing is and remains that we have a performance which is unobjectionable artistically. Good-bye till Monday at 10 o'clock at my house! Yours very sincerely Albertine Zehme.'

Monday was the 26 August. Three days after the rehearsal in Zehlendorf she sent a card putting forward the request of a young musician who wanted to attend the rehearsals. 'He is called Hermann Scherchen, plays the violin and was recommended by Göhler.' Steuermann gives a picture of the twenty-five rehearsals which preceded the first performance. 'Schoenberg's magnetic personality was always looking for enough tension and inspiration, not to mention his peculiar sense of humour. I remember very well his attempts to get the speaker away from the expression of a tragic heroine, to which she was prone. He stood behind her, when the "Sick Moon" became too tearful and said in the rhythm of her speech: "Don't despair, Frau Zehme, don't despair. There is such a thing as life insurance!".'

Gutmann had hired the Choralionsaal in the Bellevuestrasse for the Berlin performances. On a postcard of 25 September he gave Zehme the dates of the rehearsals in the hall: 5, 7 and 9 October, to be followed by a lighting rehearsal. Since 22 September the advertisements for the concert had appeared in the Sunday editions of the *Vossische Zeitung* and other Berlin papers; Wednesday, 16 October, Arnold Schoenberg *Pierrot Lunaire* (First Performance), Albertine Zehme and Ensemble, Choralionsaal. And on 6 October, in addition to the names of the players, was added: Final Rehearsal with Invited Audience; Wednesday, 9 October at 8 o'clock.

Webern followed Schoenberg's work in Berlin from Stettin with longing and burning interest. He wrote to Berg on 5 October that Alfred Hertz, the director of the New York Metropolitan Opera, had postponed his return to America in order to be able to hear a rehearsal of *Pierrot*.

The interest in the new work was also great elsewhere. The press attended the final rehearsal on 9 October, and Max Marschalk, for instance, wrote about this in great detail in the *Vossische Zeitung* on 11 October. Steuermann says of the performances: 'Frau Zehme insisted on appearing in Pierrot costume and standing alone on the stage. The instrumentalists and the conductor, Schoenberg, were behind a rather complicated screen – complicated because it was not easy on a small stage to construct the screen in such a way that the conductor could be seen by the speaker but not by the audience. Schoenberg solved this problem with the virtuosity which he so often showed in such matters.'

Webern came to the first performance on 16 October. Three days later he wrote to Berg from Stettin: 'The reception of the recitations was enthusiastic. Naturally there were a few people who hissed after the first part and one person who blew on a key. But that meant nothing. There was enthusiasm after the second part, and in the third there was one place where unrest was caused by an idiot who was laughing, so that Schoenberg stopped the performance and waited until calm was restored again. But at the end there was no trace of opposition. Schoenberg and the performers had to appear again and again on the platform, especially Schoenberg, naturally; people shouted for him in the hall over and over again. It was an unqualified success.' Steuermann confirms this account exactly.

A few of the cities which were to be visited by the tour that followed fell out, including Leipzig and Stettin. They first went to Hamburg, where the performance took place on 19 October. Unfortunately only in front of a very small public, as the critic Hermann Chevalley wrote in 'Musik'; 'hardly a hundred people', – but among them were Richard Dehmel and Otto Klemperer. Dresden followed on the 24th; here the ensemble appeared in the Künstlerhaus, and they went to Breslau on the 31st. Marya Freund, who was working at the opera house there, had already asked Schoenberg on the 20th to come and dine with his ensemble at her house after the concert: he agreed.

On 2 November the ensemble performed in Vienna in the Bösendorfersaal. Then, because of his concert engagements in Holland, Schoenberg had to hand over the conductorship to

Scherchen; Scherchen conducted the following four performances in Munich, Stuttgart, Mannheim and Frankfurt.

Now Albertine Zehme wrote seven letters about the performances and the reactions of the public and press. The first was written in Munich, where she stayed at the Christliche Hospiz, on 6 November. Steuermann had already spoken about the performance on the previous day, saying that it had been a success. There was much applause after 'Gemeinheit' and 'Parodie', and one person whistled and two people hissed, which aroused more applause. Two gentlemen and a lady who had spoken to him afterwards were disappointed that Schoenberg was not there. 'The warmth of the reception grew from Dresden to Vienna.' Full house, but no reviews yet. The organizer of the concert had given out a lot of free tickets. 'Scherchen conducted very bravely without any kind of vacillation. He lacks inspiration, but he is reliable.' She says that she would be going to Stuttgart on the 11th, and until then would be visiting museums and the theatre in Munich.

She wrote a second letter on 7 November. Munich had only brought in 300 marks, including the sale of the programme books. Eighty free tickets had been distributed. Wonderful reviews had come from Dresden and Breslau.

Among those present at the Munich performance were some painters from the 'Blaue Reiter'. Franz Marc's wife Maria wrote on 7 November to August Macke: 'We sat in a train again in order to hear Schoenberg at last . . . We were rather disappointed; the whole affair is too strongly Viennese – Egon Schiele, Klimt, – also like Schoenberg's heads with green eyes. We were naturally interested and a lot of it was certainly good. But the whole thing is not really pure. The element of sentimentality which the piece contains takes away one's confidence, even if one likes a lot of it. I prefer the futurists.' Paul Klee wrote in his diary: 'Make way, you Philistine, I think your last hour has come.'

Mathilde had remained behind with the children in Zehlendorf. On 8 November Zehme wrote to her that the music reviews were stupid and bad. Breslau had only brought in 270 marks with a full hall. Now she wrote again about a repetition of the performance in Vienna and would like Schoenberg to conduct it there on 18 or 20 January. She herself had a concert of her own in Dresden on the 22nd. 'Schoenberg has fulfilled what I have been longing for . . . It is the fulfilment of something I have wanted for a long time.'

Two letters from Stuttgart, where the performance had taken place on the day before, are dated 12 November. She asks Schoenberg to conduct the second of the two Berlin repetitions on 1 and 8 December. As Vienna had only brought in 1000 kronen in takings as against 935 kronen in expenses, she did not dare to give a second performance there. She wrote about the Stuttgart concert, saying that there had only been a small number of people there, and that some had left the hall after the first part and one person after the 'Galgenlied'. Could Schoenberg conduct in Frankfurt? Scherchen had been entirely reliable again in Stuttgart and knew his job.

The next letter was written on the 16th in Frankfurt, Hospiz Basler Hof. Mannheim on the previous evening had brought in 160 marks, Stuttgart only 50. Good reviews for Schoenberg in both cities; her performance had been criticized in Mannheim as 'crass Dilettantism'. In Frankfurt the advance sales had been small, but the demand for free tickets was enormous. She would not come to Berlin before 29 November. And again: would not Schoenberg conduct the two concerts there?

The last *Pierrot* letter came from Frankfurt, written on Sunday 17 November. 'It went really well, there was lucidity and atmosphere and good tone in the work. The public was excellent, good applause and no opposition.' He should prepare the work for Amsterdam.

Among the audience in Stuttgart on 11 November who received the work and criticized it with such lack of understanding was the ballet master of the Court Opera, Albert Burger, with his friend, the painter Oskar Schlemmer. Both were planning the creation of a new form of dance, which Schlemmer later realized in his 'Triadic Ballet'. Schoenberg's music enthralled them. Burger wrote to him that he was working on modern dance, – supported by Dalcroze's ideas – and saw in Schoenberg's music the only kind which was suitable for this. On 30 December, after his return from St. Petersburg, Schoenberg answered (the letter was published, January–February 1971):

'*If you really know my music and have to take into account its absolute avoidance of dance rhythms, and in spite of this think it possible that my music could fit your ideas, then I consider it possible too. For I myself have ideas for the theatre in this connection and it would be very interesting for me to get to know yours.*'

He was equally decisive when ten years later he turned down a plan of Leonid Massine's, the great choreographer in Diaghilev's

circle. After the first Paris performance of *Pierrot* in May 1922
Egon Wellesz wrote to him about this. Alma Werfel also gave him
some details in the summer. Schoenberg answered on 5 July:

"*I know that I am not a formalist by occupation. But it seems to me
to go too far to perform* Pierrot *without recitation but with dancing ...
In addition: I would have to make a symphonic arrangement of this
myself; in order to conduct it myself; ... I have no desire to do such
work. I would rather write something new for Massine – even if not
immediately.*'

There was also an important witness of the first performance in
Mannheim in 1912. Artur Bodanzky wrote on 20 November that
he was deeply impressed by the text and the music of *Pierrot*, but
had doubts about the melodrama as a form and about Zehme.

The reviews of her performance were very varied. Alfred Kerr,
the doyen of the Berlin theatre critics, praised her art in an article
in 'Pan'. Marschalk in the *Vossische Zeitung* completely rejected
her. Arno Nadel wrote in the 'Musik' enthusiastically, Rudolf
Louis from Munich was horrified. Scherchen, who decades later
spoke of Zehme with high esteem, wanted to perform *Pierrot* in
1920 with Tilla Durieux. He asked Schoenberg if Frau Zehme
had the copyright of the work. In that case he would not be able
to do it, as she herself, according to his own experience, had only
spoilt the effect of it.

The two Berlin repetitions took place on 1 and 8 December as
Sunday matinées in the Choralionsaal. Gutmann's advertisements
announced Scherchen as conductor of the first and Schoenberg of
the second. On 8 December Stravinsky was in the audience. We
know his judgement: Aestheticism, return to the Beardsley culture
which was long out of date. However, the perfection of the instrumentation was unquestioned. And in a letter to the St. Petersburg
critic V. G. Karatygin of 13 December 1912, he said that in
Pierrot Lunaire by Schoenberg 'the whole unusual stamp of his
creative genius comes to light at its most intensive.'

The work was also given in its original form on 24 February in
Prague and on 4 April 1914 in Regensburg. The Prague performance took place in the Rudolfinum-Saal, put on by the
Chamber Music Society. Rudolph F. Procházka wrote about it in
the 'Prague Chamber Music Society' (Prague 1926). In 1910
and 1912 the members of the Society had got to know Schoenberg's two quartets through the Rosé Ensemble. Marie Gutheil-
Schoder also sang songs, and asked that there should be no
demonstrations of any kind. 'The hereditary superior reserve of

the very conservatively-minded audience now had its victory. Fury broke out with re-doubled force on 24 February. And the pleasant Rudolphinumsaal witnessed the greatest concert scandal which Prague has yet experienced.' This quotation is taken from Dr. Ernst Rychnovsky's description in 'Musik'. He rejected it, and so did Dr. Richard von Batka in the *Prager Tagblatt* and the critic of the *Prager Abendblatt*. In 'Bohemia' Felix Adler wrote at great length and with approbation about the concert: after his purely factual account of the performance there is a description of what went before it:

'One could already see from the external picture presented by the hall that something unusual was expected. Many of those personalities who either act as stirrers-up of trouble or as cultural leaders in Prague, gave the evening the benefit of their presence. Young and old musicians sat there together, – one cannot say harmoniously. The conductor von Zemlinsky followed the performance in a box; Herr von Keussler, the conductors from Stermich, Dr. Götz, Horwitz and Pringsheim were there. Professor Rietsch, counsellor Rzach, the Director of the Conservatory Kaan von Albest, the elderly piano teacher Hohlfeld, were all there, also the former pupil of Liszt, Frau Sofie von Herget, and the grey eminence of Prague music life, Frau Gabriele von Zdekauer, were present. Naturally young Prague had sent its most violent representatives as well, and Czech musical circles were also strongly represented.

At the very first notes of the composition the lips of many people were seen to wear a half amazed, half amused smile; however, peace was kept for the moment. Even at the end of the first part of the work the opposition did not dare to show itself, and the composer had a great deal of applause. However there was now a run on the programmes with the text, which many people had not provided themselves with at the beginning. The programme-sellers were besieged and were asked with entreaties and the offer of larger tips in order to buy a programme, so that the supply ran out in a moment.

After the second part things got worse. The hissers had plucked up courage and would no longer allow themselves to be outvoted. Naturally this opposition irritated the supporters of this new art, and they answered with a storm of applause and cries of 'Bravo' which went shrilly through the hall. In one poem in the third part the Speaker, Frau Zehme, had to say the words '*Wischt und wischt*'. This was the signal for part of the audience to shout their hissing sounds and disturb the performance in a most inconsiderate manner. Schoenberg went pale and immediately rapped on the stand. One could see that he was in a trembling state of excitement. There was a painful pause, during which even the hissers were quiet. Then Schoenberg had the whole poem repeated; however, this did not prevent some particularly tasteful wits from interrupting again.

Before the next poem there was again a good deal of unrest. An epidemic of coughing had suddenly seized certain members of the audience. Schoenberg stood in outward calm, his hands crossed behind his back, in front of his conducting desk and waited nearly ten minutes until the last cougher was silent. Also Frau Zehme, by energetic movements towards the organ loft, had to protest against the continuing unrest. When finally the last of the poems was nearly finished, one heard from a single individual a cry "Stop!" Now a storm began between the holders of different opinions, during which the last notes of the composition went unheard. Not only the excited young people, but also the musically educated part of the public were on the side of those who applauded after the last poems. The opposition was also prepared. They blew shrill whistles, and the door key came into its uncultivated rights as an instrument of criticism. Cries of *"Pfui"* tried to drown the loud Bravos, and the battle between the parties went on uninterruptedly until the lights were put out and the tumult gave way to silence.

Immediately after the performance Schoenberg had put down his bâton with disapproving shakes of his head and had gone off. Now he appeared, greeted with jubilation by his supporters, and went on to the platform many times; he was able to give thanks for the applause, which was indeed disputed but really enthusiastic, with a smile. It was a moral victory won by the applauders. The victory of the lovers of progress and cultural enterprise. The victory of all those who are young enough to be moved by it and intelligent enough at least to allow it to have its say.'

A strong friendship grew up between Schoenberg and Albertine Zehme, to whom he dedicated *Pierrot Lunaire*. At the end of May 1913 he left the Villa Lepcke in Zehlendorf with his family, and moved into Berlin-Südende, Berliner Strasse 17a, of which Frau Zehme was part owner. The Schoenbergs lived on the first floor, and Zehme on the ground floor when she was in Berlin.

For a long time she had been directing her whole artistic interest to reciting in the first performance of the 'Gurrelieder', which took place in Vienna, without her, on the day before the *Pierrot* scandal in Prague; she had always hoped to be able to speak the recitation in the third part. Her efforts were in vain. Schoenberg had been negotiating with Schreker, who wanted to perform the work in Vienna with the Philharmonic Chorus. In Leipzig she spoke to the publishers Hinrichsen and Eulenburg. On 17 January she reminded Schoenberg to suggest her as the speaker for Vienna. However, he had doubts about this, and the first performance on 23 February in the large Musikvereinssaal took place with the actor from the Burgtheater Ferdinand Gregori. She was planning a performance in Leipzig. On 2 March she told Schoenberg that her husband would contribute 3000 marks to the costs and also pay her fee of 1000 marks. Then she announced that she would visit him on Saturday, the 8th, at 'the usual time, 4 o'clock.'

We do not know what was discussed then. However, in Schoenberg's legacy there were two undated, very offended letters in which she spoke about jewels, the speaking part in the 'Gurrelieder' and the suspicion that she had wanted to buy the part for herself. She said that Schreker had wanted her but that Schoenberg had asked for someone else to do the part. 'Can you really think of money when for me it is a question of the most holy things: – my *work*, for which I have given up my house, my husband, my kingdom and my comfortable life like dust under my feet.'

Their reconciliation resulted in the invitation to the whole Schoenberg family to occupy the first floor of the house in South End. Here Alban Berg visited his master and friend at the beginning of June 1913. He wrote enthusiastically to Webern that Schoenberg has splendid living quarters, good relations with his publisher, had put on a special *Pierrot* rehearsal for him and was going to spend the summer months on Zehme's estate. In fact Schoenberg did inform his brother-in-law Zemlinsky on 14 July 1913 about a visit to Leipzig-Gautzsch, where the Zehmes had a villa in the Charlottenstrasse 18. It is a handsome house in the style of Art Nouveau with a large music room. However, the Schoenbergs spent the summer with their children at Göhren on the island of Rügen on the Baltic; their pension was called Burg Neudeck.

Through her position in society Frau Zehme was not without influence in Leipzig. She used this untiringly to work for Schoenberg's compositions. Otto Lohse (1858–1925), an excellent and internationally known conductor, had been chief of the Leipzig Opera since 1912. She got him interested in the two Schoenberg operas and he planned to give the first performances of them. However, he had to write on 18 September 1913 to Schoenberg that the *Glückliche Hand* demanded too much in the way of material resources. At the same time he asked him to reserve *Erwartung* for him. The principal producer and dramaturgist of the theatre, Dr. Ernst Lert, was shown manuscripts of both pieces by Zehme, and he later put them on when he was principal producer at the Frankfurt Theatre. A letter of Lert to Schoenberg of 4 November 1920 shows the lively interest which this excellent producer and Mozart expert (1883–1955) had in these pieces.

Meanwhile Zehme was studying the recitation of the 'Gurre-lieder' with Schoenberg, although the work was conceived for a male voice. The first German performance was given during the Easter Fair on 4 March 1914 at the Leipzig Albert Hall; this had been financed by Dr. Felix Zehme. Schoenberg conducted the enormous forces, which had been brought together from the Leipzig Male Voice Choir, the Singing Academy and the enlarged Winderstein Orchestra. The main parts were sung by the same soloists as the year before under Schreker in Vienna. Hans Nachod sang Waldemar, Martha Winternitz-Dorda Tove, Marya Freund the Wood Dove and Alfred Boruttau Klaus the Fool. The recitation was spoken by Albertine Zehme. The critic Dr. Max Unger wrote about it in the first April number of 'Musik' and spoke of a musical sensation. In Schoenberg's correspondence with conductors, publishers and friends the enthusiastic reception of his choral work in Leipzig is often mentioned.

Soon after this important event the Schoenbergs accepted the invitation of their rich friend, which she had often repeated. 'We were invited for fourteen days to Gautzsch at Frau Zehme's house', he wrote on 16 April 1914 to his brother-in-law Zemlinsky in Prague. At this time the study score of *Pierrot* was published by Universal Edition.

In June Alexander Siloti wrote from St. Petersburg to Schoenberg about a second appearance as guest conductor with the Chamber Symphony and his own planned performance of *Pierrot* with Zehme. Schoenberg was very pleased about the Chamber Symphony and asked for dates for four rehearsals, which he would need in order to prepare it. However, his letter of 15 June contains a striking second paragraph about *Pierrot*. He asked for the performance to be postponed until 1915 or 1916;

he would rather not put his reasons in writing, but would tell
Siloti personally in St. Petersburg. 'For the moment I can only
say this: it is at least as much in your interest as in mine, that you
don't do it this year. You can certainly write to Frau Zehme that
unfortunately it is not possible this year. *Pierrot* would be a mistake
this year, and it might spoil the success of the Chamber Symphony.'

This letter could only mean one thing: that Schoenberg had
doubts about the interpreter, who had the sole performing rights
of the work for a limited time. Probably the time was due to
expire in 1915, but all these plans came to nothing because of
world history. At the beginning of August Germany declared
war on Russia and France. Schoenberg, at the age of 39, had to
be ready for military service as an Austrian, and for a time returned to South End. Zehme decided to leave her house and live
permanently in Gautzsch; on 1 October she asked him to do some
practical things regarding the move. Her letter ends patriotically
with hopes of German victories on the Marne and in Lwow.

As a result of the outbreak of war Schoenberg lost all his pupils.
Zehme gave up her own house in South End to him, and by letting
part of it he was able to obtain an income of 1400 marks. In the
middle of September 1915 the Schoenbergs moved from Berlin
South End to Vienna-Hietzing to the house of Frau Lieser,
Gloriettegasse 43. Schoenberg was called up for military service
in the same year, from which he was finally released at the end of
1917 after a fairly long period of leave. In a legal battle with
Marschalk and the Dreililienverlag between 1917 and 1918 Dr.
Felix Zehme's law office represented him. (Letter from law office
of 26 May 1918.)

In 1918 Zehme spent a New Year's holiday in Oberhof, Thur-
ingia. On 5 January she asked Schoenberg for the text of the
Jacob's Ladder. She would like to speak the recitation at his
'Gurrelieder' performances in Zurich, Berne and Basle. She only
hoped that he would not use Gregori again as in Vienna; she
would not forgive him for this on her death bed! In Leipzig she
had played the leader of the chorus in Hofmannsthal's *Alkestis*.
The producer Dr. Ernst Lert had been very pleased with her.

Schoenberg asked her to return the material of *Pierrot Lunaire*.
She reacted on 20 January with a furious letter from Gautzsch,
called him a satan and a sadist, spoke of stab wounds which he
was giving her, and appealed to the wife of Ambassador von
Nostitz as a witness of her performances. And again on a postcard
of 20 February she refused to give him back the *Pierrot* parts.

However, two weeks later she had calmed down. On 4 March she wrote that *Verklärte Nacht* would be performed on the 14th in the Gewandhaus. She was pleased about it. She herself was preparing an evening of recitations, including Schiller's 'Bride of Corinth' and 'Tanz', and was delighted by the piano accompaniment of the 18-year-old Mitja Nikisch. After the performance of *Verklärte Nacht* in its orchestral version she wrote on the 26th praising Arthur Nikisch's performance and advised Schoenberg to speak to him about *Pelléas* and 'Gurrelieder'.

A card of 7 June announces that she had read *Jacob's Ladder*. She asks about the music. She is delighted about Schoenberg's idea of giving public rehearsals of the Chamber Symphony. And she returns again and again to the speaking part of 'Gurrelieder', for instance in a letter of 7 August. On 17 September she announces that she will be visiting Vienna after the 20th. She only has to arrange a passport. A Dr. Meyer from the theatre was going to rehearse with her; otherwise possibly Siegfried Karg-Elert. She was sad that 'Gurrelieder' had been postponed until March 1919.

There was a further correspondence on 26 February 1919. She had read Paul Stefan's article in the *Neue Zürcher Zeitung* about Schoenberg's rehearsals and his Society for Private Musical Performances. She asked about the music for *Jacob's Ladder* and – as always – about the 'Gurrelieder' in Zurich. What was his Mödling apartment like? She herself had a cow, six hens and three rabbits. She had recently reminded Nikisch about *Pelléas* and the 'Gurrelieder'. – On 3 September she sent congratulations to Schoenberg for his birthday, too early. She says she has read about him again, this time in the *Neue Freie Presse*, and imagines him surrounded by friends and pupils anxious to learn from him. She is going to give recitation lectures with Karg-Elert, who accompanies her on the harmonium. Does Schoenberg know the pianist Walter Gieseking? He is a marvellous player of Debussy, Busoni, all modern composers, and is studying Schoenberg's piano pieces. She writes on a card that Steuermann's sister Salome is now at the Leipzig Theatre.

Is it true, she asks on 18 September, that he is going to conduct the 'Gurrelieder' in October in Zurich? She is in good form and ready to go there.

On a Christmas card of 23 December she tells him about the teaching which she has begun with some pupils in artistic speaking and singing.

Steuermann had two sisters who were both actresses, Salome (who later married the poet and producer Berthold Viertel) and Rosa (who later married the producer Josef Gielen). In the summer of 1919 Steuermann had begun to work on *Pierrot* with Rosa, and he laid special emphasis on rhythmical precision and avoidance of singing tone. In a letter of 31 July he asks Schoenberg if he has got Scherchen's query about Albertine Zehme's exclusive right to perform *Pierrot*. In April 1920 Steuermann gave a piano recital in Leipzig. 'I was with Frau Zehme a few days ago', he wrote to Schoenberg on the 18th; 'outwardly she is not very much changed; she naturally asked me about everything possible which concerns us, but seems to have become relatively apathetic to things which earlier filled her with enthusiasm.'

Zehme too wrote about Steuermann's visit on a card of 5 May. Meanwhile Schoenberg had conducted two performances of the 'Gurrelieder' in the State Opera in Vienna. She asked how Wilhelm Klitsch (an actor from the Vienna German Folk Theatre) had managed the role of the Speaker. A card from her on 7 August speaks of her joy in teaching, on the method of her master, King Clark, who had died in 1915. Among her pupils were a Tove and a born Waldemar, who were to sing to Steuermann. Steuermann had played wonderfully, with a greater depth and experience.

Meanwhile she wrote her book, which she intended to be a memorial to her teacher Clark. A letter of 20 August 1920 speaks about this and about her happy work with pupils. She was alone in Gautzsch; Dr. Zehme had been in Malcesine on Lake Garda, where they owned a house, since March. Could she meet Schoenberg in Berlin between 10 and 15 September? Five days later she altered her plans. She wanted the Schoenberg family to come to her; then he could hear her pupils sing.

But Schoenberg had other things to do and was preparing for his journey to Holland. She wrote to him there on 5 November that her booklet had come out.

'The Foundations of Artistic Speaking and Singing' is the title of this brochure, only forty pages long, which was published by Carl Merseburger in Leipzig. The ambitious title is enlarged by the sub-title: 'with the complete use of the larynx'. It is intended for self-instruction and is dedicated to the memory of King Clark. The first part, twenty-five pages long, deals with technical matters. The use of consonants should be controlled by taking up again the Italian method of speaking. Breathing, support, functions of the tongue, lips and nose are important. And naturally the author attacks all other methods. However, the exercises and remarks of Clark's quoted by her are conventional and also sectarian.

The last few pages contain some remarks of her own. 'The chief thing is always the word – it is the *leading thought*, which the word imparts to us.' This is near the aesthetic of *Pierrot Lunaire*. And here is an important thought: 'Even in lyrical speech there are "Leitmotives". The melody of speech is like a freer sister of strict vocal music, like a shadow of it, and will not allow itself to be bound by the iron rules to which vocal music is subjected.'

Now Schoenberg's name appears for the first time with a fairly long quotation from the foreword to *Pierrot*. With examples from classical poetry and a poem of Stefan George (whom she mentions together with Dehmel, Hofmannsthal, Heine and Goethe) Zehme describes what she means by rhythmical delivery and speech-tempo. And she adds requisites about what she calls tonality and pitch in recitation. Bright and dark, high and low, no sing-song, not too much and not too little – these are important. Anyone who does not possess musical gifts and education should not try recitations. She had herself 'studied Schoenberg's two melodramas, *Pierrot Lunaire* and the Speaker in the 'Gurrelieder' under his strictest guidance in Berlin.'

In an apology for stage fright Zehme recognizes the 'increased sense of being which whips up all one's nerves before appearing and . . . is necessary for the success of a performance.' One should never appear before an audience with a book or music paper in one's hands. The brochure ends with a belief in 'true art and humanity', in intellect, nobility of soul and the value of culture.

Schoenberg never spoke about her book, and it was not to be found in his library in 1971. Zehme kept up her connection with him. She sent him a New Year's greeting in 1921, and in the summer a card from Malcesine, where she was swimming every day. On 12 November she congratulated Schoenberg on the marriage of his daughter Trudi to the composer Felix Greissle. In this she did not forget to ask about Erika Wagner and her performance of *Pierrot*. She herself had been arranging Rilke poems for a pupil as recitations. – That Christmas 1921 she sent her usual greetings, dated 12 December. In this she praises the pianist Theodor Szanto, who had played Schoenberg's Piano Pieces in Paris.

Each time that she read or heard about a new interpreter of

Pierrot, she wanted to know all about it. On 5 September 1922 she asks if Schoenberg has worked on the recitations with Marie Gutheil-Schoder. She is still moved by his music. After Wilhelm Furtwängler had conducted the Five Orchestral Pieces opus 16 in the Gewandhaus she wrote on 8 December about the deep impression made by them. She says that Furtwängler had announced that he would also perform *Pelléas.*

After that the contact became looser. She did not write again until after the news of Frau Schoenberg's death on 22 October 1923. 'An angel has left you', she wrote in her letter of condolence on 21 December. And a few weeks later she herself had a loss: on 8 January 1924 her husband Dr. Zehme died. 'Shall I come to Vienna, or you to Gautzsch?' she asked.

On 10 February another letter arrived with a request for a meeting. The Hindemith-Amar Quartet was playing Schoenberg's opus 7 in Leipzig on the 19th. Perhaps Schoenberg would like to come to Gautzsch. Her worries about her husband's will had been taken away from her, and her son and her son-in-law had been made executors.

Perhaps she could come to Mödling with her housekeeper and look after his household for a few weeks. But it would be better if he would come to Gautzsch.

Her last attempt at a meeting was made when she heard that he was going to conduct two performances of *Pierrot Lunaire* in Hamburg. A card of 29 February suggests that he should come from Hamburg to Gautzsch. Schoenberg did not go, but on 30 July 1924 he wrote to her about a plan of making a tour of fifteen or twenty cities with the Chamber Symphony, *Pierrot* and his Serenade and he invited her to Mödling. Then the personal relationship between him and the first interpreter of *Pierrot Lunaire* ended. Zehme continued with her teaching and made further experiments in the field of speech accompanied by music. Her next musical god was Emil Mattiesen (1875–1939), a philosopher, professor of religion and parapsychologist, who had travelled all over the world and had studied Asiatic languages. His extensive musical output consists mainly of songs and ballads, of which Schoenberg possessed some. Zehme herself gave courses in Leipzig as an introduction to the work of Mattiesen; these lectures could be attended free. – The problems of performance which Schoenberg's 'Sprechstimme' brought with it were not solved by her. But she continued to have a passionate interest in the work, as can be seen in her letters. Interpreters such as Marie

Gutheil-Schoder, Erika Wagner and Marya Freund found little less difficulty in interpreting this work.

The most brilliant performance from the public point of view took place on 5 January 1924 with Gutheil-Schoder in the Berlin Singakademie, which was filled to capacity. The conductor was Fritz Stiedry, the violinist Boris Kroyt, the cellist Gregor Piati-gorsky, the flautist Bose and the clarinettist Alfred Richter. Artur Schnabel was at the piano. The performance had been put on by the 'Melos' Musical Society directed by Philipp Jarnach and Heinz Tiessen. The former director, Fritz Windisch, saw to it that the evening began with a scandal. He jumped on to the platform protesting and had to be seized and taken away.

Albertine Zehme died on 11 May 1946 in her house in Naum-burg, Spechtsart 5, at the age of nearly ninety. The entry in the funeral book (Register Number 615) in the Registrar's office gives her maiden name as Aman, her date of birth Vienna, 7 January 1857, and the date of her marriage to Dr. Zehme as 20 October 1881.

SCHOENBERG AND BUSONI

Ferruccio Busoni had lived in Berlin since 1894. He liked the capital of the revived German Empire, which had grown rapidly since its foundation and was progressive in cultural affairs; and he always returned there gladly after his European and Transatlantic tours as a piano virtuoso. However, he was interested in other things besides playing the piano. He himself was a fruitful, imaginative composer who was interested in new means of expression, and he observed the development of music since Brahms carefully and critically; he had met Brahms in his childhood in Vienna.

In spite of great material expense Berlin music left him unsatisfied. He wanted a methodical and regular cult of contemporary music, especially in the concerts of the Berlin Philharmonic, which at that time attracted the best public and those who were most able to pay. As a pianist he himself kept to the normal virtuoso repertoire; the reasons for this were both psychological and financial. However, with his increasing insight into the situation of modern music he found it necessary to put his artistic and financial resources at its service.

Busoni had already conducted in Helsinki on occasions. He liked working with orchestras. He regarded it as a counterweight to the limited freedom of public piano recitals. He needed partnership, and looked for collaborators who were on the same technical level as himself, to whom he could translate his considered formal ideas. About 1900 he got the idea of giving a series of orchestral concerts with modern programmes. The first two took place on 8 and 15 November 1902 in the Beethovensaal. Busoni conducted the Philharmonic. The programmes included, among other first performances, works by Elgar, Guy Ropartz, Saint-Saëns, Christian Sinding, Sibelius and Delius.

Schoenberg had lived in Berlin since 1901. He must have known of Busoni's concerts, and perhaps went to one or two of them. They did not know each other yet personally, although in 1902 they were both living in the Augsburgerstrasse in the newly built Bavarian district, Busoni at No. 55, Schoenberg at No. 48. In the spring of 1903 Schoenberg must have written to Busoni, who answered him on 14 May: 'Your letter has pleased and interested me and made me very curious to see your score. So I would be grateful if you would send me the manuscript. Perhaps it will be my lot, as a new Siegfried, to step through the circle of fire which makes your work unapproachable and to wake it from the sleep of the unperformed.'

Which score? Schoenberg had finished the composition of the symphonic poem *Pelléas and Mélisande* on 28 February, suggested by Richard Strauss's reference to Maeterlinck's drama. As there were no other scores at the time it must have been this one. We do not know why Busoni did not perform it – Schoenberg conducted the first performance himself in 1905 in Vienna. But we can imagine that the enormous orchestra was too costly for the means which Busoni had at his disposal for his cycle of concerts.

However, Schoenberg's name appeared on the programme of the next orchestral concert, which Busoni conducted on 5 November 1903. But in this case it was only as an orchestrator: these were Syrian Dances by Heinrich Schenker in Schoenberg's orchestration, of which Busoni gave the first performance. Edward Dent says in his biography of Busoni that Schenker had sent Schoenberg to Busoni in September 1903. He does not say where the meeting was supposed to have taken place. However we know that Busoni spent the month of September in Berlin, in order to orchestrate his Piano Concerto. Schoenberg had returned to Vienna that summer, where he began his teaching work at the Schwarzwald Schools in the autumn. Perhaps it had been Heinrich Schenker's idea to send Schoenberg with the score to Busoni; however the project was not fulfilled.

There does not seem to have been any correspondence between the two musicians in the following years. However, during this time Busoni was developing the ideas of his extremely revolutionary approach to music, which were brought together in his *A New Aesthetic of Music*. This little book was published in 1907 by the Trieste publisher Schmidl. A copy was sent to Vienna with the dedication: 'To the Composer Arnold Schoenberg for understanding F. Busoni'.

In 1909 the correspondence started again. Busoni had continued his orchestral concerts since then steadily but irregularly and besides works by Debussy, Carl Nielsen, Hans Pfitzner, Vincent d'Indy and other composers he performed some of his own. The twelfth programme on 2 January 1909 contained an orchestral scherzo by Bartók. On 16 July he wrote to Schoenberg that he would like to perform the Chamber Symphony but had had to cancel the concerts for the season of 1909/10 and they would not be continued later. But in the same letter Busoni asks about the Piano Pieces which Schoenberg must have told him about. These are the first two of opus 11, which has been finished in February; the third one was written later and finished on 7 August 1909.

Before this the first two pieces had been sent off to Busoni. He reacted very positively and in detail on 26 July:

Honoured Herr Schoenberg; I have received your pieces and the letter with them. Both testify to a person who thinks and feels, which I have already recognized in you. Of your works I know a quartet, some songs and at one time I had the score of Pelléas *and* Mélisande *in my hand. The instrumentation of Schenker's dances (which I performed in Berlin) testified to your admirable orchestral virtuosity. Starting from this standpoint, your piano pieces were no surprise to me – i.e. I knew more or less what to expect. I knew naturally that I would be dealing with an art which is subjective, individual and founded on feeling – and that these would be refined artistic structures with which you will bring me in contact. All this has been fulfilled and I am extremely glad at such an event.*

However, my impression as a pianist is different; I cannot get away from this, perhaps because of my education or because of my onesidedness as a specialist. – The first doubts about your music 'as piano pieces' arose because of the small span of the writing in the circumference of time and space. The piano is a short-breathed instrument and one can't help it enough. However, I will work through the pieces again until they really get in to my blood – and then perhaps I will think differently.

This is not meant to be a judgement or a criticism – I would not presume to give you either of these, especially in face of such individuality as yours, but simply a report of the impression I received and my opinion as a pianist.

Meanwhile, I thank you and greet you in friendly terms. I would like to continue to have your confidence, and please tell me if there is anything I could do. Yours very sincerely Ferruccio Busoni.

A postscript follows:

I have now had your pieces with me for five days and have worked on them every day. I understand your intentions and have tried, after some preparation, to produce the sounds and moods which you expect. However, the task is made more difficult by too great conciseness – that is the word. So that I am not misunderstood by you, I'll take the liberty of giving you a little illustration of my words – in my own defence. You write:

in order to translate orchestral writing into pianistic writing:

But perhaps that does not correspond with your intentions at all.

Schoenberg received this letter in Steinakirchen, where he was working intensively on the Orchestral Pieces opus 16. He interrupted these, perhaps provoked by Busoni's remarks, and wrote the third piano piece. It is different from the other two in style and technique and shows an avoidance of thematic and motivic working in the same way Schoenberg used this method in the monodrama *Erwartung*, which he wrote shortly afterwards. However, there is no trace of an enlargement of the writing in space and time, – Busoni had complained of its concentration. It is only 35 bars long (as against 64 and 66 in Nos. 1 and 2) and it is the shortest of the pieces; the upper and lower registers of the instrument are hardly used more in it than in the others.

However, Busoni did not content himself with expressing his doubts. On 9 August his letter of July was followed by a further pianistic criticism of opus 11. And finally he 'confessed' to Schoenberg that he had 're-orchestrated' No. 2. He said it was a private idea of his own, but he did not want to conceal it, even if Schoenberg was angry with him.

Schoenberg was not angry. Busoni was so attracted by the pieces that he recommended them to his own publisher, Breitkopf and Härtel in Leipzig. In the letter in which he wrote about Schoenberg on 26 August, he said that he knew the composer by correspondence and not personally. So the hypothesis of their first meeting in 1903 is wrong.

Breitkopf and Härtel seem to have had no interest in Busoni's proposal. Immediately after his return from Steinakirchen Schoenberg arranged a visit to Universal Edition at the beginning of October at which his Piano Pieces and works by Webern were played. On 30 November Busoni met Emil Hertzka on a night journey from Berlin to Vienna. As well as other plans, the publication of his 'Concert Interpretation' of the second piece of Schoenberg's opus 11 was arranged. This appeared at the same time as opus 11 at the end of 1910, after Schoenberg had again complained on 28 September about the delay in their printing.

Busoni's occupation with Schoenberg's piano music (which he never played in public) had been stimulating to him. 'Your pieces have given me the idea of a new "Piano notation", which – as I believe – is a "find" ', he writes in a postscript to a letter of 7 October 1909, which also said: 'I am always on your side when anyone ever talks about you or whenever the possibility of such a conversation can be created'.

In the summer of 1910 there was a further correspondence about opus 11. Schoenberg hurt Busoni by supposing that the latter did not understand his pieces. This was more than Busoni could bear. He had tears of laughter in his eyes when he read the letter, so comic did he find Schoenberg's doubts: 'Your means of expression is new, but not your piano writing, which is poorer. I believe that you write much better for the orchestra, for instance.'

In 1911 they had a personal meeting. Busoni had spoken strongly on Schoenberg's behalf to his influential friends, when Edward Clark was trying to arrange Schoenberg's move to Berlin. He went to two of Schoenberg's lectures at the Stern Conservatorium, introduced Steuermann to him as a pupil, and heard Schoenberg's concert of first performances in the Harmoniumsaal. Schoenberg for his part was so excited by Busoni's 'Berceuse Élégiaque', that he wrote in his diary that he had done him an injustice. In 1920 he arranged the piece for use by his Vienna Society for Private Musical Performances; the combination was flute, clarinet, harmonium, piano and string quintet.

In the Harmony Book too Schoenberg acknowledged him as a superior and intelligent artist whom he admired very much. He only said 'he could save himself the trouble of working out hundreds of scales'. This is the first reference to *A New Aesthetic of Music*, where 113 seven-note scales are mentioned which are possible within the twelve-note octave. On 29 January Schoenberg wrote in his diary:

> *Lecture yesterday. Busoni was there. Thanked me very warmly for my letter and was really very nice. I think it is possible that we will meet again. He certainly wanted it himself. For he is without doubt a man of genius. In any case far the best person whom I have met here. In the lecture I proposed my ideas about genius and talent. Especially the one that genius is the future form of humanity. This seems to have pleased Busoni very much. (I am very glad about this!) He wants me to give a lecture at his house in front of many guests. I am not opposed to this.*

Two temperaments of this kind could not always remain at peace. And there were intermediaries, who with the best intentions created misunderstandings and frictions. Busoni spent the summer of 1912 composing in his fine Berlin apartment on the Viktoria Luiseplatz. In a conversation with Edward Clark he devised a plan for a music school in which he and Schoenberg were to collaborate. Schoenberg was spending his summer holidays in Carlshagen on the Usedom and was told by Clark about this conversation. He understood that the Institute would be run by him. Busoni, who spent eight months every year on concert tours, would hold master classes. Busoni wrote a mocking letter about this proposed relationship on 27 July, in which he said that Schoenberg had taken up an idea which he had let fall and enriched it by his imagination. Schoenberg replied by return of post. He, Schoenberg, had only reproduced what Clark had told him. He defended himself against his 'reprimand for my presumption in wishing to be in a position of superior authority to you, this being a product of my vivid imagination'. However, earlier in the letter there is an important remark: 'My imagination is myself, for I myself am but a creature of this imagination'.

In 1910 the Leipzig Insel-Verlag took over the half-forgotten *New Aesthetic*, which Busoni had entrusted to the obscure publisher Schmidl. It now appeared as No. 65 in the famous Insel Library, a kind of predecessor of our pocket Books and paperbacks. Each of the volumes, which were of a high standard both literarily and in their printing, only cost 50 pfennig. In 1916, during the First World War, when Italy was already fighting against the Central Powers and Busoni was living in neutral Switzerland, the little book was published again, this time as No. 202. Schoenberg possessed this edition of it. It became one of the most important features of his library. Schoenberg sometimes made marginal comments in books, as in his **Karl Kraus** volumes and in the German translation of Balzac's *Seraphita*. In Busoni's *Aesthetic* marginal notes took on the proportions of a large dissertation which cannot really be separated from the text to which it belongs.

The marginal notes are not dated. We don't know whether they were written shortly after each other or over a long period of time. One passage is devoted to thoughts about Hans Pfitzner, who in 1917 had published a little pamphlet attacking Busoni's book under the title *Danger of Futurism*. Schoenberg also possessed this booklet, and as we shall see later on, occupied himself with it in detail. So his notes on Busoni were not written before 1917.

It does not matter when they were written; the thoughts in these marginal notes show Schoenberg's aesthetic position in such a remarkable way that they are worth going into in detail.

There is agreement about the distinction between historical and theoretical forms in music. On Busoni's sentence: 'Our law-givers have retained the Form as a symbol, and made it into a fetish, a religion' Schoenberg remarks 'Very good', and he gives the same praise to the final sentence on the same page: 'Is it not singular, to demand of a composer originality in all things, and to forbid it as regards form? No wonder that, once he becomes original he is accused of formlessness.'

Schoenberg also agreed with Busoni's idea that music sets in vibration our human moods, but not that the moving course causes of itself these spiritual affections: 'Is it possible to imagine how a poor, but contented man could be represented by music? The contentment, the state of his soul, can be interpreted by music; where does the poverty appear or the important ethical problem . . . This is due to the fact that "poor" denotes a phase of terrestrial and social conditions which cannot be found in the eternal harmony'.

Schoenberg's praise rises to a 'splendid!', where Busoni speaks about new theatre music and says that it seeks to repeat scenes passing on the stage instead of 'fulfilling its own proper mission of interpreting the soul states of the persons represented'. And Busoni says further: 'The storm is visible and audible without aid from music; it is the invisible and inaudible, the spiritual processes of the personages portrayed, which music should render intelligible'.

The statement of a dramatic aesthetic of this kind makes Schoenberg add two sentences which go far beyond Busoni's thoughts and formulate an important part of his artistic creed: 'The real task of the art of the theatre is different: it is to use the means of the theatre for the external representation of inner events. For the artist the theatre is exactly the same as an orchestra and the drama is a symphony, for there is only one kind of art.'

And his comment is 'more or less right!' on Busoni's doubts about singing words on the stage and his idea that singing pieces should be about something unbelievable, so that 'one impossibility supports the other and so both become possible and acceptable'.

This is where the two points of view divide more and more. When Busoni asks where music is indispensable on the stage, Schoenberg replies: 'Nowhere'. When Busoni suggests dances, marches, songs and supernatural phenomena as reasons for using music, Schoenberg contradicts him: 'These are purely formal reasons'. Busoni wants the opera to be a world of appearance which gives what cannot be found in real life, and Schoenberg, a greater believer in the future than Busoni, comments: cannot *yet* be found in life. But above all they diverge in their idea of the position of the audience. Busoni, who thus anticipates Bertolt Brecht's entire artistic position, would like the audience not to devote itself to a charming illusion as if it was an experience, and Schoenberg remarks: 'Oh, no!!'

To Busoni's anti-illusionist demand '. . . If the listener wants to taste the theatrical effect, he should never regard it as reality, and artistic enjoyment should not sink to the level of human participation' Schoenberg remarks: 'Artistic enjoyment is the highest form of human participation'.

The two disagree on the question of notation. For Busoni it is an ingenious method of putting an improvisation into a fixed form, and is related to the improvisation as the portrait is to the living model. Schoenberg finds 'that the portrait has the higher artistic life, while the model has only a lower life'. And he says that the performance will be all the greater if one follows the indications in the score. The interpreter should be a spiritual servant of the work, not its educator or tutor. 'He must read every wish from its lips'. There are two imperfections which stand in its way – that of notation and that of the interpreter, whose individuality wants to lead a full life instead of getting inside the work: 'And so the interpreter mostly becomes a parasite on the exterior, when he could be the artery in the circulation of the blood'. Hard words in a discussion with a great pianist!

Later he comes on Busoni's criticism of the concept of 'depth', which he ascribes to the apostles of the Ninth Symphony. This is the point on which Pfitzner attacked him violently. Schoenberg, too, has doubts. The cheerfulness of the Champagne Aria in *Don Giovanni*, to which Busoni ascribes more depth than many funeral marches or nocturnes, comes just as much from the depths of human nature as the overflow of a deep intimacy. However, one looks for depth usually on the side of seriousness rather than on the cheerful side. One speaks indeed of the deepest and highest seriousness, but not of high but only of deep sadness, which is also called depression.

Busoni's comment on Wagner's remark. 'It is my misfortune to possess no routine', makes Schonberg defend both Wagner and a technical facility which he regards as inborn and part of one's nature: 'It is obvious that a hand can grip better than a foot, that a drill will make a deep hole more quickly than a hammer, that, in a word, inborn characteristics which were set in advance make a personal or object suitable for a certain purpose, whereas on the contrary the lack of these make him unsuitable. If a composer – somebody who is fitted to compose, possesses these means together with the force of his expression, Wagner, although he had something new to say was also able to say it; this is not routine but a kind of animal safety will always provide an organ in the right place. Wagner could do this; but he could not do anything mechanical!'

Busoni says that the development of music is wrecked by our musical instruments. Schoenberg sees in this an over-appraisal of the apparatus of sound. He says that a C major chord in mixed scoring works in a similar way when it is written for strings. 'Important differences in sound come less from their position than from the actual writing. The kind, the number, the character and the relationship, the rhythm, the accents and other dynamics in the composed parts which take part in the music have a much greater influence'. So the positions of the two are clearly described: on one side that of the great instrumentalist, who at the same time was a creative musician. On the other side that of a creator who does not regard the instrument any higher than Beethoven did the 'miserable violin' of his interpreter Schuppanzigh.

Busoni regards alterations of musical character by transposition as imaginary: 'When a well-known face looks out of a window it does not matter whether it gazes down from the first storey or from the third'. Schoenberg counters: 'One can think for instance of the Wanderer motif (musical example, 4 chords) two octaves higher, then the difference in character is felt . . . Certainly: the proportions remain the same. But 'in art two times two is not always four and sixteen divided by two is not immediately eight', as Kandinsky once replied to me quite rightly, when I asked him whether he needed such a large format for his pictures, whether it was necessary?'

Kandinsky's reply is in a letter of 13 January 1912, which Josef Rufer published in his catalogue of Schoenberg's works on page 186. The passage runs: 'Mathematically 4 is to 2 as 8 is to 4. Artistically – no. Mathematically, $1+1=2$, artistically $1—1$ can also be 2'. So Schoenberg was quoting from memory. However, the question of transposition led him to further thoughts and comments. Transposed keys are to a certain extent foreign keys, if they are treated as such. If this happened in a logical manner, it could be an artistic advantage. And he draws an example from optics. One can get powerful effects in a watercolour by painting parts of it in oil. But if one gets perfect effects in watercolour only then it would be unnecessary to do any more.

The comparison with human relationships is less convincing: 'I can regard my brother as my true friend and intimate, and act according to this. But I can also say: I choose my friends myself according to my own nature; this relation is near to me through the accident of birth, I have not chosen him myself, he is neither my friend nor my intimate'.

He makes a detailed attack on the 113 keys, which Busoni worked out as possible seven-note series within the octave. Schoenberg regarded the medieval modes as a primeval error of the human spirit; Busoni's keys were due to a dry method of construction. In view of the many rules which applied to these 113 scales and which a musician must learn in order to use them – what happened to the freedom demanded by Busoni? And he quotes ironically the appearance of the music at the beginning of Busoni's exposition, regarding it as that of a child strumming on the keyboard. With a keynote of C, the relationships for instance in a key C–D flat–E flat–F flat–G flat–A–B–C must be worked out with great difficulty. 'For otherwise I would have here only a misty exotic character, but no artistic character.'

At this point Schoenberg inserts the flute solo which begins the 'Sick Moon' in *Pierrot Lunaire*. 'Whether this melody is beautiful or good is not the point; I don't affirm that it is good, but I believe it is. But it does not correspond to the godlike freedom of the strumming child, which springs out of the prison of its keys! Here is no procedure but the idea itself (if anyone can find one, I will give my oath against it)! I did not have to work out a keynote or any other note, I was able to use all the twelve notes, and I did not have to put myself into the Procrustean bed of motivic phrasing, I didn't need any cadences, sections, or beginnings and ends of phrases. As I say: this melody may displease many people, but everybody will agree that it is 'freer' than many of those written in one of the 113 keys. Perhaps it is the preference for freedom which destroys Busoni. He lacks the freedom, of which he speaks, and is in fact the law-giver . . .'

The revolutionary ideas at the end of Busoni's book, the thirds and sixths of a tone, the electronic musical instrument of Thaddeus Cahill are not discussed by Schoenberg in detail. His last marginal note only discusses summarily the 'unusual material' welcomed by Busoni. After remarking that Busoni over-valued and Pfitzner undervalued the worth of this material, his commentary on the New Aesthetic of Music ends with eulogy of craftsmanship, which confirms and varies what had been said in the first chapter of the Harmony Book, where theory is contrasted with craftsmanship: 'What good craftsman is not pleased with fine material. And what good musician does not also take pride in being a good craftsman. The joiner and the violinmaker are overjoyed by a fine piece of wood, the shoemaker by leather, the painter by colours, brush and canvas, the sculptor by marble – they all foresee the work to come – it stands before their eyes. Everybody knows: something is necessary in addition; it first has to be created. But they already see in the material its own future. The spirit is aroused – it doesn't matter who arouses it – but as long as it is there one can shout Hallelujah'.

This completes a circle of thought. For Schoenberg had already introduced the conception of the material in quite another connection. Busoni explains that we admire Mozart as a seeker and inventor, but not his tonics, dominants, developments and codas. 'Yes!', says Schoenberg on this. 'The material which is destined for the shaping of timeless things, attracts it; it is worthy of honour for us. It is the material vestibule of the spirit'.

Respect for material. Respect for craftsmanship. Schoenberg had had these feelings from his youth onwards. He loved to work with leather, canvas, paper and string if he wanted to bind books and music artistically. As a carpenter he made book-shelves, tables, chairs and a little ladder on wheels with wood. He cut curtains from material, stretched them on a wooden frame and painted them. He tinkered and sketched. He worked as a painter with oil, crayon, watercolours, drew with charcoal, pen and pencil. Everything practical was important to him, and he hated all theoretical science. 'Who dares to ask for theory here!', was the last sentence in the Harmony Book.

His interpretation of the concept of the material separates him radically from Busoni. For Schoenberg material is the note which is still unformed, for Busoni it is the unusual sound.

As in his copy of Busoni's book, Schoenberg also wrote in Pfitzner's *Danger of the Futurists* many marginal notes, some of which are quite long. This was the basis of a larger essay entitled 'False Alarm'. This consists of more than seven closely written pages, but was left unfinished. Schoenberg later noted on the manuscript that he had found Pfitzner's brochure worse and worse as he read it and he finally regarded it unnecessary to reply to it. However, both the marginal notes and the essay contain some important thoughts. Schoenberg first attacks Pfitzner's polemical method. Then he affirms that his own answer is not the expression of a party point of view. As he and his works are mentioned neither by Busoni nor by Pfitzner, he should not feel that he is aimed at. He says: 'If party standpoints were the rule for me, so Pfitzner *and* Busoni, would be my party, as they seem to be two of the less important musical characters of our time'. Then he defends Busoni against Pfitzner's reproaches of 'leaps and zig-zag motion'. Although Busoni's book is not divided cleanly into main sections 1, 2, 3 and subsidiary sections A, B, C, his purpose and plan seem very simple and clear. Busoni had seen a picture of the future of music and had aimed to set forth what he had seen with the most suitable means. He regarded spirit and feeling as imperishable, technique and tastes in performance as perishable. He subjected the changeable element to a criticism, which did not remain negative, 'but in the sense of the picture which Busoni had seen often succeeds, with a great many ideas, in setting up, if not "aesthetic laws", at least, "comprehensible theses",' – which Pfitzner had denied. He then cites Busoni's main ideas and objects: notation, transcription, musicality, feeling, taste, style, depth, routine and technical instruments. Perhaps, says Schoenberg, Busoni would have done better to call his book *Suggestions for a New Aesthetic.*

He says that Pfitzner's polemic was founded on his rejection of innovations in music which no longer used traditional elements. He regarded this new movement as futuristic and spoke of the danger of futurists and of futurist trash. As Pfitzner did not mention any composers by name, he, Schoenberg, would gladly volunteer to be one of them. He didn't know the music of the Italian futurists, but assumed that Pfitzner meant composers like Busoni, Scriabin, Stravinsky 'and another young Russian, whose name I have forgotten', and himself. (Probably Schoenberg meant Prokofiev as the other young Russian).

The last section of the fragment shows us Schoenberg's position and view of art. It runs: 'To say that art has no purpose is a remark which was right so long as not everybody knew it. Today it is a commonplace and therefore can be regarded as relatively false. (That is futuristic arguing, Pfitzner would surely say). But no, it works like this: this remark, like all human perceptions, was never entirely right, and one must recognize when it is no longer new. For art has at least a purpose in the one moment where it does not reach its purpose. But if all the previous happenings which show a purpose fulfilled, if these show that the art was directed towards this purpose so that it could reach it, then art is on its way to fulfil this purpose, and as it never remains stationary has always had this purpose. As we can see, it is now almost illogical to speak about the aims of art at all. In considering a long period of time one can find the abstract concept of development from the fulfilment of many small aims. If we say that this development must lead upwards, in the worst case this is a sentimental mistake full of wrong feeling'. In general Schoenberg finds that Pfitzner has misunderstood Busoni. He also dislikes him for using concepts like 'sympathetic' and 'unsympathetic' in such a serious discussion. He expresses this above everything else in his marginal notes in Pfitzner's libellous script.

THE FAITH OF THE DISILLUSIONED MAN

On the blank side of a letter from Hermann Bahr Schoenberg doodled, as he often did, a shape which represented nothing and next to it in large letters the two names AUGUST STRIND-BERG – ARNOLD SCHOENBERG. It was the first time that he mentioned the Swedish poet. Bahr's letter is dated: 10 April 1909. In the spring of this year Mahler came back from his second visit to America. Paul Stefan has described the evening in which Mahler, who had returned for a short stay in Vienna, spent with Schoenberg and his pupils and friends. They were talking about Dostoyevsky. Mahler was surprised that the young people knew nothing about the Russian novelist and said to Schoenberg that he should read Dostoyevsky with them, and that this was more important than counterpoint. At this Webern, as if in school, stood up and said: 'Please, we have got Strindberg'.

Alban Berg was enthusiastic about this 'gigantic great man' in a passionate letter of 25 July 1909 to his fiancée Helene Nahowsky. This contains seven pages of spiritual 'altitude flight', which always leads back to Strindberg from *Tristan*, Mahler, Strauss, Schoenberg and Webern, from Karl Kraus, Nietzsche, Hamsun, and Hermann Hesse, from Max Oppenheimer and Kokoschka; he defends and praises his literary works untiringly. In 1910 Berg was so much obsessed by the poet, that he dreamt of visiting him.

Strindberg's works were published by Georg Müller in Munich in Emil Schering's translation from 1902 onwards; Schoenberg possessed them all in 1912 and added the ones which appeared later. The gloomy light of the Scandinavian prophet fitted the landscape of emancipated music about 1909. Schoenberg's spiritual development had grown in a similar way to Strindberg's. Their youth was liberal but still religious, and their religious doubts were confirmed by enlightenment. Strindberg, the Protestant, had turned when young to the belief of the omnipotence of science. Later he described how in 1867 'all religious discussion ceased among educated people and God disappeared from literature' (Postscript to the *Legends* of 1898). Dissatisfied with science and with his own experiments, which were concerned with alchemy and the production of gold, he found access to a new spiritual life seventeen years later. In 1894 he lost his scepticism, which 'had threatened to devastate all intellectual life', and began 'to put himself experimentally in the position of a believer'. Tertullian's 'Credo quia absurdum' was his motto.

The dismal path, often on the borders of madness, surrounded by imaginary threats from supernatural powers, was described impressively by Strindberg in his *Inferno*. On Palm Sunday 1896 Strindberg found a copy of Balzac's *Seraphita* in a bookstall in the arcades of the Paris Théâtre de l'Odéon. It became his gospel. In September of the same year he visited his divorced wife, the writer Frida Uhl, in the Lower Austrian village of Klam. Here and in Saxony he read an edition of Swedenborg. He saw his ideas confirmed: 'Where are we going? To the beliefs of our fathers. To Catholicism. Occultism has played its part, miracles have been explained by science. Theosophy, Karma and Buddhism lead indirectly to Golgotha.'

In 1897 Strindberg had the experiences which are described in the fragment 'Jacob Wrestling' at the end of the *Legends*. In Saint Sulpice the poet was greatly impressed by Eugène Delacroix's picture 'Jacob wrestling with the Angel'. This led to imaginary meetings with an unknown person, delusions of the senses which were rooted in puritan self-reproach; 'When in thoughts, words or writings I approach material which is inflammatory or indecent, I hear a mighty bass note as if from an organ or from the trunk of an elephant when he trumpets and is angry'. The motive of immediate punishment or warning after a sin or a sin of thought dominates Strindberg's life about this time in a manic manner. It is the predominating content of 'Jacob Wrestling', combined with a firm belief in God, in the 'Mechanic' who has set in motion the mechanism of the world proclaimed by science.

This fragment by Strindberg moved Schoenberg deeply and stimulated him creatively for years. He spoke about it to his most trusted friends, not only Berg and Webern, but also Erwin Stein, Heinrich Jalowetz and Karl Linke.

Balzac's *Seraphita* had an even stronger effect on him. Schoenberg, who had admired the French poet all his life and had read many of his works, found in the philosophical novel, which belongs to the cycle of *Human Comedy*, not only a definition of prayer which he repeats in his own writings, but also a figure which was raised like an angel above the earthly world, the hermaphrodite Seraphitus–Seraphita, a synthesis of masculine intelligence and feminine beauty. Balzac's visions were based on Swedenborg's doctrine of the 'Angel Spirits', who form a transitional stage between man and angel. According to this God did not create any angels which had not grown out of the earthly human form. They go through three stages of love – always in the formula which Balzac puts in the mouth of the old pastor and admirer of Swedenborg Becker; love to one's own ego, to the world and to heaven. The idea of stepwise development, also proclaimed by Theosophy and Anthroposophy, was illuminating both for Schoenberg's artistic position and his logical thought.

Swedenborg's paradoxical conviction that his Angelology was based on mathematics also illuminated him. The self-love of the angel-man, of which the highest form incorporates genius, was familiar to him. The step to the next higher level, from the genius to the prophet as an incarnation of world-love, followed logically.

He was also taken with the grandiose scene where Balzac had set his Seraphita novel, the enormous Nordic landscape with rocky peaks and gorges on the Norwegian coast between Oslo and Trondheim, where organic life struggles against the winter. This went beyond Jacobsen's Wild Hunt in the Danish Gurre and also beyond the rocky landscape of the *Glückliche Hand*. In Schoenberg's imagination Balzac's mystic action formed a trilogy.

In the spring of 1911 he spoke to Alban Berg about a plan of setting 'Jacob's Wrestling' to music. 'He wanted at that time to write to Strindberg in detail, and even had the idea of asking Strindberg for a text'; this was Berg's answer to Webern, who had told him on 27 July 1912 about Schoenberg's project of making a stage work lasting three evenings from Balzac's *Seraphita*. On 8 August Webern wrote about this again. The beginning of the stage work was to be the scene where Seraphitus climbs the Fallberg with Minna Becker. The idea of combining 'Jacob Wrestling' with *Seraphita* was given up meanwhile. Webern was able to tell Berg that Strindberg's fragment should act as a kind of previous history of the figure of Wilfried, the young man whom Balzac opposed to Minna as an earthly pendant. So the two texts were mixed up together firmly in Schoenberg's plan.

He wanted to set the conversations and monologues from Balzac's novel as verbally as possible. The Ascension, in which

Seraphitus-Seraphita keeps the two earthly lovers, Minna and Wilfried, on the earth, was to end the trilogy. This would demand 'very large massive choirs and an enormous orchestra', as Webern described it. In Balzac's text myriads of angels appear at the ascension of the Seraph. He mentions a hymn, heavenly sounds and an exalted Hallelujah.

At the first performance in Hamburg of *Pierrot Lunaire* in 1912 Schoenberg met Richard Dehmel, whose poems he admired and many of which he had set since 1899, even before Dehmel's 'Verklärte Nacht', which gave the programme of his string sextet of the same name. A correspondence started between the two men, in which Schoenberg outlined the plan of an oratorio on 13 December. The description of the 'Men of To-day' is an autobiographical confession. The way of the path of the atheist who still has some residue of the old belief in the form of superstition leads through materialism, socialism and anarchy to a new meeting with God. He struggles with him, and finally succeeds in finding him and becomes religious. He learns to pray. In describing the fight with God Schoenberg mentions 'Jacob Wrestling'; the phrase 'Learn to pray' comes from Balzac's *Seraphita*.

Schoenberg confesses to the Hamburg poet that he had wanted to write this oratorio for a long time.

> '*Originally I intended to write the words myself. But I no longer think myself equal to it. Then I thought of adapting Strindberg's* "Jacob Wrestling". *Finally I came to the idea of beginning with positive religious belief and intended adapting the final chapter, the Ascension, from Balzac's* Seraphita. *But I could never shake off the thought of:* "The Modern Man's Prayer", *and I often thought: If only Dehmel . . . !*'

The poet sent him by return of post a text he had written in 1911, which described his path to 'a new belief in God', the 'Feast of Creation' with the sub-title 'Oratorium natale'. Schoenberg was interested and sketched out a duet with the titles 'Mother-Soul' and 'Father-Spirit' from Dehmel's text, but then made other attempts at composition. Many sketches were put together, and became a complete work as 'Symphony for Soloists, Mixed Choir and Orchestra'. Josef Rufer found all the sketches and notes for this among the manuscripts after Schoenberg's death in Brentwood Park. The work had to be put together from several sections and movements, the order of which was not entirely clear. Schoenberg called the first movement 'Turning-point in Life'; the commentary shows him looking back to the past and forward to the future and describes his character: gloomy, obstinate, self-contained.

The second movement is a scherzo, 'The Joy of Life', in two parts, and the first part has two trios. 'All motifs which are of importance later' are contained in this, according to Schoenberg's commentary. The third movement, 'Allegretto', he called 'The Bourgeois God'. The titles of the following two movements were later crossed out, but come in this order: 4. 'Interlude' and 5. 'Psalm on Biblical Words'.

Between the second and third movements a section called '1st Part' is inserted, a 'Reprise of the Whole with Song', divided into three parts on three poems by Dehmel from *Beautiful Wild World*, the 'Shout of Joy', the 'Marriage of the Gods' and the 'Aeonic Hour'. The Allegretto is also based on a text by Dehmel, partly from *Beautiful Wild World*, partly from the Oratorium Natale 'Feast of Creation'. This dates the sketch: *Beautiful Wild World* was published in 1913.

The fourth movement has two sub-divisions. 'Dissatisfied. The bourgeois god is not enough' is one of them. The other only mentions the name of the Indian poet Rabindranath Tagore and then three of his poems: 'Death of the Servant', 'Divinity of the Ruined Temple' and – as a quartet for solo singers, 'I know that a Day will come.' On the fifth movement Schoenberg notes: 'No. 100, I plunge in the depths of the sea', a verse which comes neither in the hundredth psalm nor in any other one.

The synopsis comes to a second part, which begins with 'Dance of Death of the Principles', a text written by Schoenberg himself; a bracket below the title adds 'basic movements'. Then follows 'Funeral' and 'Funeral Oration' (as it were). Also 'Dance of Death' and finally 'Prayer'. The funeral speech contains a 'short sketch of events which come in between', the insertion 'Tagore No. 88' and the addition: 'with distant orchestra: from Shout of Joy' (a reference to the Dehmel poem in the first part).

In the prayer Schoenberg notes references to Isaiah 58 and 66, and Jeremiah 7 and 17, prophetic books about punishment for false religion, hypocrisy and idolatry, and also the Last Judgment.

Then comes, as the last section of this synopsis, the most important title, in No. 5: 'The Belief of the Disillusioned Man': the combination of sober and sceptical consciousness of reality and belief. The Mystic is contained in the Simple'.

This 'Belief of the Disillusioned Man' is another way of describing Strindberg's conversion, which is set out in the play

After Damascus, and also stems from Dehmel's 'New Belief in God'.

In the last year but one of his life Schoenberg wrote an article 'My attitude towards politics' which described the influences to which he was subjected in his youth and his view of the world. At the age of twenty he had been introduced to Marxist theories by friends, doubtless Oscar Adler and David J. Bach. At that time he sympathized strongly with the Social Democrats, took part in their struggle for the broadening of their right to free votes, and as conductor of male choruses was called 'Comrade'. But even before he was twenty-five the difference between himself and the workers became clear to him.

Austrian social democracy was anti-religious at that time, and even if Schoenberg told Kandinsky in a letter of 1922 that he had never been free from religious feelings, one can be sure that the atheistical side of the socialist-materialist creed was not unknown to him. He wrote to Dehmel about the atheist with a remnant of the old belief.

The sketches for the symphony of 1912 to 1914 are unfinished. However, thoughts and musical revisions from the last part were taken over into the *Jacob's Ladder*. Twenty-five years later Schoenberg revealed this connection in his celebrated letter to Nicolas Slonimsky (3 June 1937). There he mentions a theme in the scherzo in which the twelve notes are used for the first time: D–G–E flat–A–G sharp–E–F–B–C–G flat–D flat–E flat.

This theme can also be found in the sketches for the symphony. It is dated 27 May 1914 (Schoenberg wrongly put it rather later, at the end of 1914 or at the beginning of 1915) and is used as an introduction to Dehmel's 'Shout of Joy', and then in many other ways. The three mirror forms of it, inversion, retrograde and retrograde inversion, are also written down. It is first repeated monotonously in regular quaver movement in a presto with a metronome marking $3/4 = 84$–90, and it is accompanied by three-part chords in fourths.

Schoenberg occupied himself with Strindberg and Balzac right up to his death. In the preface to the Harmony Book, written in July 1911, Strindberg is mentioned togetherwith Maeterlinck and Weininger as thinkers who had touched on unsolved problems. Schoenberg's diary of 28 January 1912 mentions the Swedish poet's thanks for congratulations on his birthday:

Just my feelings and my experiences: Devotion and confusion in the face of praise of which one receives too little; and on the other side pride and indignation when one is deprived of deserved recognition.

Strindberg was sixty-three on 22 January. His early death in May 1912 deprived Schoenberg of the hope of sending proposals for working together with the man whom he admired.

An idea from Balzac's *Seraphita* emerged again in 1941 in connection with composition. On 26 March Schoenberg gave a lecture at the University of California in Los Angeles on 'Composition with 12 notes'. As in all his theoretical writings since 1911 he mentions the recognition of the connection of musical logic in all directions. 'The two – or – more dimensional space in which musical ideas are presented is a unit', he says. And later on he pursues this: 'The unity of musical space demands an absolute and unitary perception'. As an example he mentions Swedenborg's heaven, as described in Balzac's novel, where there is no absolute below, no right or left, no forwards or backwards.

Of all the fundamental views of his theory this is the most innovatory and revolutionary. It not only explains the four forms in which twelve-tone melodies appear, i.e. their inversion, retrograde and retrograde inversion as mirror forms of the basic form: It also reveals the analytical methods with which Schoenberg enlarged all conventional formal musical theories in his interpretation of master-works from Bach to Brahms. Swedenborg – through Balzac and Strindberg – showed him the way to this. But the transference of this idea of heaven to musical forms is an act of creative intuition.

In the years before the First World War Schoenberg experienced the same disillusionment with the materialist-positive view of the world as almost all the great thinkers of the time. For him, who was so often erroneously treated and rejected as a purely intellectual musical music-constructor, there were no differences in principle between feeling and understanding. He quoted with pleasure Balzac's remark: 'the heart must be in the region of the head'. Among the axioms of his teaching what he called feeling for form was always important from at least 1911 onwards.

For a while he gave up work on the symphony. His move to Vienna cost time and energy. On 20 May he reported for military service and was sent back home. But on 29 July 1915 a letter of his to Zemlinsky gives new information about his plan for the symphony. He said that he had written something for it himself which was better than the poems by Dehmel which were originally meant for it. And a good deal of the music had already been sketched.

In August Schoenberg went to Semmering, where he was the guest of Frau Lieser. Alma Mahler was living near by. But the situation was full of tension. Erwin Stein, who visited Schoenberg here, heard of a terrible quarrel between Frau Lieser and her guest, and Alban Berg gave a dramatic description of it to Helene. Stein was even brought into these scenes. It was a situation of general nervousness, caused by the war, by the fact that all men were threatened with military service, and in Schoenberg's case by worry about his financial situation as well. Alma Mahler was fighting with an inner decision; on 18 August she married Walter Gropius.

In November Schoenberg was found fit for military service at his second call-up. As a volunteer for the last year he was allowed to choose his own regiment and on 15 December he entered the Hoch- und Deutschmeister-Regiment in Vienna. Next day a request went from the Vienna Society of Musicians to the Royal Hungarian Honved Ministry to set him free. As Schoenberg's father came from the province of Bratislava his sons – and also their families, were regarded as domiciled there and were Hungarian subjects. In 1916 Schoenberg was sent for training to the Officers' School in Bruck on the Leitha.

Now the Society of Hungarian Musicians entered the affair. Dr. Josef Polnauer, who was then secretary of the Society, wrote to Béla Bartók in Budapest saying that at the end of May, after finishing at the Officers' School, Schoenberg could be expected to be sent to the front. He said that Dr. Julius Bittner's attempts with the Austrian authorities had been frustrated by purely personal intrigues. What Bartók was able to do is unknown. But in June 1916 Schoenberg was released from service. (The few letters on the subject which have been discovered were published in Documenta Bartókiana, Vol. 2, and commented on by Professor Denis Dille.) Schoenberg still had to undergo a short, taxing period of service in Vienna, where he arrived on 17 May from Bruck. He had to be in the Prater at 6 o'clock every morning and did not get home till seven-thirty at night. This service ended in June. Schoenberg knew nothing about the efforts of his friends. He would have protested energetically against them. As he often said, he was proud to be called up and took his duties as a soldier seriously.

Romola Nijinsky, the widow of the great Russian dancer, describes a visit to Schoenberg in the Gloriettegasse in her memoirs. Frau Lieser brought her and Vaslav Nijinsky to

Schoenberg, for whom the dancer had had a great sympathy ever since he had heard *Pierrot Lunaire*. There was a heated discussion between the two men about instruction in art, until they agreed that in both their arts education was indispensible. The visit seems to have taken place in 1916, when the Nijinskys came to Vienna. They stayed there from January until the end of March. As Schoenberg was at Bruck on the Leitha until May, the meeting could only have taken place during one of his leaves. Romola Nijinsky emphasizes the warmth with which the Schoenbergs received her and her husband; she also spoke of the curious attraction of his bizarre and mystical paintings.

In the summer of 1916 he worked on the fourth of the Songs with Orchestra opus 22 on a text 'Vorgefühl', from Rilke's *Buch der Bilder*. This was begun on 19 July and finished on the 28th, and in November it was copied for Universal Edition by another hand. At the end of November the Schoenbergs went to visit Zemlinsky in Prague for a week, remaining there till 3 December. On returning to Vienna Schoenberg told his friend that he had decided to finish the second chamber symphony of 1907. However, this plan was given up in favour of work on the big choral symphony; Schoenberg did not finish the work until he reached America, at the suggestion of Fritz Stiedry. His relations with Zemlinsky were as close and friendly as in his youthful years. Zemlinsky had finished an opera on Oscar Wilde's *Florentine Tragedy*, which had its first performance in Stuttgart on 30 January 1917 and was to be performed soon afterwards in Prague and Vienna. Schoenberg and Webern went to the Prague première on 4 March; he stayed with Jalowetz and Webern with Zemlinsky. Dr. Marie Pappenheim was also there. On 27 April the same circle of friends, with Franz Schreker in addition, attended the first performance in Vienna. Zemlinsky stayed with Schoenberg, who called the opera a splendid work. He wrote in a letter of 5 May 1917 to Albertine Zehme: 'Meanwhile I am uncalled-for and not called up. – I am working on some theoretical works, and still on a text for a big work for chorus, soloists and orchestra. In addition I hold courses which are not badly attended.'

Meanwhile the position in the world had changed. Schoenberg's optimism and his belief in a quick, victorious end to the war was shaken more and more. Because of the hunger blockade provisions in Germany and Austria became more difficult to obtain in 1916. The allies turned down a peace offer by the

Central Powers. As Germany reacted with more intensive submarine warfare, the United States declared war on 6 April 1917. The Austrian Emperor Franz Josef died on 21 November. In March revolution broke out in Russia.

Austria had to call up her last reserves of men. In the summer Schoenberg was called up again. He was working on the sketches for *Jacob's Ladder*. On page 96 of the fourth sketch book he notes: 'Entering military service! 19 September 1917'. But on 7 December he was released from the light service to which he had been assigned, this time for good.

He had begun to write the text of *Jacob's Ladder* on 18 January 1915. However, the poem was not finished until two years later, on 26 May 1917, and was published the same summer by Universal Edition. Schoenberg began the composition on 19 June. When the Weberns visited him in August, he showed his friend some music from the oratorio.

About this time his financial position became serious. A ray of hope was brought by the arrival of a mysterious American called Köhler, who was sent to Vienna on a commercial and political mission. He took up Hertzka's plan of performing the 'Gurre-lieder' in New York with the composer conducting. Alban Berg met him for a meal in Hietzing. There was talk of ten performances and a fee of 5000 dollars. Schoenberg, whom Berg visited on the same evening (17 July 1917), was sceptical. Nothing more was heard of Köhler. Owing to Schoenberg's second call-up the whole plan could not be carried out.

Eugenie Schwarzwald met Berg and Erwin Stein on 6 September. 'She has taken Schoenberg's entire affairs in hand and is trying with a wonderful readiness to help to end Schoenberg's liability to military service and also to get rid of his financial trouble', Berg wrote to Helene. Now other pupils and friends joined in as well. Webern offered 1000 kronen, Jalowetz 2000, Stein a monthly contribution of several hundred. Schwarzwald wanted to ask rich friends for patronage, and sought help from the Arts Charity, the Society of Musicians and the Ministry of Education. Stein wanted to ask Alma Mahler for an honorarium from the Mahler Foundation.

Schoenberg's poverty continued. On 10 September Berg met Marie Pappenheim at Schoenberg's apartment. They spoke about a planned periodical and about the approaching end of the war. Schoenberg had to leave Frau Lieser's house on 1 October. For a short time he went to the Pension Astra, 9th District, Alserstrasse 32. Then he went to the 3rd District, Rechte Bahngasse 10. It was his last apartment in Vienna.

The text of *Jacob's Ladder* aroused a great sensation among Schoenberg's friends. Webern was enthusiastic: 'This gospel, this judgement of God, this synthesis of an enormous experience, and incredible belief. The last great speech of Gabriel is the solution of everything. The peak of human understanding up till now'. Zemlinsky too was deeply impressed.

Gabriel the Archangel, whose name means the strength of God, in Christian doctrine brings heavenly messages to man and interprets them. Webern was able to find the Balzacian interpretation of Swedenborg's heaven in the first words of the beginning of the *Jacob's Ladder*, and these also describe the nature of the music for Schoenberg: 'Whether right, left, forward or backwards, up or down – one has to go on without asking what lies before or behind one.' Gabriel gives every person information and advice about himself. The figures, One of the Called, a Protester, One Wrestling, the Chosen One, the Monk, One Dying, embody stages of maturity and completion. They have autobiographical traits. Their incarnations lead to God, who stands at the top of the heavenly ladder. This idea from the first book of Moses had many literary successors, up to Richard Beer-Hofmann and Thomas Mann. It is clear that Strindberg's Jacob fragment had an influence on Schoenberg's text. Schoenberg regards the ladder as a direct communication between man and heaven. Berthold Viertel said in an analysis that life and death are not opposites here but are shown in counterpoint.

Quotations appear in three places. The Wrestling Man strives for Arthur Schopenhauer's 'Painlessness', and he says with Luke 18, that he knows the Commandments and has kept them from his youth up. In Gabriel's great final speech there is a sentence from Balzac's *Seraphita*: 'He who prays has become at one with God.'

Schoenberg found it hard to bear the loss of his illusions. The destruction of all values which he experienced during the war showed him the uselessness of thought, invention and energy. In these years, he wrote in 1922 to Kandinsky, religion was his only support. The *Jacob's Ladder* text demonstrates the way to 'higher belief'. It is the belief of the disillusioned man.

We do not know if the study of Theosophical texts contributed to this belief. In 1971 there was no book by Helene Blavatsky in Schoenberg's library; and Rudolf Steiner's anthroposophical writings were not there either. However, in his article 'The Theosophical Element in Schoenberg's view of the world' in the symposium for Schoenberg's fiftieth birthday in 1924 Walter Klein explains that it is conviction which makes man a Theosopher. To this belongs 'the belief that the way of humanity leads through countless rebirths to higher and higher forms of being.'

Schoenberg felt the threatened defeat of Germany and Austria as a danger to many things which were dear to him through education and knowledge. From Karl Kraus, whom he had often admired and often criticised he was separated by his national pride, which was unwilling to admit the weaknesses of his own people. He lacked the caustic criticism of society, which Kraus had already written about in the summer of 1915 in the prologue of his apocalyptic drama *The Last Days of Humanity*.

Schoenberg asked for a second ticket for a reading by the poet. His letter of 14 November 1916 tells of a deep spiritual crisis: 'I hope I will soon find an opportunity of meeting you in the coffee house. *I am thirsting . . . for a conversation with you.* In the sight of unbearable depressions, since the beginning of the war, your words have often been a consolation to me.'

However, Schoenberg while a soldier set naïve poems like 'German Michel' by Otto Kernstock and in Bruck on the Leitha in 1916 he wrote the march 'The Iron Brigade' for piano and string quartet for a celebration evening of his one year's service. On 29 January he wrote on a card to Jemnitz in Budapest: 'You can imagine that I am not a particularly good soldier. However, the rank which I have reached – lance-corporal – did not fulfil my military ambitions. I like a fool thought that if I was going to be a soldier I should at least be a general. However, I have to stand in awe of every full corporal.' Jemnitz was also given information about Schoenberg's works and printed compositions.

Official art from 1914 to 1918 was far removed from metaphysical considerations. Independently from Schoenberg Alexander Scriabin was working in Moscow on a theosophical 'Mysterium', until his early death on 24 May 1915. The sketches of it contain twelve-tone melodies and chord complexes.

The theatres continued to play, but did not perform any works by living French, Italian, Russian or English authors. The novelties in the Vienna Volksoper in 1915 were *Marja* by Josef Bohuslav Foerster, who was a friend of Mahler's and also knew and admired Schoenberg, and in 1917 Julius Bittner's *Lieber*

Augustin. Frankfurt performed Schreker's *Die Gezeichneten* on 25 April 1918. Schoenberg's two one-act operas *Erwartung* and *Die Glückliche Hand* remained unperformed.

Alban Berg, who had been in the army since 1915, but was transferred at the end of May 1916 to the Ministry of War in Vienna, had been working since the summer of 1917 on his setting of George Büchner's *Wozzeck*. Schoenberg, whom he informed of this, did not agree with his choice of text. One should not set batmen to music but angels, he said censoriously, as Karl Rankl informed us in 'The Score' in 1952. Webern, who had also been in the army since 1915, was more or less unable to compose owing to his life as a soldier; up to 1918 he only wrote ten songs on texts of Strindberg, Karl Kraus, George Trakl and Bethge's 'Chinese Flute'; these were incorporated into op. 12 to 14. The folksong 'Der Tag ist Vergangen' in opus 12 of 1915 began his series of religious songs, which show his increasingly deeper religious convictions.

Foreign friends had left Germany; Kandinsky was in Russia, Busoni in neutral Switzerland. Scherchen sent postcards from a Russian prison camp. Schoenberg recognized the danger of isolation of the intellectuals. In Vienna a group of painters planned the foundation of a society of artists of all kinds. Schoenberg and Webern took part in a discussion about this. As nothing came of the plan, Schoenberg had the idea of founding a colony to which Webern and Berg also were to belong.

These thoughts were related to his wish to form spiritual communities, and also to his desire to teach. In the spring of 1917 Schoenberg gave lectures in Eugenie Schwarzwald's schools; in the middle of April he made notes about composition as regards motives and pitches. He wrote fourteen pages of a text about orchestration.

Then at the end of 1917 came his final demobilization. In Vienna conditions of life became more and more difficult. In 1918 Schoenberg decided to leave the capital, which was expensive and lacked provisions. On 1 April he moved to Mödling, where an apartment was free on the upper ground floor in Bernhardgasse 6. He knew the little town, where Beethoven had once lived, from his work as conductor of the male voice chorus there in the nineties. In 1904 he had spent the summer there with Mathilde and Trudi.

On 4 January 1918 he again took up work on the *Jacob's Ladder* and began the big interlude. In March he worked on it again and also on a string septet. These were the last compositions which he worked on in Vienna. His main work on his mighty creed, showing the belief of the disillusioned man, was finished. New tasks confronted him.

In 1955, four years after Schoenberg's death, Frau Gertrud Schoenberg entrusted Winfried Zillig with the work of making the unfinished composition into a performable shape. Schoenberg had written his last composition sketches in June 1921 and on 18 April 1922; these were concerned with the final chorus of the *Jacob's Ladder*. Zillig had at his disposal a short score and a sketchbook. Frau Schoenberg had a photocopy made of the 39 pages of short score. Zillig's work consisted essentially of producing from the short score and the sketches an appearance of the work which had been in the composer's mind, and setting out the result in full score. The first 120 bars of this score were performed for the first time in January 1958 by Hans Rosbaud in the Hamburg 'Neue Werk', i.e. before the whole score had been completed. The final result was performed in June 1961 under Rafael Kubelik at the I.S.C.M. Music Festival in Vienna at a special concert given by the Cologne Radio.

In Schoenberg's original plan there was to be a gigantic orchestra consisting of 20 flutes (10 also playing piccolo), 20 oboes (10 also playing English horn), 24 clarinets (6 in E flat, 12 in B flat, 6 bass clarinets), 20 bassoons (10 of them also playing contra-bassoon), 12 horns, 10 trumpets (2 of which were bass trumpets), 8 trombones (of which 2 were alto and 2 were bass), 6 contrabass tubas, 8 harps, celesta, percussion, 50 violins, 30 each of violas, celli and basses, 13 solo singers and a chorus of 720. Later sketches reduced these enormous forces to a normal size. So Zillig chose a symphony orchestra of the Richard Strauss type.

The Oratorio represents a simplification in its melodic and harmonic language in contrast to the works of 1908 to 1914, but it does not give up the fundamental emancipation of the dissonance or return to tonality in any way. It is a compendium of Schoenberg's language, from the early songs with their 'vagrant harmonies' through the fourth-chords of the First Chamber Symphony, the fluctuating melody of *Erwartung*, the song-speech of *Pierrot Lunaire* up to the mirror procedures of the Piano Pieces opus 23. Its construction is like that of the classical oratorio with speakers, chorus and solo singers; but the music is continuous with transitions between the individual sections. However, recitatives and recitations are differentiated from pure arias and ensembles, and there are also passages in which recitative and aria are mixed, and the speaking voice often introduces a new musical texture. The spoken choruses are written in up to twelve parts.

As well as the main part of Gabriel (baritone) there are three tenors (One of the Called, a Protester, a Monk), a lyrical baritone (the Chosen One), a deep speaking voice (One Wrestling) and a coloratura-soprano (One Dying). There are also declamatory conversations between Gabriel and the Called One and the Wrestling One as well as lyrically flowing and dramatically impulsive arias like those of the Chosen One and the Monk. The turning-point is the whispering of the Dying Soul, followed by an unearthly ensemble of high womens' voices. In the great interlude which follows the orchestra plays alone. Schoenberg develops an imaginative use of colour of unmistakable individuality. There are the well-known colours; solo strings in remote registers, deep woodwind, muted brass, chords in harmonics, celesta, harps, harmonium, unusual percussion, tremolos on the bridge, cantilenas on the fingerboard, as in *Erwartung* and in *Glückliche Hand*, the Orchestral Pieces opus 16 and the Songs with Orchestra opus 22. But there is also writing in many layers, a kind of polyphony in chords and parallel movement.

There are innovations in the structure of the music. The germ-cell is a series of six notes, D–C sharp–E–F–G–A flat and its permutation C sharp–D–F–E–G sharp–G. This is joined right at the beginning by the supplementary six notes C–E flat–B–B flat–F sharp–A, giving total chromaticism. The law of the avoidance of repetitions of notes had already appeared in Schoenberg's earlier works. However, the roots of the later twelve-tone technique are exposed here.

The beginning, with its six-note ostinato on the cellos, the contrast of colours in the orchestra which is divided into groups, the melodramatic curve of Gabriel's speech, the passionate cries of the chorus increase the range of expression of this very dramatic music to a vast extent. The musical vision in the second part, after the interlude, is astonishing. Schoenberg works with the sound of spatially separated loudspeakers, from which the soprano answers itself in a ghostly manner in giant intervals at the end.

In the short score Schoenberg had spoken of 'some off-stage music' (Orchestra, chorus, etc.); 'this should be placed partly high up and partly in the distance'. In 1921 he wrote at the end: 'Entry of Chorus and Soloist, first chiefly on the platform, but then more and more with off-stage choruses and orchestra, so that at the end the music pours into the hall from all sides'. This vision, which can only be completely realized by the modern technical means of magnetic tape, anticipates developments of a later generation of composers in the Fifties. This torso of 700 bars, lasting 43 minutes, made an extremely strong impression at the Viennese performance. It completes Schoenberg's picture as a composer for the first time. The *Jacob's Ladder* has a key position in the complicated development from free atonality to serial and twelve-note methods.

MÖDLING, NEW CONDITIONS AND NEW LIFE

Austria-Hungary, in the form of the Hapsburg Monarchy which had become a model of Utopian European dreams, had been broken up long before the end of the First World War. The material poverty which dominated Central Europe, the hunger, the death in the war of millions of men who left behind them families without means, the increasing feeling of national guilt-consciousness: all of this was a nightmare to Schoenberg, as to many other cultural people. The apocalyptic visions of his pre-war works had been outdone by reality; all the unresolved dissonances in his music, the 'vitriolizing' power of his aesthetics, the incompatibility of lines and movements in his counterpoint, came to reality in this time, which Karl Kraus described as the last days of humanity.

If one wanted to survive the only solution was flight. Schoenberg had recognized this for some time, when he turned to the metaphysical ideas of *Jacob's Ladder*. This was already a flight in the area of the creative spirit. In his personal life there were several ways out. One of them led away from publicity and his 'business' to the closed circle of people who were connected with his private life or his work. These were his family, friends and pupils. When Schoenberg decided to move from Vienna to Mödling, he took the measures which were necessary for his flight.

Above everything else Schoenberg had to continue the lectures which had been taking place for a short time in Eugenie Schwarz-wald's school, Wallnerstrasse 9. On 28 September 1917 Berg wrote to Helene that he had attended the opening lecture of this 'Seminar for Composition' a few days before. It was attended by between 90 and 100 people ('mainly women'), but the financial results were very meagre. Schoenberg had left it to those taking part themselves to decide what fee they would pay him.

Those who attended the lectures, which began in January

1918, did not know about Schoenberg's move to Mödling; he travelled twice a week to Vienna in order to teach in the Wallnerstrasse. On the other hand his private pupils had to go out to Mödling, which meant a financial problem for some of them.

His move was prepared long in advance and carefully. On 23 February Schoenberg gave his friend Adolf Loos his new address. In March he continued with the catalogue of his books which he had begun in 1912. His new purchases included works by Emile Zola, Jean Jacques Rousseau, Lord Byron, Goethe, Tieck, Uhland and Balzac, whom he still admired increasingly.

Schoenberg wrote a long letter to Zemlinsky on the important question as to whether cuts were permissible in his work; Zemlinsky wanted to conduct a shortened version of Schoenberg's *Pelléas* in Prague. Schoenberg had little time for composition. Apart from fragments of *Jacob's Ladder* and the string septet he wrote the opening bars of a piano piece. His move to Mödling and his arrangement of the Mödling apartment had priority at this stage. Georg Schoenberg describes the apartment on the upper floor of Bernhardgasse 6: 'A bathroom, a hall, and a glassed-in verandah were arranged and put in by my father. He had his own workroom, in which there was a piano, a harmonium, violins, viola and cello, his whole library, a writing-table; he worked standing up at a desk.' The piano, an Ibach, which Schoenberg bought in 1917, later followed him to Berlin and finally to his California house in Brentwood Park.

A new plan came into being, arising out of his teaching activity. Schoenberg wanted to develop a kind of practical analysis, in which he would bring a work alive step by step in rehearsals. So the rehearsals were an end in themselves, and the performance was of secondary importance. Erwin Ratz, who began as one who attended Schoenberg's lectures in the Schwarzwald schools, became one of his most eager pupils, and was enthusiastic about this plan. He made all arrangements to bring it into operation by himself, raised the necessary money and had a four-page prospectus printed on hand-made paper. In April 1918 the 'Concert Direction' Hugo Heller, more popularly known as the bookshop of the same name, which was a centre of modern literature in the 1st district of Vienna, sent out the prospectus with the invitation to subscribers: 'Arnold Schoenberg at the request of the Concert Direction Hugo Heller has declared himself prepared to perform his Chamber Symphony, which was given its first performance in Vienna several years ago by the Rosé Quartet and the Wind

Ensemble of the Royal and Imperial Court Opera – to perform it in a new way in our present-day concert life. Arnold Schoenberg intends, instead of a single concert, to give a series of ten public rehearsals. In the final rehearsal the work will by played at least once through without a break. In this way the listener will be offered the possibility of hearing the work so often that he can understand it as a whole and in its details.' Subscribers were able to buy scores of the Chamber Symphony at half price. The first eight rehearsals were to take place in the second half of May in the afternoon, the last two in the evening at seven-thirty. The project became reality in June. On Tuesday, 4 June, a large number of friends met at three-thirty in the Musikvereinssaal. Alban Berg had had lunch beforehand with Schoenberg and his daughter Trudi at the Werfels. At the rehearsal, among other people, there were Adolf Loos with a dancer friend of his, the painter Johannes Itten, President Dr. Karl Wiener, Hugo Kauder and Erwin Ratz. Afterwards Berg, Ernst Bachrich and Josef Polnauer went to Schoenberg's seminar.

There were also rehearsals on 6 and 8 June. On the 9th, a Sunday, Schoenberg had his usual regular day for afternoon coffee. There was talk of a new magazine 'Friede', for which he was to work. He was planning an analysis of Mahler's Ninth Symphony. Webern, who in spite of Zemlinsky's indulgence could bear his work in the Prague Opera no longer, was also in Mödling. Schoenberg's friends were worried about his livelihood and secretly collected money for provisions for him.

On Wednesday, 12 June, there was a final rehearsal in the small room of the Concert House; on Sunday the 16th was the last of the ten rehearsals. After this an unknown lady went up to Schoenberg and gave him an envelope. In it were 10,000 kronen and a note: 'To the great artist, an admirer, a Jew'. Berg wrote to Helene that he should now be relieved of all worries, for another anonymous person had given him 1000 kronen, and Josef Redlich sent him 2520 kronen from the Mahler Foundation, for which Schoenberg thanked him on 19 May.

Berg went to Mödling every Sunday. The 23rd of June was his great day; all his life he regarded 23 as his lucky number. He went by the electric railway and the steam tram out to Mödling, and at Schoenberg's house, as well as the two Weberns, he met Eduard and Salka Steuermann and Paul Königer's wife. After the 'Party', the coffee with cakes, Trudi's little piano was brought into the music room and Schoenberg, Webern, Berg and Steuermann played the eight-hand version of the Five Orchestral Pieces. In the evening they all went home, except Berg, whom Schoenberg had invited to stay to supper. Over a glass of Rhine wine from the provisions which had been paid for by those who attended Schoenberg's lectures, the Master asked for Berg to address him in the second person, six years after he had done the same to Webern. Before Berg left at 10 o'clock he gave him three photographs of Prague.

On 30 June, another Sunday, there was another great day in Mödling; Berg met Webern with his middle child, whom he found charming, and also Dr. Ernst Bachrich and Erwin Ratz. They played quartets with Schoenberg. On this day he worked out the important plan for a Society for Performances of Contemporary Music, from Mahler up till then. A week later Berg, Stein and Webern went for a two-hour walk to Hinterbrühl with the Master.

In August Berg was in Trahütten. Webern had found an apartment quite near Schoenberg in Mödling, in Neusiedlerstrasse 58. 'I have been to Schoenberg every day', he wrote to his friend, 'I go to him at 5 o'clock in the afternoon. Then we go for a walk or play piano four hands. After the evening meal we are always together. We play cards now (Whist or Tarock).'

But there was a tension between him and the Master, which soon rose to the level of discord. Webern was disappointed by the conditions of life in Mödling and had financial worries. His hatred of working in the theatre unexpectedly resulted in a wish to return to Prague. Schoenberg, with whom he discussed it in July, was against this. He made Webern hope for some work in the society which he was planning, even if it was not very well paid, orchestration of operettas and paid collaboration in his seminar. Webern listened to this in silence. He soon went on a journey to Mürzzuschlag and wrote to Schoenberg that he still wanted to go back to Prague. Schoenberg answered abruptly that he would not interfere further with his decisions. He was touchy in matters of this kind; Steuermann and Berg also had to endure similar difficulties with him. The situation was easier for Berg now, because he was still working in the Ministry of War and used every opportunity to travel to Mödling.

On the first Sunday in September he met at Schoenberg's house for coffee Frau Dr. Marie Pappenheim, her later husband Dr. Hermann Frischauf, Ernst Bachrich, Eduard Steuermann, Erwin Ratz and Selma Stampfer. The 13th was Schoenberg's forty-fourth birthday. Berg brought him tobacco and a copy of his String Quartet opus 3. Schoenberg spoke about a planned 'Gurrelieder' performance in Zurich, which he was to conduct. But he did not have a valid passport. As he was a Hungarian citizen he intended to see about this in Budapest. He asked Jemnitz to arrange a hotel for him.

Webern was not present at the birthday party. Schoenberg was disappointed and opened his heart to Berg, whom he accompanied in the train to Vienna in the afternoon. Shortly afterwards a laconic letter came from Webern which acted like a clap of thunder. He assured Schoenberg of his friendship. Nothing was happening in Prague and he was going back to Vienna. Berg, to whom Schoenberg showed the letter, thought that he had gone mad.

The position in Mödling, which Webern had to return to after all, was painful. The two couples did not greet each other. This remained so for several weeks. Their reconciliation did not take place until November.

Meanwhile Schoenberg had new work to do. He had conducted his seminar in the Schwarzwald schools from Mödling up till the end of June. After the end of the first period of studies on 19 September he again asked for a discussion about 'Explanations, answering questions, giving of information, arrangement of hours of instruction etc.'. The subjects of study were harmony, counterpoint, form, orchestration and analysis, with beginners and more advanced students treated separately. The lectures took place from 4 till 8 in the afternoon. They were attended by professional musicians, amateurs and lovers of art, and these could be either listeners or pupils. A pupil was one who took an examination at the end of the year. Listeners were only taken in small numbers and were entitled, but not compelled, to take the examination. The study year began at the end of September 1918 and ended on 30 June 1919.

Fifty-five people entered for the course, of which twenty-seven were women and twenty-eight were men (two of them under twenty-one years old). The list, which Schoenberg kept, contains names which can be found again among his close collaborators. Max Deutsch, Hanns Jellinek, Olga Novakovic, Erwin Ratz, the sister and brother Dolly and Viktor Schlichter, Josef Travnicek (Trauneck) and Viktor Ullmann were on this list. Ernest Bachrich performed as a pianist in Schoenberg's 'Society for Private Musical Performances'. The soprano Selma Stampfer sang in

Schoenberg's house in Mödling and played for the Society. Gottfried Kassowitz became a pupil of Alban Berg. Roland Tenschert (1894–1970) took his Doctorate of Philosophy in 1921 and later became a respected writer on music and a biographer of Mozart.

On 23 November 1918, a Saturday, the 'Society for Private Musical Performances' was founded. Schoenberg made his pupils Webern, Berg and Steuermann leaders of events, the secretary was Dr. Paul Amadeus Pisk, the treasurer Dr. Prager, the Archivist Dr. Josef Polnauer, and the writing side was looked after by Dr. Ernst Bachrich and Josef Travnicek (Trauneck). The institution arose out of the discussions at the 'Seminar for Composition', and Schoenberg built up the practice from his ten rehearsals of the Chamber Symphony in a methodical manner. The aim was to educate people in listening and understanding modern music. The choice of works to be performed was independent of styles. All modern music, 'everything that has a name or a physiognomy or a character', from Mahler and Strauss up to the youngest composers, was the object of its presentation. In rehearsal the chief aims were care and thoroughness, clarity and precision of performance. The performances took place every week as closed society evenings. Only people who had membership passes were admitted. Applause and demonstrations of displeasure were forbidden. The first evening took place on Sunday, 29 December 1918. The programme consisted of the Fourth and Seventh Piano Sonatas of Alexander Scriabin, 'Proses Lyriques' by Debussy and Mahler's Seventh Symphony, for piano four hands. The performers were Felicie Hüni-Mihacsek (Debussy), Eduard Steuermann (Scriabin, Mahler) and Dr. Ernst Bachrich (Debussy, Mahler).

The first season of the Society lasted till June 1919. In twenty-six weekly concerts forty-five works were performed. There were between ten and thirty rehearsals before the performances. From the Schwarzwald school the concerts moved on occasions to the Merchants' Society, the Musikverein and the Concert House, and finally in September 1920 to the Club of Austrian Railway Employees.

As president Schoenberg had 'an entirely free hand in running the Society'. In 1938 he described his authoritarian and absolute principle of direction in a 'Four Point Programme for Jewry', Chapter 2. He said that in 1920 he had become a kind of dictator in a musical society, which he had built up according to his own feelings, and in general it had been extremely successful. Suddenly some political extremists had aroused strong opposition to his plans. He had tried in vain to overcome them and to show them that the idea would founder if they continued their opposition. But they pressed to get a majority against his principles. Instead of giving into them he had done something which under other conditions could be called illegal: he had dissolved the society, and founded a new one which only contained members who agreed entirely with him and cut out the entire opposition. Some sentimental people had regarded this as wrong. But it was the only healthy means of preventing the entrance of inartistic principles into artistic affairs.

No work by Schoenberg himself was played during the 1918/19 season at the Society. By April 1921 the number of works played had risen to 226. They were repeated up to five times (i.e. played up to six times); in the prospectus there was a distinction between works and numbers, that means that a work which was played six times had a number in the list of works, but in the catalogue of numbers it had six numbers.

Schoenberg suffered a disappointment in the autumn of 1918; the journey he had planned to Zurich, where he was to conduct the 'Gurrelieder', did not take place, although he got a passport unexpectedly from the Vienna Police Presidency.

On 1 November the quarrel with Webern was finally ended; Schoenberg wrote a letter to his old friend thanking him, – Webern had found his way back to him by writing a letter himself. As Schoenberg put it, 'they succeeded in clearing the table of friendship' and the two hot-headed people sat down gladly at it again.

The World War was over. Life in Austria began to return to normal very slowly. But material conditions of life were extremely difficult. The quick fall in value of German and Austrian currencies, the continual inflation and the isolation of Austria from abroad reduced cultural life too. Those who had taken part in the war came back home slowly and friendly contacts were renewed, although the post worked limpingly and extremely unreliably. In correspondence for the 'Society' it was recommended to use registered letters, as otherwise delivery was uncertain.

In Mödling, apart from the musicians in his circle, Schoenberg saw many old friends again, including David Joseph Bach, Dr. Marie Pappenheim, Oskar Kokoschka, the critic Dr. Paul Stefan, the architect Adolf Loos and the poet Peter Altenberg, whom he

Schoenberg's time-table (comp. table on p.257)

had met through Karl Kraus. He visited the Villa Mandl, which Loos had built for the composer Richard Mandl in Döbling; when he was asked to sign the Visitors' Book, he wrote: 'The Visitors' Book? In a house by Loos I am not a visitor but a good acquaintance. I feel free to write something which would otherwise be ununderstandable.' This was followed by three bars from the *Jacob's Ladder* with the words of the Chosen One: 'I should not approach, for I . . .'

At the end of 1918 Hanns Eisler, Karl Rankl and Joseph Travnicek returned to Vienna as demobilized soldiers. They became Schoenberg's pupils more or less at the same time at the beginning of 1919. About this time a young demobilized officer came from Prague to Mödling with a letter of recommendation from Zemlinsky: Josef Rufer. He first of all studied harmony in the lectures at the Schwarzwald School, which took place on Tuesdays and Fridays from 4.30 to 5.30. He also took private lessons in counterpoint and composition, which were given in Mödling on Wednesdays and Saturdays. In February he took over the secretaryship of the 'Society' in succession to Dr. Pisk. Paul Amadeus Pisk had been sent back from the front for reasons of ill-health; he became a pupil of Schoenberg's in 1916 and remained with him until 1919.

In Brentwood Park a sheet of paper was found, signed by Schoenberg, which gave all his hours of work from Monday at 8 in the morning to 6 o'clock on Saturday afternoon. It is not dated. But its date can more or less be discovered from the names of the pupils. It cannot be before 1919, for this was the year in which Eisler and Rufer went to Schoenberg for the first time. And it cannot be after 1919 because Pisk's lessons ended then. Here is the timetable:

	Monday 8–11.45	Tuesday	Wednesday 7.45	Thursday	Friday	Saturday
8– 9	Rankl Novakovics	Kalten-born	Pisk	Rankl	Kalten-born	Society Rehearsal
9–10	Deutsch Travnicek	Seligmann	Neumann 9.45	Novakovics Deutsch	Seligmann	
10–11	Hein	Medicus	Kolisch 10.45	Travnicek Hein	Medicus	
11–12	Eisler		Rufer	Eisler		
2– 3	Committee Meeting	1.30–2.30 Willenberg		Society		Rufer
3– 4		2.30–3.30 Counterpoint		Rehearsal	2.30 Counterpoint	Kolisch Willenberg

	Monday	Tuesday	Wednesday	Thursday	Friday	Saturday
4- 5	4-5.30	4.30-5.30			3.30	
	Lecture	Analysis I			Analysis II	
5- 6	Consul-	Harmony	5.45		4.30-5.30	Neumann
	tations		Osterreicher		Harmony	

It can hardly be expected that this plan of work, which only left Wednesday afternoon and Sunday free, afforded Schoenberg much time or strength for creative activity. So he wrote no compositions in 1919. On the other hand he began to paint again; the two water-colours the 'Conquered' and the 'Conqueror' are dated April, and the water-colour self-portrait of 1919, which was very like them stylistically can be dated from about the same time. Schoenberg's literary works consisted only of small occasional pieces and fragments: the contribution to Adolf Loos's 'Richtlinien für ein Kunstamt', an article in praise of Mengelberg for a Dutch paper, a contribution to the collection *Creative Confessions*, which the publisher Kasimir Edschmid in Darmstadt asked him for, but sent him no proofs or fee. He also wrote a fragment 'Gewissheit' in 1919. In November the German Musicians' Magazine published Schoenberg's article 'The Question of Modern Composition Teaching' in No. 21 of its 27th volume.

Several people who took part in Schoenberg's lessons in Mödling reported on them in 1971, including Max Deutsch, Erwin Ratz, Josef Rufer, Hans Erich Apostel and Hans Swarowsky. Deutsch writes: 'After the end of the war there was often no coal or light in Vienna, no tramways and no railway. So we had to walk 15 kilometres to Mödling on foot, going there and back in one day, in order to have our lessons with Schoenberg. The lessons were collective, and there were at least two of them a week. Schoenberg sat at the piano, we stood behind him in a semi-circle and showed him our work, which he corrected and discussed. One reached his apartment up a staircase; the hall was guarded by the great shepherd-dog Wulli (who in any case only used to bite idiots, but not intelligent people). In Schoenberg's workroom almost all the furniture – except the piano and the divan – had been made by Schoenberg himself: the bookshelves, the binding of his books and music, and the standing desk at which he worked.'

The shepherd-dog Wulli was the first of a series of four-footed companions which Schoenberg had in his house all his life.

Interest in Schoenberg began to be aroused in many places in Germany. Music life recovered as the first of the public manifestations of art after the collapse of 1918. Erwin Stein, who had worked in many German opera houses since 1912, wrote on 30 January 1919 from Darmstadt, where Michael Balling as a conductor of Wagner was carrying on the good tradition of the old Court Theatre, and the young Erich Kleiber had begun his career as a conductor. Stein informed Schoenberg that a very good musician was the first conductor in Mannheim, and wanted to invite Schoenberg to conduct *Pelléas* or another work of his own. This conductor was Wilhelm Furtwängler, who had also aroused attention in Vienna. The invitation to Schoenberg followed on 9 August – In January and March the Rebner-Quartet from Frankfurt, in which the 24-year-old Paul Hindemith played the viola, performed the F sharp minor Quartet opus 10 with the soprano Anna Kaempfert in several cities such as Frankfurt, Marburg and Mannheim. On 31 July Steuermann wrote from Berlin about Hermann Scherchen's plans to perform *Pelléas* and the 'Gurrelieder' in his subscription concerts, and also to perform *Pierrot Lunaire* with Tilla Durieux, the producer Dr. Ernst Lert was planning the first performances of *Erwartung* and *Die Glückliche Hand* at the Albert Hall in Leipzig. In Cologne Otto Klemperer announced a performance of *Pelléas*.

Even in Vienna people began to think about their disturbing fellow-citizen, about whom the whole world of music was talking. The Concert House Society and even the conservative Society of Friends of Music decided to perform the 'Gurrelieder', which had not been heard since the triumph of its first performance in 1913. In March Schoenberg rehearsed with the Concert Society Orchestra for a performance in which *Verklärte Nacht* with large forces and the F sharp minor Quartet were to be performed.

Franz Schalk, a pupil of Bruckner and the chief of the Vienna Staatsoper, wanted to conduct the 'Gurrelieder' performance with the Philharmonic; it was to take place in February 1920. Schoenberg, who was to conduct the work himself in the autumn of 1919 with the Concert Society, protested against this to Universal Edition. He had reasons to fear that Schalk would not give the work the twelve rehearsals which it needed. For the first performance of Richard Strauss's *Frau ohne Schatten* was being prepared for 10 October in the State Opera. The project ended with Schoenberg conducting two performances of the works in the State Opera in 1920. The heated preliminary discussions can be appreciated from the letters which he sent on 13 March to his friend Dr. Hugo Botstiber, the General Secretary of the Concert

House, and on 30 April to Universal Edition; they are contained in the volume of Schoenberg's letters.

Meanwhile the 'Society for Private Musical Performances' took up the lion's share of Schoenberg's activity. He kept strictly to the rule made by himself to consider all characteristic tendencies of contemporary music. On 8 February Webern told his friend Berg – certainly not without doubts – that the Master had decided to perform works by Josef Marx, Carl Prohaska, Felix Weingartner and Egon Wellesz. This happened after one of the Saturday rehearsals in which Max Deutsch also took part. In the end songs by Marx and Wellesz, string quartets by Wellesz and Weingartner were performed with the greatest care. To the question, why he needed so many rehearsals for Weingartner's quartet, Schoenberg answered: 'Such music cannot be exposed enough.'

On 27 April Eduard Steuermann and Dr. Ernst Bachrich played an arrangement of Mahler's Sixth Symphony for piano four hands made by Alexander von Zemlinsky. Berg wrote to Webern about one of the rehearsals, which took place on the 19th, Good Friday.

Schoenberg also wanted to make contacts with composers abroad. One of the first of these was Stravinsky, whom Schoenberg asked for a new work on 24 April. His answer on 27 May runs:

Honoured Master, I thank you for your letter of 24.4.19. I am sending to you a copy of my '3 pièces pour quatuor à cordes' by my brother-in-law. I ask you to send this work back to me immediately after its performance. My address is

2, Place Saint Louis, a Morges (Suisse).

With best wishes Igor Stravinsky.

Two works of Stravinsky's, planned since February, were performed in the Society's programmes in June: the *Berceuses du chat* for voice and three clarinets, and *Pribaoutki* for voice, four strings and four wind. The soloist was Emmy Heim. Webern wrote to Berg transported by this (card of 9 June): 'There was no more room in the hall. Completely sold out. Stravinsky was wonderful. These songs are marvellous. This music is very close to me. I love it quite especially. There is something unmentionably moving, these cradle songs. How these three clarinets sound! And *Pribaoutki*. Ah, my friend, something quite marvellous. This realism leads us to the metaphysical.'

Two works by Berg were performed on the same evening.

Steuermann played the Piano Sonata opus 1, and also together with Rudolf Serkin, Ida Hartungen (a sister of Bodanzky) and Selma Stampfer, played an eight-hand arrangement of the 'Reigen' from Berg's Three Orchestral Pieces opus 6.

In the next programme, still in June, Josef Suk's piano pieces *Erlebtes und Erträumtes* were played by Rudolf Serkin, and also the Second String Quartet of Zemlinsky. Like all string quartets in the first years of the Society, it was played by the Feist Quartet, which also offered to give up their summer holidays in 1919 in order to rehearse new works. As well as quartets by Stravinsky, Reger, Ravel and Bartók, Berg's opus 3 were performed, and also Webern's opus 5, which should have already been played in the autumn.

Schoenberg spent the summer quietly in Mödling. His friends Berg and Webern were in the country. There were hardly any posts. The 'Gurrelieder' performance had been postponed. Only a letter from a Herr E. Fromaigeat in Winterthur aroused thoughts in him which he had long suppressed. It concerned negotiations to found a new Internationale of the mind in Paris. Schoenberg felt very German in these affairs. His long letter in answer of 22 July shows all the bitterness which the attitude of men like Maeterlinck, Paul Claudel, Camille Saint-Saëns and Edouard Lalo had aroused in him. He did not overlook what the balance sheet of war psychosis had added up behind both fronts. But by spending a prospectus of his Society he was able to show that he had already started in August 1918 to do what the leading sentence in his letter formulated:

'*No one can feel more deeply than I do the need to see equality once more prevailing in the republic of the mind.*'

In August 1919 the news of the death of his uncle Fritz Nachod on the 10th caused him great sorrow. He had been the protective spirit of his childhood and youth, a man who loved Schiller, wrote poems and sang.

Steuermann wrote from Berlin, and later from Hellerau near Dresden; he had heard from Max Deutsch that the Society wanted to take up his work again on 9 September; he did not want to miss it but he had a concert in Dresden first.

On 10 September Berg returned from Carinthia. Schoenberg invited him to a meal shortly afterwards. 'We chattered from 12 till 2.30', he wrote to his wife Helene, 'then Rufer came, and there was a great discussion with a hundred plans for the Society, which lasted till 6.30.' And further: 'Schoenberg has moved very much away from social democracy. But he doesn't really know what political position to adopt. He says: It is better to hang on to old things as much as possible but to improve them. So he is almost a monarchist.'

The Society had performed the second symphony by Franz Schmidt,played in a four-hand arrangement by Selma Stampfer and Dr. Pisk, and also Mahler's 'Lieder eines fahrenden Gesellen', sung by Stefanie Bruck-Zimmer. Berg, as concert director, rehearsed the Beethoven Variations by Reger with Olga Nova-kovics and Dr. Bachrich. On a visit to Mödling he found the Schoenberg family fairly well, but the meal was bad except for the coffee. Frau Schoenberg and the seventeen-year-old Trudi were knitting stockings. Georg, who was now thirteen, was wearing a cast-off shirt of his father's.

Their material conditions were bearable, because a couple of foreign students – these were the German Fritz Kaltenborn and Walter Seligmann from a banker's family in Frankfurt, paid well. But these two were threatened by the law of the expulsion of foreigners, which also applied to Steuermann and even to Schoenberg himself, as his father was a citizen of Bratislava and he himself was therefore stateless at this time.

On 13 September a large company assembled in Mödling for Schoenberg's forty-fifth birthday. About thirty friends and pupils brought flowers and gifts, 'a whole delicatessen shop of the finest kind', as the gourmet Berg described it. Berg gave Schoenberg a volume of Maeterlinck, and others gave ties, an ink-stand and books. In the afternoon congratulations and telegrams arrived. Adolf Loos, who was always brilliant at parties, dominated the conversation for hours. Sixteen of the large company stayed on for supper. They sat till 10 drinking a Gumpoldskirchener 1917, and Webern was the last to go at 10.30; Berg spent the night with the Schoenbergs.

The rehearsals continued. The first concert took place on 18 September and included works by Reger and Strauss; on 17 October Berg's Pieces for Clarinet and Piano, the cause of a quarrel between him and Schoenberg in 1913, were played with Steuermann at the piano.

Schoenberg was also in correspondence with Béla Bartók concerning the Society. On 31 October he wrote to him that the 14 Bagatelles for Piano had been played in their first season and the Rumanian Folk Songs and Dances in the current one; the Second Quartet was to follow. He was planning to give the

Rhapsody for Piano and Orchestra in January 1920. Would Bartók make an arrangement for the standard ensemble of the Society (Piano, harmonium, string quartet, flute and clarinet)? He also asked for information as to which of Bartók's songs and orchestral pieces had been published. He added a postscript: '*Your piano works have given me extraordinary pleasure. I am eager to see your new works. With best wishes ArnSch.*'
Altogether seven works of Bartók were performed before October 1920; his answer to Schoenberg's letter is unknown.

Some news which Schoenberg received with mixed feelings concerned the foundation of the Bauhaus in Weimar by Walter Gropius. Though he had great sympathy with the architect, whose short-lived marriage to Alma Mahler had just been dissolved, Adolf Loos was the one authority for him in all questions of architecture. And Loos's radical dislike of ornament regarded the efforts of the Bauhaus as a reaction against his own aesthetics. The Swiss painter Johannes Itten arranged the transfer to Weimar in October. He was interested in modern music, and was also a friend of Josef Matthias Hauer, whom he had met in May 1919 at an exhibition of his paintings in Vienna. Berg also told Helene in September about a meeting with Itten, who was one of the first professors ('Masters' as they were called) at the Bauhaus.

Hauer was introduced to Schoenberg by Adolf Loos. In the Society five of his piano works were played, two by Steuermann, two by Dr. Rudolf Réti, and one by himself. In August 1919 Hauer discovered the 12-tone rule, which Schoenberg had first used unconsciously in 1914. It now became Hauer's chief method in the formation of melodies, which he formulated in 1920 in the booklet *Vom Wesen des Musikalischen*. He did not draw any consequences for composition from the elementary statement that an 'atonal' melody must contain all twelve notes of the tempered scale without recognition. This makes a difference between his twelve-tone music and Schoenberg's, which was more ambitious in composition, independently of the question of priority. The changing relations between the two men will be discussed later.

On 1 November the first number of a twice-monthly magazine was published; it was used by Universal Edition as a propaganda vehicle for contemporary music. It was called 'Musikblätter des Anbruch'; the editor was Dr. Otto Schneider. Guido Adler wrote the introductory article, Schreker, who next to Mahler, Strauss and Reger was in the forefront of the discussion of aesthetics, wrote an article 'My Music – Dramatic Ideas', Egon Wellesz wrote about Strauss's *Frau ohne Schatten*. Bartók's 'Allegro barbaro' was printed as a musical example. Schoenberg's name was not mentioned. He appeared for the first time in the second number in the middle of November, in the advertisement section.

The most important project of the publishers at this time was the promotion of Franz Schreker's operas. *Die Gezeichneten*, which was given a successful first performance in 1918 in Frankfurt, appeared in February 1920 on the programme of the Vienna State Opera (this was the name of the former Imperial and Royal Austro-Hungarian Opera after the revolution of November 1918.) Schoenberg was somewhat sceptical about Schreker, who had helped him by conducting the first performances of 'Gurrelieder' and the chorus 'Friede auf Erden'; he was more sceptical in any case than Alban Berg, who was friendly with Schreker. The first special number of the 'Anbruch' appeared at the beginning of January 1920 and was dedicated to Schreker. Meanwhile new efforts were being made in Berlin for the promotion of modern music. Their passionate advocate and untiring organizer was Hermann Scherchen. Since he had worked on the rehearsals of *Pierrot Lunaire* he had had an enthusiastic admiration for Schoenberg. Even from his Russian prison camp he sent him postcards[1] in order not to lose contact with the Master, who sent him an answer. In February 1920 Scherchen began to publish a twice-monthly magazine about music, which he called 'Melos'. The expressionistic title page, designed by César Klein, announced as contributors among others Béla Bartók, Ferruccio Busoni and Arnold Schoenberg. On 26 January Scherchen sent Schoenberg news about the planned Berlin performances of the Chamber Symphony in the Volksbühne and also of the great success that *Pelléas and Mélisande* and the F sharp minor Quartet had had. He also asked Schoenberg, Berg and Webern to contribute to his magazine. His letter ended with hymn-like words: 'And now I would like to thank you yet once again; you, as a creative person are *the* experience of my life, as Russia was to me in a different way. I would like to thank you for the glowing power of a pure and entirely devoted humanity before whose ethos I bow in deep homage'. As long as Scherchen directed 'Melos' this magazine was of service to Schoenberg's works.

A few days before this another great conductor had taken up correspondence of 1919 with Schoenberg again; this was Wilhelm Furtwängler in Mannheim. He said that he was sorry not to have met Schoenberg on any of his visits to Vienna, but he

[1] 21. 8. 1917: 'Your card of 31. 3. has given me great pleasure'.

hoped to be able to meet him at his performance of *Verklärte Nacht*. He was going to start shortly on the rehearsals for *Pelléas and Mélisande* in Mannheim, so that Schoenberg, whom he had invited as guest conductor, would only need two more rehearsals for the concert; the performance was arranged for 3 March.

There were also more and more signs of interest from other countries. The old-established Copenhagen publisher Wilhelm Hansen asked if Schoenberg would let him have some of his works. In Prague Zemlinsky had founded a kind of branch of the Vienna Schoenberg Society. He was preparing four concerts, with the Society making guest appearances, for the first half of March. In Vienna itself the Society was making propaganda for itself by giving an irregular series of special public concerts. The first one was arranged for 25 February. Schoenberg asked Peters in Leipzig to let him have the performance material of Webern's piano arrangement of his Five Orchestral Pieces for the Society.

However, Schoenberg's most important connection was with the Amsterdam Concertgebouw and its director Willem Mengelberg. The Dutch public, which had been prepared by Mengelberg's cult of Mahler and by Schoenberg's guest appearances ever since 1912, showed him more understanding than any other public in Europe. And so in March 1920 Schoenberg planned to travel from Mannheim via Berlin to Prague, where he directed four concerts of the Society between the 7th and the 14th; from there he went to Amsterdam and Utrecht for performances of *Verklärte Nacht* and the first two orchestral pieces from opus 16. As the result of a railway strike in Germany the Dutch concerts were postponed till later and took place with fewer rehearsals than had been arranged. On 12 April Schoenberg returned to Mödling, carrying in his pocket an invitation to the big two-week Mahler Festival which Mengelberg was arranging in Amsterdam.

For the Festival of the General German Music Society in June, which took place this year in Weimar, the jury had made an important advance in the field of modern music. So Schoenberg's opus 16 was performed, conducted by Peter Raabe. Egon Wellesz wrote about the journey to Amsterdam to the Mahler Festival in the preface to the English edition of his little biography. The Schoenberg family, Wellesz, Frau Wellesz and Anton von Webern all sat together in the train. All were in cheerful mood and happy to be able to escape for the time from between 6 and 22 May from the misery of Central Europe, the shortages and bad food. Arriving at the Dutch frontier Webern laughingly threw an empty tin out of the window and said: 'No more corned beef' – it was the only meat that one was able to get in Austria.

At this time Wellesz was again as close to Schoenberg as he had been in 1905 at the beginning of his studies with the Master. Emil Hertzka, the Director of Universal Edition, had been planning to publish a book about Schoenberg for a long time by the firm of E. P. Tal, who was a friend of his. Alban Berg was to write the book. Berg was in a difficult position personally. He had to look after the legal business concerning his family property in Carinthia, the 'Berghof', and arrange to sell it. He could not get out of this task. He wrote in the middle of January to Schoenberg that he was not able to write the book and asked him to release him temporarily from his duties in preparing the concerts of the Society. As a result the contract for the book was given to Egon Wellesz, who meanwhile had obtained international recognition as a musical scholar and the decipherer of the Byzantine neumes. He tackled this important task with energy, obtained the necessary material from Schoenberg in many conversations, studied the latter's sketch books and unpublished works and finished the manuscript at the beginning of August.

Alma Maria Mahler-Werfel described the Mahler Festival in Amsterdam in her autobiography. At the official dinner, given by the Prince Consort on 8 May after the Resurrection Symphony, she sat between Mengelberg and Schoenberg. Schoenberg, a heavy smoker, craved a cigarette during the endless meal. Alma spoke quietly to the Prince Consort, whereupon the latter said: 'Schoenberg, have you by any chance got a cigarette? If so please give me one.' As the Prince was smoking the others had no need to refrain themselves. During his whole life Schoenberg had a strong taste for tobacco, and sometimes also alcoholic drinks. Because of his asthmatic condition, however, he often had to give up his beloved cigarettes for long periods, especially in the later years of his American exile.

However the most important experience of the year for him was the long-planned, many-times-postponed rehearsal and performance of the 'Gurrelieder' under his direction. This took place on 12 and 13 June – more than seven years after its première – in two concerts one after the other in the State Opera. Schoenberg conducted the Vienna Philharmonic, whom he thanked in an admiring letter, and the Singverein. The solo parts were sung by Berta Kiurina (Soprano), Olga Bauer-Pilecka (Alto), Carl Oestvig (Tenor), Josef von Manowarda (Bass) and Hubert Leuer.

The recitation was spoken by the Volkstheater actor Wilhelm Klitsch. In spite of the positioning of the singers in the orchestra and the bad contact with the chorus on the stage, which caused difficulties for the conductor, it was a performance which was generally regarded on both evenings as the climax of the Vienna Festival. Schoenberg was given ovations, and even the critics praised the work and the performance which he gave of it.

Since the war Schoenberg had had to give up his usual summer holidays. However Mödling itself, where he and his family were happy to live, had maintained its rustic character since Beethoven's time. One could work in peace there. Schoenberg, who had written no large works since 1917, began to write music again in March. On the 5th he wrote ten bars of a Passacaglia for Orchestra on a twelve-tone theme. It remained unfinished. However, he continued to work again in July 1920. In the fifth of his sketchbooks he wrote sketches for a piano piece. This was on 8 July. A few days later another piano piece was finished, and a third one on the 27th. These two were later put into the collection opus 23. They were played in the same year by Eduard Steuermann for the first time at a Society concert.

In Amsterdam Mengelberg had discussed two projects with Schoenberg. Mengelberg wanted to invite him for six months for composition lectures and concerts in Holland. In addition he wished to found a Gustav Mahler Society, whose statutes Schoenberg was to draw up. The contract for the guest conductorship was sent off from the Amsterdam Concertgebouw on 12 August. It said that Schoenberg was to conduct nine concerts including his own works in the season of 1920 to 21. The dates were Amsterdam on 28 and 31 October 1920 and on 6 January 1921: The Hague 30 October and 8 January, Harlem 2 November, Nijmegen 3 November, Arnhem 22 November and Rotterdam 24 November. Schoenberg was also asked to be present at the 'Gurrelieder' rehearsals in February 1921. For the composition lectures, which were not mentioned in the contract, but which were to start at the beginning of October, Schoenberg was allowed to bring two assistants with him.

There were differences of opinion about the statutes for the Mahler Society. Curt Rudolf Mengelberg, a pupil and a cousin of the conductor, acknowledged the receipt of Schoenberg's plan on 25 August, but regretted that Schoenberg had already sent 25 copies of it to other people. A month later Schoenberg received a thirty-two-line-long telegram from Willem Mengelberg. He was in hospital. He said that Schoenberg's conception of the Mahler Society seemed too German to him and too much based on local Viennese conditions. He was proposing to form an international society, which would arouse as much interest in America, England and France as in German speaking countries: 'Please do not abandon me because of the great importance of this matter but support me and add your name to the Society – it will have great international fame among all progressive musicians in the whole world of music – and devote your outstanding powers to the Society'. And he was also annoyed that Schoenberg had shown the statutes to other people while they were still in the state of sketches. He said that he could not be in Amsterdam by the end of September because of his illness.

Meanwhile Wellesz announced the completion of the Schoenberg book on 8 August. At the same time he asked Schoenberg for a contribution to a Debussy Memorial number of the Paris 'Revue Musicale'. He told Schoenberg about a young Finnish singer, the tenor Helge Lindberg, who had rehearsed Schoenberg's George songs extremely well with Steuermann in Aussee. Schoenberg refused the Paris request for reasons of national conviction. Although he regarded Debussy extremely highly, he was annoyed by some chauvinistic remarks made by the French master during the war. Wellesz argued against this that many French composers, especially Ravel, had reacted quite differently and had courageously supported 'enemy aliens' like Schoenberg and Bartók. But Schoenberg did not write the contribution.

His composition work continued. At the end of July he began another piano piece, which was later included in opus 23 as No. 4. On 6 August he made sketches for the second movement of the Serenade opus 24. In the middle of September Schoenberg was still in Vienna for the opening of the third Society season. Before his departure to Amsterdam he wrote several letters on Society matters, one to his publisher and friend Hinrichsen about Max Reger's violin concerto, and another to the widow of the composer, whom he greatly admired. She answered gratefully and at length in November.

Before Schoenberg went to Holland he had to write a letter to the housing authorities in Mödling. During the first years after the war there was a great shortage of housing in Austria. If a tenant left his place of residence for a fairly long time he had to send a request to the authorities, so that the apartmen twas not confiscated. The housing authorities granted his request till 1 May 1921.

Albertine Zehme had heard about Schoenberg's travel plans. She asked if they could meet when he passed through Berlin or if he could bring his family to Leipzig to see her and hear her pupils sing. The meeting did not take place. Schoenberg arrived in Amsterdam at the end of September and hired an apartment for the next six months in Zandvoort, a coastal resort in Northern Holland. He took Max Deutsch and Hanns Eisler as assistants for his composition course and its preparation. All were happy with their stay in Holland, which lasted till the end of March 1921. Life had not been affected by the war, and the small family, with Frau Mathilde, who was still somewhat ill, the eighteen-year-old Trudi and the fourteen-year-old Georg were well fed and clothed for the first time for years. Deutsch and Eisler were also happy about their stay for several months in this little country, and found that it strengthened their health which had been shaken by war service and post-war hunger. Among Schoenberg's visitors in Zandvoort was Klemperer.

Schoenberg was kept in touch with the work of the Vienna Society by his friends and pupils. On 9 October 1920 the first propaganda concert was given in the Little Musikvereinssaal. It began with Max Reger's 'Romantic Suite' in an arrangement for chamber orchestra by Rudolf Kolisch, who played the first violin himself. The conductor was Erwin Stein. Then followed the first performance of two new piano pieces by Schoenberg, played by Eduard Steuermann. They were not described more exactly; they were in fact the first two pieces of opus 23. After Debussy's Sonata for flute, viola and harp Béla Bartók's Rhapsody for piano and orchestra in the arrangement for two pianos ended the evening. This was the work about which Schoenberg had corresponded with the Hungarian composer.

Fourteen days later there was a concert in honour of Maurice Ravel. The French composer had come to Vienna for three weeks and was staying with Alma Mahler-Werfel. The Society concert in his honour began with *Gaspard de la nuit*, played by Steuermann. Then Helge Lindberg sang five of Schoenberg's George songs. Kolisch and Steuermann played the Four Pieces for violin and piano by Webern, and a clarinettist from the State Opera, Karl Gaudriot, played Alban Berg's Clarinet Pieces. Another well-known foreign composer was also a guest of Alma Mahler-Werfel's, Alfredo Casella from Rome. With Ravel he played the latter's *Valses nobles et sentimentales* on two pianos. After Schoenberg's ballade 'Jane Grey' the concert ended with Ravel's String

Quartet. Stein wrote to Schoenberg: 'Ravel wanted to hear some Schoenberg above all. That was difficult for us, as we did not have any large piece of yours'. Stein was somewhat disappointed by Ravel and Casella as pianists; against this he praised Steuermann's performances.

At the beginning of November a big prospectus was published by the Society with a list of all the works played up to 27 October 1920 and those planned for the next season, 189 in all. The tirelessly communicative Erwin Stein wrote on 3 November that his work with Kolisch and Rudolf Serkin was ideal. On the 13th he wrote:

'Serkin is very annoyed about the fee he was offered and will not understand that the Society has no money. When I put it to him that he didn't have to play to people for nothing, he said that he didn't have to play to people at all. A fine fellow!'

In the same letter he wrote:

'We liked Ravel very much. I was not able to get much from him in detail, because I speak and understand French too badly. In any case Ravel was in a very excited mood. After the song "Als wir hinter dem beblümten Tore".[1] Ravel and Casella said some French superlative to me. After the piano pieces I asked Ravel if he liked them and if he understood them. Yes, he liked them extraordinarily well and he could also understand them very well, as he knows your music very well, and he could see in the first bar that it was Schoenberg. There was nobody else who wrote like that. And then he admired Steuermann's performance . . . "C'est un musicien".'

About this time there must have been a crisis within the Society, of which Schoenberg said that he overcame it in a dictatorial way. Among his most faithful collaborators, whom he chose himself, was Erwin Stein. The latter had rehearsed *Pierrot Lunaire* with Erika Wagner (the wife of the director Dr. Fritz Stiedry), Eduard Steuermann (piano), Franz Wangler (flute), Viktor Polatschek (clarinet), Rudolf Kolisch (violin) and Wilhelm Winkler (cello). Schoenberg empowered him to perform *Pierrot* everywhere with this ensemble, but only with written permission outside the Society.

Performances of *Pierrot* were also planned in Paris. On 12 November Marya Freund wrote that Ravel was so sorry not to have met Schoenberg in Vienna. He asked him through her to be allowed to perform *Pierrot* in Paris, with her and in French.

[1] No. 11 of the George Songs opus 15.

The plan came to fruition in November 1923, but without Ravel, and conducted by Darius Milhaud.

Schoenberg finished the eventful year of 1920 in Holland, in the small town on the coast. This year had brought him success such as had only come previously in 1912 in Berlin. New contacts had been taken up. An admiring letter came from Leopold Stokowski in New York. Schoenberg's meeting with Furt-wängler started a strong attachment of the two men to each other, which was only occasionally troubled by political and cultural-political disturbances.

Apart from the fragments of opus 23 and 24 Schoenberg's new work in this year included a treatise on orchestration, the first sketch of the curious text of the Requiem and a fragment on the theme 'Art and Revolution'. A second edition of the Harmony Book became necessary. Schoenberg worked on the expansion and clarification of some chapters.

He learnt what was happening in Vienna from the *Neue Wiener Journal*, to which he subscribed. It did not fill him with any great desire to return home.

The Society began the New Year of 1921 with a further propaganda concert. Eduard Steuermann wrote from Dresden, where he was visiting his sister Salka and wanted to play his arrangement of the Chamber Symphony in the programme of a piano recital. He said he had been working in Vienna since October with Marie Gutheil-Schoder on *Pierrot*, but she had now given precedence to Erika Wagner. Erwin Stein wrote about new plans for the Society on 3 February. They needed a quartet for the rehearsals and performances, and they also needed singers. Serkin would not be able to work with them from March onwards. He, Stein, was continually pressing Rudolf Kolisch to form a quartet, and Kolisch was attempting to do this. There were difficulties at the rehearsals, because they were not well enough paid. Max Deutsch informed Schoenberg about the pupils whom he had left behind in Vienna, and at the same time thanked him for his four months in Holland.

In the middle of March Schoenberg was preparing for his departure from Zandvoort. On the 22nd he sent a telegram from Berlin saying that he would arrive on Wednesday at the West Station in Vienna. Berg asked his friend Webern to take some flowers into the house for Schoenberg's arrival on the 23rd. When the family were home again, they were still feeling the impression of the phenomenal success which the 'Gurrelieder' had had in

Amsterdam on the 19th and 20th of March. It was the beginning of spring and the first buds were coming out in the garden at Mödling. Schoenberg was happy, and for the first time for many years was not worrying about distant prospects. His duties, his daily round, his teaching, and the rehearsals for the Society could start again. He had gathered strength.

But first he continued his work in the Society for Private Musical Performances. While he was still in Holland a second propaganda concert had been given. Erwin Stein conducted Mahler's Fourth Symphony in his arrangement for chamber orchestra. Before this there were performances of two songs by Schoenberg from his opus 8, also arranged for chamber orchestra, and the two songs opus 14. No less than four performances of *Pierrot Lunaire* were given between 9 and 12 of May. On 22 May the text of the *Jacob's Ladder* was read by the actor Wilhelm Klitsch from the German Volkstheater.

On the 27th there was a specially unusual and attractive performance. It was an 'extraordinary evening' in the Festsaal of the Schwarzwald Schools containing four waltzes by Johann Strauss. The chamber orchestra was the usual combination in the Society: piano, harmonium, two violins, viola and cello. Schoenberg was the conductor. He made two of the arrangements: 'Roses from the South' and 'Lagoon Waltz'. Webern had arranged the 'Treasure Waltz' from the *Gypsy Baron*, and Berg had arranged 'Wine, Woman and Song'. The instrumentalists were the élite of the Society. Schoenberg and Kolisch played first violin in turns, Karl Rankl played the second violin, Othmar Steinbauer viola, Anton von Webern cello. Steuermann played the piano part, and Alban Berg the harmonium. After the concert, which was received enthusiastically, the original manuscripts of the arrangements were auctioned.

The season of the Society ended on 9 June 1921 with a programme which included Stravinsky's 'Piano Rag Music' and three sets of piano pieces by Erik Satie (*Vieux Séquins et Veilles Cuirasses, Chapitres tournés en tous sens* and *Descriptionns Automatiques*), all played by Steuermann. After this came Webern's Violin Pieces with Kolisch and Steuermann, and finally Busoni's Toccata, played by Hilda Merinsky, Steuermann's wife.

After many years Schoenberg at last had a summer holiday in the country. His brother Heinrich, who had been a member of the Prague German Opera Company under the direction of Zemlinsky, had married Bertel Ott, the daughter of the mayor of

VEREIN FÜR MUSIKALISCHE PRIVATAUFFÜHRUNGEN IN WIEN

Leitung: Arnold Schönberg

AUSSERORDENTLICHER ABEND

Freitag, den 27. Mai 1921, 7 Uhr abends, im Festsaale der Schwarzwald'schen Schulanstalten.

VIER WALZER VON JOHANN STRAUSS

Bearbeitung für Kammerorchester.

Besetzung: Klavier: Eduard Steuermann, Harmonium: Alban Berg, 1. Geige Rudolf Kolisch und Arnold Schönberg, 2. Geige: Karl Rankl, Bratsche: Othmar Steinbauer, Cello: Anton von Webern.

SCHATZWALZER (Zigeunerbaron) Bearbeitung von Anton von Webern

WEIN, WEIB UND GESANG Op. 333, Bearbeitung von Alban Berg

ROSEN AUS DEM SÜDEN Op. 388, Bearbeitung von Arnold Schönberg

LAGUNENWALZER Op. 411, Bearbeitung von Arnold Schönberg

Nach dem Konzert: Versteigerung der Originalmanuskripte der Bearbeitungen.

Konzertflügel Steinway & Son; beigestellt von der Firma Bernhard Kohn, Wien

---

Zuschriften an den Sekretär Herrn Felix Greißle, V. Rainergasse Nr. 32. Anmeldungen an den wöchentlichen Vereinsabenden jeden Montag abends 7 Uhr im Festsaale der Schwarzwald'schen Schulanstalten, I. Wallnerstr. 9 (Eingang Regierungsgasse)

Preis 7 Kronen.

Programme of Johann Strauss Concert, 27 May 1921

Salzburg, in 1917 in Vienna. They decided to spend the summer together in Mattsee near Salzburg. The family from Mödling· arrived there at the beginning of June and they felt very well in this beautiful place. Schoenberg always preferred to spend his summer holiday near the water. He was passionately keen on swimming and enjoyed the pleasure, this year especially, of which he had long been deprived. Apart from his family he had a number of pupils with him. He liked his personal contact with these young people, whom he helped not only as musicians. On 24 June he finished his work on the second edition of the Harmony Book.

The idyll on the Mattsee was suddenly destroyed by antisemitic demonstrations. The campaign against Jews in Austria and Germany was pursued at the beginning of the Twenties by a certain type of Russian immigrants. One day a placard went up on the walls in Mattsee demanding that all Jews present should leave the place. The Schoenberg family had indeed been baptized in the Evangelical church. However, Schoenberg felt insulted by the demand of the local authorities to prove his Christianity. They first of all decided to return to Vienna and pretend that the climate did not suit Schoenberg. However, the affair leaked out. An article appeared in the *Neuer Freie Presse*: Salzburg Papers make Polemics against Schoenberg. Schoenberg's friends tried to find another holiday resort in the Salzkammergut. At the beginning of July Rufer found the Villa Josef in Traunkirchen, which belonged to Baroness Anka Löwenthal. The Schoenbergs had the whole house, their own beach, boat and bathing hut. Rooms were also found for his friends and pupils. Traunkirchen is on the same Traunsee as Gmunden, where Schoenberg had been in 1905, 1907 and 1908. Hugo Wolf lived there in 1891 and many times in the following years in the Pfarrhof, until he went mad in 1898.

Schoenberg's holiday period was fruitful. He had already heard in Mattsee of the great success of the Prague performance of the 'Gurrelieder' (on 9 and 10 June under Zemlinsky), and he had worked on the final chorus of the *Jacob's Ladder*. In Traunkirchen he continued to make entries in his fifth sketch-book. This contains two pieces from the Piano Suite opus 25, the Prelude (24 to 29 July) and the Intermezzo. The post brought welcome news. Willem Mengelberg was planning to give the first part of the 'Gurrelieder' in Amsterdam. Hanns Eisler and Karl Rankl wrote a letter together. All was going well for them, they were making music together, they were planning a walking tour at the end of August through the Salzkammergut and would be glad to come to Traunkirchen one day. Eisler added that he was composing a great deal, and following Schoenberg's advice, had studied Brahms and learnt a lot from him in piano writing and harmonic things. The programme of the first Contemporary Music Festival in Donaueschingen arrived; it began on 31 July but did not yet contain any work by Schoenberg. A young musician from Karlsruhe, Hans Erich Apostel, was accepted among Schoenberg's pupils. Schoenberg gave him a positive answer on 16 August.

In Traunkirchen there were a number of aristocrats who were interested in music, and with whom Schoenberg played chamber music. Many years later Baron Hermann Roner remembered him playing quartets together, and this was continued in the following years. An enormous number of friends and pupils visited him. On 20 August a general postcard was sent to Alban Berg. It was signed by Schoenberg, his wife Mathilde and daughter Trudi, by Webern, who was there for three days, by Felix Greissle, Rudolf Kaltenborn, Olga Novakovic, and Josef Rufer. At the end of August Alban Berg came for three days.

In September there was a small family event to celebrate; Greissle became engaged to the nineteen-year-old Trudi Schoenberg. Schoenberg spent the 13 September, his forty-seventh birthday, with his family and friends, which included Webern. The Master was only distressed by the alarming news from Berlin. His mother, who had lived there since 1914, was very ill. Among his birthday presents was a set of lithographs by Gustav Klimt, whom Schoenberg very much admired; this was given to him by Webern. Rudolf Kolisch was also there; on 22 September he wrote from Karlsbad thanking Schoenberg for his stay in Traunkirchen. He said that he was enthusiastically following up the carrying out of the task which had been set him of forming the quartet which later bore his name.

The most important creative result of Schoenberg's holiday was the first movement of the Serenade opus 24 for clarinet, bass clarinet, mandolin, guitar, violin, viola, cello and a deep male voice. Schoenberg wrote it between 27 September and 6 October. Emil Hertzka came for a short visit about problems connected with the publishing firm. Pauline Schoenberg, née Nachod, died on 12 October in Berlin. Among those who wrote letters of condolence was Dr. Heinrich Jalowetz. A long letter came from

Villa Josef in Traunkirchen. Here the prelude of the Piano Suite op. 25 was composed in July 1921, the first composition to follow the canon of Schoenberg's 12-tone technique

Marie Gutheil-Schoder from Vienna; she wrote on 23 October
that she was going to perform *Pierrot Lunaire* in Copenhagen on 9
November, conducted by Paul von Klenau, and was working on
it with Rankl and Stein. She said that Klemperer had invited her
to sing the George songs in Cologne. She said that her work in
the summer with a speech trainer had helped her very much; the
main subjects of her study were now mood and expression.

Alban Berg had finished the composition of *Wozzeck* in
October. He showed the work to Schoenberg after the latter's
return. On the 24th Schoenberg emphatically recommended the
work to Universal Edition. His daily work began again in Mödling. Old and new pupils came and went. Two cards of 29
November gave news of the performance of *Pierrot* in Prague;
these were signed by Zemlinsky and his wife Ida, Erika von
Wagner, Dr. Heinrich Jalowetz, Viktor Polatschek, Eduard
Steuermann, the banker Otto Freund, the critic Felix Adler,
the Schoenberg pupil Viktor Ullmann and others.

The year 1921 is of great importance because Schoenberg made
the famous remark to Josef Rufer which the latter reported as
follows: 'I have made a discovery which will ensure the supremacy
of German music for the next hundred years'. What he meant was
the method of composition with 12 notes related only to each
other, popularly called the 12-tone technique. The preliminary
stages are described partly in the letter quoted above to Nicolas
Slonimsky, and partly in a lecture by Webern which he gave on
15 January 1932, noted down by Willi Reich: 'But already in the
spring of 1917 – at that time Schoenberg lived in the Gloriette-
Gasse and I was living in the neighbourhood – I went to him one
fine morning . . . I found that I had really disturbed him by
coming, and he explained to me that he was "on the way to quite
a new idea" . . . (the first beginnings of it can be found in the
music of *Jacob's Ladder*)'. The first strict results of this technique
were the two pieces mentioned above from the Suite opus 25, the
Prelude and Intermezzo.

In the news letter of the Society, No. 27 of 18 September 1921,
a printed programme announced the *Glückliche Hand*, a ballet
scene by Berg and Songs with Orchestra by Webern. None of these
were performed. In the season of 1921/22 the Society handed over
its activity to its Prague branch. The external reason for its
dissolution was inflation.

In 1922 Schoenberg continued the work which he had begun
and partly finished it. In February he received a letter from Henri

Hinrichsen, who was very pleased about the many performances of the Orchestral Pieces, and announced his conviction that they would become part of the classical repertoire; he sent the Master a special fee of 3000 marks 'as a sign of joy'. Schoenberg thanked him warmly on 1 March and told him that Rudolf Kolisch would perform Reger's Violin Concerto on the 9th in an arrangement for chamber orchestra. Hinrichsen said that he was sorry that he could not come to the performance, but was interested in the chamber orchestra arrangement and asked Schoenberg if he knew Mussorgsky's *Pictures from an Exhibition*.

In the same month Schoenberg received a moving letter from Eisler. He said that he would never forget that Schoenberg had obtained work for him at Universal Edition in the frightful winter of 1919/20; otherwise he would have literally starved. And his stay in Holland had prevented him from suffering physical catastrophe: 'So I thank you for everything (perhaps even more than my poor parents)'. On 18 April Schoenberg was working on the final chorus of *Jacob's Ladder*, which he had begun in June 1921.

Marya Freund sent an excited letter from Paris. She wrote on the late evening of 22 April, still entirely under the impact of the Pasdeloup concert in which André Caplet had conducted the Five Orchestral Pieces. There had been so much noise and excitement that one could hear very little. After the fourth piece some people had started to fight. Florent Schmitt had defended the music like a lion and at the end of the concert had a swollen face from a blow. Maurice Ravel, Francis Poulenc, Roland-Manuel, Henri Prunières and Maurice Delage had been present. Schoenberg returned to the incident on 20 June in a letter to Wellesz and called the blow which Florent Schmitt had received 'a blow in the face of humanity'.

Zemlinsky wrote as chairman of the newly constituted Society in Prague and invited Schoenberg to performances there. The latter gladly accepted the invitation. After many years Artur Schnabel again made contact with Schoenberg in a letter of 14 May: 'I will be very glad to meet you often!' Egon Wellesz wrote about the great success of *Pierrot Lunaire* in Paris on the 17th, saying that the dancer and choreographer Leonid Massine had said to Darius Milhaud that he wanted to make choreography for the work; Schoenberg was to conduct the première and Milhaud other performances.

Interesting visitors came from Paris. Two of the composers from the famous group 'Les Six' wanted to get to know the city and also to meet Schoenberg before they took part in the Inter-national Music Festival in Salzburg from 7–10 August. These were Darius Milhaud and Francis Poulenc. Alma Mahler-Werfel, who describes Milhaud with great admiration in her auto-biography, took over the social entertainment of the two guests. Marya Freund came with them. In the red music salon in her house the guests met Schoenberg, Alban Berg, Anton von Webern, Egon Wellesz and Hugo von Hofmannsthal. Alma Mahler-Werfel suggested that *Pierrot Lunaire* should be performed on one evening in two different versions and languages. The first one, with Erika von Wagner, was conducted by Schoenberg; the other one was performed in French by Marya Freund, more singing than speaking, and was conducted by Milhaud. The instrumen-talists came from the Vienna Society with Steuermann at the piano. Milhaud reports: 'It was a most exciting experience; Schoenberg's conducting brought out the dramatic qualities of his work, making it harsher, wilder, more intense; my reading on the other hand emphasized the music's sensuous qualities, all the sweetness, subtlety and translucency of it. Erika Wagner spoke the German words in a strident tone and with less respect for the notes as written than Marya Freund, who if anything erred on the side of observing them too carefully. I realized on that occasion that the problem of recitation was probably insoluble.'

Poulenc was also very moved by his impressions. Schoenberg invited the two composers to a meal in Mödling. The food situ-ation in Austria was still catastrophic, and Frau Mathilde had trouble in finding something to put before their guests. When she brought in the steaming bowl of soup a football flew through the open window from the garden into the middle of it; her son Georg was playing with it and was even more alarmed by this accident than the laughing guests. Poulenc, who took a couple of good photos during this visit, told me this story.

In the afternoon Milhaud played his second Piano Suite, Poulenc his *Promenades*, and both of them together finally played Milhaud's *Boeuf sur le toit* for four hands. Schoenberg was charmed by it; twenty-three years later, when Dimitri Mitropulos had conducted the piece in Los Angeles, he wrote spontaneously to Milhaud and reminded him of his visit of 1922.

In July the Schoenbergs again went to Traunkirchen. They lived in the Villa Spaun, which was even more comfortable than the Villa Josef. Schoenberg was convalescing; he had a gastric fever in Vienna.

Mathilde and Arnold Schoenberg in June 1922 at Mödling.
Photographed by Francis Poulenc

Francis Poulenc and Schoenberg

He had hardly reached Traunkirchen when he began to catch up with the correspondence which had piled up during his illness. Alma Mahler-Werfel, who had acted as a mediator in Milhaud's query about the choreography of *Pierrot Lunaire*, received a negative answer on 5 July. Dance without recitation – that was going too far. He would rather write something new for Massine. If Milhaud would like to have him in Paris, he would conduct the first performances of *Erwartung* and the *Glückliche Hand*.

On 20 July he supported Alban Berg's plan of having the score of *Wozzeck* printed himself; as far as his work was concerned he was on the *Jacob's Ladder*. Vassily Kandinsky wrote to him from Berlin on 3 July. Schoenberg answered on the 20th in a long important letter. He said that the worst things in the years since 1918 had been the destruction of things which one believed in. In the text of *Jacob's Ladder* he had expressed again what religion meant for him; it was his only means of support. He was not at all sympathetic to the modern movements in art which surprised Kandinsky; they would quickly come to a standstill. He found the atonalists disgusting. As well as *Jacob's Ladder* he was planning a 'Theory of Musical Unity', chamber music and a theory of composition.

Other letters were sent to Paul Scheinpflug, the General Music Director in Duisburg, who had produced the 'Gurrelieder' with a number of rehearsals which were even beyond Schoenberg's demands; Schoenberg thanked him, and wished him a 'reward worthy of a king' for service worthy of a king to art; the letter, of 29 July, was published in Stein's collection. Schoenberg also answered Webern and the editor of the Berlin magazine 'Musik'. The Weberns came for a visit on 17 July. A small literary work, *Thoughts about a German Art Golem* was noted down on 15 July. The interlude in *Jacob's Ladder* was written in July.

How much Schoenberg worried about the inhabitants of Traunkirchen is shown by a letter of his of 1 August to Erika Wagner. In 1921 he had already promised to put on a charity concert to raise funds for new church bells. Now he said he had been trying for ten days to ask her to collaborate. There was no money for her but only entertainment. She is singing in Salzburg. She could choose one of five dates in August. He had looked up the trains and sent her the timetable. He asked her to send him a telegram. For the programme:

Something good for summer holidays, singing and speaking; or just speaking!? Style, songs that win the war. Please suggest something and leave me to choose from it. In any case (unfortunately) no Pierrot, for my sake, Waldsonne.

On 7 August he was able to thank her for agreeing to this. Erika Wagner even brought her accompanist with her, a Dr. Paul Weingarten. Schoenberg returned to the programme, for which she had made suggestions. He said:

2–3 Brahms, 1 Wolf, 1–2 Schubert, possibly 1 Mahler as well. If you agree to this I will put it like this on the programme. As for spoken pieces: isn't Wallfahrt von Kevelaer[1] *a bit worn? I don't know the other two. Could you do a not too long recitation (not* Pierrot*)?* She could put some more serious items into the programme, as there were many interesting people in the resort; not too *beautiful* but *effective*'. As Weingarten was playing with her he would not allow Fraulein Novakovic to play any solo pieces but she would play two movements from Beethoven's B flat Trio with Kolisch and Winkler.

The concert took place on 12 August 1922. If Traunkirchen got new bells in the Twenties, this was due to the circumstances that their thoughts were more humanistic than those of the nearby Mondsee; for very few people who took part in the charity concert would have been able to bring with them their passes as Aryans!

Sounds of admiration came from Paris. Poulenc thanked Schoenberg for his stay in Vienna. Arthur Honegger wrote a letter on 1 August and, at the suggestion of Wellesz, wanted to send Schoenberg reviews of the Paris *Pierrot* performance. He stated his admiration for the Master, who was unknown to him personally, and promised to do anything for him which he needed. Schoenberg thanked him and gave Honegger a few small tasks.

In Donaueschingen the Chamber Music Festival had taken place for the second time without any music by Schoenberg. In Salzburg there was an International Festival of Contemporary Music from 7–10 August 1922. At the end of it there was a performance of Schoenberg's Second Quartet in the Mozarteum. Played by the Amar-Hindemith Quartet, the work was received with great enthusiasm. The writer and patron from Winterthur Hans Reinhart was present and wrote to Schoenberg eagerly about it on 18 August. On the day after the final concert there was a meeting in Salzburg to found the International Society for Contemporary Music. The Cambridge professor Dr. Edward J.

[1] A recitation by Franz Krinninger which was much loved at that time.

Dent, an old friend of Busoni and later his biographer, was chosen as President.

Schoenberg wrote letters to Marie Gutheil-Schoder and Marya Freund, who appeared for a short time in Traunkirchen at the end of August. Both had their problems with *Pierrot*, Gutheil, because she did not have enough time for rehearsals with Stein and therefore had to hand over the part to Erika Wagner. Freund, because at the Paris performances with Milhaud (Paris, Spring 1922) she sang the part more than Schoenberg wanted.

There are a number of things regarding the performance of my works which I would like to talk over with you. I am anxious to explain to you why I cannot allow any will but mine to prevail in realizing the musical thoughts which I have recorded on paper, and why realizing them must be done in such deadly earnest, with such inexcrable severity, because the composing was done in just that way. I should very much like to do some thorough rehearsing with you, so that you should get to know the way to solve the musical picture-puzzles that my works constitute.

Thus he wrote to the singer on 16 August. In spite of his admiration for her, he did not get a very favourable impression of her *Pierrot* performance in Alma Mahler-Werfel's house a month before.

Joseph Stransky, the conductor of the New York Philharmonic Society, had come to Mödling during his summer holidays. He was interested in a work which Schoenberg had begun in April 1922 and had finished provisionally on 24 June in Traunkirchen. It was the orchestration of Bach Chorale preludes 'Come, God, Creator, Holy Ghost' and 'Adorn thyself, O my Soul'. Schoenberg was ready to let him have the first performance of these in New York, although Zemlinsky in Prague and Webern in Vienna had also wanted to perform them. He answered Stransky's question about other modern works with recommendations of Webern's Passacaglia and the Three Orchestral Pieces by Berg; he said these were 'two real musicians – not Bolshevik illiterates, but men with a musically educated ear!' In fact Stransky conducted the first performance of the Bach arrangements with the New York Philharmonic on 7 December 1922.

On 24 August Schoenberg began a short correspondence with Hinrichsen in Leipzig about corrections to the Orchestral Pieces. Eisler wrote on the 26th a letter which renewed his request for himself and Rankl to continue their studies with Schoenberg. At the end of August Schoenberg had a letter from Edgar Varèse, who had been in New York since the war and was now on a visit to Halensee, where he was staying with the painter Eugen Spiro. He asked Schoenberg, whom he had met for a short time in 1912, to join the committee of the International Composers' Guild, to which Busoni and Ravel already belonged. He said that he would begin the season in New York with a performance of *Pierrot Lunaire*. Schoenberg reacted unexpectedly harshly with a telegram saying that he did not know Varèse's aims and therefore could not accept his proposal. On 23 October he followed his impulse and gave Varèse a further rebuff. He said from Varèse's manifesto and the programmes of the first three concerts he found no German names among twenty-seven composers. He concluded from this that German music was not important to Varèse. Secondly he was annoyed that Varèse had simply put on *Pierrot Lunaire* without asking Schoenberg whether he could do it or was allowed to. Had he a speaker, a violinist, a pianist, a conductor etc.? How many rehearsals would he hold?

In Vienna with everyone starving and shivering, something like a hundred rehearsals were held and an impeccable ensemble achieved with my collaboration. But you people simply fix a date and think that's all there is to it! Have you any inklings of the difficulties; of the style; of the declamation; of the tempi; of the dynamics and all that? And you expect me to associate myself with it? No, I am not smart [in English] *enough for that! If you want to have anything to do with me, you must set about it quite differently. What I want to know is: 1. How many rehearsals? 2. Who is in charge of the rehearsals? 3. Who does the speaking voice? 4. Who are the players? If all this is to my satisfaction, I shall give my blessing. But for the rest I am, of course powerless and you can do as you like. But then kindly refrain from asking me about it!*

A human document!

Schoenberg's forty-eighth birthday approached. He celebrated it among his friends. Webern was missing this year. Was there a quarrel between them again? On 29 September the Schoenbergs were back again at Mödling, where he began to teach several pupils, including some new ones. On 4 October Rollo H. Myers, the English writer on music who had come to Vienna on a short visit, asked him for a conversation. Casella gave a concert which Schoenberg attended. Marya Freund wrote from Paris that she wanted to get going on the first performance of *Erwartung*.

About this time Schoenberg received a letter from a young Berlin musician who wanted to study with him: Max Butting. Schoenberg received him in his workroom in Mödling, where he was writing at a standing desk. Butting found him unfriendly. But it was clear that Schoenberg knew the two string quartets which his visitor had sent him and recognized a capacity for self-expression in them. He had no judgement about the extent of Butting's gifts. Butting expressed himself thoroughly. Schoenberg remained cool. The first part of their conversation lasted two hours. When the visitor, depressed and disappointed, wanted to leave Schoenberg said to him in a very friendly manner: 'Now, don't go away straight away, I'm sure you still have some time? What are you doing in Vienna at all? Have you seen or heard anything here?' To Butting's answer that the Opera had only unfortunately put on *Pagliacci* or *Cavalleria* and a ballet, Schoenberg said: 'Why unfortunately only?' The Vienna State Opera could not arrange its programme for the visit of a young Berliner. And Butting's judgement of the ballet did not show that he had a high balletic culture.

Butting, annoyed for the second time, wanted to go out. Then Schoenberg said to him earnestly: 'Sit down again and let me give you some advice, to think over fundamentally all that we two have spoken about together . . . your conflict is not that of a pupil, but of a creative human being, and in such a position there is no other possibility than to test oneself and think about oneself. Perhaps you don't agree with me now, you certainly will do so when the years have gone by.' Butting admits that he had seldom seen such an amiable and a nice person as in these moments. When he finally left after five hours, Schoenberg winked at him 'And you have made yourself so elegant.'

On 30 November 1922 Schoenberg conducted a performance of *Pierrot* as a guest of the music college of Winterthur, with Erika Wagner, Steuermann and the rest of the Vienna Ensemble; Hans Reinhart thanked him for his stay in the Swiss town. On 7 December Furtwängler conducted the Five Orchestral Pieces in the Leipzig Gewandhaus and also on the 10th and 11th in the Berlin Philharmonic.

His friends and pupils had a surprise for him at Christmas. They gave the Master, who had to answer all letters by hand, a typewriter, which he immediately began to use and soon mastered. He had a conversation with Berg about *Wozzeck*, specially about Marie's lullaby.

A letter from Marya Freund with good wishes for the New Year disturbed him. She said that there had been religious objections to some of the texts of *Pierrot* in Paris. He said that he had noticed similar manifestations in Geneva and Amsterdam at performances there. There 'Madonna' (the image of the blood from the lean breasts of the mother of God), 'Red Mass' (with Pierrot's heart as dripping red holy water) and 'Crosses' ('On their bodies swords have feasted, bathing in the scarlet blood-stream') had been regarded as blasphemous. Schoenberg protested his innocence, '. . . As I have never at any time in my life been anti-religious, indeed have never really been unreligious either. I seem to have had an altogether much naïver view of these poems than most people have and still am not quite uncertain that this is entirely unjustified. Anyway I am not responsible for what people make up their minds to read into the words.' And then he continues with the characteristic thought: 'If they were musical, not a single one of them would give a damn for the words. Instead they would go away whistling the tunes.'

He was also naïve in this; he believed that in fifty years the music of *Pierrot* would be like a folk-song. But how far even the beginning of the Twenties was removed from the spirit of *Pierrot*! The atonal freedom of his music since 1908 could contain no other connection of melody and harmony except to the chromatic scale. Through the removal of the old rules some of the traditional forms also seem to be weakened and without purpose. However, Schoenberg took them up again in part in the 21 recitations; through the different tensions and relaxations they took on a new meaning. So, for instance, the ostinato form of the passacaglia 'Night', which begins the second part of *Pierrot*, is developed in a more logical manner than it could be on a tonal basis. Alban Berg also understood the form with this meaning and used it in *Wozzeck* as the basis of a musico-dramatic scene. Similarly the imitative, canonic movement, 'Moon-spot', which is based on a strict mirror canon, is used in a more radical way than the laws of the tonal style would permit.

After his experiments in the traditional forms with free tonal thinking, in 1921 Schoenberg began his first work with twelve-tone rows and their mirror forms. We must regard the earliest of these as the prelude of the Piano Suite opus 25, dated Traun-kirchen, July 1921, as long as the waltz opus 23 No. 5 cannot be dated. From the relative freedom in form of the prelude Schoen-berg – clearly because of the effect of his first experiments with rows – went on later to strict dance forms with reprises, and finally returned to classical procedures in sonata movements, scherzos and rondos.

In 1923 he began the experiments which led to the complete formulation of the new method of writing.

The first performance of *Erwartung* had finally been arranged. Zemlinsky felt that he was strong enough in Prague both with the public and in his control of orchestral and scenic material, so that he could give Schoenberg a firm agreement. His only worry was whether Schoenberg had previous engagements, as there were many mistakes in the piano score, and also there was the question of the singer. Schoenberg replied to Zemlinsky on 8 January 1923. He said that he did not feel bound any more to Ernst Lert, who had tried in vain to arrange the première in Frankfurt and Leipzig. He said that the piano score would be completely corrected. Regarding Marya Freund, whom he had recommended, as the result of a wish which she had expressed to him many times, he did not insist on having her if Zemlinsky knew of somebody who would be better for the part. 'I only know that she is a very gifted person, rather capricious, but with great taste, good performing qualities and originality, but all this slightly tempered to suit "Latin" smoothness.' He was glad that Zemlinsky would conduct the work; he could entrust it to him. He arranged for Universal Edition to send the material to Prague the same day. The performance took place in June 1924.

At the end of January the composer Paul von Klenau invited Schoenberg to rehearse and conduct the Chamber Symphony in Copenhagen. The latter stated his conditions: 'especially that I can hold as many rehearsals as are necessary! Could I perhaps even have ten? But if the gentlemen prepare their parts first of all very well by themselves, then I can certainly manage with fewer (perhaps seven to eight). In any case all the rhythms must be worked out most exactly (mathematically!) and all dynamic and technical matters must be perfect, and they must be able to play with ease and very pure intonation.' The performance took place on 30 January, according to his wishes. The publisher Wilhelm Hansen used the opportunity of confirming the contact which he had initiated in 1920 with Schoenberg by letter. A contract was drawn up and an advance payment made to Schoenberg. In May 1923 Hansen received the manuscripts of the Piano Pieces opus 23 and the Serenade opus 24. He sent the rest of Schoenberg's fee of 13,000 kronen to his account in Amsterdam. (The central European currency chaos caused Schoenberg to open a secret account in 1923 at the Mödling Mercurbank, under the pseudonym of 'Waldemar Gurre'!)

Through his contract with Hansen Schoenberg was put under double pressure of time. For Hertzka would only release opus 23 and 24 if he got two other new works simultaneously. No work was ready for the publisher. Schoenberg undertook to finish the Five Piano Pieces and the Serenade before the end of April, and the Suite opus 25 and the Wind Quintet opus 26, which he had not yet begun, by the end of July. So he had to save time drastically. He cancelled several journeys which he had planned, including one to Zemlinsky in Prague. Then he took up the fifth sketch book, which he had begun in Traunkirchen on 6 June 1922 with the motto 'With God'. It is the longest, and also the largest in size (34 by 25.5 cm) of its kind, and the first 85 of its 200 pages show a kind of balance sheet which can only be compared with the diary of 1912.

Between 6 and 17 February he began sketches for opus 23, Nos. 3, 4 and 5. Then follow the Intermezzo of the Suite opus 25 (finished 23 February), the Gavotte (finished 27 February), the Musette (finished 2 March), the Minuet (finished, including the trio, 3 March) and the Gigue (finished 8 March).

On 11 March part of the Serenade opus 24 appears in the sketchbook for the first time, the end of the Variations (3rd Movement). On 16 March the Minuet and Trio were completely sketched out and the Petrarch Sonnet, which had been begun in 1922, was continued and finished on the 29th. On 30 March Schoenberg made a new arrangement of the 5th movement (Dance Scene), which he had already begun in 1920, and also the complete sketch of the 6th movement (Song without Words). The Finale (also called Potpourri) was begun on 11 April and finished on the 14th, and on the same day Schoenberg began work on the Wind Quintet.

As well as these sketches Schoenberg made fair copies for the publishers in February, March and April, often alternating between ops 23, 24 and 25.

The concentration and the many levels of Schoenberg's thought are shown by the fact that he was working almost at the same time on the non-tonal pieces of opus 23, which, however, are developed from tone rows and their mirror forms, the strictly 12-tone movements of the Suite opus 25 and the gay rhythmical dance forms of the Serenade. After this the classical and symphonic movements of the quintet form a kind of summing-up of Schoenberg's first experiences in serial technique.

In the *Seranade* opus 24 a new spirit appears in Schoenberg's music. This piece, written for clarinet, bass clarinet, mandoline, guitar, violin, viola and cello, is in seven movements, of which the fourth, 'Sonnet of Petrarch', adds a baritone voice. The most remarkable points are the rhythmical ideas in the work, especially in the first and last movements, where the four-beat march metre is interrupted by counter-rhythms and sometimes removed altogether. It is a method of writing showing Schoenberg surprisingly close to Stravinsky. This rhythmical impetus also has a character of irony and roguery which corresponds well to the gay spirit of the classical serenade. The song movement shows a primitive kind of 12-tone writing. Each line of the Petrarch Sonnet, which is set to a single tone row, has only eleven syllables. One note of the series is left over each time and it is not until the thirteenth line that a line begins again with the first note. The intervals of the row are altered by moving the notes an octave up or down. Together with rhythmical alterations this made a radical variation of the course of the melody, so that the row can hardly be recognized by the ear.

The other six movements are written in a panchromatic manner which uses mirror techniques; they are not bound to complete 12-tone rows. The 'Dance Scene' (5th movement) has a Ländler episode in the trio, with cheerful falling fourths in the clarinet which remind one of old post horn melodies. The finale develops the themes of the March (1st movement).

The peculiar colour of the ensemble of the Serenade is achieved by the combination of clarinets and string trio with mandoline and guitar. (Curiously enough the title-page in two languages published by Hansen in Copenhagen calls the bass clarinet a 'basset horn' in English.)

On 30 May Schoenberg finished the first movement of the quintet, which he had begun in April. It was the day before he left Traunkirchen, and the page also contains the beginning of the adagio. Under this Schoenberg wrote: 'I believe that Goethe would have been quite pleased with me'. Perhaps he meant that through this new law and the use of old forms he had imposed limitations upon himself, which Goethe had mentioned in the remark which Schoenberg once opposed, that the Master only shows himself in limitations?

Jean Cocteau, who had already greeted the composer of *Pierrot Lunaire* in 1920 in his magazine 'Le Coq', sent him his new book *Le Grand Ecart* with the dedication

à Arnold Schoenberg
son ami dévoué
en
France
Jean Cocteau
Mai 1923.

In Germany inflation was nearing its peak. Many artists were suffering a great deal from its effects. Help was offered from America. Schoenberg was glad to be a member of the honorary committee for the American Aid Fund; he was suggested for this by the Berlin theoretician Wilhelm Klatte. As musicians in need of help in Vienna he named Alban Berg and Josef Matthias Hauer. About this time he recommended Hanns Eisler's works to Universal Edition.

On 15 April Kandinsky wrote from Weimar. The Music High School was looking for a new Director. Kandinsky had mentioned Schoenberg's name and asked him to reply at once if he was interested. Schoenberg was mistrustful. Alma Mahler-Werfel had told him about a conversation with the Kandinskys which she clearly interpreted as one-sided. She said that she could detect anti-semitic tendencies in it, and that many emigrés from Russia had brought these feelings with them to Central Europe. There were also rumours from another quarter[1] about the anti-semitic attitude of some of the Bauhaus masters, and these had reached Schoenberg. His experiences in Mattsee in 1921 had made him doubly sensitive and clairvoyant. He answered Kandinsky shortly and clearly. The latter answered by return of post on 24 April, defended himself against Schoenberg's accusation and confirmed his old friendship. He said it was bad to be a Jew, a German, a Russian, or a European. It was more important to be a human being, a desirable person, a superman.

This was followed by a long, important letter from the composer, dated Mödling, 4 May 1923. It shows an astonishing insight into the political and ideological situation of the period. The letter, which is printed in Erwin Stein's collection, is one of Schoenberg's most important pronouncements and puts forward his political position quite clearly. He was equally hostile to communism and to American super-capitalism. Because of his experiences in the World War and the post-war period the former free-thinker had become a religious man who was conservative in

[1]   Perhaps from Erwin Ratz, who had become Secretary of the Direction of the Bauhaus in 1923.

the highest sense. One can see here the preparatory ideas for Schoenberg's play *Der biblische Weg*, which he finished in July 1927 and which led to the innumerable spiritual threads in the text of *Moses and Aaron*. Schoenberg also wrote to Alma Mahler-Werfel in this connection; here he mentioned Kandinsky by name and one of his friends at the Bauhaus.

The plan of an Austrian Music Week, which was to take place at the beginning of June in Berlin, had gone so far in May that Schoenberg had to reply to a letter which invited him to take part in it. The main works in the programme were Mahler's Eighth Symphony and the 'Gurrelieder' (in three performances one after another). He answered, slightly annoyed, that his previous refusal had not been taken seriously. He also found it provoking that only one tendency was represented. He suggested that works by Bittner, Marx, Schmidt or Prohaska should also be included. The programme of new works on 5 June finally included works by Bittner, Berg, Webern and Zemlinsky. The conductor of this concert was Webern; Paul Pella conducted the Mahler Symphony – he was also responsible for the organization and arrangements for the Festival. Schoenberg's pupil and friend Dr. Heinrich Jalowetz conducted the three performances of the 'Gurrelieder'. In the same month there was a chamber music week at Frankfurt, in which Hermann Scherchen conducted the chorus 'Friede auf Erden'; Martha Winternitz-Dorda sang the George songs with Eduard Erdmann at the piano.

In the spring Schoenberg had asked Baron and Baroness Roner to arrange an apartment for him in Traunkirchen. The family went there on 1 June and again lived in the Villa Spaun. The summer was one of the most fruitful for a long time. The chief composition was the Wind Quintet opus 26. But Schoenberg also wrote a large number of notes, theoretical works and historical discussions. On 6 June he directed a polemic against Heinrich Schenker, whom Schoenberg normally esteemed very highly, and another one against Oswald Spengler's 'Decline-Pessimism' on the 9th. On 5 July he made notes about the problem of 'Israelites and Jews'; four days later he wrote a comment on a criticism by Julius Korngold under the title 'Theoretician's Brain'. A few small notes on 11 and 26 June were devoted to polyphonic writing and notation. In July he wrote notes on his technique of marking indications for performance, the question of repetition, misunderstanding of counterpoint, directions for performance, and slurs as well as construction. In August he wrote notes about Hugo

Riemann's metrics, the law of parallel fifths and octaves, about young people and about his imitators; on 5 September he wrote about historical parallels and on the 9th about Hauer's theories. All these small notes were later used in larger articles.

Alban Berg appeared on 8 and 9 August; he came from Salzburg and wrote later to his friend Webern that Schoenberg was in good form and was working on the Quintet. With Schoenberg he met Adolf Loos and Josef Rufer. Webern came at the beginning of September and stayed in Traunkirchen from the 8th to the 11th. Frau Mathilde had been in bed for weeks; she was suffering from gall and liver trouble and was very weak. On 20 September she was admitted to the Auersperg Sanatorium in Vienna. Schoenberg's birthday on the 13th was naturally influenced by his worry about her. Berg, who could not come, sent Schoenberg the second volume of Spengler's *Decline of the West*.

In Vienna Mathilde's condition rapidly worsened. She died on 22 October, exactly two years after Schoenberg had lost his mother.

There had been some ill-feeling between Schoenberg and Eduard Steuermann which brought Schoenberg's admiring friend and great pianist almost to despair. A letter of 26 May shows this tension, and also shows that Steuermann was pleased that Schoenberg had given him the new piano pieces opus 23 and 25 to perform. Steuermann and his wife, Hilda Merinsky, visited Traunkirchen in the summer. After Mathilde's death in October tension again built up between the two men, in which Hilda played a certain part.

News came from Paris from Marya Freund, who was rehearsing *Pierrot Lunaire* in a new way. The performances on the 8th, 14th and 16th in London, Brussels and Paris were great successes.

In the autumn of 1923 Josef Rufer and I started a cycle of concerts of new music in Hamburg; their programmes and performance practice was modelled on that of the Vienna Society. Max Sauerlandt put the hall of the Museum of Industrial Art, of which he was a director, at our disposal. A group of patrons, headed by Emanuel Fehling, the brother of the producer Jürgen Fehling, financed the concerts. Works were performed by Schoenberg, Berg and Webern, Mahler, Bartók, Busoni, Milhaud, Poulenc, Ravel, Stravinsky and others. Among the performers were Martha Winternitz-Dorda, who sang Schoenberg's George songs, Eduard Steuermann, who played opus 23 and 25, the singer Jenny Jungbauer, the violinist Erika Besserer, the pianist

Ilse Fromm-Michaels, violinist and leader Heinrich Bandler, solo cellist Jakob Sakom and other soloists from the Hamburg Philharmonic. Rufer conducted Mahler's 'Lieder eines Fahrenden Gesellen' and Busoni's *Berceuse Elégiaque*, both in Schoenberg's arrangement for chamber orchestra. He also rehearsed *Pierrot Lunaire* with Erika Beilke; Schoenberg himself conducted this in the Hamburg Kammerspiele. The concerts had to be given up on 13 February 1924 owing to lack of money.

At the end of November Schoenberg received a letter of thanks from Hauer, to whom he had given 350,000 Austrian kronen (the value of five dollars!) from the American Aid Fund. Hauer said that if there was going to be an 'atonal school' he asked Schoenberg for a 'position with you as a music teacher and I promise with good conscience to be able to do something'. However an angry letter, in which Hauer describes a visit to Schoenberg in Mödling, shows that Hauer was not uninfluenced by the antisemitic tendencies of the time. Schoenberg had invited him on 1 and 7 December to work together, as Hauer had arrived at similar results in 12-tone music by a different way. Originally he suggested that they should write a book together in order to show the world that 'music if nothing else would not have advanced had it not been for the Austrians'. But Hauer's plan for a school seemed to him even better. He greeted the opportuhity of putting misunderstandings and anger aside in conversations together, and asked Hauer to visit him on 10 December. Their work together did not take place; their misunderstandings became greater rather than smaller, although Schoenberg in the second edition of his Harmony Book expressly referred to Hauer as the exception among the fashionable atonalists.

With regard to the coming year Schoenberg had already written some letters from Traunkirchen in the summer to several patrons in Switzerland and Holland, to whom he recommended Anton von Webern especially.

Through the introduction of the Rentenmark industrial chaos and the complete depreciation of the currency was finally overcome. So the situation of composers whose works were performed in Germany was immediately improved.

Schoenberg's somewhat worsened relations with Universal Edition, who had taken his side-leap to the Copenhagen publisher Hansen badly, were improved by a Christmas gift from Hertzka. Between 6 and 23 February Schoenberg rehearsed *Verklärte Nacht* in Vienna. At the end of February he conducted performances of *Pierrot Lunaire* in the Hamburg Kammerspiele and the Temming private house; this had been rehearsed and also conducted by Rufer. Casella wrote from Rome that the Italian *Pierrot* tour had been arranged. Schoenberg left on 19 March, conducted on the 28th and 29th in Rome, on the 30th in Naples, on 1 April in Florence, on 3rd, 4th and 6th in Venice, Padua and Turin, and the tour ended on 7th and 8th with concerts in Milan. It brought great success to Schoenberg, the speaker Erika Wagner, and the players Steuermann, Louis Fleury, Henri Delacroix and the Pro Arte Quartet. He was proud that Puccini, whose operas he loved, had taken six hours to travel to the performance in Florence and had asked Casella to introduce him to Schoenberg. The young Luigi Dallapiccola was also present at this concert.

Before *Pierrot Lunaire* the Pro Arte Quartet played Casella's Concerto for two violins, viola and cello, which received its première in the first concert of the tour on Friday, 28 March in the concert hall of the Accademia di St. Cecilia.

In April Schoenberg received an invitation from Prince Max Egon Fürstenberg to conduct his Serenade in the summer music festival in Donaueschingen. He thanked him in a letter of old Frankonian politeness, which shows his admiration for artistically minded princes, not without naïveté. The first contacts had already been made by the Artistic Director of Donaueschingen Festival with him on 5 March 1921; however, it was not until 1924 that he was able to offer the Serenade so that it could receive its first performance there. The première took place on 20 July under his direction. A private very first performance had already been given on 2 May in the Vienna house of the music patron Dr. Norbert Schwarzmann.

At that time Vienna was preparing a big international Theatre and Music Festival, during which several works of Schoenberg, for instance 'Friede auf Erden,' were performed under Anton von Webern.

At this time the Master began a friendly relationship with Kolisch's sister Gertrud. The pretty and gifted daughter of a famous doctor had been interested in drama production and in music, had attended many performances and rehearsals of the Society, and had quickly charmed Schoenberg with her dry, rather pert Viennese wit.

He now often went to Vienna for several days and gradually began to get interested in things with which he had been little occupied before. With friends, especially Adolf Loos, he often visited the elegant bars in the central part of Vienna. He found pleasure in jazz music, of which rhythmical traces can already be found in the Serenade. His improved financial position, especially as the result of the German Rentenmark, allowed him to buy provisions and to assume an elegance in his clothes which he had not been able to afford for many years.

Webern accompanied him to Donaueschingen, where he himself was the guest of the Prince in the castle. Two works by Webern were also performed at the Festival – the six Bagatelles for String Quartet opus 9 and 6 Songs opus 14 on poems of George Trakl for voice, clarinet, bass clarinet, violin and cello. Here they also met Scherchen, Klemperer, Rudolf Schulz-Dornburg, Stein and the composers Butting, Jemnitz and Hauer, who also had works performed. Before and after the Festival Schoenberg spent a few days in Salzkammergut. Mitzi Seligmann, the sister of Rudolf and Gertrud Kolisch, offered him accommodation in the crowded Aussee. He went back to Vienna on 1 August.

In the summer of 1924 he took up work again on the Quintet for flute, oboe, clarinet, bassoon and horn which he had begun a year earlier (Sketchbook 5 on 14 June 1923), and he finished it on 26 July. The copy sent to the publisher bears the date of completion 27 August 1924.

The dedication 'To Baby Arnold' refers to Schoenberg's grandson, the newly born son of Felix and Trudi Greissle. Schoenberg's idea seems to have been that when the baby grew up he would have ears for the secrets of the score, as Schoenberg always believed that his music would become generally understandable and intelligible in a near or distant future.

In fact the Wind Quintet is Schoenberg's most conservative attempt to combine strict 12-tone technique with classical methods of writing and forms. The four movements of the work, which lasts 40 minutes, follow the classical types exactly: Sonata movement, Scherzo and Trio, three-part song form, Rondo.

The series, the basic form of which, with its three mirror forms (Retrograde, inversion, retrograde inversion) exclusively provides the material for all the themes in the four movements, is purposely invented in such a way that its two halves relate to each other like tonic to dominant: E flat–G–A–B–C–sharp–C=B flat–D–E–F sharp–G sharp–F. This makes answers at the fifth above possible, and Schoenberg makes a great deal of use of this. The pseudo-tonal character of these passages makes a paradoxical

EINLADUNG

zur

Uraufführung

der Serenade

von

ARNOLD SCHÖNBERG,

die am 2. Mai 1924, 9 Uhr abds. unter persön-
licher Leitung des Komponisten im Hause
I., Krugerstraße 17 stattfindet.

Gesangsstimme	Kammersänger Alfred Jerger
Violine	Rudolf Kolisch
Viola	Marcel Dick
Cello	Wilhelm Winkler
Clarinette	Prof. Viktor Pollatschek
Bass-Clarinette	Leopold Wlach
Mandoline	Fanni Slezak
Guitarre	Hans Schlagradl

The private première of the Serenade took place at
Dr. Schwarzmann's home in Vienna before the première at
Donaueschingen

contrast to the strict 12-tone construction which excludes consonance and tonality.

The first performance of the Quintet opus 26 was conducted by Felix Greissle in Vienna on Schoenberg's fiftieth birthday.

The famous Frankfurt music critic Paul Bekker, an advocate of Schoenberg for many years, who was also at the Viennese private performance of the Serenade in May, received a letter from Schoenberg written on 1 August, in which he thanks him for the respect which Bekker had always shown for him and says at the same time that he was no longer the wild man he was before. He says that he also finds association with the aristocracy very pleasant: 'to one who thinks something of himself'. Similar thoughts appear in a letter written a few days later to Adolf Loos. On 21 August Schoenberg told his friend Zemlinsky, who was the first to hear of this, that he was going to marry Trude Kolisch. Their marriage took place on the 28th.

Meanwhile preparations had been made in Vienna to celebrate his fiftieth birthday on 13 September worthily. The 'Musikblätter des Anbruch' prepared a special issue of seventy-two pages, to which the contributors were, besides Schoenberg's pupils and friends (Anton Webern, Erwin Stein, Karl Horwitz, Rudolf Kolisch, Hanns Eisler, Josef Polnauer, Paul A. Pisk, Alban Berg, as well as Adolf Loos, G. F. Malipiero, Alfredo Casella, Franz Schreker, Rudolf Réti, and Dr. J. Bach), the performers Marya Freund, Marie Gutheil-Schoder, Erika Wagner, Rudolf Schulz-Dornburg, Paul Scheinpflug, Fritz Stiedry, Paul von Klenau, Hermann Scherchen and Artur Schnabel, the critics Paul Bekker, Adolf Weissmann and Max Graf, and, as an outsider, the theosophist Walther Klein. The most important theoretical article was by Erwin Stein; under the title 'New Formal Principles' it deals with the basic methods of the 12-tone technique, about which Schoenberg had spoken in 1921 to Rufer and in 1923 to a larger number of his pupils. On the evening before the birthday there was a party of Schoenberg's friends in Mödling. At this Webern presented to him a leather briefcase which he had bought with Kolisch which contained a large collection of photos of Schoenberg and his friends and relations. The following morning there was an official festival in the Town Hall, at which the Mayor Karl Seitz gave the address. Later the Wind Quintet was given its first performance – In a preface, which Schoenberg wrote himself for the special birthday number, he speaks in typical self-irony as a symbol of old age: 'I cannot hate as much

Gertrud Kolisch, Vienna 1924

as I used to; and what is still worse: I can sometimes understand things without despising them.'

The performances of his works during the year showed him how much he was understood and admired by an ever larger number of people. The most important to him was the première of *Erwartung* in Prague. Since the completion of the monodrama in September 1909 there were continual disappointments with regard to its planned performances. When in 1914 Count Seebach and Ernst von Schuch had planned its première for the Dresden Court Opera, the World War destroyed all projects of that kind. The Mannheim performance foundered on the fact that the orchestra there was not large enough for Schoenberg's demands. And the attempts of the producer Dr. Ernst Lert to arrange performances in Dresden or Frankfurt were in vain.

The Prague première took place on 6 June, conducted by Zemlinsky and produced by Louis Laber, with Marie Gutheil-Schoder as soloist in the Prague German Opera House. It was the final performance of the second festival of the International Society for Contemporary Music, and was regarded as the crown of it. Soon after his birthday, Schoenberg was able to take part in a series of festival performances in Frankfurt which had been arranged for him by Scherchen. Among the young musicians who admired him was Paul Hindemith. He had already supported Schoenberg in Donaueschingen, where he had had an influence on the programmes from the beginning. It was due to him that the Serenade was performed there; in January 1924 he had written to Burkard:

'*If you have this piece, Donaueschingen will stand high in morality above all other music festivals in this year*'.

In the Frankfurt concerts which Schoenberg attended, the Amar Quartet, with Hindemith as the viola player, took part in performances of both string quartets.

Finally, a few months after *Erwartung*, Schoenberg's second opera *Die Glückliche Hand* was also played for the first time. The première took place on 14 October 1924 in the Vienna Volksoper. Fritz Stiedry conducted, Josef Turnau was the producer; the Man was sung by Alfred Jerger, the Woman was danced by prima ballerina Hedy Pfundtmayr. This première too brought success for Schoenberg. But his malicious enemies maintained that the cost of the production had ruined the Volksoper. In fact on 5 November the décor for the *Glückliche Hand* was impounded. But it was not Schoenberg's work which was the reason for this, but the rivalry between the Volksoper and the State Opera and the ban on performing works by Verdi and Puccini in future.

At this time Schoenberg seems also to have been interested in modern scientific discoveries. On 2 October he asked Emil Hertzka to arrange a conversation between himself and the physicist Albert Einstein. On 22 October Walter Gropius thanked him in the name of the Weimar Bauhaus, of which he was the Director, for the fact that his name could be included among the members of the trustees, called 'Circle of the Friends of the Bauhaus'. It was an illustrious body, to which Peter Behrens Adolf Busch, Marc Chagall, Albert Einstein, Herbert Eulenberg, Edwin Fischer, Gerhart Hauptmann, Josef Hoffmann, Oskar Kokoschka, Hans Poelzig and Franz Werfel all belonged.

The newly married couple were planning a visit to the South at the beginning of the next year. Problems had to be solved which were connected with Schoenberg's children and the household in Mödling. Purchases had to be made. The new family connection also brought social duties with itself. And finally Schoenberg was continuing to work with his pupils. It should be mentioned merely as a curiosity that on 11 December Schoenberg resigned from the Austrian Association of Teachers of Music, because the newly published magazine of the Society had immediately made a powerful attack on him in their first number. By the side of the high honours which he had received in the whole world for his fiftieth birthday, this knavish trick must take the prize for originality.

In the autumn of 1924 Oskar Kokoschka, who had given up his professorship in Dresden, came back to Vienna for a short time after all kinds of adventures in Italy. He painted Schoenberg in his surroundings in Mödling at a musical session at home. The position of the hands, especially the left hand at a high angle, is remarkable in the picture. Kokoschka left out the cello, whose finger-board and bow were manipulated by Schoenberg. The suggestive look, the bald patch, the jacket hanging loosely round the shoulders are typical of the subject of the portrait.

Music at home played an important part in the Schoenberg family during their years in Mödling. Mathilde, who should have been able to play the piano well, hardly ever took part in it. But Gertrud was a good pianist, Georg learned to play the horn, and the Schoenberg's friends and pupils gladly took part in quartet playing, in which Schoenberg played the cello part. He also wrote small movements for the domestic circle which were preserved in his legacy; for Christmas 1921 music for two violins, cello and piano (or harmonium); at the beginning of November 1923 a fragment with the enigmatic name 'Gerpa', a theme with variations for horn, two violins and harmonium.

When Rufer once went to Mödling Schoenberg and his daughter Trudi played Grieg's Cello Sonata. Schoenberg said that one could learn from Grieg how to write gratefully for an instrument. But after Mathilde's death and Trudi's marriage the family had diminished. At the end of 1924 domestic music-making was replaced by other interests. Kokoschka's picture captured the spirit of this chamber music in Mödling.

THE GREAT CALL

For a long time there had been no leisure in Schoenberg's life. Now came the time to relax. On the *Pierrot* tour in 1924 Italy had aroused his longing for Southern cities and coasts. In January 1925 the married couple travelled to Venice, where they spent their honeymoon. Then they journeyed to Milan, heard performances at La Scala and wanted to go to the Mediterranean coast. On 28 January Schoenberg wrote to Gian Francesco Malipiero, whom he had known since 1923. He wanted to visit him with his young wife in Asolo near Venice. He said he would await a reply in San Remo. At the same time he suggested a meeting to Alfredo Casella, without knowing that the latter was also in Milan. They met the same evening. Schoenberg thanked Casella for an article in 'Anbruch', which described Puccini's visit to hear *Pierrot* in Florence and the meeting of the two great masters. Puccini's death in September of the previous year had moved Schoenberg very much. 'I would never have thought', he wrote to Casella, 'that I would not see this great man again! And I am proud to have aroused his interest and am thankful to you for telling my enemies about this event, which does me a great deal of honour.'

At that time Malipiero and Casella were the leading Italian modern composers. In 1923, under the honorary presidency of the poet Gabriele d'Annunzio, they had formed an Italian Society for Modern Music, the Corporazione delle Nuove Musiche, the initial letters of which, C. F. N. M., also symbolized the Latin name Concentus Decimae Nuncius Musae. The Society invited Bartók and Hindemith to visit Italy for the first time, and put on the first performances of Stravinsky's *Tale of the Soldier* and Octet and also the tour of *Pierrot Lunaire* mentioned above.

From Milan the Schoenbergs went to San Remo, where they spent fourteen days in the Hotel Mediterranée. Malipiero invited them to visit him in Asolo on their way back. They spent the evening of 16 February in his beautiful house with its valuable art treasures. Schoenberg signed the new visitors' book with a witty sentence full of plays on words.

They also had a quiet time in Mödling and Vienna. Franz Neumann, the operatic director of the Czech National Theatre in Brno, invited Schoenberg to attend his performance of the 'Gurrelieder'. It was the first one in the Czech language. 500 performers took part in the Sunday matinée in the City Theatre.

In April the Schoenbergs travelled to Barcelona. His pupil who lived there, Roberto Gerhard (1896–1970), had arranged a 'Festival de la Musica Viennesa' with a Schoenberg concert in addition at the Catalan Associació de Música 'Da Camera' de Barcelona. The programme of Viennese music was played on 26 and 28 April. It contained chamber music by Schubert, Beethoven, Mozart and the Emperor Waltz by Johann Strauss, which Schoenberg had arranged for the ensemble of *Pierrot Lunaire* (Flute, clarinet, violin, cello and piano) and conducted it himself. When the concert was repeated in other Catalan cities such as Gerona, Figueras, Reus and Palamos Marya Freund sang some additional songs by Schubert and Mahler. The Schoenberg programme followed on 29 April and consisted of the Chamber Symphony opus 9, the songs 'Verlassen', 'Der Wanderer', 'Traumleben' and 'Am Wegrand' as well as *Pierrot Lunaire*. The programme book contained these sentences by Schoenberg in German and Catalan: 'Modern art must certainly count on becoming fashionable at some time. However, art has always had fashion behind itself, next to itself and especially against it: it is only at a certain period in time that this relationship can be clearly observed.'

The ensemble was different from the usual one. Its basis was the 'Viennese String Quartet', founded in 1924 with Rudolf Kolisch, Fritz Rothschild, Marcel Dick and Joachim Stutschewsky. They were joined by the clarinettist Viktor Polatschek, the flautist Franz Wangler and, instead of Steuermann who was prevented by other concert engagements, the pianist Friedrich Wührer. Marya Freund spoke and sang *Pierrot Lunaire* and the Songs. The cellist Stutschewsky remembers the concerts, which according to Spanish custom began late in the evening; only the Schoenberg programme was given as a Sunday matinée. As people were afraid of hostile reactions from the audience Stutschewsky asked Roberto Gerhard to sit on the rostrum with them during *Pierrot* and appease the public if necessary. These precautions turned out to be unnecessary.

Schoenberg in 1925

Casals was shortly going on a concert tour, so that they were only able to have a brief meeting. Schoenberg felt very well in Barcelona. He wrote a letter of thanks from there to Malipiero and invited the latter to visit him in Vienna.

In these cheerful spring months of 1925 he planned a new composition, the first sketch of which was written down in the fifth sketch book on 28 October 1924. These were his first thoughts for his Suite opus 29 for piano, E flat clarinet, clarinet, bass clarinet, violin, viola and cello. A piece of paper glued on to the sketch book and typewritten gives the following somewhat enigmatic indications:

1. (Movement) 6/8 light, elegant, gay, bluff.
2. Jo-Jo-Foxtrot.
3. Fl. Kschw. Waltz.
4. AS Adagio.
5. ibeB Muartsch Var.
6. Film Dva.
7. Tenn Ski.

The final version of the work, which was reduced to four movements, preserves little of these sportive and intentionally modish titles. However the first movement resembles the sketch quite closely. It is an allegretto in 6/8 time with the indication very gay'. The ironic name 'bluff' was altered to Overture. In form it is a sonata movement with two themes and a development, reprise and coda. In June Schoenberg started working on the Suite again, first of all on the 2nd movement, 'Dance Steps', on the Overture and on the 3rd movement in July. The 'Dance Steps' are a scherzo in a very free form and with continual changes of character. In the 3rd movement, the famous 'Theme and Variations', one can see the idea of the work, of using tonality as a special case of 12-tone thinking. Schoenberg wrote variations on Friedrich Silcher's *Ännchen von Tharau* song and varies it in four ways so that each note is complemented as part of the basic row.

This variation movement was not finished until August 1925. After another long interruption the final date of 1 May 1926 was written under the last movement, the Gigue. It is an ingenious combination of sonata movement and fugue, the model for which was the finale of Mozart's Jupiter Symphony.

The row is a series of twelve notes, of which the first and last groups of four notes mirror each other in a transposed retrograde form, while the middle of the series combines two two-note groups in the relation of retrograde mirror forms. Webern preferred rows of this kind from 1928 onwards. The intervals are: major third, minor third and semitone and their complementary octave relations. The work, which bears the dedication: 'To my dear Wife', was his first love-gift to Gertrud Schoenberg. Her initials E flat–G (S–G in German) begin and end each of the movements so that they have a kind of tonal bracket.

As in many other compositions of the time after the World War, a tone of ironic gaiety predominates in the Suite opus 29, in a paradoxical contrast to the strength of its construction. The relaxation of Schoenberg's conditions of life, his desire for gay company and visits to bars with the stimulation of tobacco and alcohol, corresponds to his spiritual feeling of this kind. At that time he also grew a small moustache for a short period.

Schoenberg also did a good deal of literary work of all kinds. In 1924 Erwin Stein had founded a new magazine, 'Pult und Taktstock', which came out monthly and dealt with technical musical problems, especially those of contemporary music. Schoenberg was one of the contributors to it. His articles appeared under the pseudonym 'Jens Quer', an abbreviation of 'Jenseitiger Querkopf' (A crank on the other side). But his larger theoretical works bore his real name. There are some important ones among them, like the article on 'Mechanical musical instruments', which appeared in April 1926. On 6 June 1925 Schoenberg noted down nine sentences about musical thoughts, their presentation and formulation. At the time he was visiting Dr. Kolisch in Vienna. Webern complained in a letter to Berg of 7 July that he had not seen Schoenberg since Sunday, 28 June.

At the beginning of September the annual Festival of the International Society for Contemporary Music took place in Venice. The Schoenbergs did not want to live in the city itself but on the Lido, and on 17 August Schoenberg asked Malipiero to recommend them a hotel there. They also planned to spend the autumn and winter in Italy. They fled from the heat of the Viennese summer this year to Altaussee.

Owing to the death of Busoni there was a vacancy for a teacher of a Master Class in Composition in the Berlin Academy of Arts. Professor Leo Kestenberg, who had been the representative of Music in the Prussian Ministry of Culture in 1918, and had already appointed Franz Schreker as Director of the High School of Music, wanted to have Schoenberg as Busoni's successor. He suggested to the very progressively minded Minister of Culture, Carl Heinrich Becker, that they should appoint the much-debated

Viennese composer, and obtained his agreement. On 28 August 1925 he met Schoenberg in Vienna. The contract was signed by both parties the same day. It contained seven clauses which made Schoenberg responsible for holding a Master Class in composition in Berlin, for the moment from 1 October 1925 to 30 September 1930, to teach six months of every year in Berlin and to make up any time lost through concert or lecture tours in the following year. He was entitled to a salary of at least 16,800 marks and the title of Professor. The Education Authorities would also see about getting him an apartment and providing all the material he needed for teaching. The news of this appointment aroused a great deal of excitement in Vienna among both Schoenberg's friends and his enemies. The Master Classes in Berlin were the highest grade in the hierarchy of music teaching. Men like Richard Strauss, Hans Pfitzner and Busoni had undertaken this work or were still doing so. Such an appointment was more important for prestige than a class in the Hochschule für Musik.

However, on 29 August, immediately after his conversation with Kestenberg, the Schoenbergs went to Venice. At the beginning of September the rehearsals for the Serenade began, which Schoenberg was to conduct there. The Festival began on 3 September and lasted till the 8th. Among other works there were compositions by Fauré, Villa-Lobos, Hindemith, Max Butting, Hanns Eisler, Janácek, Korngold, Honegger, Roussel, Ravel, Schnabel, Vaughan Williams, Szymanowski, Malipiero, Carl Ruggles, Stravinsky and Louis Grünberg. Schoenberg's Serenade was to be performed on 7 September in the fifth programme.

At that time the cultural and personal tensions between the chief representatives of modern music had reached a climax. Schoenberg and Stravinsky were regarded as opposites, whose points of view were irreconcilable. In spite of its sturdy rhythms Schoenberg's Serenade was regarded as leading to the new methods of the technique of composition, in the direction of 12-tone music. On the other side Stravinsky's Piano Sonata, which he played himself, was typical of neo-classicism, which went back to models of the eighteenth century. Professor Edward Dent, the English President of the Society, described the atmosphere of these hot summer days in Venice with great humour. At the head of the many German musicians and critics Adolf Weissmann appeared in a heavy knickerbocker suit and mountain boots to walk across the Piazza. When Schoenberg had over-run his rehearsal time for the Serenade Dent asked him if he thought that he was the only composer in this festival. Schoenberg said yes. In spite of all his work in Venice he still had time to begin a string quartet, after the Wind Quintet opus 26, and to send greetings to friends.

On 24 September the Schoenbergs returned to Mödling. Webern spent the next evening with Schoenberg and wrote to his friend Berg: 'He told me about the disaster of "modern Music" including Stravinsky, of whom he said that he had had his hair cropped close; he "bachelts" (Bach Imitation).' He said that Schoenberg would not go to Berlin till January and would remain in Mödling for the present.

Immediately after his return from Venice Schoenberg wrote the two official letters to the Prussian Minister of Culture and to Kestenberg. He refused an interview to a curious journalist from the *Neue Wiener Journal*: 'I don't want any accusations, any attacks, any defences, any advertisements, any triumph! Only: calm!'

Kestenberg answered some of Schoenberg's questions on 2 October. He said it was not necessary to interrupt his work in order to come to Berlin. The end of November or the beginning of December would do perfectly well. Only he would like to know the date soon. Schoenberg was not in a hurry, as Webern's letter to Berg shows. He spent a large part of October in the Vienna house of Dr. Kolisch. One of the first people to congratulate him was Henri Hinrichsen in Leipzig, who meanwhile had published Felix Greissle's chamber orchestra arrangement of the Orchestral Pieces opus 16. The friend of his youth Walter Pieau, who was then an operatic baritone in Osnabruck, recommended him an apartment in Berlin.

In November Schoenberg developed appendicitis. He went into the Rudolf Hospital and was operated on. Alban Berg sent him Franz Kafka's collection of stories *The Country Doctor* to read in bed; Webern congratulated him on his successful operation on 18 November. This operation prevented Schoenberg from being present at the first performance of Berg's *Wozzeck*, which Erich Kleiber gave on 14 December at the Berlin State Opera. One day later Schoenberg was made an honorary member of the Accademia di Santa Cecilia in Rome.

In 1926 a new epoch in Schoenberg's life began. The children from his first marriage stayed in Vienna and Mödling. He himself and Frau Gertrud moved to Berlin on 10 January and stayed, to begin with, in the Pension Bavaria. In his composition class at the

Academy he found a number of new pupils, including Walter
Goehr, Walter Gronostay and the American Adolphe Weiss.
Winfried Zillig had followed the Master to Berlin, and Roberto
Gerhard came from Barcelona – Schoenberg already knew him
from Vienna. Among his older friends Josef Rufer had been living
in Berlin for some months; Schoenberg made him his assistant,
and he had to teach the pupils harmony, counterpoint and other
pre-compositional studies.

On 19 January Schoenberg finished in the Berlin pension a
work which was to make him many enemies: the Three Satires
for mixed chorus opus 28. Stylistically they are similar to the
Four Pieces for mixed chorus opus 27. Schoenberg had been
working on both compositions since the end of September 1925.
The impressions of the Music Festival in Venice certainly
contributed to their conception. Two of the texts of opus 27 are
by Schoenberg himself. The second one, 'You should not, you
must' is nearer in thought to *Jacob's Ladder* and the later text of
Moses and Aaron. It runs:

You must not make an image for yourself!
For an image limits,
Sets bounds
To what must remain unlimited and unpresented
An image wants to have a name:
You can only take it from small things;
You must not honour small things!
You must believe in the spirit!
Immediate, without feeling
And without self.
You must, you chosen one, you must, you must remain
  yourself!

Schoenberg composed it on 16 and 17 October, soon after
'Unentrinnbar'. In October and November two poems from
Hans Bethge's *Chinesische Flöte*, the collection which Mahler also
used for his 'Lied von der Erde', followed. The Satires were begun
immediately afterwards. 'Am Scheideweg' is dated 12 November
1925; the third piece, 'Der neue Klassizismus', has the remark:
'begun still with appendicitis 13 November 1925' and '15
November 1925!! in the night!' The second piece, 'Vielseitig-
keit', was finished on the last day of the year. Nos. 1 and 2 are
unaccompanied choruses; No. 3 is a little cantata for mixed
chorus, viola, cello and piano. Schoenberg added three canons

as an appendix. The first is a maxim with two variations; the second and third were written in Berlin.

If one reads the texts of the Satires, the influence of an unmistakeable Viennese irony is clearly to be found; Gertrud Schoenberg-Kolisch was a master of this. In the much more serious preface, which Schoenberg put in front of opus 28, he mentions the addressees on whom he turns his mockery: 'All . . . , who seek their personal salvation in a middle way', the 'seeming tonalists', the 'back to – people', the 'folklorists' and finally all '. . . ists', who for him are mannerists. The bitter cheerfulness of these mocking songs is linked in language to the Serenade and the Suite opus 29, against which the four pieces for mixed chorus are nearer to the Wind Quintet. Exceptionally the last one, 'Der Wunsch des Liebhabers', has an accompaniment of mandoline, clarinet, violin and cello. Here Schoenberg works with a 12-note series which allows combinations of tonal chords. This gives rise to a kind of polytonality, which is also used even more ingeniously in the Satires, especially in the cantata about classicism. The third of the canons was dedicated to Bernard Shaw on his seventieth birthday in admiration; the text shows Schoenberg's attitude:

> LEGITIMATION AS A CANON.
> He who gives honour,
> must possess honour himself;
> otherwise it is not great enough.
> So musicians of honour
> revere the canon:
> to show that they have honour through it.

He showed this dedicatory piece to his friend Alban Berg on 7 June 1926. At the end of the music he wrote: 'For ever – without end! End only if necessary'. And Schoenberg says 'that he can bring many things together with only seven notes; this may not be very much valued, but it certainly counts as difficult'.

In March there had been a short correspondence between Schoenberg and Zemlinsky about Eisler. In a train conversation Eisler, who was then under the new influence of radical left political ideas, had raised objections to 12-tone music. He affirmed his point of view in a letter of about the same time:

Modern music bores me, it does not interest me, I hate much of it and even despise it. I will in fact have nothing to do with the 'modern'. If possible I try to avoid hearing it and reading it.

(I must unfortunately count even my own works of the last year among this) . . . also I don't understand anything (even external elements) about 12-tone technique and music. But I am enthusiastic about your 12-tone works (like for instance the Piano Suite) and I have studied it in great detail.

Schoenberg answered on 10 March extremely critically and strictly, but not without hope of a reconciliation for the future. Eisler replied at once, and Schoenberg wrote to him again on 12 March, that he reproached him especially for having made critical utterances to Zemlinsky, who at this time had a divergence of views with Schoenberg. The quarrel with Zemlinsky was soon cleared up. With Eisler, who was then going in a direction of which Schoenberg could not approve, it took a longer time. It was not till their Californian emigration that their old friendship was re-established.

Heinrich Burkard sent an enquiry about the 'Four Pieces for Mixed Choir' opus 27 and the 'Three Satires' opus 28. Schoenberg answered on 7 April 1926 that unfortunately he could not accept the friendly invitation to give the first performances of these works in Donaueschingen. He had been told that the Stuttgart Madrigal Choir was too small:

'*For my choruses I must have four to five singers to each part. And then I must certainly conduct a first performance myself, if not rehearse it, and that is quite impossible at this distance. Also I don't think it is right for me to take the place of younger and still struggling composers.*'

On 3 June the Berlin Academy of Arts gave a concert in honour of Schoenberg, in which among other works the F sharp minor String Quartet was played by the Havemann Quartet and Margot Hinnenberg-Lefèbre. On 27 May Schoenberg had been sworn in as a state official. The Schoenbergs led a social life which was rich in artistic events. One could meet them at Furtwängler's Philharmonic concerts, at premières at the State Opera and the brilliant Berlin theatres. – Unfortunately the climate caused difficulties. Schoenberg's old tendency towards asthma became worse because of the cold winter and the raw spring. We know his condition from his own medical history which he wrote in 1950 in America. There he wrote:

'*1923 to 1924, before I married my second wife, I drank again and inhaled sixty cigarettes a day. In order to overcome the consequences of this I behaved very foolishly. Besides liquor I drank three litres of strong coffee every day and took codein and pantopon. This helped me a little, though basically I was getting worse. But during my honeymoon in*

*Venice I acquired the will-power to give up all my sins described above;
as the result of this I obtained a pause of breath which lasted about two
years.'*

In Vienna Schoenberg had been treated by Professor D.
Gustav Singer. Schoenberg wrote to him from Berlin on 7 July
1926:

> *'I now have less difficulty in breathing when going to sleep, and I don't
> so often start up gasping for breath. The cough is less frequent and does
> not cause such shattering spasms . . . on the other hand in the morning . . .
> I feel somewhat exhausted and breathless, and at other times too I tend
> to get out of breath more than before. So this strikes me as somewhat less
> good now. Recently I have not been running so many temperatures, but I
> am not sure whether it is not merely the deadening effect of habit and that
> I have lost my sensitivity to it.'*

In August the Schoenbergs went to Dubrovnik, then to
Pörtschach in Carinthia, where they spent several weeks at the
Hotel Werzer which lies on the lake. There they met Franz and
Maria Schreker; the two musicians played tennis together every
day.

In this summer Schoenberg again took up religious ideas, for
which he had made notes since 1922. The work took the form of a
drama. It is called *Der biblische Weg* and is a very individual
document showing his position in questions of the Jewish faith.
Schoenberg had said that he did not agree with many details of
Zionism. But he was a passionate fighter for the idea of giving the
Jewish people a homeland. All Schoenberg's later religious texts
are linked immediately to the ideas of the *biblische Weg*, which up
till now has only been published in an Italian translation.

Even before going away on his summer holidays, Schoenberg
made a suggestion on 14 June to the President of the Berlin Academy, the painter Professor Max Liebermann, about the plan of
giving a medal to specially gifted graduates of the Prussian Art
and Music High Schools. Schoenberg suggested that any such
students should be given them, 'whose talent and ability are such
to warrant the expectation that their future achievements will
surpass the average'.

A series of notes and fragments shows Schoenberg again
occupied with the direction taken by contemporary music, which
struck him as hostile. So he attacked Stravinsky, who had declared that he only wanted to write music for the present day,
while others were trying to write the music of the future. He also
criticized an article by Ernst Krenek, who supported light music.

On 29 September 1926 Gertrud Fuhrman, the piano and composition teacher, recognized by the State, asked the Prussian Minister for Culture to be allowed to attend Schoenberg's lectures: 'I would like to further my education, I particularly want to get to know the latest "atonal" music and its development.' At the Academy's request Schoenberg replied.

This was in the Yearbook *25 Years of New Music*, which Universal Edition published as a kind of balance-sheet of twenty-five years of their activity. Schoenberg himself wrote the introductory article 'Gessinnung oder Erkenntnis?', which is especially concerned with the question 'tonal or atonal'. As in the Harmony Book he maintained that tonality was not an end in itself, but a means to an end. And he gives an answer to the question which is often posed, why consonances are suppressed in his music. 'It is in fact a *question of economy*. According to my feeling for form (and I am immodest enough to allow this alone to have control of my composition) the playing of even one tonal triad will bring its own consequences and demand a certain space, which cannot be allowed inside my form. A tonal chord arouses expectations of what is to follow, and, working backwards, also has influence on everything that has gone before it; one can't demand that I should overthrow everything that has gone before it because a triad has by chance been introduced.' And further: 'From the beginning I was clear that a substitute must be found for the disappearance of tonal means of construction, which allows larger forms to be built again . . . starting from this point I have come to composition with 12 notes'. The article ends with the important sentence: 'Thought has no time, so it can wait in peace; language must hurry up!'

The Schoenbergs celebrated his fifty-second birthday in Pörtschach. Alban Berg sent a hymn-like letter of good wishes, which protested that the celebrations of the births of all living and dead poets did not affect him as much as that of Schoenberg, 'without whose birth I would not have come into the world, or at least that part of me which was worth being born!'

Schoenberg wrote to Webern at the end of September that they were going to stay in the hotel as long as it stayed open. At the beginning of October they went to Vienna; Berg, who had not spoken to Schoenberg for nine months, could hardly wait to see him again on 9 October. On the 14th he invited the Schoenbergs and the Weberns to afternoon coffee in their house at Hietzing.

In the middle of October the Schoenbergs went back to Berlin. On 25 September Schoenberg had informed the Academy from Pörtschach that for reasons of health he would start his teaching again in November instead of October. The Academy was planning a concert for the middle of January 1927. Schreker had suggested Schoenberg's mixed Choruses opus 27 and 28 for this. He was asked if he was agreeable to this.

There was a lot of trouble with Universal Edition in Vienna. In September Schoenberg had to complain strongly that the Choral Satires and the Suite opus 29 had not yet been published. At the beginning of December their relations became so cool that the publishers released Schoenberg from his contract for the duration of a year at his own wish. However, their correspondence continued. In January 1927 there were discussions about the plan of putting on a stage performance of 'Gurrelieder' in Berlin. In order to clear up the differences of opinion Dr. Hans Heinsheimer, the young, very active director of the operatic department, came to Berlin later and discussed this with Schoenberg. Before this Alban and Helene Berg had come for a short stay, because Kleiber was putting on a new production of *Wozzeck* at the State Opera. They spent a lot of time with the Schoenbergs and also attended the lecture which he gave on 19 January in the Academy on 'Problems of Harmony'. On 20 January Schoenberg was elected to the Senate; on 3 February the Academy wrote to him: 'Through your appointment you have obtained Prussian nationality from now on.' A greeting came from Zurich from the 'Vienna String Quartet' (Kolisch Quartet) which had given a highly successful performance of the F sharp minor Quartet with Margot Hinnenberg-Lefèbre.

Between 4 February and 8 March Schoenberg wrote his third String Quartet opus 30, which was commissioned by the American patroness Elizabeth Sprague-Coolidge and is dedicated to her. He had already made sketches for it at the end of January.

Like the second quartet it is in four movements and lasts about half an hour. The 12-tone row, on which it is built and the identification of which Rudolf Kolisch took so much trouble about, is already used in the first movement with its mirror forms. This movement, a Moderato alla breve, is in the form of a sonata movement. Schoenberg said in his commentary for the record album of 1939, that this movement, with its idée fixe-like repetitions of a quaver figure was caused by nightmare memories of the picture of the Captain in Wilhelm Hauff's 'Ghost Ship', who had been nailed to the mast through his forehead by the mutinous sailors. The second movement, an Adagio, combines variation form with that of a rondo. The rondo form also appears in the Intermezzo in the form of a scherzo and trio and in the final *molto moderato*, which also contains the development, reprise and coda of a sonata movement. Schoenberg finally justifies the many variations of the serial thematic material as are made necessary by the modern ear, which does not want so many unaltered repetitions as in classical music, where recognition of the themes is a basic principle. 'If a theme appears often in a rondo and the composer has to make do with little thematic material, the conciseness of this economy must be compensated for by many variations of all the material at the composer's disposal.'

Schoenberg used his release from his contract with Universal Edition and offered this work to Hinrichsen in Leipzig, also mentioned the Variations opus 31 for Orchestra, which he had hardly begun. Hinrichsen was interested in the quartet and offered a fee of 3000 marks, which Schoenberg regarded as too little. The publisher's laconic letter in answer on 14 February said that it had been a general principle of the House of Peters not to discuss questions of money any more. So this ended this attempt to develop Schoenberg's old relations with the Leipzig publishers.

The Berlin Radio, which called itself 'Funkstunde', carried out a progressive programme under the musical direction of Hans von Benda. Schoenberg was often invited to conduct his own works and on 8 April 1927, after three rehearsals with an excellent orchestra, he conducted a performance of *Pelléas and Mélisande*. In the spring of 1927 he also wrote notes about the foundation of an international school for stylistic education; he had already made similar proposals in 1920 to the Dutch Mahler Society.

Correspondence with Mitzi Seligmann continued in a cheerful manner. Gertrud Schoenberg kept her sister informed about work and the daily round, diversions and reading. 'Have you yet read *Gentlemen prefer Blondes* by Anita Loos?', she asked in a letter. 'If not, I will send it to you'. This harmless but cheerful book was very much liked all over Europe, and was what one would call a bestseller today.

At the end of July the Paris publisher Leduc asked if Schoenberg would write a contribution to a collection of modern vocalises, vocal exercises without texts. He asked Universal Edition for their permission, and they agreed. However, the plan seems to have foundered on the fact that the Paris publisher was worried whether a vocalise by Schoenberg would fit the style of the collection.

The Schoenbergs again spent the summer in Pörtschach from the end of June. Here Schoenberg met Kandinsky and his wife Nina after many years. Their old friendship was renewed; a picture of the side of the Wörthersee testifies to the cheerful atmos-

Rudolf Kolisch, Vienna 1926

phere of these weeks together. On 1 August Schoenberg sent
suggestions about the proofs of the 3rd String Quartet to Universal
Edition, to whom he had now handed over the new work. Berg
received news from him and wrote to Webern on 10 August:
'Very nice letter from Schoenberg. He has worked a lot (without
finishing anything), plays tennis, and wants to spend his summer
holiday elsewhere (Upper Bolzanb? Sea?)'. Webern replied that
he had had two letters from Pörtschach where his friends were
going to stay till about 20 September – An interesting enquiry
came from Breslau, where the Intendant Josef Turnau was
planning a performance of *Glückliche Hand*, Universal Edition
wanted to know whether Schoenberg agreed to this. He answered
in the affirmative.

Schoenberg wrote on 21 July from Pörtschach, sending his
views to the Academy of Arts, who wanted to make it compulsory
for students at the Academy of Art to participate in gymnastics.
He says that as a rule students need to earn their living, and this
measure might well be damaging to them. Also most of them are
at an age and a stage of development which makes such compulsion appear scarcely suitable. Also compulsion would be quite
unnecessary if a modern sport such as boxing, rowing, swimming,
football, hockey, tennis or polo were introduced. Then the
students would be able to behave as they do in England and
America and regard it as a matter of prestige to produce good
teams: 'For ambition is an authority to which obedience is
accorded voluntarily and spontaneously!'

Schoenberg spent his fifty-third birthday in Vienna. There
Kolisch and his colleagues gave the first performance of the 3rd
Quartet on 19 September. Elizabeth Sprague Coolidge, who had
commissioned it, came from America, accompanied by the
conductor Hans Kindler, and sat with her hearing-aid in the
front row. Schoenberg wrote to Rufer that he would come to
Berlin on 6 or 7 October. As they still had no apartment there
they would go to the Hotel Knie.

The term began again. Newly arrived students were Nikos
Skalkottas, Alfred Keller and Peter Schacht. Schoenberg heard
from Universal Edition that he had been invited to take part at a
festival with two concerts in his honour in December in Paris.
The Suite opus 29 would have its first performance there. On 10
November he recommended Winfried Zillig to his publishers;
Zillig had become one of his favourite students and several of his
works had been published by Universal Edition as a result.

The extremely difficult piano part in the Suite was undertaken by Zillig, with whom the Schoenbergs travelled to Paris, in order to prepare for the first performance on 15 December. More than 20 years later Schoenberg remembered this period in a letter written more than 20 years later:

'*I think with special pleasure of our journey to Paris, where you really helped me so much in rehearsing the Suite. You remember that at that time I was always with my dear friend Adolf Loos in restaurants; he insisted on showing me all the places to have pleasure and eat well and showed how good it tasted. So I ate chicken everywhere and didn't get to bed till late at night. This made me so tired that I couldn't study my score. Without you I would not have been able to put on this performance.*'

After Schoenberg's great success in Paris he and his wife went to Cannes, where they spent Christmas and New Year. A card sent to Webern on 30 December gives news about the Paris concerts. His relations with the eldest of his pupils and friends had again become very warm. He had already written to him in detail in Mödling in October 1927. Schoenberg was occupied by a number of plans, which prevented his work in composition. There was to be a performance of the 'Gurrelieder' in London on 27 January, and the Schoenbergs left on the 14th for rehearsals. Basle and Berne wanted to put on *Pierrot*, and he was to give a lecture in French at the Sorbonne in Paris. He needed about two hours a day for letters; otherwise he was pleased about a concert in Berlin with Webern's new String Trio (which the latter had sent to him on 25 November), Berg's *Lyric Suite* and his own 3rd String Quartet.

The question of lodging had not yet been settled. The Schoenbergs lived in three furnished rooms, in October 1927 in Charlottenburg, Kantstrasse 4, later with a Frau Cohn at Kurfürstendamm 203. Because of this situation Schoenberg sent a request for help to the Academy on 8 February 1928; he said he still had no house and his furniture was in storage, for which he had to pay 55 marks a month. Besides he had to set up his own library, which he needed for teaching, at great cost, for there was no library available at the Academy. He had to pay more than a third of his salary for a few badly furnished rooms.

For the fiftieth birthday of Franz Schreker on 23 March 1928 Universal Edition brought out a special number of the 'Musikblätter des Anbruch'. Schoenberg sent his birthday wishes on 7 March; these introduced the book. He remembered the old times when he and Schreker spoke a new language, and asked himself

why they were now called romantics. In fact the modern youth
was turning away from Schoenberg and Schreker, the former
revolutionaries. The ideal of objectivity, embodied at that time in
the music of Hindemith, confirmed the young in their dislike of
all artistic rhetoric. Hindemith himself, who had been teaching
composition as a professor at the Berlin High School since 1927,
was less orthodox in this than his followers. – In February Paul
Bekker, who was General Intendant in Wiesbaden, performed
Erwartung. Schoenberg was not there.

On 24 March the *Glückliche Hand* was given in Breslau for the
first time since its Vienna première. The performance was conducted by Fritz Cortolezis, Herbert Graf was the producer and
the scenery was by Wildermann. Before this there was an irritable
correspondence with the producer, who was afraid of Schoenberg
being present at the rehearsals. Finally Schoenberg's minimum
demand was fulfilled: a rehearsal on the day before the performance, which was to last until he was satisfied with it.

Schoenberg was extremely satisfied and thanked the General
Intendant Josef Turnau on the 29th. He said that he had never
had the feeling so strongly that people regarded his work with
respect, even with warmth. One would think that one was in a
capital city of art. In fact the performance, which was repeated
after a short commentary by Schoenberg, was very good musically
and scenically. For this difficult work, which according to Schoenberg 'makes music with the means of the theatre' and was
cleverly placed between Rameau and Handel, the performance
had the same significance as that of Berg's *Wozzeck* in Oldenburg;
one knew now that Schoenberg's stage works were also possible
to do in smaller theatres.

In Vienna there were rumours that Emil Hertzka wanted to
resign from the direction of Universal Edition. Schoenberg and
Schreker were unhappy and planned a common action by the
chief composers who were published by the firm. On 10 April
Schoenberg wrote to Berg:

> '*If you would agree to take part in the enclosed manifesto – don't force
> yourself to do it – then sign yourself as a proposer and send it to me
> straight away. Perhaps you could also persuade Frau Mahler and
> Bittner to take part. Of course I ask you to ask Webern (I haven't got
> any more copies), and Schreker is joining in too.*'

Berg did not take part. Hertzka remained Director of the firm.
So the plan was fruitless.

On 17 April Webern wrote about the first performance of

'Herzgewächse', which he had conducted in a subscription concert put on by Kolisch's 'Vienna String Quartet' in the season of 1927/28. The soloist was the Leipzig soprano Marianne Rau-Hoeglauer who had the necessary compass from low G sharp up to F in alt. The success was tumultous.

In May 1926 Schoenberg had written down the sketch of a theme, which he then developed further experimentally and sketched out possibilities for variations. After several months he wanted to finish the Variations. In vain. The work was broken off, taken up again several times and put aside. It was planned for orchestra.

The plan was mentioned in a conversation between Schoenberg and Erwin Stein. Stein spoke about it to Furtwängler, whom he had known since his work in Darmstadt in 1919. Furtwängler immediately asked Schoenberg to let him have the first performance with the Vienna Philharmonic. Schoenberg answered on 30 May: it would take 14 days to finish the piece; he could not say whether he could spare the time. He would write to Furtwängler. But: under no circumstances did he want a first performance in Vienna; he was the one composer with a name who had never been played by the Philharmonic there. And it should stay like that.

On 1 June 1928 the Schoenbergs finally got an apartment of their own. It was in Neu-Westend, Nussbaumallee 17, fairly far from the centre, but near the Reichskanzlerplatz, where Hans Poelzig built the great Radio House. In the middle of the month the Schoenbergs went to Vienna. They took their fox terrier Witz with them. Schoenberg had discussions with his publishers. Felix Greissle had less work there than Schoenberg could have wished. He looked for a practical activity for his son Georg. Hertzka recommended him to the music engraver Hirsch, where he obtained a post on 1 July.

From Vienna they went to the Riviera, where the warm sea air improved Schoenberg's asthma. He needed rest. Even his friends received no news from him. Gertrud wrote a letter of thanks to Maria Schreker who had sent photos of her dogs; 'Witz, our dog, arouses general admiration here and is terribly spoilt.' In Roquebrune-Cap Martin, between Monte Carlo and Menton, Schoenberg continued work on the Orchestral Variations in the Pavillon Sévigné. He was able to tell Universal Edition on 28 August that the composition was finished; he would need another month to finish the score.

Josef Rufer and Arnold Schoenberg on the Steinplatz,
Berlin, 1927

Oskar Kokoschka, Gertrud and Arnold Schoenberg and
Adolf Loos in the Bristol Bar, Berlin 1927

The Schoenbergs went to Vienna again for his birthday. A joint postcard shows how many of his followers and friends met together for this in the Rathauskeller. After returning to Roquebrune-Cap Martin Schoenberg told Furtwängler on 21 September that it would be a great pleasure for him to let him have the first performance of the Variations which were now ready.

Schoenberg took yet another work with him to France the orchestration of Bach's Organ Prelude and Fugue in E flat. Universal Edition was interested. Schoenberg aimed to finish the score by the end of 1928, but had already finished it on 11 October. As his plans he mentioned the orchestration of his Serenade, the Wind Quintet and the Clarinet Suite opus 29. He said nothing about a project for a new opera. Instead of returning to Berlin in October he took six months' leave. On 12 October he sent the scores of the Variations opus 31 and the Bach arrangement to Vienna. His accompanying letter speaks of the beginning of a new work.

A new Academy prize winner wanted to introduce herself. She was called Anna Pravossudovitch and sent a letter of recommendation from Alexander Glazunov, who had left Leningrad and his post as Director of the Conservatorium on 15 June. Schoenberg took her into his class.

On 5 November Universal Edition informed him that the General German Music Society had accepted the *Glückliche Hand* for its music festival in Duisburg in June 1929. They asked Schoenberg to name his conditions. On the 14th the Schoenbergs went on an expedition to Monte Carlo; Edward Clark, who was again planning performances in London, was sent greetings on a card. Two days later, on 16 November, Schoenberg wrote to Vienna that he had begun composing the text of an opera *Moses and Aaron* which he had written between 3 and 16 October. He also mentioned the text of a comic opera.

Furtwängler had invited Schoenberg to go to the first performance of the Variations opus 31 at the Berlin Philharmonic concert on 2 December. But Schoenberg did not dare to make the journey in the northern winter. So he was spared the icy silence of the public and the conflict between two hostile groups in the Philharmonic, which was unused to scandals. His publishers told him about the première. However, they did not tell him what part of the Berlin press had dared to write about it. Paul Schwers demanded in the *Allgemeine Musikzeitung*, an influential and revered Berlin weekly, that the composer should be removed from his teaching post at the Academy, so that he could not do untold harm to the guiltless youth.

More has been written about opus 31 than any other work by Schoenberg. He himself wrote an analysis for the Frankfurt Radio in 1931 in which he gives complete information about the plan and the execution of the work. In René Leibowitz's *Introduction à la Musique de Douze Sons* (1949) the whole second part of 115 pages is dedicated to the work, to which Carl Dahlhaus devoted a small summary brochure in 1968. The ingenious manipulation of the 12-tone row and the themes derived from it in the nine variations, plus introduction and finale, need no further commentary. Even the quotation of B–A–C–H in three places in the score hardly offers the ear a bridge to the very complex world of this work. In performances in modern times, for instance by Herbert von Karajan and Lorin Maazel, it became clear that both players and audience can grasp the structure and sound of this score almost without any preparation.

The Schoenbergs again spent their New Year celebrations on the Riviera. Universal Edition had raised a charity fund for Webern, who had had to give up his conducting work because of serious stomach trouble and had to go into a sanatorium at Semmering; Schoenberg contributed a fairly large sum.

In 1928 he had a few new contacts. The pianist Paul Aron corresponded with him about the programme of a cycle of modern music arranged by him in Dresden. The 'State Commission for the Folk Song Book for Youth' had asked him through Karl Lütge in May and again in July if he would like to arrange old folk songs. Schoenberg agreed and on 4 February 1929, two days before his return to Berlin, he sent four songs from the fifteenth and sixteenth century with piano accompaniment; Lütge had sent him copies of these. In 1948 he returned to three of the melodies and arranged them for mixed chorus in four parts unaccompanied. Altogether he arranged six such melodies, though he was doubtful of their status as folk songs.

He received two letters from the Academy. One contained his tax form for 1928. Schoenberg had been paid 17,123.98 marks, of which he had to pay 1712.05 in tax. The other invited him to the election of new members on 2 January. Schoenberg had to excuse himself, but wrote his proposals for election in the margin. Foreigners: Alban Berg, Josef Hauer, Heinrich Kaminski, Ernst Krenek and Anton von Webern; Berliners: Alexander von Zemlinsky, Heinz Tiessen and Kurt Weill. Zemlinsky had been engaged by Klemperer in 1927 at the newly founded Kroll Opera. Tiessen was the most important supporter of the modern Berlin school, a friend of Scherchen's, an admirer of Schoenberg's, about whom he had written extraordinarily important and admiring articles many times since 1920 in 'Melos' and on Schoenberg's fiftieth birthday in the Hamburg 'Musikwelt'. Schoenberg liked Weill's first operas; after his change of style i n the *Dreigroschenoper* he became more scepical about him: 'What has he done? He has given us back the three-four bar', he said scornfully. He was also unsympathetic to Krenek's new development in the operetta-like 'Time Operas' like *Der Sprung über den Schatten* and *Jonny spielt auf.* But he recognized his gifts sufficiently to recommend him to the Academy.

No one had been informed about the work which chiefly occupied him on the Riviera. There were vague mentions in his correspondence with Universal Edition of a comic opera. It was not till April, when he had returned to Berlin, that he unveiled the mystery. On 1 January 1929, at 3.15 in the afternoon, he had finished the first draft of the music for a comic text. The piece is called *Von heute auf morgen*; the pseudonymous author's name of Max Blonda conceals the identity of Gertrud Schoenberg. As usual Schoenberg wrote the work down in a form of a short score, a kind of larger and more detailed piano score with indications of the orchestration. The transference of the 1131 bars into full score and the preparation of a playable piano score for two hands followed later; the music was hardly changed at all in this.

In March 1929 Erich Kleiber asked Alban Berg to enquire from Schoenberg whether he could have the first performance of the opera for the State Opera in the Unter den Linden. The answer was in the negative, as Schoenberg felt that he was bound to Klemperer for Berlin; the latter wanted to give *Erwartung* and *Die Glückliche Hand* at the Kroll Opera. Also Berg said that Schoenberg was annoyed because the Unter den Linden Opera had not yet performed anything by him. – The next person who enquired about the first performance of the piece was Dr. Heinrich Jalowetz, who had been first conductor at the Cologne Opera since 1924. Schoenberg gave him information in a letter of 18 April 1929: one act, no change of scene, duration 45–55 minutes, modern dress. Only four characters:

'*A soprano, like Gutheil-Schoder, but a bit brighter and lighter; a second soprano, higher and still lighter, perhaps like Lotte Schöne; a baritone, like Duhan in Vienna, but I have nothing against Bohnen;*

Von heute auf morgen. First page of the piano score, 1929
(Facsimile of Schoenberg's writing)

then a sweet, thin, lyric tenor, like Tauber or Naval, who could have an unconsciously comic effect through the sweetness of his voice; that is, if he is not able to make a comic effect in spite of it.'

Four days later Schoenberg offered the piece for performance to Paul Bekker, who had been Intendant at Wiesbaden since 1927. But not the only performance.

'As I have been having a quarrel with Universal Edition, I cannot approach any publisher for the moment, and so I must have the material prepared myself and would like to divide the high costs of this among several theatres; therefore, I don't want to have a real première, but will try to give about ten theatres the performing rights for the duration of a year without setting a definite date, in return for the hire of the material.'

Hertzka, to whom the composer had offered the work, wrote in a letter of 15 February 1929 to Monte Carlo, Hotel Bristol, that he could not pay a large sum for the opera. Firmly convinced that his comic opera would have a similar success to the earlier ones by Krenek, Schoenberg dared to publish it himself. He began a piano score, which was finished by Karl Rankl, and he had this reproduced photographically. A young merchant, Benno Balan, who was keen and enterprising and had taken it into his head to publish modern music, undertook the delivery and distribution of the work. This whole affair gave Schoenberg worries for a long time. There was endless correspondence and corrections with the Berlin Photographic Institute, Rud. Oskar Schmidt, Bülow-strasse, who were printing the piece. On 27 August there was a bill of 1868.10 marks to pay, which was more than Schoenberg's monthly income at the Academy. Even in a late summer holiday, which the Schoenbergs spent at Katwijk on the Dutch coast, there were a lot of proofs to be read. On 20 September Berg wrote to Webern that Kolisch was also with the Schoenbergs and had done some corrections for the new opera.

All these practical worries did not leave Schoenberg much time for composition. However, a letter of 15 April informed Universal Edition about a new piano piece, which was sent to them on the 25th.

This was opus 33a, a strict 12-tone composition, the first sketch of which bears the date 25 December 1928. Shortly before Wilhelm Furtwängler had asked Schoenberg if he could give the first performance of Schoenberg's arrangement of Bach's Organ Prelude and Fugue in E flat for large orchestra. The answer shows Schoenberg's great admiration for the conductor and is fundamentally positive. However, he does not hide his disappointment that Furtwängler had never played the Variations again after the concert which caused a scandal: 'Frankly, I expected that you would repeat the piece at the next concert, showing the rabble that *you only do what you consider right!*'

There was an unexpectedly great success when the *Glückliche Hand* was performed at the Musicians' Festival in Duisburg. The traditional Festival of the General German Music Society, which took place from 2 to 7 July 1929, mostly consisted of operas. None of the works performed – except for Julius Weismann's *Dream Play* after August Strindberg – made such a strong impression on the public and the press as Schoenberg's. He was invited by telegram to a second performance, which was decided on spontaneously and took place on 8 July. The Frankfurt critic Karl Holl wrote extremely laudably about the work and praised the organisers as well as the Music Committee of the Society, which included Alban Berg, Philipp Jarnach and E. N. von Reznicek, among others. Schoenberg must have been convinced by this how strongly his intrepid and incorruptible personality had found roots in the consciousness of musicians and lovers of music.

On 20 September 1929 the Schoenbergs returned to Berlin; a week later he told the Academy that he would begin his teaching at the beginning of October and asked them to inform his pupils about this if they enquired.

The Berlin Radio, which performed works by Schoenberg with a certain regularity, annoyed him because in a repeat of the First String Quartet two cuts were made. At the beginning of October there was a correspondence about this with the Intendant Dr. Hans Flesch (who incidentally was a brother-in-law of Hindemith) with the result that the latter apologized to Schoenberg.

Schoenberg's son Georg had finished his work with the music engraver Hirsch; Schoenberg asked Universal Edition if they could employ him. A question from Dr. Pisk in Vienna was answered negatively; he had asked Schoenberg to add his signature to a proclamation for the Workers' Symphony Concerts. In his reply Schoenberg said that in principle he never gave signatures of this kind. However, he sent greetings to Dr. D. J. Bach on the occasion of the jubilee of these concerts. Richard Strauss, Felix Weingartner and Franz Schalk were not so concerned with them. Schoenberg was often represented as a composer in the programmes of the concerts.

Josef Turnau, who had become the Intendant in Frankfurt, was interested in giving the first performance of the new opera

Von heute auf morgen. He had a very gifted, ambitious young opera director, Hans Wilhelm Steinberg, who took over the rehearsals and to whom Schoenberg sent his wishes in detail on 4 October. He was insistent that the singers should sing between pianissimo and mezzo-forte and not shout out the text, as usually happened in Germany. 'My opera is a song-work from a to z; and for this reason there are hardly any interludes.' Apart from this the singers undertaking the principal roles must be able to sing from music and have absolute pitch. The letter deals in detail with the characters of the four parts. In this the Wife, who is supposed to be a portrait of Gertrud Schoenberg, comes out best. Naturalness and intimate feelings are required for her. She must never appear to be comic and must show warmth throughout, without being sentimental. The other three figures, the Man, the Singer and the Girl Friend are all regarded as 'modern'. For orchestral rehearsals Schoenberg recommended using very small groups, as Zemlinsky had done with *Erwartung* in Prague and Stiedry with *Glückliche Hand* in Vienna. And finally the letter says:

'*The tone of the whole thing must be really* light. *But one must feel or should be able to realize that behind the simplicity of these events something is concealed: that by means of day-to-day characters and events, beyond this simple story of a married couple the modern feelings, the fashionable feelings only live "from today till tomorrow", from an unsteady hand into a greedy mouth, in marriage no less than in art, politics and attitudes to life.*'

The chief difficulty of *Von heute auf morgen* lies in the gap which divides the operetta-like text from the highly contrapuntal and dissonant 12-tone music. The première in Frankfurt on 1 February 1930 could not bridge this contrast. The text is a satire on the instability of the present in matters of love and art. The married couple have spent an exciting evening with friends. At home the Man attacks, in an obstinate manner, marriage, house-keeping, work, childrens' cries. His wife, in her reliability seems to him charmless in comparison with the girlfriend who is doing something artistic. Then comes the turn to the field of operetta. The Woman makes herself very worldly with every kind of make-up and ornaments, plays the great lady, and thereby immediately wins back the Man's affection. Now the friends ring up: the Singer, of whose voice and lack of spirituality the husband is jealous, announces an improvised visit. This does not seem right to the Man, although his enthusiastic girl friend is coming as well. Meanwhile he has realized the transitory nature of worldly charm.

When the two friends appear they find a married couple in love, and their child. The friends retire angrily, not without attacking this state of affairs as old-fashioned. The married couple agree about the difference between fashion and love and remark that modern people alter between to-day and tomorrow. The child's query 'What are modern people?' is answered by the fall of the curtain.

Schoenberg draws these characters musically in such a sensitive way that a coarser ear will understand little about them. In this self-willed aesthetic the greatness of the composer lies, yet it produces objections which a socially conscious generation could raise against the work. Conducted by Steinberg and again produced by Dr. Herbert Graf, the performance (with Else Gentner-Fischer, Elisabeth Friedrich, Benno Ziegler and the tenor A. M. Topitz) was true in style and good.

Meanwhile Schoenberg had also negotiated with other publishers about the work. Schott in Mainz turned it down. Bote and Bock in Berlin finally offered the large sum of 30,000 marks on 14 January 1930. Schoenberg wanted more, stuck to his demands and later lost a good deal of money through publishing the work himself and the incompetence of Benno Balan.

At the beginning of January Schoenberg had conducted again for Edward Clark in London. The rehearsals in Frankfurt began shortly afterwards; friends from Vienna and Berlin came to the final rehearsal. The circle of Schoenberg's friends was almost complete, and there were pleasant meetings and conversations. The artist B. F. Dolbin, an admirer of the Master since his Vienna years, made dozens of his famous caricatures. Music critics appeared from the whole of Germany and Austria and were as divided over the new work as they had been before. In spite of the good efforts of Steinberg and his singers, Schoenberg was not entirely happy about the musical side of the performance. He conducted the piece himself on 27 February on the Berlin Radio. The chief parts were sung by Margot Hinnenberg-Lefèbre and Gerhard Pechner. After the performance Schoenberg suggested something to the Intendant Dr. Hans Flesch which was later put into practise on many radio stations: a night programme of modern music, partly using available records, partly with orchestra, ensembles and soloists, partly with piano, with spoken elucidations, performance of passages and a final performance of the work which had been discussed. He was aiming at a propaganda for modern music, and also the possibility of altering orchestrations and the ensembles at the rehearsal. He himself was ready to bring the institution to life and to direct it.

His pupils in the Academy gave him a great deal of pleasure. He arranged in necessary cases for them to receive grants. So on 12 March Natalie Pravossudovitch, Hansjörg Dammert, Nikos Skalkottas, Peter Schacht, Alfred Keller, Helmut Rothweiler and Fried Walter received an increase of grants toward their fees; Norbert von Hannenheim from the Seven Mountains obtained a place without fee.

During their fortnight's stay in Frankfurt for rehearsals of the opera, the Schoenbergs went at the end of January 1930 to a concert of the section of the International Society for Contemporary Music which was established there. After this they were invited to the Seligmanns. There a Sonatina for violin and piano by the Swiss composer Erich Schmid, who later became conductor of the Zurich Tonhalle Orchestra, was performed. Schoenberg heard it, was pleased by it, and encouraged Schmid, who wanted to become his pupil, to send him some of his works. In June the plan came to fruition: Schoenberg took him into his class. On 13 November Schmid came to his first lesson in the apartment on the Nürnburger Platz, where Schoenberg received his pupils once a week from 9 till 1. Schmid studied with him until May 1931 and wrote a fine descriptive picture of his experiences. On 14 November 1930 he wrote to his parents in Switzerland about his first meeting with Schoenberg and his first lesson:

'Schoenberg himself received us in a very friendly manner and entertained us for two hours in a most lively way. Hardly a word about music, but he spoke about architecture, painting and sculpture. All ot these had some relation to his art. Then he also spoke about his own works. He insisted that his creative work was developed entirely from tradition. He had a great respect for the Masters! Brahms and Beethoven were his formal models, and Wagner was his harmonic starting point . . . Externally he is a small person, with remarkable features, very mobile. He walks up and down all the time during the conversation. He has humour and can be extremely sarcastic.'

Schmid wrote about Schoenberg's teaching in the same letter:

'Yesterday I brought my orchestral pieces. The first piece was looked at and played. Then we had a discussion. In general he liked it, but he could not entirely understand it. I was supposed to explain it. This was the fatal thing, for first of all I did not know exactly what I meant, and in my embarrassment

I said things which were quite wrong. Now Schoenberg became extremely strict. Concepts with false contents or wrongly expressed! That can make him angry. Now he expressed his aim in teaching. To lead the pupil to knowledge of himself, to make him express every phrase, and to make him regard things from a fundamental point of view. And even to chase up the pupil in his own conflict. Quite unintentionally one learns an enormous amount, one sharpens ones feeling about other works and about oneself.'

Schmid's very exact description of his studies shows how firm Schoenberg's instruction was. Why he was always in movement in mind and body, including cutting chess-men for the super-chess which he had invented. He never preached, but always thought out things anew. Compositions which were discussed had to be played on the piano. Classical and romantic masters were used as models, and occasionally some of his own works, like the first Chamber Symphony or the Wind Quintet, but never modern works, except for Reger. He never spoke about 12-tone technique; it was all the same to him whether his pupil wrote tonally, atonally or used the 12-tone method.

In a Berlin private house (probably that of Frau Dr. Kallenbach-Greller) Schmid heard the Suite opus 29 conducted by Fritz Stiedry and Schoenberg's complete piano works played by Else C. Kraus. This pianist worked tirelessly for Schoenberg's music, played the pieces publicly in many countries, and also wrote a basic commentary about them in the 1932 Year-Book of the Berlin Academy for Church and School Music. On 30 January 1931 she gave the first performance of opus 33a, and also took part in a concert of the Master-School in the Academy on 2 June 1931, in which works by Schmid, Natalie Pravossudovitch, Norbert von Hannenheim, Peter Schacht and Nikos Skalkottas were performed, some of them conducted by Schmid. Schoenberg was away. His experiences at the first performance of the comic opera in Frankfurt must have aroused the thoughts which were written down in his article for the April number of 'Querschnitt'. It is called 'My public' and begins with the confession that Schoenberg believes that he has none. After 1918 in each large city there were a few young people who expressed their convictions by a confession to all around them. They had soon fallen away from him. The reason why the larger public has not much relation to him he ascribed to the influence of conductors who have a lack of understanding. As regards his hissing enemies, they had always been small in numbers. And then Schoenberg speaks quite naïvely about his experiences with ordinary people. On his military service a sergeant had treated him extremely well because of his musical performances and gave him more joy by praising his works than with praise of his exercises. A night porter in his hotel and a taxi driver told him that they were enthusiastic applauders of the 'Gurrelieder'; a servant in an Amsterdam hotel had sung in the Leipzig chorus in the performance of the work, and a lift attendant had heard the first performance of *Pierrot Lunaire*. And Schoenberg ends: 'I will not give up my belief in those who have a smattering and those who are experts, I will think merely of them that they do not have any notion of what I am doing. But sometimes it seems to me very doubtful if I am really so disliked by the public as the experts keep on saying, and if the public is really so very much frightened of my music'. – The negotiations about the opera with Bote and Bock which had foundered had a positive result: the Berlin publisher took over Schoenberg's Six Pieces for Male chorus unaccompanied opus 35, which he wrote between 16 June 1929 and 9 March 1930 from texts of his own. The poems, 'Hemmung', 'Das Gesetz', 'Ausdrucksweise', 'Glück', 'Landsknechte' and 'Verbundenheit' have a philosophical content and are typical of Schoenberg's spiritual position around about the time which preceded his work on the biblical opera *Moses and Aaron*.

The Schoenbergs went for a cure in April and May at the Sanatorium Allee-Kurhaus in Baden-Baden. Then they returned to Berlin, where an important première took place. The Kroll Opera had decided to put on Schoenberg's two one-acters *Erwartung* and *Die Glückliche Hand*. Zemlinsky conducted the monodrama and Klemperer *Die Glückliche Hand*. Both pieces were produced by Arthur Maria Rabenalt, the décor for *Erwartung* was designed by Teo Otto, who was then still young and unknown, in the form of a dissolving view. Oskar Schlemmer from the Weimar Bauhaus had designed the two scenes of *Die Glückliche Hand*; he had been an admirer of Schoenberg since the Stuttgart performance of *Pierrot* in 1912. The Monodrama was sung by the soprano Moje Forbach, who later became an actress. She described the performance and the final rehearsal. 'I kept on being dragged across the stage on a conveyor belt, then I rushed like a mad woman behind the scene, stood on the belt again and went on singing. And when I got this behind me and was happy, then Herr Schoenberg said to me: "And now the whole thing once again". And then I said: "No, I can't do it. I'm sorry." And then he attacked me violently and said that I had no idea what an honour it was to sing a Schoenberg work and: "You will find out one day that you will be thankful to have sung Schoenberg"; and then I sang it once again.' Schoenberg was not happy with Oskar Schlemmer's work. Dr. Hans Curjel, the chief dramaturgist and one of the leading spirits of the Kroll Opera, remembers how the composer left the last rehearsal but one, which was still not working properly, under protest. So they arranged a special night rehearsal before the final rehearsal, at which Schoenberg appeared. They worked from midnight till 4 in the morning; Schoenberg was satisfied. The performance on 7 June 1930 was attended by Berlin's cultural élite. But the press was partly very spiteful, blaming Klemperer for going to such great expense for two pieces of which one only lasted twenty-eight minutes, and the other twenty-one. After the third performance on 17 June *Die Glückliche Hand* was withdrawn from the repertory, and *Erwartung* after the fourth performance on 20 September.

In a conversation with the director of the publishers Bote and Bock Schoenberg had mentioned a new big oratorio he was planning, without giving further details. The publishers turned down his proposal on 23 June. This was *Moses and Aaron*, which Schoenberg later cast in its final form as an opera.

In the spring there were discussions in the Berlin High School for Music about a teacher for a composition class. Franz Schreker thought of Alban Berg, but did not want to approach him himself, and wanted him to be sounded by someone else. He telephoned Schoenberg and asked him to invite his friend over. Schoenberg's letter, written on 10 April 1930 in Baden Baden, shows with what exactitude and conscientiousness Schoenberg carried out a task of this kind. He advised his friend seriously to accept the offer which carried a salary of 800 to 900 marks a month. He advised Berg to insist on a guarantee of somewhere to live, and to ask for payment for the cost of his move and also for a mortgage, and further another 200 to 300 marks a month as long as he could not find an apartment of his own. The letter ends with congratulations on the success of *Wozzeck*, which had been put on in many theatres in Austria and abroad. Regarding his own work, besides the male choruses mentioned above, Schoenberg writes of his Accompaniment Music to a Film Scene opus 34, which he had written between 15 October 1929 and 14 January 1930. This score was not published by Universal Edition, but by the Magdeburg publisher Heinrichshofen. The first performance took place on 6 November 1930 in a symphony concert at the Kroll Opera conducted by Klemperer. Schoenberg had influenza and was not able to be present.

In the letter to Berg Schoenberg mentioned plans for an opera to his own text. He was also thinking of a libretto based on Franz Werfel, and he thanked Berg for sending him a novel by Werfel which he liked very much. It is unknown which novel he meant; in his library in Los Angeles there was a copy of *Abituriententag*, which was published in 1928.

He also wrote a letter from Baden-Baden on 14 April to the Intendant of the Kroll Opera, Ernst Legal, with detailed proposals for the staging of both operas. And on the same day he wrote a letter to the Radio Intendant Flesch on the question of criticism on the radio. He suggested that one should have a confrontation of diverging opinions and the author's remarks on them. Three critics should talk first of all for three minutes each, and then the author, who will have been shown the critics' manuscripts, should reply for five or six minutes. Then there should be a free discussion, and the whole affair should not last more than half an hour. The radio later put on broadcasts in this form. – In Baden-Baden the Schoenbergs met an old acquaintance from their Viennese period, the operetta composer Franz Lehár. Immediately after their departure Schoenberg sent him a work of his own, the receipt of which Lehár acknowledged in a telegram from Baden-Baden on 20 May 1930:

> *Warm thanks for the kind despatch of your latest very interesting creation we had great joy and we must unfortunately go to Vienna directly tomorrow but hope to see you again soon all best wishes your good friend* Franz Lehar.

This 'very interesting creation' can only be the opera *Von heute auf morgen*, of which the piano score was published in 1929 and which had its first performance in February 1930. Schoenberg's next two works of 1930, the male choruses and the Accompaniment Music were published later than the date of Lehár's telegram. Like most great operetta composers Lehár too had begun with serious works. Schoenberg addressed him in a letter as 'Master', and that was certainly not an empty flourish. His opera *Von Heute auf Morgen* is close in time to the operetta-like text of Lehár's *Friederike*, in which the operetta composer set a text based on Goethe's life and also set some of Goethe's poems to music.

The Schoenbergs spent the summer in the South, first of all in Lugano, later in Merano. On 5 August Schoenberg wrote to Alban Berg, who had adapted Wedekind's *Erdgeist* and *Pandora's Box* for his planned opera *Lulu*. The second part of the letter rejects an allusion in which Berg had found likenesses between Schoenberg's text for *Moses and Aaron* and Strindberg's *Moses*. He said that his ideas were so much tied up with his own personality that it was impossible for Strindberg to have presented anything that could have even an external similarity. 'Today I can really scarcely remember what belongs to me: but one thing must be granted me (I won't let myself be deprived of it): everything I have written has a certain likeness to myself.'

From Lugano-Besso, Via Seminario 2, Gertrud wrote to her sister on 23 July saying that she was happy with their conditions although they were some distance from the lake. She asked how Mitzi's gall was getting on; hers was better, but they could perhaps go together to Karlsbad in the spring. Rudi would also like to go there. Her sister knew that she had already got a new apartment in Berlin at Nürenburg Platz 3, telephone Bavaria 4466. And Schoenberg added that he had to miss tennis: 'There is no opportunity for me here – far too many good players'.

Schoenberg had been a passionate lover of tennis since his time in Mödling. In Berlin he was a member of the superior Borussia Club and mostly appeared with his wife at 9 o'clock, when the courts were opened. In Chautauqua he wanted to take part in a tournament in 1934, but gave up after practice play. This passion was inherited by his son Ronny. The latter had the success as a child which his father had longed for. Schoenberg was proud of his son's diplomas and prizes and said that the boy at twelve years old was already more famous in Los Angeles than he was at seventy-five.

Schoenberg finished the second scene of *Moses and Aaron* on 22 August. In the middle of September Gertrud Schoenberg wrote to her sister that they would accept an invitation from RAVAG (the Austrian radio) to go to Vienna at the end of the month. Schoenberg was expecting his sister-in-law to partner him in tennis, as she herself was not allowed to play yet. But in Berlin they had a ping-pong room, where there would be tournaments.

After their stay in Merano the Schoenbergs went to Vienna, where they arrived on 13 October, and then on to Prague on the 22nd. Meanwhile Schoenberg caught influenza, from which he had not recovered on 6 November. He arrived in Berlin on 1

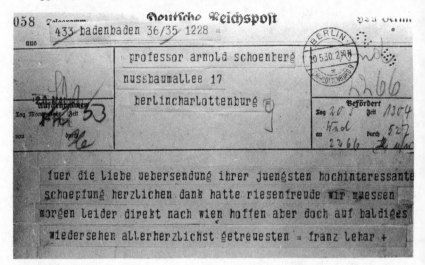

Telegram from Franz Lehàr with thanks for *Von heute auf morgen*,
20 May 1930

The Schoenberg couple bathing in Lake Lugano-Besso, July 1930

November, eagerly awaited by his pupils. He had heard in Vienna with a great deal of worry that Adolf Loos was seriously ill in the Lakatos Sanatorium at Baden. Schoenberg knew how much the great architect wanted a teaching post. For this reason he wrote to Thomas Mann, who was as yet unknown to him personally, with a request for him to sign an appeal for a foundation for a Loos school. The external reason was the sixtieth birthday of the architect in the following December. Schoenberg also wrote to Professor Amersdorfer, the General Secretary of the Prussian Academy of Arts, asking him to honour Loos and to help him.

Schoenberg was able to begin his teaching again on 13 November. Besides his class with the composition pupils he also held a course of musical analysis in his house, in which outsiders also took part. There, besides his inner circle of pupils, one could meet men like Henry Cowell, Marc Blitzstein and the author of this book. An analysis of Brahms Fourth Symphony was especially impressive; Schoenberg called it the symphony of the falling thirds. In fact he showed thematic and motivic connections with the original figure of falling thirds and their octave complements.

There were frequent discussions about musical terminology. Schoenberg always tried to clear up concepts which musicians used every day without understanding their real meaning. There was a conversation about the value of the fermata or pause. Schoenberg took the view that it demanded the lengthening of the value of the note by a half.

Since 1925 the young philosopher and sociologist Dr. Theodor Wiesengrund-Adorno had been one of Berg's composition pupils. He had discussions with Schoenberg from time to time about such questions of terminology. In a letter of 6 December Schoenberg suggested to Wiesengrund that he should compile a dictionary of music (aesthetics) or theory, in which he differentiated between historical and more modern concepts. Among the exponents of this Schoenberg mentioned not only himself, his pupils Wellesz and Erwin Stein, and Hauer and Wiesengrund, but also Walter Howard, Hans Mersmann and Heinrich Schenker. The plan was not carried out.

On the first day of the Christmas holiday in 1930 the Schoenbergs invited the Schrekers and Margot Hinnenberg-Lefèbre to a turkey dinner; the latter had been studying *Erwartung* for weeks with Schoenberg's pupil Fried Walter. Edward Clark had engaged Schoenberg to conduct the monodrama in a public radio concert. On New Year's Day the Schoenbergs travelled to

London, where they enjoyed staying in the Strand Palace Hotel. The first rehearsals were on 3 and 6 January 1931. Margot Hinnenberg-Lefèbre arrived on the 7th from Nuremberg, where she had sung Tove in a 'Gurrelieder' performance under Bertil Wetzelsberger. The London *Erwartung* was a great success and produced enthusiastic notices. Schoenberg himself was very satisfied. He wrote on 22 January from Berlin to Webern:

> '*What a pity you didn't hear* Erwartung. *I think it was very good. I have never before worked so well with an orchestra, never before rehearsed so well, heard so well, kept such a good beat, as this time. Admittedly I was (not unmindful of your curtain lecture) much better prepared this time than usual.*'

He had already written to his friend and doctor, Dr. Georg Wolfsohn, from London that Frau Hinnenberg had 'sung wonderfully'.

In Berlin Schoenberg, to whom the raw winter of this year had brought great difficulties in breathing, was busy with the manuscript of a lecture about problems of modern music which he gave on 21 January 1931 in the hall of the High School. Frau Dr. Kolisch, Gertrud Schoenberg's mother, came for another visit. She was an excellent housewife of the old Viennese type. She helped in the house and the kitchen and amused herself with Witz, the wire-haired fox terrier who had belonged to the family for a few years.

In February Schoenberg worked on an important article on 'National Music' which was first published by Rufer in 1959. It is a creed in Bach and Mozart, and in a lower place in Beethoven, Wagner and Brahms, whom he regarded as the masters from whom he had learnt. He said he had also learnt much from Schubert, Mahler, Strauss and Reger. What is remarkable in this creed is the differentiation in second place of Latin and Slavonic music, even of Debussy, whom he valued highly. The whole article shows his bitterness about the cultural battle which was fought against German music in the First World War. But it does not mention the laudable exception of Ravel who protested strongly against the musical nationalism of his fellow countrymen and protected Bartók as well as Schoenberg against attempts to boycott them. The manuscript, dated 24 February 1931, mentions the important characteristics which come from Bach: 'The art of finding phrases which can accompany themselves; the art of extracting everything from one thing and of leading the phrases from the one to the other; the independence of the section of the bar.' From Mozart he had learnt: 'the asymmetry of the phrase-lengths: the binding together of heterogeneous characters into a thematic unity; the avoidance of regular bar-lines in his themes and parts of them; the art of the formation of subsidiary ideas; the art of introduction and transition.'

What is meant by thematic working and variation, the art of development, Schoenberg derived from Beethoven, also the mastery of the greater or shorter length of movements and their variety in their larger structure and – as a development of Bach's independence of the beat – the displacement of rhythmical accents.

What he learnt from Wagner was the expressive pliability of themes, the relationship of notes and chords and 'the possibility of concealing themes and motives in such a manner that they can be placed in a dissonant manner against harmonies'.

Brahms was his model in the system of writing, which also appears in Mozart's tendency to asymmetry, to working on a large scale and to economy.

At the beginning and the end the article speaks about tradition, which to Schoenberg always means German tradition.

The small but extremely important article ended with the analysis of the Orchestral Variations, which Hans Rosbaud performed on the Frankfurt Radio for the first time after Furt-wängler. Schoenberg's lecture on the 22nd preceded the concert on 24 March. The young composer Erich Itor Kahn, Rosbaud's assistant, wrote about it enthusiastically to Erich Schmid, who felt very happy in Schoenberg's Berlin class. Immediately after the journey to Frankfurt Schoenberg returned to Berlin. On 30 March the Berlin Radio, following Schoenberg's suggestion to their Intendant Dr. Hans Flesch, had a discussion between the Master and two critics, who supported other directions in modern music. Dr. Heinrich Strobel, editor of 'Melos' and the music critic of the *Berliner Börsen-Courier,* and Dr. Eberhard Preussner, lecturer in music at the Central Institute for Education and Instruction. There was a violent discussion. Schoenberg ended it in a lapidary manner: 'Herr Strobel, don't undervalue the size of the circle which surrounds me. It will grow through the curiosity of an idealistic youth, which feels itself more attracted by the mysterious than by everyday matters. But however this may happen I cannot either think or say anything different from what my task prescribes for me.

Do not call this pride, gentlemen, I would be glad to have

greater success. It is in no way my wish to stand there as a solitary saint on a pillar. However, as long as I am allowed to regard my thoughts and imagination as right, I cannot believe in anything else except that thoughts must be thought and expressed, even if they are not understood, and even if they never can be understood.

I myself do not believe that I am so unintelligible. But let us consider: supposing unquestionably great thoughts like those of a Kant were not allowed to be thought or said, because even today sincere people must agree that they cannot follow them? Whoever God has entrusted with the task of saying something unpopular, he has also given him the possibilities of satisfying himself that there would always be others who will understand'.

This important concluding passage shows Schoenberg's firm conviction that he had been given a task by God. It is the same thought which runs through the texts of his *Jacob's Ladder*, and especially in the *Biblical Way* and in *Moses and Aaron*. But in addition to the Old Testamentary belief in being chosen Schoenberg also had a pride in suffering of a very Christian kind. In a letter to his sister-in-law Mitzi Seligmann, who had been pursued by mishaps (undated, but probably from Monte Carlo in the spring of 1929), he wrote:

'The Lord alway looks for people whom he allows to suffer! People who are less worthy, who cannot bear it and will not be able to find improvement through it, are spared everything unpleasant! So be proud! One is chosen to suffer! If people are allowed to make themselves comfortable this is done at the cost of a higher blessedness!'

The term came to an end. The Schoenbergs made plans for travel. They first of all wanted to found a tennis club somewhere with Rudolf Kolisch, his quartet and Mitzi Seligmann. But Schoenberg's sister-in-law had rented a place in Aussee, which was not possible for Schoenberg climatically. They thought about Karlsbad, possibly with Kolisch. Schoenberg's asthmatic troubles demanded a more southern atmosphere. They were always searching for summer resorts. After Dubrovnik and Pörtschach, Lugano and Merano it was now the lake of Geneva, where Schoenberg hoped to be able to breathe more freely. In May the couple went to Montreux-Territet, where they stayed till September. Here his interrupted work on *Moses and Aaron* thrived. However his optimistic wish, expressed to Stiedry on 2 June, of finishing the first act in three weeks was not fulfilled. It was finally completed on 14 July.

His only contact with friends and former pupils was by correspondence. Webern, who was planning an analytical course in Mondsee near Salzburg for the summer, asked for and received advice about this: what Schoenberg suggested to him came to fruition in the lectures in Vienna which he gave in 1933, and which Willi Reich later published under the title *The Way to New Music*. Heinrich Jalowetz had written about his Cologne performance of the Accompaniment Music to a Film Scene, and the Master thanked him for this in a cheerful letter. Alexander Jemnitz too, who had given *Verklärte Nacht* in Budapest and was planning to give *Pierrot*, received a reply and sceptical advice: '*Pierrot* must not be sung, which he already had had to say to Marya Freund. Schoenberg thanked the General Music Director Johannes Schüler for a performance of *Pierrot* in Oldenburg with Erika Wagner; Schüler was an unswerving supporter of the Viennese school.

He had to miss two important performances in Berlin: the Academy concert of works by his pupils on 2 June and the 'Gurrelieder' in the High School for Music, conducted by Franz Schreker on 5 June with students, the Charlottenburg Teachers' Choral Society and the male chorus of the Church Music Academy.

Fritz Stiedry felt that he was not properly recognized in Berlin, where he had a lot of difficulties as a conductor, and opened his heart to Schoenberg. The latter answered his friend from Territet, saying that he had signed an appeal that Stiedry should be given the 'proper position'. He was sorry that the Stiedrys were not coming to the Lake of Geneva. 'I am working very hard and have now got into the circle of thought of my work again; this is always a difficulty.'

He was annoyed by the royalty account of the Society of German Composers. He wrote about this in detail to the President Max Butting. He said that the number of his performances had doubled twice up till 1931. He was also annoyed by an article in the 'Schaffende Musiker' (The Musician at Work, the magazine of the society) with attacks on 'intellectual constructivism' in his music.

He wrote a long letter to Alban Berg about his experiences in composing *Moses and Aaron*; Berg had written to him about the first act of *Lulu*, which he had just finished. 'The libretto is only definitely finished during the composing, some of it even afterwards. This proves an extremely good method.'

He also wrote to Webern about *Moses and Aaron*, especially about the 'Dance round the Golden Calf'.

Unfortunately the summer was rainy and cold, even on the Lake of Geneva. Schoenberg's difficulty in breathing increased: the doctor dissuaded him from returning to Berlin on 1 October, when the courses were supposed to start again. In the middle of October the Schoenbergs went to Barcelona, and on the 17th he asked the General Secretary of the Academy, Professor Amersdorfer, to give him an extended leave.

He felt well in the Catalan capital. In the finely situated Bajada de Briz they found an apartment with a view of the Mediterranean. Pablo Casals, a friend of his from earlier years in Vienna, greeted the Master with some of his colleagues and his famous orchestra. Schoenberg was very moved by this honour and replied to it on 3 November with a letter full of warmth.

Stiedry had conducted the Chamber Symphony and the Serenade in October, with great success. Schoenberg congratulated his friend on his success; the latter's Berlin situation had become stronger, and he had been asked to join the Städtische Oper by the new Intendant Carl Ebert. In the *Vossische Zeitung*, which had been sent to him while he was abroad, and in the *B.Z.* (*Berliner Zeitung*) *am Mittag* he had read glowing criticisms by Marschalk and myself about Stiedry. Their correspondence became regular. On 20 October Schoenberg explained why they had gone to Barcelona, and was sorry that nothing came of the Glasgow performance of *Pierrot* with Erika Wagner-Stiedry; he also said that his own London concert had to be cancelled because of the devaluation of the English pound. He wrote on 13 November that Gertrud had had influenza for a fortnight. How was Hans Pfitzner's *Herz* (which the Staatsoper had performed for the first time on 12 November)? On 19 December he asked Stiedry to remind the Radio Station about the recording of his Symphony and his Serenade. He said that it was cold in Barcelona; he had also had influenza and was going out that day for the first time.

In spite of bad weather and illness Schoenberg continued to work. On 8 and 10 October he wrote the piano piece opus 33b, which Henry Cowell published in April 1932 in his collection 'New Music'. At the end of November Schoenberg wrote seven pages about orchestration and two pages about the disposition of a manual of counterpoint. In December he wrote notes about Manuel de Falla, about phrasing and eight pages about linear counter-point according to the theory of Ernst Kurth. 'It has always been clear to me,' he wrote, 'that there is something which looks like counterpoint and also sounds like it and yet is not counterpoint.'

At this time he wrote a letter – probably to Pablo Casals – about the composition of a cello piece which Casals had suggested to him, perhaps an arrangement of Bach, and also a seven-page article 'Stuckenschmidt', which deals with an article of mine about Brecht's remarks about opera which had appeared in the *Vossische Zeitung*.

For the philanthropist Hermann Abraham, the creator of school meals, Schoenberg wrote a two-part mirror canon for his eighty-fifth birthday; this is written down in the form of a puzzle canon and the solution of it is given in Schoenberg's text:

> Mirror yourself in your own work:
> It rewards you doubly, what you do simply,
> It radiates back, what you gave cordially in a straight line.
> The deep opens slowly,
> Then the height comes quickly.

1931 brought Schoenberg a lot of health troubles. Even in Barcelona it was colder and more rainy than usual. The Schoenbergs had been on their travels since May, first on the lake of Geneva and then on the Catalan coast. Both were liable to colds. In addition there was hope and also worry that Gertrud was pregnant. The birth was expected in the New Year.

Among the people who had taken the trouble to improve their life in the foreign city was the Swiss-Catalan composer Roberto Gerhard. As early as 1923 he had written to Schoenberg in Vienna to ask if he could become his pupil. It was he who recommended Barcelona in 1931 as a place which was good both climatically and culturally. He found the fine apartment in the Bajada de Briz. Although he was already a mature and well-known musician Gerhard became a pupil of Schoenberg and soon his friend too. The Schoenbergs celebrated Christmas with him and his wife.

Hans Rosbaud was planning to give the première of the Songs with Orchestra opus 22 in Frankfurt. This work, which had been written in Berlin and Vienna between 1913 and 1916 had remained unnoticed, perhaps because of its difficulties. Now Winfried Zillig's young wife, the soprano Hertha Reinecke, had learnt it. Schoenberg, who had been very pleased with Rosbaud's performance of the Orchestral Variations, was happy with the plan. He doubted if he would be able to accept the invitation to give an introductory lecture to the work in Frankfurt. So he asked on 19 January 1932 that Rosbaud should cancel this, although he was sorry to miss the performance. Rosbaud persevered with his request, and on 30 January Schoenberg had half agreed to his plan. He said that if he could get a score from Rosbaud and something occurred to him about it he would be ready to come.

Schoenberg wrote the text of the lecture, a twenty-page-long manuscript with seventy-five musical examples. On 13 February he sent two copies to Rosbaud. But it had been snowing in Barcelona for three days; his old troubles, from fever to breathlessness, began again. The journey was more than questionable. Schoenberg suggested that Dr. Theodor Wiesengrund or Erich Itor Kahn should read the manuscript in case he could not come himself. The performance was on 21 February. Schoenberg had to stay in Barcelona; his lecture was read for him.

In the New Year Webern sent Schoenberg his quartet opus 22. Schoenberg thanked him for the 'fabulous piece' with 'great pleasure and pride!' He was surprised at the news that his friend was leaving Mödling and moving to Vienna.

In the summer of 1932 the Music Festival of the I.S.C.M. was to take place in Vienna for the first time on the occasion of their tenth anniversary. Webern, as President of the Austrian section, was responsible for the arrangements of programmes and the organization. He asked Schoenberg for a representative work for performance. Schoenberg, annoyed about the events in Venice in 1925, and being hostile towards a member of the Viennese committee, refused to collaborate in any way.

In Berlin his long absence was regarded with distrust. The pupils in his master class felt that they had been abandoned. There were complaints and impatient demands to the Academy and to Rufer, who as Schoenberg's assistant was regarded as Schoenberg's scapegoat. Kestenberg, who was responsible for music in the Ministry, took Rufer into his confidence. The latter wrote excitedly to Barcelona that Kestenberg was being attacked from all sides, 'that it was such an important teaching post, which was filled and paid for, but that the teacher has not been in Berlin for three-quarters of a year.'

Schoenberg defended himself in a letter, which explained to Kestenberg that since his influenza in October 1930 he had not been able to go out during the whole winter, and then after seven months' teaching he had gone to Montreux, where his emphysema had at first got worse, but then gradually became better. In any case he said that his contract allowed him to choose the months himself which he was going to spend teaching in Berlin. He did not want to sacrifice his health because of some envious people making mischief.

Formally he was in the right. But Kestenberg knew the political situation more clearly than Schoenberg did. The growing group of reactionaries regarded Schoenberg as a modernist and a baptized Jew and therefore an object of attack. Kestenberg had to be doubly careful. Kestenberg's friendly answer did not satisfy Schoenberg. He wrote on 13 February that his condition had got worse. He had had to give up the lecture in Frankfurt, because of the entirely unusual snowy weather in Barcelona, he was suffering from coughing, a rise in temperature and difficulty in breathing.

In spite of illness and worry Schoenberg continued to work. On 10 March he finished the second act of *Moses and Aaron* with the resigned words of Moses 'O Word, thou Word, that I lack' accompanied in unison. – Two documents from doctors give information about Schoenberg's state of health at this time. On 30 March 1932 Dr. Ramón Sarró, a member of the Doctors' Chamber of Barcelona, confirmed that he was suffering from bronchial asthma, 'characterized by typical paroxistic attacks, which take place under the influence of lowering of temperature and influenza-like colds. For this reason Schoenberg is advised not to remain in northern countries during the cold months'. He said that a transfer to the north would cause a considerable worsening of his emphysema and his general illness.

The report which Dr. W. Minnich gave on 3 April 1932 in Montreux is similar. He had treated Schoenberg in the autumn of 1931. 'He was suffering then from a very definite emphysema of both lungs, combined with very obstinate feverish bronchitis and . . . asthmatic conditions which gave him sleepless nights. With regard to the obstinate long-lasting subfebrile rising of the temperatures I regarded the possibility of a tuberculous condition of his illness as likely. I feel very definitely that Herr Schoenberg should stay for the whole winter far from Berlin; where and if possible this will fit in with his work, he should arrange his life so that he should live as much as possible in a mild climate. Among the various places which I suggested to Herr Schoenberg he chose Barcelona, which I regarded suitable for the purpose and I hope he will stay there as long as it is possible for him'. Schoenberg told Josef Rufer on 15 April about sending this report to Kestenberg. He said that they would have to move in June, as their landlord on the Nürnberger Platz was bankrupt. Could Rufer find an apartment in Grunewald with about five rooms, near the Red-White Club?

In April Webern visited Barcelona. Schoenberg and he were invited to give concerts by Casals. The orchestra surprised Webern; *Pelléas*, which Schoenberg conducted, he had never heard done so well, and he wrote this on a card to Berg.

Early on 7 May Gertrud Schoenberg had labour pains. At half-past 8 she gave birth to a daughter, Nuria. A detailed account by her father was sent to Mitzi Seligmann. A few days later a shadow fell on their happiness: Emil Hertzka had died on 9 May in Vienna.

The Schoenbergs' journey home, which had been planned for the end of April, had to be postponed because of the birth. Strict currency controls had been introduced in Germany and they were worried about their money for the journey. In the middle of May Schoenberg wrote an urgent letter about this to Kestenberg. Finally everything was arranged so that they could leave on 1 June. The Schoenbergs flew from Barcelona to Stuttgart, in order not to disturb the child. They were very pleased by this new experience. On 2 June they saw their apartment on the Nürnberger Platz after more than a year's absence. Schoenberg did not attend the Vienna Festival from 16 to 21 June. On the final day of it Webern had arranged a special concert of the Workers' Symphony Concert under his direction. In the programme were 'Friede auf Erden' and the 'Accompaniment Music to a Film Scene' as well as Berg's 'Wein' aria and Mahler's 'Resurrection Symphony'.

The 12-tone technique of the works published since 1924 had evoked a new kind of technical analysis with which Schoenberg did not agree. In July 1932 Kolisch, who next to Berg and Webern had the most fundamental knowledge of his music, had sent Schoenberg an analysis of the Third String Quartet. Schoenberg appreciated the great trouble which his brother-in-law and friend had taken in finding the series which he had used in it: 'I can't utter too many warnings against over-rating these analyses, since after all they only lead to what I have always been dead against: seeing how it is done; whereas I have always helped people to see: what it is! I have repeatedly tried to make Wiesengrund understand this, and also Berg and Webern. But they won't believe me. I can't say it often enough: my works are 12-tone *compositions*, not *12-tone* compositions: in this respect people go on confusing me with Hauer, to whom composition is of only secondary importance'.

This very definite warning and Schoenberg's dislike of orthodoxy has not prevented two of his most enthusiastic apostles, Theodor Wiesengrund and René Leibowitz, from transmitting this kind of analysis to a whole generation of musicians and theoreticians, who dictate the means of approach to his music up to the present day through this.

As well as the remark that he and Frau Gertrud had joined the Borussia Tennis Club, Schoenberg's letter to Kolisch (and also one to Webern on 12 August) contains some important news: Schoenberg was collecting his literary work and putting it in order. He seemed astonished himself at how much he had piled up in fifteen years in the way of printed articles and manuscripts. In fact hardly a year went by without some literary work. Schoenberg estimated the size of the collection – as he wrote on 2 September to Berg – at 1500 printed pages.

In 1932 Schoenberg also wrote many short articles, about language, morals, politics, power, majority and fascism, and also about tonality, developments, in July one on Bach and the twelve notes and an attack on the conductor Carl Muck. His wish to see all these articles in print remained unfulfilled. It was not until near the end of his life, in 1950, that the Philosophical Library in New York published a selection of mainly musical articles under the title *Style and Idea*. However, there was no German edition of this work until 1973; the articles were mostly written in Schoenberg's native language and translated into English for their first publication.

In the letter to Webern on 12 August 1932 Schoenberg thanked his friend for the two concerts which he had conducted in Barcelona. He said that everyone was very impressed with his work at the Vienna Music Festival, and he could not understand why Webern had not yet conducted in Berlin. (Schoenberg had forgotten that Webern had taken part in 1923 in the Berlin Austrian Music Festival).

On his birthday Schoenberg received greetings and gifts from all his friends. Only Adolf Loos, to whom Schoenberg had sent a letter of recommendation in June for his sister-in-law Mitzi Seligmann, remained silent. He had been ill for some time, and Schoenberg, disquieted by all kinds of rumours about the great architect, asked himself if he were in danger. Rudolf Kolisch arrived for a few weeks' visit in the house and was Schoenberg's excellent tennis partner. In September the quarrel with the amateur publisher Benno Balan reached its climax. Schoenberg only dealt with him through a lawyer; Balan arranged the delivery of all the remaining scores and piano scores of the opera *Von heute auf morgen* to the Vienna Universal Edition.

Schoenberg's sister Ottilie lived with her husband, the writer Oskar Felix, in Berlin, only a few minutes distance from the Nürnberger Platz. Felix had made a name as an author of comedies and operetta texts. He was aware that Schoenberg knew Franz Lehár well, and asked him to arrange a meeting for him with the famous man. Schoenberg had already expressed this wish on 8 May in Barcelona:

'Honoured, dear Meister Lehár, my brother-in-law, Herr Oskar Felix, who is probably known to you as the author of the text of so many successful operettas, asked me to arrange a meeting with you for him. With best wishes yours sincerely Arnold Schoenberg.'

Oskar Felix's attempts to write a libretto for Lehár remained unsuccessful.

On 27 October the Kolisch Quartet gave a concert in Berlin, in which the F sharp minor Quartet was performed with extraordinary success for the last time before the coming of the Third Reich. In the morning Schoenberg had written a letter to the President of the Academy, Max von Schillings, about questions of copyright. He wanted to find a sufficiently adequate writer who could translate his Harmony Book into English. He had been warned by the example of Strindberg, whose style had not been properly represented in the German translations by Emil Schering.

At the beginning of November Norbert Hannenheim, who had been ill in his home country of Rumania for a long time, returned to Schoenberg's class. Among his other pupils Schoenberg was pleased with Peter Schacht from Bremen because of his intelligence and detailed work in chamber music. There were also important discussions in the analysis courses. These were not always only concerned with music, but now also with questions of the National Socialistic politics which were becoming more threatening and expanding. Schoenberg suffered in this political atmosphere more than he would allow himself to notice. Certainly it was chiefly reasons of health which had kept him in the south for so long. But a letter which he wrote in Barcelona on 24 May to

Dr. Joseph Asch, who was living in New York, allows one to see the truth. He says there that it was also because of political conditions that he was very reluctant to return to Germany at this juncture. As the currency restrictions made it impossible for him to stay longer abroad, he asked Dr. Asch 'as the only composer of my standing who could not live on what he made from his creative work, without having to eke out his income by teaching' for help. He suggested that a few rich people should give him from 2000 to 4000 dollars a year. 'Will you make the attempt to get some rich Jews to provide for me so that I don't have to go back to Berlin among the swastika-swaggerers and pogromists?' In his letter of 23 September to Alban Berg he speaks of a certain depression, which is connected with his stay in Berlin and which takes all the joy out of his work. He knows where he belongs; but such a change of place would be more difficult to arrange than one can imagine: 'Today I am proud to call myself a Jew; but I know the difficulties of really being one'.

In November Roberto Gerhard wrote from Barcelona, asking if Schoenberg would come there again. The latter replied on 15 November, that in 1933 he had lectures in Vienna, Brno and Frankfurt and a concert in London. In order to live in Spain again he must be able to earn a living there. He would like to live near the tennis club. In the same month he began to work on a cello concerto by the Viennese pre-classic composer Georg Matthias Monn, which was dedicated to Pablo Casals. It was a free, very virtuoso transcription of the work, which because of its great difficulties is not often played even today. He continued the work in December, and finished it on 4 January 1933.

The painter Carl Moll, the stepfather of Alma-Maria Werfel, sent Schoenberg a picture as a present. Schoenberg thanked him with a double canon at the lower fifth, a four-part little masterpiece of eight bars, of the kind he often wrote in similar circumstances. The first sketch was written down on 17 December, and it was finished on the 27th. Among new meetings was one with the American composer Roger Sessions, who at his own earnest wish had been brought to see Schoenberg, whom he admired very much. In Schoenberg's American exile he found Sessions an active and always helpful friend.

All people who were concerned with modern culture were looking anxiously at the coming year of 1933. Schoenberg seemed to keep to his usual activities for the present. On 7 January he suggested to Hans Rosbaud that he should perform the new cello concerto after Monn with Casals in Frankfurt. For a lecture, which Rosbaud had asked him for, he suggested: 'Style and Idea or Outmoded and New Music', or perhaps a lecture on Brahms. At the end of January there was a session at the Academy, at which new members were to be elected. Schoenberg excused himself to Heinz Tiessen because of his illness and asked him to take over his representation; he suggested that Anton von Webern should be elected as a new member. In the Städtische Oper there was a *Salome* performance under Fritz Stiedry, which Schoenberg attended, and at which he caught a severe cold. In February he went to Vienna, where on the 15th he spoke in the middle Konzerthaussaal at the invitation of the Cultural Society about 'New and outmoded music or style and idea', and from there he went to Frankfurt, where he gave the Brahms lecture. Both these texts were published in the collection, *Style and Idea* in 1950, after Dika Newlin had translated them into English.

Schoenberg's desire to finish the composition of *Moses and Aaron* under the mild south European sun was not fulfilled. The libretto, of which the third act was not set to music, is a poem of confession, a powerful series of pictures in dramatic form, a real Schoenbergian product, which cannot be judged by purely literary criteria any more than the text of the Bible, on which it is based. It concerns the spiritual conflict between the two brothers Moses and Aaron, as described in the Second Book of Moses, and Schoenberg's vision reaches from almost verbal quotations of the Lutheran text to the demonic events of an erotic orgy, a dance of slaughterers and a blood sacrifice, in which four naked girls are embraced by four priests and stabbed at the moment of highest ecstasy. The scenes of the first act come from the Bible: the calling of Moses before the burning bush, the meetings and conversations of the brothers, the handing of God's message to the people of Israel, the three miracles (snake, leprosy, the changing of water into blood), and the exodus of the people into the desert.

The second act is essentially Schoenberg's own invention. He shows Aaron and the people awaiting the distant Moses, who seeks revelation on Mount Sinai. Aaron gives the doubters the Golden Calf, before which an idolatrous orgy of drunkenness, madness and unbridled sexuality breaks out. After this is over Moses returns, and then follows the long dramatic argument between the two brothers. Moses, the bearer of the Word, has the tablet of the law in his hand. He must recognize that Aaron, whose mouth announces ideas, corrupts them by making them visible. And Moses regards the pillar of fire and the pillar of cloud as idolatrous too, and diverting man from the pure, unpresentable form of God. He destroys the tablets of the Lord; now it seems to him that all he has thought of is madness. With the sentence: 'O Word, thou Word, that I lack', he sinks despairingly to the ground.

Schoenberg's composition ends here. The text of the last act consists of a single scene, at the end of which Aaron, the betrayer of ideas to images, falls dead, when Moses gives him his freedom. There are only musical sketches for this final act.

With all its confused and brutal details the text has Biblical greatness. Schoenberg writes not literature but a creed; the artist has become a prophet. In the description of crude drunkenness the text is similar to Hieronymus Bosch's pictures of hell; one can find analogies with Paul Claudel in its panoramic breadth and the aesthetic objectivity of the drama. In order to express the character of the text, which is a synthesis of the characteristics of oratorio and highly dramatic opera Schoenberg used an unusual combination of instruments. As well as an enlarged classical orchestra he uses piano, harp, celesta, mandolines and much percussion. The voices consist of six singing soloists, a speaker, and both singing and speaking choruses. The characteristic of the style is a frequent combination of singing and rhythmically organized declamation. Moses is a speaking part, Aaron a lyrical tenor, which may symbolize the fact that the bearer of the idea, Moses himself, is deprived of song.

The glowing, orgiastic colours which Schoenberg distils from the orchestra go beyond everything which one knows from his own earlier stage works, *Erwartung*, the *Glückliche Hand* and *Von heute auf morgen*. It is only necessary to mention one passage: the oriental dance, which suddenly starts at the procession round the golden calf. Violins and violas beat with the wood of their bows on the open strings, lower strings play a chord in harmonics, and, accompanied by tambourine and triangle, two mandolines, harp, piano, celesta and xylophone intone a rhythmically subtle melody, which is later taken up by trombone and piccolo and grows to an unusually dense polyphony. This is followed by the powerful contrast of the dance of the slaughterers with its horrifying huge four-part glissandos on three trombones and tuba.

The orchestral sound is unmistakably expressivo music, with frequent soloistic appearances of single tone-colours of solo instruments.

No less characteristic is Schoenberg's method of treating the human voices. Right from the beginning, when God's voice is heard coming from the burning bush, he expresses it with a fantastic combination of six singing choral soloists and a speaking chorus. The second scene, a great discussion between the brothers Moses and Aaron, musically is a kind of duet for speaking voice and tenor. Recitatives, arioso passages, whispered choruses, response-like sections for solo singer and speaking choir follow each other in continually changing vocal shapes. It almost goes beyond human power to describe the variety of these events and to understand them in terms of musical form. However, it is impossible to escape their uneasy effect.

Each of the singing parts is characterized by a separate style of handling the voices, the sick woman as a tired alto dragging herself along slowly, who is brought into higher states by increasing animation. The girl fascinated by the golden god is characterized by an almost monomaniac repetition of small motivic phrases, which are sung in quick tempo in the soprano register. The Ephraimite is characterized by a slow circling round central notes in the middle baritone range which return again and again. The youth is characterized by a changing melody, which is always rising to the higher regions with powerful tenor expression; it is the voice of the idealist, which separates itself ardently from all the others.

But all these are minor characters. The big important singing part in the work is Aaron. In contrast to the thinking Moses, who clings to eternity, metaphysics and real values, Aaron is a materialist, down to earth, attracted by the tinsel of gold and the success of the moment. The part is written for lyric tenor. Following the character of Aaron, it often takes powerful turns in the manner of cantilenas. The chief interval is the fourth, sometimes falling, sometimes rising, and also often reached by means of a major third, which precedes it in the manner of a leading note. This motif of major third followed by a semitone accompanies Aaron throughout the whole opera, as well as melodies formed from broken major and minor chords. Schoenberg also uses the principle of octave transposition and so increases the number of intervals at his disposal, so that the semitone of the Aaron motive often becomes a major seventh; all this is natural in the expressivo style. Before the variety of intervals which appear increases the means of the melodic cantabile expression and so serves the purpose of the perfect interpretation of the action.

Shortly before Schoenberg's death Hermann Scherchen gave the première of the 'Dance round the Golden Calf' in Darmstadt. The first two acts were given in concert form on 12 March 1954 in the Hamburg Musikhalle for the first time. The performance was put on by the North-West German Radio and Hans Rosbaud conducted. A microfilm had been made of Schoenberg's short score, and from this Scherchen made the full score. Gertrud and Nuria Schoenberg attended the concert, which was received with enthusiastic applause.

The first stage performance – Schoenberg was by no means convinced of the possibility of this – took place in the Zurich Stadttheater in 1957. It was also conducted by Rosbaud, and was the final work in the 31st Festival of the International Society for Contemporary Music on 6 June; its great success proved the stage efficacy of the work. The next theatre to produce it was the Städtische Oper in West Berlin on 10 October 1959 in a production by Gustav Rudolf Sellner, conducted by Hermann Scherchen. The attempt to speak the words of the third act with music from the first act underneath it was argued about. However, the performance had a great success in Vienna, Paris, and other cities where it was played as a guest performance. Since then many theatres in both the Old and the New World have experienced the powerful effect of this work.

A CREED IN BRAHMS

Apart from the juvenile attempts at composition for two and three violins, which were written under the influence of Viotti and Playel, Schoenberg's first great model was Johannes Brahms. He said himself that he had known Brahms's chamber music since about 1890. He was twenty-two years old when Brahms died in 1897. Among the Viennese performances of Brahms's works Schoenberg may have heard the Fourth Symphony in 1886, and certainly the piano pieces opus 116–119. He probably also knew the clarinet sonatas, which were played in 1895. Brahms's last work, the 'Four Serious Songs' of 1896, were well-known to him in his youth and are an important subject of examination in the manuscript of a lecture which Schoenberg gave for Brahms's 100th birthday on the Frankfurt Radio on 12 February 1933. This essay was given its final form on the occasion of the fiftieth anniversary of Brahms's death in 1947; in English, under the title

MOSES UND ARON

OPER VON ARNOLD SCHÖNBERG

Uraufführung

Moses	Hans Herbert Fiedler
Aron	Helmut Krebs
Ein Mädchen	Ilona Steingruber-Wildgans
Ein Jüngling	Helmut Kretschmar
Ein Mann	Horst Günter
Ein Priester und Ephraimit	Hermann Rieth
Eine Kranke	Ursula Zollenkopf

Vier Jungfrauen

Dorothea Förster-Georgi, Karla Maria Pfeffer-Düring
Annemarie Tamm, Charlotte Betcke

Sechs Stimmen aus dem Orchester

Dorothea Förster-Georgi, Maria Hüger, Ursula Zollenkopf
Hartwig Stuckmann, Horst Sellentin, Ernst-Max Lühr

Stimme aus dem Dornbusch

Der Chor der Hamburger Staatlichen Hochschule für Musik
Einstudierung Adolf Detel

Die Ältesten, Jünglinge, Greise, Bettler und Bettlerinnen
Stammesfürsten, mehrere ältere Frauen, Volk

Der Chor des NWDR Köln
Einstudierung Bernhard Zimmermann und Otto Maier
Der Chor des NWDR Hamburg
Einstudierung Max Thurn und Otto Franze

Das Sinfonieorchester des NWDR Hamburg
Leitung Hans Rosbaud

Moses and Aaron programme of the first performance in the
Hamburg Musikhalle, 12 March 1954

'Brahms the Progressive', it forms a chapter in the collection *Style and Idea*.

Schoenberg as a very young man learnt from Brahms what one can call the 'chamber music' way of thinking. At that time he played the cello or the viola in Brahms's quartets or quintets. Thinking and hearing in independent parts, which dominates Brahms music in all strata, from the basses which are important melodically through the region of the middle voices up to the highest register (which is not always the leading melody) is a characteristic of Schoenberg's music through all the phases of the development of his sixty years' long creative career. And even when he got to know the music of Wagner, which is organized in a different way, this did not change him. Even in those works of Schoenberg which are nearest to Wagner in their exterior sound, such as the gigantic score of the 'Gurrelieder', if one looks at them more closely one can see their spirit of chamber music written in different parts, which goes back to Brahms' method of thinking.

In Schoenberg's youth it was usual to regard the relation between Wagner's and Brahms's music as an irreconcilable aesthetic hostility. This was not altered by the fact that both composers, who were twenty years apart in age, regarded each other highly. Wagner, the elder of the two, believed that all traditional musical forms were exhausted. To him absolute music, both symphonic and chamber music, belonged to a cultural epoch which was past and gone. He said that his own complete art-work would supersede in the future the individual life of arts such as music, poetry, painting, plastic art, dance and theatre and make them unnecessary. This highly individual view of art and the world has not lasted well. Simultaneously with Wagner and especially after him cultural forces continued to live which he in his splendid isolation could not recognize and also did not want to recognize.

In this sense Brahms was never a 'universal creator'. He yielded nothing to his older contemporary in cultural and general education. We know that in his cultural position he was much more 'modern' than Wagner. He was seriously interested in the painting of his time, which he not only saw embodied in the work of his personal friend Adolph von Menzel, but also in many pictures of the much abused French impressionists and of those painters who were regarded as ultra-modern, such as Arnold Böcklin and Max Klinger. The novels of Émile Zola, which were regarded as unpleasant and disagreeable in Bayreuth circles, were owned by Brahms in his small, well chosen library. But as a creative artist he confined himself throughout his whole life to music, apart from some small textual additions to the 'German Requiem'. And in music it was the absolute forms, symphonies, chamber music, piano sonatas which formed the real centre of his creative work. For him the sonata movement was as living as the rondo, the fugue as the chaconne, the canon as the variation.

Wagner was musician enough to respect this mastery. When Brahms played him his first symphony when Wagner was visiting Vienna, Wagner is supposed to have said that with such mastery the old forms could still be fertile. If he, on occasions, ironically referred to Brahms as the 'wooden Johannes', there was no real contradiction in this.

We know that Brahms always admired Wagner and recognized him without reservations. His excellent biographer Walter Niemann has collected some passages from letters and remarks which show this admiration. For example: 'Wagner, he is the leading man now. No one comes near him. Everything else disappears in a moment before his importance, which nobody understands or admires as much as I and certainly least of all do the Wagnerians.' And in a conversation with Richard Specht: 'Do you think that I am so limited that I can't also be charmed by the joyousness and greatness of *Meistersinger*? Or so dishonourable that I cannot be silent about my view that I regard a few bars of this work as worth more than all operas that have been composed since.'

Schoenberg had written about the relationship of the two antipodes with reference to the time of his youth and in Vienna, where the gulf was especially impassable, saying that those who disliked Wagner clung to Brahms, and vice versa. There were many who disliked both, and these were perhaps the only non-partisans. Only a small number were able to disregard the polarity of these two contrasting figures and enjoyed the beauties of both of them. In 1883, the year of Wagner's death, the gulf still seemed impassable; in 1897, the year of Brahms's death, the problem existed no longer.

Schoenberg regards Brahms, the supposed classicist and academic, as a great inventor in the field of musical language. So in his G minor Rhapsody opus 79, No. 2 he almost avoids fixed tonality. In his later book *Structural Functions of Harmony* Schoenberg quotes Brahms's harmonic progressions as examples of expanded tonality. However, more important than the harmonic inventions was what he calls the organization of a work conceived in advance by Brahms. In this he sees the composer not as in opposition to Wagner but as a kind of fellow-fighter for new methods and forms. He gives the Wagnerian method of leitmotiv the highest artistic rank; this represents the grandiose intention of the unification of the thematic material of an entire opera, and even of an entire tetralogy. But he thinks it wrong if similar procedures in Brahms are called formalistic. Both start from the same point of view, which conceives a whole work in one creative moment and acts correspondingly.

Writing in 1947, Schoenberg says that this principle had begun to dominate his musical thought and the formulation of his ideas forty years before. He says it played a decisive role in self-criticism. He, Schoenberg, was probably the first to announce this principle. And he continues somewhat ironically that the progress in which Brahms was operative should have stimulated composers to write music for adults. Mature people think in complexes, and the higher their intelligence the greater is the number of unities with which they are familiar. Instead of, as in former times, saying over and over again all that one has to say one should now use whole complexes in a condensed form.

Next the essay contains a slight attack on Reinhard Keiser, Telemann and Mattheson, who wanted to write themes which would seem to be familiar to everybody, 'in the light manner of the French'. As so often with mediocrity, they had a greater success than the really great men, especially Johann Sebastian Bach. And he does not fail to take this opportunity of cocking snooks at the musicologists whom he hardly respected at all: 'So these musicians live only because of the musicologists' interest in dead, decayed matter.'

Schoenberg gives examples of building larger forms and form-cycles like the four-movement symphonies from small thematic and motivic cells. He is also extremely interested in Brahms's liking for asymmetrical shapes. He finds connections of phrases of unequal lengths, of groups and bars which cannot be divided by academic rules into 8, 4 or 2, even in quite early works like the String Sextet in B flat opus 18, and the scherzo of the G major String Sextet opus 36. Then he turns to an examination of Brahms's most popular compositions, the songs. And he finds in 'Feldeinsamkeit' the reflection of verse-metres in music. He then says that in other cases Brahms goes even beyond such reflections and gives as an example for this 'An die Nachtigall'. The Brahms essay gives him an opportunity of confirming these methods not only in works of Mozart and Beethoven, but also in those of Bruckner and Mahler. For many of these compositional refinements he invents the formula of 'subcutaneous beauties'.

Then he comes to certain rhythmical innovations which Brahms took over from Beethoven and Mozart and developed further. On this he says that the idea cannot be rejected that the mental pleasure caused by structural beauty can be tantamount to the pleasure deriving from emotional qualities. Brahms has done the immeasurable service of surpassing purely technical procedures in these matters. And then he mentions as an example the third of the Four Serious Songs 'O Tod, wie bitter bist du', in which intuition and perfection are creatively united.

Schoenberg says that there is no doubt that Brahms believed in working out the ideas which he called 'gifts of grace'. Hard labour is no torture to a trained mind, rather a pleasure. If a mathematician's or a chess player's mind can perform such miracles of the brain, why should a musician's mind not be able to do it? After all an improviser must anticipate before playing, and composing is a slowed-down improvisation; often one cannot write fast enough to keep up with the stream of ideas. But a craftsman likes to be conscious of what he produces; he is proud of the ability of his hands, of the flexibility of his mind, of his subtle sense of balance, of his never-failing logic, of the multitude of variations, and last but not least of the profundity of his idea and his capacity of penetrating to the most remote consequences of an idea. It is important to realize that at a time when all believed in 'expression', Brahms, without renouncing beauty and emotion, proved to be a progressive in a field which had not been cultivated for half a century.

Surprisingly enough Schoenberg ends the Brahms essay, which at fifty pages is one of his most important theoretical articles, with a vision. What, he thinks, would have happened, if Brahms had written dramatic works as well as his songs, chamber music and symphonies? His contributions to an unrestricted musical language would enable the opera composer to overcome the metrical handicaps of his libretto's prose. The singer would be granted the opportunity to sing and to be heard; he would not be forced to recite on a single note, but would be offered melodic lines of interest. This conclusion attacks some weaknesses in Wagner's declamation and the relative over-instrumentation of his music dramas. So Schoenberg gives Brahms the prospect of influencing later dramatic compositions through his stylistic model.

Schoenberg clearly did not know that Brahms had sometimes thought of writing operas, and that he regarded Calderon's *The Secret* and Carlo Gozzi's *King Stag* (which was later set by Hans Werner Henze) as possible libretti.

Schoenberg was occupied with Brahms from 1920 onwards in other connections. First of all in the plan for a book on orchestration, which he later gave up, because he found that orchestration was a part of composition. In the sketch for this the andante from Brahms's Quartet in G minor was quoted. He also was occupied with this work later in a more detailed way. Among notes which he wrote between 1930 and 1934 there was also a text about 'Triplets and Four-Note Figures in Bach and Brahms'. In 1931 he wrote the article on 'National Music', which we have already discussed as the expression of Schoenberg's cultural nationalism. He mentions as the composers from whom he has learnt most, Bach and Mozart, and secondly Beethoven, Brahms and Wagner. What he learnt from Brahms was:

1. Much of what came to me unconsciously through Mozart, especially unevenness of bars, development and condensation of phrases.
2. Flexibility of form: not niggardly when clarity demands a larger space; and carrying each idea through to the end.
3. Systematic method of writing.
4. Economy and in spite of this: richness of ideas.

In this important article the following formula appears: 'My originality comes from the fact that I have immediately imitated any good thing which I have ever seen'.

The first sketch of the Brahms essay which was discussed in detail above was written in 1933. Four years later, from 2 May to 19 September 1937, Schoenberg orchestrated the G minor Quartet opus 25.

Little is altered in Brahms's score. Schoenberg simply transcribed the parts of the three strings and the piano for a large orchestra of Brahms's usual size. The result has a real symphonic character; Schoenberg himself spoke jokingly about Brahms's 'Fifth'. The first performance took place on 7 May 1938 in Los Angeles, conducted by Otto Klemperer. To the critic Alfred V. Frankenstein of the San Francisco *Chronicle*, who had asked Schoenberg questions about this arrangement, he answered on 18 March 1939:

'My reasons:

1. I like this piece.
2. It is seldom played.
3. It is always **very** badly played, because the better the pianist, the louder he plays and you hear nothing from the strings. I want at once to hear everything, and this I achieved.

My intentions:

1. To remain strictly within the style of Brahms and not go further than he himself would have gone if he lived today.
2. To watch carefully all these laws which Brahms had made and not to violate any of those which are only known to musicians educated in his environment.

How I did it:

For almost fifty years I have been very thoroughly acquainted with Brahms's style and his principles. I have analysed many of his works for myself and for my pupils. I have played this work as violist and cellist and many others numerous times: I, therefore, knew how it should sound. I had only to transpose this sound to the orchestra and this is in fact what I did.

Of course there are weighty problems. Brahms likes very low basses, of which the orchestra possesses only a small number of instruments. He likes the full accompaniment with broken chord figures, often in different rhythms. And most of these figures cannot easily be changed, because generally they have a structural meaning in his style. I think I have resolved these problems, but this merit of mine will not mean very much to our present-day musicians because they did not know about them, and if you tell them there are such, they do not care. But to me it means something.'

Brahms is also mentioned in later articles from the 1940s. 'Ear training through Composing', written at the end of 1939, contains the remark that in Mozart and Brahms many extensions are produced by movement of the harmony contradictory to the melody; an effect which is lost on anyone who listens to the melody alone. In the same article Schoenberg mentions the theme of Brahms's Haydn Variations, the first section of which consists of a period of ten bars, characteristically sub-divided at the fifth bar. It is difficult not to recognize this in the Variations. Furthermore the third section is unusual in that it was prolonged by means of an extension. Meanwhile at a first hearing no one can grasp all the fine points of Brahms's variation technique, the harmonic and contrapuntal combinations, the many ways in which he treats the unevenness of his five-bar sections.

In the article 'Criteria for the Evaluation of Music' Schoenberg reminds us that the Brahmsian school fought violently against the new German school. Their attitude was based on the viewpoint that unvaried repetition is cheap. Schoenberg blames the Russian composers such as Rimsky-Korsakov and Tschaikovsky, who through using the sequence had made an improper application of an otherwise acceptable technique. In connection with popular American music Schoenberg finds a friendly word for the composers who had shown their respect for traditional standards with popular themes just as Brahms had done in another way in his symphonies. And then finally he mentions Brahms's gipsy themes in the article 'Folkloristic Symphonies', which he wrote in 1947 for the magazine 'Stimmen' edited by Josef Rufer and myself. 'Whenever Brahms incorporates such a melody in a composition the structure ordinarily will not surpass the implications of a set of waltzes or of a quadrille. In works of higher organization he adds only the flavour to his own themes. But he is not forced to enter into foreign territory to express unusual melodic types, as is proved by the last movement of the G major String Quartet'.

Later on in this article Schoenberg deals with a concept which was very dear to him, that of 'developing variation'. As an example of this he mentions the beginning of Beethoven's C minor Symphony, and musical examples illustrate what he means. But from the connection it is clear how much Brahms was influenced by this method of writing.

The Niemann generation saw Brahms's music as a transition from pure symphonic procedures to techniques of variation. Beethoven had also given precedents for this: the finale of the *Eroica* and, as a much more complex one, the Choral Finale of the Ninth Symphony.

HOMELESS AND SPEECHLESSNESS

In spite of his earlier premonitions it was difficult for Schoenberg to realize the danger in which he was living. On 30 January 1933 Adolf Hitler came to power. Anti-semitism, which up till then had been a private affair in Germany, now had an official status. On his return from Vienna and Frankfurt Schoenberg found a cultural-political situation in which the fight of everyone against everyone came to a head. Even on 20 February he sent a calm and cheerful letter to Casals, offering the great cellist the first performance of the Monn Concerto:

> 'In certain respects the piece is less soloistic than a concerto of Monn's would be; for very often the cello's function is rather like a chamber music soloist's, whose brilliant playing produces very beautiful and interesting sounds. For the worst, I was mainly intent on removing the defects of the Handelian style . . . Just as Mozart did with Handel's Messiah, I have got rid of whole handfuls of sequences . . . replacing them with real substance. I also did my best to deal with the other main defect of the Handelian style, which is that the theme is always best when it first appears and grows steadily more insignificant and trivial in the course of the piece.'

These ideas correspond exactly to what Schoenberg said when analysing works by Handel. He was furious if one mentioned Handel in the same breath as Bach or even Haydn and Mozart.

In January and February Schoenberg wrote three songs, the texts of which were taken from a volume of poems by Jan Jakob Haringer; these are 'Mädchenlied', 'Sommermüd' and 'Tot'. As the American publisher Bomart Music Publications stated, Schoenberg had completely forgotten these three strict 12-tone pieces; only some of his friends remembered them. When they were published in 1948 they were given the opus number 48.

On 8 February, when Schoenberg was away, there was a concert of works by the composition class of Walter Gmeindl in the High School for Music. They played a string quartet by Max

Jarcyzk (who later went over to light music and became extremely successful under the name of Michael Jary). After this was played, the old composer Paul Graener stood up and shouted (according to an account in the *Völkische Beobachter* of 10 February 1933) 'Ladies and Gentlemen! They dare to offer you this lamentable mumbling as German art at a German high school for music. I protest against this as a German artist'. Professor Georg Schünemann reported this at the next meeting of the Senate of the Prussian Academy of Arts on 16 February. The Senate took notice of this with surprise and deplored the attitude of Graener, who had left the High School Hall after his interruption, accompanied by six like-minded people. But as early as 1 March President Max von Schillings declared in a session at the same academy that Jewish influences must be broken. Schoenberg left the session, and on 20 March offered his voluntary resignation from the Academy. He simply asked for fulfilment of his contract, which ran till 30 September 1935, payment of his costs for his return to Vienna and permission to take money abroad.

A letter of Gertrud Schoenberg's of 11 March to her sister Mitzi apparently sounds carefree. She said there was marvellous weather in Berlin, that little Nuria was going out every day; she herself wanted to go to the Italian Music Festival which was arranged for May in Florence. They had given notice for their apartment at the end of March, and did not know whether they were going to take another one now or look for another one in the autumn. Perhaps they would come to some arrangement with the landlord. Besides that Kolisch wanted to give a concert with his quartet on 17 March, but it was not yet certain if it would take place. It did not take place. In a postscript Schoenberg added that his few days in Vienna were entirely unclouded and they wanted to meet Mitzi in the summer. This plan also proved illusory.

In spite of his bitter experiences, but perhaps merely in order to protect himself and his family, Schoenberg sent an open card to Universal Edition on 31 March, in which he criticized the 'Horror Propaganda' abroad. It was only when he received a warning from his brother-in-law Kolisch, who sent a telegram from Florence recommending 'a change of air', that he decided to leave Berlin. On 17 May he travelled with Gertrud and his little daughter Nuria, who was just a year old, to Paris. As soon as he arrived on 18 May he wrote to the Academy:

'*As I had to come here on a matter concerned with my publishers I have decided to combine my leave for this year with this visit. I will probably stay in Spain again because of my asthma. I will send you an address for there later on.*

This time I have been uninterrupted in Berlin from 1 June 1932 to 16 May of this year, and as I have a surplus of two months "owing to me" from my earlier years of service, my long absence, owing to illness, in the year 1931 is fully made up for by this. Yours very faithfully, Arnold Schoenberg. *N.B. Letters can be sent to me via Berlin.'*

In Paris he received the registered letter which had been sent on from Berlin, in which the Academy informed him on 23 May that the Minister of Culture had empowered them to 'allow him leave as the Director of a Masters' School for Musical Composition with immediate effect'. The minister reserved future decisions. Wilhelm Furtwängler protested in vain in an open letter to the Propaganda Minister Dr. Josef Goebbels in the *Vossische Zeitung* on 11 April against the removal of leading Jewish artists.

Schoenberg's departure was like a flight. They only took travel articles with them. His sister Ottilie and her husband, the writer Oskar Felix, undertook to wind up the household on the Nürnberger Platz and to get the necessary permission for removing the furniture. Schoenberg's movable property was sent much later to California.

In Paris the family stayed at the Hotel Regina, 192 Rue de Rivoli. At the end of May Schoenberg asked Fritz and Erika Stiedry on a card what they were planning. He said that the Schoenbergs wanted to stay for the length of his leave (!) 'possibly to go further south, possibly to Spain again'. As the nurse was not coming till the next day they had seen nothing of Paris so far, but found it very beautiful. They stayed in Paris till the end of July. About this time Schoenberg began a correspondence with Universal Edition again. On 14 July he sent a telegram to Vienna:

'Owing to blocked bank urgently need 1500 marks advance or loan' and on 20 July:

'Great need of money, already two hotel bills unpaid'.

The reply from the publishers that they had succeeded in obtaining 3000 francs followed on the same day.

On 24 July Schoenberg took a step which had been prepared spiritually for many years. The poem of 'Jacob's Ladder', of which the first sketch was written down on 18 January 1915 and the fair copy bears the date 26 May 1917, is based on biblical foundations. The title and elements of the content come from the first book of Moses. In 1917 Schoenberg wrote large sections of the score, with which he was occupied many times until 1922, but which remained unfinished.

Jewish questions were discussed in the drama *The Biblical Way*, which was sketched on 17 and 18 June 1926 and the second version of which was written on 12 July 1927. A year later, on 3 October 1928, Schoenberg began the text of the opera *Moses and Aaron*, and finished it on 16 October; this is based on the second and fourth books of Moses. The music of the first two acts of the opera was written between 1930 and 1932.

Schoenberg had had premonitions about the events of 1933 and the following years when he wrote to Vassily Kandinsky on 4 May 1923: 'But what is anti-semitism to lead to if not to acts of violence? Is it so difficult to imagine that?' Now he was informed by the President of the Academy, who had entrusted him with a master class, that he was no longer wanted and he had drawn the consequences from this. The logical next step was to re-enter the religious community which he had left in Vienna on 21 March 1898. Thirty-five years later he again became a Jew in Paris. A witness of the ceremony was Marc Chagall.

Shortly afterwards the family moved to Arcachon, an Atlantic bathing resort in the Gironde, not far from Bordeaux. They lived in the Villa Stresa, Avenue Rapp.

Schoenberg now occupied himself methodically with the Jewish question. On 12 and 13 August he wrote a sketch for a Jewish Unity Party, which later became part of his big article about a Jewish Four Points Programme. Several other articles about the Jewish question were written in these first months of his exile. He wrote to his cousin Hans Nachod in London from Arcachon on 18 September 1933, that he was trying to unite Jewry in a common action. He believed that it would be better to do this first of all through a Jewish press; 'the question of money, otherwise I would rather travel as a speaker at public meetings. Naturally I would very much like to start with a large daily paper'. He asked Nachod if he knew any rich people, publishers, or idealists who could help in this. He said that the paper should appear in several languages, German, Yiddish and Hebrew, perhaps also in English, French and Russian.

In a later letter to Nachod he declared that he was no Zionist, but wanted to found a Jewish Unity Party. He formulated this even more clearly on 4 August 1933 to Webern.

'You are right that it is difficult to remain inactive at this time. In any

UNION LIBÉRALE ISRAÉLITE

24, Rue Copernic (XVIᵉ)
(PLACE VICTOR-HUGO)
PASSY 35-76

Devant nous, Louis Germain Lévy, Rabbin de l'Union Libérale Israélite, 24 rue Copernic, à Paris, s'est présenté le vingt-quatre juillet 1933 Monsieur Arnold Schoenberg, né à Vienne le 13 septembre 1874, pour nous exprimer son désir formel de rentrer dans la Communauté d'Israël.

Après avoir donné lecture de la présente Déclaration à M. Arnold Schoenberg, celui-ci a déclaré qu'elle était bien l'expression de sa pensée et de sa volonté.

Fait à Paris à mon cabinet, 24 Rue Copernic, le vingt quatre juillet 1933.

Lu et approuvé !

Louis-Germain Lévy
Rabbin

Arnold Schœnberg

Témoins : Dr Marianoff.

Marc Chagall

Document showing Schoenberg's re-entry into the Jewish religious community, Paris 1933. One of the witnesses was Marc Chagall *case the reasons for activity are different for me than for you. I have prepared for fourteen years for what has happened now. In this long time I have been able to make further preparations, even if with difficulty, and with many vacillations, I have definitely separated myself from whatever binds me to the Occident. I have decided for a long time to become a Jew, and you must have heard me speak many times of a piece, about which I couldn't say more in detail at the time, in which I have shown the way to an activity of national Jewry. Now for the last week I have officially returned to the Jewish religious community, although it is not the religion which separates me from them (as my 'Moses and Aaron' will show) but my view of the necessity of the adaptability of the Church to the demands of modern life.*

It is my intention to take an active part in efforts of this kind. I regard it as more important for me than my art, and I am decided – if I am fitted for such activity – only to work in future for the national state of Jewry. I have already begun this, and have found support for my idea, practically everywhere in Paris. My immediate plan is to do a big tour of America, which might become a world tour, in order to raise help for the Jews in Germany. I have been promised an important amount of support. It goes forward rather slowly. For this has always happened to me: the person who has gained an impression from what I have said to him and has believed me is seldom in the position of handing on this impression to a third person and moving him to believe it: for it is not just a question of the sound of the words but of the manner in which they were spoken which makes it so difficult to reproduce; and so the third person remains sceptical until he has actually spoken to me himself. I must speak at large meetings and on the radio.'

Webern sent this letter to Berg, who gave it back to him on 26 August and said of it: 'He has shaken me deeply. Even if I regard his departure from the Occident *humanly* as possible (I don't believe it, or at least I don't regard his turning to the *Orient* as possible) there remains for me the unshakeable fact of his musical works, for which there is only one description: German.'

Composition work was not entirely halted by these political plans. At the beginning of May in Berlin Schoenberg had started a 'free arrangement' of the Seventh Concerto Grosso of Handel's opus 6 as a concerto for string quartet and orchestra. The first two movements were finished on 10 and 12 May. Schoenberg wrote a card to Alban Berg on 15 September saying that he had taken up work on this transcription again:

'It is very tiring work. I need from four to five times as long as I

thought I would and about eight to ten times as long as I have time for. But finally it will be a very good piece, and I can say that it is not because of Handel. I liked the piece better when I started it.'

He added that he had received money again from Berlin: nothing was happening abroad.

Over and above the disappointments of this difficult time he received a negative answer from Pablo Casals, whom Schoenberg asked on 22 September to bring forward the planned first performance of the Cello Concerto after Matthias Monn which had been dedicated to him from October in London to 29 September. Schoenberg, who was to conduct it, expected to get further engagements from this. The whole affair collapsed. Casals only played the work once at a private performance in his house in Barcelona; the first public performance was given on 7 December 1935 by Emanuel Feuermann at the B.B.C. in London. – Of his German pupils Winifred Zillig was the most faithful to Schoenberg during these years. Schoenberg thanked him on 23 September in a very depressed letter. He had heard a few days earlier from Berlin the announcement of the Academy that his employment there was to be terminated on 31 October 1933. He received his last salary cheque on 1 October.

Further worries were added to his own now. His son Georg wanted to leave Mödling. He had corresponded about this with Schoenberg's former pupil Walter Goehr, who lived in Paris, and looked after Schoenberg in a friendly way. He had work for Georg, whose father immediately sent him his travel money through Universal Edition. 'I am very glad that you can use Görgi', Schoenberg wrote on 25 September to Goehr, and asked him whether he might be able to rent a furnished apartment in Goehr's house, where other acquaintances were also living, with two or three bedrooms, *salle à manger, petit salon*. But on 30 September Schoenberg returned to the Hotel Regina; the apartment was too expensive.

However, now something was happening abroad. Schoenberg had already told Zillig about a small prospect in America. The cellist Joseph Malkin, one of the brothers who had founded a famous piano trio in the Twenties, started a conservatorium in Boston. He had heard of Schoenberg's plight from Berlin. He eventually obtained his address from the critic Olin Downes. He offered Schoenberg a composition class. Schoenberg agreed. On 6 September he received Malkin's happy telegram in

Arcachon, which announced that he was sending a letter with a contract. On the 28th a further telegram arrived, in which Malkin agreed on receiving the signed contract from Schoenberg to deposit money in a bank. He asked for the date of Schoenberg's arrival in New York and for permission to arrange a big reception for him. Schoenberg hesitated over his reply. Malkin asked if he would travel on the *Degrasse* on 18 October. On 5 October came a final telegram, this time in German (the others were in English or French):

'Contract one year agreed 75% for you if more than thirty-six pupils for single lessons likewise mass lectures possible to be organized at any time 100% for you stop journey will be paid extra with best will impossible to arrange advance for journey here best cabins Degrasse *arranged for special price send telegraphic answer immediately also confirm ship and day of departure* Malkin.'

Now Schoenberg's decision was firm. There was not much to keep him in Europe. Only Edward Clark, who represented contemporary music on the B.B.C., and to whom Schoenberg had sent a despairing card from Paris, had made some offers. On 24 November *Pierrot Lunaire* and the Suite opus 29 were to be given in a public concert, which would be repeated on the 29th in the Queen's Hall. Under Schoenberg's direction Erika Wagner, the Kolisch Quartet, Eduard Steuermann, the flautist Murchie and the best clarinettists would be performing. Schoenberg turned the offer down, arranged what had to be arranged, and prepared for his departure from the Old World. He wrote his farewell letter to Josef Rufer in Paris on 24 October. He began his journey on the *Ile de France* on the 25th. He arrived in New York on the 31st.

Now events piled up on each other. From the very first day Schoenberg was drawn into the world of two large cities, which both claimed him. For after the signing of the contract Malkin had agreed that Schoenberg should teach in both Boston and New York. His conservatory had taken over a beautiful small patrician house in Boston's Beacon Street, No. 299, at the corner of Exeter Street.

The Schoenbergs found comfortable quarters in the continuation of this Beacon Street to the suburb of Brookline. The house No. 1284, called Pelham Hall, had been built in 1925 and consisted of modern furnished apartments. The smallest with one room and bath cost 25–30 dollars a month. Schoenberg rented Apartment 720. Pelham Hall was considered then as one of the three apartment houses of its kind in Greater Boston. It had hotel service with a porter, maid, laundry and a telephone in every apartment. Here the Schoenberg family lived, after spending the first days in the Copley Plaza Hotel, till 26 March 1934. At the same time they rented a suite in the New York Ansonia Hotel, Broadway, at the corner of 73rd Street, on the West Side, not far from Central Park. Malkin relates in his memoirs:

'The sensation at the news of the arrival of the great Master on 31 October 1933 was hardly believable. For months all the papers in America and Europe were full of stories about him . . .

In order to introduce Schoenberg to New York, we put on a public lecture at popular prices in the New School for Social Research. In contrast to the scandals in Vienna Schoenberg's lecture was a source of merriment and laughter. First of all his English was by no means perfect. My attempt to correct his text was rejected by him. He wanted to be Schoenberg and nothing else. When he went on to the stage he was greeted by a big ovation. The air was full of expectation. Everybody wanted to hear him speak. Trusting to the loudspeaker, he spoke very quietly. I realized with unease that the loudspeaker was not functioning, and we could not hear him. "Louder, louder", came from all sides of the room. As Schoenberg had not got a stentorian voice he asked the people to come as near to the podium as possible. Towards the end of his speech the loudspeaker worked, and to everybody's delight we heard the following story. After a concert in Rome, where Schoenberg was conducting his own works, a gentleman went into the artists' room and complained that he had travelled for twenty-four hours in order to hear the concert. He was utterly disappointed, for during two hours he hadn't heard a single triad. Schoenberg answered that he had been foolish to travel twenty-four hours for the sake of a triad; he could surely have been able to hear that at home. At which the gentleman turned round without a word and left the room.

On founding the Malkin Conservatory among other things I had the problem of creating a scholarship fund for gifted students without means. George Gershwin, excited that a young American composer could have the chance of studying with Schoenberg, was the first to give his cheque for a scholarship. Leopold Stokowski was the next.'

Right at the beginning of November Schoenberg had to go with Malkin to Washington and New York:

'*You can imagine,*' he wrote to Gertrud's sister Mitzi Seligmann-Kolisch, '*how tiring it is to do two train journeys one of five hours and one of ten hours from between twelve midday and nine in the evening on the next day, that is to say within thirty-three hours.*'

On the journey from Washington he heard from Malkin that the conservatory had no orchestra. He was disappointed by the little music school 'with perhaps five or six classrooms'. – His salary for the first year of contract was 4800 dollars.

Malkin's school was in fact a small enterprise, especially in a state which, besides Harvard University and the Massachusetts Institute for Technology, possessed the oldest Music High School in the United States, the New England Conservatory. The idea of a new foundation was based on the conviction that music must be treated as a living art, and that in teaching nothing was more important than the right atmosphere and the right attitude to this art. In the prospectus of the second scholastic year it was stated that the teachers consisted without exception of members who had a professional interest in music, especially practising artists. And the students were also asked to take an active part in public performances.

Besides Joseph Malkin and his brother, the pianist Manfred Malkin, the teachers in the first year of the school were the pianist Egon Petri and the composer and theoretician Nicolas Slonimsky. The advisory committee contained the names of Harold Bauer, Ernest Bloch, Arthur Bodanzky, Ernest Schelling, Arthur Fiedler, Ossip Gabrilowitsch, George Gershwin and Frederick Stock.

Schoenberg's flight from Germany did not remain concealed from the world. It is harder to understand that the larger music schools and the universities took no notice of any kind of it for months. And it was due to Joseph Malkin that the great composer and eminent teacher was brought to America. Schoenberg wrote in a letter from France that there were tendencies in Japan to ask him to go there; however, we can find no trace of an appointment or even a query. It was not until after his decision to go to Boston, and even after his arrival in America, that he was approached by two large educational establishments. Ernest Hutcheson, the Director of the Juilliard School in New York, asked Schoenberg to give a lecture. Princeton University followed.

Schoenberg first had to develop his activity at Malkin. He had already sent a sketch from Paris on 11 October, based on his Viennese course in the Schwarzwald Schools of 1918/19 which was published by Josef Rufer in his cataloque *The Work of Arnold*

Schoenberg in 1959. He suggested four courses, of which two –
about elements of form and an analysis of Bach – could be
attended by a larger public, a consultation period and a course
in general analysis.

He spoke about these courses in the first interviews which he
gave in November to the daily press and the magazine 'Musical
America'. He could not anticipate what a small number of
students was awaiting him.

The interest of the music critics and the American composers in
Schoenberg as a person was lively. The first organization to
honour him was the League of Composers, which gave a chamber
concert in New York with a reception afterwards on 11 November. Schoenberg made a short speech. Harvard University in
Cambridge near Boston also gave a welcoming reception, which
Schoenberg, however, had to miss owing to a sudden asthmatic
attack. On 19 November he gave his first speech in English on
the radio.

He kept Webern informed by telegram of all these things, and
later sent a card to Berg. He did not have time for longer letters
till January 1934.

His start at the Boston Conservatorium was a great disappointment. Malkin had arranged a competition, the winner of
which would have a scholarship to study with Schoenberg for
a year. Participants had to send in a composition; the jury had to
find the best one and award it the prize.

The prize was won by a woman, Lois Lautner. She had grown
up in Colorado as an infant prodigy on the violin, took her degree
in New York at the later Juilliard School in composition and
married a singer, who studied in Boston and from 1934–36 at the
Berlin High School for Music, where he was interested in
studying song performance. More than thirty years later the
'Michigan Quarterly Review' published, in January 1967, a
long article which Mrs. Lautner had written about her recollections of the time of her study with Schoenberg. It gives a
partly comic and a partly tragic picture of the difficulties with
which Schoenberg had to contend in this first American year.
– They first met early on a Friday – in the middle of November
1933 – in the Conservatorium. Schoenberg was hoarse, and
wore a scarf round his neck and asked with whom she had
studied composition. It was Dr. Percy Goetschius, an American
who had been educated in Stuttgart and who had taught in
Boston and New York (1853–1943). 'You have learnt something

from this man', said Schoenberg, looking at Mrs. Lautner's piano sonata which had won her the scholarship. Then he made her modulate at the piano, harmonize melodies and play some figured bass. He gave her a counterpoint exercise for her next lesson. When later on she brought him the beginning of a string quartet, he had some objections to it, but could not find the English words for it. Finally he thought for some time and closed his eyes and took pencil and paper. Then he began to write with 'incredible quickness'. When she could not play from his writing at sight he became annoyed. 'He made a gesture of defiance and of exasperation, which I saw many many times, in the course of the year . . . Whenever he was exposed to the obstinacy of inanimate objects, thick-headed students and the senselessness of American customs.'

His study of the quartet went on for a long time. Outside the classroom on the ground floor the secretary of the Conservatorium asked Mrs. Lautner to see in future that the lessons did not last longer than thirty minutes. For during his teaching Schoenberg would not allow any other noises in the school. In addition she was his only pupil. When Mrs. Lautner asked why, she was told that at 30 dollars Schoenberg's lessons were too expensive. However, there was no question of discussing the shortening of her lessons with him. So he was given a room on the top floor. But when a soprano started to practice in a room beneath him the sensitive Schoenberg protested. After this he taught in his apartment.

In the second semester, in February 1934, three new pupils were admitted into the Boston class. One of them was Lowndes Maury. He has sent me his reminiscences of Schoenberg in two letters. Here is a shortened version of them:

'I came into the class in January 1934, when Schoenberg was still in Boston. I only studied composition with him. The greatest impression was made on me by his analyses of Brahms's works, and once he allowed us to look at his own 1st Quartet. He never mentioned the 12-tone method, except to tell us that we must be fully grounded in traditional composition before we tried to write serially. While I was studying with him I didn't write anything of value; he intimidated me and hindered my creative powers. I discussed with him the pedal markings of his piano pieces; he said: "Only pedal when it is written". One of his great sayings, which has stayed with me and influenced all my later works: write what is POSSIBLE for the instruments, not what is PROBABLE.

My experience with him lasted for only five short months; I honour him as the greatest musical person with whom I have ever been in contact. Also as a very sweet man, as the following story shows. In 1948, when I was living in Hollywood as a commercial musician, I was asked by my friend and my other composition teacher Wesley La Violette, if I would like to hear a rehearsal of the Fourth Quartet with him at Schoenberg's house. Naturally I jumped at the chance. Schoenberg opened the door when we rang the bell. He had not seen me for fourteen years and did not know I was coming. Without hesitating a moment he thrust out his hand and said: "Mr. Maury, what a pleasure to see you!" '

Maury also relates how in the Boston rehearsal of his *Pelléas* Schoenberg heard a mistake in the fourth bassoon in the enormous orchestra. Asked why he had chosen this work, he answered that the public was not ready to hear his latest works as they did not understand the evolution of his musical thinking.

The New York class was larger. It came every week to a large room in the top storey of the Ansonia Hotel. Schoenberg suffered from these journeys; five and a half hours there, five and a half back, – his letters are full of complaints about his tiredness. And it was not only the length of the journeys which embittered him. In New York – so Mrs. Lautner says – there was fine weather. The train was like a crematorium, over-heated like all American trains. When he alighted in Boston he found snow, clouds and cold. His asthma increased so much that at the end of March he gave up his apartment in Boston and only taught in New York at the Hotel Ansonia. 'He completely left our little class, and the Malkins were compelled to send us to his teaching in New York by ship – the cheapest way of travelling.'

Mrs. Lautner's article contains many more details about Schoenberg's teaching, partly of a personal kind, partly of a professional kind. So, as we are told, many pupils, who showed him their compositions, were reprimanded by Schoenberg, who said that they should work at harmony. Or that he objected when a fugue began in a movement without a logical reason.

As examples of the technique in composition with older masters Schoenberg preferred Brahms's writing to Mozart's because – as Lois Lautner quotes 'In Mozart one can't see only hear. – Brahms is much easier to see.'

He practically never prescribed a style; only once when Mrs.

Lautner brought an invention and a fugue, he said: 'You are a modern woman, aren't you? Why are you writing like Bach?' Otherwise it was all the same to him whether a pupil wrote in a simple song style or symphonic jazz; only he would not allow anachronisms within a chosen language.

He always suffered from the great heat in the over-heated American rooms; even when there was an icy wind the doors to the balcony of the room in the Ansonia Hotel, where he taught, were left open.

Schoenberg's condition gradually became one of chronic bronchitis. When in early spring the New York streets were half-frozen rivers and the air was a poisonous cloud, he said: 'I cannot breathe. Is there no area in your land where the air is dry and warm?' Mrs. Lautner suggested Arizona to him, but he himself decided on California.

As a characteristic of his readiness to help she mentions a testimonial for her as a teacher, which she asked for after only knowing him a short time. He gave it without delay and in 1933 recommended her as the best and most gifted of his American pupils. This recommendation helped her a great deal. She says that the pupils were much more interested in 12-tone rows than in what Schoenberg taught her; this was a very detailed analysis of classical sonata movement form; instrumental writing which demands what is apparently impossible from the player; scores in which instruments are written as they sound.

Mrs. Lautner recognizes herself that her memory, after more than thirty years, has often led her astray. Her article should be read with critical reservations. But it confirms impressions which show many sides of Schoenberg's character and the details of which could not have been invented by anybody who had not known him well.

Joseph Malkin had telegraphed Schoenberg in September that the Boston Symphony Orchestra would offer him concerts. Schoenberg had known Sergei Koussevitzky, the chief conductor of the famous orchestra, since a meeting in Berlin in 1912. During the last twenty-one years Koussevitzky had become the prophet of Russian music in Paris and America, especially Stravinsky's. Therefore to Schoenberg he belonged to the opposite party, and his programmes, in their contemporary sections, were almost totally devoted to the non-Schoenbergian moderns.

But Schoenberg found no trace of opposition by Koussevitzky in Boston. The invitation for him to conduct was sent to him soon after his arrival. Koussevitzky suggested three dates in Boston and Cambridge on 11, 12 and 13 January 1934. The programme was to consist entirely of Schoenberg's music, beginning with Bach's Prelude and Fugue in E flat, orchestrated by Schoenberg in 1928; then *Pelléas and Mélisande* and finally *Verklärte Nacht*. Lois Lautner has described the *Pelléas* rehearsal to which she went with Gertrud Schoenberg. He had clearly got a bad cold – he had been coughing since December – Schoenberg conducted in a long, thick pullover. At a bassoon passage he stopped the orchestra, turned round to the two women who were sitting up in the balcony, and wanted to know whether the bassoon could be heard.

His over-exerted body gave-up. On 11 January Schoenberg conducted the final rehearsal in Cambridge. Then he became extremely ill. In a letter to Walter Goehr on 20 February he described what happened on the afternoon of 12 January, a really black Friday:

'*Immediately before the second concert (after I had been continually ill for six weeks) on the way to the concert hall I had such a violent attack of coughing that a muscle in my back was torn. Because of the unbearable pain (in spite of bandaging, from which I still have unhealed wounds on my back and front) I not only had to give up the two remaining concerts, but also a lecture in English, on which I had been working for more than two weeks. I was going to give it at Princeton University. The theme: composition with 12-tones – my first pronouncement on the subject!*'

The orchestra was informed about the event by telegram. Koussevitzky, who was in the hall, put on an improvised performance of the 1st Symphony of Brahms. It was not till 16 March that Schoenberg was able to repair the damage which was not his fault, and give a performance of *Pelléas* in Boston with the orchestra, which he praised as 'extraordinarily good'. The first clarinet was an old acquaintance from the Vienna Philharmonic, Viktor Polatschek.

And another project, from which he had promised himself a great deal, also foundered. On 24 January in the New York Madison Square Garden, a hall with ten thousand seats, Schoenberg was to conduct at a charity concert an orchestra of four hundred men and perform a work of his own. He had written to Webern about this at the beginning of January. Disappointedly he later wrote to Goehr that the whole concert had been called off for unknown reasons.

He was active again at the beginning of February. On the 8th and 9th he conducted in Chicago. On the 10th he gave at the Chicago University the lecture on 12-tone technique which he had had to cancel at Princeton. On the 11th there was a chamber concert with a reception afterwards. His composition courses at the Malkin Institute started immediately afterwards, in New York on the 12th, in Boston on the 14th. For a man who was severely asthmatic and worn down by the climate of the East coast it was a gigantic effort.

Schoenberg's work at the Malkin Conservatory ended on 31 May. The term was to go on till the end of June, but Joseph Malkin and Schoenberg had agreed that the latter should leave rather earlier, just as the beginning of his work there did not take place till 1 November, twenty days after that of the academic year. (In America the academic year is arranged differently from that in Europe. For instance from 1935–36 at the Malkin Conservatory it ran as follows: Beginning 19 September. Christmas holidays 23 December–1 January. Winter examinations 13–20 January. End of term 5 February. Beginning of the second term 6 February. Spring holidays 6–13 April. Final examinations 5–14 June. End of academic year 25 June.)

The school did not have a very long life. The Boston address book shows it from 1934–1941 at 299 Beacon Street, and in 1942 at 267 Commonwealth Avenue; afterwards no more. Joseph Malkin (born in Proipoisk on 12 September 1879) died on 1 September 1969 in New York. His brother Manfred, the pianist and co-director of the Boston Conservatory (born on 30 July 1884 in Odessa) had already died on 9 January 1966 in New York.

In a circular letter to his friends, which will be discussed later, Schoenberg said that the school had been nourished by the hope in himself; it had been '. . . announced by too late publicity, and also demanded fees that were more than double those that were available in a time of depression, and (he) stood in a crossfire of intrigue from lack of money and hatred of art.' He never said a bad word about Malkin: 'I do not wish to slander the proprietor', he said in a letter to me on 21 May 1947, 'he did his best'.

So far as Schoenberg found time for it and his strength allowed it, he kept up contact by letter and sometimes by telegram with his friends in Europe. Berg and Webern were kept in the picture about all his plans, successes, disasters, and illnesses. But the correspondence has an undertone of mistrust by Schoenberg, of mistrust of the European side. So for instance Webern wrote to Berg on 15 January 1934 that Schoenberg had indeed written him a nice letter, and wanted to dedicate a large work to him, Webern, for his fiftieth birthday, but had fears for them both. As early as 21 November Berg received a warning with ironic allusions from Boston because of his long silence, upon which Berg took up the ironic note and answered that he had written no variations on the Horst Wessel song.

Schoenberg had become so mistrustful because of his experiences of this year, that he suspected a change of thought as a result of political influences even in his most devoted friends. At the end of January Berg told Webern about 'fearful suppositions' in a short letter from Schoenberg. This was, as we know today, about anti-semitic characteristics in the text of the opera *Lulu* by Frank Wedekind, which Berg was setting to music. And Schoenberg did not always shut his ears to gossip, which had been brought to him by acquaintances from Europe and concerned Webern's supposed sympathies with some things in National Socialist Germany.

Anyone who lived outside Germany during the Nazi years knows the understandable mistrust which immigrants felt of all those who remained in the country. Schoenberg himself in March in Berlin had criticized Albert Einstein's political position. Now he was on the other side, and his passionate partisanship for Jewry made him understandably over-sensitive to every word which came from Germany. Austria indeed was still a moderately free land in 1934 with a parliamentary government. But the National Socialist anti-semitic tendencies were living in all sorts of corners and were waiting for the right moment to come out openly against liberalism. Four years later it came to this.

However, the ill-feeling soon changed to a better atmosphere. Convinced by Berg's and Webern's attitude and correspondence, Schoenberg sent to the older of his friends a letter which Berg called a 'valuable document of a, no of *the* fate of an artist, of friendship', and also important as a discussion about the U.S.A., the time and their circumstances, 'about whose real meaning' – so Schoenberg wrote – 'no living man can form a judgement'.

Meanwhile the two friends exchanged ideas about a planned celebration book for Schoenberg's sixtieth birthday. David Joseph Bach, the friend of his youth, wanted to start a new magazine with this, but it came to nothing. The contributions were collected together in July. 'Werfel should certainly be invited', Berg wrote to Webern, 'This is right for Schoenberg, after having corresponded with him about circumstances in the Third Reich. Frau Mahler should also be invited.' Now articles came in from all directions. Universal Edition had decided to publish the book, as it had done in 1924 with the special number of 'Anbruch' on Schoenberg's fiftieth birthday.

Among the contributions was an article by the poet Arnold Zweig, whose novel *Sergeant Grischa* Schoenberg esteemed highly. Zweig was an old admirer of the Master and in 1913 had written a story 'Quartet Movement by Schoenberg'. His contribution was so aggressive politically that D. J. Bach turned it down after discussions with the publishers. Webern too found the piece offensive. The book was ready on 26 August. As well as Schoenberg's oldest friends Oskar Adler, David Joseph Bach, Alexander von Zemlinsky and Alma Maria Mahler, the first generation pupils such as Alban Berg, Heinrich Jalowetz, Josef Polnauer, Erwin Stein, Anton von Webern and Egon Wellesz, the younger Hans Erich Apostel, Olga Novakovic, Paul A. Pisk and Eduard Steuermann, there were friendly composers such as Alois Haba, Josef Koffler and Darius Milhaud, writers like Hermann Broch, Hildegard Jone, Franz Werfel and Theodor Wiesengrund-Adorno, the critics Willi Reich and Paul Stefan; Erhard Buschbeck and Rudolf Ploderer, Schoenberg's friends from Vienna, and the conductor Willem Mengelberg from Holland.

The most important piece in the seventy-six-page-long book is Polnauer's analysis of the chorus 'Verbundenheit' from opus 35, the text of which, by Schoenberg himself, was put at the head of the book as a motto. The unusual quality of this homage lies in the fact that Polnauer made an exemplary use of the method of analysis developed by Schoenberg in the spirit of universal musical relations.

Remarkable evidence of how importantly Schoenberg's thinking worked on people who were outside artistic and intellectual circles is the article by the nineteen-year-old metal worker Karl Schulhofer. He had been introduced to Schoenberg's work by Dr. Pisk, and bought a copy of the Harmony Book. It gave him the greatest pleasure in his life; he said that from it he had learnt to think for himself, and to be able to be left on his own.

Walter Goehr in France had informed Schoenberg about the troubles of his son's life in Mödling. Georg 'Görgi' was and remained his problem child. Money was often sent to him by

Universal Edition at the request of his father, who also stepped in when he had incurred debts. Schoenberg's letters to Goehr sound like justifications. For Schoenberg's income was much less than the prospects which they had foreseen in Europe. Princeton University offered him a hundred dollars for his 12-tone lecture, out of which he had to pay his travel expenses. The industrial depression, which had dominated the U.S.A. since 1930, had led to the collapse of countless industrial and commercial firms and had an indirect effect on cultural life and the existence of schools and high schools. Schoenberg's income from the Malkin Conservatory certainly made it possible for himself and his small family to live. But he had to pay for the journey from Europe for Gertrud and himself out of the advance which Malkin had given him.

All these troubles and the serious asthmatic coughing, from which he had been suffering from since December, and in addition his important social engagements in New York, which led to many valuable meetings with people, prevented him for some time from working on larger compositions. On 10 December he wrote a mirror canon. And the next work which he wrote down on 10 March 1934, was also contrapuntal: a puzzle canon in three parts.

Schoenberg had to postpone answering letters which reached him in New York in the autumn of 1933. Sir Adrian Boult, the conductor of the B.B.C. Orchestra, was planning to give the concerts which had been cancelled earlier. Schoenberg wrote to him on 14 April 1934 that he would be prepared to come to Europe in June or between 15 September and 10 October in order to conduct. He would prefer to hear his new works such as the Cello Concerto with Feuermann and the String Quartet Concerto with the Kolisch Quartet performed by Boult, as the latter had performed his Orchestral Variations in such a clear, beautiful and vital way. However, he was compelled to earn money by conducting. Schoenberg's journey did not take place.

Also in April 1934 he answered a query from Dr. Walter E. Koons of the National Broadcasting Corporation in New York, who wanted a definition for a book which he was planning, of what music meant to Schoenberg. His reply was:

> *'Music is a simultaneous and a successiveness of tones and tonal-combinations, which are so organized that its impression on the ear is agreeable, and its impression on the intelligence is comprehensible, and that these impressions have the power to influence occult parts of our*

soul and of our sentimental spheres and that this influence makes us live in a dreamland of fulfilled desires, or in a dreamed hell.'

The letters to Boult and Koons are contained in the selection of letters published by Erwin Stein in 1958.

Through meeting prominent exiles in New York the Jewish problem had again become alive for Schoenberg. Among his unpublished manuscripts one is called 'Forward to a Jewish Unitary Party' and is dated 1 December 1933.

His most important new acquaintance was a man who had been living in America since 1905, after completing his studies as a composer and musicologist in Strasburg and Munich. Carl Engel, born in 1883 in Paris, one of the leading American musicologists and President of the music publishers G. Schirmer in New York since 1932, with a short interruption, became a devoted friend of Schoenberg's and one of his most active supporters up to his death on 6 May 1944.

Clearly Schoenberg discussed work plans with Engel. He chose the form of a letter to offer him a book on 6 June 1934. It was one of the theoretical writings on which he had been working for twenty years and would have the title *The Musical Thought and its Presentation*. Schoenberg called it a key book, probably because with it he wanted to open the door to artistic perceptions.

'*This book,*' he wrote to Engel, '*should show the fundamental basis of the whole teaching of composition. I estimate that it would consist of from 240–300 pages and contain many musical examples and would probably be ready for printing in October, as my previous work on it goes back for two decades. I think that this book will interest all teachers of composition and music. I am wondering, however, whether perhaps I should first write a treatise on counterpoint, also partly theoretical, chiefly practical, a teaching book. This could be published in two or three books of medium size. I think that I could have this ready by the end of the year.'*

Engel, who was about to go away, answered on the same day. He could not decide about this interesting proposal without consulting his colleagues. Did Schoenberg want to keep the copyright himself? Would Schirmers' merely have the English language rights? Would it be possible to make a contract in common with a European publisher?

Above all, however: the publishers must see the manuscript, in order to know if its production could be harmonized with other commitments which had already been made.

And then came the important sentence: 'As you are planning to spend the summer in finishing your opera, I hesitate to press you to write a book, which Schirmers' would at least have to see part of, in order to be able to decide definitely what its production would demand.'

In New York Schoenberg had published an article on 'Problems of Harmony' in the magazine 'Modern Music', edited by Minna Lederman, in the May–June issue; this was based on his Berlin lectures in the High School for Music of 1927. The Polish musical theoretician Joseph Yasser (born in Lodz 1893, had lived in New York since 1923, and in 1930 was a co-founder of the New York Musicological Society, and the author of *A Theory of evolving Tonality* in 1932 and *Medieval Quartal Harmony* in 1938) wrote Schoenberg a letter which he answered in detail on 10 June 1934. His answer is important in so far as it defends the point of view which he had put forward in the Harmony Book of 1911: that Schoenberg never produced a theory and its scientific formulation, but was interested in the clarification of musical events. In his lecture and the article based on it he started from the thesis that 'the connection of notes depends on their relationship and that even the chromatic scale is justified by natural conditions.' He illustrated this thesis with a small table of overtones. He said that he wanted to show 'that the chromatic scale is caused by relationships in the overtones which come upon the ear unconsciously, as for instance a painter is aroused by a model, or a prototype of his picture, to make a free imitation of it, while the photographer copies the original as exactly as his lens allows him to (he corrects the mistakes of this by "atmosphere"), while a scientist must endeavour to reproduce the pure truth, even if the mistakes are more beautiful, more pleasant or more useful.'

A second important fundamental idea mentioned in the letter is the insistence of tempered tuning. 'A musical ear must have assimilated the tempered scale. And a singer who produces natural pitches is unmusical, as anyone can have bad habits who behaves "naturally" in the street.'

The problem of natural intonation and non-tempered instruments occupied Schoenberg several times. In 1913 in Berlin's South End he sent Alexander Jemnitz on 20 October a piece of paper with the puzzling words: 'You can spit on my grave if a hundred years after my death there is still a usable untempered instrument.' In his Harmony Book he wrote about the C major scale: 'The overtone series, which has led the ear to follow it, contains many problems which need explanation. And if we run away from these problems, this is due almost exclusively to a compromise between the natural intervals and our incapability of using them. This compromise, which is called the tempered system, presents an armistice for an indefinite period.' Schoenberg then quotes a letter from Dr. Robert Neumann which mentions the 53-note scale as a new system of tempering, and combines pure sounds and the intervals derived from the 12-note tempered system. (Attempts to overcome the tempered system were undertaken in 1920 in Soviet Russia by Boris Krassin and Arseny Avramov. This ended in 1927 in Avramov's Universal Tone System with 175 notes to the octave, but this was regarded as undesirable in Stalin's time). Schoenberg comments on the 53-note system: 'It is clear that the overtones, in the way that they have led to the division of the simplest consonants, the octave, into 12, will also produce a further differentiation of sound some time.' But as the piece of paper sent to Jemnitz shows, he gives this period of development far more than a hundred years after his death.

A conversation with Thomas Mann in December 1945 is connected with this. A poet wanted to describe an imaginary chorus by the hero Adrian Leverkühn in his novel *Doctor Faustus*: this was to be sung in the untempered scale. Schoenberg replied: 'I would not do it myself. It is theoretically possible.' His letter to Yasser shows how much Schoenberg was occupied with theoretical musical ideas in 1934. In spite of Engel's objection he did not let himself be put off his plan for a book.

Later he wrote to Berg about the preliminary work on this which had occupied 200 pages since June. But he was also occupied with *Moses and Aaron*; on 21 June he finished new versions of the text of the third act. However the injurious effect of the climate again threatened his health. In summer the New York atmosphere was so humid that the warmth was even more burdensome than the cold in winter. In a letter to the author of this book Schoenberg describes his condition at the time. He quotes the doctor, who thought he was consoling Frau Gertrud: 'Why do you get so excited? He will live another fortnight, and that is time enough to arrange everything (he meant inheritance and insurance).' And Schoenberg adds: 'But he was wrong; he obviously thought that I was going to continue to be treated by him. Then it certainly would have been only a fortnight. So I went away.'

The Schoenbergs left the city with its dangerous climate in

July. On 3 August Webern received a card from Chautauqua, Vincent Avenue 26, on which Schoenberg wrote that they were living in a health resort for religious workers; he had not coughed for four days, and had lazed for ten. Now he wanted to work again.

Chautauqua, which lies on a large lake in the western part of New York State (about halfway between Cleveland and the Niagara Falls) is an American conception. From summer meetings of New York methodists a summer school for adults was founded in 1874 which gave academic courses for eight weeks and so became the model for numerous similar institutions in the way of universities and colleges. Among the famous Americans who had given lectures there were Theodore and Franklin D. Roosevelt, James W. Riley and Mark Twain. By building concert halls, a theatre, hotels, club houses, apartments and a library, the fishing village became a large centre of cultural education. From early days on music was one of the most important elements in the many-sided programme.

Schoenberg gave no lectures in Chautauqua. He rested, recovered, and played tennis or ping-pong. He also found his sense of humour again; on a postcard he told Alban Berg that he had taken part in tennis tournaments, but 'was put out in the first round . . . I didn't even win any points.'

Carl Engel had tried on his own initiative to help Schoenberg as a lecturer. In June he sent a letter of recommendation to forty-seven universities and other teaching establishments. As fee he demanded 200 dollars for one lecture, 500 for three. Schoenberg was thankful for the 'fabulous' recommendation, but had doubts about the size of the fee, due to his own experiences. The themes he suggested were:

1. My method of composing with twelve tones, which are only related with one another.
2. Problems of Harmony.
3. Tonal or atonal music.
4. Analysis of my Variations for orchestra.
5. Analysis of my orchestra Songs opus 22.
6. Brahms.
7. Extracts from the book *The Musical Idea and its Presentation*, which he was intending to write in the summer.

Engel reduced the fee demanded to 150 dollars for a single lecture, 400 for three. He simplified the title of the first in agreement with Schoenberg to 'My Method of Composing with

Twelve Inter-related Tones'. But the whole affair ended in a fiasco. On 27 July Engel had to write to Chautauqua that of the forty-seven bodies he had approached twenty-two had not replied, ten had politely declined, and the others remained undecided. The Peabody Conservatory in Baltimore aroused some hope, saying that it was planning a performance of *Verklärte Nacht* in February 1935 and a lecture of Schoenberg's round about that time. The New York University was also considering a series of lectures. As a little consolation Engel had a 100-dollar cheque ready for Schoenberg, if the latter would give him a musical autograph. The buyer was Claire M. Reis, the rich co-founder of the International Composers' Guild, and a supporter of the International Society for Contemporary Music. Schoenberg sent her a page of a sketch for *Moses and Aaron*. He answered Engel's news about his unfortunate enterprise with outward calm on 31 July:

'Perhaps the universities really don't have enough money for something so inessential as music or even a lecture on it by me; perhaps I also have personal enemies; perhaps it is this fine weather, in which one puts off the inevitable (namely me) as long as possible and where one would rather hear something bad from somebody else than something good from me.'

Schoenberg was much occupied with thoughts of old friends. As long as they were living in Germany it was difficult to keep in contact with them. In March 1934 Franz Schreker became very ill in Berlin. In order not to make political difficulties for him Schoenberg sent a card without giving his name or signature and asked after his state of health. His friend died on 21 March. Schoenberg did not dare to send condolences to Maria Schreker; however the loss of the man who had given the first performance of the 'Gurrelieder' in 1913 and had been close to him during his last years in Berlin must have moved him very deeply.

David Josef Bach's sixtieth birthday on 13 August was approaching. On 30 June Schoenberg wrote a three-part canon for him. The text had been written in 1926 for a planned chorus and runs:

He who will run with the world,
Must have time: or he runs too fast.
He who will fight as a hero,
Must bear pain: or he is cradled too easily.
He who would buy worth with money,
Must ask in many places: or he gives too much!

Schoenberg did not take part in the cultural life of Chautauqua, but got to know people – partly through tennis – of whom some became important to him. One of these was Ernest Hutcheson, the pianist born in Australia in 1871, who had finished his studies in the Eighties at the Leipzig Conservatory with Carl Reinecke and in Weimar with Bernhard Stavenhagen. After a brilliant career as a pianist and piano teacher Hutcheson had been Director of the Piano Department at the Chautauqua Summer School since 1911 and since 1927 had been Dean of the Juilliard School. Schoenberg took a warm liking to the slightly older man, whose German musical education was similar to his own.

The other man was Martin Bernstein, a twenty-nine-year-old double-bass player in the Chautauqua Symphony Orchestra, who was admired as the conductor of Henry Purcell's operas *King Arthur* and *Diocletian* and also as a teacher at the New York University and at Hunter College. It was Bernstein who showed Schoenberg the importance of the American High School orchestra.

'*I have the conviction,*' wrote Schoenberg, '*that all composers, especially all modern composers and very especially I should be interested in the promotion of such endeavours. For here one can lay the foundations of a new artistic culture, here young people can be given possibilities of understanding the new fields of expression and the means which are suitable for these.*'

These ideas gave birth to a work which surprised Schoenberg's friends and enemies in equal proportions. Not because it was written for a practical purpose, and so is similar to Paul Hindemith's music written for amateurs and his *Plöner Musiktag*, but because for the first time since 1909 it was written in keys. It is the 'Suite written in the old style for string orchestra'. Of its five movements: Overture, Adagio, Minuet, Gavotte and Gigue, two were written in October, the Gavotte on the 11th, the minuet on the 23rd. A sketch for the stretto of the fugue in the overture is dated 7 September 1934. The adagio was finished on 6 November and the whole work on 26 December.

The Suite for String Orchestra is the first of a small number of compositions by Schoenberg in which the tonal cadence is introduced, similarly to Mozart's and Beethoven's occasional use of the medieval modes. In spite of all kinds of freedom in permanent modulation and the use of altered chords, in spite of all the chromatic tendrils which wind round the cadences, the tonality of the five movements is clear. The overture, following Lully's scheme of slow-fast-slow, is in D major; its middle section is a five-part fugue including every kind of stretto. The beautiful adagio movement in E minor is developed in many parts. The B flat major gavotte has a broad architecture with a trio and a coda. The minuet and the final gigue are again in the original key of G major. The gestures and the form of baroque music are imitated in a virtuoso manner. The handling of the string orchestra, with many different kinds of playing and passages for solo instruments, contributes considerably to the tonal colour of the texture. In its ramification of the motivic and thematic material the score shows Schoenberg's hand unmistakably. Harmonically there is a relationship with Reger.

If one compares this first consciously archaic work of Schoenberg with Stravinsky's neo-classical attempts such as *Pulcinella* of 1919 or the octet of 1923, the latter are seen to be aesthetic copies of the style of Pergolesi and Bach, against which Schoenberg searches out the technical sources of this style.

Until the middle of September the Schoenbergs remained in Chautauqua. Schoenberg began working on the Suite, which was later continued and finished in California. Almost at the same time he wrote the first movement of the Violin Concerto opus 36 in Chautauqua, ending the movement on 11 September. The language of the two works are extremely different. The methods of writing show unmistakable likenesses.

We do not know why both works were interrupted, and the Violin Concerto was not finished until 1935–1936. Schoenberg felt both pleased and uprooted by the book which his friends had sent him for his sixtieth birthday on the 13 September. Over and above this he was having thoughts about his situation in America. The failure of Engel's attempts to assure his existence by lectures in universities and high schools was a severe disappointment for his material prospects and also for his self-confidence. Certainly Hutcheson and Alfred Stoessel, another leading teacher at the Juilliard School whom he had often met in Chautauqua, had given him hopes of a position at this important high school. But there were still reasons for scepticism, not only on the grounds of climate and health.

Hanns Eisler, who had gone from Paris in February 1934 to Copenhagen and then to London, had met Georg Schoenberg in Paris and had asked the latter to enquire from his father whether he would go to Russia. As a result Schoenberg sent him a sketch for the establishment of a music institute, which Eisler was to pass on to the Soviet authorities. Schoenberg asked his friend Stiedry, the conductor of the Leningrad Philharmonic, for advice about this plan.

'*I would only like to ask you if you are in the position to further these ideas. In fact I have not much to lose here. People would like to engage me everywhere and I have negotiated with many people. But no one has any money today and no one can offer me a salary . . . , large institutes have even given up their composition department altogether the crisis here is so serious.*' This letter was written on 12 September, the day before Schoenberg's sixtieth birthday, in Chautauqua.

The plan and two exposés of a musical institute are preserved in manuscript and are dated 'beginning of August 1934'. Stiedry did not answer until 7 February 1935, when he was on three weeks' leave in Vienna. He could not 'write freely about Russian conditions' from Russia itself. He had spoken a great deal about Schoenberg's plan and had found both enthusiasm and fear of seeing Schoenberg working in Russia, as the mediocre people were more afraid of him than they wished to have him. He, Stiedry, did not think that Schoenberg would like it there.

Meanwhile the idea was buried. The Schoenbergs had quickly decided to move to California, and left Chautauqua on Saturday 15 September. After a short stay in Pasadena they found a furnished house in Hollywood, Canyon Cove 5860, where they moved in on 1 October, felt well and lived there till the spring of 1936. 'House, food, traffic (in the sense of being able to drive!) are ideal here', Gertrud Schoenberg wrote to the Stiedrys in November, 'everything that we call luxury are regarded here as necessities of life. That is what makes life so pleasant for one here . . .'

Meanwhile good news still came from the Old World. On 6 October the Kolisch Quartet telegraphed from Stockholm:

After brilliantly successful premixre we thank you happily for opportunity virtuoso bravura please send account number repeat Prague 5 November proves success.

The signature 'Kokulehei' is formed from the first syllables of the members of the quartet, Kolisch, Khuner, Lehner, Heifetz (Benar). This telegram concerned the Prague première of the Concerto Grosso of Handel arranged by Schoenberg for string quartet and orchestra; this was given on 26 September under K. B. Jirák. The first Stockholm performance was conducted by Václav Talich.

Schoenberg's first year of exile was ending. It was a terrible year for him; from his first months from Boston on he suffered unspeakably in health. He could not get rid of breathlessness and spasms of coughing, although he gave up his beloved cigarette-smoking completely and did not take it up again till 1935. Money worries and disappointments of many kinds piled up, as hardly ever before in his life. Gertrud Schoenberg needed all her strength in order to remove the practical problems of existence from him, and herself struggled with the uncertainty of living and the bad winter of 1933/34. Only the child remained a source of pleasure and consolation. Nuria was two years old in the spring of 1934. 'She has grown up perfectly', Gertrud wrote in a letter of November to Erika and Fritz Stiedry, 'she speaks English and German equally well and gives us and everybody much pleasure.'

Schoenberg had no intention of going to Europe again. News from there was almost entirely unpleasant. Even the International Society for Contemporary Music did not perform any works of his in the Festival at Florence at the beginning of April, although his school was represented by Alban Berg's *Lyric Suite*, interpreted by the Kolisch Quartet, Five Lyrical Pieces by Hans Erich Apostel and a Quartettino by a Webern pupil, Leopold Spinner. On Schoenberg's sixtieth birthday no European radio played any work of his. But Richard Strauss was presented on his seventieth birthday in June with signed photographs by Hitler and Goebbels. Strauss's name was also on the list of members of an institution which was founded on 6 June 1934 in Wiesbaden (in opposition to the International Society for Contemporary Music, which was forbidden in Germany), the Permanent Council for the International Collaboration of Composers. Later Strauss also fell into disgrace.

'Die Musik', Germany's leading musical journal and once the first one which had supported Schoenberg since its foundation, had been 'co-ordinated' and gave space to the fanatics of the circle round Alfred Rosenberg. In its November number Dr. Herbert Gerigk wrote a pamphlet attacking Schoenberg with the maliciously joyful remark that even Jews rejected his music.

Among musical events in Germany he was possibly interested in what Paul Hindemith was doing. In spite of their differences in their approach to art, Schoenberg had more sympathy for Hindemith's gifts than the orthodox Schoenbergians liked. He had heard of the fight of the Nazis against Hindemith and the demonstrative success of the premiére of the symphony *Mathis der Maler*, which Furtwängler insisted pertinaciously on giving and conducting on 12 March 1934 in the Berlin Philharmonic. He regularly read the monthly paper 'Musical America', which contained reliable reports from Europe and America. So he was informed of the Paris premiére of Stravinsky's *Persephone* and also about the American novelty *Four Saints in Three Acts*, an opera by Gertrude Stein and Virgil Thomson, who later on, as the critic of the New York Herald Tribune, often wrote enthusiastically about Schoenberg.

Schoenberg looked back on the year. He wrote to thank and informed his friends and all who had not forgotten the 13 September. In a little circular letter of November 1934 he wrote this bitter sentence:

'Indeed I parted from the Old World not without feeling a wrench in my very bones, for I was not prepared for the fact that it would render me not only homeless *but* speechless (roman by the author of this book), *so that to all but my old friends I could now only say it in English; supposing they should wish to hear it at all. On the other hand here one lives like the Lord God in France (like a fighting cock), where he would have even more difficulty in getting a labour permit than here.'*

Much gloomier and full of complaints is the tone of a big, untitled report which because of its intimate nature was only sent to a small number of friends. Schoenberg was writing on 25 November, a Sunday, at an open window with the room full of sunshine. Anyone who knows the Californian autumn will understand how much he enjoyed this climate after his stay on the East coast. After looking back thankfully to his fiftieth birthday in 1924 in Vienna and the speech of the then social-democratic mayor Karl Seitz, he writes about the last few weeks:

'On 13 September we had already partly packed our luggage for travelling. Sometime before we had come to the conclusion that it was better for me to go to Hollywood, or California, and in the last days of August we took a definite decision. I will now give a small account of my first year in America, which ended on 31 October:

I can't conceal the fact that the disappointments, worries and ill health surpassed everything that I had had before. We already had our first disappointment in Paris, when nothing came after the news that I had to leave Berlin, and we were looking forward to a very difficult winter in France with a good deal of worries. After the expectations of mountains of gold which were offered to me at the time, I no longer expected to get so much from an American engagement. But the Malkin Conservatory offered me less than a quarter of what I expected as compensation for my Berlin salary, and which I regarded as a minimum; so I had to give in after a few hours of thought and take up this one single offer.'

What Schoenberg meant by compensation for his Berlin salary is not clear. As Director of the master class at the Prussian Academy he received about 18,000 marks a year. 4800 dollars were 20,160 marks. So the minimum sum which Schoenberg expected would have been 20,000 dollars or 84,000 marks. Probably Schoenberg meant what he had lost through the illegal non-fulfilment of his contract. This contract ran till 30 November 1935. But the Academy dismissed him on 31 October 1933. When one compares the purchasing power (in Marxist terms, real value) of the two salaries one comes nearer to seeing Schoenberg's moral demands on the land in which he was exiled. He had been injured and robbed by the powers of illegality; he expected to be indemnified by the powers of legality.

The report angrily castigates the unhelpfulness of conductors and especially Sergei Koussevitzky, who in ten years of work at Boston had not performed a note of his. With the exception of Frederick Stock in Chicago the conductors had rejected him from the beginning. They conducted a lot of Stravinsky, Ravel and Respighi, but of his works at the most *Verklärte Nacht* or a Bach arrangement. In Los Angeles Eugene Goossens, Arthur Rodzinsky and Nicolas Slonimsky had made attempts to perform his music (on 23 July 1933 Slonimsky performed the Accompaniment Music to a Film Scene in a Sunday concert at the Hollywood Bowl). But the public had only been strengthened thereby in their rejection of his music.

As a teacher, however, he had many friends. He said that he was getting only a third to two fifths of his New York salary. (This was 30 dollars; a third or two fifths of this would be 10–12 dollars.) But apart from a class of ten pupils he had some private pupils and was expecting to exist well in Los Angeles. In the summer he would give two lessons every day for six weeks, except for Saturdays and Sundays. The salary was not princely, but would cover three summer months.

Schoenberg had to turn down an offer from Ernest Hutcheson to go to the Juilliard School, because of the New York climate. He said that perhaps he would be well enough in 1935 to take up the offer. (Back in August Schoenberg also had to turn down an offer from Chicago on physical and financial grounds: Rudolf Ganz, an old friend of Busoni, wanted to engage him at his musical college for 4000 dollars.) Schoenberg accompanied his refusal with a joke canon.

The report says 'I have not been able to work any further on my opera, but I am writing a suite for string orchestra, tonal, a piece for student orchestra. I am writing this as the result of a request from a musician who teaches at New York University, conducts a students' orchestra there and has told me a lot of good news about these American school orchestras, of which there are many hundreds. This has convinced me that the fight against this wicked conservatism has to begin here. And so this piece will be an example for any progress that is possible within tonality, if one is really a musician and knows one's job; a real preparation, not only from the harmonic point of view, but also in the fields of melody, counterpoint and technically . . .'

Homeless and languageless; this was Schoenberg's situation in his American exile. The linguistic text-books in his library showed with what energy he stormed these barriers of speech. This is also shown by his letters in English, which he wrote from 1933 onwards, the manuscripts of his lectures and his sketches for readings in the foreign language which he had indeed known since his schooldays but had not mastered by any means. This is also shown by the records and tapes which have preserved the sound of his voice.

In the summer of 1933 he gave up the German cursive hand, which he used to use, in favour of Latin script. And on 16 September in Arcachon he signed a postcard to the Stiedrys for the first time with the internationally used oe instead of the umlaut ü: Arnold Schoenberg. And he stuck to this.

The first large literary work with which Schoenberg was occupied in Los Angeles was of a theoretical, cultural and political nature. It was written at the turn of the year 1934/5 and was linked in thought with another article which was eight to nine years older, based on similar foundations and had its origin through the same person, Alfredo Casella. Although these were separated by a fairly long period, they are both discussions about the Italian composer which have so far remained unpublished, and cannot be separated in their matter. They form part of the defensive battle which Schoenberg had fought since the Twenties against some tendencies in contemporary music, and which had borne musical fruit in the Three Satires for mixed chorus, opus 28.

Alfredo Casella was a man of many facets. Pianist, composer, conductor and critic, he completed his musical education at the Paris Conservatoire, where he also taught the piano until 1915. In contrast to the majority of Italian musicians, he was influenced when quite young by the music of Richard Strauss and Gustav Mahler, and supported these as a critic in Paris and Rome. He was given to speculation, and followed new paths in his music, especially harmonically. In a song which he wrote in 1915 'Mort, ta servante est à ma porte' (text by André Gide after a poem by Rabindranath Tagore) there is a chord of twelve different notes at the end. His piano style was influenced by Debussy's experiments. Spiritually he aimed for a combination of contemporary ideas and developed from an international world citizen to an Italian nationalist, to whom, however, chauvinistic limitations were repugnant.

After the First World War he was one of the most authoritative men in the International Society for Contemporary Music. His preferences were divided almost equally between the Viennese school of Schoenberg and the classical stylistic ideas of the young French musicians round Igor Stravinsky. And it was he who organized Schoenberg's Italian tour of *Pierrot Lunaire* in 1924. He wrote an enthusiastic article in the programme as an introduction to it.

In 1926 the American magazine 'Pro Musica' published his article 'Harmony, Counterpoint, etc.' in its March–June number. Schoenberg found in this article, which was only five pages long, ideas which led him to contradict them. In the margin he wrote his remarks, which were developed into a voluminous polemic. Casella explained the great crisis in modern music during the last thirty years (more or less since the beginning of the twentieth century) as a struggle with romanticism, with which he coupled the names of Wagner, Schoenberg and Scriabin. He referred to the description of romanticism as 'the sickness of human thought' and spoke of the discrepancies and mistakes of the new 'storm and stress', the power of which was now beginning to be recognized. He said that romanticism was an attack on counterpoint and form. Romanticism had made it impossible to present ideas in the forms used in previous centuries, and was responsible for the over-appraisal of harmonic experiments. It wanted to leave all questions of form on one side and merely concern itself with the problems of polyphony, both harmonic and contrapuntal. He said that the time of the great harmonic difficulties had begun with Beethoven, Schubert and Weber. However, Beethoven himself had been hindered by his deafness from developing harmony beyond that of Haydn and Mozart.

As his name was mentioned several times Schoenberg felt that he was attacked both in his ideas and personally. He hesitated about answering, especially as Casella was a redoubtable opponent, and so changeable in his ideas that one only had to wait for the moment when he again agreed with something which he had previously attacked. Then Schoenberg defined the concept of 'Musical Architecture', of which Casella said that it was impossible without tonality. Schoenberg himself defined tonality as the totality of tonal relations, which are very near to each other in the seven diatonic notes of the scale, but only indirect in the remaining five.

On the question of articulation and architecture Schoenberg says: 'Anyone who thinks in terms of head and limbs has no problem with articulation; it is an obvious characteristic of a natural form, and he need not worry about it any more than a mother has to worry whether her child has limbs. Naturally it will be articulated. Casella may have written music which seems to him unarticulated (and to me too) – but I have never done this!' – Casella had written: 'And Schoenbergian atonality seems as venerable as those rebus paintings composed of geometrical figures, which were the merriment of pre-war art exhibits. – '

Schoenberg says to this: 'That is very unfriendly. But he should not forget that he has also written things of this kind. And if he will only take a sharp look for a moment and not support himself by the parable of the repentant sheep, he must recognize that there would only be a repentant sheep if it became a sinful wolf.' And in another place in the annotations he wrote: 'Casella only occupies himself with making superficial art fashionable. As soon as something new appears the old art becomes laughable . . . But in art we know that the appearance of a new technique does not attack the old one, in so far as the thoughts presented in the latter are worthy of being thought.'

Towards the end of the annotations: 'I do not understand at all why Casella attacks me. Because I compose badly? All the better for him. Or the easier for him to compose better . . . To say that one would laugh at my music as at the Cubists and Futurists is to all intents and purposes a prophecy . . . But Casella, at the time when he imitated my music, made a different prophecy, so he hardly seems to be honourable . . .'

Finally Schoenberg notes after a performance of the ballet 'La Giara', that now he had heard Casella's Music of the Future and it was just as he expected: a potpourri, against which Josef Bayer with his 'Puppenfee' would be a great symphonist. 'His ideas are due to his memory; the only thing of his own is the architecture.' Schoenberg dates his notes 29 May 1926. At that time he was living in Berlin.

The second discussion about Casella, more important from a cultural-political point of view, comes from Schoenberg's first years in California. The quarterly of the League of Composers, edited by Minna Lederman in New York, 'Modern Music', published Casella's article 'Modern Music in Modern Italy' at the end of 1934. Schoenberg's undated marginal notes were written in Los Angeles. The English is not without mistakes. The brief marginal notes became a voluminous article. Schoenberg begins it with a quotation from Mussolini: 'Fascism is not exportable.' In this sentence, says Schoenberg, Mussolini was right in that he regarded the Fascist government as only suitable for the Italian people. He had also shown himself to be a clever politician, knowing that, like Bismarck, he did not have to dispose for eternity, only for the immediate future. And his remark calmed the fears of countries where the Soviet Union had raised the spectre of international fascism.

The quotation from Mussolini shows that Schoenberg regarded Casella's cultural politics as fascist. The latter described the Italian public as independent and anti-European. Schoenberg found that this was a variation of Mussolini's remark, and could also be expressed as: 'Italian music is not exportable.' However, he said that Casella not only exports his own music but wants – as he puts it himself – general return to artistic normality.

Meanwhile, says Schoenberg, fascism has become exportable. The return to normality has found the support of those who had waited for a long time for the destruction of modernism. Then he parries Casella's ironical remark about the disappearance of many works which were once regarded as bold and revolutionary, but had never been loved by the Italian public. 'What a famous victory!' says Schoenberg. He remembers the battles about Bach and his work which was forgotten for generations, about Schubert's symphonies which had to be unearthed thirty years after his death from hunger, about Wagner's *Lohengrin*, whom Liszt was the first to perform. He was very sorry not to be able to agree with Casella. But he is happy about Casella's great admiration for his friend and former pupil Alban Berg: 'I am happy that I am not in the position to solve the contradiction, which consists of his "strong opposition to atonality" and his appraisal of an atonal work, and the only explanation seems to be found in the smart variability of his ideas, which allowed him to take part in every artistic movement in the last thirty years, and which allows me to hope that perhaps one day I may see him as a partisan of atonality – naturally supported by a favourable turn in public circumstances.'

Then Schoenberg makes fun of the obvious influence of his own works on Casella's *Serenade*; in it he sees a tangible offer of peace, 'a clear hand of peace in my pockets'.

Casella had described atonality as the final consequence of German chromaticism in the previous century, the influence of which in Italy was small. Schoenberg finds a differentiation between German and Italian chromaticism as absurd as Casella's remark that Italy had never been influenced by any kind of chromaticism. He remembers that Italy at one time was the leader in chromaticism through Gesualdo and his contemporaries. And then he shows examples of chromatic and atonal passages in Casella's own Serenade. He continues: 'And the more Casella's music today seems to be "co-ordinated" with some political principles, the more this music will appear to coming generations to be "co-ordinated" with my style, so that creative capability alone will show the difference.' – As regards the Italian 'weakness for beauty and perfection' praised by Casella, Schoenberg remembered that on their tour together through Italy in 1924 his *Pierrot Lunaire* was not hissed or laughed at any more than Casella's String Quartet.

A fugato in Casella's Serenade leads him to a detailed examination of contrapuntal and homophonic composition. To put a fugue into a sonata form is not very sensible. This method seemed to him like an attempt to draw a haycart by an aeroplane. With reference to Beethoven's F major String Quartet opus 135 he then defines the difference between contrapuntal and homophonic methods, calling them 'Methods of developing through variation'. 'But unfortunately modern composers don't only write fugatos in sonata form but also independent fugues simply because of the contrasts in atmosphere and expression. This is as laughable as using a machine gun to spray sugar.' The modern method of writing several unconnected parts without any particular meaning was explained to him by an anecdote in a paper. In this the producer had asked the actor to speak very quickly and without any accent, so that the public would have no time to think about it or examine the words for their inner meaning.

Schoenberg gives an example on the question of atonality and tonality. When seven adjacent white keys on the piano are struck simultaneously the ear recognizes them as the seven notes of C major. But they do not express the tonality of C major. For this the tonic must be emphasized. 'Higher art demands a well organized struggle between the various degrees of the scale as to which is to be predominant, and the victory of tonality only has a deeper meaning when these usurpers are brought down.' If one looks at a chorale by Bach one can see that chromaticism does not impair the tonality. It is only when one looks at chromaticism superficially that one could regard national independence in artistic matters as possible, and think of a return to an artistic normality which had never been a norm. 'Peoples have always gained an advantage from the discoveries of other peoples. One can't despise the weapons used by an enemy if one wants to win a war. We can't stop telegraphic communications, because we would not know in time if the enemy was bringing his troops up to our frontier. Our aeroplanes have to use the airports of foreign countries if they need petrol, our ships have to enter foreign harbours if they need coal or want to sell their wares.'

Fifteen years earlier the decline of atonality had been prophesied and its similarity to futuristic painting was censured; this painting today was supposed to be 'laughable'. Schoenberg ends his fragment with an ironic attack on a prophet, a seer, whose pictures are produced from models by other people.

Casella's artistic position from the beginning of the twentieth century up to his death in 1947 was of a remarkable flexibility. Schoenberg recognized this correctly and castigated it rightly at the moment when his former Italian friend turned himself into an enemy. An enemy, however, whom Schoenberg respected, although he knew his artistic deficiencies when he was still his friend and when Casella even accepted corrections in his compositions (for example in the string quartet mentioned above).

The question of 'co-ordination' brings a point into Schoenberg's polemic which is also made clear by the Mussolini quotation at the beginning of his reply. To define Casella as co-ordinated in a fascist manner is a simplification of the circumstances. Neo-classic and anti-romantic convictions had been entertained since about 1920 by many European intellectuals and artists, even by those who supported the socialist side politically more than the fascists.

In fact Schöenberg keeps his polemic on an entirely artistic level. Beyond the external occasion of the two articles about Casella it is important because they expose the means of musical construction and forms as no one before Schoenberg has explained them. The individual and often drastic technique of comparison (haycart and aeroplane, machine gun and sugar-caster) are typical of the way in which Schoenberg co-ordinated artistic phenomena with those of practical life.

Compared with the cultural politics of the National Socialists those of the Italian fascists were tolerant. Certainly performances of Schoenberg's music were fairly rare after 1933 in Italy, where they had never been common, but some were given. Even in 1942, in the middle of the Second World War, the Royal Opera in Rome put on a production of Berg's *Wozzeck*, which was kept in the repertoire even when the German troops invaded Italy. It was Casella who suggested this production.

LOS ANGELES

The hope of improvement in Schoenberg's health was not fulfilled to the extent that he had expected. So for the moment he gave up the idea of accepting the offer from New York of a professorship at the Juilliard School. There were enough possibilities of work in Los Angeles, where the family felt very well from nearly every point of view. Schoenberg did not lack acquaintances and even friends from the Old World. Among them Hugo Riesenfeld, who had played chamber music with him in 1898, was the most helpful. Since 1933 Otto Klemperer had been conducting the Los Angeles Philharmonic Orchestra and was happy that Schoenberg had come there. Since their first meeting in 1911 the two men had a remarkable love-hate relationship with each other. Both recognized the greatness of the other, but neither of them had the gift of diplomacy. So they always had differences and violent collisions. Schoenberg found that Klemperer did not perform him enough, and the latter was imprudent enough to speak his mind when he had difficulty in understanding Schoenberg's music. In November 1934 a banquet was given in honour of Klemperer. Schoenberg wrote to Klemperer that he had refused the invitation.

'*I consider it unspeakable that these people, who have been suppressing my works in this part of the world for the last twenty-five years, now want to use me as a decoration, to give me a walking-on part on this occasion, because I simply happen, entirely at my own pleasure, to be here . . . . This refusal is not directed at you, for I esteem your talents sufficiently to adopt much sharper weapons against you. These are jests; please do not misunderstand. With, despite all, very kind regards to you.*'
One can see that Schoenberg had not changed in America. To wiseacres who prophesied that he too would hang on the Cross he replied: 'I will destroy America first!'

He remained in contact by letter with the Director of the Juilliard School, Ernest Hutcheson. On 28 March Schoenberg wrote to his friend in detail about his experiences in America, and above all about his disappointment in finding students so badly educated. He said that in Europe there was a certain knowledge of master works which predominated, in America this was mostly not the case. It seems that the reason for this was the high price of printed music, 'which for most students makes it impossible to own the rudimentary little collection of something like 200 volumes that all but the very poorest had in Austria'. In addition concert and opera tickets were too expensive.

Alban Berg was one of the most faithful correspondents with Schoenberg after his exile. He had written to his friend in January 1934 about the difficulties of Austrian cultural life, and also about his own worries and pains. He described his work on the opera *Lulu* in detail; he had finished the second act of it. A larger and more important letter of 4 November 1934 is somewhat more pessimistic in tone, perhaps because Berg felt increasingly ill and was fighting this illness with a large number of medicaments. Shortly before Christmas he sent the score of the symphonic pieces from *Lulu*, which are dedicated to Schoenberg and which had just been published; in spite of all the intrigues by the National Socialists these had their very successful première in November at the Berlin Staatskapelle under Erich Kleiber. He had already sent the manuscript of the prologue of *Lulu* in September to Schoenberg for his birthday.

Schoenberg answered Berg's Christmas letter on 2 January 1935. He suggested to Berg a plan for the foundation of a 'Protective Society'. Berg agreed in a letter of 30 January, as the Austrian artists, in so far as they did not write in a 'down to earth' manner, were threatened by the fight against 'cultural bolshevism':

'We think and talk about nothing else except how we can counter this mentality. Unfortunately we are handicapped in this, and for the reason that at the moment we cannot do anything without being mixed up in politics from the enemy point of view: that is something which we do *not* want (and have never wanted). So this makes a cultural organization of an unpolitical nature all the more necessary for us "threatened people". We will discuss this here in great detail and I hope that Rudi will be able to get over in order to tell you about this personally.'

Rudi (Rudolf Kolisch) had returned from America in the autumn and had given four concerts with his quartet in Vienna in which he had played all the three quartets of Schoenberg as well as classical works.

On 9 February, for Berg's fiftieth birthday, a parcel came from Hollywood which made Berg very happy. Schoenberg had written a canon for him to words of his own, containing motives from the *Lulu* music, and also a record of his voice giving him good wishes. Berg described in a letter of 11 March, how he stood with the Kolisch Quartet, Paul von Klenau, Anna Mahler and Willi Reich and his wife in front of the gramophone in order to hear the beloved voice, whose bright and always rather hoarse quality was never forgotten by anyone who had heard it once.

Owing to his exile Schoenberg had lost his membership of the Society of German Composers. He now wanted to join the Austrian sister organization, the AKM (Society of Authors, Composers and Publishers) in Vienna. Berg was a member of the committee of this. In a letter of 4 May 1935 Schoenberg asked Berg to propose him. He asked him to see that his case was considered on its proper merits, including appreciation of the fact that he had not received any royalties for two years. Berg's answer of 23 June was despairing and angry. The AKM had turned down the proposal completely. And the reason was – as Berg wrote to his friend Webern on 15 July – 'that Schoenberg as a member would make difficulties for them – as he did many years before when he found faults with their accounts and resigned'.

Berg spoke about the affair twice more, as the 'greatest scandal that I have experienced for decades in the artistic life of Vienna'.

The picture which Schoenberg's Viennese friends had of his life in California was rosier than the truth. Certainly the Schoenbergs felt well in the Californian climate and the usual luxurious conditions. But the medal had an obverse side. Schoenberg wrote on 13 March to the friend of his youth David Joseph Bach in New York that the golden times were over. It was difficult to keep on smiling when one wanted to spit fire.

'*One must never tell the truth, not even when I wanted to warn someone of a danger. Here in the partly (the greater part) still wild West, one sees warnings like one I saw written up on a house: "If you want to shoot, do it now, otherwise you won't ever shoot again!"* . . . *Here everything wants to be praised* . . . *here, where everything is all wrong, there is uncertainty and fear of exposure which can only endure praise* . . .

But I won't fall into European mistakes and merely grouse . . . *I have found very many people whom I like . . . Really the best people here are the English, while those who have only lived here from thirty to fifty years are mostly inferior, although often very kindly and even helpful.'*

Carl Engel in New York was one of the most helpful. Schoenberg corresponded with him about everything that concerned his life and his work in his exile. The preparation of the performance material of the String Suite gave him a lot of worry. He had arranged with Engel that his son Georg should make the copies for printing in Vienna. But the loss of time as the result of the great distance frustrated this plan. In a letter of 20 January Schoenberg also spoke about Rudolf Kolisch and Pablo Casals, who still had not performed the Cello Concerto after Monn. Clearly Casals had financial difficulties, about which Schoenberg said:

'Regarding Casals, considering his important personality I would ask you to write to him once again and allow him to have the piece for any price which he himself finds suitable. In fact conditions in Spain are such that there is no question of sums in dollars. The dearest seats there cost 4 pesetas, that is 45 cents! The Casals Orchestra is supported by subsidies, which Casals mainly pays himself. As Casals won't play in Germany any longer, he has lost an important source of income and as there are younger cellists, he doesn't earn enough any more in order to be able to contribute so much from his own pocket.'

On 28 March Engel reported to Schoenberg about the two New York performances of the String Quartet Concerto after Handel. Werner Janssen conducted the Philharmonic. Engel also wrote that D. J. Bach was with him and had brought an article about Schoenberg which he would publish in the 'Musical Quarterly.' In this way the October number would give an additional news-value to Schoenberg's taking-up his post at the Juilliard School.

At the beginning of March Schoenberg had conducted *Pierrot Lunaire* and the Chamber Symphony in San Francisco. On the 21st he conducted a concert of the Los Angeles Philharmonic, which was to have given the première of the String Suite. This was, as he wrote to his friend Bach, his first properly paid engagement in America. Because of the number of mistakes in the material of the Suite the programme had to be altered; it now consisted of the 3rd Symphony of Brahms, *Verklärte Nacht* and Schoenberg's Bach arrangements. He wrote about this in a letter to Engel of 7 April 1935, which is also concerned with the project of the Juilliard School. He liked New York very much, but he also knew the opposition which threatened him there, especially from Toscanini, whom he disliked, and he would not be able to conceal this dislike. Apart from that he had a lot to do in Los Angeles; besides his private pupils he was teaching a class of twenty-four listeners, chiefly music teachers. Life in California was very much cheaper than in New York. So if the Juilliard School could not pay him enough so that he could compose without worry for six or seven months, apart from the costs of travel and the necessity of keeping up two houses, he would not be able to remain in Los Angeles. He also wrote to this effect to Hutcheson. He said that he would soon finish the orchestral version of the 1st Chamber Symphony and he then wanted to compose the last act of his opera.

The orchestration of the Chamber Symphony was finished on 18 April. Before this Schoenberg received a long letter from Engel which confirmed him in all his thoughts about Juilliard. 'In spite of the pleasant life in California he should not forget the "strategic" advantages of New York. New York was the best centre for teaching with intelligent students. Also in New York he would have a considerable number of people who supported him.'

Financially Engel clearly offered the greatest amount that the publishers Schirmer could give Schoenberg: 1500 dollars in five monthly instalments between March and July. On 3 May Schoenberg suggested to his friend that he should take over *Verklärte Nacht* and the Chamber Symphony for America and give him further payments for that. Could not Engel also have the Harmony Book translated into English and published, as had been planned many years before? As regards Juilliard, he had only been offered 5000 dollars for a year's salary from there, the value of which was less than the 4000 which he could safely rely on in Los Angeles. If it had been 10,000 he might have been tempted into the venture. Now Engel brought in the powerful John Erskine, President of the Juilliard School and a key figure in many New York musical positions of power, including the Metropolitan Opera. On 27 May they had a long conversation and Engel found Erskine as keen and willing to get Schoenberg for Juilliard as Hutcheson was. However, he had to write to his friend on 4 June that the School could not fulfil his demands as long as the 'Senior Teacher in Composition' was still working there in spite of his failing powers. Now Schoenberg finally gave up the plan. He wrote on 18 June to Engel that his summer courses had begun the day before and would last six weeks. He had signed a contract with the UCLA (University of California at Los Angeles) for two years, from 1 July 1935 to 30 June 1937. The yearly salary was 4800 dollars. It was increased in 1930 to 5100 and in 1942 to 5400.

On 18 May the première of the Suite for String Orchestra took place with the Los Angeles Philharmonic under Otto Klemperer. Schoenberg was very pleased and now was on friendly relations with the conductor again. The summer courses, which were visited by many students, gave him pleasure but wore him out more than he thought that they would. Among those who were present was the twenty-two-year-old John Cage, who had an enthusiastic admiration for Schoenberg from this time on. Now Californian publicity began to get interested in the legendary man who had chosen to live in Los Angeles. Radio stations asked him to do broadcasts. On 7 September he spoke on the radio of the University of Southern California about: 'What have people to expect from music?', another time about 'Success and Value'. Max van Leuwen Swarthout interviewed him. He also gave public lectures at the universities, the first on 29 March with the title: 'When we young Austrian Jewish Artists', and another on 9 October with the original name 'Driven into Paradise'. Schoenberg had to wrestle with many of these speeches in spite of his health, which was continually getting worse. Finally he collapsed on 15 September. The doctors diagnosed diabetes. In a letter to Engel on 2 October Schoenberg said that the main trouble was over-exertion of body and mind. For the moment he had to stay in bed and could not begin his classes at the university till the following week. Among many expressions of friendship and gifts for his birthday on 13 September a long letter came from Alban Berg, written on 28 August. He spoke about his work on the violin concerto, which he had finished in the middle of August, with its 'tonal' 12-tone row, and ending with a motif from the Bach Chorale 'Es ist genug'. With Helene Berg, he was, as he had been every summer, in his forest hut on the Wörthersee. But he had worries about his health and told Schoenberg about a carbuncle on his backbone which would not heal. This was the beginning of Berg's fatal illness; the birthday letter was the penultimate one which Schoenberg was to receive from him.

On 3 October he again began work for eight days on the violin concerto which he had already started in 1934. The manuscript has some remarkable entries in it. On page 13 is written in Indian ink: 'Here I stopped when I had to fill in 29 bars which were merely sketched out, and had to go to bed on 15 September for almost three weeks (up till today it is nineteen days already): page 13 Arnold Schoenberg – 3.10.1953 I am going to try (!) to work on it again today Arnold Schoenberg.' On the lower edge of this page is written in ink: 'No one would believe that when I wrote the number of bar 222 in the score I thought to myself: 'Up till now this time I have not yet made a mistake in the numbering of the bars, and immediately I thought 'now it is finished' and discover a minute later I have left out the number of bar 223 and on *page 13*! The same place where I broke off work! 11.10.1935.' On an earlier page in the manuscript Schoenberg discovered that 169 – the number of the bar he had just finished – is 13 times 13. We know that he was superstitious and was already afraid of the number 13 in his Viennese days. In the title of the opera *Moses and Aaron*, contrary to usual practice, Aaron is spelt with only one A, because otherwise the title would contain 13 letters! This superstition increased in his old age.

Carl Engel was interested in the Violin Concerto and asked on 14 October if Schoenberg had a soloist for the first performance. The composer answered on the 18th that he had been in touch with Yasha Heifetz, but did not think that he would be successful. Heifetz turned down the offer of the first performance, which was not given until 6 December 1940 in Philadelphia with the city orchestra under Leopold Stokowski and with Louis Krasner as soloist.

On 21 October Schoenberg received Engel's report about the first performance in New York of the String Suite under Klemperer. 'I had the feeling that you had brought together everything that has been learnt and known in the last three centuries, and adorned it with new art and new beauty.' The New York critics were not so strongly impressed. Schoenberg wrote a long letter with the title 'Analysis by Ear' to the critic Olin Downes about his review in the New York Times. The recommendation which Schoenberg had given to his son-in-law Felix Greissle to the publisher Schirmer was accepted in principle by Engel. But Greissle did not leave Vienna until 1938, after the occupation of Austria by the Nazis.

At the end of October Schoenberg found time for a long letter to Anton von Webern. He told him about his contract with the UCLA, about Klemperer and about the latter's very good

performance of the String Suite and also about his own health:
'I am better, although unfortunately I am smoking again.'

Schoenberg kept silent about one of his principal troubles in
his correspondence with his friends. The Schoenbergs had come
to America in 1930 on a visitors' visa. In order to remain permanently they needed an immigration visa. At the end of 1935
the time which they could stay legally in the country was due to
run out. In the autumn Schoenberg sketched out a telegraphic
appeal for help to Artur Schnabel in London. It reads:

> *Although engaged as University professor, can get neither quota
> number[1] nor prolongation of my visa and will have to leave this country
> in a few weeks. Stop. Can you ask if your friends can arrange for me a
> position as teacher in England or a number of concerts or some other
> means of help, so that I can earn enough to live in England or another
> country. Stop. Am in despair and cannot see any chance for my future
> or even present.*

At the end of 1935 his visa was prolonged.

We are informed about his activities as a teacher at the
Californian universities by a letter of his to a 'Mrs. F'. She was
one of a number of prominent ladies who had a great influence on
cultural life in the United States. Schoenberg asked her to dine
with him one evening and then to come about 7.30 to his class on
musical criticism at the University of Southern California. He
says that among his listeners are professors of both universities
who are not musicians but professors of philosophy. In spite of
these enthusiastic listeners he was very disappointed that his
expectation of finding a class of at least fifty to sixty listeners was
not fulfilled. What he was trying to do in his class was to con-
centrate on the *work*: 'Everybody who is listening to me will be a
listener who knows what he likes and why he likes it.' He wanted
to educate the musical public of Los Angeles no longer to go to a
concert because So-and-so is playing, conducting or singing, but
because this or that work is to be performed. He would like to get
Mrs F and many other society people among his audience. It
was his first and last attempt to interest rich American society in
his work

On 15 November 1935 Schoenberg wrote a four-part mirror
canon with the title 'für Frau Charlotte Dieterle' and also the

---

[1] In the U.S.A. there was a law that the number of people who want to
become American citizens, being citizens of another country, is controlled.
Clearly the quota for Czechoslovak immigrants for 1935 had already been
filled.

texts: 'One can think what one likes about Schoenberg' and 'Credit may sometimes be based on a statement like that. Creed and credit.'

The fine Californian November days drew to an end. On 7 December the first performance of the Cello Concerto after Monn was at last given in London. Edward Clark had put it on at the B.B.C. However, it was not Casals who was the soloist, but Emanuel Feuermann. Letters came in advance for the festivals of Christmas and the New Year, including one from Baron Hermann Roner in Traunkirchen, who reminded Schoenberg of their playing quartets together in the summers of 1921 to 1923. After a long period of interruption the pianist Else C. Kraus, a zealous advocate and performer of Schoenberg's piano works, also renewed her correspondence with him.

Alban Berg had written on 30 November. He had returned to Vienna and was full of his impressions of the 'Gurrelieder':

'We went to the first performance the day before yesterday and heard yesterday's one on the radio. It was naturally a very great sensation again and it was an overwhelming victory from every point of view, which was even shared by the vice-chancellor Prince Starhemberg in an almost demonstrative way.

Bruno Walter, who normally drips with sweetness, made music in a more elegant and a more winged manner, so that many songs went too fast . . . As it was well rehearsed, and performed by singers of talent, the performances were on a high level and transmitted . . . a real, overpowering impression to all who were present in the sold-out hall.'

Berg's letter again complains about his health troubles, furuncles and carbuncles. He was also feeling low in morale, for he had to discover that he was not permanently resident in his home country, but at least he was still living in his homeland and was able to speak his native language, unlike Schoenberg. Berg's Christmas letter was sent from the Crown Prince Rudolf Hospital and was written by Helene. Alban's condition had worsened threateningly. They hoped he might be healed by a blood transfusion which had taken place yesterday, 16 December. A week later, on 24 December 1935, Berg was dead. The news affected Schoenberg deeply. He had lost one of his nearest and most devoted friends, and he knew how hard Berg's struggle with death had been. – In his letter of condolence to Helene Berg he offered to undertake the orchestration of the third act of *Lulu*. She thanked him with happiness about this proposal on 14 January 1936: '. . . the first ray of light in my darkness!'

Schoenberg immediately arranged for Associated Music Publishers, the American agents of the Vienna Universal Edition, to send him the material of Berg's opera. It arrived on 11 March. After a detailed study of the music and especially of the text he explained that he was not in a position to undertake the work. He gave as his official reason that it was harder and more time-consuming than he had imagined. In reality he was hurt by the description of a Jewish character in the text, whom Wedekind called Puntschu. In a detailed letter to Erwin Stein, which was begun on 9 March and finished on the 11th after Schoenberg had received the material – he gives a detailed account of his decision.

Helene Berg saw in this an act of fate and has refused since then to give permission to many friends of Berg's and people who had competent knowledge of his work to carry out the work which Schoenberg did not want to do himself. So *Lulu* has remained a fragment.

In Europe Schoenberg had been a frequent cinema-goer; he admired and loved, in quite a naïve way, the beauty and perfection of American films which he later despised. Now he himself was living in Hollywood, not far from the studios of the dream factories. The managers of this millionaire industry would not let such a famous man escape from them so easily. Schoenberg himself did not think of writing a commissioned composition for a film. But one of the most powerful tycoons in Hollywood, Irving Thalberg, heard a performance of *Verklärte Nacht* on the radio and was so enthusiastic that he considered asking Schoenberg to write music for the film *The Good Earth* after the famous novel by Pearl S. Buck. The events which now followed have since become legendary, and were described in 1947 by H. W. Heinshemer in *Menagerie in F Sharp* and also by Salka Viertel in her book of memoirs *Das unbelehrbare Herz*. Schoenberg himself wrote about them in a letter to Alma Mahler-Werfel on 23 January 1936:

> '*Then I almost agreed to write music for a film, but fortunately asked 50,000 dollars, which, likewise fortunately, was much too much, for it would have been the end of me; and the only thing is that if I had somehow survived it we should have been able to live on it – even if modestly – for a number of years, which would have meant at last being able to finish in my lifetime at least those compositions and theoretical works that I have already begun, even if not beginning any more new things. And for that I should gladly have sacrificed my life and even my*

*reputation, although I know that others, who have held their own in less
strict regard than I mine, would not have failed to seize the chance of
despising me for it.'*

Gertrud Schoenberg said about this: 'The M.G.M. company
promised him to alter nothing (a promise which naturally they
would never have kept!) but the fee of 50,000 dollars was as we
had hoped (!), too high and we got out of it with relief!' However, Schoenberg wrote down sketches for this music in two note-
books. Gertrud Schoenberg says that they were written shortly
after the negotiations 'purely from artistic interest in the solution
of a problem of this kind'. Two themes served to describe Uncle
Wang and are of a lively, cheerful, and even comic character. A
slow description of a landscape uses the Chinese pentatonic scale,
in a not dissimilar way to that in Gustav Mahler's 'Lied von der
Erde'. The third theme is a cheerful folkdance scene; the fifth a
passionate love motive. All these ideas are written in a developed
tonality. The accompaniment, in so far as it is written down, consists of three- or four-part chords.

After Schoenberg's contracts with the Prussian Academy of
Arts had expired, he had no further official connection with
Berlin. However, the German Bank and Disconto Gesellschaft,
Foreign Section (America) sent him a statement of account on 15
January 1936, showing he had a balance of 1065 marks 50. As an
immigrant Schoenberg could only make use of the money in
Germany. He used it partly to buy books. So on 10 December
1936 he ordered from the bookshop Mittler and Sons the second
and third volumes of the Philosophical Dictionary by Rudolf
Eisler.

In January Schoenberg had formed the bold plan – perhaps
while he was expecting other film contracts – of building a house
in Hollywood. His admired friend Adolf Loos had died on 23
August 1933 in a sanatorium near Vienna. However, one of his
best pupils, Karl Kulka, was alive. Schoenberg wrote to him on
24 January that he was in contact with Richard Neutra, who also
came from Loos's circle and did very nice houses himself. He says
he has Viennese taste and knows what a writer needs. What he did
not know was the art of using marble as a wall covering. Loos
had said to Schoenberg that marble was the cheapest wall paper.
It had to be cut in sheets only a millimetre thick and cemented to
the wall. This method was unknown in America. Schoenberg
wanted to know where it was done in Europe and how far Loos
carried the marble up the walls and how the transition was made

to ceiling or wall. The plan, which Loos had carried out in many houses, was not fulfilled, as Schoenberg soon found a house which he bought himself. – Hermann Scherchen, who had left Germany in 1933 and was working in Switzerland and Brussels, sent Schoenberg the programme of the fourteenth I.S.C.M. Festival in Barcelona from 19–25 April. Schoenberg thanked him on 16 March, saying that it was a 'very big affair' and was only sorry that Webern was missing from the programme. As regards *Erwartung*, this was not a mimodrama (as the programme said), but a monodrama. He said that artistically he was more dissatisfied than ever; he was teaching at one university and would go to the other one in 1937. 'But unfortunately the material I get has had such an inadequate grounding that my work is as much a waste of time as if Einstein were having to teach mathematics at a secondary school.'

On 27 April Schoenberg began to work on his fourth string quartet; on the first page was written: 'fulfilling with pleasure the commission of the great patroness of music Mrs. Elizabeth Sprague-Coolidge'. However, the work had to be interrupted on 30 April at the twenty-second bar. The Schoenbergs had found a charming, fairly new house in the Spanish colonial style in Brentwood Park, 116 North Rockingham Avenue, and they bought this by instalments. Now they had to pack and move. By 9 May they were so much installed that the composition could be continued. The first two movements were both partly written at the same time. On 24 May Schoenberg began the second movement, which was finished on 20 June; two days later he wrote the final bars of the first. Then followed the third movement, which was finished on 18 June. He began the fourth movement on the same day, interrupted work on it on the 25th and continued it again on 8 July. The work was finished on 26 July 1936.

It bears the dedication 'To the ideal patron of chamber music ELIZABETH SPRAGUE COOLIDGE and to the ideal interpreters of it THE KOLISCH QUARTET'. It is in four movements and lasts half an hour like the Third Quartet, but it differs from the latter in its greater lightness and mastery of the treatment of the twelve-note technique. The third quartet notably avoids great variation of sound colours which are obtained by out-of-the-way methods of playing, through variation between harmonics, pizzicato, tremolo on the bridge, playing on the fingerboard and suchlike. In the fourth quartet these colour effects are used much more frequently, especially in the first movement, an allegro molto energico, which shows the characteristics of a sonata form in a rondo-like shape. The second movement, which is like a minuet, is a commoso of an intermezzo type in A–B–A form; the most original movement is the third, a largo. It combines two recitatives of rhapsodic character and dramatic expression, between which there is a lyrical section, which returns in a varied form after the second recitative and leads to the end. The quick final movement is again rondo-like with variations. – Meanwhile Schoenberg had to carry out day-to-day tasks as well as his teaching. For Willi Reich's Alban Berg book he wrote a seven-page article which he later withdrew. He also wrote notes for an article for the twenty-fifth anniversary of Mahler's death.

At Carl Engel's suggestion the publisher Schirmer prepared a collected volume of articles about and tributes to Schoenberg, which appeared in 1937. It not only contains articles which had already appeared between 1929 and 1935 in other places, written by the Master himself as well as by Roger Sessions, Ernst Krenek, César Saerchinger, Paul Amadeus Pisk, Boris de Schloezer, Paul Stefan, Franz Werfel, Erwin Stein and Adolphe Weiss. The authors of articles which were specially written for this volume were Leopold Stokowski, who contributed the preface, Richard Buhlig, Louis Danz, Carl Engel, Otto Klemperer, Ernst Krenek, José Rodriguez, Nicolas Slonimsky, Eduard Steuermann, Berthold Viertel and Merle Armitage. The latter edited the book. He was a former engineer who lived in Los Angeles as an impresario; between 1911 and 1921 he had arranged world tours, including those of the Diaghilev Ballet. He founded the Los Angeles Opera Association and directed it from 1924 to 1936, and in 1936 he published a book on Stravinsky. The Schoenberg book, which was dedicated to the memory of Alban Berg, is a volume of 319 pages. Besides some photographs of the Master and two pages in facsimile from the Fourth String Quartet, it contains a reproduction of the fine oil painting which George Gershwin had painted of him; it now hangs in the Washington Library of Congress. Schoenberg and Gershwin had met through tennis and had become friends.

Next to swimming and rowing tennis was Schoenberg's great sporting passion. In California there were excellent players for whom he was hardly a match. When his sister-in-law Mitzi Seligmann had moved to New York, Schoenberg wanted to play with her again. On 30 January 1936 Gertrud wrote to her sister telling her to come soon. She recommended her not to travel by railway but by a Greyhound bus and by the southern route, in order not to come across one of the snowstorms which occur every week or two up till May in the north. Schoenberg added a post-script in which he warned his sister-in-law about travel acquaintances.

'Don't let yourself be influenced by elegant, amiable or sympathetic appearances. All Americans look honest and are amiable and helpful, but . . . they immediately recognize a greenhorn! Such an attitude is quite normal. Be entirely mistrustful.'

Among German theatrical people in Hollywood Wilhelm Dieterle and his wife Charlotte were Schoenberg's closest friends. They were planning a film about Beethoven and asked Schoenberg to act as adviser, but were unable to accept his invitation to supper and a discussion of the project at the end of July. So on 30 July Schoenberg wrote giving them his decision. He suggested Klemperer for them as an adviser.

'He does know and understand Beethoven to a really quite exceptional degree; has the ability to feel his heroic quality, himself having fire and spirit enough not to fail in the task; and though he is a tyrant, that would only be an advantage to the undertaking as a whole; for a slave cannot portray a hero.'

He said that he himself was ready to advise Klemperer on problems of style and composition.

After finishing the Fourth String Quartet he wrote to Elizabeth Sprague-Coolidge that he was very content with it and thought that it would be much more pleasant than the Third. He said she could not imagine how much work they had had through the arrival of their furniture from Berlin. The letter is dated 3 August 1936.

'I have lost four weeks and have not yet arranged my library and my manuscripts. Besides I had to teach. Private lessons and those terrible summer sessions at USC.'

In Pasadena, the elegant eastern suburb of Los Angeles, Mrs. Sprague-Coolidge had arranged a chamber music festival in June, in which Kolisch with his three colleagues performed the first three quartets by Schoenberg. Immediately afterwards the packing cases of furniture, music and books arrived, and there was a great deal to do to set the house in Brentwood Park in order. Near the entrance door on the ground floor they arranged his workroom. This contained bookshelves and pigeonholes for his library, the great Bach Edition. In front of it, in the full light of the bow window, was Schoenberg's writing-table, which he had

Arnold and Gertrud Schoenberg outside their house in
Brentwood Park, Los Angeles, 1935

made himself, with all his little trays and pigeonholes for pens, pencils, erasers, paperclips and ink. There was also a workshop for his practical work. It was not until he had arranged his books and manuscripts that he was able to work on the Violin Concerto again; the second movement of this was finished on 27 August and the third on 23 September.

Through the piling up of practical and teaching work Schoenberg had to interrupt his correspondence with his friends in Europe and America. After a long time he resumed his connection with Carl Engel on 10 October. After eight months his enormous amount of work had made him so tired that he was not able to write any letters. Apart from his private lessons and the exhausting summer sessions at the University of Southern California his position as head of the newly formed music department at the University of California at Los Angeles (UCLA) had given him a lot to do. So he could not take any leave. Engels should not be disappointed by the slow progress of the success of the works which Schirmer had published. Their fate did not depend on day-to-day progress. – As regards health he was very well; he was playing tennis twice a week.

Engel answered on 11 November that he had spent two of the summer months in Europe, partly to take a cure at Hofgastein, partly to visit the eighty-two-year-old Guido Adler in Vienna. On his daily walks with the latter he had talked a lot about Schoenberg and Berg.

Engel said that the firm had not had much luck with the String Suite, the Monn Cello Concerto and the Handel arrangement for string quartet and orchestra. However, he would dare to publish the Fourth Quartet and the Violin Concerto, provided that Schoenberg did not ask for any further advances. At the beginning of December Schoenberg sent him a short letter in manuscript on the headed notepaper of the UCLA with a suggestion that the firm of Schirmer should publish miniature editions of classical music or sell the normal, very expensive editions to students at a reduced price.

Since the middle of November Schoenberg had been working on a treatise on counterpoint. His class at the UCLA, which he had begun to teach at the beginning of October, included an excellent young pianist called Leonard Stein. He made such progress in theory and counterpoint as well that in 1938 he became Schoenberg's assistant. In 1961, ten years after the Master's death, he published the work which had been finished in 1942 as

Preliminary Exercises in Counterpoint. Schoenberg had done preliminary work on this in 1911 and 1926. Schoenberg's first
assistant at the UCLA was Gerald Strang from 1936/38; Strang
also helped him in the compiling of the Counterpoint book.

José Rodriguez asked him for a conversation for Merle
Armitage's book, which was due to appear in the spring of 1937.
Rodriguez had been an admirer since 1917, when a young
officer played Schoenberg's opus 2 to him when he was in the
army. The conversation took place at the beginning of January
1937 by the fireside in the house at Brentwood Park, after little
Nuria had been sent to bed. It concerned the traditional roots of
Schoenberg's language and method of writing. The Master called
himself a creature of inspiration. He said that he composed and
painted by instinct. Rodriguez asked him to explain his method of
work. 'I see the work as a whole first', answered Schoenberg.
'Then I compose the details. In working them out, I always lose
something. This cannot be avoided. There is always some loss
when we materialize. But there is a compensating gain in vitality.
We all have technical difficulties, which arise, not from inability
to handle the material, but from some inherent quality in the
idea. And it is this idea, this first thought, that must dictate the
structure and the texture of the work.' The conversation ranged
from the new Violin Concerto to questions of study and finally to
problems of tonality and form. On this theme Schoenberg said,
ending the interview with this, that he had himself written something for Armitage's book and he did not want to repeat himself.

By this he meant an article on 'Tonality and Form'. Harmony,
he wrote, was not the only thing which influenced form. One
could use it as an aid to form. His pupils would agree that he, as a
teacher above all things always wanted to make clear the difference between the formative potentialities of principal and
secondary subjects, introductions, transitions and codas. And he
had always maintained that most living composers were only able
to write introductions, able only to place one thing next to another.

Today most people strove for 'style, technique and sound',
meaning something purely external. The old culture was neglected
in the presentation of a thought. In a novel by Dickens one can
see from the complex structure and the cleverly woven threads
how necessary knowledge is for a work of art. For one must not
believe that one can reach a higher artistic means of expression
only by the use of a certain technique. He had worked for ten
years on settling these differences theoretically, with the success-

ful result that the work concerning it would shortly be written. Artistic expression was only possible in the mental realm. The unthinking did not demand it and did not even allow it.

In his youth people still felt how a principal subject was to be formed. Brahms had mastered this art, Mahler and Strauss had inherited it. He had showed in his Harmony Book that tonality not only served a composer but on the contrary demanded to be served. This was not so simple as the 'decreeing committee' believed. (By this Schoenberg meant the clique who decided on the style of the day.)

He himself was the last modern composer who occupied himself with tonal harmony in the sense of the old masters. If he heard one of the pieces in which all possible tonal non-relationships are avoided, right up to their end through a C major or an F sharp major triad, according to the mood, then he always had to think of those savage potentates who wore only a cravat and a top hat.

The form of a composition is achieved because (1) a body exists and because (2) the members exercise different functions and are created for these functions. If anyone forces through a function on them from outside it reminded him of the bad craftsmen who conceal faulty construction by lacquer or nickel.

Who can say today how a principal subject must be built up and made to hold together? How a fluid form is solidified? How an introduction, or a development must be evolved? Anyone who knows these things will not doubt whether or not tonality must be restored to achieve form. Construction, formation, superstructure, in short: artistic expression does not depend on any technical trick but lies rather in the musical thought itself. He who really thinks and thinks deeply will produce different expressions with different musical ideas.

Elizabeth Sprague-Coolidge had arranged a very important framework for the first performance of the Fourth String Quartet which she had commissioned. She financed a four-day cycle of concerts by the Kolisch Quartet put on by the UCLA. This took place in the concert hall of the Joseah Royce Hall on 4, 6, 7 and 8 January. Invitations were sent out personally to a number of prominent musicians and people interested in music. Each programme consisted of only two quartets, one by Beethoven and one by Schoenberg. Schoenberg's D minor Quartet followed Beethoven's E flat Quartet, opus 127; the F sharp minor Quartet (with Clemence Gifford as soprano) preceded Beethoven's opus 130 and the Grosse Fuge opus 133; Schoenberg's Third Quartet was played before Beethoven's C sharp minor Quartet opus 131. The last programme began with the first performance of Schoenberg's opus 37, followed by Beethoven's A minor Quartet opus 132. Schoenberg sent a programme book with a short note to Stiedry; he said that he would very much like to have Erika Wagner-Stiedry for the *Pierrot* performance planned for Los Angeles. However, at the moment he was only giving a performance of *Pelléas* in Los Angeles with the Federal Music Project Symphony Orchestra, formed by out of work musicians. This took place on 17 February. A week before this Louis Krasner had asked for the music of the new Violin Concerto. Krasner, a virtuoso Russian violinist born in 1903, who had studied first of all in Boston and then with Flesch, Capet and Sevcik, was a supporter of the new Viennese school and had commissioned Alban Berg's Violin Concerto in 1934; he gave the first performance of it two years later in Barcelona – Berg had died. At this time he came into close contact with Webern, who, however, had inhibitions shortly before the première and handed over the conducting of the work to Scherchen.

Between 7 January and 10 February 1937 Schoenberg made sketches on six loose sheets of music paper for a symphony in four movements. Rufer found the beginnings of the movements, thirty to fifty bars long each, in short score in his legacy. Each movement bears a title, some of which are concerned with Jewish affairs. These are:

1st Movement:	Predominance (superiority) provokes envy.
2nd Movement:	a) What they think about us.
Scherzo	b) What we think about them.
	c) Conclusion.
3rd Movement:	The sacred feasts and costumes
4th Movement:	The day will come.

The Kolisch Quartet used their stay in California to record all four quartets of Schoenberg. On 5 February 1937 the Master told his patroness, Mrs. Sprague-Coolidge, that the little edition was meant as a private gift to his friends, and the album cost 71,50 dollars. It also contained commentaries and analyses by himself of each of the quartets.

From Germany Schoenberg only received occasional news from his sister and some of his faithful pupils. It all sounded miserable. The magazine 'Die Musik', which had once been a leading promoter of his ideas, had been completly 'co-ordinated' and in

1936 had brought out an extremely anti-semitic special edition with a distorted portrait of him. Leo Kestenberg, who had built up a large music institute in Prague with state help after 1933, now left Europe. He wrote on 25 May that he wanted to put on a Schoenberg Festival in Tel-Aviv.

In May 1937 Armitage's big book was published. In it Schoenberg found articles which must have made him happy, and testimonials from an illustrious circle of old and new friends. About this time he made one of his arrangements of classical works. He orchestrated Brahms's Piano Quartet in G minor, opus 25, for large orchestra. He altered little in the composition. The work was begun on 2 May and finished on 19 September. Meanwhile he corresponded with Gustav Reese, the American musical scholar, who had a leading position in the firm of Schirmer. This correspondence discussed details of the contracts concerning the works of Schoenberg which had been taken over by Schirmer.

In an often quoted letter of 3 June 1937 to Nicolas Slonimsky Schoenberg mentions a scherzo theme from his unfinished symphony as the first example of twelve-tone writing in his own work:
'*The method of composing with twelve tones had many 'first steps'. The first step happened about December 1914 or at the beginning of 1915, when I sketched a symphony, the last part of which later became* Jacob's Ladder, *but which has never been continued. The Scherzo of this symphony was based on a theme which consisted of the twelve tones.*'
Schoenberg made a mistake about the date; the theme was written down on 27 May 1914. It is: D–G–E flat–A–G sharp–E–F–B–C–G flat–D flat–B flat.

George Gershwin, who had again been living in Los Angeles since 1936, recommenced playing regular games of tennis with Schoenberg, and a warm friendship arose between the two men. One morning, on 26 May 1937, Schoenberg told his friend that his wife had just borne him a child. This was Rudolf Ronald, who gave his father great pleasure as an infant prodigy at tennis, won many prizes and is living today in Los Angeles as a successful lawyer. Gershwin, who had painted his portrait of Schoenberg a few months before, was writing film music for M.G.M. at that time. In the middle of his work at the studio he had a nervous collapse. The doctors believed that he was exhausted by overwork. In fact Gershwin soon recovered, but suffered from continual headaches. As well as carrying out his film work he was doing an intensive study of the system of Joseph Schillinger, a kind of technical, mathematical method of writing music. On 10 July

1937 he had a second collapse. The doctors diagnosed a tumour on the brain which was operated on at once. But it was of no avail. On 11 July Gershwin died. Schoenberg, who felt an almost paternal love for the composer who was only thirty-eight, was deeply moved and spoke an obituary for him on the radio, in which he called him a great musician. He also contributed to the Gershwin Memorial Book, which Merle Armitage published in 1938. In it he described Gershwin as an innovator, an artist who expressed musical thoughts. Perhaps – he could not prophesy – the history of music will regard him as a sort of Johann Strauss or Debussy, Offenbach or Brahms, Lehár or Puccini.

There was some discord in his correspondence with Webern. Schoenberg had been informed that his friend, who remained in Austria but had been deprived of practically all his active work, had been impressed by some of the National Socialist achievements in their régime in Germany. Schoenberg asked Webern about this. The latter was shocked: 'Who dares to come between you and me?' he answered in a letter of 15 July. The waves calmed down. There was no doubt that after the Austrian Anschluss of 1938 Webern remained honest and honourable in all questions which concerned Schoenberg. This affair probably arose from a conversation which Webern had with Louis Krasner in 1936 on a railway journey through Germany.

The summer and autumn of 1937 were mainly devoted to the extensive teaching activity which Schoenberg had to undertake at the UCLA. At this time he wrote the sketches, mostly in the form of notes and musical examples with commentaries, which were later published as *Fundamentals of Musical Composition* in book form. Gerald Strang, who edited the book, was working closely with Schoenberg as his assistant in this work. Schoenberg asked Strang to co-ordinate the various versions and work on them with the aim of publication. The work continued until 1948 with long interruptions. Strang also had the task of translating Schoenberg's very personal terminology into practical English words. If Schoenberg spoke of 'tonality' he meant 'key', if he said 'measure' that meant 'bar', 'tone' meant 'note' and more things of the same kind. From the fact that this book was dealing with the fundamentals of musical composition one can see from what a modest level of knowledge Schoenberg had to start with these students.

The President of the UCLA, Dr. Robert G. Sproul, wanted to have a report on his teaching plans. He received a detailed answer from Schoenberg on 2 October. A teacher for counter-point and analysis was necessary for the less talented classes. Then he himself would be able to teach the more talented students in advanced classes. All the classes were much too big at present. Sixty counterpoint pupils, forty-five for analysis and twenty-five for composition made teaching extremely difficult. And merely a not very careful correction of the written work needed twenty hours every week.

He suggested that Gerald Strang, his assistant, should be given a contract and then the counterpoint classes should be divided into two or three groups. He would take over the more talented students himself. He thought that the composition and analysis classes should be altered in the same way. As the number of students was increasing, an adjustment was imperative. A library for the students would need 150 to 200 dollars a year.

The enticements of the Californian dream factory had not escaped the notice of the poet Else Lasker-Schüler. She had known Schoenberg in his Viennese years and with her husband, the chess player Dr. Emanuel Lasker, had visited the Schoenbergs in their Berlin apartment in the Nuremberg Platz. In 1933 she emigrated to Jerusalem. Now she asked Schoenberg if he would write music for a film version of a play of hers. He replied: 'Certainly, if I am asked to do it and if what has to be presented is within the limits of my means of expression; it will be a pleasure and I will fall upon the composition.' Then he warned her not to expect too much. He said that the cultural standards in Hollywood were incredibly low. He himself had hardly any relations with producers or directors, although they had tried to 'buy my name in order to conceal some horrible infamies.' If she sent him a book, that would not do her any harm, as anyway no one took any notice of an author's ideas. As an exception he mentioned Wilhelm Dieterle, and gave the poet his address in Hollywood. He said that if she would send him a copy of the piece he would try to show it to Dieterle or someone else.

Carl Engel had again spent a few weeks of the summer in Austria, three of them together with old Professor Guido Adler in Hofgastein. He wrote to Schoenberg about this on 6 October, and also spoke about the plans for contracts which Schoenberg had discussed with Professor Gustav Reese. He said that Felix Greissle had been given the task of making a piano score of the Violin Concerto. A repetition of the Schoenberg-Beethoven cycle with the Kolisch Quartet had been planned for the East Coast, i.e.

Schoenberg with his daughter Nuria, 1937

in New York and Boston; this had been arranged by the Coolidge Foundation of the Library of Congress in Washington. Schoenberg's answer came by return on 9 October. He said that he was travelling that day to Denver for a Schoenberg Festival of four concerts, where he would give a lecture on the theme on 'How one becomes lonely'. He asked Engel to put on the Violin Concerto the dedication: 'To my dear friend Anton von Webern with my warmest thanks for his unsurpassable loyalty.' From this one can see that all misunderstandings between him and Webern had been resolved.

Among old friends Schoenberg heard again from Marya Freund in Paris and from the artist B. F. Dolbin in Vienna. He also received a long letter from Fritz Stiedry in Vienna on 8 December. The conductor said that he had performed *Pierrot Lunaire* in Berne, Zurich and Basle with Erika Stiedry and young musicians who had already performed it with him in Vienna in June. In Berne three of the pieces had to be repeated. In the small Tonhalle-Saal in Zurich there was a sensational success:

'Even after the second part there was a unison applause of the kind which usually only tenors get. At the end there was if possible, even more noise. We repeated five pieces. After this the people came to see us and said that they would like to have heard all the twenty-one numbers once more. Ansermet and Vollkmar-Andrae[1] came in as excited as the young people and said that we must do a world tour with the piece.'

The same thing had happened in Basle. At last the right time had come for the piece, as it had for *Tristan* forty years ago and the Ninth Symphony fifty years ago.

He said that he had been thrown out of Russia, as in 1933 he had been thrown out of Germany, both times because of so-called general regulations. He had seen it all coming, although he still had a great deal to do there: forty opera performances and eighty symphony concerts in Moscow and Leningrad. Even at the end of May the Moscow Radio had offered him a contract as Musical Director. But at the end of August a piece of paper arrived from Leningrad with the brief information that his contract was invalidated for reasons of principle. As all positions in Europe had been occupied since 1933 and his colleagues Kleiber and Busch had diligently picked up what remained, he could only come to America. He said that he would arrive in New York at the begin-

---

[1] The conductor and composer.

ning of February 1938. He asked Schoenberg, and also Klemperer, for advice and help. He and his wife had been very pleased about the 'latest Schoenberg' (meaning Rudolf Ronald).

At Christmas Schoenberg gave himself a present. He bought the twenty volumes of the Encyclopaedia Britannica. His old Knaur Lexicon had not been sufficient for him for some time. He had written many marginal notes in it, especially next to the articles on music, painting and architecture. Reference books, of which only a few had any musical content, formed as an important part of his library as language manuals and books about his various hobbies.

Political difficulties in Austria grew greater every year. They had an immediate effect on cultural and artistic life, and narrowed the space in which modern and unconventional ideas could live more and more. The pessimism in Alban Berg's letters was justified. Webern was also affected by these events. Dr. Willi Reich, a pupil and friend of Berg's, had been editing a little magazine since January 1932, the unusual title of which, '23', referred to the paragraphs of corrections in the Austrian press laws. Like Karl Kraus's 'Fackel' it carried on a battle against corruption and lack of culture in Austrian magazines, and fought for everything that stemmed from the musical circle of the Schoenberg school. Among Reich's collaborators were Ernst Krenek, Rudolf Ploderer, Alexander Jemnitz, Theodor Wiesengrund-Adorno, Hans F. Redlich, Artur Schnabel and the novelist Joseph Roth. The last number appeared on 15 September 1937. When Vienna was occupied by the Germans they destroyed the remainder of the magazine.

11 March 1938 was a sad day for Schoenberg. He knew how many of his friends in Austria were threatened in their existence and their life. He knew of the power and the influence of the reactionary musical circles which now began to rule. What would happen to Universal Edition, which had published the greater part of his works? What would happen to his son Georg and his family? Soon the first dreadful reports came, the first letters from old friends asking for advice and help. The pianist and theoretician Moritz Violin had turned to Schoenberg, who was a friend from boyhood, asking for an introduction to Dr. Alfred Hertz, the conductor of the San Francisco Symphony Orchestra. Schoenberg wrote to Hertz saying that if he had more money at the UCLA he would engage Violin at once. He said that it was so sad that all these people with the finest musical culture there was in

Europe should be cast out and have to spend their old age in anxiety and hardship and grief.

Schoenberg's son-in-law Felix Greissle arrived with his family in New York at the beginning of July 1938. Schoenberg promised to send him an affidavit and advised him to get himself a quota visa. Schirmers knew Greissle as a Viennese collaborator of the firm. There was a hope that he would find work there.

Clearly Engel had advised Greissle to go to Hollywood. Schoenberg warned the latter:

'So far there has been absolutely no chance of anything here, otherwise I should obviously have seized it. On the contrary many excellent musicians who have to spend a year here without being allowed to earn a cent are now leaving Hollywood again. For instance my former pupil Adolphe Weiss, who happens to be one of the best bassoonists in America. At present he is playing in a Federal (unemployed musicians) Orchestra. And if he can't get an engagement by September he means to try New York again. I am now earning two-fifths of what I was earning about fifteen months ago and see no hope of improvement.'

Then he warned Greissle not to say anything he did not have to say about his experiences of the last few weeks, especially not to journalists. He knew that the Nazis took revenge on relatives and friends who were still in their power. He should be reserved and not get mixed up in politics. He, Schoenberg, had always observed this rule very strictly, out of consideration for his friends and relatives in Germany.

In Vevey on the lake of Geneva lived the philosopher Dr. Jakob Klatzkin, who had already written to Schoenberg in May 1933 and asked for his help. Now their correspondence was renewed. Schoenberg wrote to Klatzkin on 19 July 1938 saying that he was better, but because of too much other work he had not composed for two years:

'And anyway: who should one write for? The non-Jews are "conservative", and the Jews have never shown any interest in my music. And now, into the bargain, in Palestine they are out to develop, artificially, an authentically Jewish kind of music, which rejects what I have achieved. I am now working – in so far as I am not occupied with answering letters from unfortunate people in Germany and Austria, and in so far as I don't give way to unbearable depression – at a "practical" handbook of composition. For more then twenty years I have been wanting to write a theoretical book, but now I must decant the results of my work and all my knowledge and skill into a practical textbook.'

Schoenberg knew Albert Einstein, the creator of the Theory of

Relativity, well from his Berlin days. On 29 August Einstein wrote to him about the friend of Schoenberg's youth Oskar Adler. Adler was not only an excellent violinist and a well-trained philosopher, but also a supporter of scientific astrology. He had published a book on this in 1937. Einstein had received this from acquaintances who enclosed a recommendation by Schoenberg. He had read the book, found it very well written and valuable for supporters of astrology. But it was quite impossible for him to support the ideas expressed in the book, as he regarded them as incorrect. He even believed that the work, because of its good style, might constitute a danger to innocent people. His view was that one should give Adler an affidavit and try to find him work as a musician. Because of the widespread interest in astrology he would then perhaps be able to find something else. He, Einstein, would gladly support Adler, but he would not, even indirectly, support astrology.

Schoenberg's cousin, the tenor Hans Nachod, was still in Vienna, but was thinking of leaving Austria soon. Another cousin, Malva Bodanzky, he told Schoenberg, had sold her villa in Hietzing and was going to Brazil with her four children.

Schoenberg read carefully what was written about him in America. He did not take most of the American music critics seriously. But Olin Downes, the chief critic of the *New York Times*, impressed him by the courage of his judgements and the intuitive nature of his views. He often disagreed with him and in that case did not hide his opinions. On 30 October 1938 Downes published an article in which he wrongly called Schoenberg's Variations for Orchestra variations on B–A–C–H. Schoenberg protested against this and corrected Downes; it was only a question of quotations, of a 'hommage à Bach', like Beethoven's quotation of Mozart's 'Keine Ruh bei Tag und Nacht' (from *Don Giovanni*) in the Diabelli Variations.

The musicologist Hugo Leichtentritt, an old acquaintance from Berlin and a not always favourable critic of Schoenberg's music, was professor at Harvard University in Cambridge near Boston. He asked Schoenberg what German music books interested him. The answer, of 3 December 1938, is interesting because it contains judgement of value and shows on what strict and traditional foundations Schoenberg's theory was based, and which tendencies in modern music were important for him. He gives the counterpoint book of Heinrich Bellermann, with which he taught himself, no fewer than eight exclamation marks. In the first line he mentions Heinrich Schenker's complete works. Then follow Wilhelm Werker's book on the symmetrical structure of the fugues in Bach's Well-Tempered Klavier, Alois Hába's new harmony book, Fritz Cassirer's *Beethoven und die Gestalt*, Robert Mayrhofer's *Der Kunstklang*, Walter Howard's *Auf dem Wege zur Musik* and Lotte Kallenbach-Greller's *Grundlagen der neuen Musik*. Then he mentions Paul Stefan's books on Mahler and Guido Adler's Mahler biography. And finally A. B. Marx's Composition book and Hermann Erpf's *Studien zur Harmonie*. It is striking in that an author like Erpf was not regarded as at all friendly to Schoenberg, and Schoenberg himself had had many disagreements with Paul Stefan. Heinrich Schenker, a good acquaintance from Schoenberg's youth in Vienna, fundamentally rejected his methods of writing and theoretical position. Among the other authors mentioned only two were real supporters of Schoenberg; the Czech composer Hába, who practised and theorized about quartet-, sixth- and twelfths of a tone, and Lotte Kallenbach-Greller, whose house on the Kurfürstendamm Schoenberg used to visit at one time.

'*Perhaps the names of some more of my opponents will occur to me, then I'll write again.*'

he added.

'*I think many of these books ought to be brought to the Americans' attention. It might help to convert them away from their fossilized aesthetics: for, in spite of the generally pompous and affected style in which most of these works are written, they do put forward views of a quite different sort from those one finds in English and American books on theory.*'

How many plans Schoenberg was occupied with at that time is shown by a small batch of notes which he sent to Carl Engel between 12 and 14 December. He not only talks about the practical work of copying the Brahms arrangement, but also about the book which he had begun about the Fundamentals of Musical Composition, about his wish that his Harmony Book should be translated into English, an idea with which Adolphe Weiss was also concerned, and again about his plan for a cheap edition of scores for students. Schoenberg gives a list of classical and romantic works. Of Bach he mentions the Well-Tempered Clavier and the Clavier suites, Haydn's piano sonatas, string quartets and symphonies, the same three categories of works by Mozart, Beethoven and Schubert, in addition Schubert's songs. Of Mendelssohn the Songs without Words and symphonies, of

Schumann the piano works and songs, of Brahms piano works, string quartets and symphonies.

In addition he wants to have some operatic music in piano scores with the text, Wagner's *Meistersinger* and *Tristan*, Beethoven's *Fidelio*, Mozart's *Figaro* and *Magic Flute*, Verdi's *Aida*, Auber's *Fra Diavolo* and Bizet's *Carmen*. Perhaps one or two Bruckner or Tchaikovsky symphonies as well. Historical dates and short analyses could be inserted in the scores.

In the last part of the letter of 14 December Schoenberg mentioned the contract for the Chamber Symphony and questions about recordings. Finally he expresses a wish. He would like to conduct some of his own works at one of the two great New York World Exhibitions (these exhibitions took place in 1939 and 1940). He could not believe that mediocrity would prevent him from taking part in a musical world exhibition. 'In any case: what a world!'

He was very worried about the fate of the Greissle family. Their existence in America was on the edge of legality; they had not gone the right way about getting a resident's permit. Finally a confidence trickster had even taken their money and aroused hopes in them for weeks which were not fulfilled. Schoenberg was furious and made his daughter swear not to undertake anything more without his permission.

Schoenberg had reason to be displeased with the world, the brilliant exterior which was displayed by the International Exhibition. In Europe his works were hardly played, and his music was rarely bought. In fascist countries the music of the Vienna school was officially regarded as decadent and hostile to the people, though the Italian fascists showed a certain tolerance towards it. In the communist world the situation was not very different. Stiedry had certainly performed the Orchestral Variations in 1937 in Leningrad as the first twelve-tone work to be played in the Soviet Union. Shostakovitch went to all the rehearsals of the work as a regular guest. But the official cultural-political attitude towards music of this kind soon became sterner, so that Schoenberg and his school were frowned upon for decades and – as with the fascist régimes – were branded as inimical to the people and decadent. In Germany this development went even further. On 22 May 1938 the notorious exhibition of 'Decadent Music' was opened in Düsseldorf; Schoenberg had the first place among the leaders.

In addition Schoenberg was worried about the situation of his son Georg – Görgi – and his wife and daughter. There were hardly any direct reports about them, but alarming rumours instead. It was reported that his wife and daughter were ill, that Georg himself had been in prison and was threatened with being called up into the army. There was not enough money to keep the three people alive. In fact the family were living in Mödling in the poorest conditions. Georg Schoenberg, as a non-Aryan, was not allowed to join the army, but had to work as a kind of packer and porter in a wholesale vegetable business and was miserably paid for hard physical work. It was only sacrifices made by some friends of the Schoenberg circle, especially Erwin Ratz, which helped the three people to survive the difficult war years.

The events in Germany brought Schoenberg's thoughts back more and more to the Jewish problem. In the summer of 1938 the rabbi Dr. Jakob Sonderling in Los Angeles asked him to arrange the old traditional melody 'Kol Nidre'. Schoenberg began the work on 1 August and finished it on 22 September. In a much later letter to Paul Dessau on 22 November 1941 he said how horrified he was on reading the text. The cancellation of all the obligations which had been assumed during the year was diametrically opposed to the lofty morality of all the Jewish commandments. Then he realized that the situation of the Jews in Spain, from which 'Kol Nidre' came, justified this special cancellation. For there the Jews were compelled to appear to adopt the Christian belief, and through this prayer these oaths were cancelled.

Schoenberg arranged the melody in a strictly tonal manner and made use of its motivic elements. The piece had its first performance on 4 October 1938 in Los Angeles under his direction. A few weeks later the demonstrations, dictated from above, took place against Jewish businesses in Germany. There were pogroms on 9 and 10 November, synagogues were burnt, dwellings and firms owned by Jews were destroyed and plundered. Schoenberg had already foreseen these events in 1923 and mentioned them in detail in his famous letter to Kandinsky. He now returned to his ideas about a four-point programme for Jewry, which he had worked out in France in 1933. His main idea was a collaboration of all Jews beyond all bounds of class and ideology.

Schoenberg's teaching work continued. As he normally spoke without a script when teaching, his pile of pieces of paper with headings increased, which were used by him and which his assistant, Gerald Strang, collected and evaluated for the manuscript of the composition book which he was planning. He gave a lecture, based only on headings, on the theme 'What is good music?' at a congress of American organists.

A letter of 19 December to Emanuel Feuermann mentions a plan for a Bach arrangement. Feuermann answered enthusiastically. It was a question of a sonata for gamba and cembalo, from which Schoenberg wanted to make a concerto for cello and orchestra. He began working on it on 3 January 1939; the work was broken off after five bars and was never completed.

Fritz and Erika Stiedry were well received in New York. At the suggestion of the conductor a society of 'New friends of music' was formed, which comprised a small orchestra of which he undertook the direction. On 25 March 1939 Stiedry informed Schoenberg about his plans. The orchestra consisted of 28 strings, 8 woodwind, 2 each of horns and trumpets and a pair of timpani. Six concerts under Stiedry's direction in the New York Carnegie Hall had had a great success. The programmes were classical. Now Stiedry wanted to perform a work by Schoenberg. He said that he had thought of the Chamber Symphony and the Quartet Concerto after Handel, but would prefer a first performance. Would Schoenberg be willing to write a piece of from 20–25 minutes for the New Friends? The very idealistic, but not rich director of the society, Mr. Hirshman, had no money for an extra fee. Schoenberg delayed his answer. There was a telephone conversation at the end of March, in which he suggested completing the fragment of the Second Chamber Symphony for a fee of a 1000 dollars. Schoenberg had begun to write this on a holiday in Egern-Rottach on the Tegernsee at the beginning of August 1906, but then had abandoned it. In 1911 and 1916 he took up the composition again, without finishing it. The difficulty of writing in the style of developed tonality of 1906 was so great that the fragment had remained undisturbed for decades.

Stiedry was enthusiastic about the proposal, and he advised Schoenberg not to demand such a large sum of money. Hirshman was not a wealthy man and was not supported in any way by the moneyed aristocracy. The most which he could afford as a fee would be less than half of the sum demanded by Schoenberg. However, the first performance of the planned piece would arouse attention which would only be possible there. Also the chief of the R.C.A. Victor Company, the principal American gramophone firm, Charles O'Connell, was extremely interested in a recording of the Second Chamber Symphony. Schoenberg had doubts about interrupting his current work for a commission which was so badly paid. He said that he would need at least two months to finish the Chamber Symphony. On the other hand he could orchestrate the Suite opus 29 or the Wind Quintet in a shorter time for a fee of 500 dollars. He said that Stiedry should take some notice of his.position; he worked very hard in order to live.

They arrived at a provisional agreement. On 19 May Schoenberg wrote that his university teaching would end in a week and then he would probably 'tinker with the chamber symphony – for recreation'. The next undated letter to Stiedry informs him that he had been working on the piece for a month. The first movement was finished and hardly altered, only the ending was new and the instrumentation. He was very pleased with the movement, which lasted from $7\frac{1}{2}$–8 minutes and was easy to play. Now he was working on the second movement, a very effective, lively allegro. He did not know if there would be a third one. It was too hot to look up the old sketches. For the present he was planning a heroic maestoso as a finale to the work. For the contract with Hirshman he suggested:

1. He agreed to finish the Second Chamber Symphony before 31 January 1940. It would have at least two movements.
2. The work would be scored for the ensemble mentioned by Stiedry and would last 15–20 minutes.
3. He gave Stiedry the rights of first performance and a number of repetitions given immediately afterwards in New York by the New Friends of Music.
4. Within a year Stiedry should give four further performances of it in New York.
5. After this Schoenberg would get the material back and further performances must be paid for.
6. For obtaining these rights Hirshman must pay six monthly instalments of 100 dollars, beginning in August, ending in January of next year.
7. The finished first movement was at the disposal of the Society.
8. The parts should be made at the expense of the 'New Friends of Music', but after the expiry of the contract should be Schoenberg's property. The agreement should end on 31 January 1941.

From the content of this letter it is clear that it was written before August 1939 in the hot Californian season, therefore in July. On 28 July Stiedry, who was spending the summer on Long

Island, answered that Schoenberg's suggestion had made a fantastic sensation in New York. He *must* keep to it. Although he, Stiedry, was interested in arrangements and orchestrations of Schoenberg's own works or those of Bach, he must consider the practical present. And with great self-consciousness he continues:

At last you have a conductor in New York who not only has been performing your works for decades, and understands them very well, but has the conviction and the wish to perform them . . . Your Chamber Symphony, especially after a first performance which will be useful halfway, and in New York, will be played by every symphony orchestra in the world.

But he thought it questionable to write only two movements. The performance could be postponed till March. The parts which were ready he would rehearse wet from the printers, so that Schoenberg would have almost seven months' time to finish it.

Stiedry had no typewriter; from his sketches, which were difficult to read, the young clarinettist Erich Simon, who was a friend of his, wrote out the letters to Schoenberg. He also telephoned Brentwood Park. Mrs. Schoenberg answered the call. Schoenberg was feeling ill and had not yet received a contract from Hirshman.

The two movements of the Second Chamber Symphony – the third one was never composed – were finished on 15 August and 21 October 1939. The first performance of the work, which was given the opus number 38, had to be postponed for some time. It finally took place on 14 November 1940 under Stiedry in New York.

In the summer of 1939 events in Europe led to the outbreak of the Second World War. Schoenberg followed the events with great attention. Friends and followers wrote to him. The physicist Dr. Friedrich Eichberg, Schoenberg's school friend, had already come to America in 1937. Things went well for him, as General Electric had bought a new invention from him. On 16 July 1939 he wrote to Schoenberg that he wanted to find a position for the latter's cousin. Arthur Schoenberg had become a highly respected man in Munich, but had not been spared the persecution of the Jews. An architect and an engineer, he had built the German Museum in Munich with Oscar von Miller and had received high Bavarian orders for this. Now, at the age of sixty-five, he wanted to emigrate to America. Among Schoenberg's old friends and pupils Dr. Heinrich Jalowetz and his family had come to the USA. Schoenberg recommended him to the Black Mountain College, which was very ambitious and modern artistically, where he found a position as a teacher and continued his work till his death on 2 February 1946.

In 1939 Thomas Mann, who had been a professor at Princeton University for a year, moved to Los Angeles, as the climate agreed with him better than that of the East Coast. He soon met Schoenberg, who outlined to the poet his theories about the Jewish unity party. Mann reacted respectfully but reservedly.

In Europe the position was miserable. Hitler's troops had occupied Czechoslovakia in March – a year after Austria's 'Anschluss'. Friends of Schoenberg's and his cousin Arthur, who had fled from Munich, were not able to escape and ended up in concentration camps. Poland seemed safe for the time being. Between 14 and 21 April the seventeenth Music Festival of the ISCM took place in Warsaw. Schoenberg was not represented in the six programmes; but Webern's String Quartet opus 28, written to a comisssion by Elizabeth Sprague-Coolidge and first performed in 1938 at the Berkshire Festival in Pittsfield, worthily represented his school.

At the beginning of September, after the fateful pact between Hitler and Stalin, German troops invaded Poland. Britain and France declared war on Germany. With this all immigrants from Central Europe began a new chapter in their lives.

CHANGES DUE TO WAR

The sea and air war between Germany and England interrupted almost all mail correspondence between America and the Old World. Therefore, Schoenberg's relations with old and new friends in New York and Los Angeles became closer. He corresponded in detail with Fritz Stiedry in New York about the plan of finishing the Second Chamber Symphony. However, there were financial difficulties, as he had different views about the amount of payment from Hirshman, his partner in the contract. In this connection Schoenberg mentioned the fee of 1000 dollars which Elizabeth Sprague-Coolidge had paid him for the Fourth String Quartet. Stiedry continued to try to mediate and eventually managed to see that the opposing points of view were brought together by compromises on both sides. In their correspondence they spoke about mutual friends, such as Arthur Bodanzky, who had had a great success as conductor at the Metropolitan Opera, and whose death on 23 November 1939 was a blow to Stiedry. Alexander von Zemlinsky too had travelled with his wife from Prague to New York in 1938 and was a member of Stiedry's circle. His speech and his left hand had been afflicted by paralysis. He could no longer think of conducting.

Ernst Krenek, who had a teaching job at Vassar College, New York, sent Schoenberg his book *Music here and now*, which deals with almost all problems of contemporary music in a very subjective way and also has literary merit. Schoenberg thanked him in a letter of 1 December 1939, which he did not finish till the 12th. He said that he was very interested in Krenek's views about American students, whom they were both teaching.

'*They are extremely good at getting hold of principles, but then want to apply them too much "on principle". And in art that's wrong. This is what distinguishes art from science.*'

Schoenberg's nationality was of importance when he tried to become an American citizen. Born in Vienna, he was an Austrian.

However, his father, who came from Slovakia, was a citizen of Bratislavia. According to an old Austrian law this citizenship was transferred automatically to all his descendants. As Austria was included in Hitler's German Reich in 1938, there was no longer any Austrian nationality. The authorities in Prague behaved in a helpful and friendly manner. Schoenberg had often seen the cultural attaché of the Czechoslovak Embassy in Berlin, the well-known lyric writer Dr. Camill Hoffmann. In 1933 the latter had already arranged for him to have a Czech passport, with which he emigrated to America.

On 14 November 1939 he sent a telegram to the director of Schirmers', Professor Dr. Gustav Reese, saying that he now had the 'First Papers' (the necessary papers for becoming an American citizen) and would get the further documents by December 1940.

In spite of his personal worries Schoenberg did not forget his children. Through Schirmers' he sent his son Georg (who received 150 marks a month from Universal Edition out of Schoenberg's fees) 50 dollars by telegram. At Christmas the Greissles were sent a record with one of his works and his voice talking about it. Schoenberg offered his son and the latter's family an affidavit. However, Georg could not decide about emigration. He was afraid of an increase in anti-semitism in America as well. And he did not want to use the affidavit without having a fixed job. Schoenberg could not assure him of this.

Between 28 and 30 December 1939 the sixty-first annual conference of the Music Teachers' National Association (MTNA) took place in Kansas City. Schoenberg was invited to give two lectures, one 'How can a music student earn a living?' on the opening afternoon, and the other 'Ear training through composing' on 30 December in the afternoon. He wrote both texts in Los Angeles: 'Ear training through composing' was published in 1950 in the collection *Style and Idea*. The other text has only been printed in the report of the congress, the 'MTNA Proceedings, 1939'. Schoenberg recommends students to earn their living while they are studying. He recommends that they take up work which is closely connected with music. 'There is perhaps no field of human activity on which one has to spend more time than music; even he who modestly aims for only a moderate knowledge must spend years of work. In fact eight or ten years are not much. But he who wants to become an expert, excellent or even brilliant, cannot be sure that a whole lifetime will suffice'. A student should have a good musical handwriting and be able to write without error. By this he could earn a living as a copyist and proof-reader. By being a calligrapher of music he could earn 20 dollars a month and more by two hours of daily work. Advanced students should try to arrange music, for instance for piano two or four hands. Coaching and teaching singers and instrumentalists also furthers their knowledge. A student could teach his own instrument, if he finds somebody who knows less than he himself and regards him as an authority. Finally money could also be earned by teaching theory. Then he recommends music students to write about music.

A young music student could also use his knowledge to make money by working in music and instrument shops, and do various jobs in publishing. Printing, engraving and photocopying of music also required the capacity of a musically educated person. He had noticed with pleasure that more and more musicians were working for radio and gramophone. 'The soundman of the future will be a perfect musician with a physio-mechanical education'.

The numerous lectures and discussions at this congress were interspersed with concerts. Among those taking part was the pianist Egon Petri, a pupil of Busoni and an acquaintance of Schoenberg's from his time in Berlin about 1912. In the programmes of these concerts, besides classical and romantic composers, contemporary composers such as Igor Stravinsky, Maurice Ravel and Sergey Prokofiev were also represented. No works by Schoenberg were performed.

From the spring of 1939 onwards Schoenberg continued to receive invitations to the musical evenings which were called 'Evenings on the Roof'. This rather curious name can be explained as follows: Peter Yates, who at that time was working at the California Department of Employment, and today is Professor of the State University College at Buffalo and Director of the Music Department there, had married the concert pianist Frances Mullen. In 1938 the couple bought a small bungalow with a view over Los Angeles. The Viennese architect R. M. Schindler built a storey on the roof of this with a big studio which could contain two pianos and an audience of about seventy-five. The 'Evenings on the Roof' took place there, beginning in April 1939 with a Bartók programme. The concerts mostly consisted of piano music, songs and chamber music, two-thirds old music to one-third contemporary. In the first year Busoni, Ives and Schoenberg were represented by whole programmes. Arnold and Gertrud Schoenberg went to the concert devoted to his works on

28 January 1940. The piano pieces opus 11, 19, 25 and 33a were performed, the last by Leonard Stein. Some of Schoenberg's songs were also performed. Schoenberg did not go to the later concerts, but he heard the 'Roof' programme on the radio in which Ingolf Dahl conducted *Pierrot Lunaire* (in an English translation by Beyer-Dahl) on his seventieth birthday as well as his String Trio.

At the 'Roof' concerts one could meet Igor Stravinsky, Aldous Huxley, Ernst Krenek and Otto Klemperer; among those taking part was Robert Craft, who conducted several works by Schoenberg and Webern.

Peter Yates was one of the advocates of Schoenberg and his American contemporary Charles Ives in Los Angeles. At one of the first receptions which were given for Schoenberg after his arrival in New York in 1933 Ives was among the guests invited. The two men do not seem to have met again. Schoenberg did not hear music by Ives at the 'Roof' concerts, but probably did so in radio transmissions of these concerts.

In 1940 Schoenberg's work as a composer had to give way to teaching and practical work. However, he wrote some important articles and sketches. An article 'Art and the Moving Pictures' appeared in the April number of 'California Arts and Architecture'. Schoenberg writes that he had dreamed of a dramatization of Balzac's *Seraphita*, of Strindberg's *To Damascus*, of the second part of Goethe's *Faust* and even of Wagner's *Parsifal*. (He naturally means a film version). What one could find and must find would be a production of plays and operas to satisfy the demands of the more highly educated, plus the demands of art. He did not assume that the industry which at present produced moving pictures could, or would care to start such a move towards pure art. This could only be done by new men. Further he did not assume that the theatres which were owned by the industry should be used for such works of art. Art did not need so much pomp. Its own splendour created a scene of dignity, which could not be surpassed by materialistic profusion. There were, of course, many problems involved, which did not need to be discussed at present. There would be time enough to do this, especially as the industry might shortly be forced to consider some problems of its own, imposed on it by the advent of television. Perhaps people might then come to realize that art is less expensive than amusement, and more profitable. At this point Schoenberg again shows himself to be a prophet. In 1940 no one would have believed it pòssible to foresee what happened in the Fifties and Sixties to the once so powerful Californian film industry: its severe throttling, through the arrival of television.

Stiedry used his good relations with the gramophone industry to arrange a recording of *Pierrot Lunaire*. He did not want to undertake the conductorship. He said that Schoenberg himself should conduct. The record was made in the autumn of 1940. The correspondence about this between Schoenberg and Stiedry had begun as early as March. There was a small difficulty about a planned New York performance of *Pierrot*, which Schoenberg wrote about on 2 April. He had had a bitter quarrel with Klemperer in the spring of 1939, because the latter neglected Schoenberg's music. Klemperer replied that Schoenberg's music had become alien to him. This led to the breaking point. However, Schoenberg was soon reconciled with the conductor, because the latter became critically ill. And now, Schoenberg writes in his letter to Stiedry, Klemperer had just told him that he was going to conduct *Pierrot Lunaire* in New York. Could Stiedry stop this? For he wanted to perform *Pierrot* himself with Erika Wagner-Stiedry, Kolisch, Steuermann, Benar Heifetz and Polatschek, not only in New York but also in Boston and Philadelphia. This was a difficult task for Stiedry, and he felt he could not undertake it because of Klemperer's severe illness. The negotiations continued for months backwards and forwards, until finally the recording project was arranged. Schoenberg returned to this subject in a letter to Stiedry of 31 August and asked for a definite decision, as his university lectures were to begin in the middle of September. He said that it would certainly take more than a week to rehearse the ensemble:

'*We must freshen up the speaking part fundamentally – at least I am going to try this time to see if I can bring out perfectly the light, ironic and satirical tone in which the piece was really conceived. In addition times and our perceptions have changed very much, so that what we perhaps regarded as Wagnerian or at the worst as Tchaikovskian, today suggests Puccini, Lehár or worse composers. It is difficult to arrange to immortalize the authentic performance on records in two weeks.*'

The recording was made in September-October in Los Angeles. Schoenberg wrote a note for the record sleeve. In this he mentioned the most important interpreters of the work since 1912, and especially Rudolf Kolisch: 'I have to discount that he is my brother-in-law; what counts more is, that he was my pupil, what counts still more, is that he now – with Erika Stiedry and Eduard

Steuermann, plays the violin and viola part since 1921; and what counts most, that he has participated in every of the perhaps hundred rehearsals from the very beginning to the very end – though, after the first five rehearsals, he did not need more of them for himself. He knows the music better than I myself know it, and, thus, I was happy that he was the one who prepared the new ensemble for the recording.'

Nuria, who was eight at the time, remembers the weeks of the *Pierrot* rehearsals in Schoenberg's house as a happy, wonderful time.

In the summer of 1940 Schoenberg concerned himself with the personality of Anton Webern again. In a series of 'memorials' which he devoted to some of his contemporaries, he collected together all the notes which he had made about Webern for years. Here it was chiefly a question of priorities. Schoenberg remembers: '1906. Webern returned from vacation, sees chamber symphony (written Rottach-Egern), says he had thought about how modern music should look. He sees chamber symphony fulfils that idea. Chamber symphony still influenced by Strauss's *Salome*. – 1907 new style. Told Webern about short pieces. One of the piano pieces should consist of only three to four measures. – Webern starts writing shorter and shorter pieces – follows all my developments. Always tries to surpass everything (exaggerates). 1914 (5) I start a symphony, wrote about it to Webern – mention: singing *without words* (*Jacob's Ladder*) – mention: Scherzo theme including all twelve tones.

After 1915: Webern seems to have used twelve tones in some of his compositions – *without telling me*.

'From 1910–1921. I was always thinking of replacing the structural effects of the harmony.

'Several attempts: (a) using the "tones" of the beginning of a theme for new themes, (b) *Jacob's Ladder*: main themes build from a row of six tones, etc.

'1921 found out that the greater distance between a tone and its repetition can be produced if twelve tones lay between. Started twelve-tone composition. Told Erwin Stein. I had now a way I wanted to keep all my imitators at a distance because I am annoyed by them: I even do not know any more what is mine and what is theirs. – Webern jealous about Berg, had suggested me to tell Berg he (in about 1908 or 9) should not write in the new style – he has no right to do it – it does not fit to his style – but it fitted to Webern's!!!

'Webern committed at this period (1908–1918) many acts of infidelity with the intention of making himself the innovator.

'In about 1920 I had written one of the Five Piano Pieces opus 23 and some of the Serenade opus 24. Here is to be found what at this time I called "working with the tones of the main theme". One important step toward the permanent use of one row of twelve tones.

'About 1919 or 1920 Berg brought me a composition of Klein.[1] I think it was called "Musical Machine" and dealt with twelve tones. I did not pay much attention to it. It did not impress me as music and probably I was still unconscious of where to my own attempts might lead me. So forgot entirely having seen something in twelve tones.

'Now there is one important difference between me, Klein and Hauer. I came to my method for compositional and structural reasons. I was not looking out for a new mannerism, but for a better structural foundation, replacing the structural effect of harmony.

' "Harmony is not to be discussed" I had said between 1908 and 1918. But I was unconscious that the harmonies I wrote at this time were not used haphazardly but were of necessity. Later I discovered that they had a melodic function – vertical melody.

'It must have been about 1920 that I saw first something of Hauer and heard him speak of atonal music. (In 1924 I asked him why he called it "atonal" – to which I was opposed. He answered he had the term from my *Harmonielehre* – which I could not find – I still do not know where I used it.

'But in his first book he had really taken something out of my *Harmonielehre* – about the danger of one note becoming the key-note. – (This sentence was eliminated in the second edition of Hauer's book! Without any excuse!)

'In 1924 I had become aware that Hauer had also written twelve-tone music. Up to this time I had kept it a secret that I do it. But in order to make clear that I had not been influenced by Hauer, but had gone my own way, I called a meeting of all my

[1]   Fritz Heinrich Klein, born in Budapest in 1892, pupil of Albanberg, a music teacher in Linz since 1932. Borrowing the name of Terence's comedy 'Heautontimoroumenos' (The self-torturer) he published a volume in 1921 called 'The Machine, an extonal self-satire'. This contains 12 tone themes and chords, including a 'mother chord' of twelve different notes and eleven different interva alss well as a rhythmical series.

students and friends where I explained this new method and the way which I had gone.

'Curiously when I had shown the four basic forms, Webern confessed that he had written also something in twelve tones (probably suggested by the Scherzo of my symphony of 1915), and he said: "I never knew what to do after the twelve tones" meaning that the three inversions now could follow and the transpositions.

'One thing had become clear to all of them: that the permanent use of only *one* twelve-tone set in one work was something quite different from everything else others might have attempted.

'My way meant: UNITY. My way derived from compositorial necessities. – N.B. Hauer afterwards accepted this method of using only one set – while formerly he used a different set in every measure, which – if it was really admissible – would not correspond to my desire of repeating a tone as late as possible.'

To this collection in English of notes about priority in matters of twelve-tone music Schoenberg added a postscript in German on 10 August 1940: 'One may be surprised to find so many lines directed against Webern. It looks awful and throws a bad light on me, especially if one compares Webern's letters to me with these. I must unfortunately say, while Webern – in spite of Hitler – shows an admirable attitude towards myself, that his position then was very wavering. However, he has wavered back to me and this shows that he was always stirred up against me by a third party, though this could not destroy his love for me. It would fill me with deep sorrow if I had to think otherwise.'

Calls for help came from many parts of Europe. Walter Goehr, who had been living in France since 1933, was endangered by the German military occupation of the country and wrote to Schoenberg asking him to intervene for him and send him an affidavit. Schoenberg was powerless and could only write to Goehr's wife in Paris on 12 July, when he was already interned in the Eastern Pyrennees, saying that he would do what he could and that she must put her trust in God. He intervened without success with the State Department in Washington for Karl Rankl. When Paul Dessau asked him to intervene for the liberation of René Leibowitz, who was also interned in France, Schoenberg answered that Dessau could use his name but that he was too busy to find out what musical importance there was in René Leibowitz's work. 'The main thing is that it should be of some use, and I feel no sense of responsibility whatsoever towards the enemy, who in any case are destroying our values without examining them.'

The Stiedrys spent a long holiday in Colorado Springs, where they rented a house from the beginning of August till 20 September. The beautiful mountain resort is about twice as far from New York as from the Pacific Coast. They had chosen it thinking of the possible *Pierrot* recording in Los Angeles. On returning to New York Stiedry said that he would give the first performance of the Second Chamber Symphony on 15 December; in the programme he would play the first Brandenburg Concerto of Bach before it and the fourth after it. He tried once again, using all means of persuasion, to get the master to write a further movement. A discussion about this in Brentwood Park was fruitless. Stiedry declared 'in all friendship and admiration', that Schoenberg was wrong and would not help himself by the publication of a fragment in two movements. He entreated him to think quietly whether he could write a middle movement of five minutes' length. A musician of his calibre could do this in a few weeks. It would still be possible to rehearse the movement at the beginning of December in time.

Even the 'enthusiastic admiration for these two masterly movements', as Stiedry protested, could not make Schoenberg change his mind. He remained with the work as it was. And even with the best of will he had no leisure for composition. He had begun his teaching at the UCLA. On 13 November he travelled to New York, where he conducted *Pierrot Lunaire* in the Town Hall four days later and gave a lecture. Many friends were there or sent greetings, including Hanns and Lou Eisler who wished him luck by telegram. The success was remarkable. Even the New York press recognized him. Since October 1940 Virgil Thomson had been one of the leading critics. He wrote for the *Herald Tribune*, and in spite of his often one-sidedly Francophile position he was an admirer of Schoenberg's.

As Carl Engel's house guest Schoenberg, who was alone, was very much pampered. On 22 November Schirmer's gave a reception for him. But all the friendship and admiration could not reconcile him to the New York climate. He returned to Los Angeles, Gertrud was pregnant and her confinement was expected in a few weeks.

So Schoenberg did not attend the two premières which took place after one another in December 1940. On the 6th Krasner played the new Violin Concerto in Philadelphia with Stokowski and his famous orchestra for the first time. The conservative public of the city, with its old cultural tradition, received the new work with mixed reactions. The local press mostly rejected it crudely. 'Time Magazine' printed an arrogant, apparently objective article about the 'bald-headed, parchment-faced Austrian', who had plunged the world of music into a war to the knife.

Following classical usage, the work is in three movements. It lasts thirty-five minutes. It begins with a poco allegro movement of 265 bars in 4/4 times with a vivace middle section in 3/4. Between bars 233 and 234 a long virtuoso solo cadenza is interpolated (adagio), which continues with accompaniment by the orchestra up till bar 249. Then follow quickly one after another: stretto, poco allargando, a presto reprise of the beginning and a slow ending.

This, the longest of the three movements, is followed by a 208-bar Andante grazioso in 2/4 time. The finale is a 4/4 Allegro of 261 bars. Shortly before the end, after a short 'quasi Cadenza' there is a Cadenza of seventy bars accompanied by the orchestra. The character of this finale is that of a march, and the energetic main theme, which circles round the note D, comes 'alla marcia' in a somewhat calmer tempo after the 'quasi Cadenza' interpolation. Like all the thematic material in the piece it is derived from a twelve-tone row, of which the first three notes A–B flat– E flat (a–b–es in German) form Schoenberg's initials, and the characteristic intervals of it are formed by the three tritones F sharp–C=D flat–G=A flat–D. The themes, which are always exposed by the solo instrument, complement the series played by the orchestra, which is often an accompaniment; so these are selected out of the series.

Sonata form is only hinted at in the first and third movements. Schoenberg has not used the principle of developing variation with such superior mastery since his opus 31 as he does here. This also causes the frequent changes of character in all three movements.

In spite of polyphonic and serial crossings with the orchestral parts the solo violin is predominant throughout. Its part is a synthesis of all possible combinations of colour, double-, triple-, quadruple stops and harmonics. Schoenberg spoke jokingly of a sixth finger which was needed for the piece. But he worked out all the fingerings in practice before he wrote them down.

The musical language of the work shows signs of more tranquillity and – as René Leibowitz remarks – archaisms. It ends with a

Eduard Steuermann, New York 1940

polytonal sequence of chords over the fifth in the bass C–G, three times repeated, crossing with D major and the fifths E flat–B flat, D flat–A flat and E–B, which leaves out only the final note of the row, F, which was obstinately repeated previously.

Nine days after the première in Philadelphia the first performance of the Second Chamber Symphony took place in the New York Carnegie Hall under Stiedry. Greissle wrote a clever commentary for the programme. Next morning Stiedry, at 3 East 63. Street, received a letter-telegram from Los Angeles:

Our living room full of friends and pupils admire you and your orchestra in the excellent performance of my chamber symphony many congratulations and thanks to all of you please write soon more details best greetings the Schoenbergs and family.

The details which Schoenberg requested arrived quickly. Stiedry wrote him a long letter on 17 December. He said he had had six rehearsals apart from the final rehearsal, which had gone extremely well. Among those who attended the rehearsals were Greissle, Steuermann and Wiesengrund-Adorno. There had been some mishaps at the performance; he himself was not entirely happy about his tempi. The majority of the listeners found that the piece was complete; he and some friends believed, as they had done before, that it needed a slow middle movement.

1940 was ending. Schoenberg saw the coming year without illusions. Seven years in America had made him sceptical about mountains of gold. Hitler's European war aroused his political consciousness against dictatorship and terror. His relations and friends were in danger if they had not found safety by going abroad. Max Deutsch was interned in France; one of the many help organizations, the New York Emergency Rescue Committee asked him to intervene. Another one, the Jewish Club of 1933, asked him to become a member. His first name was missing on the address of the letter and in the letter itself. Schoenberg wrote on the piece of paper: 'Jews have not yet acknowledged that my first name is Arnold. But they certainly know the first names: Paul, Béla, Igor and Jan. Probably my activity is not a credit to Jewry'. (He always regarded himself as neglected in America compared with Paul Hindemith, Béla Bartók, Igor Stravinsky and Jan Sibelius.)

On 27 January 1941 – Schoenberg was sixty-six – Gertrud Schoenberg brought a son into the world. She wrote about this in detail to her friend: 'Two months before the birth I lost five pounds through excitement and an inflamation of the intestines which resulted from it. In the last month I had been waiting almost every day for the happy event, which did not help my nerves. I worked out the way to the hospital by stopwatch and calculated exactly how long and in favourable conditions how short a time it would take to get me to the hospital. I asked the doctor not to get mad at me and really to come (again on the 27th as far as I had worked out) when I rang him up. On the 26 January, the day which I had regarded as the last chance for a good birth, I rang up a friend in order to find the address of a baby's nurse from her. I said to her that my only worry was that I would have the baby again without a doctor, and as I had no chauffeur in the house I did not know how I could get to the hospital. I was worried about calling a passing taxi and more by the ambulance which Arnold suggested to me. As you will see I was right. My friend Mrs. Thorsten calmed me down and reminded me that she had done a midwife's course in Switzerland and could be with me in seven minutes.'

Then there follows the cheerful description of the birth, which had to be improvised at home owing to lack of transport, after a doctor had arrived at the last moment: 'At 10 o'clock exactly on my watch (Arnold's was two minutes faster) the little fellow of 7 pounds 2 ounces was there. In the first two weeks he put on 1 pound 2 ounces, although he would not take mother's milk at first. He has legs already (see picture) and can crawl. So he is a wonder-child.' The wonder-child was called Lawrence Adam.

Among those who asked Schoenberg for help for friends was Thomas Mann's second daughter Monika in Princeton. She herself had had a bitter experience. Her husband, the art historian Jenö Lányi, had been drowned in 1940 in front of her eyes with other passengers of the *City of Benares* which had been torpedoed by a German submarine. She did not know Schoenberg, but was a friend of the pianist Peter Stadlen from the Viennese Schoenberg circle. Stadlen was interned in Australia, and Monika Mann-Lányi asked the Master for a letter of recommendation for his release. The composer Marc Brunswick, a former pupil of Webern, was right when he wrote on 16 January 1941 that Schoenberg had done something for refugees all the time. Relations also wrote from Vienna. Felix Nachod, a cousin, asked for affidavits for himself and his brother Walter, which they both obtained.

In March 1941 there was a serious quarrel with Schirmer's which lasted for months. Schoenberg had sent one of his 'nasty letters' to Engel. It was a question of differences of interpretation about the payment contract which the Master had made in October 1940. Now he sent hard words and suspicions. Engel, who answered quietly and carefully on 15 March, had to defend himself against the suspicion of having harmed Schoenberg. As regards the rude words which the Master had not spared him, he would ignore them and answer them with friendship 'in the manner of the New Testament.' (Engel was also of Jewish origin and so could allow himself this little remark.) Financially Schirmers' could not go any further. 'Kol Nidre' and the Folk Song arrangements were sent back to the composer.

The correspondence with the New York firm was not resumed till October; Schoenberg was only informed by Greissle, and about his success in the firm.

Dental treatment worried Schoenberg from the spring of 1941 onwards for the whole summer. He had to have two plates made, for which several teeth had to be extracted. On 27 October he wrote to Greissle about his worries, which also concerned his son Georg. His letter was full of bitterness about Schirmer's and speaks of attempts at extortion and breach of contract. On the same day Schoenberg missed the manuscript of the Volkslieder and asked Schirmer about it; they told him that it had been sent back to him together with 'Kol Nidre'. Schoenberg had put the packet on one side, angry about the refusal of the work, without even opening it. Now he apologized to Gustav Reese on 18 November. But the differences of opinion, this time about a contract for an older work, the First Chamber Symphony, did not cease, even if the tone was calmer.

There was also more cheerful correspondence. On 23 March 1941 Erwin Stein wrote to him from London; the publisher Leslie Boosey of the firm Boosey and Hawkes had removed him from internment. Now he was writing an English translation of the text of *Pierrot*. Max Deutsch's younger brother Friedrich, who called himself Frederick Dorian in America, had conducted the chorus 'Friede auf Erden' in Pittsburgh, with great success; he taught at the Carnegie Institute of Technology there.

The correspondence took on dimensions which Schoenberg could hardly cope with. He wrote to Stein that there was already an English translation of *Pierrot*. It had been made by a young American composer, Dika Newlin, who had been a pupil of Schoenberg's since 1938 and who enjoyed his special confidence.

In August, during the university vacation, Schoenberg began

writing a piece for organ commissioned by the New York publisher H. W. Gray and Co. He called it 'Variations on a Recitative'. The work, opus 40, was finished on 12 October. It is a
tonal piece, begins in D minor and ends with a D major chord.
The ten Variations, which are very rich harmonically and
contrapuntally, and are followed by a four-part piano fugue, are
in the tradition of Max Reger. The publishers printed them with
a plan of registration which was meant for the organ of Princeton
University. Schoenberg was not happy with this, although he had
corresponded with the arranger, Carl Weinrich. He wrote in a letter:

> '*I always write a pitch which I want to hear . . . I do not like
> unnecessary octave doublings. It is clear to me that the organ can sound
> louder to a certain extent if one adds octaves above or below. I know that
> one must allow an organist to do this if there is no better way of bringing
> out the parts according to their structural importance. I would like to
> see such doublings avoided, if clarity and transparency can be reached
> without additional octaves.*'

Schoenberg spoke about the piece many times in later years, for
instance in a letter of 4 July 1947 to Leibowitz. He describes it
there as an equivalent of Bach's French and English Suites, of
Wagner's *Meistersinger* Quintet and *Tristan* duet, Beethoven and
Mozart's Fugues and Reger's 'Pieces in the ancient style'.

He wrote to Dr. Werner David in Berlin-Zehlendorf on 10 May
1949, that he had made his position regarding the organ clear
more than forty years earlier in an unfinished and unpublished
article: 'There I have demanded among other things that such a
gigantic instrument should be able to be played by at least two to
four players at once. Perhaps a second, third or fourth console
could be attached to it.'

Then he describes his idea of a future organ, which should not
be bigger than one and a half portable typewriters. He imagined
that lovers of music would play duets, trios and quartets on such
instruments in the evening, and reproduce the content of symphonies.

The Organ Variations were performed for the first time on 10
April 1944 at a concert given by the ISCM in the New York
Church of the Blessed Virgin Mary.

A Sonata for Organ, which Schoenberg began on 7 August
1941, remains a fragment of fifty-three bars. And a composition
for two pianos, which was begun on 21 January, was put aside
after seventeen bars. – On 11 April 1941 the Schoenbergs were
finally invited to go the the Federal Building in Santa Monica to
take the oath of American citizenship.

A handwritten time-table gives an indication of the examinations held at the UCLA towards the end of the winter term 1940/41:

Structural Functions	Wednesday June 4	3
Composition I	Thursday May 29	12
Counterpoint II	Tuesday June 3	1
Composition II		
Concert	Friday June 6	12–4

Meanwhile people asking for help from Europe were joined by others from America, who believed themselves for one reason or another to have solidarity with Schoenberg as a member of a minority. The Negro boxer heavyweight world champion, Joe Louis, was planning to retire from the ring. But before this he wanted to put on a fight in the New York Yankee Stadium which would be dedicated to the oppressed in the country. He asked Schoenberg on 27 September to buy a seat or a box: 'The hardest fight which I have ever had was against prejudice and intolerance. My people know what I mean.'

On 7 December 1941 the United States were brought into the war by the unexpected attack by the Japanese on the American fleet in Pearl Harbour. Schoenberg followed the events of the war with tension and with convinced partisanship for the country to which he now belonged. The atmosphere in his house was described by Salka Viertel, the actress, Eduard Steuermann's sister and the wife of the poet and producer Berthold Viertel, in her memoirs *Das unbelehrbare Herz*. Los Angeles, like all Californian cities, was full of Japanese. Now they were all interned, including the gardener Yoshida, whose wife Mio did the cleaning and washing at the Schoenbergs and at Max Reinhardt's. Salka Viertel was sitting one evening in the Schoenberg's house when the two boys, Ronny and Larry, and the rather older Nuria appeared with a white rabbit. It was a gift from Mio. Schoenberg hesitated to take a Japanese rabbit into the house. After a long palaver with the children Nuria explained that the animal had been born in America, and so was not Japanese and it should stay in the house. It was called Emperor Franz Josef.

In March 1942 there was further news from Erwin Stein in London. He was getting on with the preparations for the planned *Pierrot* performances, but was now using another translation which had been made in England.

On 9 April a telegram came from New York. The Director of the Ballet Theatre, German Sevastianov, had given the first performance of a choreographed version of *Verklärte Nacht* on the previous day under the title *Pillar of Fire*. It had been received with ovations in the Metropolitan Opera such as had never before been experienced, and the uniformly enthusiastic reports in the press confirmed its success. Schoenberg was congratulated and invited to conduct the ballet himself when it was performed in Los Angeles and in San Francisco in January 1943.

Meanwhile he was working on a piece which for the first time shows him as politically engaged. It is the 'Ode to Napoleon Buonaparte' on a text by Lord Byron for string quartet, piano and speaker, opus 41. It was begun on 12 March and finished on 12 June 1942. The music, which was filled with emotional and dramatic spirit, is strictly constructed from a twelve-tone row which, however, allows of triads, so that the work ends with a kind of cadence in E flat major. Schoenberg had recognized similarities in the figures of Napoleon and Hitler, and in this melodrama gave expressions to tensions and feelings which were aroused within him by world events. In a letter to me of 15 January 1948 he wrote:

> '*Lord Byron, who had previously admired Napoleon very much, was so disappointed by his resignation that he overwhelmed him with the sharpest scorn; and I believe not to have missed this element in my composition.*'

He wrote in the same letter:

> '*I believe that the speaker for the Ode must be a very musical singer. The declamation is not so difficult as in* Pierrot. *But if possible the speaker should remain strictly in tempo where there is no "colla parte". Much in the music, which continuously depicts, underlines and illustrates, would remain unintelligible, even senseless, if word and note do not appear together at the right moment. I joke about the clown, who first falls to the ground, and then lifts up his arm with a pistol and then one hears the shot.*'

The League of Composers had asked him to compose the Ode. Schoenberg offered the piece to Schirmer in May 1942 in New York, and they later published it.

In May they had domestic worries with the severe illness of the older boy Ronny, who was five. The necessary operation was a burden on the family budget. But he was better by the beginning of June, and Schoenberg could now concern himself with matters of publication. He also exchanged letters again with Stiedry. The latter had been enthusiastic about a private performance of the Violin Concerto by Louis Krasner. He pressed Schoenberg to finish *Moses and Aaron* and the *Jacob's Ladder*. For this reason, in order to strike while the iron was hot, he wanted to spend the summer in Los Angeles.

Schoenberg had a lot of work on the summer courses of the UCLA. It bore important fruit in the small book *Models for Beginners in Composition*, a collection of examples of problems of melody, harmony and form, which was published in the same year by Schirmer. On 25 August he found time for a long letter to Stiedry. In this he spoke about the illness of the children and about Ronny's operation. The letter – differently from his previous ones – was written in English.

'*The children are now all well. Nuria is on holiday and helps her mother a good deal in the house, kitchen, garden and with young Larry. Ronny is a very sweet child; he is musical like Nuria and Larry, but won't practise his violin. My wife has no help, or only occasionally and has to do everything by herself – my help in washing up is not very great. In July I finished the "Ode to Napoleon Buonaparte" by Lord Byron for speaker and piano quintet. Now I have to write a piano concert, which Oscar Levant[1] has commissioned from me. But at the moment I am so tired and my eyes hurt so much (from writing on small music paper) that I have to interrupt my work. Though I have time to write to you. Otherwise I would be composing or was too tired for letters. In addition I have been commissioned to write a string quartet through Mr. Shriver, a former pupil of mine. I wanted to finish* Jacob's Ladder *and* Moses and Aaron *but now that must be postponed. And you will understand how happy I am to have got such help from these commissions. So that at least I can be calm and peaceful for the immediate future. My vacation lasts till 8 or 10 October. But I must at least finish the piano concerto before the school begins again. I hope I will find time to write the string quartet and other works which I have promised: Orchestration.*'

He did not write the quartet. On the other hand he dedicated the piano concerto, which he wrote between 5 July and 29 December, to Henry Shriver instead of Oscar Levant.

On 12 September 1942 he sent a letter to Carl Engel. He said that yesterday, two days before his sixty-eighth birthday, he had finished the *Models for Beginners in Composition* and had sent it by air immediately after receiving the contract. He was happy to be on good relations with Schirmer again; they had sent him 500 dollars in June. He said that his eyes were bad and that he had not

---

[1]   Levant, born in 1906, was a pupil of Schoenberg and Schillinger. In 1940 he published his very witty book of memoirs *A Smattering of Ignorance*.

been able to work for a week. The doctor said it was only tiredness.

On 2 October Schoenberg thanked Erwin Stein for the latter's
birthday letter and asked him, as his oldest pupil and friend, to
address him in the second person. On 13 September they had had
a party and he had been given nothing but alcohol; 'And right
now I do not drink – but if I give up smoking again drinking will
give me some pleasure'. Schoenberg failed many times in his
attempts to give up smoking.

Stein answered on 30 November that they had had two sold
out *Pierrot* performances in London and were planning others now
in Oxford and Cambridge. The record of it conducted by Schoenberg himself had arrived in London. There had been a long
discussion about it with Walter Legge (the gramophone magnate),
Cecil Gray (the writer on music) and Stein, in which Stein
defended Erika Wagner. The British speaker Hedli Anderson had
achieved almost perfect intonation, to Karl Rankl's delight. Stein
wanted to know if the voice-pitches in the work were to be
sustained.

At the end of the year Schoenberg finished his piano concerto.
He seems to have thought of a personal programme, which he
wrote down on a piece of paper:

> Life was so easy
> suddenly hatred broke out (Presto .l=72)
> a grave situation was created (Adagio)
> But life goes on (Rondo).

Schoenberg also addressed Carl Engel in the second person
from the autumn onwards. An unusually long letter from him was
dated 27 November 1942 and then again 9 and 10 December. It
speaks of the fifteen pupils in his composition class, and Schoenberg was sorry that Engel's planned visit to California did not take
place. He advised him not to let himself be got down by bad
health.

'*When I have my asthmatic condition every six or nine months, because
I am still smoking and drinking, I feel near to death, just as you do. But
if I abstain for only two weeks I have the prospect of living till at least
eighty.*'

He said that his eyes were better, since he no longer wore his
three last, very expensive pairs of spectacles, except for deciphering small writing. However, he could not yet write music without
them. In spite of this he had started a counterpoint book on 25

November, and this was occupying him from three to four days a week. Should he accept the invitation of the Society for Esthetics to give a lecture on 'Beauty and logic in music'? Engel said that if anyone was to speak about it it should be Schoenberg, and he advised him to do it. But the lecture did not take place.

The Piano Concerto was completed in the last days of December 1942. Schoenberg had offered it to Schirmers' as well as the 'Ode to Napoleon', and Engel was interested. He said that one should try to find an occasion for a performance of the Ode, if the League of Composers could not guarantee this.

Since the fall of France in 1940 Los Angeles was increasingly overrun by German, Austrian and French refugees. On 1 January 1941 Franz and Alma Werfel had come from New York on their first visit to California to sound out the possibilities of living there, and a year later they finally took up residence in California. On 21 July 1941 Bertolt Brecht arrived, after a sea voyage from Vladivostok, lasting many weeks in San Pedro, the harbour of Los Angeles. He settled a few miles from Brentwood Park in Santa Monica on the Pacific coast. He was followed there on 20 April 1942 by Hanns Eisler. A few days later Brecht and Eisler met again at Dr. Wiesengrund-Adorno's house and had a long discussion about Schoenberg. Brecht did not know the composer at that time. Eisler took Brecht with him when he visited Brentwood Park. On the way he warned Brecht not to interrupt anything that Schoenberg said. He even threatened to break off his friendship with Brecht if the latter did not respect the Master unconditionally.

They arrived at the house shortly after Ronny's operation. Eisler realized that Schoenberg had money worries. He offered him 300 dollars as a contribution towards the costs of the operation. When Schoenberg hesitated to take the gift, he suggested that he should give him a few lessons for it. To which Schoenberg said: 'If you haven't learnt it yet, I can't teach you any more.'

Brecht was very impressed by the 'birdlike' man. On 29 July he went with Eisler to one of his lectures at the UCLA, which was also attended by Thomas Mann and was on the subject of modern composition. Without understanding the theoretical ideas, he found the formulations clear and convincing.

On 13 September 1942 Schoenberg's sixty-eighth birthday was celebrated with a large number of friends, as we know from the letter to Erwin Stein. Brecht was one of those invited. 'Unfortunately a swollen cheek prevents me from accepting your very friendly invitation', Brecht answered 'So I must send you my warm good wishes in writing.' And he enclosed a copy of one of his Svendborg poems which had been written in Denmark between 1933 and 1939. 'In unserem Lande zur Jahreswende . . . ', to which he added: 'To Arnold Schoenberg in admiration.'

The Werfels were frequent guests. At the beginning of September 1942 they had bought a little house in Berverly Hills. Among the Schoenberg circle, apart from his pupils such as Leonard Stein, Gerald Strang and Dika Newlin there were not many musicians. Arthur Rubinstein, the great Polish pianist, invited the Schoenbergs to a meal, at which Thomas Mann and his family were also present. Monika Lányi-Mann sat next to Schoenberg, without knowing who he was. She only realized this in the course of the conversation. 'However', she wrote later (in a letter of 30 July 1972 to me), 'it was a "nice" experience. Schoenberg kept shovelling marvellous things on to my plate and looked like a tennis coach (in white), who was also a sly fellow.'

Later she was invited with her parents to Brentwood Park. 'He made coffee with his own hands with whipped cream in tall glasses and showed me the secret, that the whipped cream must be at the bottom of the glass and the hot coffee poured on top ot it'. Thomas Mann and Salka Steuermann also spoke admiringly of Schoenberg's coffee. This belonged to his Viennese way of life.

Schoenberg's reconciliation with Schirmer's took a long time. On 17 May 1942 he decided to write to Carl Engel again. He offered him the 'Ode to Napoleon Buonaparte' on which he was working, and which he hoped to finish on 1 August. Besides that he had made a two-piano arrangement of the Second Chamber Symphony. He was ready to negotiate about his works which were still unpublished, if he received a sufficient fee or an advance on royalties. The answer came by telegram on 26 May: the publishers were not in a position at the moment to negotiate with him under conditions which would interest him. But he was free to negotiate with other publishers. This was a blow to Schoenberg.

However, the ice was finally broken when Engel assured Schoenberg on 29 May of his collaboration and readiness to help with the problems which had arisen through Ronny's illness. Schoenberg's warm answer came by return of post. He had always felt that Engel was not really responsible for his commercial relationship with Schirmer's. The publishers had denied him publicity; that was why his works had had such little success. He said that it was the first time in his career as a composer that publishers had not brought out his works within a few years. *Verklärte Nacht*, 'Gurrelieder' and *Pierrot*, thirty to forty years old, were being played with growing success. Columbia had sold 960 copies of the *Pierrot* records in six months. The letter ended with a protestation of friendship.

They arrived at a new form of contract which gave the publishers a share of performance royalties. When Schoenberg told Engel apout his worries the latter sent him 500 dollars by telegram. On the day before his birthday Schoenberg told him about the completion of *Models for Beginners in Composition*. The printing of it was started at once. Both friends had trouble with their health, Schoenberg especially with his eyes. He was smoking again.

Carl Engel had often told Schoenberg about the great number of good wind orchestras in the USA. These had a strong influence on American musical culture, but there were very few original works for them, so that they had to content themselves with arrangements of well-known works which were often mediocre ones. Engel said that Schoenberg should write a piece for wind orchestra. At the beginning of 1943 he took up this idea.

The year began with work and illnesses of all kinds. In a letter to Trudi Greissle of 2 March Schoenberg complains that he could only write a few words because he had to work very hard without even one day's interruption. As well as his university classes and the work at his writing desk he also had to help in the house: he had to make breakfast and a packed lunch for Nuria and Ronny, wash dishes, prepare lunch, – and once even supper as well. He got up daily between 6.30 and 7. Gertrud had hardly half an hour in which to rest.

Schoenberg sent Carl Engel a parcel containing two new works: the Ode and the Piano Concerto. He wrote to his friend on 11 March that at the beginning he had had many difficulties with the nineteen verses of Byron's poem. It was all hatred, contempt, satire, scorn, and one must not make it monotonous! He had found many possibilities of contrasts and variations and it was a well constructed piece. He had come across the poem in almost miraculous circumstances, – it had chosen him, not the other way round.

He said that he had seen Mr. Schirmer at a meeting of the Californian ASCAP at a distance, but the latter had not recognized him. Apart from this he was trying to write as much as possible of the counterpoint book and the Variations for Wind Orchestra, but could not make much progress during the semester. On 15 March Engel confirmed that he would go through the new pieces as soon as possible with Greissle and Carl Deis (a music editor at Schirmer's).

Engel told Schoenberg confidentially about a conversation with a member of the committee for financial help to composers. Shortly after this Steuermann played the new piano concerto at Schirmer's; Engel was full of admiration and said that Steuermann should play the Concerto as well as the 'Ode' to Stokowski. Schoenberg at once agreed with this. He had also always thought of Steuermann for the première. If Steuermann could not play it, he would like to have Schnabel. He said that Engel should 'read the riot act' to Schnabel because he never played modern works. He said in the letter of 6 April 1943:

'His standpoint to me seems not only foolish but almost criminal. I believe it is the first duty of a real artist to play contemporary music. If all interpreters had behaved as he had done the works of the greatest masters would never have reached the ears of the public.'

On 17 April Schoenberg began work on his *Master Copy Book* with a preface and seventy-seven typewritten pages of the text of the Counterpoint treatise in its fourth version. As well as this Schoenberg, who loved tinkering with things, made two models for a 'Rastrál', a device for drawing the five lines of a music stave simultaneously; he sent this off on 25 April to Engel, so that Schirmers' could put it on the market.

In the middle of May Schoenberg received a really despairing letter from Stiedry. He said that he had been ill for some time and had had trouble with his career. He could not find enough work as a conductor or as a teacher. Only the performance of Verdi's *Macbeth* by the New Opera Company had helped him a little.

Schoenberg had told him about the Piano Concerto and the string quartet which he was planning; Stiedry urged him to finish *Jacob's Ladder* and *Moses and Aaron*, the beginnings of which he had lived through in a small room in Lugano together with Schoenberg. He had spoken briefly to Schnabel; Schnabel was working on his Second Symphony. Stiedry said that he had also written to the Werfels a few days earlier about his problems.

Schoenberg was on friendly terms with the Werfels. In May 1943 Thomas Mann wrote in his diary, in which the name of the composer had often occurred before: 'Party at the Werfels with the Schoenbergs. Drew him out a good deal about music and a composer's existence, and it is lucky that he himself wants to return the compliment.' It was the time when he was writing the novel *Dr. Faustus*. Schoenberg had often been interested in the trilogy *Joseph and his Brethren*, which has points of contact with his Biblical texts.

Now Engel made new offers about Schoenberg's fees for his latest works. Schirmer's were prepared to pay him 2400 dollars in twelve monthly instalments of 200. The Master agreed to this, but asked at the same time whether he could accept the offer of another publisher to arrange Beethoven's String Trio opus 8 for string orchestra. (This is the D major Serenade; the plan was not completed). He said that he was very busy with teaching and with preparing examination papers which had to be duplicated for the final examinations of his classes.

The short summer holidays began. On 7 June Schoenberg wrote a four-part mirror canon and on the 20th he took up his interrupted work on the Variations for wind orchestra again. He had to hurry. The summer sessions began on 5 July. On the 10th a letter to Engel announced the completion of the Variations, the orchestration of which would be finished in two to three weeks.

On 21 July Carl Engel was sixty. Gustav Reese was preparing a 'Birthday Offering' as a private print by the firm of Schirmer's. Schoenberg offered it two three-part canons of the most refined construction. These had been written without any special purpose on 14 April 1933 in Berlin, together with two four-part canons. Now he wrote a text for them together with an English translation. This goes: 'It happens to everyone; no one can remain twenty forever. Suddenly one is sixty, and is dismayed and is astonished, and asks oneself: What is suddenly wrong with me? What have I done that I can't skip about like I used to?

Even the notes are too quick; I am out of breath! Wouldn't it be better for me to sing this slower part?

This has happened to me, but I comforted myself quickly and have revelled in the enjoyment of wisdom, which I should have had at forty, but which is now very gradually coming to me, now when I haven't got any more of it!

Don't believe it! It's all a swindle. Those who have always been old, and never dared to do youthful pranks, only they speak with wisdom; we others still dare to blame ourselves, for we believe firmly: Life begins at sixty.'

And as a postscript Schoenberg wrote a two-part combination of C–E and A–E flat–C–B (in German ASCH) as well as a perpetual, chromatically rising cadence as a symbol of 'many happy returns!'

Engel, who did not like celebrations, had fled to the sea with his dog. Deeply moved, he thanked his friend on 6 August for the 'real masterpiece of contrapuntal art', which would assure immortality for him, Engel.

The score of the wind orchestra work was finished later than had been planned, on 24 August. Schoenberg celebrated his sixty-ninth birthday three weeks afterwards with one of the large parties which he liked on such occasions, much in contrast to his friend Engel! Thomas Mann was invited, but did not know about the birthday and shortly afterwards sent Schoenberg his *Magic Mountain* with the dedication: 'To Arnold Schoenberg, the daring master, for 13 September 1943 from somebody who also tries to build music Thomas Mann'. He wrote in his diary: 'Buffet dinner at Schoenberg's to celebrate his sixty-ninth birthday. Many guests. Sat down with Gustav Arlt, Klemperer, Frau Heims-Reinhardt. Spent a long time with Klemperer and Schoenberg. Spoke too much . . .'

Then Schoenberg sent the poet the text of his *Jacob's Ladder* and his Harmony treatise. Mann found the oratorio undigested religious poetry. 'So his remarkable treatise struck me all the more strongly, for its pedagogic position is apparently conservative; the most extraordinary mixture of pious tradition and revolution'.

A letter o꜀ 19 September 1943 answering an invitation to a congress of Californian school supervisors, shows how the Master himself regarded his spiritual position at that time. Schoenberg was asked to conduct his own works at it. He wrote to the Director of the Division of Elementary Education at the Department of Education in Sacramento, Miss Helen Hefferman, that he had always believed that a composer should concern himself with the problems of mankind. But this happened in a symbolical way, without definite words expressing matters of philosophy, economy, or problems of labour, society or morals. The 'release of the creative spirit' was always the subject of music, regardless of the standard and the spiritual level of the composer.

There were new negotiations with Engel. The Variations opus 43 were seen to be too difficult to be playable by a sufficient number of the 20,000 American High School bands in order to cover the cost. Schoenberg said that they would also be in demand in Europe after the war. One could also insert a Hammond organ part and if necessary leave out a few of the difficult variations. He said that at Greissle's suggestion he had already half finished a version for large orchestra, which he could send in ten or fourteen days. The letter, dated 6 October, then deals with 'Kol Nidre', which Schoenberg wanted to assign to the publishers under favourable conditions.

The autumn examinations at the UCLA included tests of orchestration. These took place on 19 October from one o'clock to five in the afternoon. Schoenberg noted on this: 'Given a four-hand piano score and a record – orchestrate about 24 measures – Mahler Schoenberg – secure music paper with instruments on the margin.' The pupils had to listen to a chosen work and orchestrate it from a four-hand piano score, as much like the original as possible. He had already used this method in 1920 (but without records), and so did Busoni, who however confined himself to works of Mozart.

He had a letter from an old admirer in New York: Edgar Varèse. Varèse had lived in Los Angeles up till 1940 and had been to the house in North Rockingham Avenue. He performed works of Schoenberg with the 'Greater New York Chorus', which was founded in 1941. Now he wanted to give a lecture about him and asked for biographical material in a letter of 23 October.

Erwin Stein and Karl Rankl had telegraphed Schoenberg from London on his sixty-ninth birthday. Schoenberg thanked them on 22 November. He said he was having his last semester at the UCLA, and had to retire at seventy. His last classes would be in February 1944. Then he wanted to finish a few theoretical books as well as *Moses and Aaron* and *Jacob's Ladder* if possible.

'*I have begun a book on counterpoint. It will consist of three volumes. 1. Preliminary exercises, 2. Contrapuntal composition, 3. Counterpoint in the homophonic compositions of the nineteenth century (from about 1770 to the present day). This last volume, of which I have made a good sketch many years ago, will be something completely new. At least I don't know of any book on this subject.*'

He said that the family were well apart from colds. His wife had to work very hard as she had no servant. He was helping to wash dishes and make breakfast. It would be better for him if he didn't smoke. Then he adds a greeting to Professor Edward Dent.

Bruno Walter had put down *Verklärte Nacht* on a programme with the Philharmonic Orchestra in New York. On 10 December he suggested a cut of fifty-four bars (338–391). Schoenberg refused this.

The annual Christmas letter to the Greissles was sent on 18 December 1943. It said that a parcel had arrived from Trudi, but had not yet been opened. They hoped that their parcel with gifts for Felix and Trudi had also arrived. They would like to have more news of the two grandsons, Arnold and Hermann, who were American soldiers; Arnold had sent a card with a picture of Naples.

'*A few days ago*,' Schoenberg writes: '*I sent Arnold two pocket chess games. Two boards and one set of chessmen I made myself. I hope he can use them. Hermann seems to be an excellent soldier. That is very good. I hope he is lucky.*'

The sentence about Hermann as a soldier was written in German in the middle of a letter written in English. Schoenberg had often made chessmen earlier.

The rest of the letter is concerned with preparations for the performance of the 'Ode', which Basil Rathbone was studying with Hanns Eisler and also with the Piano Concerto which Steuermann was working on with Clara Silvers.

Towards the end of the year Steuermann came to Los Angeles. He played Schoenberg his concerto with Leonard Stein. Friends listened to this, including Alma Werfel; the poet was in his bungalow in Santa Barbara, working on his play *Jacobowsky and the Colonel*. She remembers the performance: 'I heard some real old-fashioned Schoenberg "de laboratoire" as Ravel would say – but it was all very interesting and always Schoenberg'. Alma says that Schoenberg remarked afterwards that he himself would need forty-five rehearsals in order to get to know his work.

The work, which is in one movement clearly divided into four sections, is strictly based on a twelve-tone row (A–E–G sharp–B–B flat–F sharp–C–D–G–E flat–F–D flat) and avoids the tonal effects which occurred in the 'Ode to Napoleon' because of the nature of the row chosen by the composer. Only the final Giocoso-Rondo begins with a theme which for twelve bars circles round the note F sharp. In the division of emphasis between the solo part and the orchestra the work continues the tradition of Brahms, which can also be recognized in the virtuoso fullness of writing. The first, ländler-like-theme starts in a Viennese manner, softly cheerful, and the finale returns to cheerful feelings. However, in the Molto allegro darker regions are approached and the shadowy harmonics on the piano (an effect which Schoenberg had introduced into his opus 11 in 1909) leads in to a ghostly world. In the Adagio, after a purely orchestral section, the music leads to more and more threatening and exciting ideas, calms down for a short time in a solo cadenza for the piano, and then splits up the web of sound into molecular figures. To pour so much drama, lyrical expression, anguish and uneasiness into a completely coherent form can only be done by a master like Schoenberg.

On 7 January Richard Buhlig, the sixty-three-year-old pianist, who had given the first performance of opus 11 before the First World War in Berlin and was now teaching in Los Angeles, invited Schoenberg to a cycle of subscription concerts. On 3 and 4 February *Verklärte Nacht* had a stormy success in New York under Bruno Walter, who wrote enthusiastically about the work and its reception.

On the 6th Leopold Stokowski gave the première of the Piano Concerto with Steuermann and the NBC Orchestra. This afternoon concert in 8-H-Studio at Radio City was the cause of the NBC not renewing his contract. The broadcast was financed by General Motors. Virgil Thomson, who had now become the leading American critic, reported on it in the New York *Herald Tribune*. He said that it was an honour which Stokowski had paid not only to one of the great living masters of music, but also to the American public; General Motors could be proud of it. In its romantic and deeply felt expressiveness Schoenberg's work corresponded to the best Viennese tradition. As characteristics of it he praised the delicate orchestration, the change from one instrument to another. It sounded like chamber music for a hundred players. The combination of rhythmical methods and contrapuntal development reminded one of Bach. Thomson's criticism was the most fundamental and positive which Schoenberg had found up till then in America. It counteracted a mass of foolish reviews.

Thomson also gave a positive review of the New York performance of the Organ Variations by Carl Weinrich on 10 April 1944, although they affected him more through their impressionistic richness of ideas than by their construction.

On 6 May Schoenberg lost his devoted and most helpful friend in America, Carl Engel; he had been ill and exhausted for some time and died hardly more than six months after his sixtieth birthday. From the beginning of 1944 on their correspondence was very close and warm. Under the impression of the concert given by Stokowski and Steuermann Engel wrote on 7 February with unusual enthusiasm:

'Dearest friend, it does not often happen in my old days that a new piece of music puts me into ecstatic confusion. Your Piano Concerto succeeded in doing this . . . I have only really understood what the work has in it when I heard the phenomenal instrumentation.'

Engel had heard two rehearsals and the radio broadcast. A month later he regretted that the première of the 'Ode' had been postponed. He had hoped to 'import' Schoenberg to New York on this occasion. On 5 April he asked about the best piano teacher in Los Angeles. Schoenberg was suffering from one of his heavy colds, but answered on 10 April. He recommended as the most cultivated pianist Richard Buhlig, as a good virtuoso the Steuermann pupil Jakob Gimpel, and also mentioned Edward Wolfgang Rebner and Ignace Hilsberg. Arthur Rubinstein lived near him, but he did not know whether he taught. Engel was disquieted by his friends' illness, because Schoenberg was suffering from giddy fits, and advised him to have a proper examination of his stomach and intestines. He said that the 'Models' were selling slowly but steadily. Unfortunately he had not been able to hear the Organ Variations, about which he had heard glowing reports. The New York critics came very near to the Beethoven concept of 'prize oxen'.

In March 1943 Engel had already spoken to Koussevitzky about a composition commission for Schoenberg. But the Master could not overcome his illwill against the conductor. On 27 April Engel telegraphed him:

'Strongly and urgently advise you reconsider Koussevitzky situation stop please do not send him any further message stop refer you to my letter of March fifteenth last year second paragraph which you will now understand stop should be terribly disappointed if you refuse commission stop think variations would be ideal work for the occasion and greatly hope it will be accepted stop affectionate regards.'

That was the last sign of life from his friend. His intervention with Koussevitzky was at least successful in that the Variations were given their première in the arrangement for large orchestra on 20 October 1944 in Boston by their élite orchestra under the Russian conductor. Schoenberg was very deeply moved by Engel's death. When Schirmer's asked if he would arrange his friend's 'Triptychon' for violin and piano in an orchestral version, he answered at once, agreeing to do it and did not ask for a fee for this work, which would not have been easy for him. Felix Greissle and Gustav Reese were informed about this in these terms.

Owing to illness there were many domestic worries in Brentwood Park. A letter to Trudi Greissle of 7 April 1944 complains.
about these. Gertrud had fallen on the stairs in February. At the
same time Ronny and Nuria became ill. Finally Schoenberg himself got a cold in the middle of February and had to spend two
days in bed, but finished his lessons and examinations. He had a
fever in March, with coughing and pains all over his body. His
stomach was affected; his weight went down about eight pounds
in a few days. X-ray photographs on 18 and 23 March confirmed
that there was no cancer or affection of the lungs. On 1 April
Schoenberg was examined for diabetes. He was given insulin and
a diet. His heart was in order. He himself did not believe he had
diabetes, but thought that the whole thing was one of those
mysterious kinds of influenza. But he was still suffering from
giddiness. Through her over-exertions in looking after him and
the children Gertrud had a collapse just when Lou Eisler was
visiting her.

Then he asked Trudi to come and help until Gertrud was well
again. He said that he would soon be able to help her himself.
Nuria was also helping. The children were independent; Larry
at the age of three was frying bacon for himself. But they were
American children. Their school and school friends undermined
discipline.

On the other hand he was sure that Trudi would like the three
children. For a third of the day they were really very nice. They
spent a quarter of it at school. Apart from sleep there were two
hours for each of them in which they could be a good deal of
trouble. However, they changed when a new person appeared.

But Trudi was ill herself and was being treated for a tumour.
On 3 May Gertrud wrote to her that her father was better, that
diabetes had been avoided; only his blood pressure was too
high at 205. She herself could not afford the luxury of being ill,
although the doctor had said that she was the illest of them all.

In June 1944 the success of Hitler's armies was halted. American troops landed in Brittany. Soon afterwards the Russian
offensive began, which led to an irresistible forward march by
Stalin's troops.

Schoenberg had a letter from New York from Kurt List, a
writer on music and publisher, who had been an energetic
advocate of Schoenberg in the magazine 'Listen, Guide to Good
Music'. List wanted a photo of him. An old acquaintance wrote
from Beverly Hills, a suburb of Los Angeles. It was Josef Reitler,

who at one time had been the music critic of the *Neue Freie Presse* in Vienna together with Julius Korngold. He said that perhaps Schoenberg might still remember him, because round about 1903 he had made 'his first attempts to walk' in Harmony with him.

All those who had been driven out of Europe followed the events in France, Italy and Russia with passion. Schoenberg regarded the retreat without resistance of the Germans on the Eastern front sceptically. On 7 July 1944 Minsk was evacuated, on the 27th Lwow, on the 28th Brest-Litovsk. 'Schoenberg', Thomas Mann wrote in the *Creation of Dr. Faustus*, 'and not he alone among my acquaintances, believed at that time firmly in a concerted game, in an arrangement.'

In September Schoenberg completed the seventieth year of his life and thereby was irrevocably compelled to retire from academic work.

The Viennese art historian Dr. Otto Kallir, who was now the owner of the New York Galerie St. Etienne, wrote on the 9th about Richard Gerstl, the painter who had played such a fatal rôle in Schoenberg's life, clearly without realizing what memories he was reawakening. Schoenberg noted in the margin of the letter: 'Talent is fate – very full of talent, to remind me of this just now.' Schoenberg's old school companion Arnold Steiner wrote from Buenos Aires. He reminded Schoenberg of the Volksschule in the Second District, of the teacher Starek and of some curious events. Julius Korngold, once the feared critic of the *Neue Freie Presse* in Vienna, had come to Los Angeles in 1938 with his son Erich Wolfgang. Schoenberg entered on a friendly relationship with his former enemy; Korngold thanked him for two letters on 15 October.

As a present for Schoenberg's seventieth birthday Hanns Eisler dedicated to him the 'Fourteen ways of describing the rain' in the *Pierrot Lunaire* combination of flute, clarinet, violin, cello and piano. To reply to the homage which he received from all sides, Schoenberg had a circular letter printed on 3 October, which was sent to those who had congratulated him. He says in it that for more than a week he had tried to write a letter of thanks. But it was terribly difficult to produce anything, as everybody expected something unusual on such an occasion. In reality one should be pleased if somebody of his age was still capable of giving a sign of life at all. To his great astonishment so many people had been surprised at the première of his Piano Concerto that he still had something to say. Or perhaps that he was not stopping saying it, and was not yet wise enough to keep it to himself or to be silent altogether. The Stiedrys and the Greissles were also sent the circular letter, but with detailed additions in manuscript. Schoenberg told them both that he would perhaps come to the performances in New York in November.

Schoenberg now had more time for social life than he had had previously. Eisler took Brecht and Paul Dessau round to see him again. Brecht noted in his diary that he felt in tune when Schoenberg complained that there was no 'purely musical conceptual material' in music. On 21 October Schoenberg again continued working on *Jacob's Ladder*, which also occupied him on 3 December.

The première of the Orchestral Variations opus 43b was given in Boston on 20 October; on 23 November the 'Ode to Napoleon' followed in New York, arranged for string orchestra and piano at the request of the conductor Arthur Rodzinsky. Mack Harrell undertook the speaking part, and Eduard Steuermann the piano part. Rodzinsky directed the New York Philharmonic.

In November Thomas Mann made entries in his diary which recur in the *Creation of Dr. Faustus*. He affirms that Schoenberg and Adorno did not meet each other, and imagines that 'the Master scented a critical element in the younger man's admiration for him'. A conversation about Wagner with Eisler in Schoenberg's house amused him very much. After a dispute about the harmonies of *Parsifal* the Master sent him an autograph letter with music and figures.

At Christmas Schoenberg received a parcel of gifts from the Greissles in New York; he was sent a belt, which he put on at once and found very nice. On 3 January 1945 he wrote an unusually long letter to Felix and Trudi. He began with eleven questions concerning the publishing firm, and ended with the most personal matters which Gertrud then augmented. Schoenberg wanted to know from Felix Greissle whether for instance Fritz Reiner would conduct the Wind Variations, what the criticisms and the general reception of the performances up to date had been, whether the Goldman Band would play the piece and whether he would have parts for a military band. He was also interested in the critical reception of the 'Ode to Napoleon' and its further performances in Chicago and Madison with Kolisch. Finally he wanted to know whether William Schuman would become Carl Engel's successor and whether Schuman was for or against him.

The rest of the letter, which alternates between English and

German, was partly written by Gertrud and partly by Arnold in his own hand, and is chiefly addressed to his daughter. Schoenberg writes that he had not been teaching since February and had been retired since 13 September. The pension which he was getting brought him in 28,50 dollars a month. Luckily he had two pupils who paid well, and since he had not been teaching in the university enquiries about private lessons were increasing. Then he wrote about the children. He said that he himself was planning to finish *Jacob's Ladder* and *Moses and Aaron*; 'for my legacy, for I don't think that Schirmer's will take anything more from me.'

Gertrud ended that she had enjoyed their gift of bath salts. Now she often indulged in the luxury of a hot bath, while otherwise only showers were allowed in the house. They could see how well Arnold was by the fact that he had been with her up till 5.30 in the morning at a New Year party.

Much has been written about the shamefully small pension which Schoenberg received from the UCLA. There can be no excuse for the fact that somebody like Schoenberg was retired on such a tiny sum. But there is an explanation. The American universities (like other institutions in the USA except for government posts) do not have the kind of pension scheme which is common in Europe and makes the retirement years viable. The pensions of retired professors are calculated according to the number of years of service, and on the basis of a very modest percentage. Schoenberg had taught at the UCLA since 1 July 1935 and directed the music department. His final salary up till his retirement in the autumn of 1944 was 5400 dollars. His pension, originally 28,50, then 29,80 and 38, was increased to 40,38 dollars on 3 March 1945.

More shameful was the attitude of the millionaire John Simon Guggenheim Memorial Foundation, which since the early 1930s had given their heavily endowed fellowships to many American composers, including George Antheil, Samuel Barber, Ruth Crawford, Lou Harrison and Harold Shapero. On 22 January 1945 Schoenberg, who had often acted as a referee for them for other candidates, sent an application to their general secretary Henry Allen Moe. He wrote about his difficult financial situation since his retirement, of his very small pension of 38 dollars a month, of his three young children and of the small number of his private pupils.

It was his desire to finish if possible without the necessity of teaching two important compositions and three text books, one of which would be in three volumes. He would need six to nine months for *Moses and Aaron*, and one and a half to two years for *Jacob's Ladder*.

The theoretical works included a treatise on counterpoint, of which only the first of three volumes was ready; with regards to the contents of the planned third volume, counterpoint and semi-counterpoint in the music of the masters after Bach, no literature existed at all. The textbook *Structural Functions of Harmony*, could be finished in a few months. A further textbook, either about fundamentals of musical composition or about orchestration would be based on sketches which were partly four to five years old, partly twenty-eight years old.

His application was rejected. One of the greatest geniuses of the age had to keep his head above water for a further six years, up till his death, by teaching and occasional small composition commissions.

On 8 February the long-planned performance of the ballet *Pillar of Fire* with Antony Tudor's choreography of Schoenberg's *Verklärte Nacht* finally took place in San Francisco. Schoenberg conducted it with great success. He spent the following day with Gertrud and Nuria in Oakland with Darius Milhaud, who was teaching at Mills College there and invited the three of them to lunch. Their old good contact of 1922 was strengthened. In March he again met Thomas Mann at Gottfried Reinhardt's house. Gottfried was the son of Max Reinhardt. Arthur Schnabel and Otto Klemperer were present. Thomas Mann reports a discussion about music after the meal.

Schoenberg never accepted academic titles and honours. Two American universities had decided to give him an honorary doctorate. He refused. In April 1945, shortly after his retirement, a similar request came from UCLA. Schoenberg hesitated about answering it, and finally wrote on 14 May to the President Dr. Robert G. Sproul:

'*Your letter regarding the intention of the Regents of the University of California to give me an honorary doctorate in jurisprudence is very embarrassing for me.*

For: I have been offered a similar honour by other institutions on two occasions and, according to my principles, I had to thank them for it very politely and asked them to understand that I do not wish to accept such honours.

I think that if I now accepted a degree from the University of California it would be an insult to those who were the first to offer me such an honour. So I thank you and the Regents of the University warmly, but I must again decline it.'

Three and a half years after his death, on 21 January 1955, the UCLA gave him another honour. They officially named the concert hall in the new university building on the campus of Los Angeles 'Arnold Schoenberg Hall'.

Schoenberg began a correspondence with Serge Frank (a relation of Anne Frank, who became tragically famous through her diary). This was concerned with a translation of Schoenberg's texts, which this pupil of the Master was undertaking.

In May Schoenberg received a circular letter from Dr. Roy Harris, the chief of the music section of the Office of War Information in New York. It was about American composers. Schoenberg answered that he hesitated to give a list of the ten composers which Harris wanted. However, he mentioned Harris himself, in addition Aaron Copland, Roger Sessions, William Schuman, David Diamond, Louis Gruenberg, Walter Piston, Anis Fuleihan, Henry Cowell, Adolphe Weiss, Gerald Strang, Lou Harrison, and Miss Dika Newlin. He said that in these persons' compositions – he gave thirteen of them! – he had found talent and originality; in many cases the technical performance was not on the same level as the talent.

To his friend Leopold Stokowski, who had asked him for an opening fanfare for his concerts in the Hollywood Bowl, Schoenberg offered a choice of fragments from the Dance round the Golden Calf in *Moses and Aaron* or a combination of three 'Gurrelieder' motifs; the C major ending of the dawn passage was not right for the time of day, but would be right for the atmosphere of the Bowl concerts. This last remained a fragment, but was sent by Leonard Stein to Stokowski.

For Thomas Mann's seventieth birthday on 6 June 1945 Schoenberg wrote a double canon for string quartet, the sketches of which also have a text:

> *Depth: on the surface if often looks like mere*
> *Riches or even extravagance.*

The manuscript also had a commentary: 'Probably to show you in a special way how I value you, I made it specially hard for myself in this canon, in fact almost impossible. It sounds impossible too, and I hope you will not want to hear it. (Therefore I notated it in the old "clefs".)

'It is not without "honest" egotism that I wish we may remain good contemporaries of one another for many years. Most cordially your Arnold Schoenberg.'

The publisher William Schlamm asked him in June to contribute to his 'New Magazine'. Schoenberg was pleased and developed one of his ideas 'I believe in the right of the smallest minority'. He wrote:

'Because democracy often acts in a manner resembling dangerously something like a Dictatorship of the (very often extremely small majority), it is impossible, in spite of the freedom of the press, to publish ideas which do not fit into the frame of one of the greater parties; ideas whose truth might manifest itself only in five, ten, thirty, a hundred years; perhaps only at a time when to their author they have already become obsolete!' He said that he wrote a good deal about the theory, technique, aesthetics and ethics of composers, and had recently begun an essay on 'Theory of Performance', which could grow into a book. A shorter article would be called 'Form in music serves for comprehensibility', denying form the effect of beauty. An article which he had started shows how critics misled listeners into overestimating performers at the expense of creators. Another plan was concerned with the injustice of the American copyright laws, and another on mistakes in musicology. His letter to Schlamm was not finished till 1 July, and its key phrases are:

> If it is art it is not for the masses.
> And if it is for the masses it is not art.

These ideas show something of the tension wrought by events in the Old World. In May the Hitler regime had surrendered unconditionally in Berlin. The dictator and his mouthpiece Joseph Goebbels had committed suicide. The war was over. The concentration camps were opened. It was time to begin the great clearing up, in which it was often not easy to decide who was guilty and who was guiltless. Gradually correspondence with Europe became possible again. Schoenberg watched all this with lively understanding and the keenest interest.

LAST YEARS AND DEATH

The summer of 1945 ran its course calmly and without any important creative work. On 3 August Schoenberg met Berthold Brecht by chance in a drug store. In the writer's diary is a note that Schoenberg, during the conversation which naturally was concerned with European and political questions, had stated his support for monarchy, 'as republics have hardly produced stability for more than a few hundred years.' This is similar to his thoughts which he had formulated in 1950 in a small unpublished article 'My attitude towards politics'. Schoenberg had turned away from the socialist ideas of his youth and had become conservative in a very individual manner. In the time of the massive German unemployment and the radical ideas which had been evoked by this in all directions about 1930, he adopted the point of view of a social capitalism, which would pay its workers well and look after them for the whole of their lives.

In these matters he agreed with Brecht as little as he did with the more liberal ideas of Thomas Mann and Franz Werfel. Alma and Franz Werfel were among his most trusted friends. In the spring of 1945 Werfel was taken ill, but recovered temporarily in Santa Barbara. In the middle of August he had attacks of fever; he died on the 26th. Schoenberg, who had thought of writing an opera with him in 1930 and had had many conversations with him about music in their Californian exile, took a sincere part in Alma's mourning. But Werfel's musical views were those of an opera lover to whom all modern music appeared to be a cerebral production made by sectarians of the kind of Mathias Fischböck in his Verdi novel, and not compatible with his ideas. It was only in their love of Gustav Mahler that the two unlike men came together.

On 23 August Schoenberg had written down ideas for a fragment 'To all my critics'. Then the composer and conductor Nathaniel Shilkret approached him, Stravinsky, Toch, Milhaud,

Castelnuovo-Tedesco and Alexander Tansman with a proposal. Each of them should, for a fee of 300 dollars, write a short piece on a text from the Biblical story of the Creation. Schoenberg accepted the commission and chose the prelude to the Creation, which he composed as 'Prelude' for mixed chorus and orchestra, and finished in on 30 September 1945. The whole Suite, to which Shilkret also contributed a piece, was given its premiere on 18 November in Los Angeles under the direction of Werner Janssen.

On 29 September Dimitri Mitropulos invited both the Schoenbergs to attend his performance of the Violin Concerto in Minneapolis with the Symphony Orchestra and Louis Krasner. Schoenberg accepted the invitation, but could not be present because of his illness.

Among his old friends in Europe Erwin Stein had written to him from London. Schoenberg suggested that Stein should write his biography. But Stein did not think that he was the right author. He was more interested in analysis. A few days later Schoenberg received a letter from Hermann Scherchen, which he answered on 12 November. He regretted that Scherchen had not gone to America ('though it was gallant of you to stay in Europe'), as only Mitropulos dared to stand up for modern European music here. The last question in his letter was concerned with the death of Anton von Webern. Schoenberg knew that Webern had been killed on 15 September in Mittersill through the tragic mistake of an American soldier.

In December Thomas Mann consulted the Master about an idea in *Dr. Faustus*. He was thinking of choruses that sang without orchestral accompaniment in the non-tempered scale, so that the intervals did not agree with those of the piano. In the *Creation of Dr. Faustus* he wrote: 'I was so in love with the idea that I even went behind Adorno's back to ask for Schoenberg's advice; he answered "I would not do it. But theoretically it is possible." In spite of this permission from the highest level I finally gave up the idea . . .'

1945 was approaching its end and with it the time of the hardest troubles for all people who had been near to Schoenberg in Europe.

In 1946 Schoenberg received the news in January that he had been appointed Honorary President of the International Society for Contemporary Music. Winfried Zillig wrote from Salzburg, where he had performed Schoenberg's opus 19 on the radio in September 1945. On 24 January Schoenberg received another letter from Kurt List, who had been occupying himself with the case of Wilhelm Furtwängler. Like Schoenberg he took the point of view that the great conductor had never been a Nazi and was not anti-semitic either. Then Schoenberg formulated his views about Richard Strauss and Furtwängler (see appendix). He was convinced that the American ban on Furtwängler was due to Arturo Toscanini alone. He also vindicated Pfitzner's standpoint.

On 8 March the President of the Austrian Cultural Society, Dr. Egon Seefehlner, wrote that people wanted Schoenberg to return to Vienna in order to teach at the Academy. Schoenberg was not opposed in principle, but delayed his decision. When the Lord Mayor of Vienna repeated the invitation in April 1946 he showed that he was deeply moved by the latter's 'magnanimity in calling on me to return from exile, the flattering manner in which you convey the summons, and the honourable task which you assign to me: that of helping in the work of reconstruction'. He thanked the Lord Mayor with the hope that circumstances might make his return possible.

In April Schoenberg heard a statement in a quiz that other musicians had collaborated with Wagner in writing his scores. He protested energetically against this untruth, and the *New York Times* critic Olin Downes thanked him on 15 April for his protest.

For a long time Schoenberg had had trouble with his eyes. They got tired when reading more quickly than before, and he could not read small writing any more. It was hardly possible for him to use normal music paper. So he used music sheets with much increased spaces between the lines. Even writing of normal size was difficult for him to read.

The University of Chicago invited him to give three lectures. Schoenberg wanted to reject the offer because he was afraid of difficulties in deciphering the typewritten texts. At that time, 1946, Paul Dessau was employed by the film company Warner Brothers. In his office was a typewriter with extra large letters which was not being used. He heard about Schoenberg's troubles and offered to lend him the machine. Schoenberg was pleased about this, because he depended on the fees for the three lectures in Chicago. His financial situation was very tricky at that time, and for this reason he sold his friends photo-copies of the piano score of the *Glückliche Hand* which was then unobtainable commercially. The normal price was ten dollars; Dessau paid a hundred dollars for his copy. As a dedication Schoenberg wrote in it: 'This is my/lucky handwriting as/my thanks for your lucky handwriting, which now/made my lectures legible to me./ Cordially Arnold Schoenberg 1946.'

In May the University of Chicago asked him through its Chancellor Robert Maynard Hutchins about the organization of the music department. Schoenberg gave detailed information and suggested three possibilities of organization. The first section would be a clean-cut musicological department which would have the right of promotion. The second he thought of as a complete conservatory, in which musicians would be educated; the third would be an academy of music, where practical musicianship would be taught in master classes, as well as composition of all kinds in connection with records, radio and films. He ended with suggestions about some problems in the musicological department; these included ideas from his previous theoretical writings, especially his treatise on form. The letter was dated 2 June 1946. Five days later he wrote down a twelve-tone row which he later used in the Trio.

Schoenberg's sister Ottilie Blumauer lived in Berlin, but after the violent bombardment of the capital she fled to Elstra near Kamenz in Saxony with her two daughters, and spent the last days of the war and several months after the end of the war there. Schoenberg answered a letter from her in detail on 3 June 1946. He wrote about his relations and friends, about Rudolf Gold-schmied, Arthur Schoenberg and his wife, about Hans and Walter Nachod in London, about the sons of Uncle Gottlieb, a daughter of Aunt Kläre Waitzner in Budapest, about Webern, Jalowetz, D. J. Bach, Rufer, Polnauer, Ratz and Olga Novakovic. He said that Georg as well as Trudi and Felix Greissle had survived. The death of his brother Heinrich seems to have taken place after an operation. After that Schoenberg remained in contact by correspondence with his sister and her daughter Susanne Remus.

German music life had been deprived of all works of Jewish origin during the Hitler régime with increasing severity. The need for reconstruction after the collapse of 1945 was enormous. This concerned the music of Mendelssohn as well as Mayerbeer, Gustav Mahler and Schoenberg. Even in the first months after the collapse, that is since the summer of 1945 onwards, a quickly developing music and theatre life began again from the ruins of the Austrian towns. Members of orchestras and opera theatres, who had been scattered in all directions, came together and gradually

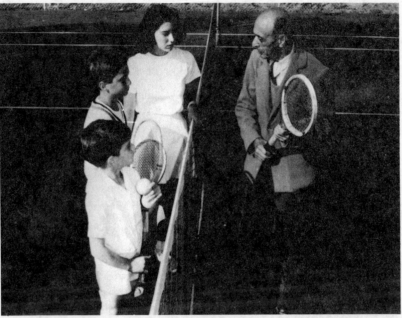

Schoenberg with his three children at tennis, Los Angeles, 1946

The whole family in Brentwood Park, 1946

built up a repertoire, often with the most primitive means. The difficulties, for instance of finding musical material, can hardly be realized in normal times.

The four occupying powers helped in all activities concerning cultural reconstruction. At that time Berlin was divided into four sectors, ruled by the American, English, French and Russian occupying powers. They fostered the re-introduction of music which had been forbidden during the Nazi régime, often with a certain rivalry against each other. The Berlin Radio, in the beautiful Radio House of Hans Poelzig in the Masurenallee, was in the British sector, but was directed by the Russians. The Americans put up a transmitter in their sector, at that time in the Winterfeldstrasse in Schöneberg, which was first relayed by telephone and was called Telephone Radio in the American Sector, DIAS for short. When the transmissions took place without telephone wires this name was altered to RIAS. The Russian and American directors of radio encouraged the performance of music which had been forbidden. So as early as 1946 the Russian-directed Berlin Radio gave a performance of Schoenberg's F sharp minor Quartet, the quartet led by the excellent violinist Rudolf Schulz with Margot Hinnenberg-Lefèbre as the singer. The latter had been singing in public again since 1946, especially in the house on the Waldsee belonging to the district of Zehlendorf, of which Josef Rufer was the musical counsellor; she sang Schoenberg's Stefan George Lieder with Helmut Roloff at the piano. Through Rufer's activity West Berlin soon became familiar again with Schoenberg's complete chamber music and piano works. In Leipzig too, which was in the Russian occupation zone, there was a strong interest in modern music. In the summer of 1947 the city put on a modern music festival, in which Paul Schmitz conducted the Chamber Symphony opus 9, Margot Hinnenberg-Lefèbre sang the George songs with Klaus Billing and I gave a lecture on Schoenberg. All these events were sold out and were received with tumultous success.

Schoenberg was informed about these events and their effect on the public by his friends and was happy in the thought that his work was living in the place where he had been condemned to silence for twelve years.

There were similar efforts in other German cities, mostly supported by the big radio organizations. One of the first was the 'Musica Viva', founded in Munich by Karl Amadeus Hartmann. Hamburg and Cologne put on similar music series later. And everywhere where modern music was promoted the works of Schoenberg were in the vanguard.

Schoenberg was pleased to receive a letter from Oskar Kokoschka from New York. He answered in detail on 3 June; his letter, written by hand, is published in Stein's collection and contains bitter complaints about the 'lack of culture in this amusement arcade world'.

In August Schoenberg was taken seriously ill. He was given injections for violent pains in the chest. After one of these he became unconscious. His pulse and breathing stopped. The doctor injected into the heart itself and brought Schoenberg back to life. 'I have risen from a real death and now find myself quite well', he wrote in a letter to me. Gertrud Schoenberg describes the events in detail in a letter to Ottilie Blumauer of 9 December 1946: 'We worked with adrenalin, oxygen and hot water bottles till five in the morning. In the early morning things had gone so far that he wanted to get up. He didn't know anything about his whole collapse. The cardiogram showed an irregular rhythm but no heart attack. On the tenth day he got his usual inflammation of the lungs, but after three weeks he was able to get up and then he recovered with surprising quickness . . . his only trouble is his eyes. He becomes giddy if he reads or writes.'

While still in hospital Schoenberg began the composition of his String Trio opus 45, which was finished on 23 September. Shortly afterwards he met Thomas Mann and told him that his piece described his illness and his medical treatment.

Hanns Eisler told Schoenberg that it was a grandiose composition, to which Schoenberg answered: 'Do you know, that I was so weak that I don't know at all how I wrote it. I just pushed something together.' And he showed Eisler how some chords represented injections.

The work is in three sections without any breaks. The first two sections are again subdivided, so that an episode follows each main complex. The main complex in the first part consists of fifty-one bars and the first episode of eighty-one. The main complex in the second part, beginning as a slow waltz with falling sixths on the violins, with its length of forty-seven bars more or less corresponds to that of the first part; against this the second episode, only twenty-four bars long, is approximately a third of the length of the first episode. The first episode begins in an almost Tristan-like romantic style with a dolce phrase in the violin over a held third A and C sharp in the viola and cello; this is followed by a short song-like section in the lower registers, which is resolved into an increasingly unquiet movement and ends with a rising violin passage in the highest harmonic regions. A recitative passage which contains a falling glissando is transposed up a semitone twenty-five bars later. The second episode is characterized by a strictly worked-out canon and the glissandi which follow, now played fortissimo and falling to a feroce figure which is obstinately repeated. A unison passage also arises out of the style, which is otherwise very complex. The third section, eighty-six bars long, begins with an exact reprise of the beginning but only for one bar; there are already variations in the second bar, the third bar is left out entirely, but the fourth and fifth are repeated unaltered. After this two bars are left out, the next two bars are repeated unaltered, then the next two left out, then an exact reprise of the two following bars. Finally there is an idea consisting of sevenths and ninths, led by the violin, which goes into a somewhat concentrated variation of the beginning.

The whole formal course of the first main section is shortened and compressed, through simple omission or through refined syntheses of ideas; and so the reprise of the episode which begins in the 'Tristan romantic' style appears much earlier than in the first section. This is also shortened by leaving out two bars. So what we have here is a very ingenious form of what is called 'shortened reprise'. And shortly before the final section the recitative from the first episode occurs again, now in the inversion, with the glissando upwards and the arpeggio which follows downwards.

These clearly perceptible repetitions make the form of the whole work very clear. Here they give the effect of connection, of relation to previous events, which however do not become mechanical repetitions of things already said, but through the easily traceable omissions takes on the appearance of a montage of building blocks. In connection with Schoenberg's later music people have often spoken of athematism, which he himself energetically denied. Of course this music is not thematic in the sense of classical procedures. This is prevented by the special dialectic of the twelve-tone method. But it produces a montage of ideas in a technique which can be followed thematically and motivically throughout, which are often grouped like figures in a kaleidoscope with new and surprising combinations of previously known elements in different ways.

This also affects the harmonic side of the work. The harmonies are developed from the row and often become independent in the texture, which otherwise is highly contrapuntal. For instance, after the middle of the first main section, when various six-part chords are played nine times for four bars in semiquavers. But before this these chords were as it were developed in different combinations of three major sevenths, shaken up in different forms, till all the possibilities of tension in sound had been exhausted. Each repetition is widely removed from the pleasant 'once upon a time', through contraction, variation, mirror forms, permutation and transposition, and becomes so unlike the form in which it first appeared that it can be regarded more as a surrealistic event produced by psychical automatism and not as an 'Act of convention'. And here lies the inner affinity between this style and the attempts at denaturalization which Stravinsky undertook with the forms of classical music in his so-called neo-classical works.

Of the style of the Trio it remains to say that it contains an entirely exorbitant piling up of varying tone colours for the three instruments, unusual even for Schoenberg, an alternation of harmonics, pizzicato, struck and bowed co legno, sharpening of the character of the sound by playing on the bridge, and a juxtaposition of dynamic opposites, which in its general sound contradicts all previous musical experience. The shock effect of the first minutes is unescapable; it stamps the work as a product of genius arising from anguish and oppressiveness, from which strange ideas, melodies, sounds and rhythms present us unexpectedly with a realm of unearthly and dreamlike truth.

In New York an honorary committee of the Jewish Music Council had been formed, the President of which, Frederick Jacobi, asked Schoenberg to be an honorary member. Koussevitzky, Milhaud, Pierre Monteux, Gregor Piatigorsky, Jascha Heifetz and Ernest Bloch had accepted; Schoenberg did not react to two telegraphic appeals.

In 1946 Schoenberg began a correspondence with Robert D. W. Adams of the University of Kansas City about the translation of the Harmony Book. The famous university of Princeton wanted to give him an honorary doctorate and invited him to a reception for this purpose; Schoenberg sent a formal refusal because of illness.

Next to the String Trio the most important fruit of the year was the book *Structural Functions of Harmony*, which he finished in 1948, but was not published until 1954, after his death.

The Schoenbergs were again in contact with all their relations who had survived Hitler's Reich. They sent parcels to Otti and Susi Blumauer, who had not been handed over in the Soviet Zone, but came back. There was an occasional correspondence with Schoenberg's son Georg, who was also sent 'care parcels'. The widow and daughter of Schoenberg's brother Heinrich wrote from Mattsee near Salzburg. Now Schoenberg finally learnt that the reason for Heinrich's death was not an operation; he had been killed by an injection in a Salzburg hospital. The Nazis called it euthanasia. Gitty, Heinrich's daughter, had the balance of her mind disturbed for the rest of her life by this frightful experience.

On 2 February Schoenberg's circle of old friends and pupils was again diminished. In Black Mountain, North Carolina, Dr. Heinrich Jalowetz had died at the age of sixty-three; he had been Schoenberg's pupil since 1905, and both as a conductor and a writer had been one of the most faithful and knowledgeable advocates of his work. His articles about the Harmony Book and about Schoenberg's methods of teaching were some of the best in the collection published by Piper in 1912. In 1923 Jalowetz conducted the first complete performance of the 'Gurrelieder' in Berlin. He was an opera conductor in Danzig, Stettin, Prague, at the Vienna Volksoper, in Cologne and in Reichenberg. On Schoenberg's recommendation Jalowetz, who had been a student in Guido Adler's school, became professor at Black Mountain College in 1939. Many of the old friends from Schoenberg's circle who had immigrated met here again when he held lectures on modern music in 1944. Among those who took part were Mark Brunswick, Marcel Dick, Rudolf Kolisch, Ernst Krenek, Roger Sessions and Eduard Steuermann. Schoenberg, who was then seventy, could not accept the invitation himself because of his health. However, in the six years up to Jalowetz's death he remained in constant contact with him.

In 1947 a young relation from New Zealand came to America. His father, Richard Hoffmann, an uncle of Gertrud Schoenberg's who had emigrated there, had started a correspondence with Schoenberg in 1944. Schoenberg answered on 17 October that he had always been very interested in the islands of New Zealand, perhaps because of their fine stamps. After his retirement he had thought of moving to a country where the dollar would buy more than in America itself. He asked about the conditions of immigration, the price of buying or renting a house or flat and the cost of living. He said that Hoffmann's sister, Mrs. Henriette Kolisch (née Hoffmann), was living with them in the family. He had read with interest that Hoffmann's younger son Richard, called Dick, was a musician. He, Schoenberg, would be able to help him if he came to America.

This plan for a second immigration foundered because of Gertrud Schoenberg's determination not to give up the Californian house and her contacts there. Instead of this Richard Hoffmann Junior came to Los Angeles. Born in Vienna in 1925, he became Schoenberg's pupil and secretary at the age of twenty-two. Since 1966 he has been Professor of Theory and Composition at Oberlin College.

The String Trio, which Schoenberg had written in August and September 1946 immediately after his illness, had been occasioned by a commission. Harvard University was preparing a symposium on music criticism for the spring of 1947; this was to last three days and was to help large numbers of listeners to music by a certain number of authoritative guides. For this meeting three composers were given commissions; the Czech Bohuslav Martinů (Sixth String Quartet), the Harvard professor Walter Piston (Third String Quartet) and Arnold Schoenberg. His Trio was given its première there on 2 May 1947.

In April Schoenberg had received a high honour. The American Academy of Arts and Letters gave him the prize for outstanding achievements. It carried an award of 1000 dollars. Schoenberg thanked the Academy in a letter which was one of the most original of which we know of his (see appendix). Among the first people in Germany to congratulate him was the actor Wolfgang Jarnach, a son of the composer Philipp Jarnach, the friend and pupil of Busoni. When the latter, Philipp Jarnach, later approached Schoenberg, asking him to give lectures at the Hamburg Music High School (of which he was the director) and to conduct on the radio, Schoenberg answered Jarnach with a very bitter letter. He had heard that Jarnach had become a supporter of the Hitler régime, and this would explain the doubtful honour which Jarnach had prepared for him by performing five songs and two choruses. However, he still hoped that this was a calumny; Jarnach had been so friendly with Jalowetz that it would be difficult for him to believe such rumours. The rumours were without foundation. During the Hitler régime Jarnach had completely retired from politics.

In May Schoenberg received news and programmes from Hans Rosbaud, who was the conductor of the Munich Philharmonic

Orchestra. He had conducted the First Chamber Symphony there and Professor Dr. Hans Mersmann had given an analysis of it. 'This strikes me as an even more important contribution than the preceding (Schoenberg means a similar attempt in 1933 in Frankfurt with his Variations), for understanding that my music *still* goes on suffering from the fact that the musicians do not regard me as a normal, common or garden composer who expresses his more or less good and new themes and melodies in a not entirely inadequate musical language – but as a modern dissonant twelve-note experimenter. But there is nothing I long for more intensely (if for anything), than to be taken for a better sort of Tchaikovsky – for heaven's sake: a bit better, but really that's all. Or if anything more, than that people should know my tunes and whistle them.'

I had returned to Berlin in May 1946. At the beginning of 1947 I wrote to Schoenberg, who answered me on 21 May. He was deeply moved by the news that my wife, who had interpreted and closely collaborated with Schoenberg as a singer from 1926 till 1933 under the name of Margot Hinnenberg-Lefèbre, had taken the score of the F sharp minor quartet with Schoenberg's dedication among her indispensible possessions on her flight from Prague in 1945. Because of an illness Schoenberg's letter was not finished until 26 August 1947.

Tennis was still a game in which Schoenberg was interested, although he could not play it any more. We know that his friendship with Gershwin was founded on games of tennis played together. He also used at times to play tennis with one of the Marx Brothers. Charlie Chaplin, who had lived for many years in Beverly Hills, writes in his memoirs that he had often seen Schoenberg – whose music he admired very much – sitting at tennis tournaments in white clothes and cap in the cheap seats. One day Hanns Eisler appeared in Chaplin's studio and brought Schoenberg with him. Chaplin describes him as a small man, scant of words but sincere. For Schoenberg had said to the much admired actor, director and producer that he liked the film *Modern Times* very much but he had found the music very bad. The star was not used to so much sincerity.

Schoenberg wrote about a tennis teacher for Ronny in a letter of 6 June 1947 to Dr. Perry Jones, the President of the Tennis Association of Los Angeles.

'. . . *the boy, Ronald, is always called a "natural" tennis player. He started alone practising against our windows, at six dollars a glass,*

and it was perhaps this that developed him technically. But he possesses also the mind of a fighter and – what I call the "field sense".'
Ronny needed a partner. Should they try a club? Soon Ronny found the partner he needed. His career as a young tennis champion began when he was twelve and his father was enormously pleased at his success.

In the short time between 11 and 23 August 1947 Schoenberg wrote a work which had been commissioned from him by the Koussevitzky Foundation. The original manuscript called it *A Survivor of Warsaw*; later Schoenberg altered the title, changing the 'of' to 'from'. It is a melodrama for a speaker, male chorus and orchestra and was given the number opus 46. Schoenberg wrote it in short score, from which René Leibowitz made a full score in December. Apart from the 'Ode to Napoleon' it is the only score which adopts a political position. The text, written by Schoenberg himself, is based on stories which he had heard directly or indirectly from the appalling days of the Warsaw ghetto. The first performance took place on 4 November 1948 in Albuquerque with the symphony orchestra of the city conducted by Kurt Frederick, during a concert put on by the University of New Mexico. This work, which only lasts seven minutes, was performed twice running. After the first time the audience of 1500 sat in astonished silence; after the second the applause was stormy. Schoenberg was not able to be present at the performance.

The *Survivor* is written in a free, dramatically exciting and cumulative form, which includes short recitative-like episodes. Everything aims towards the exciting conclusion, where the male chorus raises its mighty voice. The whole work, ninety-nine bars long, is based on a twelve-note series, which Schoenberg uses in continual variation with its mirror forms. It is presented right at the beginning by a fanfare of two trumpets and the tremolos in sevenths of high violins and low double basses. The song 'Sch'ma Jisroel' which appears at the end is also sung to this twelve-tone row and its inversions.

The work has a spontaneous effect of arousing feelings, it goes beyond the graveness of the dark scene in an immediate way so that it works as a release in its heroic conclusion; a harsh musical reflection from days in which the sun seemed to be covered.

The artistic methods are very different from each other in effect. A drum roll, a cymbal clash, the clacking of castanets, the sigh of a chord in string harmonics, the twittering of a wind flutter-tongue illumine situations as it were by lightning, and are witness of Schoenberg's mastery, as well as the hymn-like ending with the Biblical demand to love God. There are not many musical scenes which can compare with this in power of expression. Beethoven aroused similar feelings in the prison scene in *Fidelio*. But there at least the trumpet of salvation could sound, which was denied to the victims of this modern apocalypse. Gertrud von Le Fort wrote on a similar theme in her story *Die Letzte am Schaffott*, when the Carmelite nuns, resigned to the will of God, go to their death.

Among Schoenberg's old Viennese pupils Hans Erich Apostel wrote on 28 October; he was happy about the choice of Schoenberg as Honorary President of the ISCM.

Bad news came from New York. Trudi Greissle had had an operation on her womb in October and had not recovered from it. Gertrud Schoenberg wrote about this on 3 November to Schoenberg's sister Ottilie in Saxony. The letter describes domestic life in Brentwood Park. Nuria, now fifteen years old, has a free place in a school two hours' distance from her parents' house and only comes home at weekends. Ronny is playing successfully in tennis tournaments. Gertrud Schoenberg's mother is living in the house, where she helps a great deal. She is the best preserved of them all and earns herself money by cooking for rich people. "Cooking is very well paid here, better than composing".'

A certain Dr. Aram wanted to get money for Schoenberg from the patron Henry Reichold. Reichold was an emigrant from Berlin who helped many cultural institutions financially and through whose generosity the West Berlin Academy of Arts was built in 1960. To the question, what Reichold could do for him, Schoenberg answered that the most natural thing was to see that his music was performed. In addition Reichold should prevent the musical profiteers from obtaining unfettered power.

Schoenberg reacted extremely irritably to stylistic alterations which Serge Frank had made in the English text of some articles by him for a collection which had been planned and was being edited by Frank. He wrote on 3 December to New York that all his words must be put back in their original form, and that Frank should show his translations to a third party to be read. He did not fail to mention that Richard Hoffmann and René Leibowitz had found Frank's translation of the Mahler lecture very good, and he himself found that of 'The Relationship to the Text' good.

Even harsher words were sent in a letter to Erwin Stein of 15 December. Schoenberg's friend and former pupil had annoyed

Schoenberg by an article in which some English composers were praised immoderately, to the neglect of Schoenberg's own work. 'Do you know if I am still alive? And if so: who told you? I would rather say that I belong to those people whom people already want to forget.'

Schoenberg had regular contact with his friends in Berlin, even if the post often took a long time to cross the Atlantic Ocean. Josef Rufer and I had founded a monthly magazine about music, called 'Stimmen'. Schoenberg at once agreed to collaborate. So I was able to open the first number in November 1947 with his article 'Folkloristic Symphonies', written on 10 January and which had already been published in English in New York.

I had been commissioned by the Atlantis Publishers of Zurich to write a small book about Schoenberg, and in August and at the beginning of September he sent me material for this. He had an even closer relationship with Rufer, who was preparing his book on twelve-note music. Schoenberg wrote to him on 18 December not only about musical problems but also about his worries regarding Berlin. He mistrusted the Russians, whom he regarded as destroyers of world peace. Although he had never been a communist himself, he had credited the leaders of this party with more political understanding. He would like to have more information about Hanns and Gerhard Eisler. He found it stupid that men who have better things to say were going in for theories about reforming the world. He had always regarded Hanns Eisler's tirades as a means of showing off. If he wanted to appear important let him compose important music.

Another old pupil wrote from Santiago in Chile, Dr. Victor Krüger. In Krüger's letter of 23 December 1947 he said: 'I recall it as if it was today, the day when Guido Adler sent me to you and I addressed you with "Good morning, Herr Professor". And you answered me: "Professor? I am not a professor. One is only a professor and a doctor as long as one is nothing. Goethe was a doctor too and was only called Goethe. And another person signed his name with N only and the whole world knew who he was".'

Krüger's letter referred to a statement in the paper that Schoenberg had become an honorary doctor of a university. In fact Schoenberg made so little fuss of academic honours, which were often offered to him in America, as if these requests did not exist.

1947 produced some small important articles. On 21 July, long before the declaration of 'Human Rights' which the United Nations published on 10 December 1948, Schoenberg wrote an article on human rights. Its nineteen points are full of unusual and often surprisingly new ideas, which go far beyond the realms of culture. 'It is tragic that a code of human rights lacks the capacity of defending itself against attacks and annihilation to the same extent as does democracy. Everything which one might undertake in their name would violate the human rights of the attackers – just as everything is undemocratic which might protect democracy'. The article speaks about forms of faith, which also include communist and fascist states. One of the first declarations of human rights is the Ten Commandments; they assure the right to live and have possessions; they protect marriage, vows and work, but deny from the very beginning freedom of faith, because there is only One God. Schoenberg defends the 'bourgeois art' which was attacked by the Socialists, as well as the modern architecture which was called 'Palestinian' by the Nazis, and which stemmed from the great Adolf Loos. 'He who fights will and must conquer, will and must oppress the conquered. But what are the human rights of those who still believe in defeated art, in defeated ideas?' As a result, says Schoenberg, one must also recognize the rights of cannibals.

More peaceable and less sarcastic is the long article 'Heart and Brain in Music', which was written for the collection *The Works of the Mind*, published by the University of Chicago Press. This starts from the passage in Balzac's *Seraphita* about the man whose heart lies in the region of his head. Schoenberg denies the possibility of separating heart and brain in art. In examples from his own works he shows how forms which were apparently constructed by the head were produced completely spontaneously and unconsciously. Did he know Wagner's letter to Eduard Hanslick where Wagner writes: 'The work of art which is produced unconsciously belongs to cultural epochs which are long past'?

In 1938 Dr. Hans Heinsheimer, the former young director of the Vienna Universal Edition and the successor of Emil Hertzka, had come to New York. He worked there for the English firm Boosey and Hawkes, till in 1947 Schirmer made him a director. This appointment was not unimportant for Schoenberg's works, as Heinsheimer sought to maintain the old Viennese connections.

Trudi Greissle's illness was a heavy burden at the end of the year. It led to the death of Schoenberg's daughter before Christmas.

Friends of Schoenberg's from his last years in Berlin were living in Israel. The medical doctor Georg Wolfsohn, whose patient Schoenberg had been, had settled in Tel Aviv. His daughter was married to Dr. Peter Gradenwitz, who had studied musicology in Berlin and composition with Josef Rufer. He founded the Israeli Music Publications in Tel Aviv. He corresponded with Schoenberg about performances of his works in Israel and about publishing more recent works. Schoenberg told him on 10 January 1948 about the *Survivor from Warsaw*. He was worried about the 'fearful battles, which we all follow with great tension and anxiety . . . we believe firmly in victory'.

For the second International Music Festival in Vienna Dr. Egon Seefehlner, as General Secretary of the Concerthouse Society, had asked Schoenberg for permission to give a first performance of one of his works. Schoenberg hesitated, as he says in his answering letter of 10 January 1948 that he still believed that in Vienna works of art were judged more from racial than artistic points of view. 'Otherwise it would have been necessary immediately after the war to recompense me for the neglect of my works which has lasted many years'. However, he recommended Seefehlner to engage René Leibowitz as interpreter of his works; Leibowitz would also be able to make suggestions for the programmes. 'Don't say', the letter ends, 'that it would be better for me to forget the bad things which people have done to me. But it has been my fate that I have always had to do what has made me seem worse in the eyes of my colleagues, if I wanted to preserve my independence and fulfil my task'. One can see how little the humiliations of Schoenberg's years of exile had lessened his self-consciousness and his claim to be a leading spirit of the times. Also age and his long corporeal sufferings had made him distrustful. If he did not hear from a friend for a long time he thought that he had been forgotten or neglected. On 15 January 1948 (as well as the commentaries of 'Ode to Napoleon' mentioned above) he gave Rufer and me permission to print articles of his in 'Stimmen'. He said he would like to send us food, but he could not do enough even for his son Görgi and his sister Ottilie. But it is moving to read how much this old man, who was completely insecure materially, thought about the living conditions of his friends; none of them had ever dreamed of asking him for such gifts.

Much of Schoenberg's correspondence, especially within the family, was taken over by Gertrud Schoenberg. On 14 January 1948 she wrote to her sister-in-law Otti about the tragic death of

Trudi Greissle. She enclosed pictures of the children and asked for confirmation of the receipt of a parcel. She said that Arnold wanted to go to New Zealand, but she was against it. His health was better since the intervention of a doctor; he was not taking any insulin or any drugs any more. She herself had become old and shabby – work makes one disgraceful. Apart from that she had a litter of four Cocker spaniels.

The bookseller Dr. Alfred Rosenzweig wrote on 6 February from London about a Schoenberg autograph which his daughter had brought to him. It was the arrangement of the chorale 'Allein Gott in der Höh sei Ehr' for alto, violin, cello and piano. It had been written for a Christmas concert for the family in the house at Mödling, in which Schoenberg himself played the cello. Schoenberg entrusted Rosenzweig in the following spring to hold an auction in Zurich of the short scores of the operas *Glückliche Hand* and *Von heute auf morgen*. Neither of them should be sold for less than 1000 dollars.

Schoenberg was very interested in the programmes of the 'Musica Viva' concerts, which the composer Karl Amadeus Hartmann had founded in Munich. The list of twenty-five composers with perhaps equally as many ways of creating new music was astonishing, he wrote on 6 March: 'And that's without including Webern and Berg, or Zillig, Apostel and Einem, all Austrians except Zillig'. He did not know whether he would be able to send the score and parts of the String Trio as it was not published yet.

On 15 March he warmly thanked Leibowitz for an article which he had written to defend Schoenberg against the followers of Stravinsky. This contains the important remark that he found Stravinsky's present-day attitude a dignified one. Zillig wrote from Frankfurt that he had conducted the Second Chamber Symphony on the Berlin Radio and was now working (22 April) on the 'madly difficult piano part' of the Suite opus 29. He found the 'Ode' marvellous; its tone-row reminded him very much of the Suite.

After a long time Stiedry wrote again. He had been engaged to conduct in Los Angeles and asked Schoenberg about an apartment there. Visits by friends were always very welcome in Brentwood Park. The Schoenbergs went out very rarely. He liked walking in the beautiful garden, was happy to look at the flowering shrubs, and played with the dogs or the cat. Gertrud had to do housework the whole day, and in addition drove the children to school in the car. For two and a half years, she wrote in a letter to her sister-in-law Ottilie, she and Arnold had not been to the cinema or a concert. This means since the autumn of 1945!

It was friends in Los Angeles itself who kept the Master informed about many things and cultural events in the world. In the autumn of 1947 the first German edition of Thomas Mann's *Dr. Faustus* appeared. Schoenberg knew that the poet had been working for years on a book which included musical subjects. But the rumour did not reach him until 1948 that Mann's new book was connected with himself. When Rufer asked him about *Dr. Faustus* on 17 April, Schoenberg's relations with Thomas Mann were still fairly friendly. Only Alma Werfel had sown the seeds of discord, perhaps without knowing it and thinking of its consequences, when she suggested that Schoenberg should take up a position against Thomas Mann's *Dr. Faustus*. On 25 May Schoenberg answered Rufer's long letter. He first of all calmed the fears of his friend about political changes and the threatening Russian blockade of Berlin. He said that those who live in music had no place in politics and must regard them as something essentially alien. He answered Rufer's question about his new tonal compositions, saying that in all composers since Bach a yearning for the contrapuntal style occasionally wells up, whereupon they set to writing fugues and the like. 'I myself often felt an upsurge of desire for tonality, and then I have to yield to the urge. After all composing means obeying an inner urge.' And between the remarks about politics and tonality is the paragraph: 'I didn't read *Dr. Faustus* myself, owing to my nervous eye affliction. But from my wife and also from other quarters I heard that he had attributed my twelve-note method to his hero, without mentioning my name. I drew his attention to the fact that historians might make use of this in order to do me an injustice. After prolonged reluctance he declared himself prepared to insert, in all subsequent copies in all languages, a statement concerning my being the originator of this method. Whether this has been done I don't know.

The affair grew into a battle. Schoenberg carried it on bitterly. Thomas Mann persevered in a defensive attitude which irritated the angry Schoenberg even more. The quarrel began in February 1948. Schoenberg sent the poet a text which was supposed to be written by an historian, Hugo Triebsamen. Relying on an 'Encyclopaedia Americana' of 1988 (!) he confirmed that Thomas Mann was really a musician and had invented the twelve-tone technique. Going over to literature later, he had passed over the fact in silence that a composer called Schoenberg had claimed the discovery for himself. However, in the novel *Dr. Faustus* he had again claimed his spiritual and musical property (see appendix). Mann hastened to answer on 17 February. He said that the curious document, a sign of the zealousness of Schoenberg's followers, was gripping and comic at the same time. Anybody who had merely taken his book in his hand knew who had invented the twelve-tone technique, and Schoenberg's historical importance would not be lessened by the novel. What was this document indeed, a letter or an article? He himself did not feel entirely free of guilt. Schoenberg's explanation came much later. On 25 November he sent the poet a letter of reconciliation in which he explained that the text of 1988 was his own invention: 'My synthetic Hugo Triebsamen, whom I concocted from Hugo Riemann and Dr. Rubsamen . . .' was only meant to make Thomas Mann conscious of the fact that the novel represented a danger to him, Schoenberg.

Schoenberg had so much work in the summer, and so much illness, that the *Faustus* affair was shelved for months. In June he wrote new choral arrangements of three folk songs of the fifteenth and sixteenth centuries, which he had already arranged for voice and piano in 1929; 'Es gingen zwei Gespielen gut' on the 24th, 'Der Mai tritt ein mit Freuden' and 'Mein Herz in steten Treuen' on the 26th. This time these were unaccompanied movements in four parts; they were given the opus number 49. Earlier sketches for a string quartet were not carried on further.

On 12 July the family drove to Santa Barbara, two hours from Los Angeles on the Pacific Coast. The Music Academy of the West had invited Schoenberg to give lessons there. Although he felt very ill, he accepted the commission, which was well paid with the sum of 1200 dollars and free lodging for himself, Gertrud and the two boys. In spite of swollen feet, giddiness and lack of breath, he carried out his duties, had a great success with students and teachers and gained many friends, he wrote to Görgi on 8 September.

He had to pay dearly for his efforts.

'*From 24 August till now I have been under treatment,*'
he wrote in the same letter to his son.

'*I had six kilos of water in me, and through injections and the stomach and intestinal trouble which followed, through digitalis and a number of other medicines, I took off 8 kilos and now I only weigh 48 kilos altogether. But the result of all these examinations and treatments is very favourable. I had heart trouble and people were afraid of a heart attack. But my heart is good and even my asthma has improved. I have been in my bedroom for more than ten days and have mostly been in bed. I am not allowed to climb stairs.'*

Signs of life came from almost forgotten relations or people who wanted information about members of the family. In May a Monsignore Antonio Bassetti-Sani wrote from Florence enquiring about a Vladimir Schoenberg. Schoenberg replied on 28 May: Samuel Schoenberg had only two sons and a brother Ignaz. The latter's only son, Arthur, died, probably aged about seventy, in the Theresienstadt concentration camp.

Relations on Schoenberg's mother's side called Waitzner had lived in Budapest. A Waitzner grand-daughter called Berend married a Hungarian police officer, Nikolaus Vamos, nephew of the Hollywood film king Adolf Zukor. In May 1948 they wanted to emigrate and asked for affidavits; some months later they gave up these plans.

His earliest reminiscences were awakened by a letter from Rio de Janeiro. In February 1947 Schoenberg's cousin Malva Bodanzky had written a long letter from there. She said that she and her sons were getting on well in Brazil. She possessed two letters which Schoenberg had written to her when he was about sixteen. They were interesting because he – then in love with his young cousin – wrote about his formative years, his job in the bank and his compositions.

Schoenberg was not able to reply until 1 October 1948; he had lost the address. Now he was seventy-four and was glad to remember his youth. As his wife was not jealous, but was curious to read the letters which he had written to Malva fifty-eight years before, he asked her to send him the letters.

Contact was even made again with an old acquaintance from the Mödling Workers' Choral Society. This was the eighty-two-year-old Ferdinand Buchberger, a Social Democrat Mayor and local official in Mödling, who thanked Schoenberg for the receipt of a parcel on 28 June 1948. He had intervened in vain for Görgi at a critical time. Of their common acquaintances and members of the Choral Society of fifty years ago, about whom Schoenberg had enquired, none were alive any more.

In New York Mitropoulos gave a repeat performance of the Five Orchestral Pieces. The day after the concert, on 22 October, Henry Cowell wrote that he had been fascinated by the performance. John Cage had sat next to him and had been entranced. Artur Schnabel had also liked the work very much; they had all congratulated Mitropoulos afterwards. Schoenberg thanked Cowell on 5 November for his letter and for sending him the criticisms, among which the favourable one by Olin Downes had surprised him. It seemed that he had to celebrate a come-back in New York. In Los Angeles Alfred Wallenstein had not played one piece of his, although Wallenstein had been there for six years.

On the same day Schoenberg wrote to Leibowitz and Stiedry, who had sent photos and an extract from a paper. He said to Stiedry that he was now helped in the preparation of letters by Richard Hoffmann from New Zealand. In addition he had got a dictaphone. He saved himself work by this, but he made many mistakes in speaking into it. Leibowitz, who wanted to perform new works of his, was given a negative answer. Neither the symphony which he had begun many years ago nor *Jacob's Ladder* or *Moses and Aaron* had a chance of being finished. If his eyes allowed him to write he must finish the counterpoint book.

In October 1948 the *Saturday Review of Literature* asked Schoenberg for information about the *Dr. Faustus* affair. He sent the newspaper a violent attack on Mann. He said that Mann had purloined his cultural property without asking him about it. The dedication which Mann had written for him in the book 'To Arnold Schoenberg, the real owner', shows that the character in the novel, Adrian Leverkühn, was a portrait of himself. Leverkühn is described as mentally ill; Schoenberg himself, however, had reached the age of seventy-four without suffering from the paralysis from which this mental illness stems. This was an insult to himself. He had not read the book, but Alma Werfel had discovered the misuse of his property and had told Mann about it. After some pressure the poet had added an explanation to the book, which, however, committed a further crime against himself. There Mann spoke of '*a* contemporary composer and theoretician'; in two or three decades one would know who was the contemporary of whom.

Mann answered in astonishment and in grief. He complained that Schoenberg only knew his book through intermediaries. It was not true that he, Mann, had only added the note which had been demanded to the novel under pressure. *Dr. Faustus* could be called a Nietzsche novel rather than a Schoenberg novel, because the mental tragedy and the history of illness of the philosopher was similar to it. Although Mann himself was not suffering from paralysis, the hero of the book did have some characteristics of himself. Instead of regarding the book as a piece of literature, and a proof of Schoenberg's influence on modern music culture, Schoenberg had regarded it as theft and insult. 'It is a painful drama to see how an important man, in an all too understandable over-irritation because of a life which has wavered between adoration and neglect, almost wilfully burrows into ideas of persecution and theft and loses himself in poisonous quarrels. May he rise above bitterness and mistrust and find peace in the secure consciousness of his greatness and fame!'

Both articles appeared on 1 January 1949 in the *Saturday Review of Literature*. Many people who honoured both the poet and the composer were subjected to a serious conflict of conscience by this quarrel. It was easy to see where right and wrong lay on both sides and in what proportion. Schoenberg, mistrustful by nature and strengthened in this disposition by a hard life, was certainly not only annoyed by his apparent identification with Adrian Leverkühn, the fictitious inventor of his twelve-note technique. If he had known the book properly other motifs too would have been painful for him, especially the pact with the devil which Leverkühn concluded in his paralytic madness. A chief reason for Schoenberg's anger was the fact that Thomas Mann's adviser on questions of modern music had been Dr. Theodor Wiesengrund-Adorno, who was also living in Los Angeles. Schoenberg had known Adorno since the twenties. He knew how much this Frankfurt philosopher and pupil of Alban Berg had been occupied with his works. The analyses of the Serenade opus 24, the Wind Quintet and other works of Schoenberg were famous and left nothing to wish for eager disciples. However, the relations between the Master and his philosophically trained advocate had always been cold. Even in their exile in California there were no friendly relations, and indeed at meetings in houses of common friends there were battles of words between them. Wiesengrund-Adorno, who in exile had given up the German-Jewish name of his father and adopted the Italian one of his Corsican mother, irritated Schoenberg, the admirer of the clear prose of Karl Kraus, by a language which obscured simple statements of fact with complicated formulations. So the collaboration of Thomas Mann and Adorno had a disquieting effect on him; the philosophical and dialectical reproduction of his own ideas in passages of *Dr. Faustus* which he knew verbally contradicted his feeling for language. So his angry reactions against the book were not purely objective but were also strongly personal. This explains and excuses his vacillating position as regards the author.

The latter himself felt his attitude in preparing and the lengthy writing of the novel a discordant one. He knew about the tension between Schoenberg and Adorno, and if he had asked for advice from 'the top', i.e. from Schoenberg himself, he could not fail to understand the risk in the creation of a figure like that of the paralytic German composer. As Leverkühn was given the first name of Adrian, reminiscent of the first names of the Viennese school, Arnold, Anton and Alban, this appeared to justify Schoenberg's suspicion that it was really he himself who was portrayed. But in one point the author showed himself sensible; he never did anything to increase the conflict and tried to do everything in his power to get it out of the way.

In December there was a long and important correspondence with the *Times* critic Olin Downes in New York. This was about the difference of opinion about Mahler mentioned above, and also concerned the favourable account of Schoenberg's Five Orchestral Pieces which Downes had given. To Downes's question, what Schoenberg thought about composers writing criticism, the Master answered on 21 December 1948:

'*I think that they are in the first instance fighters for their own musical ideas. Their ideas of other composers are their enemies. You cannot restrict a fighter. His blows are correct when they hit hard and only then is he fair. Thus I do not resent what Schumann said about Wagner or Hugo Wolf about Brahms. But I resent what Hanslick said against Wagner and Bruckner. Wagner, Wolf, Mahler and Strauss fought for life or death for their ideas. – But you fight only for principles or rather for the application of principles.*'

An important autobiographical confession was written in the year which was now reaching its end: 'On revient toujours'. It has often been quoted since its publication in the Berlin 'Stimmen' in 1949. The final idea presents the spiritual world of the mature Schoenberg: 'A longing to return to the older style was always vigorous in me; and from time to time I had to yield to that urge. This is how and why I sometimes write tonal music. To me stylistic differences of this nature are not of special importance. I do not know which of my compositions are better; I like them all, because I liked them when I wrote them.'

Now the world was increasingly waking up to Schoenberg's works. In Germany his friends, especially Rosbaud, Zillig, Rufer and myself were arranging performances of his works, not only the old ones like the Orchestral Pieces and *Erwartung*, but also new ones like the Piano Concerto and the 'Ode to Napoleon'. When Dr. Wolfgang Steinecke started the International Summer School for Modern Music in Darmstadt in the summer of 1946, it was completely dominated by Hindemith and Stravinsky. In 1947 in the same summer school performances of the Stefan George Lieder and the Second String Quartet as well as a long lecture on Schoenberg gave the young people present an experience of Schoenberg's world of sound. Then there was a change of cultural atmosphere. In 1948 René Leibowitz and Peter Stadlen were among the teachers at Schloss Kranichstein near Darmstadt. They gave the first performance of Schoenberg's Piano Concerto. Leibowitz conducted the Second Chamber Symphony; Stadlen and the Berlin pianist Helmut Roloff played Schoenberg's piano music. In lectures on the twelve-tone method Leibowitz gave the young composers the foundations of dodecaphony. In 1949 the spreading of the influence of Schoenberg's works continued. In Paris Leibowitz and Max Deutsch rivalled each other in advocacy and live performance of his compositions. Deutsch had already told Schoenberg at the end of December 1948 about his performance of *Pierrot Lunaire* in Geneva. In his answer of 3 January 1949 he showed that he was enthusiastic that the glacial ice on the Lake of Geneva had been broken; he knew that the great conductor Ernest Ansermet had become a powerful enemy of atonality and twelve-tone music and had not conducted any of Schoenberg's works for years.

Paul Hindemith too, who taught at Yale University and was much performed in America, had turned away from Schoenberg, both in his music and in his theories. He was rearranging his own youthful and inspired works, like the 'Marienleben' on poems of Rilke, so that dissonances and free harmonic progressions were removed to a considerable extent. Schoenberg regarded these corrections with displeasure. He noted on 17 January 1949: 'Is this the New Look? No, the clothes get longer and longer and soon they will come down to the ground again; no, it is the New Antiquated, or, as P.H. would say, the Antiquated New Look. The "Marienleben" has been put on anew. Earlier, so P.H. confesses, it was only a demonstration of power. Something had to be overcome, and anyone who perhaps believes that this could be the result of inspiration was completely wrong. But today there is no shortage of material any more.' In a letter to the chemistry professor G. F. Stegmann at the University of Stellenbosch near

Cape Town in South Africa Schoenberg confirms with pleasure that his twelve-tone technique has spread. Apart from this he does not find it so bad to imitate Stravinsky, Bartók or Hindemith, but tends to oppose the instruction given by 'a woman of Russian-French descent, who is a reactionary and has had much influence on many composers'. Tactfully he does not give the name. It was the advocate of Stravinsky, who teaches in Paris and Fontainebleau, Nadia Boulanger.

Schoenberg corresponded with the viola player Eugen Lehner, who formerly had been a member of the Kolisch Quartet and was now a member of the Boston Symphony Orchestra, about the gramophone recordings of his quartets. In America the small firm of 'Dial' had made the recordings with Kolisch and his colleagues, and a new firm called 'Alco' was planning to take these over. In Schoenberg's letter of 10 February 1949 it is interesting that he finds his first quartet far the most mature and better played than the second.

An invitation had come from Darmstadt to take part in the summer school of 1949 as a teacher. Schoenberg wanted to very much, but in a letter sent to René Leibowitz on 15 March he doubted whether his health would permit it.

Schoenberg heard from the London bookseller Rosenthal about the auction of manuscripts in Zurich: '*Die Glückliche Hand* raised 5350 Swiss francs, which is about 1300 dollars, and it was bought by an American institution. I arranged an interesting event before the auction. Dr. Curjel was kind enough to speak about the manuscripts (he remembers with great pleasure the time when he knew you in Berlin) and I will send you a photograph which was taken while we were talking about your manuscript,' Rosenthal wrote in a letter of 28 February.

The Dominican College in San Rafael asked Schoenberg to give a lecture; he had hoped to go there, but had to give up the journey. This also meant that he missed a planned excursion to Oakland, where Darius Milhaud and his wife Madeleine had invited him and Gertrud.

On 7 February Zillig wrote: 'The music week in Frankfurt is now arranged and also the festival concert of your works; it is on Monday 27 June in Frankfurt and on the 26th in Darmstadt, and will include the Five Orchestral Pieces, the "Song of the Wood Dove", the Violin Concerto with Tibor Varga, a marvellous Hungarian violinist who lives in London, and the Variations opus 31.

After a long interruption Schoenberg's musical inspiration burst out again almost explosively in March 1949. Between the 3rd and the 22nd of this month he wrote the 'Phantasy' for violin and piano opus 47, on the 20th he finished 'Dreimal tausend Jahre' for mixed chorus unaccompanied on a text of Dagobert D. Runes, and between the 9th and the 15th he sketched out the first ideas of a mixed chorus with orchestral accompaniment on his own text, 'Israel exists again'. His musical idea preceded the first sketch of the text, written on 8 June, by about three months; the composition, on which he worked again on 18 May, remained unfinished.

At the end of February 1949 I travelled to the United States for two months as a guest of the American Government. Schoenberg had heard that I was in New York and wrote on 15 March in his impulsive way:

> '*It's a colossal surprise that you are in New York. Why don't you write to me? Is your wife with you? I imagine that you are the same Stuckenschmidt, and not someone else of the same name who was in my classes and visited us so often.*
>
> *How can you doubt that I would be very glad to see you? Let us hear from you and write to me when you are coming. I can't show you much here – I am a bit isolated and live in a very retired manner. But it will be a great pleasure to see you and Margot here. With warm greetings, your* Arnold Schoenberg.'

On 9 April we met in Brentwood Park. I had had lunch with Thomas Mann at San Remo Drive in Pacific Palisades, a few kilometres from Schoenberg's house. 'Will you see Schoenberg?' the writer asked. I replied that I had been invited to coffee in Brentwood Park immediately afterwards. Thomas Mann advised me not to tell Schoenberg where I had had lunch; he would take it badly. The advice was good. Arnold and Gertrud Schoenberg greeted me warmly. The *Faustus* affair was not mentioned. Schoenberg was much more interested in what his guest from Germany had to tell him. He had altered terribly in sixteen years, was thin to the bones and had deep furrows in his fine prophet's head. But his spirit and his temperament had remained the same. At this first short meeting, which only lasted an hour, he did not speak about his own work. As I was able to stay for a week in Los Angeles, I asked if I could telephone in order to arrange a longer visit. This took place four days later on 13 April. George and Böske Antheil, with whom I was staying, were invited together with me to supper. It was a small circle; only Gertrud's mother, the old Mrs. Kolisch was there. The children, of whom Nuria had grown into a pretty seventeen-year-old girl, said good-night after supper. On the question of *Moses and Aaron* Schoenberg answered that he did not think that he would be able to finish the opera now. When I told him that the work was awaited eagerly by some German opera houses for performance he gave a definite answer: 'It cannot be performed. In the blood sacrifice scene four naked girls are embraced by four priests and are stabbed by them in a moment of the highest passion. How can that be shown on a stage?' He said also that in the distant future the electronically produced tones and sounds could make the performance of this powerful unfinished work possible.

The great old man spoke with emotion and thankfulness about his friends in Europe who had remained faithful to him in spite of all difficulties during all these years. He wanted to know if American music and books could be bought in Germany. He gave me as a gift all his works which had been published since 1933. In addition he gave me his copies of Joseph Schillinger's *The Mathematical Basis of the Arts* and Nicolas Slonimsky's *Thesaurus Of Scales and Melodic Patterns*, a collection of new kinds of scales. About Schillinger's book, an important work of research into technological analysis of the arts, he said: 'I don't understand it entirely, for it contains too much mathematics. But there is something right in it.' George Antheil, who had been a fanatical admirer of Stravinsky's in his youth, was deeply impressed by his visit to Schoenberg. From that evening onwards he turned all his attention to the man whose music he had previously rejected as abstract and dry.

Between these two visits I had a surprise, when Stravinsky asked me to his house on North Wetherley Drive. Among the first questions which the composer put to me was: 'Have you seen Schoenberg?' When I replied that I had Stravinsky said how sorry he was not to see the great old man more often. They were almost neighbours, but only occasionally had short meetings in a third place. He admired Schoenberg; perhaps the difficulties between them came less from Schoenberg and Stravinsky themselves than 'from the ladies.'

On 12 April Schoenberg wrote Rudolf Kolisch a letter about American musical life and the market which the imitators of Stravinsky, Hindemith and Bartók as well as Boulanger's pupils wanted to conquer. He said that the tendency was to suppress European influences in America and to take American music to

Europe. The public was more inclined to accept his music; the rough illiterate stuff of the bad composers would teach the public to feel that there was something different in his own music. A week before he had finished a piece for 'Violin solo with piano accompaniment'; Richard Hoffmann and Leonard Stein had played it already, it was apparently difficult to play but sounded very good.

The piece he mentioned is the 'Phantasy' opus 47, finished on 22 March (three weeks before the letter to Kolisch). After Adolf Koldofsky, who had commissioned it and to whom it is dedicated, Tibor Varga was the first to play it in Europe. 'In order to write this piece entirely in the form of a solo work for violin, I first of all wrote the whole violin part and then added the piano accompaniment', the composer wrote on 5 February 1951 to Rufer. And as regards the form: 'I wanted to write a piece, the unhindered flow of which cannot be derived from any kind of formal theories.'

Leibowitz praises the very high concentration and intensity of expression of this piece, which is only 166 bars long, and mentions the quite different material in the two instrumental parts. 'The fact that each part consists entirely of segments of the row which are peculiar to it, and at the same time one part compliments the other serially all the time; this was one of the most important steps forward in modern harmony, the further consequences of which open up entirely new paths to us.' (In the special number of 'Stimmen' for Schoenberg's seventy-fifth birthday).

Glenn Gould, as the piano partner of Israel Baker, played the 'Phnatasy' for the Columbia complete recording of Schoenberg's works, says that no theme is introduced and repeated by the piano. Inspired by the poetic individuality of the piece, which he calls a long, rhapsodic speech for solo violin, Gould speaks of the waltz scene with its nocturnal character illuminated by lanterns, of the choral-like episode which follows it and of the sardonic stretta which exposes Schoenberg's expressionistic credo. The title of this opus 47, 'Phantasy for violin with piano accompaniment', expresses Schoenberg's method of procedure and also the relative hierarchy of the instruments.

The Russian sculptor Alexander Archipenko, who had lived for decades in New York, was involved in an intrigue in 1949 and among others asked Schoenberg for support, which the latter promised him.

In Palermo the 23rd Music Festival of the International Society for Contemporary Music was attended by many friends and followers of the Viennese school. On the 24th, the day after the performance, Marya Freund wrote about the enthusiasm aroused by *Pierrot Lunaire*. Luigi Dallapiccola, Mario Peragallo, Karl Amadeus Hartmann, Josef Rufer and many others sent greetings. Among Schoenberg's pupils Eisler was represented by the Quintet, dedicated to Schoenberg and written for the *Pierrot* ensemble, 'fourteen ways of describing the rain', and Hans Erich Apostel by a string quartet.

Schoenberg made new sketches for the chorus 'Israel exists again' on 18 May. But he did not feel able to accept the invitation to the summer school in Darmstadt. The doctors had certainly said that his condition was not dangerous. But subjectively he felt ill, was suffering from asthma, giddiness and stomach troubles. He was very sad not to come, he wrote finally to Rufer.

Work and correspondence increased. In Berlin Dr. David wanted information about the Organ Variations, and in New York Amadeo de Filippi wanted to know about the Satires for chorus and other works. In addition requests came from many sides on the occasion of his approaching seventy-fifth birthday to write articles for papers and to send words of greeting for performances, such as those on the Frankfurt Hessian Radio, which put on festival concerts of Schoenberg's works at the end of June. His pictures were even remembered. Dr. Ludwig Grote in Munich, later General Director of the German National Museum in Nuremberg, was planning to show them in a celebratory exhibition of the 'Blaue Reiter'. Schoenberg was pleased about this, but was not able to send any pictures because of the high costs and the risk of loss.

Again, and for the last time, he took up work on 'Israel exists again'; the text of the musical fragment was written between 8 and 10 June 1949.

In April the young London writer on music Hans Keller had written that Oskar Adler, with whom he studied viola, was longing for a sign of life. Finally on 2 July Schoenberg found the time to write to the friend of his youth. He envied the activity of this man of the same age, who was still playing quartets. Had Adler heard his latest works? Adler replied in detail, writing about common friends such as Erwin Stein, Schoenberg's nephew Hans Nachod, D. J. Bach, with whom he had been interned, Arnold Rosé and the cellist Buchsbaum, with both of whom he had recently made music, Etta Werndorff, who wanted to come from Pasadena to London, Dr. Prager, the former treasurer of Schoenberg's Society in Vienna, and Erwin Ratz, who sent him articles from Vienna from time to time.

In the Thomas Mann affair he was on Schoenberg's side: 'Your work stands and works, and your music perpetually says much more than anything, clever or stupid, which may be said or written about it.'

In the summer of 1949 Schoenberg's correspondence with Josef Rufer in Berlin increased. Rufer had mentioned to Schoenberg his plan of writing a book about twelve-tone composition. Schoenberg was extraordinarily interested in this and contributed to the substance of the work in many letters; he did not live to see the publication of Rufer's book.

'*Do not call it twelve-tone Theory, call it Composition with twelve Tones. Personally it is on the word composition that I place the emphasis. Unfortunately most would-be followers of this method do something removed from the idea of writing music.*'

He was agreeable for Rufer to use Schoenberg's lecture which he had already given on twelve-tone music as a basis for the book, but only in quotations, as the lecture was to be printed in English in his book *Style and Idea*. He found Rufer's idea of basing the book mainly on analyses excellent. But there must not be only twelve-tone analyses! 'How one can use the series for the production of basic phrases and in what way: I think that in my opinion the key note should be laid on that.' And then follows a postscript:

'*Apparently Rodzinsky performed my Violin Concerto in Venice. But he was warned beforehand to expect to have eggs and tomatoes thrown at him. Instead of this it was received enthusiastically with eight recalls.*'

The Darmstadt Summer School, in which Schoenberg had wanted to take part, was influenced by his works and his ideas in spite of his absence. For the first time the school was combined with a week of modern music put on by the Hessian Radio in Frankfurt on Main. Here Schoenberg's Organ Variations were played by Michael Schneider, the String Trio by the Walden String Quartet, the Fourth String Quartet by the Amsterdam Quartet with the cellist Maurits Frank and the Violin Concerto by Tibor Varga; all these were first performances in Germany. René Leibowitz ran a course on twelve-tone composition, which was based entirely on Schoenberg's works, while at the same time Josef Rufer spoke on the connection of Schoenberg with the Viennese classical tradition, especially with Beethoven and

Brahms. The lectures and performances, which were attended by a large international audience, took place for the first time in the Seminar Marienhöhe. On 23 June the German section of the ISCM, which had been out of action since the Nazi period, was resuscitated.

Schoenberg reacted with great pleasure to the news that the Austrian Society of Dramatists and Composers had made him an honorary member, – a late recompense for the wrong which the AKM had done him in 1935 by refusing his application for membership. In his answer of 4 July 1949, he says that he has in intensity and perhaps even in number friends in Vienna so many as to exceed the number and power of his opponents. One of these friends was Hanns Jelinek, who sent him the first volume of his *Twelve-Tone Work* on 20 July, and added: 'If I can't call myself a pupil of yours – the three months in the Schwarzwald School in 1918 don't give me the right to do this – you were certainly my model and teacher.' On the prospectus of the Institute for Peace and International Understanding, which had also been formed in Vienna, Schoenberg noted down his probable answer to a question about his musical education.

Letters to the family were now mainly written by Gertrud. On her birthday, 9 July, she wrote to her sister-in-law Otti that Arnold's health was so uncertain that one was worried about him all the time.

On 21 July Schoenberg dictated to his nephew and assistant Richard Hoffmann on the machine a long letter to Stiedry There too he complains about his health, and says he had been waiting five years for it to improve. He was annoyed about the English translation of *Pierrot*, which a Herr Beier had taken over completely from a previous translator Wachtel, which caused Schoenberg embarrassment. The Frankfurt Festival Concerts seem to have been very successful, but the critics were incredibly luke-warm. He suspected an American intrigue behind this.

On 1 August he set a curious text as a four-part canon; who can it be addressed to, if perhaps not to Schoenberg himself? 'Centre of gravity of its own solar system circled by shining satellites – so thy life appears to thy admirer'. It is his last dated composition in the strict canonic style, fifteen bars in pure C major with a brilliant, Meistersinger-like final cadence.

At the Music Festival at the Berkshire Center in Tanglewood, which had been found by Kussewitzky and lasted the whole summer, the young Juilliard String Quartet played Schoenberg's

Second and Fourth Quartets on 21 August. The performances were received with enthusiasm. Schoenberg was also very pleased with the recording of the Second Chamber Symphony, which Bernhard Herrmann had conducted in New York for Columbia. He congratulated the conductor, who later became a film composer in Hollywood, on the high quality of the performance in a letter of 30 August. He only felt that the first movement was too slow, as it had been under Stiedry also.

Gertrud was worried about Schoenberg. She told her sister-in-law Ottilie on 23 August that his seventy-fifth birthday was giving him a lot of extra work, as everybody wanted to celebrate it at his own expense. Tomorrow he had to have an X-ray. His great happiness was Ronny's success as a young tennis champion. Nuria was intelligent, full of humour and pretty. There were sometimes tensions with Mama Kolisch.

Now came September, and with it the flood of letters, gifts and honours for the seventy-fifth birthday on the 13th. Luigi Dallapiccola sent a letter full of admiration from Florence, and from Cambridge in England Professor Edward Dent sent a detailed report, telling Schoenberg about Karl Rankl, Hermann and Gustl Scherchen, Roberto Gerhard, Egon Wellesz, O. E. Deutsch and Paul Hirsch. The natural scientist and psychologist Professor Dr. Kurt Wilde in Göttingen declared in a letter of homage that he had been an admirer of Schoenberg since he was eighteen, and found him one of the five or six greatest men.

Two magazines published special numbers exclusively dedicated to Schoenberg. The Berlin 'Stimmen' opened the number with the autobiographical reminiscences which Schoenberg entitled 'On Revient Toujours'. Roger Sessions wrote about his work in America. The two editors, Josef Rufer and I, wrote long articles. René Leibowitz wrote a short piece about the literary harvest of earlier birthdays and a commentary on the violin 'Phantasy'. Peter Gradenwitz discussed Oriental parallels to the twelve-tone technique. Alfred Keller, Margot Hinnenberg-Lefèbre, Fritz Stiedry and Winfried Zillig wrote about personal meetings with Schoenberg, work at rehearsals and anecdotes. Short homages to Schoenberg were contributed by Boris Blacher, Dallapiccola, Paul Dessau, Werner Egk, Wolfgang Fortner and Karl Amadeus Hartmann. The volume also contained advertisements from two New York publishers, who had printed Schoenberg's latest works; Edward B. Marks had published the three choral arrangements of German folk songs, and Bomart Music

Publications had published 'Kol Nidre', the Trio, the *Survivor from Warsaw* and the three songs on poems of Jacob Haringer which Schoenberg had written in 1933.

The other magazine was published in Sydney. It was called 'The Canon, Australian Journal of Music'. The special number, No. 2 of its third volume, began with a letter of homage from its associate editor Wolfgang Wagner to Schoenberg. The idea of a jubilee number came from Schoenberg's American pupil Dika Newlin; she wrote about the violin fantasy herself, while Leibowitz discussed the late tonal works. Schoenberg's own lecture on Gustav Mahler was the first of the articles. Otto Klemperer wrote about him as a teacher, composer and arranger, Eduard Steuermann about Heart and Mind, Paul A. Pisk about Schoenberg's influence on his youth, Alma Maria Mahler-Werfel about her friendship with him. Many British and Australian musicians honoured Schoenberg. The most original contribution came from Rudolf Kolisch. It was called 'Schoenberg's Mission, a Birthday Homage in Twelve Tones' and consisted of five twelve-line verses in hexameters. Each line began with one note of the twelve-tone row of the 3rd Quartet. The first verse runs:

> *Gestern nur war's; da flossen die Töne des Bach's noch*
> *Eingebettet ins Ufer der Tonalität.*
> *DISsonanzen dann stürmten; Du nutztest sie mutig*
> *Aufzureissen den Damm, der hemmte die Fülle*
> *Chromatischen Stromes. Ihn nun hast Du gegliedert,*
> *Freiheit erobernd vom Zwange, Grosse und neue*
> *GEStalten hast Du geschaffen, leuchtende Zeichen.*
> *Haben sie's gleich erkannt und sind sie dankbar gefolget?*
> *Beängstigt wagen sie nicht den Sprung in die Tiefe*
> *DES chromatischen Raumes den gleich jenem krummen*
> *AStronomisch uns öffnet die neue Erkenntnis.*
> *Du aber hast uns gegeben die wahre Dodekaphonie.*

(The notes in English which form the series are: G–E–D sharp–A–C–F–G flat–B–B flat–D flat–A flat–D.)

Only yesterday the sounds of Bach were flowing,
still embedded in the banks of tonality.
Then dissonances stormed; fearlessly you wielded them
to tear open the dam that stopped the full flow
Of the chromatic stream. You have channelled it,
changing constraint into freedom.

You have created new forms, blazing signs.
Did they perceive them at once and did they gratefully follow?
Frightened, they dare not leap into the abyss
of chromatic space which opens, like a parabola,
a new astronomical perception.
Yet you have given us the true Dodecaphony.

On the birthday itself Adolf Koldofsky and Leonard Stein gave the première of the 'Phantasy' opus 47, for which Schoenberg had spoken a commentary on the radio. Slightly later Eduard Steuermann's recording of all Schoenberg's piano pieces arrived. He was worried about mistakes in the performance. Schoenberg calmed him down; 'There is no absolute purity in this world: pure water contains infusoria. But I am certain that you can play music so convincingly that it evokes the impression of purity, artistic purity, and after all that's what matters'.

He was given the freedom of the city of Vienna. When the letters of citizenship were handed over by the Austrian Consul General Harold Byrns conducted the 1st Chamber Symphony with his excellent soloists. Schoenberg thanked the Mayor of Vienna on 5 October, and expressed the wish again to be able to enter the city which he had always loved so much. It was beyond human powers to answer all the individual congratulations. Schoenberg again solved this problem by a photographically copied manuscript letter of 16 September with the title 'To gain recognition only after one's death – !'. He knew, he said in this human document, that he could not count on living to see full and sympathetic understanding of his work. He quoted his aphorism of 1912: 'The second half of this century will spoil by overestimation whatever the first half's underestimation left unspoilt.' This circular letter was also sent in an English translation to countless friends and admirers, to Stiedry, Dr. Wolfsohn in Tel Aviv, to Walter Goehr, to Rufer, to me and my wife, and often Schoenberg added a few warm lines in addition. Some of the people who congratulated him had only heard about his birthday from the newspapers and wrote too late for it, like the cellist Professor Wilhelm Winkler, who had played in the orchestra in the Leipzig 'Gurrelieder' performance; in 1911 he had studied theory with Schoenberg in Ober St. Veit and had later taken part in the performances of the Schoenberg Society in Vienna. Marya Freund wrote about her *Pierrot* performances in London, Brussels and Paris. She continued: 'Now I would like to take up "Napoleon", and I would like to *know* so much from you! Unfortunately Los Angeles is not as near as Gmunden was.' Hans Erich Apostel, rather pessimistic by nature, sent Schoenberg descriptions of Viennese musical life; Max Deutsch informed Schoenberg that he had given the first French performance of 'Erwartung' on 7 November in Paris with Lucienne Marée in his own translation.

A few months before Theodor W. Adorno's *Philosophy of Modern Music* had been published in Germany. Kurt List in New York asked Schoenberg on 16 November for his views on it. He said that he was astonished by Adorno's lack of understanding of the logic of Schoenberg's whole development. Schoenberg was angered by the book, and in his anger overlooked the fact that it was more a defence than a criticism of his work. He wrote to me on 5 December:

'So modern music has a philosophy – it would be enough if it had a philosopher. He attacks me quite vehemently in it. Another disloyal person . . . I have never been able to bear the fellow . . . now I know that he has clearly never liked my music . . . it is disgusting, by the way, how he treats Stravinsky. I am certainly no admirer of Stravinsky, although I like a piece of his here and there very much – but one should not write like that.'

And on the same day he wrote in a letter to Rufer:

'The book is very difficult to read, for it uses this quasi-philosophical jargon in which modern professors of philosophy hide the absence of an idea. They think it is profound when they produce lack of clarity by undefined new expressions . . . naturally he knows all about twelve-tone music, but he has no idea of the creative process.'

He, who as I say needs an eternity to compose a song, naturally has no idea how quickly a real composer writes down what he hears in his imagination. He doesn't know that I have written both the Third and the Fourth Quartet in six weeks each, and Von heute auf morgen *in ten weeks. And these are just a few examples, for I have always composed quickly. He seems to believe that the twelve-tone row, if it doesn't hinder thought, hinders invention – the poor fellow . . . the book will give many of my enemies a handle, especially because it is so scientifically done.'*

Schoenberg's correspondence with Luigi Dallapiccola led to a friendship between the two men who did not know each other. Schoenberg gladly accepted the dedication of the 'Tre poemi' for soprano and chamber orchestra (on poems of James Joyce, Michelangelo and Machado). He said it was an extremely original and promising idea to write variations for a singing voice and this he envied Dallapiccola.

The London magazine 'Music Survey' had asked for a statement about the quarrel with Thomas Mann. Schoenberg's anger
broke out again, perhaps stirred up by Adorno's book. He
launched new attacks on Mann and called the note added to *Dr.
Faustus* an act of revenge. The magazine published the article as a
'character document'. Mann answered on 19 December 1949 and
reminded Schoenberg of his letter of reconciliation of 15 October
1948. 'You are attacking a bugbear of your imagination, and I am
not it', the writer ended, 'so there is no desire for revenge. If you
want to be my enemy completely – you will not succeed in making
me your enemy.'

Among the few friends who received a letter of thanks for their
seventy-fifth birthday congratulations was Darius Milhaud; as
usual between immigrants in the United States Schoenberg wrote
to him in English and thanked him warmly for his extremely nice
words in the magazine 'Canon'. He said that in conversation with
German and American composers he had often upbraided them
for their lack of comradeship, because they were inclined to kill
each other out of jealousy. On the other hand he had always
praised French artists of all kinds, because they provided the
world with a selfless and friendly attitude towards their colleagues.
Although naturally they knew how to recognize greater and
smaller talents and also recognize who were superior people, this
did not lessen the friendship and friendliness of most of them; a
depreciation of a rival was ruled out. 'It is this which I have
always liked in your personality: the deeply rooted dignity of a
man who knows his worth and therefore can be friendly to
another personality for this reason.'

The ice was finally broken by Thomas Mann's letter. On 2
January 1950, probably his first letter in the New Year, Schoenberg wrote to Mann that he had been ill for two weeks and therefore had not been able to finish his first spontaneous notes on the
subject. This is what he had written:

*'If the hand that I believe I see held out is the hand of peace, that is if it
signifies an offer of peace, I shall be the last not to grasp it at once
and shake it in token of confirmation.*

*In fact I have often thought of writing to you and saying: Let us bury
the hatchet and show that on a certain level there is always a chance of peace.'*

He did not finish the letter till 9 January. In order not to hurt
the friends who had supported him in this fight he suggested an
intermediate stage of neutrality. 'Let us make do with this peace:
you have reconciled me.'

Thomas Mann answered at once on 12 January, that he was extraordinarily pleased, and was only sorry about Schoenberg's recent ill-health. He said that he entirely agreed with Schoenberg's sentiments. His first answer in the *Saturday Review* had already shown that he did not want to become Schoenberg's enemy. He was really happy that Schoenberg too wanted to bury and forget this enmity. He hoped that Schoenberg had recovered all the vigour which he had shown on his seventy-fifth birthday. He sent belated and warm congratulations. 'Where and whenever we meet again in this life it will be an honour for me to shake you again by the hand.'

On 16 February Schoenberg wrote a confession: 'My attitude towards politics' which throws a very informative light on the development of his political and religious thought (see Appendix). A day later he wrote the preface to a radio broadcast of the Capitol record of *Pélleas and Mélisande*.

At the end of March another letter was sent to Schoenberg's sister Ottilie Blumauer. Gertrud only wrote a few words, but complained about the amount of housework that she had to do, in which the children had to help her. She said that Arnold was reasonably well, but he could not see very well and they became very tired from the heat from the desert from time to time. Arnold added that he had often been ill, but as the doctors could not find anything organic, it must be his nerves. The letter also contained a list of clothes, linen, and a coat, the content of a parcel which he had sent to Ottilie.

One of his last letters to Rufer, of 8 April 1950, was about an attempt by René Leibowitz to attach the label of athematicism to Schoenberg's music. Schoenberg says of this:

'*Leibowitz' athematic music: that goes back to a time forty years ago when I had maintained something of the sort for a short time. But I soon withdrew it, as coherence in music can only depend on motifs and their metamorphoses and developments . . . so I entirely agree with you. Leibowitz, intelligent as he is, often exaggerates: not everything is not gold which does not glitter, and something can be thematic which does not in the least look like it.*'

Stiedry, who was on a visit to Los Angeles, showed Schoenberg a Patience which the latter played with pleasure. It was called Napoleon Patience, and Schoenberg sent the conductor a witty letter about it. One can see from this that his condition had improved. The letter is dated 17 April 1950.

Hermann Scherchen had founded the publishing firm Ars

Viva in Gravesano, which was entered in the commercial register in Zurich in 1950. Schoenberg negotiated with him about some works which Scherchen wanted to publish. On 22 May he wrote to him about *Jacob's Ladder*, the score of which Scherchen wanted to have by 31 August.

Among Schoenberg's American admirers was the New York conductor Robert Craft. Craft had written to Schoenberg and was received in a friendly manner in the house in Brentwood Park, on 5 July. It was not his first visit; however, he says that he walked on tiptoe and did not ring the bell and waited till Nuria saw him, brought him in and made him wait till her father came. He describes the big room with the piano, the leather chair, the picture by Kokoschka and the son Ronny's tennis cups. Schoenberg leant on Gertrud's arm while walking, bowed down and thin, but sunburnt, thinner than before, his sensitive face in pain, and thick veins sticking out on his right temple.

Three days before he had finished the last composition he was to complete. It was the setting for a six-part mixed choir un-accompanied of the 130th Psalm, 'Out of the deep, O Lord', set in Hebrew. Chemjo Vinaver, the publisher of an anthology of Jewish music, had asked him for a contribution. Schoenberg began the work on 20 June and finished it on 2 July. Schoenberg rejected Vinaver's suggestion of using one of the traditional melodies to which the text was sung. However, he studied some of these chants in order to get a feeling of the melodic inflections of the Hebrew language. He dedicated the piece – as the fore-word in the Israeli Music Publications edition tells us – to the State of Israel in admiration for its people and its cultural achievements. When Serge Koussevitzky asked him to contribute to the first King David Festival in Jerusalem, Schoenberg suggested the Psalm to him as the most suitable contribution. He suggested to Vinaver that in the performance each part, if neces-sary, should be supported by a wood-wind instrument, in order to maintain the intonation and the rhythm: 'for this is always my greatest desire and I think it more important than the so-called pure sound of the voices.' The first performance did not take place in Israel, but was given in 1954 in Cologne by the Radio Chorus under Bernhard Zimmermann.

The clear manuscript of this work does not show us with what trouble the last works were wrung from Schoenberg's ailing body. However, Gertrud's letter to Ottilie Blumauer on 18 July tells us about this; Ottilie had moved to Berlin-Zehlendorf. Gertrud says that Arnold was suffering from asthma and depressions. He could hardly ever go out or wanted to go out. But he was able to get up and down stairs without becoming breathless and he could run in the garden in order to see something. His nerves were responsible for much of his illness. His blood pressure was between 136 and 160. He was very attached to Ronny.

On 2 August 1950 he wrote a report on the history of his own illness, which Dr. Dieter Kerner quotes in his book *Illnesses of Great Musicians*. He writes at the end: 'My asthma has changed somewhat: I do not often have violent attacks, but the condition of breathlessness is more or less chronic. I only feel free from it for four or five hours a day, and every night I awake from lack of breath. Then I often cough for three or four hours, and can only go to sleep again when I am exhausted – only to go through the same sequence of events in the morning.

'For many months I have not dared to sleep in my bed any more but sleep in a chair. Various treatments have been carried out on me. I was treated for diabetes, pneumonia, kidney disease, hernia and dropsy. I suffer from lack of strength and giddiness, and my eyes, which earlier were extraordinarily good, make reading difficult for me.'

Because of Schoenberg's poor state of health his seventy-sixth birthday on 13 September 1950 was celebrated without the usual party. The Schoenbergs spread the rumour that they were not at home and so only their very closest relations and friends were able to come to them.

About this time Schoenberg wrote the codicils to the two wills which he left behind for the division of his inheritance. One of them again insists on the primary right of his three children from the second marriage, and forbids a number of people to enter his work-room and touch the objects, manuscripts, books, etc. there. It is undated. The second one, of 1 October 1950, is in the form of a letter to Gertrud and deals with the publication of unpublished manuscripts. As adviser he recommends:

'*Dr. Josef Polnauer, Josef Rufer, Erwin Stein (if he does not become my enemy), Erwin Ratz, and especially: your brother Rudolf Kolisch!, Roberto Gerhard, Karl Rankl. Görgi too can be useful in many things; also perhaps Khuner or Lehner, the latter more in instrumental problems. Rudi is the best at understanding my music. Polnauer and Rufer may be considered, and also Rankl. Rudi understands theoretical matters. I have not mentioned several people here whose capabilities come into consideration, but perhaps will not really remain my friends. Among these unfortunately is Stein, Erwin Stein. Wiesengrund should be excluded altogether. Everything is a matter of luck. But in some time our dear children, Nuria, Ronny and Larry will be mature enough. – So good luck.'*

Thoughts of death and the last things took up more and more space in Schoenberg's mind. He was now nearing the end of the path which he had entered in 1926 with the play *The Biblical Way* and which had led to *Moses and Aaron*. Soon after his seventy-sixth birthday, on 29 September 1950, he wrote the first of the texts to which he gave the provisional name 'Modern Psalms'. It was concerned with God and prayer. As in the *Biblical Way* and *Moses and Aaron*, God is again the only one, the eternal, the almighty, all-knowing and unpresentable; prayer transmits the feeling of union with him. The last lines are:

'O you my God, your mercy has left prayer to us as a connection, a blessed connection with you. As a blessing which gives us more than all fulfilment.'

Immediately after the codicils to the will Schoenberg began setting this first psalm to music on 2 October. It remained a fragment.

Schoenberg was no longer very interested in the outside world, unless the contacts with it were friendly ones. He was certainly glad to hear that Robert Craft had performed *Pierrot Lunaire* and the Suite op. 29 on 21 October in the New York Town Hall. And he must have been amused by the reminiscence made by the son of a friend of his boyhood, Richard Mandl. He wrote of a visit to the latter's villa built by Adolf Loos in Döbling and saw his signature in the visitor's book. But contacts and questionings for no purpose aroused his ill-humour. He left unanswered a letter from the American Music Center of 11 October which asked for a list of his works since 1939 with exact details of composition and publication; he wrote on the piece of paper: 'The person who demands a favour of Herr Schoenberg should first present himself with the necessary respect. For he must give a clear explanation whether this favour he demands serves a purpose which is friendly towards Herr Schoenberg. For Herr Schoenberg does not want to help his enemies.'

The first serious request for the first performance of *Moses and Aaron* came from Francesco Siciliani, the Director of the Florence May Music Festival, to whom Scherchen had suggested it. Schoenberg answered with great delight. As only the first and second acts had been composed he postulated various possibilities in a letter of 27 November 1950:

1. A performance of the first two acts either
   a) omitting the third, or
   b) having it merely spoken. (It was the dialogue between Moses and Aaron, followed after Aaron's death by a long monologue by Moses.)
2. A performance of only the Dance round the Golden Calf (from the second act).
3. Of the complete second act.

(Contrary to his custom he writes the name Aaron here with two As.) Schoenberg added that instead of this fragment, it would be better to give performances of his three one-act operas. Nothing came of this.

Some nice antiques were sent from Berlin-Zehlendorf, where Ottilie Blumauer had returned, as birthday gifts. Schoenberg's sister knew how much her brother loved pewter, silver cutlery and old jewellery. He was very pleased with the gift. He thanked her in his still astonishingly clear handwriting on 22 November 'for the wonderful antiques . . . these are really precious!' He said that they were all very busy, Gertrud with household matters and he himself with his illness, although three doctors had said that his heart, lungs, stomach and kidneys were healthy. So it must be his nerves or the results of overwork.

Dr. Heinrich Strobel, who had revived the magazine 'Melos' in 1947, wrote from Baden-Baden on 4 December. He wanted a short article on Verdi. Schoenberg noted in the margin of the letter that he was not well, and that Verdi was too important to be written about on one side of a sheet of paper. Perhaps later . . .

The Ordinarius for Musicology of the Free University in Berlin, Professor Dr. Walter Gerstenberg, thanked Schoenberg for a recommendation for Josef Rufer as a lecturer. Rufer was appointed.

There were difficulties about the recording of Schoenberg's piano music which Eduard Steuermann had begun. The all too self-critical great pianist still had scruples. Schoenberg's patience was exhausted. He wrote an angry letter, which was not dated apart from 1950; Steuermann must have surely got as far as he could with it, he says, otherwise he would never be able to do it. Perfection does not exist among human beings; he himself, Schoenberg, had had to do without it.

1950 also produced what Schoenberg called the 'Miracle Set' (or series). He had sometimes concerned himself earlier on occasions with twelve-note series, which allowed certain sub-divisions, which produced new possibilities of combinations. The 'Miracle Set' of the 1950s shows such peculiarities in its mirror forms (inversion and retrograde) which Schoenberg explained in a short text. The final sentence is typical of his whole approach to serial composition: 'Of course you have to invent your themes as ordinarily; but you have more possibilities of producing strongly related configurations, which in sound are essentially different.'

His creative powers were aroused again at Christmas time. The three following psalms were written on 25 December. He wrote another one on the 29th; and two more on the last day of the year.

On 2 January 1951 Schoenberg sent a long letter to the two Stiedrys in New York; this was clearly dictated into the machine. The Stiedrys had sent greetings for the festivities and added questions about the 'Gurrelieder', which Erika Stiedry was preparing for performance.

'*As against* Pierrot, *there are no pitches here. The only reason why I wrote notes was because I thought that I could make my phrasing, accentuation and declamation clearer. So please no speech melodies. The only likeness with* Pierrot *is in the necessity of remaining in time with the orchestra. It is also important that all accelerandi or ritardandi should be gradual ones, not like . . . Toscanini who puts slow and fast tempi together without any connection. . . . In driving a car and in music one cannot suddenly stop a tempo.*'

Then Schoenberg added questions about Stiedry's success as a conductor, about Verdi's *Don Carlos*, which Schoenberg did not know, about the *Magic Flute* and remarks about the Herculean effort of putting on the whole Wagner *Ring of the Nibelungs*. Schoenberg agreed with Stiedry that conducting from memory was risky:

'*You know perhaps that in my Society for Private Performances I did not allow playing from memory. I said: 'Our musical notation is a puzzle picture which one cannot look at often enough in order to find the right solution. Mitropoulos is an extraordinary musician. But he does too much. One cannot digest so much in a short time. Especially not my music.*'

In a postscript to Erika Stiedry he expresses his joy about her success with *Pierrot*. He said that she should not discourage young admirers of his music like Craft; he was gradually working himself into Schoenberg's music by giving many performances of it, and he would finally succeed in this. 'I would be very glad if all my friends would encourage young people like Craft and the young horn-player Günther Schuller or the Juilliard Quartet.' (He

Schoenberg and Erika Stiedry-von Wagner studying
Pierrot Lunaire, Los Angeles, 1940

With Dr. Fritz Stiedry outside the house in Brentwood Park, 1949

meant Günther Schuller, the composer, and later director of the New England Conservatory in Boston.) To rumours about an 'old Schoenberg clique' which knew everything better than any one else, he said that that was right.

Oskar Adler wrote from London that his astrological work was being printed. Schoenberg answered on 10 January with pleasure. The following correspondence with his friend of his youth contains remarks about tempo indications in Beethoven. Expressions such as allegro, andante and presto were clearly undefined, although Beethoven probably meant degrees of speed by them. On the other hand allegro energico or andante cantabile were indications of character. If one compared the metronome markings, where minuets were prescribed at one crotchet per second, any attempt at a unified explanation broke down. It was also wrong to gauge the speed from the smallest note values, as today the 'great' artists began to run like mad when the quick passages came along. 'I have thought of drawing conclusions from the motivic content. But this too is very difficult. I have used the expression "difficulties of content", but don't think that this concept can be regarded as a means of measurement.' Finally Schoenberg attacks the over accentuation of the strong beats of the bar, because they stand in the way of good phrasing. 'There should only be one strong accent in a phrase. Except when there is a special characteristic of some kind.' Finally on 3 March Schoenberg thanked Adler for the *Testament of Astrology*. He said that unfortunately his nervous affliction of the eyes prevented him from reading it himself. If he used spectacles his eyes began to swim. He would have it read to him. The last letter to Adler on 23 April announces a collection of writings: 'Psalms, prayers and other conversations with and about God'. As he also wrote to Dr. Georg Wolfsohn in Tel Aviv, this was the final title of the cycle of poems which he had originally called 'Modern Psalms' and was published under this title in 1956 by Schotts'. Since 1938 the viola player and composer Ödön Partos, who had emigrated from Budapest, was living in Israel. In 1951 he became Director of the Israel Academy of Music in Jerusalem. He had visited Schoenberg during a visit to America and told him about the new State. In April Schoenberg was made Honorary President of the Academy. Another admirer of Schoenberg, the composer, pianist and conductor Frank Pelleg, who came from Prague, and since 1950 had been Director of the music section of the Israeli Ministry of Culture, also took part in this honour. On 25 April Schoenberg sent Pelleg and Partos a long letter, which was only printed in an abbreviated form in Erwin Stein's collection of the letters and given a wrong date. He said that for more than four decades his dearest wish had been to become a resident citizen of an independent Israeli state.

'*Whether my health will allow the fulfilment of my second wish I can hardly say at the moment. But I do hope to be able to arrange that of the many compositions, poems and articles which I have written for the sake of artistic propaganda for my plans, as many as possible should pass into your possession for the Israeli National Library.*'

The letter ends with a remark about the dedication with which the real priest should approach art and about the fact that the Israelis were a chosen people. As the Israeli people had maintained pure monotheism in spite of all affliction, so the Israeli musicians must set an example to the world to which the development of humanity could orientate itself.

At Easter Schoenberg received a greeting from the pianist Else C. Kraus, who was continuing to advocate his piano works. Dr. Georg Wolfsohn wrote from Jerusalem about a festival which the Music Academy had arranged on the occasion and in honour of Schoenberg's honorary presidency. After Pelleg had read out the Master's letter of thanks his Serenade was performed on gramophone records. A young English admirer, the composer Humphrey Searle, wrote on 25 May about a talk which the British radio wanted Schoenberg to give. The latter suggested 'Advice for Beginners in Twelve-Tone Composition'. In a letter to Rufer on 13 June Schoenberg defends himself against any autobiographical interpretation in *Moses and Aaron*; he says that the subject matter and its treatment were purely of a philosophical and religious kind.

Dr. Ödön Partos in Jerusalem asked Schoenberg for advice about the teaching syllabus at his school. Schoenberg answered him on 15 June 1951 in a form which can be regarded as a creed. One cannot set up a syllabus which is valid for all time. New techniques and theories, a new aesthetic have to be considered. The material could grow in an extraordinary manner or decrease through simplification. The only principle must and can be to give the most of the best things to the students.

'*Give the students a great deal of the best reading matter and make them work through it. I hope that my writings will also be included in this.*

And now I feel compelled to do some plain speaking about the reason why I hesitated to accept the honorary presidency and what holds me back in similar circumstances. – For years I had to observe with sorrow that, among the admirers of my art, of each ten, seven or eight were Christians and at the most two to three were Jews. On the other hand most of the Jewish musicians were admirers of the Christian musicians, Stravinsky, Bartók, Hindemith. All these were also enemies of my music and theories and yet they found more support among Jews than I did.

Noblesse forbade me to take up a position against this. But now I must say: I will be very sad if this institute educates those who admire my enemies, instead of bringing up those who are ready to fight.

I cannot allow them not to take this remark as obligatory. I would have to resign, if I found an experience which was going against myself.

But I will not say that the students should not be instructed in the techniques of my contemporaries. They should not and must not lack knowledge, but they should not adopt a partisan opposition against me. If this is a programme, then I wish that you will be able to carry it through.'

Karl Rankl, who as the Director of the Covent Garden Opera held one of the principal musical posts in London, had a correspondence with Schoenberg. On 27 June Schoenberg asked Rankl if he would make a score of his *Jacob's Ladder* from his very full short score. Rankl had to give up the work, which was later carried out by Winfried Zillig. Schoenberg wrote enthusiastically to Tibor Varga, who was then living in Detmold, about the records of his performance of the Violin Concerto on 27 June. He hoped also to hear Varga's performance of the Violin Phantasy soon.

One of the last letters written by Schoenberg was sent on 29 June to Hermann Scherchen, who was planning a performance of *Moses and Aaron.*

'Dear Friend, if you look at the poem you will see that the second act can be performed alone – perhaps introduced by a few words from the first act – and this is really the only act which I want to be performed. If one performs the third act without music, – as an extra piece or just reads out the text, this reproduces the main content of the work.

So therefore I will limit the contract to the printing and performance of the complete second act.

I expect to receive a suitable advance on royalties – not less than 2000 marks, while the royalties for performances should be so divided that I should receive 75% for concert or theatrical performances (in royalties and hire fees), my share of the sales of music should be 15% to start with, and to rise to 25% after 3000 copies. Royalties and records are normally divided 50:50, for television and film performances I would demand 75%, and also for stage performances. All future contracts should be based on these terms and should be similar to normal contracts, provided that my consent is first obtained. If your firm is liquidated or sold, then I demand an irrevocable primary right of buying my works. I also note that I am excluding Associated Music Publishers, New York from dealing with my work in any circumstances. Any such agreement is invalid so far as my works are concerned. Also in the case that the firm is sold to others.

Now I wish you and me a lot of luck for the first performance – that means as great a success as possible. And in the future we will perform the whole of the second act. Many warm greetings. Your Arnold Schoenberg.'

This letter, which contained a draft of a contract, was occasioned by the forthcoming première of the 'Dance round the Golden Calf' from the second act of *Moses and Aaron* under Scherchen. The latter, who conducted it on Monday 2 July in Darmstadt, was also the publisher of this large fragment through his Ars Viva firm: this scene is the third one in the second act of the opera. Schoenberg's wish that the second act should be performed alone but complete was never fulfilled, although he had already mentioned it as a possible alternative in his letter to Siciliani of 27 November 1950.

Now Schoenberg's life was approaching its end. On 3 July he began another psalm which was concerned with the maintenance of the race: 'In breeding, incest is forbidden, because they destroy the race.

National inbreeding, national incest is as dangerous to the race as to the family and the people.'

That is the last message of the man who adopted the Jewish faith, who believed in the chosen nature of his people and felt himself to be a prophet, a mouthpiece of the divine power.

He looked forward to 13 July, a Friday, with apprehension. In the last hour of the day his heart stopped. The first telegram was sent on the following day to Ottilie in Berlin:

Our beloved Arnold passed away 11.45 p.m. Friday 13 Trude and family.

On 4 August Gertrud sent Ottilie a report of Schoenberg's last illness and the end. 'In the last few months he had had asthma again, but not in the sense of an attack, more a kind of uneasiness which went on for hours. Then he again had trouble with his foot or through constantly sitting down. And then an undescribable nervousness in his whole body and in his mind. His fear of dying had turned to resignation at the end, in the last two or three weeks. He was tired and wanted to die. Sitting alone in his bedroom without his friends and without being able to work, without taking part in the life of the children (they were too lively for him, and he could only see them for a short time without getting excited), all of this drove him to despair.

'He still had some pleasures. Ronny's honour as "outstanding in all subjects" in the school, and the scholarship for the Loyola High School made him very proud. Also Ronny's successes at tennis. Even on his last day he asked: has Ronny won? And Larry's love for him – he adored Arnold and hung on every word that Arnold gave him – I believed that he recognized this in the last time and he was moved by it! Then the successes in Europe and the respect shown him by the Library of Congress in Washington, which wanted to have his entire correspondence and manuscripts, an honour which he received during his lifetime.

'He spoke a good deal about his youth and remembered many details, especially his uncle, who apparently liked him very much. Right up to the end, though he was weak, he was perfectly young in spirit. He could curse his enemies up till his last day and care for his friends right up to the end.

'On the 13th (he and I had a great fear of this), he insisted that I should get a sitter-in for the night. He was a German doctor who was not allowed to practise here. I was very tired, but woke up every hour and we had the light on. Arnold slept restlessly but he slept. About a quarter to twelve I looked at the clock and said to myself: another quarter of an hour and then the worst is over. Then the doctor called me. Arnold's throat rattled twice, his heart gave a powerful beat and that was the end. But I couldn't believe it for a long time afterwards. His face was so relaxed and calm as if he were sleeping. No convulsions, no death struggle. I had always prayed for this end. Only not to grieve!'

Gertrud Schoenberg had told her closest friends about her husband's death. Alma Maria Mahler-Werfel arrived with her daughter, the sculptress Anna Mahler, who made a death mask of Schoenberg. In the house which had lost its soul all was silent. The workroom with its many books and music scores, the writing-table, carved by Schoenberg himself, and covered with paper, pencils, notes and magnifying glasses was no longer used.

The last photo shows the change of Schoenberg's prophet-head even more horrifyingly than Anna Mahler's death mask. The

The workroom in Brentwood Park

clear eyes stare out from its powerful skull with its high brow. The jawbones can be seen through the taut skin. The great ear seems to be listening to Utopian worlds of sound. His nose and mouth look as if they had been chiselled above his energetic chin. The white bedclothes raise his face up as if it had been spiritualized into immateriality, like that of a saint after a long martyrdom. – Schoenberg, one of the greatest men of the twentieth century, a composer whose work has influenced music for generations and set it on new paths, died in poverty. His burial took place with very few people present.

The world heard of the news of his death with mixed feelings. There were obituaries in all the leading papers and musical magazines. Only in the Socialist countries the echo was insignificant; in East Berlin Hanns Eisler was the first to give a lecture full of warmth and admiration in the German Academy of Arts, speaking of the genius of the Master.

My first small book on Schoenberg arrived on 14 July in Brentwood Park. Schoenberg, who had enlarged and corrected a chronology for it, was not to see it. Thomas Mann, to whom I sent it and to whom I asked about his relations with Schoenberg, answered in a warmhearted letter on 19 October 1951, which was prefixed to the translations and to the second edition. 'The opportunity of another possible meeting with Schoenberg, who had been ailing for some time, did not arise after all. Suffice it to say that I was absolutely determined not to increase his hostility, but to allow it to remain one-sided and never to say a bad word about him, and that this determination finally won the day.'

Gertrud Schoenberg, who died in February 1967, survived her husband by sixteen years. In this time she succeeded in convincing even those people who had been sceptical in his lifetime of the greatness of his work. She arranged the cataloguing of the legacy, which was carried out by Josef Rufer in 1956. She laid the foundation of the complete edition, which has been appearing since 1966 with Schott and Universal. She was present when the UCLA opened the Concert Hall which bears Schoenberg's name.

We cannot yet evaluate the amount of impulses which Schoenberg's work has left behind in the total picture of modern culture. The sound of his music has lost none of its novelty even for modern ears, which shocked those who were present at the premières of his works. Against this *Moses and Aaron*, especially in the West Berlin Opera production, has gripped tens of thousands of listeners in countless performances. Without becoming repertory pieces in the conventional sense his orchestral and chamber music works have found their place in the programmes of the big orchestras and quartet ensembles. In my last conversation with him in 1949 he said: 'I expect to live till 125 and then experience the beginning of my success!' Fate willed it otherwise. But perhaps in the year 2000 Schoenberg's Utopian wish will be fulfilled.

THE PRIMAL CELL

'One cannot analyse by simply looking at the notes. *I* at least hardly ever find musical relations by eye but I *hear* them', Schoenberg wrote in 1932 in his broadcast for Frankfurt Radio about his four Orchestral Songs opus 22. With this he drew a line between his conception of music and the ostensibly scientific one of all theoreticians, who relied on the reading eye. Anyone who attended his analysis courses in Berlin from 1931 onwards knows that he separated himself from the normal analysis of musical forms, even when this was used by people who belonged to the circle of his pupils and friends.

Anyone who listens to his music can discover in it some small complexes of notes which return like fixed ideas. They appear either horizontally or vertically, as melodic or chordal groups, thus entirely in the idea of 'musical space', which Schoenberg did not describe until he was a mature composer and theoretician. These complexes of notes, minimal bricks which make up minimal forms, consist of three notes. They have the peculiarities and functions of cells in an organism. They attach themselves to their likes and so develop into complexes of four or more notes.

A cell of this kind appears in 1899 in the song 'Warnung', opus 3, No. 3, which was already quoted by me in another connection. Its three notes

achieve a motivic function through the rhythm ♪♪.♪. Among the Songs opus 2 there is one, also a setting of a poem by Dehmel, 'Schenk mir deinen goldenen Kamm'. It begins with this series of notes

which affect the whole form of the piece in varying transpositions and also function motivically. From its first appearance this series is harmonized with chords of three or four notes and it achieves a modulation from F sharp minor to the most distant key of C minor in the shortest possible way.

The String sextet *Verklärte Nacht* was also written in 1899. Its slow theme in 9/8, 'etwas ruhiger', begins with the notes

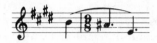

which are also used in its further development and in the final section.

In these three unlike series of notes the ear recognizes the connections which make the metamorphoses of a cell. This cell is a group which contains three intervals: a semitone, a fourth and a tritone, as well as their octave complements: a major seventh, a fifth and a diminished fifth, which is identical with the tritone in the tempered system. According to the horizontal or vertical arrangement of the three notes, two of these intervals can be clearly perceived, while the third is only perceived indirectly.

The three notes are exchanged with each other in a permutatory manner. They can be mirrored in the three forms which musical mirroring allows. They can submit to keys, but also contribute to the dissolution of tonality. They make up sections of many of the twelve-note melodies which Schoenberg used after 1914, and of the twelve-note series which he used after 1921.

The three-note cell is soon joined by a fourth note, which stands in the relation of a semitone, a fourth and a tritone to the other three. This leads beyond the boundaries of diatonicism and removes tonality. This procedure is again derived from one of the mirrorings, which are contained in the composition of the primal cell.

Of the possible transpositions, which increase the number of primal cells from one to twelve, Schoenberg prefers especially those which contain the tritone A–E flat (D sharp) or the fourth A–D (as well as its complementary fifth D–A). In the 'Gurrelieder' the group D–A–G sharp plays an important part both melodically and chordally. It first appears in Waldemar's D major song 'So tanzen die Engel' at figure 45 as a chord

THE ANGLO-AUSTRIAN MUSIC SOCIETY

Patrons: THE EARL and COUNTESS OF HAREWOOD.
Presidents: SIR ADRIAN BOULT, PROF. BRUNO WALTER.

SCHOENBERG

MEMORIAL CONCERT

PROGRAMME:

STRING QUARTET No. 4, Op. 37
PETER GIBBS QUARTET

THREE SONGS, Op. 48
(WORLD PREMIERE)
ANNE WOOD, *Contralto.*   PETER STADLEN, *Piano*

SUITE FOR SEVEN INSTRUMENTS, Op. 29
**(FIRST PERFORMANCE OF COMPOSER'S VERSION FOR
FLUTE, CLARINET, BASSOON, STRINGS AND PIANO)**
L.S.O. CHAMBER ENSEMBLE
directed from the piano by PETER STADLEN

THURSDAY, JUNE 5th, at 7.30

WIGMORE HALL, Wigmore Street, W.1

TICKETS :- 9/- 6/- and 3/- (unreserved)
Obtainable from : WIGMORE HALL Box Office (WEL. 2141)
usual Agents, and
ANGLO-AUSTRIAN MUSIC SOCIETY, (WES. 9003)

THE SECRETARY, ANGLO-AUSTRIAN MUSIC SOCIETY,
139 KENSINGTON HIGH STREET, W.8.

Please send ____tickets at _____ *for the Schoenberg Memorial
Concert at the Wigmore Hall on June 5th.*

Enclosed find £ ____ *s.* ____ *d. (Cash Cheque P.O.)*

Name BLOCK LETTERS

Address BLOCK LETTERS
Please enclose Stamped and Addressed Envelope with your order.

Programme of the Schoenberg Memorial Concert in London,
5 June 1952

in which the G sharp still works as a leading note to A; melodically it introduces Waldemar's song 'Es ist Mitternachtszeit'

three bars after 55 and returns as thematic material at the beginning of the third part of the 'Gurrelieder'. The final canon in C
major 'Farbenfroh am Himmelssaum östlich grüsst ihr Morgen-
traum' begins with the notes

six bars after 93.

In his first, tonal, creative period Schoenberg had a preference
for keys based on D. His earlier String Quartet of 1897 was
written in D major, the sextet *Verklärte Nacht*, the symphonic poem
Pelléas and *Mélisande* and the String Quartet opus 7 in D minor.
Several of the early songs, the chorus 'Friede auf Erden', and the
Ballads opus 12 are written in D. In *Pelléas and Mélisande* the chord

—Pelléas figure 32 has a motivic importance. Together with
the diminished fourth chords which also appear it introduces a
chain of development of harmonic phenomena which leads
through the First Chamber Symphony and the Stefan George
Songs to the Five Orchestral Pieces.

The chord A–D–G sharp continued to live in his world of ideas.
In the First Chamber Symphony, three bars after one, it is played
by bass clarinet, contra-bassoon, cello and contra-bass fortissimo
with the marking 'hervortreten' and becomes a motive of the
principal section.

In the last movement, 'Entrückung', of the F sharp minor quartet, one bar after twenty, it is played sforzato by all the four instruments

and gives the singer her cue for her entry on D ('Ich fühle luft von anderem planeten'). The second Orchestral Piece opus 16 begins with the G sharp played by solo cello, accompanied by the notes D–A–A–D in the trombone, trumpet, bassoons and oboe.

In the tenth of the Stefan George Songs 'Das schöne beet' the beginning sounds like a reminiscence of the 'Gurrelieder'.

The fourteenth song 'Sprich nicht immer von dem laub' begins with the notes E flat–D–A–A flat in the vocal part, in which the cell is made into a four-note one by the additional note

Forty years after the 'Gurrelieder' Schoenberg wrote his 'Variations on a recitative' on a D minor theme which begins in the bass with

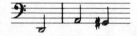

The examples quoted here are only a selection from the point of view of their motivic and thematic importance, chosen from the complete number of identical sequences of notes. The sequence G sharp–A–(E flat)–D can already be found accidentally, that is to say without any definite purpose, from the piano pieces written in 1894 onwards. In the Dehmel song 'Schenk mir deinen goldenen Kamm', as a transposition of the opening theme, this sequence dominates the middle section at the words 'Schenk mir deine schwerste Last'.

In the D minor Quartet opus 7 the main theme contains the sequence F–E–B flat in bars 2, 3 and 4, and the transposition of this A–G sharp–D in bar 5.

The fugato at A has G flat–C–D flat in the first violin followed by D–G sharp–A, answered in the second violin by G–C–C sharp–D–G–A flat, in which by putting the G down to the lower octave the characteristic step of a ninth, G to A flat, arises. This answer, which introduces a fugato, contains the primal cell three times: G–C–C sharp, C sharp–D–G and D–G–A flat. Here it becomes a four-note group, C sharp–D–G–A flat.

The same procedure is compressed in the stretto at C, Bar 34 and its effect is enhanced.

In the First Chamber Symphony the primal cell in the rising sequence C sharp–F sharp–C introduces one of the finest ideas in the work, the second theme of the first main section.

The second String Quartet in F sharp minor contains the D minor scherzo, which has already been discussed in a biographical connection, and which quotes the song 'O du lieber Augustin'. The trio section, when it appears, has an upper part with the notes F sharp–F–C–B. Against this the cello plays its transposed inversion: D–E flat–A flat–A. Both melodies contain the primal cell increased to four notes; in addition that in the cello contains the notes D, A, A flat (G sharp). These lead away from the main key of D major, in which the Augustin song nevertheless appears in the middle part.

The primal cell can also be found in the George Songs and the Piano Pieces opus 11, both melodically and chordally. Here it shows its power of compensating for tonality. The chord of augmented fourths is the chief component of the harmony in the Stefan George Songs. The first piano piece ends with the chord

the second with the chord sequence

G–D–A flat=G flat–C–F, the third piece with the simultaneous sequences of notes G–C sharp–F sharp=A–E–B flat.

The primal cell has only a minimal melodic influence in the orchestral pieces and the two stage works of the period before the First World War. But it is more important for the harmony. The beginning of opus 16 No. 2 has been mentioned. *Erwartung* has the chord G flat–C–F–B flat in its second bar, and in bar 50 the transposition of this B flat–E–A–D sharp. And the famous twelve-part (not twelve-note) chord in bar 269–270 contains the primal cell as an augmented fourth chord three times; G flat–C–F, D–G–C sharp and B flat–E flat–A. The harmony in the *Glückliche Hand* is similar, but there complexes of more than four notes are hardly ever found. In *Pierrot Lunaire* too the primal cell scarcely plays any melodic role, except for the beginning of the flute solo in 'Der kranke Mond'. However chords like C–G flat–C flat–F–B flat in No. 2 and D–G sharp–C sharp–G in No. 6 confirm the development from opus 11 up to the operas. The influence of the primal cell in the Orchestral Songs opus 22 is insignificant; they are based on combinations of major or minor seconds with major or minor thirds. *Jacob's Ladder* too, which marks the transition to serial composition with twelve notes, is substantially free from the primal cell.

In 1915 Schoenberg wrote the the first twelve-note theme, already mentioned, which was the basis of a scherzo of a symphony.

In this the primal cell is found five times: E flat–A–G sharp,
E–F–B, F–B–C, B–C–G flat and C–G flat–D flat. It also becomes
a four-note group: F–B–C–G flat. The first works which contain
twelve-note movements, the Piano Pieces opus 23 and the 'Serenade', have only unimportant traces of the primal cell. But the
primal cell makes an important contribution to the series of the
first work which was based entirely on the rules of the twelve-note
technique: the Piano Suite opus 25: E–F–G–D flat–G flat–E flat–
A flat–D–B–C–A–B flat. The primal cell appears twice running, as
G–D flat–G flat and after this as E flat–A flat–D. The comic opera
Von heute auf morgen is based on a series which begins with

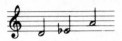

and will be discussed in another connection. The series of the
Third String Quartet shows several versions of the primal cell

and the middle section of this forms the four-note sequence C–F–F
sharp–B. *Moses and Aaron* begins with the chord which is based on
the first notes of the series: A–B flat–E. The violin part in the
Violin Concerto begins with the notes A–B flat–E flat–B. In the
String Trio the initial note D is followed by the notes B flat–E
flat–A–E, the primal cell in a four-note form. The *Survivor from
Warsaw* is based on a series which begins with F sharp–G–C,
exactly like the song of 1899 'Schenk mir deinen goldenen Kamm'.
    Schoenberg's last completed work was Psalm 130, 'De pro-
fundis'. Its first notes are: E flat–A–G sharp. I have already
mentioned the extraordinary profusion of sequences of the tritone
A–E flat (D sharp) (A–Es [Dis] in German) and its connection
with one of the neighbouring semitones. We know that plays on
words were much enjoyed in the Mödling circle, humorous
enharmonic changes like a 'Displanade' instead of an 'Esplanade'.
In a letter to Mitzi Seligmann-Kolisch Schoenberg asks her to
give greetings to (in musical notes) E–Es–C–H–A; if one reads
the first note in the Italian and French manner, one arrives at
Mischa. This was the name of Mitzi Seligmann's son. Alban
Berg used this method in the three themes of his chamber con-

certo, taking the letters from the three names Arnold Schoenberg, Anton Webern and Alban Berg which represented notes and
forming them into melodies: A–D–S–C–H–B–E–G, A–E–B–E
and A–B–A–B–E–G.

We know from the researches of Friedrich Smend that Johan
Sebastian Bach loved similar plays on letters and notes and often
concealed them in his compositions, especially the sequence
B–A–C–H. (B flat–A–C–B). Schoenberg quotes this motif in his
Orchestral Variations. But he used his own name in the form of a
monogram Es–A or A–Es (E flat–A or A–E flat) very frequently
in works which were connected with his own emotional life. The
threatening lovesong 'Warnung' begins with the monogram; the
song 'Erwartung', also composed in 1899, contains it in the lower
notes of the often quoted second chord in the second bar. And one
can find it in many other places in the songs, right up till the
Stefan George Songs. In the first bar of the F sharp minor Quartet
the A of the first violin is followed by a D sharp in the second; the
tragic biographical connections of this opus 10 with Schoenberg's
private life are as clear as the cheerful ones of the opera *Von heute
auf morgen*, in whose series the first note D is followed by the
monogram.

In 1926 Schoenberg began work on the Wind Quintet, which
was dedicated 'to baby Arnold', the recently born son of Felix
Greissle and his wife Gertrud, Schoenberg's daughter. The first
notes of the series are: Es (E flat) G and A, the initials of Schoenberg, Greissle, Gertrud and Arnold. The first work which Schoenberg dedicated to his young wife Gertrud, née Kolisch, was the
Suite opus 29. All its movements begin and end with her monogram: G–Es or Es–G (G–E flat or E flat–G).

Schoenberg continued such plays with letters of this kind in
America as well. He wrote down on a piece of paper (without any
date), sequences of notes based on the words façade, cascade,
Bachfisch, Geiss, Gasse etcetera. He was pleased and highly interested when I told him in 1949 about Smend's researches into the
counting alphabet used by Bach (A=1, B=2, C=3, etc.); this
had been published in 1947. He saw in this a confirmation of his
conviction that in music one must recognize 'what it is' and not
'how it is done'. Whenever the sequence E flat–A appears in his
works he is as it were introducing himself to the listener. When a
further note at a semitone's distance is inserted in the tritone, this
gives rise to the primal cell.

APPENDIX

LIST OF DOCUMENTS

Schoenberg's last two school reports, 1889/90   536
Schoenberg's first contract, 1901   537
Notes on Webern, after 1910   538
Income Tax Return for 1915 and supplement 1913   539
Schoenberg's pupils in Berlin, 1926–1933   540
Letter on the Jewish question, 1933   541
From a letter to Alban Berg, 1935   542
From a Notebook, 1937   543
On Strauss and Furtwängler, 1946   544
Letter of thanks to the National (American) Institute
    of Arts and Letters, 1947   545
A Text from the Third Millenium, 1948   547
Self-analysis, 1948   548
My attitude toward politics, 1950   551
Bach, 1932/1950   552

SCHOENBERG'S LAST TWO SCHOOL REPORTS

Class 5, School Year 1889/90

	1st Semester	*2nd Semester*
German	Satisfactory	Praiseworthy
French	Praiseworthy	Praiseworthy
English	Satisfactory	Satisfactory
History	Satisfactory	Praiseworthy
Mathematics	Satisfactory	Praiseworthy
Natural History (Zoology)	Sufficient	Sufficient
Chemistry	Satisfactory	Satisfactory
Practical Geometry	Sufficient	Satisfactory
Free Drawing	Satisfactory	Satisfactory
Gymnastics	Praiseworthy	Praiseworthy

Free Lessons:

Stenography	Praiseworthy	Praiseworthy
Work in Chemical Lab.	Satisfactory	Satisfactory

Outward Appearance of

Written Work	Commendable	Commendable
General Progress Class	First	First
Moral Behaviour	Satisfactory	Satisfactory
Industry	Satisfactory	Satisfactory
Number of lessons missed	Excused 17	Excused 13
Received a report	22.11.1890	5.7.1890
School Fees	Paying	Exempt
		(24 3 1890)

Schoenberg went to the Realschule in Vienna 2, Vereinsgasse, from 1885 to 1891. As he left the school in January 1891, he did not receive a report for the first semester of Class 6 in 1890/91.

SCHOENBERG'S FIRST CONTRACT

Society of Members of German Theatres.

Contract, which has been drawn up between Herr Arnold Schoenberg on one side and E. von Wolzogen's Buntes Theater Überbrettl GmbH. on the other. No. 1. Herr Arnold Schoenberg is appointed as conductor at the Buntes Theater, Berlin.

The contract begins on 16 December 1901 and ends on 31 July 1902.

It is the task of Herr Schoenberg to fulfil those duties which correspond to his artistic capabilities.

For the fulfilment of those duties Herr Schoenberg is offered by the Directors of the Theatre: (a) a salary of 300 M, (three hundred marks) monthly. In addition for travel in Germany and abroad he will receive 5 M (five marks) a day as expenses.

The salary and expenses will be paid both in Berlin and on tour in arrears on the 1st and the 16th of each month.

If this contract is extended beyond 31 July 1902 the Direction of the Buntes Theater has the right to give Herr Schoenberg leave in the summer for one to two months. During this leave he will receive a third of his salary, but must not undertake other artistic activities during this period.

It is the duty of Herr Schoenberg to take part in all the guest performances arranged by the Direction in Berlin, in Germany and abroad.

It is the duty of Herr Schoenberg to hand over his entire compositions, such as are suitable for the Buntes Theater, the decision regarding which will be made by the Buntes Theater, to the Buntes Theater, and to give the theatre the exclusive performing rights of these compositions for the duration of one year, such works as are accepted by the Direction for performance. Further Herr Schoenberg agrees to entrust the publication of these compositions to the publishers who are contractually bound to the Buntes Theater.

Breach of Contract carries a penalty of 3000 marks.

Berlin, 23 December 1901 E. von Wolzogen, Buntes Theater, Überbrettl GmbH. Signed Ernst von Wolzogen, Moritz Muszkat.

NOTE ON WEBERN

Webern
1. has confessed: Coloratura Singing without text
2. has forgotten that in the monodrama harmonics cover the whole page
3. has at once made orchestral pieces 'short piece, only a few bars'
4. has immediately imitated: chords placed heterogeneously
5. the subsidiary section of Chamber Symphony
6. early chords from Sextet, *Pelléas*, Quartet, etc.
7. has provided a piece with a date which is absolutely wrong and comes before the time in which such things were written. Replied to my remonstrances: *that is a mistake.*

TAX DECLARATION FOR 1915 AND SUPPLEMENT 1913

My income for 1914 consisted of:

1. Private subscription from February to December

11 Months at 400 Marks	4400	
Mahler Foundation	1300	5700

2. Lessons (teaching)

6 Months (January till end of June) at 220 Marks   1320

3. Conducting – Fees less expenses

London	500 Marks	250 —	250	
Amsterdam	500 Marks	200 —	300	
Leipzig	500 Marks		500	
	1500	450	1050	1050

4. Royalties from the sale of my works

July Account	500	
December Account no profit!	—	500

5. Advance from the Universal Edition   500

            9070

Since the beginning of the War I have not got a single pupil!

In this statement I ask you to take into account that my income for 1915 will be

Twelve Months of the Private subscription (in the case that this will really continue to be paid to me for this year as well)

         at 400   4800

in addition 1400 marks net profit from the letting of an apartment (Frau Dr. Zehme) who has transferred this to me   1400

            Total = 6200

As I cannot expect profits from the sale of my works, lessons or concerts, it will hardly be possible for me to pay the higher taxes in the present state of inflation. Yours faithfully Arnold Schoenberg.

Supplement to my Tax Declaration

My income consisted of the following:

1. Teaching January to July	6 × 280	1680	
	October to Dec. 3 × 220	660 Marks	2340

2. Advances from Publisher (the Universal Edition, Vienna 1)				1500
3. (a) Conducting Fee (Vienna, April) less travel expenses for 8 days	400 250			
		=150		
(b) Fee for lecture in Stettin less expenses	200 50			
		=150		300
4. Subscriptions (a) Mahler Foundation (b) Private Subscriptions	1300 1600			2900
				7040

Amsterdam: Share of Royalties
(a) Universal Edition   700 Marks
(b) Dreilinden Verlag   160 Marks

Total   860 Marks which I have already entered in the form of advances in the previous year, as they were not paid to me but were deducted from the advances mentioned under 2; so they should not be included in my income, otherwise I would have to pay tax on them twice. As my income for this year was not sufficient I was compelled to incur debts which I have to pay back next year. Therefore I ask to be put in a lower tax category. Arnold Schoenberg.

SCHOENBERG'S PUPILS IN BERLIN

Students of the Master School for Musical Composition directed by Professor Arnold Schoenberg.

1.1.1926–31.12.1928
Winfried Zillig
Walter Goehr

1.10.1927–30.9.1930
Alfred Keller
Peter Schacht

Walter Gronostay
Adolphe Weiss
Robert Gerhard Castells

1.4.1926–31.3.1929
Josef Zmigrod
Josef Rufer

1.1.1927–31.12.1929
Johannes Moenck
Max Walter
Leo Weiss
Charilaos Perpessa
Myroslaw Spiller
Marc Blitzstein

Outside Listener – 1927
Gertrud Fuhrmann

Hansjörg Dammert
Nikolaus Skalkottas

1.4.1929–31.3.1932
Natalie Prawossudowitsch

1.10.1929–30.9.1932
Helmut Rothweiler
Norbert von Hannenheim

1.10.1930–30.9.1933
Erich Schmid

1.4.1931–31.3.1933
Peter Schacht
Bernd Bergel

1.10.1932
Fritz Reich

LETTER ON THE JEWISH QUESTION

In the summer of 1933 Schoenberg sent the following letter from the Hotel Regina, in Paris, to Dr. Ernst Toch, Joachim Stutschewsky and probably other Jewish musicians:

The mistake of the Jews was always to expect help from others, like Zionism, and to have achieved a certain amount of tranquillity by the means of charity, which however is the end of all activity which aims at a goal.

Perhaps one could let this pass for the past 150 years (perhaps, *we say; the Russian and Polish Jews will not say it!*), *but today it would be the end of Judaism and of every single Jew if we go on sleeping.*

So I will start a movement which will unite the Jews again in one people and bring them together in their own country to form a state. One will have to use all the means known from history for this, without any regard for the conventional ideas which the Jews and others have about the nature of the

Jew. As against that we must think of the tasks which have been placed on the Jew in his individual position as a people chosen by God; as the God which is singled out to maintain an idea, the idea of the unpresentable God.

We need for this a man who is willing and fit to run his head against the wall and who is determined to run down anyone who merely wants to discuss, speak in Parliament, protest, support and in one word: weaken.

I have decided, lacking a better person, to begin for the moment. We all know that I have run against walls and can see that I have not perished thereby. People can follow me until they can find a better person. In any case: I do not want to be prevented in this.

Let me know your position.

Best wishes, Your: (signed) Arnold Schoenberg.

One thing more: it would be useless to write against some other affair, for instance against Germany. We only have to do what helps us: nothing against anybody. Everything for the Jews!

Toch and Stutschewsky both left the letter unanswered. They had a different attitude towards Zionism from Schoenberg, and the developments in the following decades finally showed that they were right. When Schoenberg moved to the USA at the end of 1933 he gave up this idea of dedicating himself in such an active and exclusive way to the Jewish cause. However the letter shows his way of reacting to historical events. It was commented on by Stutschewsky on 27 July 1951 in the Zurich 'Israelitische Wochenblatt für die Schweiz'.

FROM A LETTER TO ALBAN BERG, 2 JANUARY 1935

Schoenberg wrote 1934 by mistake; as the letter was sent from 5860 Canyon Cove, Hollywood, and as Schoenberg was living in Boston in 1934, it must have been written in 1935.

. . . here in the Los Angeles Times *I have read nothing about the events in Germany, but I have now been informed in detail aurally about it by some Viennese. In any case I was very pleased about your success in Berlin, which, I hear, was even a demonstrative one.* (Schoenberg meant the première of the fragments from *Lulu* on 30 November 1934 under Erich Kleiber.) *But what will happen next? What will happen to Hindemith? I hear that he had to give up his position at the Academy. Will he be exiled from Germany?*

The idea came to me that perhaps you, Webern, Krenek, Hindemith and also possibly Zillig, Hannenheim and other Germans too should get together to form a protective society. I do not know whether we will be able to achieve much, unless we are joined by other threatened people from the cultural world, scientists, scholars, inventors, painters and poets. But the day before yesterday I sketched out a little scheme for the foundation for a 'Protection Society for Culture', and if you can ask around a bit in Vienna about this and find interest in this I will work on it further and send it to you . . . I will also try to interest people in it here; this does not seem impossible, as I am thinking of the whole threatened area, from left and right, from behind and in front, excluding all political bias. For it seems to apply to the whole! In all countries! Like after the overthrow of the French revolution, where it lasted fifty years until the victory of liberalism. It seems that we may have to experience something of the kind.

FROM A NOTEBOOK

A small red notebook, clearly bound by Schoenberg himself, as the inscription says on the cover:

ARNOLD SCHOENBERG
116 N. ROCKINGHAM AVE
BRENTWOOD PARK
LOS ANGELES
CALIFORNIA
1937
AR. 35077

Inside are some small sheets of music paper. They contain a twelve-note theme and its inversion, a few bars from the third act of *Moses and Aaron*, as well as a text about caricatures, beginning with the kind of written self portrait.

The art of the Caricaturist; summing up most
characteristic features.

I am small; I have short legs, I am bald having a central bald patch and a small (crown?) of dark hair around it. My nose is big and hooked, I have dark big eyes, big eyebrows, my mouth is perhaps the best of me; I have usually my hands crossed on the back; my shoulders are round.

Some cartoonists provide for instance all their victims with a special kind of nose. (Here follow drawings of three noses: a pointed one, a lumpy one and a hooked one.)

Perhaps behind that one might find the aim of creating a type (typus) in a manner comparable to the types of 'Pierrot, Pierette, Colombine, Hanswurst the clown, the Kunstreiterin (circus rider)' etc.

But then you see some cartoonists bringing on one cartoon three or more persons and giving all of them the same nose.

Why a procedure for reasons other than lack of imagination should be applied to our species of men is difficult to understand. True, we don't distinguish the faces of bees or of monkeys of the same race.

To us even all Japanese or Savages from the Pacific Islands look alike.'

ON STRAUSS AND FURTWANGLER (1946)

I am not a friend of Richard Strauss, and, though I do not admire all of his work, I believe that he will remain one of the character- istic and outstanding figures in musical history. Works like *Salome*, *Elektra*, *Intermezzo* and others will not perish. But I do not believe that he was a Nazi, just as little as W. Furtwängler. They were both Deutsch-Nationale – Nationalistic Germans, they both loved Germany, German culture, and art, landscape, lan- guage and its citizens, their co-nationals. They both will raise their glass if a toast is brought to Germany 'Hoch Deutschland' and though estimated French and Italian music and paintings highly, they consider everything German as superior. Their enthusiasm – on a high level of course – was in nature closely related to that of the 'Bierbank' and of the 'Deutsche Männer- gesangs-Verein'. May I repeat: of course on a higher level, because both men, Strauss and Furtwängler, had a higher edu- cation. One must, however, not be blinded by this education. We know that scientists, doctors, professors, writers, poets and artists could stand the musical vulgarity of the Horst Wessel Lied and sing the horrible text with as much fire and enthusiasm as the simple man in the street. I have no information about St's and F's attitude in this respect; but it seems to me doubtless that they at least despised the music.

But; Nazi or not: that Furtwängler cannot come to America and that he has to live lonely in Switzerland without work is due to the intrigue of one man:[1] this powerful man whose word power is not great enough to explain his ideas understandably to musicians, the man who throws a golden watch to the floor in anger over his verbal impotence – this man is capable of keeping a Furtwängler, who is many times his superior, from conducting in America and in the rest of this world.

But I wanted rather to speak about Strauss.

People who do not agree that the ban on F. is justified will have to admit that there is at least consequence in a perfect ban. But even if there were truth in a ban on Strauss, there would only be consequence if his music would also be banned.

But those who allow to play his music but refuse to pay what they owe him, act as shamelessly as pirates.

I do not speak because of sentimental reasons. Of course, I regret an old man of eighty-two years, who wrote throughout his entire life and has created things which 90% of the music lovers of the earth enjoy; I regret that this old man now has lost – for the second time in his life – all his fortune; I regret that he lives at present in two rooms in Switzerland on charity which is extended to him by an eminent lover of the arts, Mr. Reinhart of Winterthur.

I do not speak as a friend of Richard Strauss; though he was helpful to me in my youth, he has later changed his attitude towards myself. I am sure that he does not like my music and in this respect I know no mercy: I consider such people as enemies.

I speak from the standpoint of honesty.

LETTER OF THANKS TO THE NATIONAL INSTITUTE OF ARTS AND LETTERS

In May 1947 Schoenberg sent thanks for the 1000 dollar prize which he had been awarded for outstanding achievements in these words:

Mr. President, ladies and gentlemen, I am proud about the formulation under which this award has been given to me. That all I have endeavoured

[1] Toscanini

to accomplish during this fifty years is now evaluated as an achievement, seems in some respects to be an overestimation. At least not before I could sum up – that is: while it still looked like a pell-mell of incoherent details – at least then did I fail to understand it as a direction leading towards an accomplishment. Personally I had the feeling as if I had fallen into an ocean of boiling water, and not knowing how to swim or to get out in another manner, I tried with my legs and arms as best I could. I did not know what saved me; why I was not drowned or cooked alive . . . I have perhaps only one merit: I never gave up. But how could I give up in the middle of an ocean? Whether my wriggling was very economical or entirely senseless, whether it helped me to survive or counteracted it – there was nobody to help me, nor were there many who would not have liked to see me succumb. I do not contend it was envy – of what was there to be envious? I doubt also that it was absence of goodwill – or worse – presence of ill-wishing. It might have been the desire to get rid of this nightmare, of this unharmonious torture, of these unintelligible ideas, of this methodical madness – and I must admit: these were not bad men who felt this way – though, of course I never understood what I had done to them to make them as malicious, as furious, as cursing, as aggressive; – I am still certain that I had never taken away from something they owned; I never interfered with their prerogatives; I never did trespass on their property; I even did not know where it was located, which were the boundaries of their lots, and who had given them the title to these possessions. Maybe I did not care enough about such problems; maybe I myself failed to understand their viewpoints, was not considerate enough, was rough when I should have been soft, was impatient when they were worried by time-pressure, was ridiculing them, when indulgence was advisable, laughed when they were distressed . . . I see only that I was always in the red – But I have one excuse: I had fallen into an ocean, into an ocean of overheated water, and it burned not only my skin, it burned also internally. And I could not swim. At least I could not swim with the tide. All I could do was swim against the tide – whether it saved me or not! I see that I was always in the red. And when you call this an achievement, so – forgive me – I do not understand of what it might consist. That I never gave up? I could not – I would have liked to. I am proud to receive this award under the assumption that I have achieved something. Please do not call it false modesty if I say: Maybe something has been achieved but it was not I who deserves the credit for that. The credit must be given to my opponents. They were the ones who really helped me. Thank you. Arnold Schoenberg.

A TEXT FROM THE THIRD MILLENNIUM
(February 1948)

The name of Arnold Schoenberg is mentioned in one of the few
letters by Anton v. (does that mean von or van?) Webern. In the
letter which he wrote a few weeks before he was killed fighting
against the Russians (1938) he spoke enthusiastically about this
Schoenberg, and called him the greatest living composer, whose
services to art would never be forgotten. How wrong he was in
this prophecy! I read through six ten-yearly volumes of the
Encyclopaedia Americana without finding a mention of his name.
It was not till I came to the edition of 1968 that I found this name
and a short biographical notice.

He must have played a part forty or fifty years before this
volume, that is to say almost a hundred years ago, because,
although not a single one of his compositions are mentioned, two
facts are of interest to me. First that he also wrote theoretical
works, and clearly had a large number of pupils. However, none
of his thoeretical writings here survived him. The biography says
that they were already out of date at the time they were written.
They dealt with traditional methods of composition, functions of
harmony, variations, musical logic, and referred to composers of
the romantic era of chromaticism. Secondly, he must have had a
kind of battle with the well-known German writer Thomas Mann,
who was clearly the inventor of the method of composing with
twelve tones, based on the emancipation of the dissonance, i.e.
the equality of the presentation of dissonances with the presentation of consonances. Webern mentions the invention of this
theory and the terminology which belongs to it as an achievement
of Schoenberg's, but this seems to be wrong, for Schoenberg was
an unscrupulous exploiter of other people's ideas.

It has been said that in his youth Mann urgently wanted to
become a musician, but turned to writing in his 20s.

Probably Mann was in contact with Schoenberg about this
time; Schoenberg was living in Vienna, only a few minutes'
flight from Munich, where Mann lived. He probably invented
the twelve-tone theory at that time (1933), and as he had given
up composing himself, he allowed Schoenberg to use it and publish it under his own name. Mann's liberal nature never mentioned this violation of his rights. But it seems that they became
enemies in the last years of their lives, and now Mann took his
property back and attributed its origin to a person whom he had

created himself (Homunculus). So the great American music came into the position o. being able to profit from Mann's theoretical invention, and this led to all the progress in American music from the fusion of this with Budia Nalanger's[1] modal methods of producing real old music which works like new music.

If this accusation of the forgotten 'theoretician' Schoenberg and his hateful crime as well as his disregard of the rights of cultural property are aggravating, the way in which Mann has presented this, his own idea, is all the more grandiose. Only a real inventor is in a position to give such an illuminating presentation. Schoenberg would never have had the *capacity for work of this kind*.

Hugo Triebsamen.

A SELF-ANALYSIS
1948

If people speak of me, they at once connect me with horror, with atonality, and with composition with twelve tones. Generally it is always forgotten that before I developed these new techniques, there were two or three periods in which I had to acquire the technical armament that enabled me to stand distinctly on my own feet, in a manner that forbade comparison with other composers, either predecessors or contemporaries.

It is seldom realized that a hand that dares to renounce so much of the achievements of our forefathers has to be exercised thoroughly in the techniques that are to be replaced by new methods. It is seldom realized that there is a link between the technique of forerunners and that of an innovator and that no new technique in the arts is created that has not had its roots in the past. And it is seldom realized that these works in which an innovator prepares – consciously or subconsciously – for the action that will distinguish him from his surroundings furnish ready information about the justification of an author's turn toward new regions.

In formulating this justification it seems as if this might be the task of a musicologist. But this is untrue, because it is just the audience to whom such recognition is important. And it is the

---

[1]　A distortion of the name Nadja Boulanger, b. 1887, teacher of composition and prophetess of Igor Stravinsky.

musicologist's duty to guide the audience in order to procure a fair evaluation of one who had the courage to risk his life for an idea. Musicologists have failed to act in favour of the truth. This is the reason why my situation with the audience is often as follows: those of my works that might interest them (that is, those they consider atonal and dissonant) they refuse to listen to, and those works that are not called atonal but are less dissonant are not interesting enough – to people who do not know them at all.

Atonality or dissonance are no yardsticks for evaluation. Superficiality might base its judgements on such qualities. True love and understanding of music will wonder: What has been said? How was it expressed? Was there a new message delivered in music? Has a new personality been discovered? Was the technical presentation adequate?

Of course, to identify the style is easier and procures for one the glory of a connoisseur. But the love of the friend of art does not derive so indirectly – if it is appreciation that it aims for.

I am sure that the works of my last style would find at least the respect they deserve if the audience were given a chance to do justice to the works of my earlier periods. It was a healthier situation when Richard Wagner's works had to struggle for recognition. Then, even the most conservative friends of music recognized the value and the beauties of Wagner's first and second periods – *Rienzi*, *The Flying Dutchman*, *Tannhäuser*, and *Lohengrin*. This recognition paved the way for the appreciation of *Tristan*, *Die Meistersinger*, *The Ring*, and *Parsifal*.

I personally do not find that atonality and dissonance are the outstanding features of my works. They certainly offer obstacles to the understanding of what is really my musical subject. But why then did even the works of my first period always meet resistance at the first few performances, only later to become appreciated?

It seems that the true cause must be found in my tendency to endow every work with an extravagant abundance of musical themes. In the works of my first period this caused extension to a length that soon began to annoy me. It was, of course, the tendency of the Wagnerian and post-Wagnerian epoch. Recall the extension of symphonies by Bruckner and Mahler and other forms by Strauss, Reger, Debussy, Tchaikovsky and many others. Much of this length, except in Mahler and Reger, was due to the technique of using numerous little-varied or even unvaried repetitions of short phrases. I became aware of the aesthetic inferiority of this technique when I composed the final section of the symphonic poem, *Pelléas and Mélisande*. In the greater part of that work, sequences made up a considerable contribution toward achieving the necessary expanse of the presentation, such as is required for easier understanding.

At the very start I knew that restriction could be achieved by two methods, condensation and juxtaposition. The first attempts that I made prior to this recognition – to use variation, often with far-reaching changes – did not satisfy me perfectly, though in 'developing variation' lies a far greater aesthetic merit than in an unvaried sequence. But even by that method the length of a piece was scarcely reduced. Thus even my First String Quartet, Op. 7, which I dislike as little as any of my earlier works, is of an unusual length – a great obstacle to the recognition of whatever beauty may be found therein.

Before I could master technically the difficulties of condensation and juxtaposition, I was forced by my destiny upon another road. By abandoning the one-movement form and returning, in my Second String Quartet, to the organization of four movements, I became the first composer in this period to write shorter compositions. Soon thereafter I wrote in the extreme short forms. Although I did not dwell very long in this style, it taught me two things: first, to formulate ideas in an aphoristic manner, which did not require continuations out of formal reasons; secondly, to link ideas together without the use of formal connectives, merely by juxtaposition.

I admit that this style of writing does not promote easy understanding. It is the style of music since about 1920, and it requires intense attention to grasp and a good memory to keep in mind what is going on. I am sure that a full understanding is difficult to acquire if one has not gradually become acquainted with my ideas in general and their special presentation.

Already my early works show some traits of my mature style, but seldom are all the so-called difficulties crowded into one single place. If, for instance, heterogeneous units of a work are juxtaposed, the unit itself might not be too condensed or its harmonic background might be rather comprehensible; in other cases, a slightly varied repetition might support the memory; in still other cases, subsequent elements might function as belated connectives. Thus, not all such procedures as are obstacles to the uninitiated listener will work in a sense-interrupting manner. And once the gate to understanding is open an emotional impression will not fail to appear.

May I venture to say that, in my belief, even works of my third period as, for example, the Three Piano Pieces, Op. 11, or the Five Orchestral Pieces, Op. 16, and especially *Pierrot Lunaire*, Op. 21, are relatively easy to understand today. And if I speak at present dispassionately about these works, one must not forget that they were written forty or more years ago. I can look upon them as if somebody else might be their composer, and I can explain their technique and their mental contents quite objectively. I see therein things that at the time of composing were still unknown to me.

May I venture to say that if in spite of my personal feeling about them I still like them, the idea that they are worth it seems somehow justified.

MY ATTITUDE TOWARD POLITICS
1950

I am at least as conservative as Edison and Ford have been. But I am, unfortunately, not quite as progressive as they were in their own fields.

In my early twenties, I had friends who introduced me to Marxian theories. When I thereafter had jobs as *Chormeister* – director of men's choruses – they called me 'Genosse' – comrade, and at this time, when the Social Democrats fought for an extension of the right of suffrage, I was strongly in sympathy with some of their aims.

But before I was twenty-five, I had already discovered the difference between me and a labourer; I then found out that I was a *bourgeois* and turned away from all political contacts

I was much too busy with my own development as a composer, and, I am sure, I could never have acquired the technical and aesthetic power I developed had I spent any space of time to politics. I never made speeches, nor propaganda, nor did I try to convert people.

When the First World War began, I was proud to be called to arms and as a soldier I did my whole duty enthusiastically as a true believer in the house of Habsburg, in its wisdom of 800 years in the art of government and in the consistency of a monarch's lifetime, as compared with the short lifetime of every republic. In other words, I became a monarchist. Also at this time and after the unfortunate ending of the war and for many years thereafter, I considered myself as a monarchist, but also then did not participate in any action. I was then and thereafter only a quiet believer in this form of government, though the chance for a restoration was at zero.

Evidently when I came to America such considerations were superfluous. My viewpoint since then has been one of gratitude for having found a refuge. And I decided that I, as only a naturalized citizen, had no right to participate in the politics of the natives. In other words, I had to stand by and to be still. This, I have always considered to be the rule of my life. But I was never a communist.

16 February 1950

BACH
1950

I

I used to say, 'Bach is the first composer with twelve tones.' This was a joke, of course. I did not even know whether somebody before him might not have deserved this title. But the truth on which this statement is based is that the Fugue No. 24 of the first volume of the Well-Tempered Clavier, in B minor, begins with a *Dux* in which all twelve tones appear. I have tried to find another example of this kind, but have not succeeded. I could, however, check only a part of his whole work.

It is an exceptional case; even in this fugue the *Comes* consists of only eleven different tones, and of the twelve repetitions and transpositions, only seven are complete, while five omit one or two of the twelve tones. Maybe an examination of the countersubjects and the episodes might exhibit more interesting facts. But what is more important here is that this fugue deserves the title of 'chromatic fugue' more rightfully than the one which is usually called so. It approaches a style of chromaticism in a manner different from Bach's ordinary procedure. In general, chromatic alterations appear as ascending or descending substitute leading-tones as in measures 1–2 of Fugue 14, vol. 1; or in half-tone progressions, as in measures 6, 12 (and others) of Fugue 22, vol. 2, or in Fugue 10, vol. 1. There are in vol. 1 two somewhat similar cases: Fugue No.

18 in G-sharp minor and, especially, Fugue No. 12 in F minor. But measures 33–34 of Fugue No. 19 are less chromatic than they look; they are in B minor, mixing features of the ascending scale with ordinary descending scales and with Bach's peculiar form of a descending minor scale.

In Fugue 24 the chromatically altered tones are neither substitutes nor parts of scales. They possess distinctly an independence resembling the unrelated tones of the chromatic scale in a basic set of a twelve-tone composition. The only essential difference between their nature and modern chromaticism is that they do not yet take advantage of their multiple meaning as a means of changing direction in a modulatory fashion.

II

I have always thought highly of the teacher Bach. Doubtless he possessed a profound insight into the hidden mysteries of tone-relations. He was certainly able to present his ideas clearly and understandably. But I am also convinced that he was not so sentimental as to renounce his contemporaries' application of *Schopfbeutler, Kopfstukeln und Ohrenreissen*,[1] if it helped to make his pupils work, practise and even only understand. And he was successful in that. One need only remember the unsurpassed excellence of so many of his sons and especially of Philipp Emanuel, who, I believe, must have possessed a tremendous knowledge of counterpoint. Probably Johann Sebastian had invested in him all his secrets of finding one's way with the hidden peculiarities of the tones. I am sure that had he not considered his father's style as obsolete, and had he possessed his inventive and expressive power and his personality, he might have become as great as his father.

Technically, I assume, he must have known the secrets that enabled the Old-One to build, in contradiction to the advice of theorists, on a broken chord, all the different themes of the *Art of the Fugue*, which admit all the canonic imitations, direct, in inversion, in augmentation and diminution.

He must have known this – and more; he also knew the contrary. He knew what to do and what not to do in order to produce a theme which would not lend itself to any treatment of this kind. For this reason I believe that he, Philipp Emanuel, was the originator of the *Royal Theme*.

Whether malice of his own induced him, or whether the 'joke' was ordered by the king, can probably be proved only psychologically; the great king knew how one feels after winning at battle and he wanted to see how another person behaves after losing a battle. He wanted to see the embarrassment of one who had experienced only battles which he won; he wanted to enjoy the helplessness of the victim of his joke, when the highly praised art of improvization could not master the difficulties of a well-prepared trap. A trap it was, Philipp Emanuel had constructed a theme that resisted Johann Sebastian's versatility. In the *Art of the Fugue* a minor triad offered many contrapuntal openings; the Royal Theme, also a minor triad, did not admit one single canonic imitation. All the miracles that the *Musical Offering* presents are achieved by counter-subjects, counter-melodies and other external additions.

The Royal joke, through Philipp Emanuel's skill, had been successful. But Johann Sebastian must have recognized the bad trick. That he calls his 'Offering', a *Musikalische Opfer* is very peculiar, because the German word *Opfer* has a double meaning: 'offering', or rather 'sacrifice' and 'victim' – Johann Sebastian knew that he had become the victim of a 'grand seigneur's' joke.

III

Many musicians today are inclined to overestimate merits which are obvious even to the lesser minds of average men, at the expense of merits which shine less brilliantly. I am not in opposition to overestimation of the art of counterpoint, nor do I overestimate other techniques. In considering such differences of style not as techniques, but as manners of expression, one will do justice also to the particularities of other ways of presentation. Wagner's balance of harmony, in a style at his time still catalogued as modulatory, the illustrative power of his orchestration, the emotional quality of his melodies; Brahms's structural finesses, the richness of his fundamental harmony, the beauty of his melodies; Beethoven's logic, the originality of his invention, his impulsive personality, the variety of his directions; Schubert's ability to use rather simple structural devices, in spite of which he could ennoble a popular touch in his melodies; Mozart's unique capacity of combining heterogeneous elements in the smallest space – all these are merits which deserve just as much praise as do contrapuntal achievements. And though one may believe me when I say that I am the last one to degrade the merits of contrapuntal writing, one must take into consideration that no real master's merits were hindered by a difficulty he had to overcome. To the real master there is no difficulty, and what a layman or a musician will call one is none to him; he speaks his native language. To the one it is counterpoint, to the other, orchestra colour and rich harmony, or logic or beauty, and so forth.

I am fortunate to have learned a few facts, reported to me by a friend. He was a composer who believed in his inspiration, whether it dictated to h'm music in agreement with theory and aesthetics or not. He told me that, in several cases, he had written at first only the melody of quite a long section. Thereafter he would add a second line, an accompanying voice, without even looking at the first line; gradually he added, by the same procedure, a sufficient number of voices to complete the setting. The result was astonishing; nobody would discover that this had been produced in such an unusual manner, under such extraordinary conditions.

He was afraid that people would believe it was mere nonsense he had written, or that the whole story was untrue. He assured me that some such passages were at least as good as others, if not better, and that he must have been in a kind of trance. He had had the feeling that he was merely copying from a model he saw – or heard – in front of him.

It seems to me that only this can explain miracles like that of the *Art of the Fugue* and all similar miracles performed by great masters. These are miracles which no human brain can produce. The artist is only the mouthpiece of a power which dictates what to do.

Born to this language, Bach translated the will of this power into terms of human counterpoint.

IV

I have speculated much about the fact that Bach writes, on the contrapuntal combinations of canons of all forms and of multiple counterpoint of counter-subjects, and, on the other hand, composes a great number in which nothing of this kind can be observed, and which seem to correspond to the most superficial concept of the several entrances of themes 'fleeing from one another'. Such examples are, among others, in vol. 1, Nos. 1, 3, 6, 9, 10, and 17 (*Well-Tempered Clavier*).

It is difficult to believe that there should not be present here the same high art which we observed in those pieces where it is quite obvious. I rather believe there is a hidden mystery which has not yet been discovered. I have frequently tried to discover such a principle therein, but in vain. Nevertheless, I always feel that something is going on that catches my attention in a peculiar way. What is it?

I want to suggest that gifted and experienced musicians should try to solve this problem. I myself have assumed that one such principle could be deduced as deriving from multiple counterpoint of the second, third, fourth, sixth and seventh. Whether such treatment is applied to a whole theme or only to parts of it, or even only to main notes, or to a counter-subject, or to the material of episodes, it may produce the themes, configurations, combinations and variants needed to produce all the contrasts, the variety and the fluency of a piece.

Research into these problems should be conducted according to viewpoints of compositorial technique, rather than according to aesthetics. Accordingly it might be of some assistance if I offer herewith my own theory of the nature of contrapuntal compositions.[2]

Music of the homophonic-melodic style of composition, that is, music with a main theme, accompanied by and based on harmony, produces its material by, as I call it, *developing variation*. This means that variation of the features of a basic unit produces all the thematic formulations which provide for fluency, contrasts, variety, logic and unity, on the one hand, and character, mood, expression, and every needed differentiation, on the other hand – thus elaborating the *idea* of the piece.

In contrast, contrapuntal composition does not produce its material by development, but by a procedure rather to be called *unravelling*. That is, a basic configuration or combination taken asunder and reassembled in a different order contains everything which will later produce a different sound than that of the original formulation. Thus, a canon of two or more voices can be written in one single line, yet furnishes various sounds. If multiple counterpoints are applied, a combination of three voices, invertible in the octave, tenth and twelfth, offers so many combinations that even longer pieces can be derived from it.[3]

According to this theory, one should not expect that new themes occur in such fugues, but that there is a basic combination which is the source of all combinations.

I cannot believe that the author of the *Art of Fugue* here composed only what most musicians perceive: piano pieces, based merely on the external and superficial characteristics of succeeding entrances of a theme. At least, if such were the case, he would not have called them fugues, but perhaps suites, inventions, partitas, etc.

March 10, 1950

NOTES
BACH

Eight typewritten pages, in English, dated March 10, 1950. Corrections by Dika Newlin.

[1] 'Hair-pulling, head-slapping, ear-pulling.'

[2] I am not sure whether all this has not already been described by competent theorists. However, as I already said in my *Harmonielehre*, I have not learned this by reading but by thinking; therefore it is my own. But it seems to me that today's musical education is not always benefited by the tradition of the great line of Viennese teachers and theorists – the line of Porpora, Fux, Albrechtsberger, Sechter, Bruckner and Schenker. It seems that only musicians five or six years older or younger than I have had part of it. Many of them are dead; curiously, none of them was an advanced composer. (AS)

[3] I have made use of such possibilities in the first movement of my Suite (in ancient style) for String Orchestra, which I had planned as a *Lehrstück* for students of composition, omitting, of course, those combinations which are not interesting enough. (AS)

CHRONOLOGICAL LIST OF WORKS AND FIRST PERFORMANCES

1894 Three Piano Pieces

1897 String Quartet in D major (17 March 1898, Vienna, Fitzner Quartet).

1897 (98?) Two Songs opus 1.

1899 Four Songs opus 2, String Sextet *Verklärte Nacht* opus 4 (18.3.1902, Vienna, Rosé Quartet and members of the Vienna Philharmonic).

1899–1903 Six Songs opus 3.

1900–1911 'Gurrelieder' (23.2.1913, Vienna, Philharmonic Choir, Franz Schreker).

1901 Seven Chansons (Brettl-Lieder).

1903 Symphonic Poem *Pelléas and Mélisande*, opus 5 (26.1.1905, Vienna, Konzertverein Orchestra, A. Schoenberg).

1903–1905 Eight Songs opus 6.

1904 Six Songs with Orchestra opus 8 (Nos. 2, 5 and 6 on 29.1 1914 Prague, soloist Hans Winkelmann, Conductor Alexander von Zemlinsky).

1905 String Quartet No. 1 in D minor opus 7 (5.2.1907, Vienna, Rosé Quartet).

1906 Chamber Symphony in E major opus 9 (8.2.1907, Vienna, Rosé Quartet and Wind ensemble of the Vienna Philharmonic).

1907 Two Ballades for Voice and Piano opus 12. 'Friede auf Erden' for mixed choir a cappella, opus 13 (9.12.1911, Vienna, Philharmonic Chorus, Franz Schreker).

1907–1908 String Quartet No. 2 in F sharp minor opus 10 (21.12.1908, Vienna, Rosé Quartet and Marie Gutheil-Schoder, Soprano).

1907–1908 Two Songs opus 14.

1908–1909 Fifteen Songs of Stefan George opus 15 (14.1.1910, Vienna, Martha Winternitz-Dorda).

1909 Three Piano Pieces opus 11 (14.1.1910, Vienna, Etta Werndorff).

1909 Five Pieces for Orchestra opus 16 (3.9.1912, London, Sir Henry Wood). *Erwartung*, Monodrama opus 17 (6.6.1924, Prague, Neues Deutsches Theater, Marie Gutheil-Schoder, Conductor A. von Zemlinsky).

1910 Three Pieces for Chamber Orchestra (unfinished) (10.10. 1957 Berlin, Members of the Berlin Philharmonic).

1911 Six little piano pieces opus 19 (4.2.1912 Berlin, Louis Closson).

1911 'Herzgewächse' for soprano, celesta, harp and harmonium opus 20.

1912 *Pierrot Lunaire*, 21 Melodramas opus 21 (16.10.1912, Berlin, Albertine Zehme, Conductor Arnold Schoenberg).

1913 *Die Glückliche Hand*, Drama with music opus 18 (14.19.1924, Vienna, Volksoper, Conductor Fritz Stiedry, Producer Josef Turnau).

1913–1916 Four Songs with Orchestra opus 22 (21.2.1932, Frankfurt, Hertha Reinecke, Conductor Hans Rosbaud).

1917–1922 *Jacob's Ladder*, Oratorio (unfinished), (First performance of the opening section 12.1.1958 Hamburg, Conductor Hans Rosbaud; of the whole work 16.6.1961 Vienna, Conductor Rafael Kubelik).

1920–1923 Five Piano Pieces opus 23 (1 and 2: 9.10.1920, Vienna, Eduard Steuermann). Serenade opus 24 (20.7.1924, Donaueschingen, Schoenberg).

1921 Suite for piano opus 25.

1922 Two Chorale Preludes by J. S. Bach arranged for orchestra (7.12.1922 New York, Conductor Joseph Stransky).

1923–1924 Wind Quintet opus 26 (13.9.1924, Vienna, Conductor Felix Greissle).

1924–1926 Suite for Piano, three woodwind and three strings opus 29 (15.12.1927, Paris, Conductor A. Schoenberg).

1925 Four Pieces for mixed chorus opus 27. Three Satires for mixed chorus, opus 28.

1925–1926 Appendix to opus 28.

1926–1928 Variations for Orchestra opus 31 (2.12.1928, Berlin, Conductor Wilhelm Furtwängler, Berlin Philharmonic).

1927 String Quartet No. 3 opus 30 (19.9.1927, Vienna, Kolisch Quartet).

1928 Prelude and Fugue in E flat by J. S. Bach, orchestrated (10.11.1929, Vienna, Conductor Anton von Webern).

Piano Piece opus 33a (30.1.1931, Hamburg, Else C. Kraus). Three German Folk Songs (15th and 16th centuries) arranged for unaccompanied mixed chorus a cappella.

1928–1929 *Von heute auf morgen*, Opera in one act opus 32 (1.2.1930, Frankfurt Opera House, Conductor Hans Wilhelm Steinberg, Producer Herbert Graf).

1929 Four German Folk Songs (15th and 16th centuries) arranged for voice and piano.

1929–1930 Accompaniment Music to a Film Scene opus 34 (6.11.1930, Berlin, Conductor Otto Klemperer).

1929–1930 Six Pieces for male chorus opus 35 (No. 4 'Glück', 3.11.1929, Berlin Radio, Erwin Lendvai Quartet; the other five: 29.11.1931, Frankfurt, South West German Radio, the thirteenth quartet of the Workers' choral Society 'Vorwärts', Hanau, Conductor Franz Schmitt).

1931 Piano Piece opus 33b.

1930–1932 *Moses and Aaron* Opera in three acts (Dance round the Golden Calf 2.7.1951, Darmstadt, Conductor Hermann Scherchen; the two completed acts in concert performance 12.3.1954, Hamburg, Conductor Hans Rosbaud; stage performance 6.6.1957, Zurich, Stadttheater, Conductor Hans Rosbaud, Producer Karl Heinz Krahl).

1932–1933 Concerto for Cello and Orchestra after the Harpsichord Concerto in D major by Georg Matthias Monn (7.12.1935, London, Emanuel Feuermann).

1933 Three Songs on texts of Jakob Haringer opus 48 (5.6.1952, London, Anne Wood and Peter Stadlen). Concerto for String Quartet and Orchestra after the Concerto Grosso in G minor by G. F. Handel (26.9.1934, Prague, Kolisch Quartet, Conductor K. B. Jirak).

1934 Suite for String Orchestra (18.5.1935, Los Angeles, Conductor Otto Klemperer).

1934–1936 Concerto for Violin and Orchestra opus 36 (6.12.1940 Philadelphia, soloist Louis Krasner, Conductor Leopold Stokowski).

1936 String Quartet No. 4 opus 37 (9.1.1937, Los Angeles, Kolisch Quartet).

1937 Brahms, Piano Quartet in G minor opus 25 arranged for orchestra (7.5.1938, Los Angeles, Conductor Otto Klemperer).

1938 'Kol Nidre' for Speaker, mixed chorus and orchestra opus 39 (4.10.1938, Los Angeles, Conductor A. Schoenberg).

1939 Chamber Symphony No. 2 opus 38 (begun 1906) (15.12. 1940, New York, Conductor Fritz Stiedry).

1941 Variations on a Recitative for Organ opus 40 (10.4.1944, New York, Carl Weinrich).

1942 'Ode to Napoleon' for Speaker, Piano and String Quartet opus 41 (24.11.1944, New York, Conductor Arthur Rodzinsky).

1942 Concerto for Piano and Orchestra opus 42 (6.2.1944, New York, Eduard Steuermann, Conductor Leopold Stokowski).

1943 Theme and Variations for Wind Orchestra (also version for full orchestra) opus 43a and b (20.10.1944, Boston, Conductor Sergei Koussevitzky).

1945 Prelude for Orchestra and mixed chorus opus 44 (1.11.1945, Los Angeles, Conductor Werner Janssen).

1946 String Trio opus 45 (May 1947, Cambridge, Mass.).

1947 *A Survivor from Warsaw* for Speaker, male chorus and orchestra opus 46 (1948, Albuquerque, Conductor Kurt Frederick).

1948 Three Folk Songs for mixed chorus unaccompanied opus 49.

1949 Phantasy for violin with piano accompaniment opus 47 (13.9.1949, Los Angeles, Adolf Koldofsky, Leonard Stein).

1949 'Dreimal tausend Jahre' for mixed chorus unaccompanied opus 50a (29.10.1949, Fylkingen, Conductor Eric Ericson).

1950 'De profundis' for mixed chorus unaccompanied opus 50b (29.1.1954, Cologne, Conductor Bernhard Zimmermann).

1950 'Modern Psalm' to Schoenberg's own text for mixed chorus, speaker and orchestra (unfinished) opus 50c (29 May 1956, Cologne, Conductor Nino Sanzogno).

WRITINGS IN BOOK FORM

Harmonielehre (Treatise on Harmony), Vienna 1911 (3rd enlarged edition 1922).

Models for Beginners in Composition, New York 1942.

Structural Functions of Harmony, London and New York 1954.

Preliminary Exercises in Counterpoint, edited and with a foreword by Leonard Stein, London 1963.

Fundamentals of Musical Composition, edited by Gerald Strang and Leonard Stein, London 1965.

Die Jakobsleiter (Jacob's Ladder), Vienna 1917.

Texts (Die Glückliche Hand, Totentanz der Prinzipien, Requiem, Die Jakobsleiter), Vienna 1926.

Der biblische Weg (The Biblical Way), Drama, (Original German version still unpublished), Italian translation, Milan 1968.

Style and Idea (a selection of articles and lectures and notes), New York 1950; enlarged edition London and New York 1975.

Moderne Psalmen (Modern Psalms) Mainz 1957.

Letters, edited by Erwin Stein, Mainz 1958; English translation London 1964.

SELECT BIBLIOGRAPHY

Arnold Schoenberg, Sympos:um with contributions by Alban Berg; Paris von Gütersloh, Heinrich Jalowetz, Vassily Kandinsky, Karl Linke, Paul Königer, Erwin Stein, Anton von Webern, Egon Wellesz and others, Munich 1912.

Egon Wellesz, *Arnold Schoenberg*, Vienna 1921; English translation London.

Paul Stefan, *Arnold Schoenberg*, Vienna 1924.

E. E. Sollertinsky, *Arnold Schoenberg*, Leningrad 1934.

Arnold Schoenberg, edited by Merle Armitage (with contributions by Carl Engel, Otto Klemperer, Ernst Krenek, Paul A. Pisk, Arnold Schoenberg, Paul Stefan, Eduard Steuermann, Leopold Stokowski, Berthold Viertel and others), New York 1937.

Luigi Rognoni, *La scuola musicale di Vienna*, Turin 1966; English translation London 1977.

Juan Carlos Paz, *Schoenberg o el fin de la era tonal*. Buenos Aires 1954.

Dika Newlin, *Bruckner, Mahler, Schoenberg*, New York, 1947.

René Leibowitz, *Schoenberg et son école*, Paris 1947; English translation New York.

H. H. Stuckenschmidt, *Arnold Schoenberg*, Zürich and Freiburg 1951, second enlarged edition 1957; English translation London 1959 (also translated into French, Hebrew, Polish, Spanish and Japanese).

Josef Rufer, *The Works of Arnold Schoenberg*, Kassel 1959; English translation London 1962.

Willi Reich, *Schoenberg oder der konservative Revolutionär*, Vienna 1969.

Special Numbers: for his 50th birthday, Anbruch, Vienna 1924.
for his 60th birthday, Anbruch, Vienna 1934.
Musical Quarterly, New York 1934.
for his 75th birthday, Stimmen, Berlin 1949,
The Canon, Sydney 1949.

Memoirs by Alma Maria Mahler, Charlie Chaplin, Salka Viertel, Bertha Zuckerkandl and Bertolt Brecht (Arbeitsjournale).

Letters from Alban Berg to Helene Berg, from Anton von Webern to Hildegard Jone and Josef Humplik.

Analytical Writings by Reinhold Brinkmann, Jan Maegaard and Karl H. Wörner.

SOURCES

Photo Florence Homolka, Los Angeles (dust cover).
Fotographische Anstalt Matzner, Vienna.
Private Photographs.
Louis P. Lochner: Fritz Kreisler.
Bibliotheca Bodmeriana, Cologne-Geneva.
Library of Congress, Washington.
Berliner Architekturwelt, Vol. 4, 1902.
Picture collection of the Austrian National Library.
Photo by Martin Müller, Stettin.
Universal Edition, Vienna.
Foto Schlosser und Wenisch, Prague.
Belmont Music Publishers, Los Angeles.
Historical Museum of the City of Leipzig, Theatrical collection.
Prussian State Library Cultural Archive, Music Department, Berlin.
Archive of the Prussian Academy of Arts, Berlin.
Photo John Graudenz.
Photo Ilse Rumpler, New York.
Phot Richard Fish.

INDEX

The names of Schoenberg's first and second wives and his five children are not included in this index, as they are referred to very often. These are Mathilde (pages 40–301), Gertrud (pages VII–534), Trudi (pages 58–477), Georg (pages 88–513), Nuria (pages VII–513), Ronny (pages VII–521), and Lawrence (pages VII–521). Anton von Webern and Alban Berg also appear from the beginning of their friendship with Schoenberg up till their deaths so often that the passages in which they are mentioned are not listed individually. Under the entry 'Arnold Schoenberg' there is an alphabetical list of works, with the help of which the works of Schoenberg mentioned in this book can be found. The chronological catalogue of works is on pages 558–61.

INDEX

Abraham, Hermann 345
Adams, Robert D. W. 481
Adler, Felix 208, 277
Adler, Guido 79, 105, 169, 179, 193, 263, 418, 424, 430
Adler, Oskar 21, 22, 238, 382, 429, 482, 487, 502, 517
Adorno, Theodor W. 339, 345, 382, 427, 448, 495, 508, 509, 512
Aeschylus 140
Aibl, Joseph 66
d'Albert, Eugen 44
Alpern, David Dr. XII
Altenberg, Peter 23, 116, 183, 184, 185, 255
Altmann, Wilhelm 59
Amar-Quartet 282, 299
Amersdorfer, Prof. 339, 344
d'Amico, Fedele XI
Ammann, Heinrich 91
Amsterdam-Quartet 503
Anderson, Hedli 455
Andrae, Volkmar 426
Anglès, Higino XIII
d'Annunzio, Gabriele 303
Ansermet, Ernest 426, 497
Ansorge, Conrad 60
Antheil, Böske 499
Antheil, Georg 469, 500
Apostel, Hans Erich 258, 274, 382, 392, 486, 490, 502, 507
Archipenko, Alexander 501
Aristotle 183
Arlt, Gustav 461
Armitage, Merle 415, 419, 422, 423, 563
Arnhold, Eduard 167
Aron, Paul 325
Asch, Joseph 351

Auber, Daniel François 431
Avraamov, Arsemy 386

Bach, David Josef 22, 29, 30, 80, 144, 238, 255, 297, 329, 381, 382, 388, 405, 430, 476, 502
Bach, Johann Sebastian 161, 168, 169, 239, 283, 309, 324, 328, 340, 341, 345, 349, 365, 375, 378, 398, 406, 408, 430, 432, 451, 464, 470, 491, 552–56
Bach, Philipp Emanuel 553
Bachrich, Ernst 251–54, 260, 262
Bahr-Mildenburg, Anna 98, 99, 130, 184, 195, 196
Bahr, Hermann 98, 99, 124, 143, 164, 233
Baker, Israel 501
Balan, Benno 328, 331
Balling, Michael 259
Balzac, Honoré 175, 224, 234–36, 239, 243, 250, 440, 488
Bandler, Heinrich 42, 293
Barber, Samuel 469
Bartók, Béla 164, 173, 221, 240, 261, 262–64, 268, 269, 292, 303, 340, 439, 448, 498, 500
Bassetti-Sani, Antonio 492
Batka, Richard von 208
Bauer, Harold 374
Bauer-Pilecka, Olga 266
Bayer, Josef 398
Beardesley, Aubrey 92
Becker, Carl Heinrich 307
Beer-Hofmann, Richard 243
Beethoven, Ludwig van 44, 74, 93, 98, 154, 162, 169, 192, 245, 262, 282, 304, 332, 340, 341, 359, 363, 389,

397, 399, 416, 420, 421, 429, 430, 451, 460, 465, 503, 516
Behrens, Peter 300
Bekker, Paul 295, 297, 321, 328
Beilcke, Erika 293
Bellermann, Heinrich 429
Belling, Sandra 181
Benda, Hans von 317
Berg, Alban VII, X, 42, 53, 64, 65, 67, 80–427, 442, 443, 490, 496, 534, 563
Berg, Charly 80
Berg, Helene 53, 97, 137, 233, 242, 249, 261, 263, 316, 408, 411, 412, 415, 563
Berg, Smaragda 147
Bergel, Bernd 541
Berger, Willhelm 91
Bergson, Henri 183
Berlioz, Hector 75, 83
Berhnardt, Sarah 60
Bernstein, Martin 389
Besserer, Erika 292
Bethge, Hans 245, 310
Bie, Oskar 92
Bien, Irene 97
Bienenfeld, Elsa 78
Bierbaum, Otto Julius 47, 49, 53, 54, 75
Billing, Klaus 478
Bittner, Julius 193, 240, 244, 291
Bizet, Georges 431
Blacher, Boris 505
Blavatsky, Helene 243
Blech, Leo 157
Blitzstein, Marc 339, 541
Bloch, Eduard, Publishing firm 52
Bloch, Ernst 374, 481
Blumauer-Schoenberg, Ottilie VIII, XII, 18, 28, 29, 40, 350, 367, 476, 479, 482, 486, 489, 491, 510, 511, 514, 520
Blumauer, Susanne 482
Böcklin, Arnold 357
Bodanzky, Arthur 27, 34, 128, 129, 130, 188, 261, 374, 437
Bodanzky-Goldschmied, Malvina XI, 25, 27, 34, 429, 493
Bodanzky, Robert 27, 31, 177, 189
Bodmer, Daniel XIII
Bohnen, Michael 328
Bomart, Publisher 365

Boosey, Leslie 450
Bopp, Wilhelm 131
Boruttau, Alfred J. 184, 211
Bosch, Hieronymus 353
Bote & Bock, Publishers 331
Botstiber, Alois 98
Botstiber, Hugo 98, 259
Boulanger, Nadja 498, 500, 548
Boult, Sir Adrian 383, 384
Bradsky, Božena 53, 56
Brahms, Johannes 30, 34, 37, 74, 75, 78, 84, 85, 98, 101, 119, 160, 188, 219, 239, 282, 332, 339, 340, 341, 352, 355–63, 376, 377, 379, 420, 421, 423, 430, 504
Brecher, Gustav 175, 178, 179
Brecht, Bertolt 345, 456, 457, 468, 473, 563
Breitkopf & Härtel, Publishers 191, 222
Brinkmann, Reinhold 563
Brioschi, Antonio 92
Broch, Hermann 382
Bruch, Max 51
Bruck-Zimmer, Stefanie 262
Bruckner, Anton 112, 549, 563
Brunswick, Marc 449, 482
Büchner, Georg 54, 245
Buck, Pearl S. 412
Buhlig, Richard 415, 464, 465
Bülow, Hans von 74
Burger, Albert 206
Burkard, Heinrich 299, 312
Busch, Adolf 300
Busch, Fritz 58, 426
Buschbeck, Erhard 151, 183, 187, 382
Busoni, Benvenuto 156
Busoni, Ferruccio VIII, 59, 60, 62, 133, 146, 148, 153–55, 158, 159, 170, 180, 213, 219–31, 264, 272, 283, 284, 292, 293, 307, 308, 439, 462
Busoni, Gerda 158
Butting, Max XI, 284, 285, 295, 308, 343
Buxbaum, Friedrich 22, 502
Byron, George Gordon Noel, Lord 250, 453, 454

Cage, John 408, 494
Cahill, Thaddäus 229

Calvocoressi, Michel Dimtri 157, 158
Capet, Lucien 421
Caplet, André 278
Carl Carl 50
Carreno, Teresa 44
Casals, Pablo 143, 161, 162, 344, 345, 351, 352, 365, 371, 406, 411
Casella, Alfredo 269, 270, 284, 294, 297, 303, 306, 395–401
Casella, Yvonne XI
Cassirer, Paul, Publisher 138, 141, 148, 159, 430
Castells see Gerhard, Roberto
Castelnuovo-Tedesco, Mario 474
Catherman, Terence XII
Chagall, Marc 300
Chaplin, Charlie 483, 563
Charpentier, Gustave 60
Chevalley, Hermann 204
Clark, Edward XIII, 134, 143, 144, 146, 150, 153, 155, 156, 157, 159, 169, 190, 223, 324, 331, 339, 372, 411
Clark, King 214/215
Claudel, Paul 261
Closson, Louis 156, 157
Cocteau, Jean 289
Cohn, Gisela 36
Conradi, Hermann 78
Copland, Aaron 471
Cortolezis, Fritz 321
Cowell, Henry 339, 344, 471, 493
Craft, Robert 440, 511, 513, 516
Crawford, Ruth 469
Csokor, Franz Theodor 164
Culp, Julia 162, 171, 179, 188
Curjel, Hans 335, 498

Dahl, Ingolf 440
Dahlhaus, Carl 325
Dallapiccola, Luigi XI, 123, 502, 505, 508
Dammert, Hansjörg 332, 541
Danz, Louis 415
David, Werner 451, 502
Debussy, Claude 73, 87, 139, 157, 213, 221, 254, 268, 269, 340, 423, 549
Dehmel, Richard 35, 36, 38, 39, 40, 41, 48, 84, 87, 116, 183, 204, 215, 237–39

Deis, Carl 459
Delacroix, Eugène 234
Delacroix, Henri 294
Delage, Maurice 278
Delius, Frederick 219
Dent, Edward J. 282–83, 308, 462, 505
Dessau, Paul XI, 444, 468, 475, 505
Deutsch, Max X, 253, 258, 260, 261, 269, 271, 448, 450, 497, 507
Deutsch, Otto Erich 505
Diamond, David 471
Dick, Marcel 304, 482
Dickens, Charles 419
Dieren, Bernard van 155, 156
Dieterle, Charlotte 410, 416
Dieterle, Wilhelm 416, 424
Dille, Denis X
Diaghilev, Serge 206, 415
Döblin, Alfred 150
Dolbin, B. 426
Dorian, Frederick (Friedrich Deutsch) 450
Dostoyevsky, Fyodor 233
Downes, Olin 109, 371, 409, 429, 475, 494
Dowson, Ernest 189
Draber, Hermann W. 152
Drachmann, Holger 42, 47
Drewett, Norah 164
Dukas, Paul 87
Durieux, Tilla 207, 259

Eberle, Gottfried XII
Ebert, Carl 344
Eckl, Heinrich 91
Edel, Edmund 53
Edison, Thomas 552
Egk, Werner 505
Ehrenstein, Albert 150, 158, 164, 414, 428, 429
Eichberg, Friedrich 20, 22, 168, 435
Einstein, Albert 300, 381
Einstein, Carl 151
Eisler, Edmund (Eysler) 31, 33, 50, 51
Eisler, Gerhard 487
Eisler, Hanns VII, 257, 269, 274, 275, 283, 297, 308, 311, 312, 390, 445, 456, 468, 479, 483, 487, 502
Eisler, Lou 445, 466
Eisler, Rudolf 412
Elgar, Edward 219

Elvers, Rudolf XII
Endell, August 55, 92
Engel, Carl XII, 384, 387, 388, 390, 406, 407, 409, 415, 418, 424, 426, 445, 449, 454, 455, 457–61, 464, 468, 563
Engländer, Richard see Altenberg, Peter
Erdmann, Eduard 291
Ernst, Otto 90
Erpf, Hermann 430
Erskine, John 407
Essberger, Karl 202, 203
Eulenberg, Herbert 300
Ewers, Hanns 49, 56
Eyken, Heinrich von 52

Falck, Edward 34
Falke, Gustav 48, 54, 75
Fall, Leo 176
de Falla, Manuel 344
Fauré, Gabriel 308
Fehling, Emanuel 292
Fehling, Jürgen 292
Felix, Oskar 350, 367
Feuermann, Emanuel 371, 411, 432
Fiedler, Arthur 374
de Filippi, Amadeo 502
Finckh, Ludwig 48
Fischer, Edwin 300
Fischer, Samuel Publisher 86
Flesch, Carl 421
Flesch, Hans 329, 331, 336, 341, 421
Fleury, Louis 294
Foerster, Josef Bohuslav 244
Forbach, Moje 334
Ford, Henry 552
Formey, Alfred 35
Fortner, Wolfgang 505
Franck, Maurits 503
Frank, Serge 471, 486
Franz Josef, Emperor 242, 452
Frederick, Kurt 485
Freund, Marya 100, 184, 204, 211, 217, 270, 278, 279, 283–85, 287, 292, 297, 304, 343, 426, 502, 507
Freund, Otto 277
Fried, Oskar 134, 140, 141, 142, 146, 148, 154, 155, 158, 162, 177
Friedberg, Carl 172
Friedberg, Gerda 172

Friedell, Egon 23, 164
Friedrich, Elisabeth 331
Frischauf, Hans 122
Frischauf, Hermann 119, 252
Fröbe, Ivan 157, 158
Fromaigeat, E. 261
Fromm-Michaels, Ilse 293
Fuchs, Robert 51
Fuhrmann, Gertrud 541
Fuleihan, Anis 471
Fürstenberg, Prince Max Egon 294
Fürstner, Adloph 167
Furtwängler, Wilhelm 216, 259, 264, 285, 312, 322, 324, 367, 393, 475, 544

Gabrilowitsch, Ossip 44, 374
Ganz, Rudolf 395
Gärtner, Eduard 37
Gaudriot, Karl 269
Gaugin, Paul 93
Geissler, Max 91
Gentner-Fischer, Else 331
George, Stefan 95, 96, 113, 116, 117, 124, 183, 189, 215
Gerhard, Roberto 304, 310, 345, 351, 505, 512, 541
Gerigk, Herbert 392
Gershwin, George 373, 374, 415, 422, 423, 484
Gerstenberg, Walter 514
Gerstl, Richard 93, 94, 95, 96, 97, 169, 467
Gesualdo, Carlo 399
Gide, André 396
Gielen, Josef XII, 214
Gielen, Michael XIII
Gielen-Steuermann, Rosa 214
Gieseking, Walter 213
Gifford, Clemence 465
Gimpel, Jakob 465
Giraud, Albert 55, 195, 198
Glazounov, Alexander 323
Gmeindl, Walter 365
Goebbels, Josef 367, 392, 472
Goehr, Walter XII, 310, 371, 379, 382, 383, 444, 507, 541
Goethe, Johann Wolfgang von 64, 65, 85, 215, 250, 289, 336 440, 487
Goetschius, Percy 375
van Gogh, Vincent 93

Göhler, Georg 202
Gold, Alfred 22, 35
Goldmark, Karl 131
Goldschmidt, Adalbert von 58
Goldschmied, Edmund 24, 26, 27
Goldschmied, Richard 128
Goldschmied, Rudolf 476
Goldschmied, Sigmund 25
Goossens, Eugene 394
Götz, Dr. 208
Gould, Glenn 501
Grädener, Hermann 51
Gradenwitz, Peter XII, 489, 505
Graener, Paul 366
Graf, Herbert 321, 331
Graf, Max 257
Gräner, Georg 151, 158, 172
Gray, Cecil 455
Gray, H. W., Publisher 451
Gregor, Hans 51
Gregori, Ferdinand 210, 212
Greissle, Felix VIII, 215, 275, 295,
    296, 309, 322, 409, 424, 428, 448,
    449, 459, 462, 463, 465, 468, 476,
    534
Grieg, Edvard 30
Gronostay, Walter 310, 541
Gropius, Manon 105
Gropius, Walter 105, 192, 240, 263,
    300
Grote, Ludwig 502
Gruenberg, Louis T. 156, 158, 308,
    471
Guilbert, Yvette 47, 56
Gürtler, Hermann 164
Gütersloh, Paris von 563
Gutheil-Schoder, Marie 97, 99, 134,
    141, 188, 195, 196, 207, 216, 217,
    271, 277, 283, 297, 299, 320
Gutmann, Emil 155, 157, 158, 162,
    179, 195, 203, 207

Hába, Alois 382, 430
Haftmann, Werner IX
Hagemann, Carl 130
Halir, Karl 59
Hamsun, Knut 112, 233
Handel, George Frederick 321, 365,
    370
Hannenheim, Norbert von 332, 350,
    541, 543

Hansen, Wilhelm, Publishers 265,
    287, 288, 293
Hanslick, Eduard 29, 30, 488
Haringer, Jakob 365, 506
Harrell, Mack 468
Harris, Roy Dr. 471
Harrison, Lou 469, 471
Hart, Heinrich 37
Hart, Julius 78
Hartleben, Otto Erich 35, 56, 195,
    198, 201
Hartmann, Karl Amadeus 478, 490,
    502, 505
Hartungen, Ida 261
Hauer, Josef Matthias 263, 289, 292,
    293, 295, 325, 339, 349, 443
Hauff, Wilhelm 17, 316
Hauptmann, Gerhart 36, 81, 85, 183,
    300
Hausegger, Siegmund von 66, 177,
    178
Haveman Quartet 312
Haydn, Joseph 74, 430
Hebbel, Friedrich 133
Hefferman, Helen 461
Heifetz, Benar 391, 441
Heifetz, Jascha 481
Heim, Emmy 260
Heine, Heinrich 51
Heinecke, Max 59
Heinsheimer, Hans W. XII, 316, 411,
    488
Heinz, Berthold 59
Heller, Hugo 134, 250
Hempel, Frieda 157
Henkel, Paul 114
Herget, Sofie von 208
Hermann, Hans 91
Herrmann, Bernhard 505
Hertz, Alfred 427
Hertzka, Emil 78, 125, 129, 138, 140,
    144, 148, 149, 151–55, 158, 162,
    170, 175, 176, 184, 189, 190, 223,
    242, 265, 275, 288, 293, 300, 321,
    322, 348, 488
Hesse, Hermann 233
Heuberger, Richard 30, 31
Heymel, Alfred Walter 48
Hilsberg, Ignace 465
Hindemith, Paul 259, 299, 303, 308,

389, 392, 448, 497, 498, 500, 542, 543
Hinnenberg-Lefèbre, Margot VII, 312, 316, 331, 339, 340, 478, 483, 505
Hinrichsen, Henri 159, 177, 178, 189, 268, 278, 283, 309, 317
Hirsch, Paul 329, 505
Hirshman, I. A. 433, 434, 437
Hitler, Adolf 392, 436, 438, 448, 453, 466, 472, 476, 482, 483
Hoess, F. W. IX
Hoffmann, Camill 438
Hoffmann, E. T. A. 112, 181
Hoffmann, Josef 300
Hoffmann, Richard XII, 482, 483, 486, 494, 501, 504
Hoffmann, Rudolf St. 66
Hofmannsthal, Hugo von 21, 38, 64, 116, 149, 212, 215, 279
Hölderlin, Friedrich 84
Holl, Karl XII, 329
Holländer, Gustav 62, 63
Holz, Arno 48
Hommel, Friedrich XII
Honneger, Arthur 308
Horwitz, Karl 97, 140, 149, 158, 161, 208, 257
Howard, Walter 339, 430
Huberman, Bronislaw 15
Huder, Walter XI
Humperdinck, Engelbert 51, 131, 196
Huneker, James 199
Hüni, Mihacsek, Felicie 254
Hutcheson, Ernest 374, 389, 390, 354, 403
Hutchins, Robert Maynard 476
Huxley, Aldous 440

Ibsen, Henrik 80, 111, 183
d'Indy, Vincent 221
Isaac, Heinrich 88
Itten, Johannes 263
Ives, Charles 439, 440

Jacobi, Frederick 481
Jacobsen, Jens Peter 111
Jalowetz, Heinrich 80, 97, 105, 140, 149, 176, 179, 180, 190, 234, 242,

275, 277, 291, 326, 343, 382, 435, 476, 482, 563
Janácek, Leos 308
Janssen, Werner 474
Jaques- Dalcroze, Emile 178
Jarczyk, Max 365/6
Jarnach, Philipp 483
Jarnach, Wolfgang 483
Jary, Michael 365
Jawlensky, Alexey von 142
Jellinek, Hanns 253, 504
Jemnitz, Alexander X, 174, 188, 244, 253, 295, 343, 384, 427
Jerger, Alfred 299
Jirák, K. B. 391
Johann Georg von Sachsen 83
Jonas-Werndorff, Etta 33
Jonasz, Marietta 97
Jone, Hildegard 382, 563
Jones, Perry 483
Joseph II, Emperor 17
Joyce, James 508
Juilliard Quartet 504, 515
Juilliard School 376, 389, 394, 403, 406, 407
Jungbauer, Jenny 292

Kaepmpfert, Anna 259
Kafka, Franz 309
Kahn, Erich Itor 341, 345
Kainer, Lene 150
Kainer, Ludwig 150
Kallenbach-Greller, Lotte 333, 430
Kallir, Otto 467
Kaltenborn, Fritz 262
Kaminski, Heinrich 325
Kandinsky, Nina 317
Kandinsky, Vassily VIII, IX, 72, 93, 141, 142, 144, 151, 152, 174, 183, 189, 190, 227–28, 238, 243, 245, 281, 290, 317, 368, 432, 563
Kant, Immanuel 183, 342
Karajan, Herbert von 325
Karatygin, W. G. 181, 207
Karg-Elert, Sigfried 192, 213
Kassowitz, Gottfried 254
Kauder, Hugo 251
Kaun, Hugo 91
Keller, Alfred 319, 332, 505, 541
Keller, Gottfried 79
Keller, Hans 502

Kerner, Dieter 512
Kernstock, Otto 244
Kerr, Alfred 49, 138, 142, 148, 207
Kestenberg, Leo 307–09, 346–48, 422
Keussler, Gerhard von 140, 161, 190, 208
Kienzl, Wilhelm 161
Kindler, Hans 202, 319
Kirchmeyer, Helmut 119
Kiurina, Berta 266
Klatte, Wilhelm 179, 290
Klatzkin, Jakob 428
Klee, Paul 205
Kleiber, Erich 259, 309, 316, 326, 404, 426, 542
Klein, César 264
Klein, Fritz Heinrich 443
Klein, Walther 244, 297
Klemperer, Otto 141, 204, 259, 269, 295, 326, 335, 336, 403, 408, 409, 415, 416, 427, 440, 441, 461, 470, 506, 563
Klemperer, Victor 91
Klenau, Paul von 100, 277, 287, 297
Klimt, Gustav 92, 93, 164, 275
Klinger, Max 357
Klitsch, Wilhelm 267, 272
Kniese, Julius 196
Koffler, Josef 382
Kokoschka, Oskar 47, 93, 94, 164, 165, 173, 183, 189, 233, 255, 300, 301, 479, 511
Koldofsky, Adolf 501, 507
Kolisch, Henriette 340, 482
Kolisch Quartet 316, 350, 372, 383, 391, 392, 414, 420, 421, 424, 498
Kolisch, Rudolf VII, VIII, XII, 269–72, 275, 278, 282, 294, 295, 297, 304, 307, 309, 316, 319, 322, 328, 337, 342, 348–50, 366, 391, 404, 416, 441, 468, 482, 498, 500, 501, 506, 512
Komzak, Karl 22
Königer, Dr. 184
Königer, Paul 161, 173, 184, 190, 251, 563
Korngold, Erich Wolfgang 60, 308, 467
Korngold, Julius 291, 467
Koons, Walter E. 383, 384
Koussevitzky, Sergy 155, 179, 378,

379, 394, 465, 481, 485, 504, 511
Kralik, Heinrich von 74
Královcová, Marketa XI
Kramer, Emil 28, 40
Kramer, Leopold 28
Kramer, Susanne 28
Krasner, Louis 421, 423, 445, 453, 474
Krassin Boris 386
Kraus, E. 131, 132
Kraus, Else C. XI, 411, 518
Kraus, Karl 99, 150, 151, 164, 183, 224, 233, 244, 245, 249, 257, 427, 495
Krebs, Carl 91
Kreisler, Fritz 44
Krenek, Ernst 73, 74, 123, 325, 326, 328, 415, 427, 437, 440, 482, 543, 563
Kretzschmar, Hermann 179
Krinninger, Franz 282
Kroyt, Boris 217
Krüger, Victor 487
Kruse, Käthe 48
Kubelik, Rafael 246
Kuhlau, Friedrich 160
Kulka, Karl 413
Kurth Ernst 344

Laber, Louis 299
Lalo, Edouard 261
Lane, Sonja XII
Langner, Thomas-M. XII
Lányi, Jenö 449
Lasker-Schüler, Else 150, 164, 424
Lasker, Emanuel 424
Lauff, Josef 90
Lautner, Lois XII, 375, 376–78
Lazarus, Gustav 91
Lederman, Minna 385, 398
Le Fort, Gertrud von 485
Legal, Ernst 336
Legge, Walter 455
Lehár, Franz 27, 53, 336, 350, 423, 441
Lehner, Eugen 391, 498
Leibowitz, René 325, 444, 446, 451, 485, 486, 489, 494, 497, 498, 501, 503, 505, 506, 510, 563
Leichentritt, Hugo 429
Lenau, Nikolaus 35
Lendvai Quartet 560

Lenneberg, Hans XII
Leopold II, Emperor 17
Lepcke, Ferdinand 145
Lepcke, Oscar 145
Lert, Ernst 211, 212, 259, 287, 299
Leuer, Hubert 266
Leuwen Swarthout, Max van 408
Levant, Oscar 454
Levetzow, Karl M. Freiherr v. 37, 164
Liebermann, Max 313
Lienau, Robert 133
Lieser, Frau 192, 193, 212, 240, 242
Lieliencron, Detlev von 35, 48, 49
Lindberg, Helge 268, 269
Lingg, Hermann 44
Linke, Karl 149, 152, 162, 234, 563
List, Kurt 466, 475, 508
Liszt, Franz 40, 60, 74, 75, 80, 83, 154, 208, 398
Lochner, Louis P. 44
Löfler, Albrecht 59
Lohse, Otto 211
Löns, Hermann 91
Loos, Anita 317
Loos, Adolf 55, 93, 150, 158, 164, 183, 193, 250, 255–56, 258, 263, 291, 295, 297, 339, 349, 413, 488, 513
Loos, Anita 316
Lortzing, Albert IX, 78
Louis, Joe 452
Louis, Rudolf 207
Louise, Crown Princess of Saxony 196
Löwe, Ferdinand 68, 131
Löwenthal, Anka 272
Ludwig, Emil 164
Ludwig II, King of Bavaria 143
Lueger, Karl 81, 144
Luft, Friedrich XII
Lütge, Karl 325
Luther, Martin 352

Maazel, Lorin 325
Machado, Antonio 508
Macke, August 141, 205
Maegaard, Jan 563
Maeterlinck, Maurice 151, 220, 238, 261, 262
Mahler, Alma Maria VIII, 66, 67, 91, 93, 101, 102, 103, 105, 106, 107, 108, 115, 137, 149, 151, 153, 170,

192, 193, 233, 240, 241, 263, 266, 269, 279, 281, 283, 290, 351, 382, 412, 415, 456, 463, 473, 494, 506, 521, 563
Mahler, Anna 521
Mahler, Gustav 35, 42, 50, 66, 70, 76, 80, 87, 88, 90–94, 98–115, 118, 124, 127, 129, 131, 134, 135, 137, 140, 143, 151, 153, 155, 162, 168, 170, 171, 173, 180, 184, 187, 192, 233, 244, 251, 254, 262, 265, 282, 291–93, 304, 340, 348, 396, 420, 473, 476, 486, 496, 506, 563
Maliniak, Jakob 203
Malipiero, Gian Francesco 297, 303, 306
Malkin, Beatrice XII
Malkin, I. XII
Malkin, Joseph XII, 371–75, 378, 379, 380, 383
Malkin Conservatory 379, 380, 383, 394
Malkin, Manfred 374, 380
Mandl, Richard 257, 513
Mandyczewski, E. 81
Mann, Monica XII, 449, 457, 459
Mann, Thomas 243, 339, 386, 436, 449, 456, 457, 459–60, 461, 467, 470, 473, 474, 479, 491, 492, 494, 495, 503, 509, 510, 523, 547
Manowarda, Josef von 266
Marc, Franz 141, 152, 153, 168, 205
Marée, Lucienne 508
Maria Theresia, Empress 17
Marks, Edward B. 505
Marlow, Mimi 164
Marschalk, Max 59, 81, 100, 129, 130, 139, 140, 159, 204, 207, 344
Marinu, Bohuslav 483
Marx, A. B. 430
Marx, Josef 260
Mascagni, Pietro 29, 51
Massine, Leonid 206, 207, 278, 281
Mattiesen, Emil 216
Maury, Lowndes XII, 376, 377
Max von Baden 83
Mayrhofer, Robert 430
Mendelssohn-Bartholdy, Felix 74, 83, 160, 476
Mengelberg, Curt Rudolf 267
Mengelberg, Willem 180, 189,

265–67, 382
Menzel, Adolph 357
Merinsky, Hilda 272, 292
Merseburger, Carl 214
Mersmann, Hans 339, 483
Meyer, Conrad Ferdinand 213
Meyer, Waldemar 59
Meyerbeer, Giacomo 128
Michaelis, Karin 150
Michelangelo Buonarroti 508
Milhaud, Darius XI, 270, 278, 279, 281, 283, 292, 382, 470, 473, 481, 498, 509
Miller, Oscar von 435
Minnich, W. 347
Mitropulos Dimitri 279, 474, 493, 515
Moe, Henry Allen 469
Moenck, Johannes 541
Moll, Carl 91, 93, 134, 149, 170, 351
Möller, Carl 151
Mombert, Alfred 133
Monn, Georg Matthias 169, 351, 352, 365, 371, 411
Monteux, Pierre 481
Morgenstern, Christian 48, 49, 56, 164
Mörtl, Wilhelmine 135
Mozart, Wolfgang Amadeus 29, 74, 93, 128, 162, 169, 254, 306, 340, 41, 359, 365, 377, 389, 397, 429–31, 451, 462
Muck, Carl 349
Mühsam, Erich 164
Mullen, Frances 439
Müller, Georg 233
Munch, Edvard 94
Münter, Gabriele 141, 142, 174
Mussolini, Benito 398
Mussorgsky, Modest 278
Muszkat, Moritz 56
Myers, Rollo H. 284
Mysz-Gmeiner, Lulu 149

Nachod, Felix 449
Nachod, Friedrich 18, 178
Nachod Gottlieb 476
Nachod, Hans 20, 31, 33, 127, 184, 211, 261, 368, 429, 476, 502
Nachod, Joseph 16
Nachold-Hutter, Karoline 28
Nachold, Walter Josef 476
Nadel, Arno 180, 207

Napoleon 453
Nedbal, Oscar 177
Nef, John Ulric XII
Neschling, John Luciano IX
Neschling-Bodanzky, Renate IX, 27
Nestroy, Johann 50
Neumann, Angelo 28
Neumann, Franz 303
Neumann, Robert 386
Neutra, Richard 413
Newlin, Dika XII, 20, 33, 84, 110, 450, 457, 471, 506, 563
Newman, Ernst 177
Nielsen, Carl 221
Niemann, Walter 358, 363
Nietzsche, Friedrich 35, 84, 116, 183, 233
Nijinsky, Romola 240
Nijinsky, Vaslav 240
Nikisch, Arthur 58, 59, 189, 213
Nikisch, Mitja 148, 213
Nolde, Ada 153
Nolde, Emil 94, 150, 153
Novák, Vitezslav 174
Novakovic, Olga 253, 262, 275, 282, 382, 476

Obrist, Aloys 68
Ochs, Sigfried 140, 188
O'Connell, Charles 433
Oestvig, Carl 266
Offenbach, Jacques 47, 50, 128
Oliven, Fritz (Rideamus) 50
Oppenheimer, Max 93, 130, 233
Orloff, Ida 164
Otto, Bertel 272
Otto, Teo 334

Panizza, Oskar 48
Pappenheim, Marie XII, 71, 119, 121, 122, 180, 183, 188, 241, 242, 252, 255
Partos, Oedön 517, 518
Paul, Adolf 192
Paz, Juan Carlos 563
Pechner, Gerhard 331
Pella, Paul 291
Pelleg, Frank 517, 518
Peragallo, Mario 502
Perelman, Leo 150, 153, 159, 178

Perpessa, Charilaos 541
Peters, Publishers 117, 189, 192, 265, 317
Petri, Egon 155, 156, 157, 439
Petri Quartet 91
Pfau, Ludwig 35
Pfitzner, Hans 63, 80, 93, 98, 221, 225, 26, 229–31, 308, 344, 495
Pfundtmayr, Hedy 299
Piatigorsky, Gregor 217, 481
Pieau, Walter 34, 79, 309
Pingoud, Ernst 181
Piper & Co., Publishers 152, 161
Pisk, Paul Amadeus 254, 257, 262, 297, 329, 382, 415, 506, 563
Piston, Walter 471, 483
Plato 154, 183
Pleyel, Ignaz 357
Ploderer, Rudolf 382, 427
Poe, Edgar Allan 181
Poelzig, Hans 300, 322, 478
Polatschek, Victor 277, 304, 441
Polgar, Alfred 164
Polnauer, Josef 139, 152, 161, 240, 251, 254, 297, 382, 476, 512
Porpora, Nicola
Possart, Ernst von 58
Poulenc, Francis XI, 278, 279, 282, 292
Prawossudowitsch, Anna Natalie 332, 541
Preussner, Eberhard 341
Pringsheim, Klaus 208
Procházka, Rudolph F. 207, 260, 291
Prokofiev, Sergey 181, 439
Prunières, Henri 278
Pryce-Jones, Alan 23
Puccini, Giacomo XI, 67, 303, 423, 441
Purcell, Henry 389
Raabe, Peter 265
Rabenalt, Arthur Maria 334
Rankl, Karl 245, 257. 272, 274, 277, 283, 328, 444, 455, 462, 505, 512, 519
Rathbone, Basil 463
Ratz, Erwin VII. X, 250, 251–53, 290, 476, 512
Ravel, Maurice 157, 261, 268–71, 278, 292, 308, 340, 439, 463
Rebner, Edward Wolfgang 465

Rebner Quartet 259
Redlich, Fritz 175
Redlich, Hans Ferdinand 251, 427
Redlich, Josef 149
Reese, Gustav 422, 424, 438, 450, 460, 465
Regenstein, Joseph XII
Reger, Max 65, 87, 114, 131, 181, 261, 262, 268, 278, 333, 340, 390, 451, 549
Reich, Fritz 541
Reich, Willi XII, 86, 277, 382, 415, 427, 563
Reichold, Henry 486
Reinecke, Carl 389
Reinecke, Hertha 345
Reiner, Fritz 468
Reinhardt, Gottfried 470
Reinhardt, Max 98, 140, 144, 151, 170, 452, 470
Reinhart, Hans 282, 285
Reis, Claire M. 388
Reitler, Josef 60, 466
Remus, Susanne XII, 476
Respighi, Ottorino 394
Réti, Rudolf 164, 179, 183, 263, 297
Reznicek, Emil Nikolaus von 329
Richter, Alfred 217
Richter, Hans 44
Rieman, Hugo 291–92, 492
Riesenfeld, Hugo 34, 403
Riley, James W. 387
Rilke, Rainer Maria 116, 183, 192, 241, 497
Rimsky-Korsakov, Nicolai 363
Ritter, Alexander 75
Roda Roda 164
Rödelberger, Philipp 91
Rodriguez, José 415, 419
Rodzinsky, Arthur 468, 503
Rognoni, Luigi 563
Roland-Manuel 278
Roller, Alfred 92, 94, 98, 164, 189
Roloff, Helmut 478, 497
Romano, Jacopo 563
Roner, Hermann 275, 291, 411
Roosevelt, Franklin D. 387
Roosevelt, Theodore 387
Ropartz, Guy 219
Rosbaud, Hans 246, 341, 345, 349, 351, 352, 355, 483, 496

Rosé, Arnold 59, 68, 78, 90, 134, 164, 168
Rosé, Justine 151
Rosé Quartet 42, 78, 91, 105, 141, 148, 149, 152, 172, 207, 250
Rosenberg, Alfred 392
Rossini, Gioacchino IX, 77–78
Roth, Joseph 427
Rothschild, Fritz 149, 304
Rothstein, James 53
Rothweiler, Helmut 332, 541
Rousseau, Jean Jacques 250
Roussel, Albert 308
Rubinstein, Arthur 457, 465
Rufer, Joseph VII, X, 29, 85, 228, 236, 257, 258, 261, 274, 277, 292–345, 347, 369, 372, 421, 476, 478, 487, 489, 491, 496, 501–03, 505, 507, 508, 510, 512, 514, 523, 541, 563
Ruggles, Carl 308
Rychnovsky, Ernst 207

Saerchinger, César 45, 415
Saint-Säens, Camille 161, 219, 261
Sakom, Jakob 293
Salis, Rodolphe, Baron de la Tour de Neintre 47
Sarasate, Pablo 100
Sarro, Ramon 347
Satie, Eric 272
Sauerlandt, Max 292
Sayn-Wittgenstein, Caroline 63
Schacht, Peter 319, 332, 350, 541
Schalk, Franz 68, 101, 259, 329
Scheinpflug, Paul 281, 297
Schelling, Ernest 374
Schenker, Heinrich 220, 291, 339, 430
Scherchen, Hermann 180, 203, 205, 206, 207, 214, 245, 259, 264, 291, 294, 297, 299, 355, 414, 474, 505, 510
Schering, Emil 233, 350
Scherl, August, Publisher 90
Schiele, Egon 205
Schiller, Friedrich 18, 261
Schillinger, Joseph 422, 454, 500
Schillings, Max von 60, 63, 91, 178, 196, 350, 366
Schindler, R. M. 101, 439

Schirmer, G. Publishers 384, 407, 409, 415, 418, 422, 428, 438, 449, 456, 457, 459, 460, 465
Schlaf, Johannes 36
Schlamm, William 472
Schlee, Alfred IX, X
Schlemmer, Oskar 206, 334, 335
Schlichter, Dolly 253
Schlichter, Viktor 253
de Schloezer, Boris 415
Schmid, Erich 332, 333, 341, 541
Schmidt, Felix 91
Schmidt, Franz 262, 291
Schmidt, Leopold 159, 171
Schmidt-Rottluff, Karl 94
Schmied, Josef 161
Schmitt, Florent 278
Schmitt, Franz 560
Schmitz, Paul 479
Schnabel, Artur 44, 45, 146, 148, 297, 308, 427, 459, 470, 494
Schneerson, Grigory XII
Schneider, Michael 503
Schneider, Otto 263
Schnitzler, Arthur 23
Schoeffer, Maria 188

Schoenberg, Arnold Compositions:
'Abschied' Song 37, 38
Accompaniment Music for a film, opus 34 335, 343, 348, 394
A Survivor from Warsaw, opus 46 485, 489, 506, 533
Ballades for voice and piano, opus 12 90, 175, 528
Brettl Songs (1901) 44, 54, 56
Canons (Appendix to opus 28) 310
Chamber Symphony No. 1 164, 246, 333, 449, 450, 531
Chamber Symphony No. 2 opus 38 90, 433, 434, 437, 445, 448, 490, 505
Chamber Symphony, opus 9 IX, 68, 86, 96, 105, 113, 129, 133, 164, 175, 183, 184, 186, 212, 216, 221, 246, 250, 254, 264, 287, 305, 333, 344, 406, 431, 433, 434, 442, 478, 483, 507, 528, 538
Choral Preludes of J. S. Bach (Arr) 283, 406
Concerto for Piano and Orchestra,

Schoenberg. Arnold
Compositions cont.

opus 42 455, 456, 459, 460, 463,
466, 467, 497
Concerto for String Quartet and
Orchestra (after G. F. Handel)
370, 391, 405, 418, 433
Concerto for Violin and Orchestra,
opus 36   390, 419, 426, 445, 497,
498, 503, 519
Concerto for Violoncello and
Orchestra (after G. M. Monn) 351,
365, 370, 383, 411, 418
'Dank' Song 37
'Darthulas Grabgesang'
(unpublished) 65
'Deinem Blick mich zu bequemen',
Song (1903), unpublished) 64
'De profundis' opus 50b   512, 533
'Der deutsche Michel', Song 244
'Dreimal tausend Jahre', opus 50a
499
'Eiserne Brigade, Die', Marsh 244
Erwartung,   opus   17   40,   71,
119–21, 123, 130, 144, 188, 189,
211, 222, 245–47, 281, 284, 287,
299. 321, 326, 330, 334, 335, 339,
340, 353, 497, 508, 532
Five Piano Pieces, opus 23   271,
288
Five Orchestral Pieces, opus 16
551
Folksong for mixed chorus a
cappella, opus 49   449
Four Pieces for mixed Choir,
opus 27   312, 315
Friede auf Erden, opus 13   140,
152, 294, 348
Glückliche Hand, Die, opus 18
122–24, 135, 136, 144, 145, 176,
188–90, 193, 211, 235, 245, 247,
259, 277, 281, 299, 319, 321, 324,
326, 329, 330, 334, 335, 353, 475,
490, 498, 532
'Gruss in die Ferne', Song (1900) 44
'Gurrelieder', 38, 42, 43, 54, 64, 85,
99, 100, 102, 111, 112, 127, 135,
146, 155, 164, 175, 176, 184, 187,
191, 193, 209, 211, 213, 214, 242,
255, 259, 261, 266, 272, 274, 281,

291, 316, 319, 320, 334, 340, 388,
411, 458, 471, 482, 510, 526, 529.
Herzgewachse opus 20   129,   151,
156, 158, 193, 322
'Im alten Style', Gavotte and
Musette for String orchestra (1897)
37, 389
'In hellen Träumen hab ich dich
oft geschaut', Song (1893) 22
'Israel exists again', (unpublished)
499
Jacob's Ladder 192, 212, 213, 238,
242, 245, 249, 257, 274, 277, 278,
281, 310. 342, 367, 422, 442, 454,
462, 468, 469, 470, 494, 511, 519,
532
Karolinenwalzer 28
'Kol Nidre', opus 39   432, 449,
450, 462, 506
Little Piano pieces, opus 19   108
'Mädchenfrühling', Song (1897) 37
'Modern Psalms', opus 50c
(fragment) 38, 513, 517
Moses and Aaron 290, 310, 324, 334,
335, 338, 342, 343, 347, 351–55,
367, 386, 388, 395, 409, 454, 455,
459, 462, 469, 470, 471, 494, 500,
513/14, 519, 523, 533, 543
Ode to Napoleon Buonaparte, opus
41   454, 456, 458, 463, 468, 485,
489, 496, 497, 507
Orchestral Pieces, opus 16   VII,
45, 106, 117, 129, 148, 156, 158,
172, 179, 188, 192, 216, 222, 247,
252, 277, 283, 285, 309, 494, 550
Pelléas and Mélisande, opus 5   52,
60, 64, 65, 75, 86, 134, 135, 146,
149, 152, 161, 162, 164, 178, 180,
181, 213, 216, 220, 259, 264, 265,
317, 379, 421, 500, 528, 550
Petrach Sonet 79, 288, 289
Phantasy for violin, opus 47   499,
501, 507, 519
Piano Pieces (1894) 30
Piano Pieces, opus 11   45, 69, 115,
119, 133, 140, 141, 163, 167, 179,
183, 220, 419, 439, 464, 531, 551
Piano Pieces, opus 19   108, 136,
157, 158, 173, 175, 183, 439
Piano Pieces, opus 23   246, 267,
268, 286, 288, 292, 442, 533

Schoenberg. Arnold,
Compositions cont.
Piano Pieces, opus 33a   328, 333,
440
Piano Pieces, opus 33b   344
Piano Sonata, opus 1   133
Piano Suite, opus 25   274, 286
Pieces for Chamber Orchestra
(1910) unfinished 137
Pieces for male chorus a cappella,
opus 35   334, 335
Pieces for mixed chorus, opus 27
310, 312, 315
Pierrot Lunaire 84, 85, 97, 100, 146,
175, 176, 180, 193, 199. 200, 203,
207, 209, 210, 214, 216, 228, 241,
246, 259, 264, 270, 271, 277, 278,
282-85, 289, 292-94, 303, 304, 319,
320, 334, 343, 396, 399, 406, 421,
426, 440-42, 445, 450, 453, 455,
458, 467, 497, 502, 504, 507, 513,
515, 532
Prelude for Orchestra and mixed
chorus, opus 44   474
Puzzle canon for 3 voices (1913)
345, 383
Satires for mixed chorus, opus 28
86, 310, 312, 315, 316, 502
Scherzo and Trio for string quartet
(1897) 37
'Schilflied' (1893) 35
Serenade for small Orchestra
(1896) 94
Serenade, opus 24   216, 268, 271,
275, 287-89, 294, 311, 344, 442,
495, 518, 533
Six pieces for male chorus, opus 35
334
Songs, opus 1   38, 52, 59, 75
Songs, opus 2   38, 39, 40, 52, 59,
75, 79, 100, 139, 525, 530, 534, 535
Songs, opus 3   38, 39, 52, 59, 75,
79, 139, 525, 534
Songs, opus 6   52, 78, 81, 84, 100,
121, 139
Songs, opus 14   114, 272
Songs after Jakob Haringer, opus 48
365, 505
Songs after Ludwig Pfau (1815,
unpublished) 36
Songs with Orchestra, opus 8   68,
79, 136, 148, 163, 188, 272
Songs with Orchestra, opus 22
188, 192, 194, 241, 247, 345, 525,
532
String Quartet in D (1897) 33, 37,
527
String Quartet No. 1 in D minor,
opus 7   33, 52, 81, 84, 90, 91, 105,
134, 139, 140, 148, 152, 168, 172,
216, 376, 404, 416, 420, 422, 498,
528, 530, 538, 420, 550
String Quartet No. 2 in F sharp
minor, opus 10   69, 90, 95, 97, 129,
134, 138, 140, 141, 152, 155, 164,
350, 404, 415, 420, 427, 478, 483,
498, 529, 531, 534, 550
String Quartet No. 3, opus 30   17,
316, 319, 349, 404, 421, 498, 504,
533
String Quartet No. 4, opus 37   69,
376, 414, 415, 418, 421, 437, 453,
498, 503, 505, 508, 533
String Septet (unfinished) 246, 250
String Trio, opus 45   479-81, 483,
503, 506
Suite for Piano, opus 25   274, 276,
277, 286, 288, 438, 533
Suite for Piano, wind and strings,
opus 29   287, 306, 316, 319, 323,
333, 490, 513, 534
Suite for String Orchestra (1934)
389, 395, 406, 408, 409, 418
Symphony for Soli, mixed chorus
and orchestra (sketch) 190, 236,
239, 240, 241, 242
Symphony in four movements
(sketches) 421, 494
Theme and Variations, opus 43a
and opus 43b   155, 459, 460, 461,
462, 468
Three Satires, opus 28   85, 310,
311, 396
Variations for orchestra, opus 31
316, 323, 324, 328, 341, 345, 428,
431, 483, 533
Variations on a recitative, opus 40
450, 451, 464, 465, 503, 530
Verklärte Nacht, opus 4   38, 40, 52,
59, 65, 75, 78, 80, 84, 86, 102, 213,
259, 265, 293, 343, 375, 394, 406,
412, 453, 458, 464, 526

Schoenberg, Arnold,
Compositions cont.
  Von heute auf morgen, opus 32   326,
    330, 336, 353, 490, 508, 533
  Wind Quintet opus 26   295, 296,
    309, 311, 324, 333, 434, 531
  Wind variations 468

Schoenberg, Arnold, Writings:
  Aus der Jugendzeit (From   my
    youth) 22
  Brahms the Progressive 357, 358
  Criteria for the Evaluation of Music 330
  The Biblical Way play 291, 313, 342,
    368, 513
  Ear training through composing 438
  Folkloristic Symphonies 487
  Fundamentals of Musical Composition
    423
  Gesinnung oder Erkenntnis? 315
  Harmonielehre 74, 88, 90, 125, 133,
    138, 151, 152, 154, 164, 224, 229,
    238, 271, 293, 314, 419, 430, 443,
    481
  Harmony, Counterpoint, etc., 396
  Heart and Mind in Music (Herz und
    Verstand in der Musik) 85, 488,
    506
  How can a music student earn a living?
    438
  Human Rights 488
  Looking Back 91
  Models for Beginners in Composition
    454, 458
  My attitude towards politics 473, 510
  *My Method of Composing with Twelve
    Inter-related Tones* 388
  National Music 340
  Preliminary Exercises in Counterpoint
    419, 458, 462, 470, 494
  Probleme des Kunstunterrichts 135
  Problems of Harmony 316, 385
  Structural Functions of Harmony 470,
    481
  Style and Idea 108, 109, 349, 352,
    357, 438, 503
  Tonality and Form 419
  *Zur Frage des modernen Kompositions
    Unterrichtes* 858

Schönberg, Arthur 435, 476

Schönberg, Bertel XII
Schönberg, Heinrich 18, 272, 482
Schönberg, Ignaz 15, 493
Schönberg-Nachod, Pauline 18, 20,
    23, 82, 275
Schönberg, Samuel 25
Schöne, Lotte 328
Schopenhauer, Arthur 183, 243
Schott, Publishers 188, 331, 517
Schreker, Franz 152, 178, 184, 210,
    241, 245, 264, 297, 313, 315, 320,
    321, 335, 343, 388
Schreker, Maria XI, 313, 388
Schröder, Rudolf Alexander 48, 53
Schubert, Franz 117, 179, 282, 304,
    397, 398, 430
Schuch, Ernst von 51, 61, 189, 190
Schuh, Willi XII
Schulhofer, Karl 382
Schuller, Gunther XII 154, 190, 515
Schultz, Sheila XII
Schulz-Dornburg, Rudolf 295, 297,
    478
Schulz-Fürstenberg, Max 59
Schulz, Wilhelm
Schuman, William 471
Schumann, Georg 91
Schumann, Robert 40, 83, 112, 117,
    119, 431, 456
Schünemann, Georg 366
Schuster, Bernhard 138
Schwab, Gustav 44
Schwarzmann, Norbert 294
Schwarzwald, Eugenie 78, 158, 242,
    245
Schwers, Paul 324
Scriabin, Alexander 88, 124, 231, 244,
    254, 396
Searle, Humphrey 518
Sechter, Simon
Seebach, Nikolaus 190
Seefehlner, Egon 475, 489
Seitz, Karl 393
Selden-Goth, Gisella 180
Seligmann-Kolisch, Maria (Mitzi)
    XI, 295, 317, 337, 342, 348, 349,
    366, 373-74, 415, 533
Seligmann, Walter 262
Sellner, Gustav Rudolf 355
Serato, Arrigo 134
Serkin, Rudolf 261, 270

Sessions, Roger 351, 415, 471, 482, 505
Sevastianov, German 452
Sevcik, Otakar 421
Shapero, Harold 469
Shaw, George Bernard 85, 164, 165
Shilkret, Nathaniel 473
Shostakovitch, Dimitri 431
Shriver, Henry Clay 454
Sibelius, Jean 219, 448
Siciliani, Francesco 519
Silcher, Friedrich 306
Siloti, Alexander 148, 149, 178, 179, 181, 182, 211–12
Simon, Erich 435
Simons, Rainer 77, 124, 130
Simrock, Hans 188
Sinding, Christian 219
Singer, Gustav 313
Sittner, Hans X
Skalkottas, Nikos 332, 541
Slonimsky, Nicolas XII, 190, 238, 277, 374, 394, 415, 422, 500
Smend, Friedrich 534
Smetana, Bedřich 40
Sollertinsky, E. E. 563
Somin, Hedda 48
Sonderling, Jakob 432
Soot, Fritz 188, 189
Specht, Richard 358
Spengler, Oswald 291, 292
Spiller, Myroslav 541
Spinner, Leopold 392
Spiro, Eugen 284
Spiwacke, Harold VIII
Sphor, Louis 74
Sporck, Ferdinand von 75
Sprague-Coolidge, Elizabeth 316, 319, 414, 416, 420, 421, 436, 437
Sproul, Robert G. 423, 470
Stadlen, Peter 449, 497
Stalin, Josef 386, 436
Stampfer, Selma 252, 253, 267
Starhemberg, Prince 411
Stefan-Grünfeld, Paul 60, 149, 151, 172, 187, 255, 382, 415, 430, 563
Stegmann, G. F. 497
Stein, Erwin 80, 85, 97, 100, 105, 140, 149, 174, 180, 183, 190, 193, 234, 242, 258, 269, 270, 277, 281, 290, 295, 297, 307, 322, 339, 382, 384,

411, 415, 442, 450, 455, 456, 462, 463, 474, 486, 502, 512, 518, 563
Stein, Gertrude 393
Stein, Leonhard XII, 252, 418, 457, 471, 501, 507
Steinbauer, Othmar 272
Steinberg, Hans Wilhelm 330, 331
Steinecke, Wolfgang 497
Steiner, Arnold 467
Steiner, Rudolf 20, 243
Stern Conservatory 56, 63, 146, 223
Steuermann, Clara XII
Steuermann, Eduard VII, 135, 150, 154, 156, 157, 160, 170, 201, 202, 204, 205, 214, 223, 252, 254, 259–62, 268–71, 277, 285, 292, 294, 382, 415, 441, 442, 448, 452, 459, 463, 464, 468, 482, 506, 507, 514, 563
Steuermann, Salome (Salka) XII, 170, 214, 251, 271, 411, 452, 457, 563
Stiedry-von Wagner, Erika X, XI, 270, 271, 277, 279, 281–83, 285, 294, 297, 343, 344, 367, 372, 391, 392, 421, 431, 432, 441, 444, 455, 468, 515
Stiedry, Fritz X, 217, 241, 270, 297, 299, 330, 343, 352, 367, 392, 432, 434, 437, 441, 444, 448, 459, 468, 490, 494, 505, 507, 510
Stock, Frederick 374, 394
Stoessel, Alfred 390
Stokowski, Leopold 271, 415, 464, 471, 563
Strang, Gerald XII, 419, 423, 424, 432, 457, 471
Stransky, Joseph 283
Strasser, István 161
Straus, Oscar 49, 50, 52, 53, 54, 55, 187
Strauss, Johann, father 17, 50, 67
Strauss, Johann, son 53, 271, 304, 423
Strauss, Alice IX
Strauss, Richard IX, 40, 42, 48, 58–77, 80, 82, 88, 90, 98, 102, 112, 114, 117, 128, 146, 170, 178, 187, 190, 196, 220, 233, 246, 254, 259, 262, 264, 308, 329, 340, 392, 396, 420, 475, 496, 543, 545, 549
Stravinsky Igor 184, 207, 231, 260–61

272, 292, 308, 309, 313, 390, 393,
396, 415, 439, 440, 448, 473, 490,
498, 500, 508, 519, 549
Strobel, Heinrich 341, 514
Stucken, Eduard 172
Stuckenschmidt, Hans Heinz 345,
499, 505, 507, 563
Stutschewsky, Joachim XI, 304, 541
Suk, Josef 261
Swarowsky, Hans X, 258
Swedenborg, Emanuel von 234, 235,
239, 457
Szanto, Theodor 215
Szymanowski, Karol 308

Tagore, Rabindranath 237, 396
Tal, E. P. Publisher 266
Talich, Václav 391
Tansman, Alexander 473
Tappert, Wilhelm 59
Tauber, Richard 327
Tenschert, Roland 254
Tertullian 234
Teweles, Heinrich 161
Thalberg, Irving 412
Thiel, Klaus X
Thomson, Virgil 393, 464
Tieck, Ludwig 250
Tiessen, Heinz 217, 325, 352
Tischer, Gerhard 159
Toch, Ernst 473, 541
Topitz, A. M. 331
Töply, Prof. 164
Toscanini, Arturo 516
Toselli, Enrico 196
Toulouse, -Lautrec, Henri de 47
Trakl, Georg 164, 187, 245, 295
Trauneck (Travnicek) Joseph X, 253,
254, 257
Tchaikovsky, Peter 363, 441, 483, 549
Tudor, Antony 470
Turnau, Josef 299, 319, 321, 329
Twain, Mark 387

Uhl, Frida 234
Uhland, Ludwig 250
Ullmann, Ludwig 151
Ullmann, Viktor 277
Unger, Max 211
Urban, Heinrich 51

Vamos, Nikolaus 492
Varèse, Edgar 283, 284, 462
Varga, Tibor 498, 501, 503, 519
Vaughan Williams, Ralph 308
Verdi, Giuseppe 128, 431, 459, 473,
514, 515
Verhaeren, Emile 164
Viertel, Berthold 164, 415, 452, 563
Viertel-Steuermann, Salka XII, see
Steuermann, Salome
Vignau, Hans von 63
Villa-Lobos Heitor 308
Vinaver, Chemjo 511
Violin, Moritz 427
Viotti, Giovanni Battista 356
Vries, H. W. de 203
Vrieslander, Otto 196

Wagner, Cosima 98, 196
Wagner, Richard 33, 37, 38, 39, 40,
42, 44, 47, 74, 75, 79, 93, 98, 101,
112, 143, 169, 227, 332, 259, 341,
357, 358, 396, 398, 431, 440, 441,
451, 468, 475, 488, 496, 549
Wagner, Siegfried 99
Wagner, Willibald 59
Wagner, Wolfgang 506
Waitzner, Kläre 476
Waldbauer Quartet 152
Walden, Herwarth 150, 183
Walden String Quartet 503
Wallenstein, Alfred 494
Walter, Bruno 149, 151, 170, 188,
411, 462, 464
Walter, Fried 98, 332, 339
Walter, Max 541
Wangler, Franz 270, 305
Webenau, Wilma von 97
Weber, Carl Maria von 397
Weber, Hildegard XII
Webern. Amalia von 158
Webern, Anton von VII, X, 40, 53,
59, 72, 79–392, 409, 423, 426, 427,
436, 440–44, 449, 474, 476, 490,
496, 534, 537, 547, 563
Webern, Carl von 173
Wedekind, Frank 48, 54, 75, 164, 165,
381, 411
Weigl, Carl 31, 33, 66
Weill, Kurt 325, 326
Weinberger, Publishers 28

Weingarten, Paul 282
Weingartner, Felix von 131, 260, 329
Weininger, Otto 96, 138, 183, 238
Weinrich, Carl 451, 464
Weirich, Rudolf 127, 128
Weismann, Julius 329
Weiss, Adolphe 310, 415, 471, 541
Weiss, Leo 541
Weissman, Adolf 297, 308
Wellesz, Egon IX, 40, 54, 67, 80, 105,
    164, 187, 207, 260, 263, 265, 266,
    268, 278, 279, 505, 563
Wendland, Waldemar 51
Werefkin, Marianne von 142
Werfel, Franz 34, 164, 251, 300, 381,
    382, 415, 456, 459, 473
Werker, Wilhelm 430
Werndorff, Etta 127, 164, 173, 502
Werner & Co., Private Bank 25
Wetzelsberger, Bertil 339
Wiener, Karl von 131, 174, 251
Wiesengrund Theodor see Adorno,
    Theodor W.
Wilde, Kurt 505
Wilde, Oscar 241,
Wilhelm II, Emperor 160
Windisch, Fritz 217
Winkelmann, Hans 190
Winkelmann, Hermann 190
Winkler, Wilhelm 270, 282
Winternitz, Arnold 127, 128
Winternitz-Dorda, Martha 127, 128,
    130, 156–58, 164–65, 184, 211, 291,
    292
Wohlbrück, Olga 51, 56
Wolf, Hugo 58, 98, 112, 496
Wolff, Erich J. 151, 171
Wolff, Hermann 148
Wolff, Louise 148, 149, 158
Wolfsohn, Georg 340, 489, 507, 517,
    518
Wolzogen, Elsa Laura von 56
Wolzogen, Ernst von 37, 42, 48, 51,

52, 53, 54, 55, 56, 59, 61, 75, 537
Wood, Henry 178, 189
Wörner, Karl H. 563
Wührer, Friedrich XII, 304
Wurth, Johannes VIII

Yasser, Joseph 385
Yates, Peter 439, 440

Zahn, Ernst 91
Zdekauer, Gabriele von 208
Zech, Paul 164
Zehme, Albertine X, 55, 56, 158, 172,
    187, 195–96, 198, 201–03, 205, 207–
    17, 241, 269
Zehme, Felix 195, 196, 211, 212, 216,
    217
Zemlinsky, Alexander von VIII, 31,
    33, 37, 38, 40, 42, 50, 52, 53, 64, 65,
    66, 67, 75, 77, 78, 79, 90, 93, 94,
    100–05, 119, 121, 130, 143, 151,
    161, 162, 176, 177, 179, 184, 185,
    188–90, 193, 208, 210, 239, 241,
    251, 260, 261, 265, 272, 277, 278,
    283, 287, 288, 297, 311, 312, 325,
    330, 382, 437,
Zemlinsky, Ida von 277
Zemlinsky, Klara von 175
Zepler, Bogumil 51, 63
Ziegler, Benno 331
Zillig, Winfried 246, 310, 319, 320,
    345, 371, 474, 490, 496, 498, 505,
    519, 541, 543
Zimmermann, Bernhard 511
Zmigrod, Josef 541
Zola, Emile 250, 357
Zuckerkandl, Bertha 563
Zuckerkandl, Emil 102
Zukor, Adolf 493
Zweig, Arnold XI, 382
Zweig, Fritz XII, 150, 160, 179
Zweig, Stefan 21, 23, 164